D0875344

CONSTITUTIONAL HISTORY OF THE AMERICAN REVOLUTION

THE AUTHORITY TO LEGISLATE

JOHN PHILLIP REID

THE UNIVERSITY OF WISCONSIN PRESS

The University of Wisconsin Press
114 North Murray Street
Madison, Wisconsin 53715

3 Henrietta Street
London WC2E 8LU, England

Printed in the United States of America

For LC CIP information see the colophon

ISBN 0-299-13070-3

For Robert J. Beckmann

and his friends of O'Gara and Copley Halls

RICHARD J. NEAGLE

JACKIE HORAN

PAUL JOHN GROSSHART

TERENCE J. MULVIHILL

JAMES D. MALONE

EARL JOSEPH WASNESKI

CONTENTS

vii

CONSTITUTIONAL
HISTORY OF THE
AMERICAN REVOLUTION

INTRODUCTION

Power was feared in the eighteenth-century British Empire: the power of government, the power of "factions," power that was arbitrary, corrupt, unchecked, and unconstitutional. Above all, political theorists, constitutionalists, and just plain citizens were apprehensive of the arbitrariness of "will and pleasure," whether it was the caprice of a single ruler, an oligarchy, or that of the fickle, unpredictable democratic majority, sometimes called the "mob."

There was in the polemical political literature of the third quarter of the eighteenth century a touch of unreality to discussions of power. Most writers seemed to think that only the Crown, that is the king, not the ministry, would ever abuse power. That was a time, the 1760s and 1770s, it should be remembered, when the monarchy retained little power to abuse. In 1750 very few constitutional theorists imagined that legislative authority could ever pose a threat to liberty. With the 1760s their numbers increased as the "radicals" of British politics—the followers of John Wilkes, parliamentarians of the opposition such as John Sawbridge, Supporters of the Bill of Rights, lawyers like Serjeant John Glynn, and those members of London's Common Council who drafted petition after petition praying George III to restore the old constitutional balance by exercising dormant prerogative checks—discovered to their horror that the

3

constitution that had been settled at the Glorious Revolution of 1688 was fading into obsolescence. A new constitution of arbitrary parliamentary sovereignty was emerging, placing English (and, therefore, British) liberty in greater jeopardy than had been known even under the Tudors and Stuarts. It was a constitutional development that American whigs would also acknowledge, despite great reluctance, within the next decade. No other legal or constitutional consideration contributed more to the coming of the American Revolution than the realization that, in the years since the reign of Queen Anne, the doctrine of parliamentary supremacy had evolved into parliamentary sovereignty, making the House of Lords and the House of Commons not only supreme over the Crown, but potentially sovereign over the people, the constitution, and, most extreme of all, over the law. Americans would rebel because they faced the spectre of arbitrary government.

This study, like its companion volumes, *The Authority to Tax* and *The Authority of Rights*, is concerned with the constitutional issues that divided Great Britain and thirteen of her North American colonies during the years from 1765 (and the Stamp Act crisis) to 1776 (and the Declaration of Independence). The first volume dealt with the most virulent of the prerevolutionary constitutional issues—Parliament's authority to lay an internal tax upon a colony for purposes of revenue. Because the English constitutional precept that there could be no taxation without representation was so widely shared and cherished, there would have been no American rebellion had taxation been the only constitutional topic of controversy. Before troops took the field, the British administration abandoned any serious claim to colonial revenue, not because the policy of taxing Americans lacked adequate political support, but because the constitutional principle had became untenable.[1]

The subject of the second volume, American enjoyment of English rights, contributed more to the drafting of state and federal constitutions than to the coming of the Revolution. The dispute with the mother country about rights and liberties would teach the framers what rights needed constitutional and judicial protection, but the lesson was learned more from seeing rights endangered at home in Great Britain than from any jeopardy they faced from British rule in the colonies.[2] With certain exceptions and occasional lapses, the British government respected American civil rights. Its treatment of rights in the colonies provided grounds for political complaint but was insufficient cause for constitutional rebellion. Had there been no other constitutional grievances, American whigs would not, indeed could not, have constructed a constitutional case for independence.

It was the exercise of legislation—the subject of this study—that cast the constitutional die for rebellion. For the constitutional history of the

American Revolution this is the gravid volume because it was Parliament's use of the authority to legislate that took the constitutional quarrel to the point of armed conflict. Due to the dynamics of the eighteenth-century British constitution, once Parliament asserted the authority by promulgating statutes intended to legitimize the right to legislate, the British imperial constitution was forever changed and Americans either had to concede the right or leave the empire. The inflexibility of constitutional principle left no room for constitutional settlement or constitutional change. The purpose of this book is to explain those constitutional dynamics and ask how the British Parliament and its leaders became entrapped by the imperatives of the constitution they were struggling to preserve.

There are notions, accepted to varying degrees by historians, regarding eighteenth-century parliamentary authority over the North American colonies that this study seeks to dispel. A few are so prevalent among scholars it would be well to avoid future confusion by stating certain premises at this point. One is the old-fashioned idea, still repeated by lawyers, that the coming of the American Revolution turned on natural-law arguments. "The colonists," a recent law-revew article contended, "premised their fight for indepedence . . . on the natural law–social contract theory expounded by numerous writers, foremost among them John Locke."[3] It is difficult to imagine a statement more erroneous. One objection is that the British constitution, not Locke, supplied American whigs with their theoretical motivation. Another is that the colonists found little utility in the social contract. They drew their contractarian arguments from the original contract, especially the second original or colonial contract with its several variations including the migration contract, the commercial contract, and the imperial contract.[4] Most pertinent of all, the Americans did not build their case on natural law. True, they mentioned it constantly—calling constitutional rights "natural" as well as "constitutional"—and believed nature an authority for all legitimate law. But they cited no principle and made no argument on the basis of natural law alone.[5] It should never have been supposed that they did. A fact well appreciated in the eighteenth century, although not sufficiently credited in the historical literature, is that legal theorists did not think of natural rights as autonomous entities enforceable on their own authority. Rather, natural rights were surrendered on entering into a state of society and, if they were secured, they were secured only through human or "positive" law. The historical record is clear: every right for which American whigs contended was located in British constitutional-law theory. Every objection they raised to parliamentary power came from the British constitution and English constitutional history.

A second assumption of current scholarship that this study challenges concerns the doctrine of sovereignty. Bernard Bailyn is too dogmatic when contending that even American whigs "were ultimately obliged to admit" that "sovereign power in the nature of things could only be absolute and indivisible, that a government that did not in the end have a monopoly of the legitimate use of coercive power was no government at all."[6] In fact, the eighteenth-century legal mind started from different premises—that law was a restraint on government—and reached opposite conclusions—that legitimate government was restrained by law and that government exercising unrestrained power was illegitimate. The jurisprudence of law as restraint rather than command was an inheritance from seventeenth-century constitutionalism that was still respectable in the 1760s and would not be repudiated by British lawyers until the middle decades of the nineteenth century.

Because of the eighteenth-century theory that law was as much government's restraint as government's command, there is an assumption commonly made by today's lawyers that also needs correction. American whigs were not compelled to undermine a long-established and entrenched British doctrine of parliamentary sovereignty by concocting an extraconstitutional theory of fundamental rights superior to legislative authority. It was, rather, the other way around. The doctrine of the sovereignty of fundamental law was older than Magna Carta. The concept of legislative supremacy supported by sovereign command was relatively new in 1765 when Parliament began the revolutionary controversy by enacting the Stamp Act.[7] Mark A. Thomson was only partly correct when he observed that American whigs "never properly appreciated the evolution of British constitutional theory and practice since 1688." But then, neither did contemporary British lawyers, not even English common lawyers residenced at the Inns of Court. Arthur M. Schlesinger, Sr., was wrong to say that "the colonists would have lost their case if the decision had turned upon an impartial consideration of the legal principles involved."[8] They might have lost but not for the reason that they misunderstood the doctrine of sovereignty, as Thomson and Schlesinger supposed. The American whig case was stronger, not because it was a new law that would be codified into the United States Constitution and into the bills of rights of the states, but because it was an old law, the not yet quite passé law of Magna Carta, the Petition of Right, and the English Bill of Rights.

To say there was still validity left to the constitution of legal restraint on government, that the constitution of parliamentary sovereignty was not yet dominant, may jar historians who have thought that the constitutional issue of legislative supremacy had been set to rest long ago by Robert Livingston Schuyler's destruction of Charles Howard McIlwain's scholarship. McIlwain in *The American Revolution* sought to demonstrate that the English Parliament never had enjoyed lawful authority to legislate for crown possessions outside the realm and, therefore, the British Parliament lacked constitutional power to legislate for North America. "Few 'verdicts of history'," Schuyler answered, "seem to be more unanimous than that which finds unwarranted the view held by many Americans on the eve of the Revolution that the Parliament of Great Britain possessed no legal authority over the colonies."[9] Very good historians once accorded Schuyler the better of the argument by a wide margin, some dismissing McIlwain's case on the double grounds of bad history and bad law.[10] Today judgment is more reserved. McIlwain may be faulted for limiting his evidence to the analogy (he called it the "precedent") of Ireland, which leaves his history questionable as the Irish analogy was a minor argument in the American constitutional case. Law that is not argued in an appellate brief usually has no bearing on the judgment and McIlwain's Irish analogy was not argued. No matter how sound it might have been in theory, and its soundness is at best doubtful, it becomes irrelevant to history when it plays no role in history—when, that is, the Americans relied upon the defenses of British constitutionalism, especially custom and representation, and used the analogy of Ireland only as alternative support.

Schuyler's scholarship can also be faulted. His history may be convincing but his law will not stand the scrutiny of critical examination. His proof from medieval times, that Parliament legislated for England's earliest dominions, is of an era when Parliament acted as a council, not a legislature, and provides shaky precedent for eighteenth-century imperial legislation.[11] His main evidence came from the period after the American Revolution, from the island colonies of the Caribbean, colonies that had not questioned Parliament's right to legislate, and whose subsequent acquiescence was not—in law—relevant to the constitution of New Jersey or North Carolina in 1776.[12] Historians may continue to be more impressed by Schuyler than by McIlwain for reasons that suit their predilections. Lawyers have no choice but to dismiss Schuyler's law out of hand, and in matters of law the conclusions of lawyers deserve some weight.

There is yet another assumption about the American Revolution to be corrected. It is a frequently stated contention that the American whig constitutional case was not consistent, that it changed over time as colonial whigs either made more bold claims to legislative autonomy or moved progressively closer to asserting outright independence. By 1775 according to the thesis, the colonists would say Parliament had no right to make laws for them, but at the time of the Stamp Act crisis, the beginning of the constitutional controversy, as Robert Middlekauff asserts, they took a less extreme stand. "They had long acknowledged Parliamentary supremacy and colonial subordination without troubling to ask exactly what these grand phrases involved," Middlekauff writes. "They continued in 1765 and 1766 to profess to believe in Parliament's absolute sovereignty and in their own subordinate place."[13]

We must be careful with legal terms. A mistake in law can lead to a mistake in history. It is wrong to confound the words "sovereignty" and "supremacy." They were not often synonyms in the eighteenth century. More to the point, it should be appreciated that these terms were generally used with precision, especially in the carefully drafted petitions and resolutions of colonial assemblies stating the official position of American whigs. It is a mistake to say that in the beginning of the controversy colonial whigs acknowledged either the sovereignty of Parliament or the supremacy of Parliament or both. Attention must be paid to the dynamics of constitutional advocacy. Although there are several ways to argue any constitutional case, the most acceptable is to limit the issues and claim no more than is necessary to establish your point, at least not to assert principles that might damage your case. This was the rule American whigs followed in the revolutionary controversy. At the start, the Stamp Act crisis, when Parliament first imposed on the colonists an internal tax for the purpose of raising a revenue, the salient constitutional issue, as whigs interpreted it, was whether Parliament had authority to impose an internal tax on the North American colonies. A secondary issue—one that did not have to be stated but could be without changing the constitutional argument—was whether Parliament had authority to impose an internal or external tax upon the North American colonies for purposes of raising a revenue. Because a respectable school of eighteenth-century constitutional theory held that the right to tax was a power separate from the authority to legislate,[14] the question of the authority of Parliament to enact nontaxation statutes controlling the internal policy of the colonies did not have to be in controversy. In constitutional advocacy failure to deny does not constitute an admission of a point that is not in contention. Many students of the American Revolution have assumed that it does, that when American whigs in 1765, denying Parliament's authority to impose the Stamp Act, failed also to deny parliamentary authority of general legislation, they were conceding the constitutionality of that authority, and that later, in 1774, after the authority had been exercised and was legally in contention, they altered their constitutional argument when they disputed its validity.

There is a different perspective regarding the "consistency" of the American constitutional case against Parliament's claim to both legislative supremacy and legislative sovereignty that will be developed in the following chapters. It is the perspective of asking whether the colonial whig argument adhered to a cohesive legal argument. It will be contended that from the beginning of the revolutionary controversy until Parliament irrevocably legislated the claim to supremacy, the American assemblies followed a strategy of constitutional avoidance. The concept of constitutional avoidance can best be introduced by paying close attention to the "legal" wording of the famed Stamp Act resolutions passed by most colonial assemblies. The question to ask is not the question usually asked, whether the resolutions denied Parliament's authority to legislate, but the question a lawyer would ask, whether the resolves were worded to avoid but not concede the issue.

Virginia spoke first. The House of Burgesses limited itself to claiming that Virginians "have without Interruption enjoyed the inestimable Right of being governed by such Laws, respecting their internal Polity and Taxation, as are derived from their own Consent, and the Approbation of their Sovereign," by which was meant the Crown, not Parliament. Rhode Island was second. Its legislature asserted that the people of that colony "enjoyed the Right of being governed by their own Assembly, in the Article of Taxes and internal Police." The Pennsylvania and Connecticut assemblies voted lengthy, strong denials of Parliament's authority to impose the Stamp Act, but on the issue of legislation limited themselves to the potentially drastic but immediately inoffensive statement "[t]hat the only legal Representatives of the Inhabitants of this Province are the Persons they annually elect to serve as Members of Assembly." The Massachusetts General Court lay claim to several rights, including the right to taxation by consent, alluding to the issue of legislative supremacy only to observe that the province's inhabitants were not represented in Parliament, that representation in Parliament was "impracticable," and that "the several subordinate Powers of Legislation in *America*, were constituted, upon the Apprehensions of this Impracticability." South Carolina's Commons House of Assembly said the same as Massachusetts, adding that "the only Representatives of the People of this Province are Persons chosen therein by themselves," a statement that the New Jersey Resolves repeated a day later. New York's resolutions are of special note as they begin with what at first glance might be taken as an admission of parliamentary supremacy if not parliamentary sovereignty: "That they owe Obedience to all Acts of Parliament not inconsistent with the essential Rights and Liberties of *Englishmen*, and are intitled to the same Rights and Liberties which his Majesty's *English* Subjects both within and without the Realm have ever enjoyed." This statement concedes less than might be thought when we recall that one of the rights and liberties of Englishmen was the right to government by consent. Maryland's Stamp Act resolves said nothing of the authority to legislate, except to observe "that it cannot with any truth or Propriety be said that the Freemen of this Province of Maryland are Represented in the British Parliament." Three months later the Marylanders adopted new resolves, repeating what New York had said about obedience to all acts of Parliament consistent with the rights of Englishmen.[15]

Maryland had not been copying from New York. Rather, both were adopting the words of the Stamp Act Congress which spoke on behalf of all the colonies. The first two articles in the Declaration of the Congress had provided:

> I. That his Majesty's Subjects in these Colonies, owe the same Allegiance to the Crown of *Great-Britain*, that is owing from his Subjects born within the Realm, and all due Subordination to that August Body the Parliament of *Great-Britain*.
>
> II. That his Majesty's Liege Subjects in these Colonies, are entitled to all the inherent Rights and Liberties of his Natural born Subjects, within the Kingdom of *Great-Britain*.

The Declaration also asserted:

> IV. That the People of these Colonies are not, and from their local Circumstances cannot be, Represented in the House of Commons in *Great-Britain*.
>
> V. That the only Representatives of the People of these Colonies, are Persons chosen therein by themselves, and that no Taxes ever have been, or can be Constitutionally imposed on them, but by their respective Legislature.

These propositions and their constitutional contentions should be marked. The first aspect to consider is the concession of "all due Subordination to that August Body the Parliament of *Great-Britain*."[16] Those words have led historians to the conclusion that the Congress did not question parliamentary sovereignty, a somewhat reasonable supposition, perhaps, had the Declaration been drafted by theoretical scholars, not by practical men intent on avoiding constitutional pitfalls. If it had been drafted by lawyers such as James Otis and John Dickinson, as we are told it was, they can be read as the words of lawyers skirting a constitutional issue that did not have to be raised. The same was true of the Stamp Act Congress's assertion that only representatives elected by the colonists could constitutionally tax Americans. It is a misreading of a constitutional argument to suppose that because the authority to legislate was not proscribed along with the authority to tax, that the Stamp Act Congress was conceding to Parliament the right to enact local statutes for purposes of colonial police regulation.

The interpretation of the Stamp Act Congress's Declaration written by William Knox deserves special attention as he was the subminister in the British administration looked to as an expert on American constitutional affairs. As a ministerial writer, it was his practice to misrepresent American arguments in order to refute them. "The title of *August Body*," he complained, "is another subterfuge for *seeming* to respect its authority, whilst they *mean* to disavow it." That was precisely what the Stamp Act Congress had not meant. The idea of the Declaration was neither to avow nor disavow parliamentary authority, but to avow a due subordination to customary constitutional practices.[17]

Some colonists worried that even the careful phrases of the Stamp Act Congress might be misunderstood or misrepresented. South Carolina's Commons House of Assembly, adopting the Congress's resolves, omitted the phrase "due subordination," explaining to its agent that in "making Laws for our own internal government or police we can by no means allow our Provincial legislatures to be subordinate to any legislative power on earth."[18] Such caution was unnecessary. The concept "due subordination" became common formulae for statements of the American constitutional understanding regarding Parliament's authority to legislate. In May 1766, Boston voters instructed their representatives "openly [to] profess . . a constitutional subordination to parliament," qualifying the expression after passage of the Townshend duties to "a reverence and due subordination to the British Parliament as the supreme Legislative in all cases of necessity, for the preservation of the whole Empire." By saying "subordination" the voters in both instances were not instructing their representatives to retreat from or add to the constitutional doctrine they had adopted in October 1765 when the Massachusetts House told Governor Francis Bernard that "[t]he parliament has a right to make all laws within the limits of their [Parliament's] own constitution."[19]

It was good polemics for Knox, writing for the ministry, to claim that "[t]he Colonies conceive the parliament to have no right to make laws for them; and due obedience to parliament is therefore, in their apprehension, no obedience at all." From Knox's perspective of the constitution, it was not obedience. Whether that perspective was correct was the salient constitutional issue leading to the American Revolution and for the moment is beside the point. What is of immediate interest is the constitutional strategy of the members of the Massachusetts House. We must remember it was a constitution they were arguing, the same constitution that the two houses of Parliament had argued in March 1642 when asking Charles I to live in London. "[F]or this we shall return to you," they pledged, "our Lives, Fortunes, and uttermost Endeavours to support your Majesty, your just Sovereignty and Power over us." The two houses had just promulgated the Militia Ordinance, putting Parliament in a state of war with the king, yet the Lords and Commons meant what they said just as the Massachusetts House would mean what it said: they would support Charles I's "Sovereignty and Power over us"—in a constitutional way.[20]

John Dickinson was speaking constitutionally when he wrote that the North American colonists were "as much dependent on Great-Britain, as a perfectly free people can be on another." "Was it really possible," Edward Countryman has asked, "to be both dependent and free at the same time?" There are several constitutional ways to answer "yes" which this book will explore, including "dependence" based on customary procedures rather than sovereign, unchecked, discretionary will and pleasure. Edmund S. Morgan had a more political, pragmatic answer. "The Stamp Act Congress," he wrote, "has frequently been treated by historians as a rather conservative body of men, possibly because it acknowledged 'all due subordination' to Parliament. But as conservatives at the time recognized, this phrase was an empty one unless you stated what subordination was due."[21]

It is really not significant that there was an occasional individual who, in a sermon, pamphlet, or letter, said that Parliament was not only supreme in imperial affairs but legislatively sovereign over the colonies in matters of police, or who thought that the only quarrel with parliamentary authority was about taxation.[22] Neither the British Parliament nor the British administration misunderstood that the authority to legislate was the issue in controversy, even when that issue was not directly asserted by the colonial whigs, although both sometimes ignored it or pretended to believe it could be limited to the authority to tax. Certainly imperial officials appreciated what the Americans were saying and reported to London that the issue was parliamentary authority to legislate as well as to tax.[23] It is well known that Parliament understood the message and acted on it. That was why colonial petitions against the Stamp Act were not read in the two houses: in the view of a majority of the members the petitions disputed the authority of Parliament.[24] Colonial assembly petitions were also denounced by the Board of Trade as exhibiting "the most indecent disrespect to the Legislature of Great Britain," and voted by the Privy Council "a Matter of the utmost Importance to the Kingdom, and the Legislature of Great Britain and of too high a

Nature for the Determination of your Majesty in your privy Council and is proper only for the Consideration of parliament."[25]

Another aspect of the colonial whig argument understood by both Parliament and administration was the need for the Americans to avoid the constitutional issue. At least the issue was better understood and its importance was better appreciated than it has been in the twentieth century. There is no other part of the constitutional controversy so little heeded in the historical literature. There were, it is true, also occasions when British officials got careless and apparently forgot it. One has to wonder what Francis Bernard was thinking of when he raised the constitutional issue of legislative authority with Massachusetts legislators in September 1765. "I trust that the supremacy of that Parliament, over all the members of their wide and diffused empire, never was and never will be denied within these walls," the governor told the General Court. "This House, sir," the representatives replied, "has too great a reverence for the supreme legislature of the nation, to question its just authority: It by no means appertains to us to presume to adjust the boundaries of the power of Parliament; but boundaries there undoubtedly are." Almost ten years later, in the last official attempt at reconciliation by an American legislature before the Continental Congress met and began to speak for all the colonies, the New York General Assembly took a stab at locating those boundaries. "Resolved . . . that his Majesty's subjects in this colony owe obedience to all the acts of parliament calculated for the general weal of the whole empire, and the due regulation of the trade and the commerce thereof, and not inconsistent with the essential rights and liberties of Englishmen, to which they are equally entitled with their fellow subjects in Great Britain." These "boundaries" will strike twentieth-century readers as imprecise —evasive. In truth, for those who were thinking of constitutional law and not economic determinism or nationalism, they were constitutionally bold. It is simply not accurate to say that colonial leaders were "unwilling" to consider the issue of parliamentary supremacy prior to 1774. It was, rather—and this is one of the most important conclusions to be developed in future chapters—too risky constitutionally, until, of course, the "coercive" legislation enacted that year by the British Parliament forced them to the issue. Even then, pamphleteers and newspaper theorists might draw boundaries, but, as the New York legislators showed, American assemblies hesitated.[26]

There are also boundaries to this study deserving brief mention so the contours of argument are not misunderstood. One boundary is defined by the word "constitutional." This is a constitutional history of the American Revolution, not a legal history. The legal history of the American

Revolution has not yet been written. The boundaries between eighteenth-century legal and constitutional history are a bit imprecise in a few areas but otherwise generally marked and may be clarified by a brief look at the British Mutiny Act for North America. In legal history interest in the Mutiny Act is mainly limited to Massachusetts Bay and concerns the problem of implementing the provisions of the act for quartering troops. Local colonial law made enforcement of Parliament's intentions very difficult, at times, even impossible.[27] The Mutiny Act raises different issues in constitutional history, such as parliamentary authority to quarter troops in North America and the suspension of the New York General Assembly for defying Parliament's authority.

As a constitutional history of the American Revolution is not a legal history, so too it is not a political history. Students looking for discussion of political matters will be disappointed to find only constitutional arguments. A constitutional history that restricts itself to constitutionalism is concerned with putative legal principle, procedure, precedent, and custom, not with legislative policy, governmental discretion, or the implementation of party programs. Ian Christie inadvertently made the distinction clear when urging historians to admit the reasonableness of British imperial policy. Alexander Hamilton, John Jay, and James Madison, he contended, proved that British imperial taxation had been reasonable when they repeated in the *Federalist Papers* many of George Grenville's arguments on behalf of the Stamp Act, and, in Hamilton's case, also acknowledged that revenue raised from voluntary requisitions, a scheme of imperial "taxation" that had been acceptable to American whigs, would have been unfair. Christie may be right, but only to the extent that the American whigs had objected to imperial taxation for purposes of revenue on political not constitutional grounds. In fact, American whigs did not say that a stamp tax or customs duties were unfair methods of taxation, or that the imperial requisition system was a fair method. They said that imperial taxes for purposes of revenue, however reasonable, were unprecedented and contrary to constitutional custom established both by historical practice and by certain expressed or implied contracts. The imperial requisition system, whether fair or unfair, was sanctioned by custom and, therefore, constitutional.[28]

A related illustration is the claim that colonial assemblies were hypocrites for objecting to taxation without representation when undertaken by Parliament, while themselves taxing people within the colonies who could not vote and hence were not represented. American whigs, however, objected to taxation without representation on British constitutional grounds. It was the British constitution, not the American constitutions that proscribed taxation without representation. American whigs were protesting not unreasonableness, but inequality, violation of precedent, and departure from English and British constitutional custom.

The quarrel of the constitutional historian with the political historian of the American Revolution is not about error but perception. Events are interpreted differently. A subtle instance is provided by Bernhard Knollenberg's argument that the British ministry's mistake was to have legislated changes in the imperial system. "[T]o act unilaterally, to change a constitutional relationship established for over a century without prior effort to negotiate a settlement and without any offer of compensation or assurance against future exploitation, was high-handed, reckless and unjust."[29] The constitutionalist's objection to Knollenberg's assertion concerns its implication that the colonial complaint was essentially political—a problem of the implementation of policy or how policy was determined. In fact, the colonial complaint was not political but constitutional. American whigs believed their security "against future exploitation" lay not in better political consultation but in constitutional safeguards, primarily by avoiding departures from constitutional custom and violations of constitutional precedent.

The distinctions that have been drawn concern the eighteenth-century British constitution, not those of the nineteenth or twentieth centuries. Political history of eighteenth-century Great Britain deals with choice and policy, whether by a representative body or another government group, making decisions and formulating programs based on the influence of interests, the immediate needs of current circumstances, or judgment concerning the general welfare. Eighteenth-century British constitutional history finds choices based on adherence to more abstract principle, to some criteria of values beyond the caprice of majority vote or the will of those who hold power: on arguments of recognized legal procedures, discernible precedents, acknowledged analogies, shared traditions, and established custom.

A final caution must be mentioned. This constitutional history is concerned only with the question of Parliament's authority to bind the North American colonies by legislation. It is not concerned with that aspect of parliamentary authority that many eighteenth-century constitutional theorists separated from the authority to legislate, the authority to tax. Taxation, with all the constitutional issues raised by the controversies of the Stamp Act, the Townshend duties, and the tea tax—the imperial contract, the commercial contract, the taxation-legislation dichotomy, the precedents of Durham and Chester—is not discussed in this study.[30] Also not part of the constitutional dispute over Parliament's authority to legislate were all the rights that American whigs claimed were constitutionally protected from parliamentary, prerogative, or imperial power:

the jury right, the rights to property, to security, and to enjoy an equality of rights, and the constitutional theories of contract, migration, purchase, inheritance, and ownership upon which the English, Scots, Welsh, Irish, and Americans based their claim to those rights.[31] Even these three topics of authority—the authority to tax, the authority of rights, and the authority to legislate—do not exhaust the issues that must be studied to complete a history of the American Revolution's constitutional controversy. Also not covered in this volume are matters more properly dealt with by examining the authority to govern, including the constitutionality of executive instructions to colonial governors, the disagreement over judicial tenure, and the authority of colonial assemblies to legislate. The right of Pennsylvania or North Carolina to legislate for themselves was quite a different constitutional issue than the authority of Parliament to legislate for Pennsylvania or North Carolina.

CHAPTER ONE

CULTURE OF CONSTITUTIONALISM

Before taking up the main topic of this book, the constitutionality of direct parliamentary legislation for the North American colonies, there are two preliminary points that deserve attention if we are to understand the issue of the authority to legislate as it was understood in the eighteenth century. The first, mentioned but not explained in the introduction, is that a distinction was clearly drawn in the eighteenth century between law and politics, a distinction that students of the American Revolution would do well to heed. The second is that eighteenth-century political rhetoric was, to a remarkable extent, phrased in the vocabulary of law, a fact students of the American Revolution can ignore at the risk of misunderstanding what was said. These points, the political culture of constitutionalism and the constitutional language of politics, are the subjects of this chapter.

E. P. Thompson has reminded scholars of the extent to which events in the eighteenth century were guided by constitutionalism. "I am insisting only upon the obvious point, which some modern Marxists have overlooked," he wrote of eighteenth-century common law, "that there is a difference between arbitrary power and the rule of law." Everything was not will, choice, policy, or result. The "rule of law," Thompson believed, meant "the imposing of effective inhibitions upon power and the defence of the citizen from power's all-intrusive claims."[1] As a measure of what Thompson meant—that constitutional values and legal fears helped determine the course of events—consider that constitutional values and fear of military power restrained the British from locating barracks in England and Wales until the last decade of the eighteenth century, constitutional values and fear of governmental power delayed the creation of a uniformed, professional police force until well into the nineteenth century, and constitutional values and fear of executive power was responsible for retaining the archaic process of private felony prosecutions until the twentieth century.[2]

There are two clues to the eighteenth-century constitutional mind that too often have been overlooked: methodology and language. The methodology can be summed up in two words, precedent and custom: adherence to precedent and conformity to custom. "[A]ll judgments derive their obligatory quality from a supposed conformity with pre-existing laws," an anonymous pamphleteer reminded the duke of Grafton in 1770.[3] He was, of course, describing the methodology of the judiciary, marking a distinction between judicial power and legislative power that would belong even more to the nineteenth century than to the age of the American Revolution. The legislature, Edmund Burke explained, "has no reference to any *rule*." It was as likely to be guided by interest, will, power, party, or result as by doctrine, analogy, precedent, principle, or custom. A judge, by contrast, should not arrive at a judgment by making a policy choice between interests, but "upon a fixed Rule, of which he has not the making, but singly and solely the *application* to the Case. The very Idea of Law [is] to exclude discretion in the judge."[4]

Today we think the principle that Burke was defending is primarily judicial. Fear of discretionary power had a wider reach in the eighteenth century. The freeholders of England's Middlesex County were speaking as eighteenth-century constitutionalists who wanted executive authority restrained when they complained to George III that evil advisors came between him and the people. Then, in two sentences, they summed up the constitutional principle that would guide American whigs in their opposition to the authority of Parliament to bind them by legislation.

> For this wicked purpose they have introduced in every part of the administration of our once happy and legal constitution a certain unlimitted and indefinite discretionary power, the prevention of which is the sole aim of all our laws, and was the sole cause of all those disturbances and revolutions, which formerly distracted this unhappy country. For our ancestors by their own fatal experience

well knew that in a state, where discretion begins, law, liberty and
safety end.

That statement concisely summarizes the essential elements of eighteenth-
century constitutionalism. If the argument does not make sense today,
we should remember that discretion in the context of the Middlesex petition meant policy choices by executive will and pleasure. "Law, liberty
and safety" meant the rule of law, which was then, unlike now, as much
the opposite of legislative discretion as it was of executive or judicial
discretion. It is a central argument of this book that most eighteenth-
century English-speaking political theorists thought the legislature restrained by the same constitutionalism that restrained the judiciary for
Edmund Burke and which the Middlesex freeholders hoped restrained
the executive.[5]

Language is the second overlooked clue to eighteenth-century constitutional thought. Writing of parliamentary power, George G. Suggs,
Jr. recently concluded that "In challenging the century-long practice of
colonial assemblies to tax their own residents and generally to govern
their own domestic affairs," the parliamentary legislation enacted between 1763 and 1776 that will be discussed in this book, "threatened the
progressive and evolutionary development of nearly 150 years of colonial
self-government."[6] This statement cannot be faulted as a historian's conclusion. It is still fair to ask, however, how much it reflects the words and
thoughts of American whigs. Read their resolutions, petitions, and protests and you will not find them talking of a threat to "the progressive and
evolutionary development of nearly 150 years of colonial self-government." American whigs, rather, objected to a new definition of law that
threatened to end 150 years of constitutional custom. To preserve it they
practiced the methodology of their traditional law ways, citing precedents, protesting innovations, and pleading prescription. Of course,
defense of self-government was a concern. What deserves as much attention is that security of constitutionalism through the rule of law provided
the vocabulary for that defense.

"[L]egalism . . . prevaded the political thought of England at the
time," Sheldon S. Wolin has written of the eighteenth century, stating a
truism as applicable to most of Great Britain and the North American
colonies as to England. "The dominant tendency was to argue issues like
electoral reform, representation, and colonial matters on the basis of law
and precedent. The influence of Hardwicke, Mansfield, and Blackstone
symbolized the alliance which had sprung up between law and politics."
We discover what Wolin meant not just in the language of lawyers and

legislators arguing constitutional points, but of farmers and schoolmasters. Dover, New Hampshire, was a small agricultural community in 1774 when its voters stated their objection against the authority of Parliament to legislate for them in terms of equality, the original contract, the British constitution, and the rule of law by consent. "Why the KING'S Subjects in Great-Britain should frame Laws for his Subjects in America, rather than the reverse, we cannot well conceive," Dover's town meeting resolved, "as we do not admit it to be drawn from any PACT made by our Ancestors, or from the Nature of the British Constitution, which makes Representation essential to Taxation." Samuel Kemp, a schoolmaster in Caroline County, Virginia, cited several other contracts in addition to the original contract when, in 1775, he publicized his opposition to "the ministerial Measures against the Rights and Liberties of America."

> Our Forefathers left *England* because they could not submit to unconstitutional arbitrary Exertions of Power; they chose rather to trust themselves with Beasts and Savages than with *Englishmen*, who had resigned themselves to Slavery. Almighty God protected them whenever they were in Danger; he was a present Help to them; under his Guardianship, what was then a howling Wilderness is now become a fruitful Field; the Labour and Blood of our Ancestors have enriched the Soil of this Country; they undauntedly exposed themselves to every Kind of Hardship, and bravely met Death in the high Places of the Field, that they might secure to us a quiet Possession of those Rights and Liberties, which, as Men, as *Englishmen*, and as Christians, they knew we were entitled to.[7]

The legal premises upon which Kemp based "the Rights and Liberties of America" were universally known and argued throughout whig North America. They included "the authority of migration" (with three supporting concepts, "the expectation of migration," "the purpose of migration," and escape from "slavery") and the "migration purchase" which meant a physical purchase through hardship, labor, or blood, either in person or by an ancestor.[8]

Perhaps the word Wolin used, "legalism," is too narrow in its connotations. Constitutionalism may be more accurate: a normative culture of constitutionalism uniting the eighteenth-century English-speaking world on both sides of the Atlantic Ocean. Caleb Evans, a dissenting British clergyman, explained the cultural heritage of the legal language which he shared with New Hampshire farmers and with that Virginia schoolmaster when, supporting Americans against parliamentary taxation, he altered the usual perspective and stated the issue in terms not of colonial but British rights.

Suppose the house of Lords were to pass a money-bill independent of the Commons, and the king should give his assent to it;—would the question be whether the bill were, simply considered, *reasonable*? Whether the tax imposed by it were *equitable*? Whether there was not a necessity that the king should have *a great revenue* to support the navy, army, and so forth? No, sir, but the previous grand question would be, is not this *unconstitutional*? . . . And if so, were it but a peppercorn that was demanded, no man that deserves the name of a BRITON, would pay it, unless compelled. However *easy* the payment might be, it would be establishing a destructive precedent, it would be throwing down the barriers betwixt liberty and slavery, and *stabbing*, as far as in us lay, the vitals of the constitution.[9]

More was at stake than the principle of taxation by representation. The vitals being stabbed were the entire conceptual framework of constitutional restraint, the constitutionalism vesting in the British and American people security in their civil rights and liberties as well as in their property.

CONSTITUTIONALISM OF POLITICS

It is not irrelevant to consider how the rhetoric of law pervaded the politics of the eighteenth century. That language after all, will provide much of the evidence for the subsequent chapters of this book. The purpose of this section is to underscore the methodology as it has not always been appreciated by scholars of the American Revolution.

It is not claimed that political language of the eighteenth century was fundamentally different from ours. The argument is that words, expressions, and manners of thought that today are heard only in common-law courts, particularly in appellate courts, in the eighteenth century saturated debates in the two houses of Parliament, and provided the dominant methodology of dispute in the polemical political pamphlets on both sides of the Atlantic. What is today the language of constitutionalism intruded upon what then was the language of politics. It was as much the practice of members of the House of Lords or the House of Commons, when urging passage of a statute or adoption of a political program, to cite precedent, apply doctrine, draw analogy, rely on custom, and discuss principle as it was to promote interest, exercise discretion, plea necessity, urge expediency, or command result. To borrow from the combined legal-political language of that time, it was as common to argue for the passage of legislation for reasons of "right" as for reasons of "power."

Perhaps the most famous instances of constitutional language and thought formulating parliamentary debate during the American Revolution controversy, were the passage and repeal of the Stamp Act, discussed elsewhere. [10] The technique can be outlined here by considering another, more easily summarized parliamentary event, the expulsion of John Wilkes from membership in the House of Commons. It deserves the attention of students of the American Revolution as it tells so much about the political language of the era and the imperspicuity of constitutional thought. Falling between the customary constitution of the past and the arbitrary constitution of the future, Wilkes's expulsion was argued as a constitutional matter in both the House of Commons and the press, yet the outcome was decided not by constitutionalism but by power. As an exercise of raw political authority, Wilkes's expulsion presaged the nineteenth-century British constitution, although to a large degree, the men expelling Wilkes spoke and reasoned as if they were deliberating under the balanced constitution of restrained power that they had learned to cherish in their youth.

The legal excuse for expelling John Wilkes from the House of Commons was that he had been convicted of crime. The real cause was political: he had offended the king. Reelected to the House by the county of Middlesex, he was expelled a second time. Again reelected, he was again expelled, declared "incapable" of reelection, and the candidate whom he soundly outpolled was ruled to have been elected in his place.

The Wilkes case was argued both in and out of Parliament on both political and constitutional premises, sometimes both in a single paragraph. An anonymous pamphleteer made a political point when complaining that the expulsion served "to gratify the rancorous resentment of an unforgiving minion." Two pages later the author raised a legal complaint when he asserted that "it is the very essence of the representation-principle, that the right of election be controulable only by the law of the land: and that even parliament itself hath not a power to make a law destructive of the liberties of the people." Even those justifying the expulsion of Wilkes as an exercise of "power" tended to put their case in terms of "right," relying on legal concepts such a "forfeiture" or wilful intent. The right of electors to select their own representative by a majority vote was seldom questioned on grounds of Parliament's sovereign power. The contention rather was that "the people of Middlesex forfeited their right of electing a certain part of the representative body, when they chose a profligate, blaspheming bankrupt," or, as the House of Commons resolved, "that Mr. Wilkes having been repeatedly expelled the House, and declared incapable of being elected to sit in this present Parliament, the freeholders, who voted for him, had wilfully and knowingly thrown away their votes, as effectually as if they had voted for a dead person."[11]

In the Commons the legal quality of the debate emerged as members on both sides of the question argued judicial cases from the 1620s and 1640s as if they were of yesterday. Historians might doubt the relevance, not common lawyers or eighteenth-century constitutionalists for whom law was set in a timeless frame. As legal authority, precedents from the Middle Ages were as valid as were precedents of just a year or two ago. A summary in the popular press of a speech by George Grenville opposing Wilkes's expulsion provides a glance at the eighteenth-century legal mind wandering through different reigns and several decades.

> Mr. *Grenville* made, this day, one of the best speeches that had been made in the House of Commons for many years. He shewed, from history, that the vote of the House of Lords respecting one of their own members, had been considered by the King's-bench as null and void, because contrary to law; and that the Judges had not been punished by the Lords for so doing (this was the case of lord Banbury, Holt chief justice). He then shewed, that in the case of Ashby and White, a vote of the House of Commons, contrary to law, had been disregarded by the courts below; and, from the premises, concluded, that a vote of the House might and did bind the House, the session it was made; but, out of the House, except in matters of privilege, had no effect on the people. If the ministry, he said, will take such headstrong measures, the vengeance of a deluded, injured people, must fall on them.

Grenville spoke April 1769. The case of the earl of Banbury had been decided in 1694. *Ashby* v. *White* was a 1703 decision.[12] Grenville's use of these old cases tells us why they were relevant. He did not treat them as historical events, place them in the context of the times when they had been litigated, or try to relate them to the political or historical circumstances of the Wilkes affair. He cited them as precedents, as authority, as timeless rather than as belonging to a historical epoch, of the same meaning and the same authority whether they had occurred yesterday or three hundred years ago.

There were a variety of legal positions from which political commentators of the day looked at the Wilkes expulsion. Grenville supposed the Commons's mistake was not to separate its judicial from its legislative functions. A pamphlet that many contemporaries thought written by William Dowdeswell, leader of the Rockinghamites in the House, but which now is attributed to a Mr. Downley, suggested that the tension was between two incompatible theories of law.

> If I were to admit this power in any case, it should be where the House exercises a criminal jurisdiction in offences properly within

the cognisance of the House, and punishes *at its discretion*. If, in support of such a case, I saw a strong uniform custom from the earliest times, I might lament the uncertainty of human discretion, which, while it punished the offender, was inattentive to the rights of the innocent. But I might deem myself precluded *now* from disputing the validity of such a custom, and might hold it safer to be consistent, and *"stare super vias antiquas,"* than to render every thing uncertain by departing from an established custom. Where the House has a power to punish *at its discretion*, it is a desirable thing that the limits of that power should be fixed by a known and well-established usage.

Today, we would think Dowdeswell or Downley contradictory, that there cannot be "a power" limited by usage that "punishes *at its discretion.*" What he said, however, was standard eighteenth-century constitutional theory, repeated over and over in parliamentary debates and polemical pamphlets, without anyone questioning the argument. It made more sense in the latter half of the eighteenth century than it does now. There were too many people then who had been educated in the values and glory of the seventeenth-century constitution of customary constraints, who could not bring themselves to admit that they lived under what we can recognize as the nineteenth-century constitution of arbitrary sovereign coercion.[13]

Rather than face constitutional reality, Dowdeswell looked backward to an earlier constitutional law, when he moved "that this House, in the exercise of its Judicature in Matters of Election, is bound to judge according to the Law of the Land, and the known and established Law and Custom of Parliament, which is part thereof." He believed the power of the Commons could be "set . . . on legal grounds" if the qualifications of members were fixed. To be constitutionally secure, these qualifications did not have to be precisely defined. It was sufficient if they were "set" by the rule of law. That was the tactic advanced by "Mr. Downley" in the pamphlet contemporaries credited to Dowdeswell, contending that they were defined by usage, custom, precedent, and analogy: "They are founded in good sense; analogous to the like restraints adjudged in other cases by the courts of law; and confirmed by usage. They are *not occasional, but fixed: to rule and govern* the question as it shall arise; not to *start up* on a sudden, and *shift from side to side*, as the caprice of the day or the fluctuation of party shall direct."[14]

Dowdeswell and Downley's law was not hopelessly anachronistic. The House of Commons alone, not the sovereign Parliament of king, Lords, and Commons had expelled Wilkes, and it was still creditable to argue that the Commons, when acting as one house, was bound by the rule of law. The bell had begun to toll for that theory of law, however. Opposing Dowdeswell's motion was a leading spokesman for the new constitution of sovereign discretion and his law carried the day. "[T]his House is competent in the case of elections," Sir William Blackstone told the Commons, "there is no appeal from its competence to the law of the land. There are cases in which the other House is competent: if the House of Lords . . . should determine contrary to the law of the land, what is the remedy?" Blackstone may have confused sovereignty over the law of the land with failure of appeal, but no matter. People knew that either way it amounted to what in the eighteenth century was called arbitrary power, and many, if not most constitutional theorists and lawyers, did not like it. The Commons now claimed "an exclusive jurisdiction *without appeal in all* matters of election," the duke of Grafton was warned. It was a power "alarming because uncontroulable." Moreover, the Wilkes expulsion violated the principle that "all judgments derive their obligatory quality from a supposed conformity with pre-existing laws." True enough, but one of the differences between the old and the new constitutionalisms was that the rule of law would no longer control.[15]

Many members of the Commons supporting Wilkes had rallied to the cause of a man they personally detested. Namierites might tell us it was politics. The participants who tell us anything say they were motivated by the rule of law and adherence to the old constitution of restraint. The issue at bar, Grenville insisted, was "whether it is conformable to the usage and law of parliament, to the practice of any other court of justice in the kingdom, or to the unalterable principles of natural equity; or whether it is a new and dangerous mode of proceeding, unsupported by any precedent or example in the Journals of parliament, or the records of any other court, calculated merely to serve a present purpose." "Mr. Wilkes's disqualification," Downley agreed, "was supported by *no custom*, nor by any *statute*; deriving its authority from a resolution of the House of Commons *only*, and that resolution taken *extrajudicially*, without hearing the parties." Forty-seven members of the House of Lords, an unusually large number, felt strongly enough to draft a protest—not in defense of John Wilkes, but in defense of the law of the land. It tells us much about constitutionalism in the 1760s that they were upset by the novel Blackstonian thesis that, no matter the ruling, if there is no appeal, that ruling is law.

> [W]e conceive ourselves called upon to give that proposition the strongest negative; for, if admitted, the law of the land (by which all courts of judicature, without exception, are equally bound to proceed) is at once overturned and resolved into the will and pleasure of

a majority of one House of Parliament, who, in assuming it, assume a power to over-rule at pleasure the fundamental right of election, which the constitution has placed in other hands, those of their constituents.

The dissentient lords were doing more than protesting the passing of the constitution of the rule of law. They did not realize it, but they were protesting the constitution of sovereign legislative authority against which American whigs would soon rebel.[16]

LANGUAGE OF CONSTITUTIONALISM

From the perspective of history the Wilkes controversy appears to delineate the eighteenth-century culture of constitutionalism. From the perspective of constitutional law, however, it is faulty. It involved, after all, only one of the two houses of Parliament. In fact, the Wilkes debate did not, properly speaking, concern legislation, but a situation in which the members of the House of Commons were both making new rules for the qualifications of members and applying those rules ex post facto to a particular member. It was, in other words, a process that can be analogized to the adjudication of a case of "first instance," making the fact less surprising that debate in the House concerned questions of "right" as well as decisions of "power."

More apt instances of the language of constitutionalism would be debates on a bill enacted by both houses of Parliament, regular legislation or what the eighteenth century called an act of "power," a command of the sovereign to be obeyed as "law." The best illustrations for our purposes are furnished by the Coercive Acts passed by the houses of Parliament in 1774. The most important legislation of the American Revolution controversy, the Coercive Acts were the strongest assertion by Parliament of its claim to the constitutional authority to legislate for the colonies in all cases whatsoever. They were the statutes promulgated in reaction to the Boston Tea Party when Massachusetts whigs, to prevent dutible tea being entered at the customs house, boarded a ship in the harbor and destroyed the tea.

Only two of the Coercive Acts need be considered, the Port of Boston Act closing Boston's harbor to all commercial business until the town paid for the tea, and the Massachusetts Government Act altering the charter of Massachusetts Bay in some principal respects. We are not here concerned with the purposes or provisions of these acts. They will be discussed together with the other Coercive Acts in another volume in this series, *The Authority of Law.* For the moment our attention is confined to the language and concepts with which the political and legal aspects of the two bills were debated both before and just after being enacted into law.

Legal and constitutional problems shaped the Port of Boston Bill. A legal problem was that the people who had staged the Boston Tea Party were not known and not even a sovereign Parliament could order prosecutions of unidentified culprits. The alternative was to punish the entire town as a corporate unit and the simplest way to do that was to close the harbor to commerce by royal proclamation. That procedure, however, raised a constitutional issue: whether the royal prerogative could constitutionally do the job. After first thinking it could, the cabinet backed away and decided that Boston had to be dealt with through the more cumbersome method of legislation.[17] An act of Parliament, the administration knew, would raise other constitutional issues about power, process, and legislative function. "The Parliament," Boston's Committee of Correspondence charged, had undertaken "to try, condemn, and by an act, to punish them [the inhabitants of Boston] unheard; which would have been in violation of natural justice, even if they had an acknowledged jurisdiction." It was a matter of confounding what was properly judicial with what was unconstitutionally legislative, Connecticut's House of Representatives resolved. The Port of Boston Act put the "lives, liberties and property" of every American "at the mercy of a tribunal, where innocence may be punished upon accusation and evidence of wicked men, without defence, and even without knowing the accuser."[18]

A similar constitutional case was made against the Massachusetts Government Act. "All charters should be proceeded against by *Quo Warranto*," William Dowdeswell asserted, also meaning that reform of the Massachusetts charter was properly judicial and not properly legislative.[19] It was a contention of constitutional law that a twentieth-century American understands, but which would not be made in a twentieth-century British Parliament. When Prime Minister Edward Heath, in 1972, told the House of Commons that he intended to suspend the Stormont Parliament and rule Northern Ireland directly from London, it is doubtful if any member of Parliament thought of judicial process.[20] True, the government of Northern Ireland rested on parliamentary legislation, not on royal or legislative charter. That distinction would have been irrelevant in the eighteenth century, however, as the doctrine of vested rights based on prescriptive usage would have allowed Northern Ireland to argue, as it was argued on behalf of Massachusetts in 1774, that there was a "peculiar impropriety . . . of condemning the colony, and taking away its charter without any form of process."[21] "[C]harters by government were sacred things," Sir George Savile had contended in the House of Commons, "and are only to be taken away by a due course of law, either as a punishment for an offence, or for a breach of the contract, and that can only be by evidence of the facts."[22] No one in 1972 said anything like that to Prime Minster Heath.

The point to heed is not just that different arguments were made in 1774 than would be made in 1974 or that there was disagreement about constitutional law and the proper division of authority. What also deserves attention is the degree that issues of law and even jurisprudence permeated the entire debate. Both sides raised questions of law and answered with defenses of law. This was so even for those saying that Parliament had the constitutional right to do as it pleased, and who today would discuss only how to exercise power, not whether power to legislate was constitutional. "I am sorry," George Byng complained raising one issue in the House of Commons, "to find that we are not now proceeding in our judicial capacity, but in our legislative one; I could wish that we instilled into the measure more judgment, and less of our power." He meant that when it came to punishing Boston and placing imperial controls on Massachusetts Bay, that Parliament, in the words of Lord John Cavendish, was "too much like judge and party to be without great care impartial." Remarkably, such questions of procedure consumed more of the reported debates than did discussion of the administration's political policy. "A court of law would not do as this House has done," Dowdeswell complained. "No, Sir, courts of law will not stir without having the parties before them." John St. John, the barrister, playwright, and placeman, who opposed any concessions to the colonists, probably gave the most authoritative answer based on the concept of legislative power. "The honourable gentleman said that, unsummoned, unheard, in one day they [the people of Massachusetts] are to lose their constitution," he replied. "What, Sir, is this but a gross misunderstanding of the very nature of Parliamentary proceedings? Are we sitting here, Sir, like judges in a court of law? Or is this a great, legislative proceeding founded on political necessity? Will it be said, that formerly when they lost their charter [in 1684], they were summoned [to the Chancery Court]? That, Sir, was a very different proceeding. That was a proceeding by *scire facias*, from the petty bag, and judgment was had in Chancery." St. John's law makes good sense in the twentieth century, but he belonged to the eighteenth century, and although his understanding of constitutional law told him that reform of the Massachusetts charter was within Parliament's competence, he did not think it a simple matter of power without reservations of right. "I grant," he concluded, "that this House ought always to govern itself, by those rules of proceeding in hearing the parties which prevail in the courts below, wherever those rules are essential to justice." It was just that Massachusetts could not have justice "in this case" "without a delay dangerous to the peace of the country." Even as political necessity took precedent over due process, claims of procedure were considered.[23]

The political-legal point was argued as it would have been in a court of law. "Every punishment is unjust that is inflicted on a party unheard," Edmund Burke insisted. "The distance of the party is no argument for not hearing." "[T]he parties should be heard, though even at a twelve-month hence," Sir George Yonge, member for Honiton, agreed. He also concurred with St. John that necessity created an exception but disagreed about how to determine necessity. St. John thought delay "dangerous to the peace of the country" proved necessity. Yonge thought the emergency had to be much more serious. "Nothing," he told the Commons, "but *fatal* necessity can countenance this measure."[24]

Sir George Savile, member for Yorkshire and one of the most persistent spokesmen for the political opposition, argued that there were much stronger grounds for establishing Massachusetts' right to be heard than by drawing analogies to common-law practice. Just to put vested rights in jeopardy, he said, required judicial process. "The case is brought to a short issue, whether this is a property," he explained. "Whether a charter is property. . . . If a property, they have a right to be heard." It did not matter whether the bill was primarily to punish or primarily to reform the government of the colony. "No charter rights should be invaded or taken away from any man or men without being admitted to a defence."[25] The members of Parliament were not only concerned with the property of vested charter rights. There was also extensive debate whether closing Boston's harbor was an unconstitutional taking of the private property in wharves, warehouses, ships, and other items of business owned by Boston merchants.

On the surface the debate seemed to be whether Boston and Massachusetts should be given the opportunity to defend themselves. In fact, it was largely a disagreement about parliamentary power and supremacy. It is possible that the former colonial secretary, Henry Seymour Conway, thought he was stating an immutable principle of law when he claimed that, "Parliament cannot break into a right without hearing the parties." "This measure before us," Savile said of the Massachusetts Government Bill, "seems to be a most extraordinary exertion of legislative power."[26] The distinction may have been stated most strongly in the protest of dissenting lords against the Bill when speaking of Parliament not as a legislature but as a judiciary that should conform to the procedures of "the courts below." "Before it can be pretended, that those rights of the colony of Massachusett's-bay . . . could with propriety be taken away," the dissentient lords contended, "notice of this adverse proceeding ought to have been given to the parties affected; and they ought to have been heard in their own defence. Such a principle of proceeding would have been inviolably observed in the courts below. . . . When therefore the *magnitude* of such a cause transfers it from the cognizance of the inferior courts, to the high judicature of parliament, the Lords are so far from being authorised to reject this equitable principle, that we are bound to an extraordinary and religious strictness in the observance of it."[27]

It may be impossible today to understand just how much this language reflected the way that members of Parliament thought of the power to legislate. We may get a hint, however, when we discover that even the ministry, who possessed the votes to command a decision of political power, spoke the language of legal right. An instance is furnished by the head of the administration, Lord North. On the day that he introduced the Port of Boston Bill, North came to House of Commons prepared for debate in a way that a twentieth-century prime minister would not be. He had researched the law and cited precedents for the bill much as he would have had he been a barrister arguing a case in King's Bench or at the Old Bailey. Some people might object to the degree or type of punishment, he pointed out, but

> it was no new thing for the whole town to be fined for such neglect; he instanced the city of London in King Charles the Second's time, when Dr. Lamb was killed by unknown persons, the city was fined for such; and the case of Edinburgh, in Captain Porteus's affair, a fine was set upon the whole; and also at Glasgow, where the house of Mr. Campbell was pulled down, part of the revenue of that town was sequestered to make good the damage. He observed that Boston did not stand in so fair a light, as either of the three before-mentioned places, for that town had been upwards of seven years in riot and confusion.[28]

If today we heard a prime minister recite these precedents when introducing a penal bill we might be surprised. In 1774, Lord North apparently did not surprise members of the parliamentary opposition. They had also come prepared, and the relevancy of North's precedents were immediately questioned both as law and as fact. The Lamb killing, it was argued, had been political in part. The incident was not well documented, but in 1774 it was believed that Dr. Lamb had been an advisor to Charles II or a "creature" of the duke of Buckingham, and that the king had interceded with the mob to save his life.[29] Moreover, the murder had been committed within the city walls, by citizens, in day time, a very relevant set of facts for during the seventeenth century a daytime killing within the walls was an offense at common law for which a town was corporately answerable if the killers were unknown or not indicted.[30] Besides, the penalty against London had been decreed by the king, not by an act of Parliament. It had been punishment by prerogative command, not by legislation. The Lamb case, therefore, was not a precedent for the Boston Port Bill. It was not even an analogy.

The cases of Edinburgh and Glasgow were better analogies for those cities had been fined by Parliament—Edinburgh because a mob lynched a crown official performing an official duty; Glasgow because a mob destroyed the house of that town's member of Parliament. There is no need to recite the numerous distinctions of fact that were drawn by the opposition to show that these were not precedents—that Edinburgh and Glasgow, unlike Boston, were walled cities which by charter were responsible for their own executive governance, that their officials testified in their defense and they were defended by counsel, and that the two cities as well as other localities in Scotland were represented in Parliament.[31]

The more persuasive argument was one of law. The cases of Edinburgh and Glasgow, the opposition in the House of Commons charged, were not precedent for punishing Boston because they had been subject to fines and once the fines were paid the prosecutions ended. Boston was not to be fined. Instead, its port was to be closed and its trade prohibited until it paid for the tea, and even then the harbor would not be reopened to commerce but at the pleasure of the crown.[32] Today the distinction might not be important in a legislative debate. In 1774 it was important enough for North to answer. He had cited Edinburgh and Glasgow as precedents not for the type of punishment, North explained, but to show that Parliament had inflicted punishment on "the whole town" for actions not committed "by the whole town."[33]

It is best not to extend this discussion. The arguments can be summarized by noting that the evidence could go on and on, for every conceivable constitutional and legal argument was raised in what we think should have been a political debate. It was alleged that the charges raised in the preambles of some of the Coercive Bills were not proven:[34] that as every American port had prevented the dutied tea from being entered at the customs houses, it was unjust, unequal,[35] and, therefore, unconstitutional to punish only Boston;[36] that Boston was being punished by ex post facto legislation;[37] that as the people of Boston had been defending their constitutional rights they had acted in constitutional self-defense and, therefore, their actions were not criminal;[38] that the town meeting was the governing body of Boston and that there had been no evidence that the town meeting sanctioned the Tea Party;[39] that the medieval English concept of collective guilt was legally inapplicable to a colonial community where the authority to enforce the law was not exclusively local, but was divided between royal, provincial, and town officials;[40] and that the punishment, which was too severe, was being inflicted on British merchants doing business with New England and on the entire province of Massachusetts Bay, not just on Bostonians.[41]

Two other arguments should be mentioned as they raised legal doctrines that are major themes in this book. The first was the contention that to proceed against Boston by legislation was arbitrary; that "by being deprived of many of the Forms which are wisely established in the Courts of ordinary Resort," Bostonians lost their constitutional "Protection against the dangerous Promptitude of arbitrary Discretion."[42] The conclusion to be developed in this book is that the American constitutional case against the authority of Parliament to legislate for the internal police of the colonies depended to a large extent on the illegitimacy of arbitrary power in English and British constitutional theory. The legal doctrine was summed up by dissentient lords when they described the Port of Boston Act as "an arbitrary Sentence" and protested that the length of the sentence was left to the arbitrary discretion of the minister advising the crown that Boston had satisfied the penalty. In a concise statement of the constitutional principle, they asserted, "The legal Condition of the Subject (standing unattainted by Conviction for Treason or Felony) ought never to depend upon the arbitrary Will of any Person whatsoever."[43] That single sentence not only sums up a legal principle dominating much of English constitutional history, a principle that will be examined more closely below, it sums up much of the American whig constitutional case against Parliament's authority to legislate.

The second legal doctrine that is central to the conclusion of this book is the principle of precedent. The Port of Boston Act was constitutionally questionable legislation, opponents contended, because it could become a precedent for future arbitrary statutes exerting unchecked parliamentary power. "If the Colonies in general permit this to pass unnoticed," Arthur Lee warned, "a precedent will be established for humbling them by degrees, until all opposition to arbitrary power is subdued."[44] Again a good deal of the material of this book is summed up in a single sentence, this time in a petition to the House of Commons protesting that, "under such a precedent, no men, or body of men in *America*, could enjoy a moment's security."[45]

There is a lesson to be drawn from these legal and constitutional arguments of principle, doctrine, precedent, and right in situations where we would expect political arguments of program, result, policy, and power.

It is the pervasiveness of the legal way of thinking: To discover what people feared constitutionally and why they feared it, should tell us more about the coming of the American Revolution than has generally been realized.

It is not just arguments made that deserve our attention. We also should heed arguments not made and how arguments were phrased. The fact usually noticed by historians who mention the debates on the Coercive Bills, is that the Port of Boston Act was condemned as tyranny. More often, more loudly, and more perspicaciously it was attacked at that time as precedent for a new constitution of legislative power. "[T]o what a deplorable state this, and all the other colonies are reduced," the General Assembly of Rhode Island lamented of the Port of Boston Act, "when, by an act of Parliament, in which the subjects in America have not a single voice, and without being heard, they may be divested of property, and deprived of liberty." The Port of Boston Act, the Georgia Congress agreed, "is contrary to our idea of the British Constitution: First, for that it in effect deprives good and lawful men of the use of their property without judgment of their peers; and, secondly, for that it is in nature of an *ex post facto* law, and indiscriminately blends, as objects of punishment, the innocent with the guilty." It can be expected that the Continental Congress made the same complaint against the Massachusetts Government Act: "Without incurring or being charged with a forfeiture of their rights, without being heard, without being tried, without law, and without justice, by an Act of Parliament, their charter is destroyed, their liberties violated, their constitution and form of government changed." The process was as objectionable as the legislation, the precedent more insufferable than the punishment.[46]

CHAPTER TWO

PASSAGE OF THE DECLARATORY ACT

The marquis of Rockingham became the king's first minister during the Stamp Act crisis. American whig refusal to pay the stamp tax was irrevocable and Rockingham knew the statute had to be modified or repealed for the colonists could not be compelled to obey except by overwhelming force. Members of his administration understood that Americans objected to the Stamp Act for constitutional reasons, not economic reasons. They also appreciated that due to the grounds of colonial opposition the Act could be modified and made constitutionally acceptable only by giving up the object of raising revenue, without which it had no purpose. The tax had to be repealed, but how without acquiescing to America's constitutional argument?[1]

Reasons of state, politics, and constitutional law prevented repeal without some formula reserving Parliament's legislative authority over the colonies. There was a constitutional need and a political need. The constitutional need was thrust upon Parliament by the substance of colonial opposition to the Stamp Act. To repeal without a constitutional saving left a precedent implying that American claims of legislative autonomy were constitutional. Repeal either had to save the right or evade the precedent. The political need was caused by the fact that there were not enough votes for any repeal that might become a tacit, implied relinquishment of Parliament's authority to legislate for North America. Members of both houses wanted to restore law and order to that part of the empire but not at the risk of weakening parliamentary authority over the colonies. Rockingham had to find a way around both the constitutional and political predicament.

The constitutional solution was easy. The Rockinghamites adopted the standard parliamentary maneuver for avoiding constitutional precedents. They repealed the Stamp Act for reasons of economic expediency. Repeal on expediency rather than on constitutional grounds converted what would have been a constitutional action into a political decision. The method was to announce that although the right was indisputable its exercise was, under present circumstances, inconvenient.[2]

It was a well-known legal tactic—shift the grounds and avoid the precedent. The Massachusetts House of Representatives, when first protesting the Sugar Act of 1764, had been persuaded by Lieutenant Governor Thomas Hutchinson to adopt the expediency excuse. It had objected to the stamp tax on the grounds of economic expediency instead of constitutional right, and then had to draft additional, "constitutional" resolutions when it found it was the only colony not to stand on the right. There were serious risks for the colonies if their leaders were too passive, as Governor Francis Bernard inadvertently explained when he urged the Massachusetts General Court to keep opposition to the Stamp Act limited to pleas of expediency.

> It is said that the gentlemen who opposed this act in the House of Commons, did not dispute the authority of Parliament to make such a law, but argued from the inexpediency of it at this time, and the inability of the colonies to bear such an imposition. . . . The power of the Parliament to tax the colonies may be admitted, and yet the expediency of exercising that power at such a time, and in such a manner, may be denied. But if the questions are blended together so as to admit of but one answer, the affirmation of the right of Parliament will conclude for the expediency of the act.

It would be well to understand just what Bernard was saying. He was the first participant in the revolutionary controversy to outline the constitutional reasons why, once Parliament exercised legislative authority, the American Revolution crisis became constitutionally insoluble. No matter the excuse of expediency or other strategy for exercising the right, the mere exercise asserted the authority. What the colonists could not afford was to ignore or fail to recognize the constitutional implications of a parliamentary statute, to "suffer," that is, "the Expediency of the Mea-

sure, to prevent their examining into it's Legality." It was such constitutional pitfalls that led the earl of Abingdon to exclaim, "*Inexpediency!*
curse on the term! What is *inexpedient* to-day, may be *expedient* tomorrow. *Inexpediency* is as the tyrant's sword, that hangs over the head,
suspended by a thread; and which *Discretion* only is to keep from falling. But are Englishmen to be thus *worded* out of their Rights?"[3]

The excuse of expediency was part of eighteenth-century British constitutional government, and if we fail to take it into account we will miss
much of the political maneuvering leading to the American Revolution.
It explains the administration's strategy for repealing the Stamp Act. The
constitutional right was shunted to the background, and hours were
spent by the House of Commons taking evidence that the stamp tax crisis
had damaged British trade.[4] The Act was repealed on several grounds,
including that it was injurious to imperial commerce, not worth the
economic hardship it caused the colonies, and that it had been too great a
constitutional shock, too great a legal innovation, too much a departure
from established customary practice. The first two, the ones everyone
mentioned, were excuses of expediency, allowing members of Parliament
to say they were removing an economic-political grievance, not repealing an unconstitutional statute.[5]

Some of the administration's opponents in Parliament, to be sure, said
that the expediency sleight of hand would not work, that a controversy
the Americans had wantonly made hyperconstitutional could not so easily become benignly political. "[T]he disgrace of departing from the
inforcing the laws by constraint, and by open rebellion of the Colonies,
can't be wiped off by the power of any words whatsoever." It was constitutionally absurd, George Grenville and Sir William Blackstone argued in the Commons, to claim a right at the same time you repeal the
only statute maintaining that right. In the upper house dissentient lords
voted against repeal, saying that Parliament "had, hath, and of right
ought to have full power and authority, to make laws and statutes of
sufficient force & validity to bind the colonies and peoples of America,
subjects of the crown of Great Britain, in all cases whatsoever."[6] This
opposition, together with a universal understanding that the right had to
be constitutionally reserved, led the ministry to accompany the expediency of repeal with the Declaratory Act. In fact, the Act had to be passed
first or there might not have been repeal.

NEED FOR DECLARATORY

"[R]epeal upon expediency is proper," Chancellor of the Exchequer
William Dowdeswell warned the Commons, "but if you let this repeal go

without an assertion of right, they [Americans] will conclude that Parliament has given up the right absolutely and confessed that it ought never to be exercised in any cases whatever." He wanted Parliament first to declare the right and then to repeal. Dowdeswell's words and Dowdeswell's constitutional strategy deserve a moment of scrutiny. They simply cannot be passed over as meaningless political propaganda. They reveal both how eighteenth-century British constitutional law was made and how aware eighteenth-century British legislators had to be of the possibility that even the repeal of a statutory innovation could create an objectionable constitutional precedent. The two chief law officers in the cabinet, the lord chancellor and the attorney general, insisted that Dowdeswell's strategy be adopted. If there was a repeal there also had to be a saving of the right, they said, and the only way was a statutory enactment, adopted by regular parliamentary procedures, asserting the authority of Parliament "in general words."[7] That solution may not have been as constitutionally certain as we might think today, for there seem to have been doubts raised in 1766. Some historians have claimed the law officers "had to be persuaded" that declaring the right would overcome whatever constitutional harm was caused by repeal.[8]

The secretary of state for the colonies told the Massachusetts agent that most ministers had not wanted a declaratory statute, but "were obliged to agree to the resolves in order to secure a majority for a Repeal." To obtain the votes needed for repeal, that is, it had to be demonstrated "that the repeal of the Stamp Act was the result of Indulgence, and not of Fear."[9] The political strategy was to win support for repeal, but the constitutional issue was Parliament's authority to legislate for the colonies.[10]

The preamble of the administration's bill stated the purpose with clarity. Several American houses of representatives had claimed "the sole and exclusive right" of taxation, it noted, and "have, in pursuance of such claim, passed certain votes, resolutions, and orders, derogatory to the legislative authority of parliament." To set the constitution straight, Parliament declared that "the said colonies and plantations in *America* have been, are, and of right ought to be, subordinate unto, and dependent upon the imperial crown and parliament of *Great Britain*," for Parliament "had, hath, and of right ought to have, full power and authority to make laws and statutes of sufficient force and validity to bind the colonies and people of *America*, subjects of the crown of *Great Britain*, in all cases whatsoever." The last four words are the ones that all commentators mark. Less noticed is the second article of the statute where Parliament reacted to the Stamp Act resolves of the American assemblies denying its authority to legislate. "[A]ll resolutions, votes, orders, and proceedings, in any of the said colonies or plantations, whereby the power and authority of the parliament of *Great Britain*, to make laws and statutes as

aforesaid, is denied, or drawn into question, are, and are hereby declared to be, utterly null and void to all intents and purposes whatsoever." The legislative theory of a declaratory statute was not to promulgate new law but to reiterate the old, to declare what the constitution,
law, or custom had always been. As far as the British administration was
concerned, the Act was a restatement of existing constitutional law. Parliament had merely affirmed what had always been the rule. The colonists, of course, insisted it stated new doctrine, otherwise, Benjamin
Franklin said, "there would have been no necessity for such an act."[11]

ENACTMENT OF DECLARATORY

For the twentieth century the striking fact of the Declaratory debate is
that the extant reports indicate that it was entirely concerned with the
constitution, law, custom, doctrine, precedent, principle, and analogy.
In the Commons, Hans Stanley, a commissioner of the admiralty and
member for Southampton, began the debate by wondering whether the
Declaratory Bill "be only to give a specious Appearance to the Neglect of
exercising the Right or the first Step tow[ar]ds the enforcing of it." Comparing the American colonists to English copyholders who also had no
direct representation in Parliament, he concluded that the colonists suffered no "hardship" by citing the argument of Oliver St. John in the ship
money case, a law suit that had taken place 128 years before. "I am
persuaded," Stanley said answering the Stamp Act resolves, "that enacting Laws and laying taxes so entirely go tog[ethe]r that if we surrender
the one we lose the others." He knew what the American assemblies had
meant in their resolves. "All their Petitions are Insults on your authority,"
he told the Commons.[12]

Attorney General Charles Yorke spoke second and went directly to the
question at bar. "I consider this as the Way of Proceeding most consistent
with your Dignity separating the Q[uestion] of Right from that of Expediency," he said of the Bill. "I w[oul]d repeal not wantonly because it is
asked, not timidly because it is resisted, but on being convinced of the
Inexpediency, but I am clear on the Right. The sovereign Legislature
must be supream." He then made a remarkable legal argument, remarkable not so much for his knowledge of law as for how well he had prepared for the debate. To supplement the analogy of Ireland that would
be often mentioned over the next few years, he discussed the analogies of
Lithuania and Holland, which may never have been referred to again
during the revolutionary controversy. "The Legislative Power of Par-
l[iamen]t extends as far as the Power of the Crown," Yorke insisted, cit-

ing the Irish analogy to refute what would become the main argument in the American whig case. At the Glorious Revolution, he pointed out, the English Parliament not only conferred the crown of Ireland on William and Mary, but it established new oaths of loyality for the Irish, sold forfeited Irish estates, paying the receipts into the English exchequer, and established an army. Yorke even cited by statutory year some of these acts. In fact, the attorney general was so well briefed that he recalled the proceedings in the House of Commons against William Molyneux whose 1698 book, *The Case of Ireland's being bound by Acts of Parliament in England stated*, challenged the authority of the English Parliament to legislate for the Irish much as American whigs were challenging the British Parliament. Parliament, he reminded his listeners, stood up for the right then. Yorke concluded the survey of Irish analogies by going back even further, to James I who "was anxious that Ireland sh[oul]d hold only of the Crown," and back further still, to a statute of 1 Philip and Mary. All these analogies proved, he concluded, that "Parl[iamen]t represent the whole Body of the Realm and all the Dominions of the same."[13]

From analogy the attorney general turned to precedent, displaying not only an impressive grasp of the constitutional history of the North American colonies, but bringing to the attention of the Commons almost all the precedents of imperial legislation the colonial whigs would cite over the next decade. George Grenville, Richard Jackson, and other members of the Commons had done much the same the first time the Stamp Bill had been debated.[14] Again we encounter striking evidence that has not received sufficient credit in our accounts of the American Revolution. The law, analogies, precedents, and customs upon which the colonists would build their constitutional case for legislative autonomy were not *sui generis*, natural law, or fabrications invented to give resistance the veneer of legitimacy. They were based on the same law, analogies, precedents, and customs that, in 1766, the attorney general of England cited as authority he believed proved Parliament's constitutional right to legislate.

First he took up the charter argument, dismissing what would have been the most farfetched legal contention of the revolutionary controversy had American whigs ever made it, that colonial charters granted absolute legislative autonomy. "The King cannot grant away the supremacy of Parliament," he contended. "The Legisl[ative] Power given to the Colonies is to be exercised after the manner of corp[oratio]ns in England. The Law can grant no other." It is not clear why Yorke raised the point. Perhaps he felt that, as it was so obvious, it would strengthen his case just to mention it. He may have thought—although more likely he hoped— that the Americans would rely on their charters as organic instruments of government. They never did, of course. Not all of their legal arguments would prove to be constitutionally sound, but they generally avoided pleading bad law.[15]

The core of Yorke's argument was drawn from the precedents of parliamentary colonial legislation that will be evaluated in this book. There is no point discussing them now, except to emphasize that they were anticipated by the Crown's chief law officer in early February, 1766. He had even researched the briefs submitted to King's Bench in the last century by Massachusetts counsel when the colony defended its first charter. "You cannot put a case for the dissolution of Governments by law," he warned. Finally, Yorke became one of the first participants in the constitutional debate to raise what would prove to be the ultimate constitutional issue for British whigs. He was afraid "for the balance of the constitution," he said, because "separating any part of the dominions of this country from the legislative power of Parliament" meant "leaving them subject to the dominion of the Crown."[16]

As soon as Yorke finished William Beckford, alderman of London, was on his feet answering him. Beckford was not a lawyer, yet was well briefed with judicial precedents. His first reference was to Lord Coke's decision in Dr. Bonham's case. He even cited the page where Coke said that the common law would judge void an act of Parliament against reason. After recounting several precedents of colonial refusal to obey Parliament, Beckford disparaged the Irish analogy, by reciting some of the differences between how the British ruled Ireland and how they ruled the colonies. "I deny your rights," he told the Commons, quite likely directly addressing the attorney general. "You have no right. Lord Coke says you have none."[17]

Robert Nugent, reading instructions he had received from his constituents in Bristol, answered Beckford. Although he referred to an Act of Henry VIII, Nugent relied more on constitutional logic than on precedent and custom. "If they can say in North America you shall bind us when we choose only," he reasoned, "they are the superior and you the subordinate legislature."[18]

As Secretary of State in charge of colonial affairs and a member of the administration, General Henry Seymour Conway had introduced the Declaratory Bill. Even so, his support was not wholehearted. He would vote for it, he said, for he had "no doubt on the Right," but did have doubts about "the Justice, Equity and Expediency." Like some other supporters of the colonial political (but not their constitutional) case, he was less interested in the bill under debate than putting on record his constitutional solution should the controversy continue. "The Americans have denied the whole," he explained, "and I say that we have a right to bind them in all," but for reasons of expediency it would be better never to bind them again.[19] Conway's law may seem odd today, but it made sense under the eighteenth-century constitution and would, in 1776, become the final solution acceptable to the British administration. By then, of course, the constitutional issue would not be Parliament's sovereignty over the colonies, but the colonies' relationship to the Crown.

Sir William Blackstone had no truck with expediency. Law was his concern, and on law he based the case of Parliament's undoubted right to legislate for every part of the empire. Going back to Magna Carta and two statutes of Elizabeth, Blackstone recited precedent after precedent to demonstrate that "Sovereignty and Legislation go always together." His primary concern was proving that Parliament had taxed the colonies, but he also considered the authority to legislate by discussing as a precedent a supposed act of 1621 dealing with fishing rights in Virginia, and pointed out that "[t]he preamble of the Navigation Act of 1650 speaks of the subordination and dependence of the colonies." "It is," he argued, "a Contrad[ictio]n to say that the inferior must send Repres[entatives] to the superior. . . . All the Dominions of G[reat] B[ritain] are bound by Acts of Parl[iamen]t—Calais, Guienne, Jersey, Guernsey, Ireland—and never contended that they must be represented." Here again we encounter an example of the common lawyer's way of thinking about history. The Duchy of Guienne had been lost to the crown in the middle of the fifteenth century. The last time the English had ruled Calais was in the reign of Mary I.[20]

Thomas Pitt was the first speaker that day not to mention a precedent nor to talk of Britain's customary colonial practices. Instead, as would become common procedure for those who believed the colonies bound by the sovereign power of Parliament, he quoted John Locke.[21]

Richard Hussey gave the best presentation of the colonial constitutional argument, although he went further than any American assembly or congress would when he claimed that George III, "by giving his consent" to the Stamp Act, "has overrode and destroyed as a limited monarch those privileges which his predecessors as absolute monarchs had granted to them." He distinguished away all precedents relied on by the other side, finding they either were not relevant, a crucial objection, or that the colonists had not consented to them, an element most of his listeners thought of no consequence. "The Parl[iamen]t," he argued, turning from precedent to custom, "never taxed Countries who had Legislatures of their own, you have therefore not imitated the wisdom of your predecessors." Hussey believed the premises of the debate were less definite than most participants assumed, which may be why he referred to "the obscurity about the Constitution" of the colonies. He had no doubt Parliament was supreme, but seemed to think that custom and the rule of law should define the parameters of supremacy. "The colonies were never heard" when the Stamp Act was passed, he pointed out. "I am for asserting the authority of the British Legislature, but in my justice I would remember merely, that I had sowed the seeds of sedition."[22]

Nothing was ambiguous to the Scots lawyer Alexander Wedderburn. Everything was clear. His concepts may have been somewhat fuzzy to those listening to him, however, for both his law and his history were questionable. He asserted, for example, that Sir Edmund Andros, serving as governor for the proprietor James, duke of York, had "by his own authority," imposed a tax on New York in 1683. This prerogative tax, Wedderburn concluded, was precedent supporting the constitutionality of parliamentary taxation. He also claimed that in an earlier era of English history the prerogative council had legislated for the colonies. Parliament was now doing the legislating and Wedderburn spoke as if there were no distinction. He equated past executive authority with present legislative authority, and would have made conciliar mandates precedents for parliamentary mandates. Wedderburn's humor was better than his law. Disparaging American whig constitutional principles, he noted that they were not new. They had been "aired by Wat Tyler in Richard 2nd's time and by the Parliament which destroyed Charles Ist and the whole constitution." "I would read a resolution of the assembly of Massachusetts Bay," he concluded. "Resolved that we will never dispute the right, unless Great Britain should ever think proper to exercise it." Wedderburn was being facetious. He may not have realized how accurately he had summed up the American constitutional argument.[23]

Edmund Burke probably did not express his true thoughts. He had to support the administration of his patron, Lord Rockingham, yet the Declaratory Bill's claim of absolute power left him with misgivings concerning the governance of the British Empire. "Without subordination, it would not be one Empire," he knew. "Without freedom, it would not be the British Empire." Burke discussed a few precedents, not to prove what the constitution currently ordained, but to show that the constitution had changed in fundamental ways. "I believe nobody misses them," he said of the king's veto and the convocation of the clergy. The implication is ambiguous, but may have been that parliamentary supremacy over the colonies would also not be missed. Although Burke did not explore colonial history for legal customs as he would often do later in the revolutionary controversy, he did say as he would continue to say over the next several years that a way out of the constitutional predicament could be found if the Commons let itself be guided by principle and practical realities. The colonies once "were meer Corporations, Fishermen and

Furriers, they are now commonwealths," Burke insisted. "Give them
. . . some Resemblance of the British Constitution, some idea of popular
Representation. Draw the Line where you please between perfect and no
Repres[entation], but draw the Line somewhere." He was saying what
the Massachusetts house had said to Governor Francis Bernard in 1765
and would say to Governor Thomas Hutchinson in 1773.[24]

It was a quarter past ten when Isaac Barré got his chance to speak and
changed the course of the debate by moving that the words "in all cases
whatsoever" be struck from the Bill. He was afraid the colonists would
read them to say that Parliament planned another stamp tax and, if they
did, it could mean civil war. "The Americans have acknowledged our
right of restriction of trade and submitted to it, but they will not be
deprived of their property which they acquire under this restriction."
More than most members of Parliament over the next decade, Barré had
a realistic sense of the limits of British power. Moreover, he seemed
trapped by the ambivalence of the two constitutional traditions of the
1760s. "The Legislature of this like that of every other Country is supream," he explained. "It cannot be controuled: but it ought to controul
itself and in that sense you have no right to lay an internal Tax on N[orth]
A[merica]." We may think it odd to use the word "right" in this sense, to
say that an uncontrollable sovereign has no "right" because of the need
for the sovereign to exercise self-control. It was, however, familiar usage
in the ambiguous context of the two contemporary constitutions. Barré is
not reported as saying—but surely he also meant—that Parliament had
no "right" to legislate for the colonies, except in the "restriction of trade."[25]

The chancellor of the exchequer opposed Barré's motion. If the words
"in all cases whatsoever" were omitted, he contended, the statute would
be "too much confined." Dowdeswell misstated the American whig constitutional position, saying they demanded only the right of taxation by
representation, they did not claim internal legislative autonomy. Then,
like the other speakers, he turned to precedents, noting that in the previous century Massachusetts had objected for seventeen years to the Navigation Act on constitutional grounds, finally resolving the issue by passing an enabling statute, adopted by the General Court in 1677. In 1748,
Dowdeswell recalled, there had been a colonial petition protesting parliamentary legislation of paper money and as late as 1764 opposition on
some ground to a statute of 4 George III. Dowdeswell used his precedents for a different purpose than most speakers—not as evidence proving some version of the constitution, but as evidence of how frequently
Americans had denied Parliament's authority to legislate. It was time, he
was saying, for a declaratory statute telling them they were wrong.[26]

George Grenville started speaking at twenty minutes past eleven. He was less interested in precedents and constitutionalism than were most of his colleagues. He had been the prime minister who had planned, drafted, and enacted the Stamp Act, and, without any reservations, wanted the statute enforced, the tax collected, and the colonists punished. "I must lament that the executive power of Gov[ernmen]t is entrusted to one who apologizes for Rebellion," he said of Rockingham. Yet even Grenville could not avoid considering the question in constitutional terms. "Antiquity [has] no appeal," Grenville claimed, and then he appealed to it, citing the precedent of 7 James I or of 8 William III requiring a colony, on penalty of forfeiting its charter, to punish pirates. Finally, like Attorney General Yorke earlier in the evening, he warned of the threat to British liberty if the colonies established legislative autonomy. "That doctrine may one day put the King out of the power of Parliament." He wished that there was not that danger, that parliamentary sovereignty did not have to be applied so rigidly. Too bad the Stamp Act did not have faults, he lamented, then Parliament "might give way to Justice and Reason not to force and Resistence." Because the Americans had objected to the right, because they looked to the authority of the Crown rather than to Parliament, there was no room for expediency.[27]

It was ten minutes after twelve when William Pitt was recognized. He was the speaker everyone wanted to hear and one member of Parliament twentieth-century scholars might expect to be ahead of his time, to shun the legalism of eighteenth-century legislative debate, and to speak of the need for imperial unity and imperial vision. Not so. He supported Barré's amendment, because he was afraid the words "in all cases whatsoever" included taxation. The authority to tax was his only concern, and, as he denied that taxation was a legislative function, Pitt paid no heed to the constitutional danger of American legislative autonomy. To prove that Parliament had no authority to tax the colonists, he went back and forth over history, citing precedents, discussing statutes, and distinguishing cases. The counties palatinate were mentioned just as they had been during the debate at the passage of the Stamp Act. They had taxed themselves and supported the Crown only by writs of requisitions, as Pitt thought the colonies should, ignoring Grenville's warning of resurgent monarchial power. He recalled a statute of Richard II acknowledging the tax status of the Cinque Ports and reminded the Commons that from the time of Edward II the clergy had taxed themselves. There was even a judicial case from "20 Harry VI" that he applied to the colonial situation. Just as striking as his respect for precedent, is the picture we obtain of William Pitt, a man history recalls as the great parliamentarian who used the House of Commons to unite the empire, contending for the constitution of legislative restraint against the constitution of parliamentary sovereignty. He could not deny that supreme authority was a reality, but wished it was not. "The noblest exercise of power is to moderate and control itself," Pitt said, expressing one of the most fundamental givens of eighteenth-century constitutionalism, almost as fundamental as the common-law dichotomy between power and right. "Power you have. I think in this case you have not the right. Authority [is] something sensible rather than visible. Consider America as an acquisition the greatest any empire ever received. Bind them with the golden cord of equity and [moderation]." "I wish this to be an Empire of Freemen: it will be stronger for it and it will be the more easily governed. Let the Premises and Conquences agree therefore, decline the Right, do not let Lenity be misapplied nor Rigour unexecuted: take not the worst of both. The Colonies are too great an object to be grasped but in the arms of affection."[28]

The last recorded speaker was Sir Fletcher Norton. The leader on the northern circuit of the common-law bar and attorney general at the time that the Stamp Act was passed, he held an authoritative view of law, defending the legality of general executive warrants, the expulsion of Wilkes, and imperial sovereignty. Even so, and despite the fact it was ten minutes before two when he rose to speak, he thought it necessary to discuss still more precedents, at one point going back to "before the Norman Period." Perhaps due to the fatigue of the hour, Norton stretched his history a bit. "Lord Coke, Lord Ch[ief] J[ustice] Anderson, and in [a] Meeting of twelve Judges, it has been determined that all the Kings Dominions sh[oul]d be subject to the Laws," he said. It was a meeting no one else was to remember over the next decade. What is most revealing for us was his constitutional theory. Norton may have understood and championed legislative sovereignty, but he did not think the Declaratory Bill would be sufficient to save it. "If you follow the Decl[aratio]n by a Repeal [of the Stamp Act] it is a Mockery of Parl[iamen]t," he warned. "I w[oul]d receive the American with open arms but I would receive him penitent and if something is not done to support this [Stamp] Law it will be the last you will pass upon North America."[29]

Norton's final sentence summed up the issue of the Stamp Act crisis as imperialist lawyers understood it. In the Lords' debates the leading lawyer of the eighteenth century, Lord Mansfield, pursued the argument: because American assemblies had objected to the stamp tax on grounds of constitutional power, the Stamp Act could not be repealed without surrendering the authority. The authority that would be lost was not only the authority to tax, but authority to legislate. "The Americans have adopted on this fatal occasion a new principle that they are not subject to the legislative authority of Great Britain," Mansfield explained. "They have refused the Law." American opposition alone, however, had not made the crisis. Blame belonged to a combination of factors including a flaw inherent to British constitutionalism. Once a statutory innovation such as the Stamp Act was promulgated by Parliament it became a precedent and the constitution was irrevocably changed. There was no way to undo an innovation or reverse a precedent except by drastic steps such as a declaratory statute. Certain legislation, therefore, could be enacted only with extreme caution. If "a Bill passes which destroys the land marks of the Constitution, it is without remedy," Mansfield explained, referring to the Stamp Act. The Lord Chief Justice was not saying the Stamp Act was unconstitutional. He knew it was constitutional. The mistake Mansfield lamented had been to enact a statute the colonists would perceive to be so unconstitutional it could not be enforced. "In this situation," Mansfield asked, "what is the effect [of] repealing this Act? It is the giving up the total Legislature of this Kingdom." The Declaratory Bill, he said, should resolve the controversy by providing another, more authoritative precedent. "It is now settled that there is no restriction to the legislative authority of Great Britain."[30] We may wonder if Mansfield said this with conviction.

CHAPTER THREE

SCOPE OF THE DECLARATORY ACT

Many months after the revolutionary war had begun, and members of Parliament were asking where British policy had gone wrong, Lord Beauchamp could not make up his mind whether repeal of the Stamp Act had been the fatal mistake. "He would not pretend to decide, whether the repeal was a wise measure," Beauchamp told the Commons, "but certainly the sovereignty of this country would have been abandoned, if the Declaratory Act had not maintained it." Beauchamp was speaking from the perspective of the jurisprudence of power. His point was not that the Declaratory Act had resolved the imperial issue of parliamentary sovereignty, but that without it the claim to the right would have been given up. Whether that was true—that without the Declaratory "saving" the right would have been lost—depended, many commentators agreed, on how one interpreted the colonial Stamp Act resolves. "[T]he Fact is," Lord Halifax told the upper house, "that it is not the Stamp Act that is opposed but the Authority of this Legislature." Lord Lyttelton had agreed. "The Point on which we are debating is no Question of Expediency, it is a Question of Sovereignty till the Americans submit to this Legislature."[1]

Whether the Declaratory Act was "necessary" is a question so dependent on definitions of the constitution it can never be answered to everyone's satisfaction.[2] When members of Parliament said that the right had to be saved, they were thinking of the constitution more in terms of customary powers than in terms of unlimited sovereignty. In constitutional advocacy the Declaratory Act would be most useful in the older constitutional tradition, as a defense against a future claim that the right had been lost by disuse, or as authority for proving that Parliament, when dealing with the colonies, was unrestrained by custom, precedent, or "law." One difficulty is that although almost every commentator in and out of Parliament, spoke of the right, hardly any defined it.[3] Worse, too many were confused or inconsistent when discussing it. The earl of Egmont, for example, was said to have gone "back to the Original of our Constitution," and, "from the Feudal Tenures, from History, and [from] the records in the Tower," to have proven to the House of Lords that "taxes were levied upon the People not by right of their having *representatives* but that of being *subjects* to the Government." "It is not, said he, to be doubted but that there exists in every Government, however extended, a Power supreme, absolute and unlimited. But this power may upon some former occasion have delegated to other subordinated powers a part of itself. In which case time will give to these subordinate powers a right of prescription; nor can the supreme recall its gift, excepting only in the utmost emergency." If we are puzzled by a "Power supreme, absolute and unlimited" against which irrevocable prescription rights can exist, so were those of Egmont's contemporaries who were more attuned to the newer legal theory that rights and privileges are grants from the sovereign. "Our friend, Lord *Egmont*, was *recondite*, but beyond me," the earl of Hardwicke wrote his brother the attorney general. "Parliament had the *right*, but if we exercised it, we deprived the Colonies of a privilege *against abuse*."[4]

Eighteenth-century constitutional jurisprudence may not have been ready for what, to us in the twentieth century, is a commonplace concept. A power to bind "in all cases whatsoever" was more difficult to comprehend in 1766 than it is today. Charles Garth, a member of the Commons, wrote Maryland legislators, of whom he served as agent, that the Declaratory Act had passed because his colleagues in Parliament "were convinced that in Point of Law, the King, Lords and Commons were undoubtedly possessed of that Power, tho' in Point of Policy, Justice or Equity, it was a Power that they ought to exercise but in the most extraordinary Cases only." By 1775, Sir William Meredith, who had served as a lord of the admiralty in Rockingham's administration, still wanted Parliament to be supreme over the colonies but not as supreme as he had wanted in 1766 when he had voted for the Declaratory Bill. "[A] power to bind, in all cases whatsoever, had never been claimed by the greatest tyrant on earth, nor by any earthly power, before the declaratory act," Meredith argued in the Commons.[5] Over the years something had happened to the legislative confidence of a Rockinghamite. Perhaps some of the values of the seventeenth-century constitution of customary restraint had been revived to intrude upon the newer constitutionalism of legislative sovereignty. The explanation depends upon the meaning of the Declaratory Act of 1766 to its framers and to the Americans who had to deal with it.

MEANING OF DECLARATORY

Thomas Pownall, member of Parliament, former governor of Massachusetts Bay, and author of *The Administration of the Colonies*, was, together with William Knox and George Johnstone, London's resident expert on the colonial constitution. His definition of the Declaratory Act was both the simplest and one of the most widely accepted. By the Act, he wrote, "the imperial crown of Great Britain, the *King, Lords and Commons, collectively taken,* is stated *as sovereign,* on the one hand, and *the Colonists as subjects* on the other." Another meaning, also generally agreed to on both sides of the Atlantic, was that the Act declared old law. "The law was not a new law," Lord Beauchamp explained, "it was only a declaration of what the law had been, and was, previous to its being passed. The law was disputed; the true constitutional connection between both countries controverted or denied; Great Britain was therefore called upon to make a declarative assertion of its ancient indubitable claim, which was the supremacy of its legislature, and the dependency and civil subordination of our colonies."[6]

Neither definition was controversial, for neither one said much—that a bill declaring Parliament sovereign stated that the colonists were subjects, and that a declaration of old law did not enact new law. Once the search for the meaning of the Declaratory Act went beyond these elementary propositions, controversy began. How one interpreted the Declaratory Act depended on how one understood the British and American constitutions.

There was not even agreement about what the American Declaratory Act owed to the Irish Declaratory Act, the statute from which it had been copied. At least many members of Parliament had thought they were copying the older law, that the Irish Act declared the same authority to legislate—"that the legislature of Great Britain had a right to make laws to bind Ireland, and all the other members and dependencies of the British empire."[7] There were, however, many students of imperial legislation who, marking differences as much as similarities, did not think the American Act a copy of the Irish. For one thing, a Philadelphia correspondent pointed out, the older law declared Ireland "subordinate unto and dependent upon the Imperial CROWN of *Great-Britain*." The words "and Parliament" were not in the Irish statute.

> Compare the Acts and you will find the Act for *America* copied from that of *Ireland;* but in the last mentioned, the annihilating Words, "in all cases whatsoever," are not to be found. The People of *Ireland* have been for several centuries bound by *English* statutes for regulating their trade, and for other Purposes, and this statute, therefore, only asserted the *usual* authority over them. Their Vitals, the exclusive Right of Taxation, and the Right of Trial by Jury, have been preserved. If it was the Intention of the *British* Parliament to exercise a "power and Authority" over that Kingdom destructive of these Rights, it is not expressed—it is not implied. Why were the unlimited words [of the American Act] omitted in that Act? Or why, when the Lords and Commons were copying a pattern, which their fathers set them, did they deform the Transcript by such Eastern Flourishes?

The Eastern flourishes were the threats of arbitrary governance that Americans found in their statute and did not see in the Irish law. Compare the two acts, colonial whigs were told, and they would discover that Parliament had intended to assert much more authority over them than it was accustomed to exercise over Ireland. "Here is no charter violated, no claim of power to deprive them [Irish] of property, or levy taxes on them without their consent," a second Pennsylvanian argued. "Their Parliament, their right and trial by jury, and the granting supplies to their King in their own way for the support of Government, administration of justice, and defence of the Kingdom, remain untouched."[8]

By "granting supplies" the author meant that the American Act declared Parliament's power to tax the colonies and that the Irish Act did not claim the right to tax Ireland. It was generally agreed the Irish Act did not, but there was less certainty about the American. The marquis of Rockingham had needed the support of William Pitt to enact the Declaratory Bill, but Pitt had posed a problem. Most members of Parliament thought the power of taxation part of the authority to legislate, Pitt not only thought them two separate powers, he insisted that Parliament had no right to tax the unrepresented colonies for purposes of revenue. To avoid antagonizing either Pitt or the majority of Parliament's members who wanted tax revenue from the colonies, the Bill had not mentioned taxation. Parliament asserted the authority "to make laws and statutes of sufficient force and validity . . . in all cases whatsoever." It could be read either way from either point of view.[9]

The meaning might have been clarified when Isaac Barré as quoted in chapter 2, moved that the words, "in all cases," be omitted to make "clear" that Parliament had no "right to tax" British subjects domiciled in the colonies. The House of Commons rejected the amendment which could be evidence that a majority of the members understood "in all cases" to include taxation, except that on the same day Robert Nugent had moved to insert "in cases of taxation." When his amendment was also rejected the meaning returned to where Rockingham wanted it, muddled.[10]

It is anyone's interpretation what Parliament intended about taxation. "What laws can be meant by 'the laws' or 'all laws' but the Stamp Act? What other law has been violently opposed?" asked William Pitt, objecting to taxation. "The general word 'all laws' cannot point out the Stamp Act particularly because all other laws were equally disobeyed, no other laws indeed are obeyed there," answered George Grenville, objecting to repeal.[11] The best guess would be that Pitt, despite himself, was correct. "The full discussion," P. D. G. Thomas has concluded, "can have left no one in any doubt that the deliberately vague phrase 'in all cases whatsoever' had been interpreted to include taxation, and the clarification of this point was the most important result of the debate." Of course, the "no one" left in doubt was limited to members of Parliament. The Act still did not mention taxation, and there was no "clarification of this point" for American whigs who, not unreasonably, could assume that Parliament had not denied their constitutional objections to the Stamp Act.[12]

Quite different from what the statute was intended to legislate was the question what legislation it was intended to bring about. "I am satisfied, that the administration, which passed that Act, never intended to inforce it at least by taxation," John Wilkes contended. He may have been correct. At least Edmund Burke thought so, despite once having described the Declaratory Act as "the bill ascertaining the right of taxing the colonies." If the Rockingham ministry first declared the right before repealing the Stamp Act, he later recalled, "it was not from any opinion they entertained of its future use in regular taxation. Their opinions were full and declared against the ordinary use of such a power." The ministers had faced the problem that the general constitutional objections which American assemblies had raised against the authority of Parliament to tax for purposes of raising revenue, "went directly to our whole legislative right; and one part of it would not be yielded to such arguments, without a virtual surrender of all the rest." In other words, to preserve the authority of legislation, it was necessary to save the taxing authority, even knowing that Parliament would never again exercise it.[13]

In summary, it can be said that some participants in the revolutionary controversy believed that the Declaratory Act had not claimed the right to tax the colonies,[14] others, including many objecting to the claim,[15] said that it had.[16]

It is not necessary to resolve the matter. Taxation is not the concern of this book and the only purpose for discussing it is to illustrate the ambiguity of the Declaratory Act. Taxation was, of course, the gravid constitutional question of the day, the reason why the Declaratory Bill had been drafted and introduced, and yet it was an authority the sponsors of the Act did not dare to clarify. It would be wrong, however, to conclude that a "desire to slur over instead of clarifying the constitutional issue led to a deliberate evasiveness in the wording of the Declaratory Bill." There was not a mere *desire* to "slur over," there was a constitutional *necessity*. The basic essence of the Declaratory Act may be that it had to be imprecise. The statute was less a legislative policy than a constitutional saving and, as Edmund Burke said, may not have presaged future legislation because the Rockingham administration had no legislation in mind.[17]

"Declaratory laws have no operation, they are poor things," William Burke asserted. "You declare that you have a doubt. It is doing something to eke, and help out your authority." But what authority? It may not have been the one we have been thinking of. The Declaratory Act, after all, was one side of two halves. Its passage was part and parcel of the repeal to the Stamp Act. One statute told American whigs that Parliament claimed the authority to legislate for them. The other told the colonists that it was inexpedient to exercise that authority in certain circumstances. The two halves of the legislative package appear inconsistent—but only if we view them from the perspective of the colonies. If we view them from the perspective of the Crown, the Declaratory Act loses ambiguity. If the saving of the authority to legislate was to reserve supremacy over the monarchy as well as over the colonies, the words "in all cases whatsoever" were, at least in respect to the king, as clear as any precisian could ask. The colonies were put on notice that their relationship to Great Britain was through the Parliament of king, Lords, and Commons, and not through the Crown alone, as the colonists claimed— mutely in 1765 and loudly by 1775.[18]

REACTION TO DECLARATORY

The Declaratory Act, a contemporary noted, "was treated with contempt." He meant that in North America it was hardly heeded at all. The statute was printed in some colonial newspapers, usually without comment. Governor William Pitkin of Connecticut thanked the secretary of state for sending a copy of the statute repealing the stamp tax, and told of the great joy and gratitude among the people, but did not mention the Declaratory Act which the secretary also had sent. Thomas Bradshaw seems to have been puzzled to discover that "the Americans are less pleased with the repeal, than displeased with the declaration of right."[19] Of course they were. The original passage of the Stamp Act and its repeal meant more in constitutional law regarding the claim of right than did passage of the Declaratory Act. When Parliament passed and then repealed the Stamp Act, it was both asserting and exercising the authority to tax the colonists for purposes of revenue. Constitutionally, the Declaratory Act was far less dangerous. It was a mere assertion of the authority to legislate.

The reaction of the colonists to the Declaratory Act would deserve little attention if it had not puzzled so many historians. A few have even suggested that Americans "misunderstood" or "disregarded" the Act and, as a result, made the mistake of not protesting its passage as they had protested passage of the Stamp Act.[20] It may be that colonial whigs, unaware of the legislative history, did not appreciate fully the Act's implications,[21] or that "gratitude and joy" over the repeal of the Stamp Act caused them to greet the other statute "without animadversion,"[22] but it is doubtful. More likely the Declaratory Act was not misunderstood. Americans did not react to the Declaratory statute as they had reacted to the stamp tax because there was no legal or constitutional grievance against which to react.[23]

We must not think of American whigs as philosophers or political scientists. We must think of them for what they were, constitutional advocates. They may not have been lawyers, but they were advocates in a constitutional dispute. Abstract theorists might say that if Americans did not treat the Declaratory Act as they did the Stamp Act, if they did not challenge it then and there without reservation, they risked conceding by acquiescence the right of Parliament's supremacy as claimed in the Act. No lawyer would agree.

American whigs, it should be remembered, did not challenge the Stamp Act as an abstract claim, but because it was about to be applied. Arguing that it was unconstitutional, they took to the streets to prevent enforcement, ensuring that the British would not have a precedent of taxation for purposes of revenue. There was no enforcement of the Declaratory Act to prevent. The Act was a declaration of constitutional principle, not the promulgation of a legislative program. Aside from the abstract claim, there was nothing in "litigation." Parliament encountered a comparable situation a year later when some members complained that, as the result of a dispute between the Massachusetts House of Representatives and Governor Francis Bernard, certain "expressions" had been entered in the journals of the House "in derogation of the authority of Parliament." A committee of the House of Commons considered the complaints and voted not to take action because the "expressions had not been carried into overt acts of disobedience to an act of Parliament." It was better "not to interpose until actual occasion was given." As with the Declaratory Act, there were words but not a controversy of substance.[24]

There was reason to believe the Act was more words than substance. On both sides of the Atlantic there was a widespread expectation that it would remain an abstract claim, that although the right might be defined and published in the *Statutes at Large,* it would never be exercised.[25] "Let the matter of right rest upon the declaratory law, and say no more about it," Governor Pownall urged the House of Commons. "Do nothing which may bring into discussion *questions of right,* which must become *mere articles of faith*—Go into no innovations in practice, and suffer no encroachments on government. . . . Continue to exercise the power, which you have already exercised, of laying subsidies, imposts, and duties—but exercise this, as you have always hitherto done, with prudence and moderation, and directed by the spirit of commercial wisdom."[26] The claim was even made by legislators in both Ireland and in America that the colonists had been "told" or "assured" that the Declaratory Act would never be put to the test. If we are certain that they were told no such thing, we still cannot rule out the possibility that they believed that were Lord Rockingham to say anything, he would give them this assurance.[27]

There was reason to believe it. The Irish Declaratory Act was a precedent—or so it was generally thought. The legislative authority claimed over Ireland, as Benjamin Franklin said, had never been exercised; it was, according to Robert Carter Nicholas, "a dead Letter, unregarded."[28] The notion of a legislative power seriously asserted but not put into practice was not farfetched or even unusual to the eighteenth-century mind. It was analogized to royal titles daily asserted in Europe: the claim of the British king to the throne of France or the Spanish king to the throne of Jerusalem.[29]

We will never know how widespread the expectation was that the Declaratory Act would ever be anything but a constitutional saving. We only know what individuals said: that Charles Carroll of Carrollton called it "an empty point of honour," that Samuel Estwick, barrister and agent for Barbadoes, called it "an act of *accommodation,*" and John Dickinson called it "a barren tree, that cast a *shade* indeed over the colonies, but yield no *fruit.*" On the other side of the constitutional controversy, George Grenville's secretary predicted the statute "will hold forth *only a delusive and nugatory affirmance of the right of the legislature of this kingdom,* if not followed by some bill which shall exert it," and Grenville complained in the Commons of "the weakness and meanness of our proceedings in repealing the [Stamp] Act and hoping to preserve our authority by naked and unsupported resolutions." Hugh Williamson summed up what seems to have been the general American expectation when arguing that the "declaratory act was a sword of state, for ornament rather than for use, it was never to be drawn for the purpose of revenue." That, moreover was the way "the Americans viewed it from the beginning," and continued to understand the Act until the question became moot with the beginning of the war.[30]

There had been a few colonial whigs who wanted to make a fuss, who warned that silence in the face of the Declaratory Act meant that Americans "*tacitly* gave up your Right," and acknowledged the right of Parliament. "If this sovereign power, which they so warmly assert, should be tamely conceded," the *Boston Evening-Post* asked, "to what trifling purpose have we exerted ourselves in our glorious opposition to the Stamp Act. At best we have but put the evil day afar off."[31]

The evil day was only put off, and not afar, yet it made constitutional sense not to litigate an issue that might remain moot. It was better for colonial whigs to do what they in fact did do, what a "British American" told them to do shortly after passage of the Declaratory Act.

> The part which I would advise the different assemblies of *America* to act, upon this occasion, is this, To take no further notice of the declaration of the *British* Parliament, should it be laid before them, than to pay it the respect of ordering it to be laid upon the table for the perusal of the members, and without mentioning any thing of the proceedings of Parliament, to enter upon their journals, as strong declarations of their own rights as words can express: Thus one declaration of rights will stand against another, and matters will remain in *statu quo,* till some future weak minister, equally a foe to *Britain* and her Colonies, shall, by aiming at popularity, think proper to revive the extinguished flame, and draw upon himself the curses of millions yet unborn.

The predicted occurred. Charles Townshend became that "weak minister" when he engineered enactment of the Townshend Duties, imposing on the colonies taxation for the purpose of revenue. It was then that American whigs had something to protest and they could base their opposition on an actual, not a theoretical grievance. "The exercise was the thing complained of, not the right itself," Charles James Fox later explained. "When the Declaratory Act was passed, asserting the right in the fullest extent, there were no tumults in America, no opposition to government in any part of that country: but when the right came to be exercised in the manner we have seen, the whole country was alarmed, and there was an unanimous determination to oppose it. The right simply is not regarded; it is the exercise of it that is the object of opposition." One need not agree with Fox to understand what he meant. The Americans did not make an issue of abstract parliamentary claims to supremacy and sovereignty, because they were not litigating theories of legislative supremacy but were defending customary constitutional government. "They only wish to hold under this supremacy those rights which they have hitherto enjoyed," Governor Pownall told the Commons, "and to exercise them in the manner in which they have been hitherto permitted to use them."[32] The American constitutional case threaded between the two constitutions of custom and power, setting itself against departures from custom, but not concerning itself with mere claims of power.

THE DECLARATORY GRIEVANCE

Had Charles Townshend not become chancellor of the exchequer the American whig interpretation of the Declaratory Act might have evolved into constitutional law. Passage of the Townshend duties in 1767, imposing customs taxes for the purpose of revenue, ended what slim likelihood there was that the authority of Parliament to legislate for the colonies could, under the imperial constitution, return to customary restraints. Even so, American whigs, still hopeful the old constitution would revive, did not raise the ultimate constitutional issue. Rather than press through assembly resolutions or petitions the grievance of parliamentary authority to legislate, colonial whig leaders limited their constitutional protests against the Townshend duties to the taxation grievance by flooding London with demands for repeal and by enforcing trade boycotts in every seaport from the district of Maine in the North to Savannah in the South. It would be five more years before they were forced by circumstances to confront the Declaratory grievance. Colonial whigs would then let the rulers of Britain know that Parliament could not constitutionally legislate for them in any case whatsoever, as the Massachusetts House of Representatives did in May 1773, when it resolved that "the admitting any Authority to make Laws binding on the People of this Province in all Cases whatsoever, saving the General Court or Assembly, is inconsistent with the Spirit of our free Constitution, and is Repugnant to one of the most essential Clauses in our Charter."[33]

The Massachusetts resolution stated the constitutional grievance as it could have been stated in 1766 had it been in controversy, and as American whigs would state it from 1773 until the Declaration of Independence. The Declaratory Act, it would be said with increasing frequency, subjected Americans "to the absolute discretion of *Great Britain*," leaving them "no right at all,"[34] "tenants at will, of our lives, liberty, and property."[35] The Act claimed "a power of so unbounded an extent," the New York General Assembly complained, it "would totally deprive us of security and reduce us to a state of the most abject servitude."[36]

Servitude was the concept most often mentioned, slavery was the favorite word. The Declaratory Act was a scheme "for enslaving the colonies," the Assembly of Jamaica told George III. "[T]he wit of man," Pennsylvania counties instructed their elected representatives, "cannot possibly form a more clear, concise, and comprehensive definition and sentence of slavery, than these expressions contain." "I defy any one to express slavery in stronger language," Richard Price added.[37] They were referring to constitutional, not chattel slavery, the eighteenth-century concept of slavery that was the opposite of liberty—subjection to arbitrary power, even if that power was benign, benevolent, or unexecuted. "Absolute and uncontrollable power in any man, or body of men," New York legislators explained, objecting to the words "in all cases whatsoever," "necessarily implies absolute slavery in those who are subject to it, even should such a power not be carried into execution."[38]

The most comprehensive analysis of the Declaratory grievance was voted by the New York General Assembly at the rather late date of March 1775. "[C]an it be a matter of surprise," the House of Commons was asked, "that we should feel the most distressing apprehensions from the act of the British Parliament, declaring their right to bind the colonies in all cases whatever?" "Incompatible as this claim is with the very idea of freedom," the House of Lords was told, "your Lordships cannot wonder that the Colonies should express an invincible repugnance to it . . . ; let it be remembered, that the liberties of an *Englishman* are his *rights*, and that freedom consists not in a mere *exemption* from oppression, but in a *right* to such exemption, founded on law and principles of the Constitution." "[U]pon these principles," the General Assembly concluded, "it is a grievance of a most alarming nature, that the parliament of Great Britain should claim a right to enact laws binding the colonies in all cases whatsoever."[39] In contrast to 1766, by 1775 the claim alone had become a grievance.

Speakers in both the House of Commons and the House of Lords praised the first Continental Congress for not making the Declaratory

Act a grievance.[40] It was impossible for the second Continental Congress to ignore it. "What is to defend us against so enormous, so unlimited a Power?" the second Congress asked. "Not a single Man of those who assume it, is chosen by us; or is subject to our Controul or Influence; but on the Contrary, they are all of them exempt from the Operation of such Laws." Considering the date, these words do not seem extreme, yet an anonymous Bristol pamphleteer thought they contained "the whole Sum and Substance of American Grievances."[41]

Lord Mansfield agreed with the Bristol author. The Americans, he argued, did not complain of "particular injuries so much" as of Parliament's claim to bind them in all cases whatsoever. "That is the true bone of contention," he is quoted as saying. "They positively deny the right not the mode of exercising it."[42] Even by 1774 not very many colonial whigs were ready to go so far, but their numbers increased as the realization spread that parliamentary notions of legislative sovereignty, not parliamentary taxation, were what threatened constitutionalism in North America. It was in 1774 that a series of resolutions passed by whigs from South Carolina to Pennsylvania blamed the imperial crisis on the Declaratory Act. "That the power assumed by the parliament of Great Britain to bind the people of these colonies, 'in all cases whatsoever,' is unconstitutional, and therefore the source of these unhappy differences." The divisiveness came not just from the abstract claim itself, but—when Parliament exercised the claim—from the constitutional necessity to resist. In July 1774 a whig convention of New Jersey counties decried the "unconstitutional and oppressive" Declaratory Act "which we think ourselves bound in duty to ourselves and our posterity, by all constitutional means in our power, to oppose."[43]

Despite the earlier ambivalence, there was American support for the charge made by John Wilkes, long after the Revolutionary War had commenced, that "This one statute, the Declaratory Act, is the fountain, from which not only waters of bitterness, but rivers of blood, have flowed."[44] Wilkes spoke symbolically, quite appropriately as the Declaratory Act had always been more symbol than substance. In 1766 it had been for imperialists a symbol of authority for what Parliament could but most likely would never do. By 1774 it had become for American whigs the symbol of their grievance against what Parliament had been doing ever since Charles Townshend enacted his duties.

EFFECTS OF DECLARATORY

Although it was never important for its substance, the Declaratory Act was, in addition to being a symbol of power, a statement of potential policy and, eventually, the basis of a legislative program. Between 1766 and 1774, it became the constitutional foundation upon which Great Britain postulated its claim of right to legislate for the colonies. Merely having the law on the statute books changed substantially how the imperial side looked at the colonies. Under Lord North's leadership the ministry got in the habit of using the Declaratory Act not just as proof that Parliament had authority to legislate for North America, but as a reason why Parliament should pass specific legislation—to preserve its sovereignty by asserting it. A discernible but elusive change occurred in the jurisprudence of parliamentary debate; at least for the exponents of the constitutionalism of power, for whom, when dealing with colonial issues, arguments of precedent and custom became less relevant than before. They had what they now thought was better authority—sovereign, statutory authority—for the right to bind the colonies in all cases by legislative will and pleasure.[45]

Sovereignty alone became justification for using power. Members of Parliament who otherwise might have been reluctant doubters, felt compelled to support the "law," and American petitions questioning the right were not received by either house.[46] In March 1767, summarizing arguments made by members of Britain's House of Commons, Charles Garth explained to South Carolina's Commons House of Assembly how the Declaratory Act had changed the way some people thought about legislative authority. "While the Question of Right, it was said, was in Doubt and in Discussion Lords and Gentlemen might with Propriety differ in Opinion, but when the Doubt was removed, and Parliament had after the most Mature Deliberation so solemnly declared the Law and Constitution of the Realm, former opinions must submit, and the Authority of Government must be maintained."[47]

Seven years later, as the constitutional controversy was winding down and in the very month that civil war was about to break out in the rural towns of eastern Massachusetts Bay, a "printed paper" was circulated among the opposition in the Commons charging that the support that "the minority" had given to the Declaratory Act was still providing the ministry with "a most powerful advantage over them and their cause." In "almost every debate," the paper complained, the ministry was reminding the minority "that they are only exercising that very authority which *they* established and declared *unlimited*."[48] It would seem that not only the Act, but the support originally given the Act, had become precedent justifying American legislation.

In the colonies the legalism was different. The Declaratory Act did not alter American constitutional notions. "[T]hese prejudices," F.B. reported of colonial whig thought, "are still so fixed and rooted in the Americans, that it is supposed not a single man among them has been convinced of his error by that act of parliament." The finality of sovereign command was a constitutional possibility that the American legal mind was not yet ready to accept. "True it is, that it has been solemnly declared by Parliament, that Parliament has such a power," John Dickinson wrote, instructing Pennsylvania's delegates to the Continental Congress. "But that declaration leaves the point just as it was before: for if Parliament had not the power before, the declaration could not give it."[49]

It is the judgment of some recent historians that the American legal mind was wrong. "After 1766," Ian Christie has written, "the legal fact was established that Parliament had power to tax the colonies by virtue of its own legislative declaration." The certainty of Christie's "legal fact" is marvelously anachronistic. From the perspective of the nineteenth-century constitution of law by command, the revolutionary controversy can be dismissed by a historian's "legal fact." For eighteenth-century participants in the controversy that law would have been no more persuasive than the law of Arthur L. Goodhart, a better lawyer than Christie. "Parliament adopted wholeheartedly the doctrine of sovereignty as stated by Hobbes, that in every state there must be a sovereign, uncontrolled by the law," Goodhart wrote of the Declaratory Act. "Thus a theory of law that had cost Charles I his head and James II his throne was about to cost Great Britain its American Colonies."[50]

Of course there were many members of Parliament, quite possibly the majority, for whom Christie's law, not Goodhart's law would have been the law—if they had thought about it. But surely legal and constitutional history cannot be written by the historian adopting one of the theories of law that were competing for supremacy during the period under study and pronouncing its premises to be "legal fact." Contemporaries who took part in the revolutionary debate, such as Alderman Beckford, the earl of Abingdon, and General Conway, would have objected. Consider what each of these three men said in Parliament. Beckford spoke to the question whether the Commons should receive a Pennsylvania petition, which Welbore Ellis moved not be read as it denigrated the Declaratory Act. A vocal opponent of the emerging constitutionalism of sovereign power, Beckford espoused an older constitutional norm. "Acts of Parliament are not like the laws of the Medes and Persians," he protested. "An Act of Parliament against common right is a nullity, so says Lord Coke." Christie's law was not Beckford's law. As late as 1778 Abingdon was still protesting the Declaratory Act. "The legislative body has done what it was not authorised by its constitution to do," he complained. "It has dared to say, that it has a right to bind in all cases whatsoever; thereby making the rights of Englishmen subject to its will, and in a limited government, establishing unlimited tyranny." For Abingdon rights existed independently of parliamentary "legal fact." Conway, as secretary of state in the Rockingham administration, had been the minister who introduced the Declaratory Bill in the Commons and moved its passage. Certainly he was one member of the Commons who knew what fact Parliament had ordained and he did not think the Act created the "legal fact" of legislative right. "It was a declaration on one side, which was never disputed, nor ever expressly acknowledged on the other," he contended. "It was a declaration that had better never been brought in question. . . . It was the unlimited use that some hungry statesmen were eager to make of it, which caused the Americans to take the alarm, and to endeavour to confine it within the line of constitutional dependence." Perhaps Conway should have realized that parliamentary sovereignty settled the legal fact, but he was not thinking as a twentieth-century historian, that is, thinking of the constitution as it would come to be in the nineteenth century. He was, instead, thinking of the constitution of customary restraint under which fewer questions were final because fewer concepts were absolute.[51]

Governor Pownall gave the constitutional dichotomy a different slant, summing up the two approaches to the Declaratory Act not as a conflict of the seventeenth-century customary constitution against the nineteenth-century constitution of command, but as a conflict of the British constitution against the American constitution. "Parliament had, by a solemn act," he noted in the fifth edition of his *Administration*, "declared, that it hath a right to make laws, which shall be binding upon the people of the Colonies, subjects of Great Britain, in *all cases whatsoever;* while the Colonists say, in *all cases which can consist with the fundamental rules of the constitution.*" Later, in the same edition, Pownall made an observation showing that even a student of the constitution such as himself, who supported parliamentary sovereignty over the colonies and knew the Americans were pleading a different constitutional theory, could not quite escape drawing conclusions from that other constitution of fundamental rights. "[T]he true intent and meaning" of the Act, he wrote, "refers only to cases of necessity, and not to the wantonly and arbitrarily interfering with, or superceding that political liberty; which they have, so long as they do not misuse it."[52] Parliament may have been supreme, but supreme in an attenuated sense.

Pownall was attempting to straddle two constitutional traditions, and there is reason to believe he thought the task hopeless. Earlier he had urged the Commons to be less insistent about its right to legislate for the colonies. There was more to be lost than gained. But no matter. "[W]hatever may be my opinion of that right . . . I know it *never* will be decided by arguments, reasonings, resolutions, or even Acts of Parliament—It will be decided by *power*."[53] A decision of power meant the constitution of sovereign command, but to understand what troubled Pownall one has to see the right through the earlier constitution of customary authority. That constitution made the decision of power almost inevitable once the Declaratory Act became law. By claiming the right in all cases whatsoever, the Act meant that Great Britain had to defend the claim even if the defense meant "subduing America."[54] Because of that fact, the Declaratory Act was not ordinary legislation. "It is like Magna Charta, or the Bill of Rights, a Fundamental Law. It is a legislative establishment of a constitutional principle; and is therefore a Law which no future Legislature, that professes a regard for the Constitution, can annul."[55] It could not be annulled, that is, unless America insisted on the older meaning of fundamental law.

CHAPTER FOUR

THE LOGIC OF SUPREMACY

"We have neither knowledge nor system nor principle," Governor Thomas Pownall complained of the governance of the British empire following passage of the Declaratory Act, "we have but one word . . . sovereignty—and it is like some word to a mad-man which, whenever mentioned, throws him into his ravings."[1] He meant that the Declaratory Act had elicited a way of arguing that was a departure from the familiar rhetoric of English jurisprudence. In the new constitutional liturgy quickened by the Act, power rather than right, expediency rather than precedent, were measures for action, and the concept of sovereignty was used to answer questions of law that usually were answered by experience, practice, precedent, and history. When Americans appealed to the traditional, familiar, English constitutionalism of custom, imperialists replied by citing the Declaratory Act, that is, the sovereignty of Parliament.

Even as late as the 1770s the concept of sovereignty seemed to many legal theorists to be a foreign, uncomfortable intrusion upon common-law thought, despite being by no means new to English constitutional jurisprudence.[2] The antiprerogative lawyer Sir James Whitelocke had defined it as early as 1610 when arguing against James I's claim to authority of promulgating new impositions by letters patent. "[I]n every Com-

mon-wealth and government there be found some rights of Soveraignty,"
he contended, "unless Custome, or the provisional ordinance of that
State doe otherwise dispose of them: which Soveraigne power is *potestas
suprema*, a power that can controule all other powers, and cannot be
controuled but by itself." It is worth emphasizing that Whitelocke be-
trayed a common-law training when he said that custom and organic
law checked sovereignty. Even as late as the age of the American Revolution, the definition of sovereignty was clouded by the reluctance of many
constitutionalists to locate arbitrary power anywhere within the con-
fines of the British constitution.[3]

The English constitution had first encountered the concept of sovereignty during the Civil War when Charles I and the House of Commons competed for the allegiance and obedience of subjects. A theory
emerged with the writings of Thomas Hobbes, Robert Filmer, John
Locke departing from the common-law tradition and from the constitutionalism that would dominate American legal thought both before the
Revolution and into the age of the early republic. Hobbes and Filmer
utilized sovereignty to place state power beyond the limitations of legalism, custom, precedent, history, and inherent individual rights, or what,
in the late eighteenth century, was known as constitutional government.
"Power," no longer constrained by "right," was free to function on behalf
of a more efficient, sensible, practical law, unencumbered by outdated
precedent and time-worn custom.[4] The concept of sovereignty had compelling attractions but did not gain indisputable acceptance in England
or Great Britain due to the threefold opposition of (1) common lawyers
trained in the legalism of a law that restrained more than it served power,
(2) theorists of liberty mindful of the doctrine of nonresistance and the
maxim of passive obedience, discredited constitutional principles that
the eighteenth century associated with the House of Stuart, and (3) constitutionalists who could not brook notions of arbitrary power.[5]

Dictionaries in the age of the American Revolution defined "sovereignty" as the "highest place, power or excellence" or the "highest place,
supremacy." There was a set formula, familiar to every reader of popular
political literature, that explained the notion in terms of ultimate, irre-
ducible authority: "there is in every civil community, some where or
other placed, a supreme power of making laws, and inforcing the observation of them."[6] The rule was so irrefragable that proof was superfluous.
"My lords, it is impossible to endeavour to prove a self evident truth,"
Lord Chancellor Northington exclaimed during the Declaratory Act debate. "Every government can arbitrarily impose laws on all its subjects;
there must be a supreme dominion in every state."[7] That was the salient
factor. Sovereignty had to be the "supreme power," a power "uncon-

troulable and irresistible" or, as Blackstone said, "a supreme, irresistible, absolute, uncontrolled authority."[8] Samuel Johnson concocted what H. L. A. Hart termed "a layman's version of Blackstone's principle."

> In sovereignty there are no gradations. . . . There must in every society be some power or other from which there is no appeal, which admits no restrictions, which pervades the whole mass of the community, regulates and adjusts all subordination, enacts laws or repeals them, erects or annuls judicatures, extends or contracts privileges, exempt itself from question and control, and bounded only by physicial necessity.[9]

LOGIC OF PARLIAMENT

"The giving of laws to a people forms the most exalted degree of human sovereignty," Richard Wooddeson wrote when Vinerian professor of law in Oxford during the American Revolution, "and is perhaps in effect, or in strict propriety of speech, the only truly supreme power of the state."[10] There are two concepts compounded by Wooddeson that must be kept separated if we are to understand the controversy over Parliament's authority to legislate for the colonies. They are the concept of legislation and the concept of supreme power. We should keep them separate because American whigs always did. Most British constitutional theorists also distinguished between them—but not all, a consideration that confuses the story.

On one crucial point there was little disagreement during the first six decades of the eighteenth century: sovereignty could not be divided. From that basic maxim the concept of supremacy sprang. "It is a fundamental principle in Government, *That Sovereign Authority must lodge somewhere,*" Jared Eliot told Connecticut legislators in that colony's 1738 election sermon.[11] There was no dispute among British political theorists where that place was. "The *summa potestas* of any State is said to consist in the Power to make Laws, and to enforce the Execution of them," an anonymous commentator on the British constitution wrote. That meant the institution that legislated, whether it was the sole person of an absolute monarch or the deliberation of an assembly, be it hereditary, representative, or elective.[12] "Why is the legislative power supreme?" Lord Bolingbroke asked. "Because what gives law to all must be supreme," he answered.[13] The reason, Blackstone explained, was that legislation "is the greatest act of superiority that can be exercised by one being over another." It was legislation, therefore, that located supremacy. "[T]he power of making laws constitutes the supreme authority, so wherever the supreme authority in any state resides, it is the right of that authority to make laws." As a result, Blackstone concluded, "[s]overeignty and legislature are indeed convertible terms; one cannot subsist without the other."[14]

The logic of supremacy in legislation led eighteenth-century British constitutional theory to the logic of parliamentary supremacy. "In all states," Blackstone reasoned, "there is an absolute supreme power, to which the right of legislation belongs; and which, by the singular constitution of these kingdoms, is vested in the king, lords, and commons."[15] What this meant in operational terms was discussed many times during the eighteenth century, but for our purposes it is enough to consider the words of the law compiler, Giles Jacob, who contended that "the Power of Parliament, for making of Laws, and proceeding by Bill, is so absolute, that it cannot be confined either for Causes or Persons within any Bounds."[16] He meant, of course, that it could not be limited by individual rights or immemorial custom. Put even more concisely, "[t]he legislative power of Britain is, and must be, as absolute and uncontroulable as any power on earth." The concept was sovereignty but generally the emphasis was on supremacy. The "supreme" power of the kingdom was in king, Lords, and Commons: "They constitute the supreme legislative authority of this country, to which every other power of the state is subordinate: they have the power of making laws, and of enforcing obedience to those laws, to which both the supreme and subjugated are bound to submit. From their jurisdiction there is no appeal: and they who resist, forfeit their protection."[17]

In the eighteenth century, thought of the authority of Parliament first brought to mind the word "supremacy," second the word "over," and third "subordinate." The supreme Parliament was "over" other branches of the government, and other "powers of the state" were "subordinate" to the supreme Parliament. There was one other word that belonged with these three, a word we in the twentieth century no longer associate with parliamentary supremacy, but which was the whole object of the concept of supremacy in the eighteenth century. That word was "Crown." Parliament was supreme over the king and the monarchy was subordinate to Parliament. The reason for being of the concept of supremacy, why the concept became dominant in eighteenth-century constitutional law, was supremacy over the Crown.

The doctrine of parliamentary supremacy over the king was not incongruous even though in constitutional language Parliament was "king, Lords, and Commons," a tripartite legislature of which the Crown was not only one third part but the part always mentioned first. That, however, was constitutional theory in 1765, not constitutional reality. It had been decades since a monarch by vetoing a bill had participated in the legislative process. Still, if the "king in Parliament" was no longer a significant legislating factor, the king outside of Parliament remained a potential threat to constitutional liberty. And liberty—the defense of liberty to be precise—was what made the concept of supremacy so central for eighteenth-century constitutionalists and why parliamentary supremacy then meant supremacy over the Crown, not as it would in the nineteenth century, supremacy over the law and the constitution, or sovereignty.

After repeal of the Stamp Act and passage of the Declaratory Act, the fact was quickly evident that a second meaning of the concept of supremacy had emerged: parliamentary supremacy over the colonies. "That is a line from which you ought never to deviate," Governor Thomas Pownall urged the House of Commons.

> The parliament hath, and must have, from the nature and essence of the constitution, has had, and ever will have, a sovereign supreme power and jurisdiction over every part of the dominions of the state, to make laws in all cases whatsoever; this is a proposition which exists of absolute necessity—its truth is intuitive, and need not be demonstrated—and yet there may be times and occasions when this ought to be declared and held forth to the eyes and notice of the subject.[18]

Pownall said that the concept of parliamentary supremacy over the colonies was constitutional, but that was one of the debatable points of the revolutionary controversy. Neither constitutional custom nor indisputable practice, after all, supported the notion. It was supported by the logic of power. The fact is revealing, therefore, that those constitutional scholars who explained parliamentary supremacy over the colonies in terms of sovereignty, did not cite common law but political theory—often John Locke's theory of legislative sovereignty.[19] Although it is premature, as that theory must be developed in detail, mention can be made here that American whigs rejected Locke in this regard and continued to reject him when they wrote their state constitutions. Or, perhaps it would be more precise to say, they respected Locke but with a reservation that made all the difference between a concept of supremacy based on theoretical sovereignty and a concept of supremacy based on the restrained constitutionalism of customary experience. "It must be acknowledged necessary," the *New Haven Gazette* explained, "that there be some supreme legislative authority, in every state whose power and jurisdiction must extend to the whole, but may not be exercised as to violate the rights, liberties, and properties of particular persons, corporations, or communities, but for their preservation and protection." That was a large qualifier and must not be thought peculiarly American. It was nonLockean, to be sure, but vintage English common law and, as late as 1776, defendable British constitutional law. In 1778, a London pamphleteer writing against the American claim to legislative autonomy and in support of Parliament's authority to legislate for the colonies, contended: "But all sovereign legislative authority must be *supreme,* while it exists, and while it preserves the bounds prescribed by its original constitution. The difference between the free and arbitrary governments is not to be sought for in their Administration, but in their Constitution, for in their executive and legislative authority, they must all be alike supreme."[20] If this had been the parliamentary supremacy for which Great Britain was contending, American whigs could have accepted it. It was a supremacy that while supreme in law would not have been sovereign over law.

Two other applications of the concept of supremacy in eighteenth-century constitutionalism must be understood as they will receive extensive attention in the remaining chapters. One was parliamentary supremacy over the constitution. "What pray is the Constitution but the Parliament?" it was asked, a question most constitutionalists probably would still have answered in the negative. More controversial, and an element of supremacy that was both a given of the doctrine of sovereignty and is a central issue of this study, was parliamentary supremacy over the law. Jeremy Bentham stated the rule that certainly was controlling for the future when he wrote: "Nothing is unlawful that is the clear intent of the Legislature. Nothing can be void: neither on account of opposition to a pretended Law of Nature, nor on any other. . . . Nothing is gained to Liberty by such language, and much is lost to common sense. Yet it is much used by the advocates for Liberty. We hear it every day. I am always sorry when I hear it." The most interesting thing Bentham said was that he "heard it every day." That fact explains why he was arguing for a legal proposition that in this century is indisputable. Perhaps we would not ask why so many of his contemporaries disagreed with him, if we recalled that the future for which he wrote was the British constitutional future, not the American future.[21]

Logic of the Revolution

British whigs and supporters of parliamentary imperial supremacy knew that the British constitutional future was irreconcilable with the

American constitutional past. When Britons looked forward with their constitutional principles, they anticipated a constitution of parliamentary sovereignty. When American whigs looked at the same constitution they were seeing it from the past or the historical perspective of customary rights, a vista stretching back over a timeless infinity to the ancient constitution of Gothic Europe. In theory, that constitution was an endless chain of custom, evolving by circumstances and changing with time, but never altered by the imposition of sovereign will and pleasure. That last notion was the rub for those theorists who were exponents of parliamentary supremacy—in other words, for the British constitutional future. For them, the American constitutional past was no unbroken line of customary rights. Sovereign will and pleasure had shifted the course of custom, not only by the numerous statutes of Parliament said to be precedents for Parliament's authority to legislate for the colonies, but most famously and dramatically by the Glorious Revolution.

The Glorious Revolution had shattered the American whig constitutional past when the English and Scottish parliaments, by legislative command, removed James II from the throne, replaced him with William and Mary, and settled the succession of the crown on a Protestant line. George III owed his throne to an act of Parliament, a constitutional rite of passage making the Lords and Commons supreme over the king and, according to an argument increasingly being voiced although not fully understood in the mother country, sovereign over the constitution. By the most extreme constitutional version, the English Parliament, which, in theory, had been a creature of the customary constitution, became the constitution when, by its institutional will and pleasure, it invested William III with the kingship over Anne who had a stronger hereditary claim than he.

> [F]rom whom did he receive it? Not from the *collective* body of the people, but from the *two Houses of Parliament*, from the House of Lords in their *own right*, and from the *House of Commons* as the immediate delegate, *the virtual representative* of the inhabitants of England and the American Colonies. The Colonists by *acknowledging* William to be their *lawful* Sovereign, did not barely *admit*, but actually *constituted* and *appointed* the House of Commons to be their virtual representative. They did not submit to the Revolution as to an act of *legal authority*, for that it could not be, since all *legal* authority was abolished by the *Abdication* of James, and could not be *restored* till William *had been acknowledged*. He received the sovereignty of the Colonies, exactly in the same manner as he received the sovereignty of England; as the *voluntary* offering of the people, and the House of Commons was considered as acting, on this solemn and important occasion, in the capacity of *trustees, dele-*

gates, virtual representatives of the *collective* body of people inhabiting the whole British [English] empire.[22]

When it replaced James II with William and Mary, Parliament not only established supremacy over the monarchy, it transmuted the customary constitution into the constitution of parliamentary command and, it was claimed, the North American colonies were then and there summoned to obey that command. Parliament had, after all, by legislating a new line of kings and queens for the colonists, exerted as high an exercise of sovereign authority as the eighteenth century could imagine, "the Zenith of its legal Omnipotence" as one South Carolinian described it, so omnipotent, in fact, its orbit had to include all the dominions of the Crown.[23]

The election of William and Mary, exponents of parliamentary supremacy contended, was not only "the most evident proofs of the supreme legislative authority of Parliament, over the Colonies," it was also the premier precedent establishing parliamentary supremacy. The argument began with the premise that "[t]he Abdication of James the Second had *dissolved* the *social compact* between England and the Colonies." It was then, at least if they had understood that the original contract (not the social contract) had been terminated, that the Americans, had they any constitutional objections to parliamentary rule, would have renegotiated a new agreement or pleaded a novation.[24] Instead, the history of the times showed that the colonists had done the opposite. Every North American assembly acquiesced in the new constitution of the Glorious Revolution, and, as a result it was claimed, *"in the plainest and clearest manner acknowledged themselves* to be virtually represented in the British Parliament, since they actually transferred their allegiance [to William and Mary] in submission to its decrees." Two crucial points of evidence that no one in the 1690s noticed became of great importance to imperialists arguing the American Revolution controversy: (1) Parliament did not ask the advice and concurrence of the colonial assemblies to the election of William; and (2) none of the assemblies passed enabling acts "for settling the crown upon King William, or the illustrious house of Hanover."[25] From these two facts followed the legal conclusion that during the Glorious Revolution the Parliament of England had acted sovereignly over North America. It had commanded and the colonial assemblies had obeyed its sovereign decision. Seen from this perspective, all that the Declaratory Act had done was codify the Glorious Revolution. "The constitution of England, as it now stands, was fixed at the Revolution, in 1688," Charles Inglis wrote, questioning American whig constancy to the ancient, customary constitution. "What is it to us, what the constitution of England was two or three hundred or a thousand years ago? That constitution, as fixed at the revolution, as it *now* stands, is what we are interested in."[26]

American whigs could not refute the historical fact of parliamentary monarchical election, but they had to limit the constitutional doctrine of supremacy that imperialists said followed from election. It was not an easy task, as Alexander Hamilton discovered when he attempted to explain it and found himself depending on a lawyer's narrow reading of a theoretical contract. "Admitting, that the King of Great Britain was enthroned by virtue of an act of parliament, and that he is King of America, because he is King of Great-Britain, yet the act of parliament is not the *efficient cause* of his being the King of America," Hamilton contended. "It is only the *occasion* of it. He is King of America, by virtue of a compact between us and the Kings of Great-Britain." Hamilton referred to the second original contract or the colonial contract made by the first settlers of the colonies with the then reigning English monarch. "So that, to disclaim, the authority of a British Parliament over us, does by no means imply the dereliction of our allegiance to British Monarchs. Our compact takes no cognizance of the manner of their accession to the throne. It is sufficient for us, that they are Kings of England."[27]

Hamilton's argument was the standard American whig defense against the constitutional implications of the Glorious Revolution. John Adams had developed it in some detail during his memorable debate with Governor Thomas Hutchinson in 1773. There was, he had argued, a constitutional autonomy stretching from current opposition to parliamentary supremacy back to the original contract negotiated with Charles I, a chain made stronger when Massachusetts staged its own rebellion of 1688.

> It is easy upon this Principle to account for the Acknowledgment of and Submission to King William and Queen Mary as Successors of Charles the First, in the Room of King James: Besides it is to be considered, that the People in the Colony as well as in England had suffered under the TYRANT James, by which he had alike forfeited his Right to reign over both. There had been a Revolution here as well as in England. The Eyes of the People here were upon William and Mary, and the News of their being proclaimed in England was as your Excellency's History[28] tells us, "the most joyful News ever received in New-England." And if they were not proclaimed here "by virtue of an Act of the Colony," it was, as we think may be concluded from the Tenor of your History, with the general or universal Consent of the People as apparently as if "such Act had passed." It is *Consent alone*, that makes any human Laws binding; and as a learned Author observes, a purely *voluntary* Submission to an Act, because it is highly in our Favor and for our Benefit, is in all

> Equity and Justice to be deemed as not at all proceeding from the
> *Right* we include in the Legislators, that they thereby obtain an
> *Authority* over us, and that ever hereafter we must obey them of
> *Duty*. We would observe that one of the first Acts of the General
> Assembly of this Province since the present Charter [granted by
> William], was an Act requiring the taking the Oaths mentioned in
> an Act of Parliament, to which you refer us: For what Purpose was
> this Act of the Assembly passed, if it was the Sense of the Legislators
> that the Act of Parliament was in Force in the Province.

The implied consent the colonists accorded William and Mary was consent to continue the original contract, not consent to a newfangled parliamentary sovereignty. An enabling act had been unnecessary because of the existing contract, and for other matters, such as oaths of allegiances, prerevolutionary American whigs could say that the Massachusetts General Court doubted Parliament's authority or it would not have enacted at least one enabling statute. "So that our allegiance to his majesty," Adams later explained, "is not due by virtue of any act of a British parliament, but by our own charter and province laws. It ought to be remembered, that there was a revolution here, as well as in England, and that we made an original, express contract with King William, as well as the people of England."[29]

That last contention was an Adams hyperbole. Other colonial whigs did not claim that a second original colonial contract had been made with William and Mary, certainly not one expressed rather than implied. After all, if Adams was right about the colonists accepting William and Mary as successor parties to the old contract, there was no need for a new contract. Adams was probably trying to protect the whigs' case even against unforeseen contingencies. If the other side did not agree that William and Mary were bound by the first original contract, to say that the second original contract was expressed rather than implied gave it the appearance of a stronger compact with, in theory, the suggestion it was one easily proven. It was a small point, but that Adams thought it worth making shows how seriously he regarded an argument that has been largely overlooked or forgotten by historians.

Perhaps too much should not be made of how the Glorious Revolution changed the constitutional connection between the colonies and Parliament. The changes wrought by the Revolution were simply not as authoritative for settling questions of legislative power and sovereignty as today's lawyers would expect.[30] The Revolution was the traumatic constitutional event of what then was recent British history and "Revolution principles" were appealed to by so many sides of so many constitutional and political debates that the answers provided by the Revolution were on many issues curiously undefinitive.[31] Moreover, by the 1770s, the realization that parliamentary supremacy meant parliamentary arbitrariness made the Glorious Revolution more controversial among constitutionalists than has generally been appreciated by scholars of the American Revolution.[32] These considerations may help explain why neither side in the American Revolution controversy took the logic of the Glorious Revolution settlement as far as it might have been taken.

Although both British imperialists and colonial whigs hesitated pushing the Glorious Revolution conclusion to the extent that theory could have pushed it, imperialist hesitancy was less pronounced than American hesitancy. More practical than constitutional, the British hesitation resulted less from a belief that the colonists had not been constitutionally included in the supreme sovereignty wrought by the Revolution, than from a realization that several other significant constitutional results of the Revolution had not been extended to Americans and that Parliament did not intend to extend them. Among these was one of the most controversial rights at issue between the colonies and the mother country, a right that the English people obtained as a direct result of the Revolution: the tenure of good behavior protecting judicial independence in the United Kingdom. American demands for equal constitutional protection was a major revolutionary grievance. There were other statutes and constitutional rights spawned by the Glorious Revolution that Parliament withheld from the colonists: the Bill of Rights, the Act of Settlement, and the Habeas Corpus Statute. Their denial was practically immaterial to Americans as each colony could have enacted its own bill of rights or habeas corpus law. But in constitutional theory it was serious, giving the Americans an inequality grievance and making the imperial argument appear inconsistent when it was contended that North America had been included within the orbit of the new sovereignty-of-Parliament constitution established at the Revolution.[33]

American whigs, by contrast, faced a serious constitutional predicament if they went too far in protesting that the supremacy established by Parliament at the Glorious Revolution did not bind them. It could lead them directly to a royalist conclusion, a conclusion they would be surprisingly willing to draw when they had no choice, but one that they were determined not to be locked into as long as it could be avoided. It is important to think of the Glorious Revolution as it was seen by eighteenth-century whigs. When they thought of the supremacy created by the Revolution they did not think of it as it would be thought of in the nineteenth century: a supremacy over the constitution, or even a supremacy over the colonies. The true constitutional achievement of the Revolution, as seen from the perspective of eighteenth-century constitu-

tionalism, had been the security obtained by the two houses of Parliament as they established supremacy over the Crown. American doubts
about this aspect of the Glorious Revolution threatened to undermine,
perhaps destroy, that security.[34]

In 1769, William Knox, believing the answer was so constitutionally
obvious there could be no other, had thrown caution to the winds and
asked American whigs how the colonies could claim a relationship to the
king independent of Parliament, when it was Parliament that had settled
the Crown on the House of Hanover. For over five years leading colonial
whigs avoided replying. Then, after Parliament enacted the Coercive
laws, John Dickinson decided that the American answer could be stated
publicly without undue risk. It did not follow, he wrote in legislative
instructions adopted by the Pennsylvania Congress, "that because the
two houses, with the consent of the nation, made a king, *therefore* the
two houses can make laws." The Revolution had not changed the constitution, or, as John Adams had said, the original colonial contract was
still in force. "The colonies have no other head than the king of *England*," Dickinson concluded. "The person, who by the laws of that
realm is king of that realm, is our king."[35]

Seeking to contest parliamentary supremacy, yet products of the same
constitutional dynamics that, at the Glorious Revolution, had made parliamentary supremacy a constitutional necessity, colonial whigs adopted
a constitutional solution that shocked British whigs but which was dictated by constitutional logic. They turned for constitutional protection
to the most feared bugbear in the liturgy of English common-law liberty,
the royal prerogative. There was little other choice once Parliament rejected their first defense of the old constitution of Cokean common law,
and of rights derived from customary authority, not from sovereign grant.
The only alternative that they had was natural law, and American whigs
would never be willing to trust their constitutional security to authority
so weak.

LOGIC OF EMPIRE

Saying that "Sovereign Authority" had to be vested in some institution,
the Reverend Mr. Eliot told the Connecticut Assembly in 1738, that
"[t]he Community have placed this in the Legislature." He meant that
supremacy, perhaps he did not mean sovereignty, was lodged in the Connecticut Assembly and the other legislatures of the North American colonies. In constitutional language what Eliot said was that supreme legisla-

tive power was located in king, council, and House of Representatives, not king, Lords, and Commons.[36]

For imperialists who gave thought to constitutional theory, as most seemed to do, logic dictated a different conclusion. "In an Empire, extended and diversified as that of *Great-Britain*, there must be a supreme Legislature, to which all other Powers must be subordinate," Governor Francis Bernard told the Massachusetts General Court. The conclusion followed from the certainty of deductive reasoning. "There cannot be two *equal* legislatures in any state; there may indeed be *one supreme*, and *others inferior.*"[37] That Parliament possessed sovereign, supreme legislative authority over every part of the empire, Governor Thomas Pownall assured the Commons, "is a proposition which exists of absolute necessity—its truth is intuitive, and need not be demonstrated." Attorney General Yorke used the expression "vital principle of empire" twice in one speech to get the idea across. "This universality of the legislative power is the vital principle of the whole Empire," he said, adding that because Americans seemed to have other notions, he was "alarmed for the vital principle of your Empire, the sovereignty of this country."[38]

The logic of an imperial legislative authority flowed from the logic of *imperium in imperio;* there could no more be a state within a state than two souls in one person or two hearts in one body.[39] The proposition was stated hundreds if not thousands of times. Sir Egerton Leigh, imperial placeman serving as admiralty judge for South Carolina, summed it up as well as anyone would:

> [A]s there must be in every State one *supreme Legislative* Jurisdiction, so the same, in like manner, has a right to an occasional exercise thereof, over the most distant and remote Branches of the Empire. And this one over-ruling Power is implied in the nature of things; for there cannot exist, at one and the same time, in the same Empire Two supreme Jurisdictions; because *Equals* can on no score controul *Equals*, and Two supreme Directions imply two distinct and separate States: I therefore hold, that in our Government this One *Supreme Legislature* is the *British Parliament*, which clearly possesses *summum imperium;* whilst our Colonies, at the same time, possess certain Subordinate Powers of Legislation, as essential to *their* Political Existence.

The old familiar constitutional theorem of sovereignty, that "there must be one unlimited and uncontroulable authority lodged somewhere," led unreservedly to the imperial truism that "[i]n every Empire a supreme legislative authority over the whole must exist somewhere, with an adequate power to controul and bind all and every part of which it consists; otherwise it would be an Empire without government, without laws, and without power."[40]

The rigidity of the logic of supremacy left little opportunity for eighteenth-century imperial constitutional thought to consider the possibilities of federalism. The doctrine of a single, controlling sovereignty made it difficult to credit the possibility of a federal union of provinces. If one were attempted, if there were a confederation without a supreme legislative power it would surely collapse into anarchy.[41] There were two imperatives demanding unified control: the imperative of the undivided state and the imperative that supreme authority must be sovereign.

"The British empire is one single undivided state; governed by the same general laws, and acknowledging one supreme authority," the argument went. "The British legislature is the great representative of this *one* state; and is, indeed, politically speaking, the state itself." If Parliament were less than sovereign for the whole, Richard Jackson explained, the British empire would not be a state. "[B]ecause an Universal Legislature is a necessary part of every intire State, the Parl[iamen]t is that Universal Legislature of the British Dominions & must be so unless it be contended either that the British Dominions do not form one Intire State or that there is some other Universal Legislature."[42] If the colonists were not subject to parliamentary supremacy, they were "no part of the British state."[43]

The concept of supremacy threatened to make federalism impossible in the eighteenth-century British empire. "Supreme power and authority must not, cannot reside equally every where throughout an empire," the reasoning went. "For this would rather suppose absolute confusion and anarchy, than any imaginable mode of government." Just as there had to be a sovereign legislature or lawmaker in the single state, so there could be no more than one. "If we admit more such assemblies than one, the power and authority of all but one must necessarily be abridged, and brought in subordination to one only as supreme. For if each assembly, in this case, were absolute they would, it is evident, form not one only, but so many different governments perfectly independent of one another."[44]

Whatever federalism could be imagined was severely curtailed by the rigidity of theory. "Local Purposes may indeed be provided for by local Powers," Thomas Whately wrote when defending the Stamp Act which he had drafted, "but general Provisions can only be made by a Council that has general Authority."[45] Colonial assemblies had undoubted authority to legislate, but they were subordinate, unequal, and not empowered to act independently of Parliament, otherwise Parliament's supremacy would be hollow, not supreme, and nonsovereign.[46] The most obvious truth was that supremacy had to be whole and could not be divided. "[T]o divide this supremacy, by allowing it to exist in some cases, and not in all,—over a part of the members, and not the whole,—is to weaken and confound the operations of the system," Pennsylvania's Joseph Galloway contended. "[T]he colonies must be considered as complete members of the state, or so many different communities . . . as independent of it, as Hanover, France, or Spain."[47] The constitutional doctrine was so uncontrovertible it answered all questions except one. "[A]ll that seems necessary to be asked," London's *Public Advertiser* thought, "is, Where shall this supreme power be lodged—at LONDON, or at BOSTON?"[48]

For a remarkable number of articulate American tories, the logic of supremacy answered enough constitutional doubts to be their constitutional explanation for remaining loyalists. Two basic constitutional theorems were irrefutable. First, there must be a supreme legislative authority lodged somewhere, and second, every member of society in each part of the single state is subordinate to the supreme legislature.[49] In his memorable constitutional plea to the first Continental Congress, Galloway made the logic of supremacy the theoretical foundation of his plan for a union between Great Britain and the colonies, with an American legislature coexisting but not coequal with the supreme legislature at Whitehall.

> The advocates for the supremacy of Parliament over the Colonies contend, that there must be one supreme legislative head in every civil society, whose authority must extend to the regulation and final decision of every matter susceptible of human direction; and that every member of the society, whether political, official, or individual, must be subordinate to its supreme will, signified in its laws: that this supremacy and subordination are essential in the constitution of all States, whatever may be their forms; that no society ever did, or could exist, without it; and that these truths are solidly established in the practice of all Governments, and confirmed by the concurrent authority of all writers on the subject of civil society.

The most extreme argument from the logic of supremacy made the British Parliament both supreme and sovereign over the colonies, the constitution, and individual rights. "The three branches of the Legislature united make daily alterations in the Constitution of Great-Britain," James Macpherson a hack in the pay of the North administration wrote; "and, if their Supremacy extends over the whole empire, they have the same right to alter the constitution of the American Colonies. If the Americans deny this position, all argument is at an end; and they avow an independence, which, in THEIR circumstances, marks them out for enemies."[50]

American whigs replied that rejection of the logic of supremacy brought them back to the old constitution; it did not propel them to independence. Spurning the logic of the analytical constitution of sovereign power, the colonial whigs sought the security of the customary constitution of restrained power. Their history, their constitutional heritage, and their education in the tradition of common-law rights taught them that there were limits to legislative command.[51] The constitutional premises by which those limits were determined will take up the next several chapters. They were summed up in the "yes, but" answers that American assemblies voted time and again when confronted by the doctrine of parliamentary supremacy. Yes, the colonies were part of one empire "in which it is necessary there should be some supreme regulating power," the New York General Assembly told the House of Lords less than one month before New England minutemen realized the hour had come to make a stand at Lexington. "But though we acknowledge the existence of such power, yet we conceive it by no means comprehends a right of binding us in all cases whatsoever; because a power of so unbounded an extent, would totally deprive us of security, and reduce us to a state of the most abject servitude."[52] Nineteenth-century Britons would not have understood what the New Yorkers meant. In 1775 there were still many, *very many* politicians and students of politics in the capital city of George III who understood why constitutional power was not the same as arbitrary power.[53]

CHAPTER FIVE

LIMITS OF SUPREMACY

There is a tendency among students of the American Revolution to isolate American political thought from British political thought. Whatever validity that practice has it would be wrong to extend it to constitutional thought. American constitutional thought was British constitutional thought because both were the direct, legitimate progeny of English constitutional thought. It is easy to forget this historical fact and to assume that American opposition to parliamentary supremacy was concocted to meet the political crisis of the 1760s. Recognizing the many "uncertainties about the nature of the constitution" then rife, Robert Middlekauff has noted that "a half-articulated constitutionalism made its appearance by 1766. It held that there were limits, outside of and independent of Parliament. Their essence might not be altogether clear and their sources might be a matter of dispute, but they existed nonetheless."[1]

Middlekauff, of course, was wrong that this constitutionalism was new,[2] but correct about the basic tenet of that constitutionalism: that it imposed "limits" on power. That is the topic of this chapter, the legal theory of limitations constraining parliamentary authority. Indeed, it is not unrealistic to call it the theme of this book and even the core constitutional contention of American whigs in their controversy with Great

Britain: that no matter how one defined the supremacy of Parliament there were limits to that supremacy.

It is not enough to know what colonial whigs argued. We must also know why they argued as they did. It is important, therefore, to guard against certain notions that have crept into the historical literature of the American Revolution. One of these is the idea that "the major task confronting the leaders of the American cause before the actual outbreak of the Revolution," was "how to qualify, undermine, or reinterpret" the doctrine of legislative sovereignty.[3] That was the task, of course, but the implication is wrong if the impression is that colonial whigs were required to formulate new constitutional arguments or that prior to the revolutionary controversy Americans would not have been familiar with those arguments.

Colonial whigs would have been familiar with up to half a dozen theories why parliamentary sovereignty had limits. These theories would have been familiar because they came directly out of British constitutional doctrine and English common-law practice. William Hicks was expressing a British constitutional-law thought when he wrote in the *Pennsylvania Journal* that "[t]he boldest advocates for the power of parliament, cannot, at this day, without blushing, assert that it is sovereign and supreme in every respect whatsoever."[4] By 1768, when Hicks wrote, the legal theory he expressed was more prevalent in the colonies than in the mother country. After reading all the New England election sermons for the eighteenth century, Alice M. Baldwin found only two clergymen, both from Connecticut, one in 1738 and the other in 1746, who attributed absolute sovereignty to the legislature.[5] More in the mainstream of colonial constitutional theory was the warning in 1768 by Daniel Shute, pastor of the third church of Hingham, who told Massachusetts legislators that they had to "assent" to "the special end of the electors in chusing" them, that is, "to secure their natural rights and privileges, and to promote their happiness." The limits of the legislators' power were inherent in their elections. Elected representatives were "vested with no authority" independent of election, "for the being chosen to a particular purpose by those in whom the right of choice is, can give no rightful power to act beside or counter to this purpose." No matter how the theory was explained, as an original contract, as vested rights, as mixed government, as natural law, as an implied trust, as temporary authority delegated by election, as constitutional custom, the underlying premise was that there was no "unlimited Power" in the legislature. "We revere the English Parliament, because by the Constitution it has no such Power," FREEMAN told the *New York Gazette*, "and those who pretend it has, are Enemies to that Constitution."[6]

That constitution, of course, belonged to the eighteenth century and it is wrong for us to say that those who grappled with it were not coherent or were inconsistent because they were capable of doing what we can no longer do, postulate a supreme legislature that was not supreme. The working constitutional concept was "limited," for unlimited power was not constitutional. The emphasis on "supremacy" belonged to the future. Governor Thomas Hutchinson was speaking from the perspective of the future and against the constitutionalism of limits when he said in 1771 "that the disorders in America must be attributed to a cause, that is common to all the colonies, a loose, false and absurd notion of the nature of government, which has been spread by designing, artful men, setting bounds to the supreme authority." Four years later Arthur Lee, speaking from the perspective of the customary constitution, wrote that Hutchinson had misrepresented the American whig position. "The general object then of the colonies was confessedly to *limit*, not to *destroy*, the supreme authority," Lee wrote. He was saying that although parliamentary authority was supreme, it had limits that were customary.[7]

What scholars have not told us is how extensively constitutionalists in contemporary Great Britain shared and agreed with the American whig theory of limited legislative authority. Jack P. Greene may be correct to say that "by the 1760s the British constitution had become the constitution of parliamentary supremacy," while "the emerging imperial constitution, like the separate constitutions of Britain's many overseas dominions, remained a customary constitution." Certainly that dichotomy is right in retrospective. But it is by no means certain that the doctrine of parliamentary sovereignty over law and the constitution had as yet been accepted in Great Britain as mainstream constitutional theory. Certainly the principle of legislative supremacy limited by customary practice was no longer as dominant in the mother country as it was in the colonies, but it is not true that it was limited to the British opposition.[8] The principle of limited legislative supremacy was widespread throughout all sectors of British political thought. Although we can no longer measure this doctrine's full reach, it is necessary to understand not just that it was respectable doctrine, but what it was—what the British as well as American whigs meant by constitutional limitations and by a supremacy harnessed by constitutional constraints.

LIMITS ON PARLIAMENT

Students of eighteenth-century politics as much as students of eighteenth-century jurisprudence would do well to give closer attention to the meaning and usage of words. Terms such as "supreme" and "supremacy" just did not mean what some scholars of the American Revolution have assumed them to mean. The "supreme Legislative Authority of Great Britain," the earl of Abingdon complained in 1780, was something "so much talked of, and yet so little understood." "Supremacy of Parliament," the earl of Mansfield was told, "is a high-sounding Word, having more Weight for Currency, as it ought to have, than intrinsic Value."[9] What was meant was that the concept of "supremacy" was more a topic of dispute than an element of definition. It was used as much to argue about constitutionalism as to explain it. "*Supremacy of Parliament* is a combination of terms unknown to the English polity," Abingdon contended, implying that the only supreme powers in British government were the House of Lords, as "the *supreme* court of Justice," and the king, "as the *supreme* Head of the Church." Parliament's supremacy was of a different quality. "The Legislative," he explained, "is a supreme, and may be called in one Sense an *absolute*, but in none an *arbitrary* Power."[10]

Abingdon was saying that Parliament was bound by the "law" or the constitution or at least by unchangeable, fundamental law. Oddly enough, even that relatively accepted notion of supremacy was too much for some constitutionalists. "[T]he word *supremacy* has not any absolute and unlimited sense (as many now affect to understand it) but [h]as its proper boundaries," *Candidus* argued. "Indeed; how else can they speak of the King's supremacy, as consistent either with the supremacy of Parliament, or the supremacy of law? Besides, if there be an *absolute* supremacy in law, it must follow, that law must be *immutable* . . . and neither be subject to the King or the Parliament, or the Legislature, or the Community at large." That fundamental law was immutable had once been respectable legal theory, but had lost much ground and in the 1760s the future was uncertain whether supremacy would be vested in the legislature which would become the undisputable British rule in the nineteenth century, or remain with the constitution which would be the American rule.[11]

Legal uncertainty and constitutional argument often occurred during the age of the American Revolution because one cherished constitutional principle would collide with a second valued constitutional principle. One plodding fundamental constitutional principle, for example, was that the government of Great Britain was a limited government, not an arbitrary government. That premise provides one of many different explanations why the doctrine of supremacy to be "constitutional" had to have limits. "It is a solecism in politics," Lord Abingdon pointed out, "to say that in a *limited* Government there can be *unlimited* Power." A competing principle was that sovereignty could have no gradations because in every government there had to be a supreme uncontrollable power vested in some person or institution. "There may be limited royalty," Samuel Johnson explained, "there may be limited consulship; but there can be no limited government."[12] It would not be for a generation or more after Johnson's death that the obvious certainty of his constitutional doctrine would obtain universal acknowledgment—on his side of the Atlantic. In the meanwhile, those who doubted the thesis were still numerous and still vocal. Of course there can be limited government, Henry Goodricke replied. Supremacy meant "nothing more,—than that it is *absolutely supreme* in command; that there is no *civil* or *legal* power in the state *superior* to it, and that its acts can not be controlled or annulled by any other *authority*. This does not preclude in the least its being limited, as to the extent of its power, either by laws of Nature, or by rules and principles of the Constitution." This practice of subordinating supremacy to constitutional law would be forgotten within about two generations. It was, however, well understood in the age of the American Revolution. "When we say that the legislature is *supreme*," *Junius* explained, "we mean that it is the highest power known to the constitution;—that it is the highest in comparison with the other subordinate powers established by the laws." The word "supreme," therefore, was still relative. It would not be until the nineteenth century that the word would become absolute. "The power of the legislature," *Junius* concluded, "is limited, not only by the general rules of natural justice, and the welfare of the community, but by the forms and principles of our particular constitution."[13]

One way to evaluate the doctrine is to consider its alternate. The logic of limited government lay more in the unacceptableness of unlimited government than in any inherent merits of limitation. "If this doctrine be not true," *Junius* concluded, "we must admit, that King, Lords, and Commons have no rule to direct their resolutions, but merely their own will and pleasure." That was the basic logic of limited government: unless government was limited it would have arbitrary power, the ultimate bugbear of British constitutionalists. Baron Rokeby called sovereignty "the doctrine of despotism" for that reason: it suggested an absolute power lodged somewhere in the government, that is, in Parliament.[14] A second imperative for resisting unlimited legislative authority was the historical premises of English and whig liberty. "If the British Legislature is the constitution, or superior to the constitution," Reverend William Gordon explained in a sermon, "*Magna Charta, the bill of rights, and the protestant succession*, these boasts of Britons, are toys to please the vulgar, and not *solid securities*."[15]

There is no need to push the argument further. It is familiar. The

American case against parliamentary supremacy, well known to historians, was, after all, not new legal theory. It was a mirror reflection of the old English constitutional doctrine of resistance to arbitrary power. The only points that must be stressed here are that even as late as the 1770s, it was as respectable in Great Britain as in the colonies,[16] was understood by British commentators to apply to the governance of the colonies as much to the governance of the home kingdom,[17] and had as much support among common lawyers as among nonlawyer constitutional scholars.[18] The Irish barrister Charles Francis Sheridan was only one of several lawyers to point out that if Parliament was limited in regard to Great Britain, it should have been even more limited in regard to other British communities. He would have left Parliament with no authority at all over the dominions, going further than American whigs would ever go or ever say they wanted to go.[19]

LIMITS OF SOVEREIGNTY

There is an aspect of eighteenth-century legal thought that was touched on before[20] and requires only the briefest expansion. Again it involves a way of looking at law from a perspective that today's British lawyers have forgotten, but which once was mainstream constitutional theory: that along with limits to parliamentary supremacy there were limits to parliamentary sovereignty. As late as 1776 the doctrine that there was not an "uncontrollable" supreme power in British government still commanded much respect. It did so, a correspondent of the *London Evening Post* explained, because of the old common-law doctrine that, "by the very principles of this constitution, the government is *bounded by law*." What twentieth-century common lawyers have forgotten is not the doctrine, but the meaning of the word "law" as it was used by the writer for the *Evening Post*. It was a meaning, however, that he could take for granted in 1776 when objecting to Samuel Johnson's opposite aphorism, quoted above, that although there "may be limited *royalty* . . . there can be no limited government."

> For if government be supreme, it is above the law; otherwise there must be two supremes in the same state; but if the law be paramount, then all other powers may be lawfully resisted. And, indeed when we suppose a supremacy in government, which on no occasion, can be lawfully resisted, we destroy the difference betwixt free and absolute governments. The idea of political and civil freedom, is to live under a government of laws, founded on natural rights,

which cannot therefore subvert those laws and rights. Supremacy is the very essence of despotism; there is only a nominal distinction between a British parliament and a Turkish divan, unless the former may be resisted lawfully.[21]

There are two possible meanings to the word "law" when it used in this context during the eighteenth century. One is the meaning of today's British constitutional law, that government was bound by the rule of law, that it had to act by its own legislative mandates. If Parliament enacted a statute changing the definition of the ownership of property, for example, the Crown and the ministry, as well as the courts, were bound to respect the statute's transferal of rights until Parliament repealed the statute or enacted different rights. The second meaning was that law, itself, was sovereign and supreme, binding not only the Crown, the ministry, and the courts, but Parliament as well. It was in the latter sense that the *London Evening Post* writer meant "law," as had the earl of Warrington when he told a Chester grand jury that, "in every Government there is a *Supreme Power* to which all are to submit, whilst that Power contains it self within the Laws." The concept of the sovereignty of law was best summed up in the distinction between "right" and "power." Law was "right." Power alone, power without right, could not make law.[22]

The issue on which the doctrine of law's sovereignty was most frequently in controversy was the question of the constitution's mutability. George Chalmers, who practiced law in Maryland for a few years before returning to London at the outbreak of the Revolution, stated what was most likely the majority British view in 1777 when he argued that "the constitution is the will of the legislature operating upon the distribution of the whole mass of power; that, so far from being any thing distinct from law, it [power] is a part of the law." During the previous generation, Chalmers's theorem had been a bone of contention between the followers of Robert Walpole and the supporters of Viscount Bolingbroke. Because the British constitution was mutable, Walpole's newspaper asserted, all law, even fundamental, organic law such as the Act of Settlement, was subject to be mutated by the legislative will and pleasure of Parliament. "There are, indeed, no human Laws *unchangeable*, nor *any Points* which bind the *Legislative Power* of the Kingdom from doing what is *at any Time* judged best for the Good of the Kingdom; for that Power is *supreme* and *absolute*."[23] Starting from the opposite premise—that the immutable constitution had created Parliament—Bolingbroke's newspaper replied that *"there is something, which a* Parliament *cannot do. A* Parliament cannot annul the *Constitution."* Thirty years later these contrary perceptions of immutability and legislative sovereignty drove the first constitutional wedge between the colonies and Great Britain. As "the supreme legislative as well as the supreme executive derives its authority from that constitution," the Massachusetts House of Representatives explained, it followed that the constitution "is fixed: it is from thence that all power in the state derives its authority: therefore, no power can exceed the bounds of it without destroying its own foundation." The conclusion was inescapable: "that there are certain original inherent rights belonging to the people, which the Parliament itself cannot divest them of, consistent with their own constitution."[24]

CHAPTER SIX

CONSTRAINTS OF TRUST

Shifts in eighteenth-century legal theory sometimes were signalled by resistance to words, and there were no words adherents to the old constitutionalism of constraints resisted more than the noun "omnipotence" and the pronoun "omnipotent."

"We ridiculously of late bewilder ourselves with frantic, highflown sonorous expressions of the omnipotence of parliament," John Wilkes complained to the House of Commons. "The omnipotence of parliament . . . seems to me a false and dangerous doctrine."[1] "[T]he Omnipotence of Parliament," Rusticus Americanus agreed, was a "pompous expression." It was "an invidious term," according to William Stevens, "the better to cast an odium on the supreme authority," a term, John Cartwright added, "bordering on blasphemy, as in 'divine right' applied to Kings," a term menacing enough to be called "a kind of popery in politics" by Granville Sharp.[2]

For constitutionalists in the second half of the eighteenth century the concept of omnipotency became what in the 1990s would be called a "buzz" word, especially after Sir William Blackstone shocked many readers when he used "omnipotent" to describe Parliament's unlimited powers. More interesting for us, the earl of Abingdon, in 1780, blamed the American Revolution on the doctrine of parliamentary omnipotency.

"[I]t hath 'divided a House against itself'," he complained of the word, *"it has severed America from Great-Britain."* Omnipotency was a doctrine, Abingdon sermonized, "which from *Heaven* took its Name; but from *Hell* received its Principles."[3]

When people claimed that governors were omnipotent, Peter Peckard observed in 1783, they meant that "there is no Liberty against them." It was a word, therefore, that could do "more in a single sentence than Filmer could in a whole volume." Omnipotent, in other words, was a different way of saying "sovereign,"—a special British way as the concept of omnipotency, even more than the concept of sovereignty, had the merit of insinuating that sovereign power was arbitrary power. "[T]herefore saith the Omnipotence of Parliament, I will enact what is *unreasonable*, and you the Collective-Body of the People of England shall receive it as *reasonable*," Abingdon wrote with his characteristic wild exaggeration that still had a knack for delineating the issue. "I will substitute Slavery for Liberty, and the Exchange shall be approved. In short, I will be *arbitrary*."[4]

If Parliament was omnipotent in Great Britain, it followed for imperialists that it was omnipotent over the colonies. "[T]ill within these few years, or few months, within the British territory of Europe, Asia, Africa, and America, Parliament was supposed omnipotent and irresistible," Adam Ferguson complained the year of the Declaration of Independence.[5] He was wrong, of course, and not just because of the resistance of American whigs. Like every other notion that smacked of arbitrariness, the concept of omnipotency had as many critics in the mother country as in the colonies.

Exponents of the concept of omnipotency treated the notion much as they treated the concepts of sovereignty and supremacy—as self-evident. "This omnipotence," Baron Rivers wrote, "must be the privilege of every state, of whatever rank, and is inseparable from the idea of government, of whatever form." He thought the concept universal, an assumption disputed by a large school of constitutional theorists who knew of at least one exception to the rule. "I might deny this whole language," the author of *Tyranny Unmasked* wrote of the contention that "there must be in every society an absolute omnipotence," "however it may be true in other places, it is not the constitution of England."[6]

Again the ultimate question was whether Parliament was supreme over the constitution or whether it was subordinate to the constitution. If you said that Parliament was subordinate, you had to be saying that Parliament's supremacy was something less than omnipotent. "For omnipotent as Parliament is . . . sometimes said to be," one observer argued, "it ought never to be forgotten, that the CONSTITUTION is above it, and bridles it: And if that curb ever loses its power, the constitution itself is no longer in being."[7]

As omnipotence, like supreme, was a word of eighteenth-century constitutional language, it could, like the word "supreme," be employed to say both that Parliament was omnipotent and that Parliament was subordinate to the constitution. Henry Goodricke did so when, as mentioned in chapter 5, he contended that even though Parliament's sovereign power was "absolute, [ir]resistable, uncontrolable, and omnipotent," it also had "limits." Omnipotence "only means that as the Parliament is the supreme power in the state, there neither is, nor can be, any appeal against its oppressions or transgression of those limits." Parliament, he added, "is always limited by *natural* law; it may be limited by *constitutional* law;—but it must be, as Mr. LOCKE observes, in all cases, as long as the government subsists, SUPREME over every other person, body, or power in the State."[8]

Goodricke made sense to many constitutional theorists of the revolutionary era, as for example a London writer who a year earlier had asked, "but does not reason, policy, and the spirit of the constitution somewhere set bounds to that omnipotence?" A question American whigs would raise with frequency by 1773 was the "line" at which the constitution set those bounds. Another question, seldom asked but often debated, was how the "line" was drawn. There were several answers to that second question. Goodricke gave one when observing that "although people may differ, more or less, about the general or constitutional limits of the supreme power of Parliament," he was confident of one: that "Parliament's Authority" did not extend "beyond the limits of the trust for which it was delegated."[9] Such, in fact, was one of the best known of the eighteenth-century theories of constitutional constraints on parliamentary supremacy. Along with the constraint of consent, the constraint of contract, the constraint of constitutionalism, the constraint of liberty, and the constraint of law, was the constraint of trust.

LIMITATIONS OF TRUST

In its most extreme expression, the theory of limitations by trust postulated that all of government "is, in the very nature of it, a TRUST; and all its powers a DELEGATION for gaining particular ends."[10] Members of Parliament, from this perspective, were best thought of as "*delegates, not principals; trustees, vested with great authority, not for their own benefit*, but for the benefit of *those who chuse them*."[11] Members of Parliament, including those in the House of Lords,[12] rather than being "representatives," were more properly called "Trustees and Guardians of the Liberties and Properties of Englishmen all over the globe," the "Trustees and Agents," or even "the *creatures* of the people."[13]

The theory of constraints through delegated trust was stated and discussed so often in the eighteenth century that it could easily be made the subject of a separate study. For our purposes one example of the argument should be sufficient, and the following seems especially pertinent as it is from the London press, reprinted in a Dublin magazine, discussing parliamentary legislation for North America. "The power of parliament," it was said, "is a power delegated by the people, to be always employed for their use and benefit, never to their disservice and injury." It was, therefore, a limited power, "bounded by the good and service of the people; and whenever such power shall be perverted to their hurt and detriment, the trust is broken, and becomes null and void."[14]

There were two major elements to the trust theory of legislative power: (1) that the delegation limited legislative authority, and (2) that legislation in violation of the trust could be challenged. "My lords," the common lawyer Earl Camden told his colleagues in the upper house when debating American affairs a month before the Battle of Lexington, "the bodies which compose the Legislature, are invested with that power for the good of the whole. We are trustees, and can exercise our powers, only in execution of the great trust reposed in us."[15]

Commentators discussed the trustees' powers in only the most general sense. The terms of the trust were important because of the rule that "[a]ll delegated power must be subordinate and limited," or, as applied to the British constitutional trust, that the trust was "limited in its own nature by the end and purposes of the civil union." In its most extreme pronouncement, limitation meant that Parliament was charged by the trust "to preserve the constitution."[16] In the eighteenth century the primary expectation of that injunction was that Parliament could not be arbitrary. One constitutional commentator, for example, who in 1776 rejected all American claims to fundamental rights immune from parliamentary alteration, maintained that Parliament had sovereign authority to do whatever it pleased, but that it could not exercise arbitrary power because arbitrary power was contrary to the trust.[17] Put in common-law agency terms, legislative authority "is only a fiduciary power to act for certain ends."[18] Those ends were as readily defined in the constitution as in the trust, Allan Ramsay explained in 1771. "Our legislative authority is, by its own nature, confined to act within the line of the constitution; and not to break through it," he wrote. The reason was "[b]ecause, the house of commons is only vested, with a trust, by the people, to the end they may protect, and defend them in their rights and privileges."[19] Put more simply, the terms of the trust were the constitution.

There was little agreement about what rule applied should Parliament step beyond its bounds and violate the constitutional trust. Many legal commentators, even those who understood that Parliament was limited by the trust and that legislation in excess of its delegated powers was "void," acknowledged that there was no constitutional remedy. Others argued that there could be a remedy depending on the nature of the violation. If horrendous enough, it might trigger a constitutional right to resist constituted authority. If the violation was not sufficiently serious to justify forceful resistance, yet clearly contrary to the fiduciary relationship, the delegation of authority would terminate, "the trust must necessarily be forfeited, and the power devolve into the hands of those that gave it."[20]

There was a second side to the concept of trust in the eighteenth century, more practical and political than the constitutional doctrine of legislative trusteeship. Rather than imposing a duty of behavior on lawmakers, it asked people to trust their legislators. The opposite of the doctrines we have been studying, it placed constraints upon the governed, rather than the governors.

This second legal trust theory may be difficult to credit, but it was widely prevalent in the second half of the eighteenth century, especially in Great Britain. It told citizens to trust an all-powerful Parliament, on no other grounds than that members of Parliament were worthy and deserving of trust. It did not matter if Parliament possessed arbitrary authority. With members of such high character it could never act arbitrarily, certainly not against the colonists who could and should "as safely trust their liberties" to the care of Parliament, "as we in the kingdom do ours; for . . . no government in the world is under a legislative power which, in all its acts, has maintained a more just and impartial regard to the interests of the several parts of the dominions, whether represented or not, than the legislative power of Great Britain."[21]

It is not clear why so indeterminable an argument became a guiding constitutional theme in the years after 1750. Perhaps it was due to the dawning realization that the old constitutional guarantees of constraints on power were slipping away, and, facing the prospect that Parliament was exercising arbitrary authority, Britons had to reassure themselves they were still a free people—as freedom was defined in the eighteenth century. If so, it was a typical English solution for a problem of government: assume the best and the problem may work itself out. A people who had always been fearful of arbitrary power were told to trust Parliament, that somehow it could be trusted to act in a way that the Crown was never trusted to act. Indeed, Parliament had obtained supremacy precisely because James II had been untrustworthy, and now, five reigns later, was saying it could as an institution be trusted to behave better. "But though the Constitution gives this Power to Parl[iamen]t," Richard Jackson explained, "yet this Power has always been exercised with great Moderation & even Abstinence, because the same Wisdom & Discretion that always governs the Proceedings of Parl[iamen]t have prescribed Moderation & Abstinence in those Cases."[22]

The theory was that although the humans who were members of Parliament might err, they could be expected to correct their wrongs—or what the historian Bernard Bailyn described as "the idea of an automatic, inner self-correction of Parliamentary error." William Knox called it "a peculiar tenderness" upon which the colonists could safely put their trust. How the theory worked in practice was explained in two ways. From the perspective of authority, Charles Yorke, the attorney general of England, told the House of Commons that there was "no boundary to the legislative power but that which the constitution itself presumes, your wisdom and your justice." From the opposite perspective, that of the consumers of authority who were to trust the "wisdom and justice" of Parliament, *Philanthropos* assured the colonists that should Parliament, "for want of proper information, lay any taxes on the inhabitants of America that are found inconvenient, oppressive, or not suited to the nature of their situation and trade, on application to the King and Parliament, they will, on being shewn so to their satisfaction, immediately make such alterations, regulations, or total repeal, as shall be found best for the whole body."[23]

Not only was trust in the goodness of Parliament not thought naive in the eighteenth century, it was more than mere theory. Imperialists attempted to make it official colonial policy, at least for the American side to adopt. Parliament could be trusted to "give due attention to all well founded complaints" the secretary of state for the colonies wrote to the governor of Massachusetts, an assurance the governor had already given to the General Court. "It is our happiness that our supreme legislature, the Parliament of Great Britain, is the sanctuary of liberty and justice," he told the Council and House of Representatives. "Surely, then, we should . . . acquiesce in a perfect confidence, that the rights of the members of the British empire will ever be safe in the hands of the conservators of the liberty of the whole."[24]

The argument did not seem farfetched to some eighteenth-century Americans, as, for example, the only two governors elected locally and not appointed from London. There was a moment when both thought that trust in Parliament could be a viable constitutional policy preserving colonial rights. Governor Thomas Fitch of Connecticut wrote that it was "to be presumed" that the "wise and vigilant" Parliament would not permit "an essential right" to be infringed. In neighboring Rhode Island Governor Stephen Hopkins urged the colonies to unite in petitioning Parliament for relief from the Sugar Act of 1733. "[I]f their Cause be good," he asked, "what have they to fear from such a Procedure? Or rather, what have they not to hope, from such an Application and Appeal to a King who delights in doing Good to all his Subjects; to a Peerage, wise, and accurate, guided by the Principles of Honor and Beneficence; and a Representative Body, penetrating and prudent, who consider the good of the Whole, and make that the Measure of their Public Resolves."[25]

Governor Hopkins published that plea in January 1764. Within a year and a half the Stamp Act had been passed and he had learned a sobering lesson in trust: the character and good intentions of legislators were one thing, their power something else. Now, he realized, it did not matter if members of Parliament "are men of the highest character for their wisdom, justice, and integrity, and therefore cannot be supposed to deal hardly, unjustly, or unequally by any." What did matter was legislative authority, not legislative goodness. "For one who is bound to obey the will of another is really a slave though he may have a good a master as if he had a bad one." All it took was one Stamp Act and one set of Townshend duties for an American whig to be purged of what *Resolutionist* called "[t]he monstrous and slavish doctrine of *trusting* to the British parliament to do us justice."[26]

If, as was suggested, the trust doctrine had been concocted in Great Britain to compensate for the decline of rule by law, American whigs soon concluded it was no substitute for the rule of law. Laws, James Iredell of North Carolina pointed out, quoting *Junius*, "are intended to guard against what men may do, not to trust to what they will do." Andrew Eliot of Boston thought what was needed was not trust in Parliament's "justice and equity" but "an American bill of rights," while James Wilson of Philadelphia thought the safest course was to revive the old constitution of constraint and control. Without what he termed "a sufficient control," Parliament, "the temple of British liberty, like a structure of ice, would instantly dissolve before the fire of oppression and despotick sway."[27]

There was yet another factor to be weighed, Wilson's fellow Pennsylvanian John Dickinson noted. The colonists were in a different legislative situation than were the people of Great Britain. Not only were members of Parliament less familiar with their local circumstances, and thus, even if trustworthy, more prone to make mistakes,[28] they could be personally and economically uneffected by legislation they enacted for the colonies while they had to share the burdens of any statutes or taxes imposed on their own constituents. "Where these laws are to bind *themselves*, it may be expected, that the house of commons will very carefully consider them," Dickinson explained. "But when they are making laws that are not designed to bind *themselves*, we cannot imagine that their deliberations will be as cautious and scrupulous, as in their own case."[29] If the British had constitutional reasons to trust Parliament, Americans had practical reasons why they could not.

THE ARTICLES OF TRUST

The instrument of the trust of authority to legislate was negotiated at the founding of a government. The theory of how the terms were set was not unique. It was, rather, a variation of the theory of compact, combining the social contract with the original contract. People, by creating government, created the sovereign power, Francis Gregor of King's College, Cambridge, explained during the 1730s, in a law publication reprinted in 1775. That power was intended not to destroy but to preserve the commonwealth. Also created were the wielders of that power, the governors who were "charged and entrusted" with "the *Sovereign Power*," and who, therefore, were limited by the grant of trust. "If it be asked, What is the Extent of the *Sovereign Power*? the Answer is easy, in one Word, that it is not more nor less than the *Public Good*."[30]

The legal theory that the trust instrument of government defined and limited the powers of legislation provided one of the explanations why eighteenth-century British constitutionalists were able to assert that although Parliament was supreme, and even was sovereign, that there could be situations in which it "exceeded" its constitutional jurisdiction and, if it did, that it acted unconstitutionally if not unlawfully.[31] The problem, eighteenth-century commentators readily admitted, was not in the theory but in the precision of application. As with so many aspects of British constitutionalism, it was a question not only better left unanswered, but better left unasked. Parliament was "supreme *in all cases whatsoever*, or, in other words, the authority of parliament" was "unlimited," John Gray explained in his critique of John Dickinson's theory of parliamentary authority,

> yet it does not from thence follow, as the factious colonists conclude, that it has *no limit*, or that the subjects have *no rights*. Where its legal authority ends, and its illegal power begins, is wisely left undecided by the constitution, which never supposes the case of its

acting to the destruction of the *community*, that is, *of itself;* but thinks it equitable to leave great discretionary powers to it, since we do not scruple often to leave great discretionary powers to ambassadors, and generals of armies, independent of their instructions, which are to them what fundamental principles are to legislators, not to be trifled with, or wantonly to be departed from.[32]

Truly, there can be few better examples of the imprecision of the eighteenth-century constitutional imagination than this statement by Gray. He not only espoused the notion of an unlimited power that was limited, he accepted as workable limitations that depended entirely on trust.

Although there may have been students of British government in the eighteenth century who believed without reservation that there were no limits on the unlimited Parliament, they are difficult to find. Almost every commentator who acknowledged Parliament's omnipotent and unlimited power thought there was at least one or two exceptions to the rule. At the very least there were the general exceptions, legally meaningless but cherished in the eighteenth century, that Parliament "hath no right to do wrong," or to be despotic, "for in Despotism the very Idea of Rights is excluded."[33] More specifically there were the duties imposed on the legislature by the trust, the duty to protect society or "the general good" or "the good and happiness of the people,"[34] or to "preserve the constitution,"[35] which meant making no laws *"inconsistent* with the *fundamental* Principles of just Government."[36] More usual the formula of limitations was expressed by saying that Parliament could not be destructive. As its task was to promote the welfare of everyone, it could neither harm the multitude nor favor the few.[37] When commentators got down to specifics of what Parliament could not do, the enumerated items were a list of horribles selected to prove the argument by their shock effect rather than demonstrate the boundaries of constitutional power. Parliament could not vote itself perpetual,[38] vest the king with its delegated power of legislation,[39] change the mode of representation even by eliminating the rotten boroughs,[40] alter the right to trial by jury, give the nation a different religion, or repeal Magna Carta.[41] Perhaps the most famous of these listings were those of Lord Camden, the leader of the common-law bar,[42] and James Otis, an American whig who believed that Parliament was sovereign over the colonies but not over the constitution.[43]

There was yet another way to state the trust theory of constitutionalism, a way that is more familiar to us as it is based on a concept that is basic American constitutional doctrine. The explanation of the legal writer William Jones is the most revealing for our purposes as he also used the eighteenth-century concepts of supremacy, power, limits, and consent to define the constitutional restraints of trust. Parliament's power was "supreme," he contended, because "there can be no political power *equal* or *superior* to it." Supreme, however, should not be confused with unlimited, not because there were enumerated powers that the supreme legislature could not exercise, but because its power, even though supreme, was delegated. "A power is therefore supreme because the powers of all are vested in it, with the implied consent of all; the consent of all is implied, upon this only motive, that the supreme power shall be exercised for the interest of all."[44] That was another way of understanding the constraints of trust. Parliament's powers were delegated. Parliament possessed the authority to legislate not only by a trust instrument such as the social contract or the original contract. It also possessed the authority to legislate by consent.

CHAPTER SEVEN

CONSTRAINTS OF CONSENT

The constitutional doctrine that the legitimacy of governmental authority came from the consent of the governed was not an American invention.[1] Although there were political commentators in Great Britain who doubted the rule's constitutionality, thought it "absurd," or questioned its antiquity,[2] legitimization by consent was ancient English legal theory, part of the common law as stated by Bracton[3] centuries before John Locke, to whom some writers have attributed the concept.[4] It had been well understood and defended in the seventeenth century[5] despite Filmer and Charles II.[6] In the eighteenth century the concept was one of the elements making up a definition of freedom popularized by the numerous political catechisms of the day. In what did British liberty consist? Viscount Bolingbroke asked in the most frequently reprinted catechism. "In laws made by the consent of the people," he answered.[7]

In the age of the American Revolution, the legitimization-through-consent principle made three important contributions to constitutional theory. The first was the notion that without consent to government there could be no liberty. If Parliament could legislate for the American colonists "without their *privity* and *consent*," a writer asked the *Boston Gazette*, "what benefit have they of any laws, liberties, and privileges granted unto them by the crown of England?" The answer: "I am loth to give their condition an *hard name;* but I have no other notion of *slavery, but being bound by a law to which I do not consent.*"8

The second contribution of consent to constitutional law was the legitimacy of government command. The right of government to require obedience to its commands was conferred by consent. "[T]he only moral foundation of government," John Adams claimed, "is, the consent of the people." One reason why consent helped to make government legitimate had been explained eighty-two years earlier by the whig divine Samuel Johnson. "What is done according to Law," he wrote, "every Body must abide by, because every Body's Consent is involved in the making of every English Law, and then it is no more than Common Honesty, to stand to one's own Act and Deed." Consent to command gave moral force to command or, as John Trenchard put it, all governments "derived their Authority from the Consent of Men, and could exercise it no further than that Consent gave them Leave."9

The third contribution was the most important. Trenchard mentioned it when he said that the power of governments was limited by consent, and added that "[w]here positive Conditions were annexed to their Power, they were certainly bound by those Conditions." The very act of legitimization constrained authority. The point was clarified by two New England clergymen preaching in 1774. Government was created by people, Samuel Lockwood told Connecticut's lawmakers. "And when this is done by free consent, and mutual compact, it . . . limits the power of the rulers—secures the rights of the people—is the standard of justice for rulers, and subjects." In other words, Nathan Fiske pointed out in a discourse delivered at Brookfield, Massachusetts, there were fundamental laws marking the boundaries between the powers of the rulers and the liberties of the people. "And those can be no other than what are mutually agreed on, and consented to. Whatever authority therefore, the supreme power has to make laws . . . being an authority derived from the community and granted by them, can be justly exercised only within certain limits, and to a certain extent, according to agreement."10

The doctrine of consent can easily be misunderstood. From the perspective of the twentieth century it has aspects of a theory of democracy. This is partly due to the word "consent," and the right we tend to associate with it, the function of electing direct representatives to serve in the legislative branch of government.

There were a few constitutional theorists in the eighteenth century who thought of consent through representation exclusively in terms of direct electoral participation in government and for whom "consent to government" was manifested only by the representation that the British people exercised in the House of Commons. That notion—that constitutional "consent" required some exercise of direct legislative representation—seems to have had little support in the earlier years of the century.[11] By the 1770s, however, it was well enough established in British legal thought that many of the constitutional plans offered for resolving the revolutionary controversy assumed that the necessity of representation for consent was established, indisputed constitutional law. By way of illustration consider one analysis of the imperial constitution that assumes consent is necessary for legitimate (or "free") government and that British constitutional consent is established through direct legislative representation (that is, people were bound by legislation because they had some role in the selection of at least part of the legislature that had authority to bind them):

> Thus although the British parliament may indeed with propriety make laws for Britain, yet it cannot with the same propriety exercise the like power with respect to America, while those parts of our dominions are not fairly represented in it. Nor, on the other hand, can our colonies make laws for themselves in their own assemblies, without thereby actually declaring themselves independent states, unless what they enact is only of force, so long as it is not inhibited or reversed by the parliament of Great Britain. And while their power stands thus limited by a superior authority, whereof they themselves have no share, they cannot be considered as a free people. For they are subject to laws and regulations not of their own making, which is the very definition of slavery.[12]

Today the striking feature of this analysis is its anticipation of how the supremacy clause of the United States Constitution would solve the conflict of two-tier legislative bodies in one federal system. For eighteenth-century Great Britain the striking feature was the suggestion that constitutional consent required legislative representation. That would become constitutional principle in nineteenth-century Great Britain and possibly it may have been established theory in many of the colonies. In England and Britain during the seventeenth century and most of the eighteenth century—the decades when the doctrine of consent was at the height of its popularity among constitutional theorists—direct participation by citizens in the process of government, even in elections, was not necessary for that government to be a government of consent. The concept of constitutional consent was, rather, first a theory of the legitimacy of authority,[13] and second a theory of restraint on power.

It would be no exaggeration to assert that the crucial value of the doctrine of consent in the eighteenth century was to provide one of the theories of constitutional law, along with theories of trust, custom, contract, and the rule of law, ensuring that the supreme power in a constitutional state—the authority to legislate—would not become arbitrary power. Richard Wooddeson, Oxford's Vinerian professor of law, blended several of these concepts together, when explaining that consent was less an action of participation than a legal condition rendering legislative command constitutional. "[G]overnment ought to be, and is generally *considered* as founded on consent," he contended. "For what gives any legislature a right to act, where no express consent can be shewn? what, but immemorial usage? and what is the intrinsic force of immemorial usage, in establishing this fundamental or any other law, but that it is evidence of common acquiescence and consent?" Do not dismiss the argument as a lawyer's professional reasoning or a law professor's thesis. In addition to being the better eighteenth-century view of constitutional consent, it was a statement of current constitutional doctrine, not of discredited theory or passé law. Wooddeson first published his lectures in 1783 and the quotation is from the edition of 1792.[14]

The consent of lawyers such as Wooddeson was a real consent, not a fiction, not a consent of the type known to historians of the American Revolution when they think of virtual representation. It was, rather, a consent manifested by the acquiescence implied by an individual living in British society and, by living in that society, freely accepting British rule and British law. A similar consent was the vicarious consent eighteenth-century Britons inherited from ancestors who, by conforming to the developing customs of an earlier day, "consented" to those customs. It was a consent, therefore, found in the doctrine of legal custom, for immemorial usage demonstrated not just the utility of a practice, but its popular acceptance over the centuries and the "consent" of generations.

The constitutional rule was both old and current, as demonstrated by a law compiler in 1775 arguing that English parliaments "never consider themselves as acting with absolute, unconditional, and uncontroulable power." To prove his contention he quoted from a statute of 25 Henry VIII freeing the English "from exactions and impositions" owed to the Holy See. The preamble—or a loose version that the compiler rendered into eighteenth-century language—provided "that the realm of England is free from subjection to all laws, but such as have been made within it for its *wealth*, or such other, as the *people* of the realm have taken to *their free liberty, by their own consent,* to be used among them; and *have bound themselves* by long *use* and *custom,* to the observance of the same; and that all the accustomed, and ancient laws of this realm, were originally established as laws by the *said sufferance, consents, and custom; and none otherwise.*" These words, from the preamble of the statute of

Henry, the law complier of 1775 asserted, "being declarative, and in affirmative of the ancient common law, will at once develop as well the nature, as power of Parliaments."[15] Parliament, it would seem, was restrained not only by the doctrine of consent, but by the existence of other law which may have been stronger than legislation because it had received a stronger consent.

LIMITATIONS BY MIGRATION

The argument has not been made that the theory of consent by direct representation was unknown or unimportant in prerevolutionary constitutional theory, only that consent was established on much wider premises. The right of representation in the law-making institution of the nation was a right more and more articulated as the eighteenth century progressed. It was, however, the American Revolution controversy that made it a prominent issue in constitutional debate, especially as it related to the authority of Great Britain to tax the colonies and to the question whether there could be constitutional taxation without *direct* consent.[16] In the matter of parliamentary supremacy, it was introduced in various disguises, one of which was the authority of migration.

The authority of migration was a major constitutional doctrine in the American whig case to establish immutable civil rights and has been extensively discussed in that regard.[17] It played a lesser role in the case against Parliament's claim of authority to legislate and may be treated briefly. The constitutional theory of migration as it applied to the authority to legislate was summed up by Virginia's House of Burgesses when it said of the colonists of North America: "[T]heir ancestors brought over with them entire, and transmitted to their descendants, the natural and constitutional rights they had enjoyed in their native country; and the first principles of the British constitution were early engrafted into the constitution of the Colonies." Among these rights, of course, was the authority to legislate, "derived, and assimilated as nearly as might be to that in England," including "the privilege of chosing their own Representatives."[18]

This doctrine of eighteenth-century constitutional law contained six elements restraining Parliament's authority to legislate for North America. The first two are so closely linked they are often treated as one. First, the original settlers of the colonies had been free subjects in their homeland, whether England, Wales, or Ireland. Second, the original settlers carried to the new world all their rights and privileges and retained them as English subjects. "The English subjects who left their *native* country to settle in the wilderness of America," Daniel Dulany explained, "had the privileges of *other* Englishmen. They knew their value, and were desirous of having them perpetuated to their posterity."[19]

Third, the rights carried to America were "engrafted into the constitution of the Colonies," retaining the primacy of constitutionalism or fundamental law.

Fourth, because the model of the colonial constitution was the then English constitution, legislation by consent "was derived, and assimilated" as near as possible to that of England. "They were aware," Dulany wrote, "that as their consent whilst they should reside in America could neither be asked nor regularly given in the national legislature, and that if they were to be bound by laws without restriction affecting the property they should earn by the utmost hazard and fatigue, they would lose every other privilege which they had enjoyed in their native country and become mere tenants at will, dependent upon the moderation of their lords and masters without any other security."[20]

Fifth, Dulany had limited consent to direct consent through representation. That was better American doctrine than British doctrine, a difference in constitutional theory that the Virginia Burgesses may have tried to resolve when saying that the first settlers had confirmed to themselves and to their posterity "the privilege of chosing their own Representatives continued to the people."

And sixth, the confirmation was both expressed and repeated. It was effectuated by the "contract" that will be outlined in the next chapter, a contract made with the Crown, not with Parliament. The theory was summed up by Thomas Jefferson whose analysis, although discussed as pathbreaking by some students of the American Revolution, was void of any jurisprudential originality. "That settlement having been made in the wilds of America," he contended, "the emigrants thought proper to adopt that system of laws under which they had hitherto lived in the mother country, and to continue their union with her by submitting themselves to the same common Sovereign, who was thereby made the central link connecting the several parts of the Empire thus newly multiplied."[21]

There were few other constitutional arguments on which American whigs were so strongly challenged by imperialists as the authority of migration. A few ridiculed the general theory,[22] while a larger number, who accepted the doctrine's validity, took exception to one or another of the American whigs' arguments of facts. To gain an idea of the flow of the debate, it would be best first to consider an instance of the general criticism. It was written by Sir William Draper, a lieutenant general in the British army, after he had taken an extended tour through the major seaports of the colonies.

> Let us suppose, that any five hundred subjects are determined to try their fortunes elsewhere, and *voluntarily* emigrate to North America; I presume that no one will deny the power of the Legislature over them at their departure, or say that they are more exempt from our *Taxes, Tribunals, Juries, Punishments*, than the rest of their fellow-subjects whom they left behind. In what part of their voyage then does the State lose its usual right over them? At thirty, three hundred, or three thousand miles? Until some advocate for American Independency will explain this to my conviction, their condition seems to be just the same in America as here; distance can make no alteration.[23]

The imperialist answer to the authority of migration could be stronger than Draper stated it. For example, a claim that could be made but generally was not was that English rights did not accompany settlers to parts outside the realm. At its most extreme, this argument said that the emigrants took with them only what the government granted, that their privileges while in America were rights by sufferance. "[T]he colonies [*sic*] could carry over with them nothing but what was immediately granted them from hence; for, it was by an act of indulgence, that they were permitted to transport even their persons," Richard Phelps argued, and his views are significant as he was under secretary of state to Lord Hillsborough.[24] His constitutional conclusion, however, owed more to political theory than to common-law constitutionalism, and was too harsh for most imperialists. To say that rights, even American rights, were granted rather than inherent made eighteenth-century constitutionalists uneasy. The preferred doctrine was that rights were personal, inherited, inalienably owned, and independent of government largess.[25] For the colonists to have enjoyed rights secured in this, the constitutional sense, the first settlers of North America had to have taken with them to the new world all of the English rights they had possessed before migrating. They also took their duties as English subjects and, possessing the same rights and duties they had possessed in England, remained in the same relationship to Parliament they had been in before their departure. After all, as Draper said and even underscored, the migration had been voluntary.

But how voluntary had it been? The answer to that question became a matter of dispute. "When the colonists first migrated, they necessarily lost, among other local privileges, the right of an actual representation in Parliament," the Reverend John Hampson is supposed to have reasoned. "This was on their part a voluntary degradation." American whigs replied that there had been several important aspects to the migration that had not been voluntary. "Because I'm obliged by the severity of my father to desert his house and settle in a desert like a hermit, shall my brethren rule and domineer over me?" a correspondent asked the *New York Gazette*. That the first settlers of Massachusetts, at least, were forced by government policy to leave was immaterial, a second writer told the *Boston Evening-Post*.

> All allow it was voluntary: 'Twas a religious squabble that occasioned it. Could they have kept themselves within any bounds marked out by prudence, they might have been as happy in Britain as any where. 'Twas their own choice that bro't them here; and if they are not in a condition to be represented in parliament, let them charge the consequences to themselves. . . . How can we refuse obedience to the British parliament, because we enjoy not a privilege we put ourselves out of the reach of?[26]

From the perspective of consent by direct representation, the causes or purposes of migration may not have been significant. The British constitution based direct representation on geography rather than population. Because members of the Commons represented specific places within the kingdom, the probative fact was the migration, not the reasons for migrating. "If they voluntarily quit the Place of their Representation for another where no Representation is, how is the State to blame?" General Draper wondered. "It cannot lose its old *Authority* over them as Subjects, because they chuse to remove to a greater distance from the seat of Government." The result of migration should be seen as the "natural effects" of migrating, and not analogized to a government policy of penalty such as forfeiture depriving the settler of some privilege, John Welsey maintained. "When a man voluntarily comes into America, he may lose what he had when in Europe. Perhaps he had a right to vote for a knight or burgess: by crossing the sea he did not *forfeit* this right. But it is plain, he has made the exercise of it no longer possible. He has reduced himself from a voter to one of the innumerable multitude that have no votes."[27]

Wesley alluded to a second issue that became a dispute of fact: whether the original settlers had been voters before migrating. "[T]hey can have no personal right of representation in the mother-country, because they are not in possession of the particular qualifications annexed to that right," Phelps insisted, meaning that they had not owned the requisite value in real property necessary for electors. "There are undoubtedly many Gentlemen in America of very good families," Draper pointed out, "but there are also some hundred thousands who were not Freeholders at the time of emigration, and of consequence gave no more consent to Taxation by Representatives, than some millions of people at this day in Great-Britain and Ireland."[28]

Even if all original settlers had been electors when they left England that fact would have been immaterial, other imperialists insisted, because by going to America the settlers knew they were losing the right. "Of this no American is ignorant at the time he leaves his native country," one pamphleteer argued, "therefore he voluntarily and deliberately . . . gives up the privilege of being represented in the British Senate, and turns his back upon every advantage he enjoyed in this kingdom, for something which he prefers to it in America."[29] Besides, the settlers who had been English electors lost only the exercise, not the substance of their right. On returning home they could still vote—if they had retained sufficient property. "They have not, by going to *America*, lost the privilege of voting which they possessed in *England;* any more than an *English* Peer going to *America*, loses the rank and dignity which he claimed in *England*." In fact, all that Americans had lost was direct consent by representation, they retained the privilege of being ruled by a government restrained by consent. In moving across the Atlantic, Allan Ramsay argued, the settlers may have given up the vote, "but, in every other respect, they may receive the full benefit of the constitution, as much as any man at home," or, as Samuel Johnson, the dictionary man, put it, because of their ancestors' migration eighteenth-century Americans could not make laws, but they still possessed "the happiness of being protected by law, and the duty of obeying it."[30]

British constitutionalists who supported American legislative autonomy objected that the imperial side was misapplying the British constitution. Answering Johnson's charge that, of course, an emigrant going to the colonies—by ceasing to be an English freeholder—could no longer vote for a member of the Commons, a London book reviewer pointed out that the emigrant would better be seen as exchanging a freehold in North America for the one he had possessed in England. "[I]f after removing to that continent his person and his new freehold were still to continue subject to the laws and taxes of parliament, every circumstance which rendered it expedient or desirable for him to be represented while he was an English freeholder, must make it expedient and desirable that he should enjoy a similar representation as a freeholder in America."[31]

Other critics of Johnson theorized that the settlers, by crossing the sea, had not forfeited constitutional rights. What they had done was make it impossible for either themselves or their descendants to exercise some of those rights as they had been exercised in the past.[32] The rights still remained and the original settlers retained all the "inherent privileges of Englishmen." "[B]ut by being prevented, by their distance, from being represented in Parliament to their advantage, they were necessarily to be so governed, as that they might have no cause to entertain apprehensions for their freedom."[33] The argument should not be given a twentieth-century constitutional meaning. It belongs to the eighteenth-century British constitution. That constitution required consent by the governed, not voting by the governed. Consent generally was expressed through direct representation of some freeholders. Americans, the argument contended, had a constitutional right to local assemblies in which some freeholders were directly represented.[34]

The constitution provided American whigs little support for the authority of migration. If the doctrine was plausible, it was no more plausible than the imperialists' counterargument. The original settlers had not migrated to form a new society, John Lind pointed out, but had intended to remain English subjects. That had not only been their understanding, it had been the understanding of the king and other rulers of England who had encouraged their migration.[35] Their domicile had changed, but their constitutional status was the same. "Subjection to the jurisdiction of the British legislature is the very circumstance which constitutes a British subject." They had been subject to parliamentary authority at the time they sailed for America, Ramsay added, and they were going to territories which were English and, therefore, also subject to Parliament. "If then the lands, and the people that were to occupy these lands, were equally subject to the authority of parliament, before their embarkation, they must be so still."[36] It did not follow that under the constitution they were entitled to local, autonomous legislatures. Quite the opposite. "It is inconsistent with all ideas of government," the argument concluded, "that a people migrating to lands *partibus exteris*, have a right to exercise a jurisdiction, separate, and independent of the parent state. . . . Or that because in Great Britain, some of them enjoyed the privilege of sharing in the legislature, that, they have a right to elect *one* of themselves."[37]

Standing alone the imperial contention was not very convincing. It was, however, effective, answering that part of the whigs' theory of the authority of migration which claimed that the mere act of migration, by making it impossible for the original settlers and their descendants to participate in one form of constitutional consent, put constitutional limitations on Parliament's supreme authority to legislate. It was necessary, therefore, to carry the American argument somewhat further, in one of two opposite directions.

One direction was popular: to place sovereignty and therefore consent in the people. The other was monarchical: to establish that their constitutional link with the mother country was solely through the Crown, that they had never been connected with Parliament. It is the second theory that was to be their ultimate constitutional argument, even though it was bizarre in eighteenth-century constitutional law. It was, however, anachronistically not theoretically bizarre as it belonged to seventeenth-century English monarchical constitutionalism, to the constitutional tradition, that is, that had existed at the time of the original settlement of the colonies. This topic must be developed in the proper places where the issue arises. For present purposes it is sufficient to quote just one instance of the conclusion as it related to the migration argument. "So long as the people of *America* resided within the Realm, shared in its Government, and were protected by it, so long they were necessarily bound to obey, and support that Government," it was argued in a letter supposed to have been written by Edmund Burke which was published in colonial newspapers. With migration, however, the authority of Parliament terminated, although the allegiance to the king continued. "[N]othing more was necessary to emancipate the people of *America* from the authority of Parliament, than to permit them to leave the Realm."[38]

Constraints of Popular Sovereignty

The popular factor of constraint of consent upon legislative authority need not be fully developed in this book. In a sense it has already been touched on for it is the reverse side of the theory of trust. The doctrine of popular sovereignty explained the origin of the trust and who created it.[39] It deserves mention because some students, unfamiliar with either English common law or eighteenth-century British constitutional law, have assumed that government from, of, and by the people is most likely an American doctrine that probably was an outgrowth of the revolutionary controversy.[40] If it was American constitutional doctrine, it was inherited whole and without reservation from the mother country.

Eighteenth-century political partisans often exaggerated the political philosophy of their opponents. The dominant whig majority especially enjoyed depicting the tories as royal absolutists. "The extreme of the one party, is absolute power in the King," a whig in 1782 wrote of what he said were tories, "the extreme of the other, is sovereignty in the people."[41] If so, the first extreme was well hidden. A casual reading of political

pamphlets and religious sermons readily brings to light numerous statements of popular sovereignty, but it is not easy to find writers attacking
the doctrine that power came from the people.[42] The better view, the one
that dominated parliamentary expression as well as the political and
constitutional literature, is summed up in the truisms that "all civil powers and authority originates from the people" and that the people "are
the only source of civil authority on earth."[43]

The doctrine of popular sovereignty was primarily an instrument for
restraining power,[44] not an explanation or justification for the exercise of
power. Perhaps the extremes of application can best be demonstrated by
two instances of the argument, one from a Briton in 1776, the second by
an American in 1768. "In every government a supreme transcendent
power must be placed somewhere, and it can be no where else but in the
people," the Briton contended. "This plentitude of power cannot subsist
in the king; his authority is delegated, and consequently defeasible." The
premise could, of course, have led to the conclusion that Parliament, as
"the people," had supreme transcendent power, but that was not the
usual conclusion. Rather, as the American asked, what would have been
the value of people delegating authority to government if that authority
was arbitrary authority?

> The people are the origin of all civil power. They are uncontrolable.
> They have it in their power therefore to institute a despotic uncon-
> trolable *legislative and executive civil power*, by vesting their gover-
> nors with all the power naturally vested in them, collectively. But
> every government they erect, is not necessarily invested with that
> plenitude of power. It belongs to the people to communicate just so
> much of it, to those in whom the government is vested, as they think
> proper. If more be assumed, it is usurpation; and may be lawfully
> resisted, except by a quiet submission, the people shall have testified
> an approbation, and usage has rendered it legal.

Here, indeed, was a marvelously full theory of popular sovereignty. Not
only was the authority to legislate delegated by the "people," if the authority was exceeded, the breach could be made legal by popular acquiescence. Everything depended upon the "people," a premise that departed only in degrees from most mainstream constitutional thought
which would have made the people if not the source of all power, at least
an independent source of power, which checked the Crown and the legislature, and was restrained in turn by those and other constitutional institutions.[45]

Following from the premise that "government is the creature of the people,"[46] eighteenth-century British popular sovereignty applied several restraints to legislative authority. One followed from the fact that, as the people created the government, they had the right to change not only the personnel of government but the form or constitution of government, including the sovereign legislature.[47] A second was that all government officials were "servants of the people," which meant that all officials from the king down had limited powers and discretion.[48] Third was that government had been "ordain'd for the Good of the *Governed*," "set up by the people to be the guardians of their rights, and to secure their persons from being injured or oppressed,—the safety of the public being the supreme law of the state."[49] Or, as several American and British clergymen pointed out, "Rulers are made for the People, and not the People for the Magistrate."[50]

Bishop Samuel Squire in 1748 outlined the theory of constraints through popular sovereignty as the whig principle of government which he contrasted with the tory theory. The tory principle, so he said, was "the divine right of kings." The whig was "that civil government was originally the institution of men, and may have its certain bounds prescribed it by the people, . . . and that in extreme necessity, where the very being of the state depended upon it, even the supreme magistrate himself might be resisted."[51] Samuel Estwick, a barrister of the Middle Temple, connected the restraint of reserved power to the concept of omnipotency, concluding that not only was no institution of government, such as Parliament, omnipotent, "but the constitution itself is not omnipotent, because it is subject to controul, by the higher power originally in, and ultimately residing with the people. That the people at large therefore, and not the constitution, nor the governing power resulting therefrom, are omnipotent."[52]

The contention was, of course, mere theory. There was no "people" except for a small group of male members of the aristocracy and the upper class of male freeholders who alone could effect political change—short of rebellion. Richard Hey, also of the Middle Temple and who was admitted into Doctors Commons, tried to qualify theory with reality when, agreeing that the legislative authority could not be omnipotent if opposed to the whole people, he pointed out that in actual fact the voice of the people was mute. It followed, Hey concluded, that "those to whom the ordinary powers of legislation in any state are committed must be considered as unconfined in the power of making laws."[53]

John Gray who published several works on political and constitutional topics, thought the theory of reserved power was valid law but without practical application. "By the principles of the British constitution," he noted, "the Parliament have no right to alter fundamental laws without the acquiescence of the people; but that they have altered them with that acquiescence is most certain," and he listed a number of instances, including the Septennial Act and the repeal of certain clauses of Magna Carta. But had the consent of the people been gathered? Yes, Gray said, but he did not mean consent in a way that the word is defined in the twentieth century. He meant consent in an eighteenth-century constitutional way. It had been supposed, not polled. "The British legislature then in assuming to itself an omnipotence . . . always supposes the acquiesence of the majority of the people."[54] Under the eighteenth-century British constitution, therefore, consent of the people was universal. It could include women as well as men, Catholics as well as Anglicans. If definitions were stretched to meet legal doctrine, it might even be called democratic.

CHAPTER EIGHT

CONSTRAINTS OF CONTRACT

Direct representation was the coming manifestation of constitutional consent in the 1770s. It would be the constitutional norm in the nineteenth century. In the age of the American Revolution the dominant manifestation of constitutional consent was still not expressed but implied, not personal but vicarious, not by elective choice but by social acquiescence. It was not by *direct* representation but by original contract.

When supposing government to be founded by consent of the people, as David Hume pointed out, the eighteenth century was supposing that there was an original contract. The sometime barrister, Richard Hey, in 1776 looked at the contract from the opposite perspective, saying that its primary utility was to explain how people, not members of the legislature, constitutionally consent to government and laws. As "all men are by nature equal," none "can claim authority over the rest," the Reverend Myles Cooper was told in an open letter the next year. "On what then can government be founded, but on the consent of the governed; that is, in other words, on compact?" Thomas Rutherforth in his law lectures at St. John's College, Cambridge, also linked consent to the contract when he asked why people who were equal to one another could be bound by law. The reason, as seen in the last chapter, "must be an act of joynt consent. Sometimes we consider this act of joynt consent as a law, and call it the law of the civil constitution. Sometimes we consider it as a compact, and say, that a king in monarchies, or the nobles in aristocracies, or the representatives of the people in democracies, which are administered by representatives, derive their power from compact."[1]

In seventeenth-century England and eighteenth-century Great Britain, many political theories and almost all constitutional theory were shaped by contractarian thought. It was adaptable to every issue and was a standard that could be used to judge every problem. When Governor Francis Bernard first arrived in Massachusetts he reported to London that much was well in the Bay colony. "This people," he wrote, "are better disposed to observe their contract with the Crown than other on the continent I have known." Sixteen years later and a month before the Declaration of Independence, New York's loyalist William Smith complained that "the present Animosities are imputable to the Pride & Avarice of Great Britain, in assuming an Authority, inconsistent with the Compact by which the Empire have been so long prosperously united." Agreeing with Smith, but on the opposite side of the constitutional controversy, the freeholders of North Carolina's Chowan County voted that the Massachusetts Government Act, one of the intolerable acts of 1774, was "an attempt to dissolve a Contract most solemnly entered into by the present Ancestors of the Massachusetts Bay with their Sovereign; a contract w[hi]ch ought to be held inviolable, without the mutual consent of King and People."[2]

During the revolutionary controversy both sides appealed to contractarian theory, making similar constitutional arguments for similar constitutional reasons. It is, of course, well known that colonial whigs argued the contract, but less well appreciated is the extent to which the other side, the parliamentary imperialists, utilized contractarian jurisprudence. Consider four imperialist claims that the contract—or that special version of the contract that can be called the second original contract or the migration contract—contained specific stipulations establishing Parliament's supreme authority over the colonies. Lord Lyttelton stated the least complicated of the four, finding the stipulation in the constitution and laws of the mother country from whence the first settlers migrated. "They went out subjects of Great Britain," he told the House of Lords, "and unless they can shew a new compact made between them and the parliament of Great Britain (for the king alone could not make a new compact with them) they still are subjects to all intents and purposes whatsoever. If they are subjects, they are liable to the laws of the country."[3]

The second argument implied the contractual stipulation of parliamentary supremacy from the circumstances of the migration. "When the first emigration took place," a parliamentary letter writer contended, quoting Vattel, "there was a tacit and implied condition on the part of the Emigrants, *'that they would continue to act, as they would have done, had they remained inhabitants within the realm of Britain;'* for it must be the very summit of error and ignorance in any Nation to tolerate Colonies on any other terms."[4]

Rejecting both Lyttelton's law and the "implied condition" of the letter writer, the third argument located the stipulation of parliamentary supremacy in the failure of the emigrants to contract a new constitutional arrangement. "[W]hen the first Settlers departed from this country to form a Colony, they ceased to be represented here, and therefore *ought* to have a new Constitution similar to that at home," he admitted. "It is a pity . . . that things of this importance were not expressed in that clear manner so as not to be left doubtful."[5]

The fourth imperialist contention explained why the burden of negotiating the stipulations of the contract had been on the original settlers and not upon the Crown. They "well knew" that, if they did not contract new provisions, the old constitution of parliamentary supremacy would have remained in force. After all, the settlers had not been foreigners but English subjects "who were previously well informed of the nature of the grant, and the terms whereon they were to occupy it. Thus they who first migrated from England to settle in America well knew, I presume, they were still to continue the subjects of the same government."[6]

The lesson to be drawn is not the flexibility of the contractarian doctrine, its adaptability to almost every aspect of constitutional litigation, or its general usefulness in explaining the legitimacy of authority in an unwritten, customary constitution. It is, rather, the wide acceptance that it enjoyed in eighteenth-century constitutional thought and the persuasiveness it was accorded by political exponents as well as legal experts. Twentieth-century students of constitutional law may find it hard to believe, but imperialists active in the revolutionary controversy took the original contract as seriously as did colonial whigs. When American whigs cited the second original contract, their opponents might argue with the whigs' interpretation and sometimes counter with interpretations of their own, but they did not disparage the concept. They seldom said there was no contract.

THE SECOND ORIGINAL CONTRACT

From the perspective of historians of the American Revolution it may appear inevitable that the colonial whigs would develop in time an argument of the authority of the constitutional contract. As John Adams pointed out, "there is no precedent in English records, no rule of common law, no provision in the English constitution, no policy in the English or British government, for the case of the colonies; and therefore . . . we derive our laws and government solely from our own compacts with Britain and her kings, and from the great legislature of the universe." In other words, according to Adams who was exaggerating the paucity of constitutional authority, had the whigs not the authority of contract, they would have either had to depend on a natural-law defense or concede Parliament's supremacy. They however did have the doctrine of contract, a theory of constitutional law that was neither new nor American, but one of the oldest concepts in European and British constitutional jurisprudence.[7]

In their case against parliamentary supremacy, colonial whigs relied on several different contracts. The least important was the social contract, the compact creating society, which they frequently referred to but hardly ever relied on to support a constitutional argument. The contract that they most often cited for authority was the original contract, the constitutional compact between the people and their rulers, the contract of the "fundamental form" of government.[8] Not only did American whigs, in contrast to later historians, seldom compound or confuse the two contacts, they were not even considered mutually supporting. Indeed, it was not unusual for a constitutional theorist to reject the possibility or disparage the significance of the social contract, yet use the original contract either to explain limits on government or to discuss the existing British government.[9]

The compelling attractiveness for constitutionalists of the original contract as a limitation on government was summed up by the Connecticut Valley lawyer Joseph Hawley in 1775:

> Does not the King of *England* hold his Crown by compact?[10] Is not the relation that is subsisting between him and his subjects in *Great Britain*, founded on compact?[11] Is not the relation that is subsisting between us and *Great Britain*, founded upon compact? Was not our Charter the evidence of this compact? Was not the sense of King *Charles* the First, and of our ancestors, the parties to this Charter, that this Colony was not a part of the Empire, and should not be subject to the authority of Parliament?[12]

Hawley was referring to the second original contract or the colonial contract, a variation of the original contract of English and British government—that is, an older contract or the contract to which he referred when saying the king "held his Crown by compact" and had a contract with his subjects in Great Britain. The American variation was implied from colonial historical facts, but the constitutional theory was not American doctrine. The second original contract had long been a staple in the formulation of Irish constitutional rights, for Ireland, like the colonies, had been settled by English adventures who had left the mother country on the understanding reached with the king that they would continue to enjoy English rights and privileges. "*They granted* the Kingdom to *him;* and CHOSE and *acknowledged him,* as *their King;* and *he,* in return, *gave them,* the *same Laws* and *Privileges,* and, in general, the *same Constitution,* with his *English Subjects,* in all Points, by *which,* and *by none other,* they should be *for ever governed.*" Among the powers stipulated in the "Compact" was the one that many Irish Protestants thought "the most valuable," the authority to legislate. "By this Agreement," the lords of Ireland had argued in 1719, "the People of *Ireland* obtained the Benefit of the *English* Laws, and many Privileges, particularly that of having a distinct Parliament here as in *England.*"[13]

The colonial original contract was an exact duplication of the Irish original contract. The reason is probably not because the Americans know of the Irish and copied it, but because both were extensions or novations of England's original contract. The English people had made their contract with their earliest kings, renewing it each reign through the coronation oath and from time to time through specific, negotiated compacts such as Magna Carta and the Petition of Right. The American contract, like the Irish contract, had been made with a king of England by the original settlers at the time of the first settlement, and it covered all aspects of colonial government including the matters in controversy in the prerevolutionary crisis––the authority to tax, the authority of rights, the authority to legislate, and the authority to govern. We are concerned only with the authority to legislate, and discussion must be limited to that question, but it is important to realize that the original contract was argued on both sides of every constitutional issue in dispute between Great Britain and the colonies. The reason why is even more significant: because, from the perspective of a very important legal theory, the original contract was the constitution.[14]

The original-contract theory made its greatest impact on the question of legislation, partly because of the way that the negotiations were always described. They were between the Crown and the original settlers, creating a relationship between king and people, not between the Americans and Parliament. "[T]he people of each Colony," the standard account explained, "either before or soon after their emigration, entered into particular compacts with the Kings of *England* to continue in allegience to them, their heirs, and successors, and also as to their particular forms of Government, which appears by Charters, royal Proclamations, and the laws and regulations in each Colony, made by mutual consent of the King and the people." James Lovell overstated the American dependence on the contract for constitutional autonomy when, in the first Boston Massacre oration, he claimed that "[i]t is in this compact that we find OUR ONLY TRUE LEGISLATIVE AUTHORITY." He meant, of course, that due to the colonial original contract, Parliament's recent assertions of supremacy were a constitutional usurpation. It was an extreme position, not often articulated by American whigs. Of the few times argued, it was perhaps best stated by the voters of the town of Pembroke, Massachusetts Bay, in 1772.

> *Resolved*, That although the British Parliament is the grand legislative of the nation, yet according to the original compact, solemnly made and entered into between the King of England and our ancestors, at the first coming into this country, and the present Royal Charter, no legislative authority can be exercised in or over this province, but that of the Great and General Court or Assembly, consisting of the King or his representative [i.e., the governor], his Majesty's Council, and the House of Representatives.[15]

It may be that no one thought an actual expressed bargain had been struck, written down, and signed, although many spoke of the colonial contract in terms of a time and place of agreement, and even "quoted" its clauses and stipulations. For them, as for many constitutionalists in the mother country and in Ireland, the original contract and the second original contract were real, and it is a very serious misunderstanding of the eighteenth-century legal mind to disparage that fact.[16] It might be an implied, rather than expressed, contract, but, as Gouverneur Morris argued, it had to exist, it had to be real, or there would have been no constitutional government.[17]

For that reason, constitutionalists of the eighteenth century did not think of the original contract as we would have expected, that is, as a legal fiction. "[W]e must not imagine that what has been here said, concerning the manner in which civil societies are formed [that is, by an original contract], is an arbitrary fiction," John Dickinson insisted when instructing members of Pennsylvania's assembly. "For since it is certain, that all civil societies had a beginning, it is impossible to conceive, how the members, of which they are composed, could unite to live together dependent on a supreme authority, without supposing the covenants," including the colonial original contract.[18]

Although implied from circumstances, custom, history, and existing governmental institutions, the original contract was no theoretical abstraction, but an entity existing in law. There were even said to be contracts between bodies politic, between two nations, or, as in the case of the colonial original contract, between sections of a nation. "That it is both possible and lawful for one corporation or body politic to submit themselves to the laws, and contribute to the supplies of another, no one will doubt," Adam Ferguson, a Scots professor of moral philosophy, assumed. "[T]hat all corporations and bodies politic belonging to the same state are actually under such a contract, no body ever questioned."[19]

What disputes occurred were not about the reality of the contract but its terms. People on the imperial side did not question that Americans had rights vested by the original contract, they questioned what those rights were and how they had been established. In one respect, the imperialists had the easier part of the argument, as they would start with the anachronistic premise that the British constitution extant in the 1770s had also been in effect at the time of the first settlement, and that Parliament was supreme under that constitution. A persistent tactic for the imperial side, therefore, was not to question but to assume the contract, basing the authority of parliamentary legislation precisely on the fact that the first settlers both had made a contract and had sought permission to leave. "[T]he express condition upon which the first adventurers to our American Settlements were *permitted* to colonize, was to maintain a constant obedience to the laws of England," one observer concluded. The reason, Governor Pownall explained, was that the settlers could not depart the realm "without leave or licence," a statement of law that is questionable, and that "they had such leave, according to the then forms of the constitution, and the terms were, that the society, community, or government which they should form, should neither act nor become any thing repugnant or contrary to the laws of the Mother Country."[20]

Pownall's reading of the contract was the exact reverse of the American whig interpretation. It would have put a contractarian restraint upon colonial assemblies. The second original contract for Americans was a legal theory clamping restraints on imperial power.

THEORY OF THE ORIGINAL CONTRACT

The original-contract doctrine had developed over the centuries as a constitutional theory explaining why there were restraints on the power of the Crown. Sir William Blackstone, who as late as 1765 wrote of the original contract entirely as if it were an agreement between king and people, called the contract "one of the principal bulwarks of civil liberty." He echoed what English commentators had always been saying, as for example Richard Claridge, the Quaker, who seventy-six years before had remarked that "where this *Agreement* is not, 'tis not properly *Government* but *Tyranny*."[21] The reason was that government could not exist without law and there could be no law without limits on power. Whether made only with kings or negotiated with other officials as well, the original contract was primarily a constitutional brake on power. The original contract, Jackson Barwis summed up, "comprehends in it all that is important to civil liberty." He meant that the contract gave rulers no authority independent of the people. "The compact, strictly speaking, on the part of the people, extends only to the intrusting of the magistrates with certain power, which are to be exercised in certain modes, with a view to attain ends which may be deemed beneficial to the community at large."[22]

Because for most citizens of the nation the exercise of consent was not direct, personal, or by elected representation, the true significance of the original contract is that it provided a stronger restraint on government in the eighteenth century than did representation, popular election, or the concept of consent. "*Humane Compact* must found *Government:* and yet be *superior* to it, so as to be its *Rule*," Bishop Benjamin Hoadly wrote in the first decade of the eighteenth century, "and so as that the whole *Society* might still have a *Right* to take *care* of themselves, *superior* to the *particular Right* of any Man to govern, which was given for the good of the whole."[23]

The doctrine of the original contract, therefore, like the doctrine of trust and the doctrine of consent, was a theory of restraint on government power. It imposed restraint in several ways. One of the most utilized has just been mentioned: imposition of the burden of proof. "As all lawful Government is founded in compact," a Philadelphian explained, "it behooves those who claim authority, to prove that they have it." Since, by the contract, power went from the people to the king, the onus had to be on the king to prove any right he claimed, not on the people to prove it had not been conveyed. "In questioned Cases," a British writer contended in 1790, "the King is to produce his Grant (for he hath no more than what was granted) and not the People to shew a Reservation; for all is presumed to be reserved, which cannot be proved to be granted away." On the matter of the authority of Parliament to legislate, the burden was easily assigned. "Is there," Joseph Hawley asked, "any proof or evidence of any surrender, compact, or consent of the people, that the Colonies should be, *in all cases*, within the legislative authority of Parliament?"[24]

A second restraint was imposed by the very fact that the original contract existed. Just to say that government had been created by contract was to claim that there were restraints on government. "[A]s no Government is lawful, but what is founded upon Compact and Agreement, between those chosen to govern, and them who condescend to be governed," Robert Ferguson reasoned, "so the Articles upon which they stipulate the one with the other, become the Fundamentals of the respective Constitutions of Nations, and together with superadded positive Laws, are both the limits of the Rulers Authority, and the Measures of the Subjects Obedience."[25] Perhaps it would be wrong to claim that Ferguson's conclusions deserve special attention because he was an expert on original contracts. But he did have more experience with them than did most people, for he tried to rewrite at least two of them. Known as "the Plotter," he served as chaplain to Monmouth's army, was an early supporter of William of Orange, and ended life a Jacobite.

The same theory of restraint by contract prevailed in the colonies. "Whatever authority therefore the supreme power has," John Tucker told Governor Hutchinson and the legislators of Massachusetts Bay in 1774, "can be justly exercised, only within certain limits, and to a certain extent, according to agreement." Tucker was referring to what he called "fundamental laws, which are the basis of government, and form the political constitution of the state." These fundamental laws, he added, "which mark out, and fix the chief lines and boundaries between the authority of Rulers, and the liberties and privileges of the people, are, and can be no other, in a free state, than what are mutually agreed upon and consented to." Samuel Estwick, barrister of the Middle Temple, expressed the theory in more legal terms. "From compact arises certain primary, or fundamental laws, which form the constitution; and which are called, the principles of the constitution," he wrote. "These principles of the constitution establish the government that follows from thence, and, for the execution of which, place the governing power in the hands of king, lords, and commons."[26]

Today the concept of the original contract could easily be misinterpreted. From the perspective of our constitutional values, it might be thought that Tucker and Estwick were expounding a theory of civil rights. They were, of course, but there is a distinction. In the eighteenth century in contrast to the twentieth century, the emphasis was less on the creation or expansion of rights, than on preserving what were perceived as immemorial, unchanging rights by maintaining and even strengthening constitutional restraints on governmental authority. As Charles Turner told Massachusetts lawmakers just two years after Tucker preached, the "people" have the right "to fix on certain regulations, which if we please we may call a *constitution*, as the standing measure of the proceedings of government; so determining what powers they will invest their rulers with, and what privileges they will retain in their own hands."[27]

It would not be too many years after the American Revolution that educated people in Great Britain would find arguments about the original contract fantastic. It may be assumed that they might have smiled if someone was bold enough to suggest that the contract could limit Parliament's sovereignty. It is well to note, therefore, that in 1785, after the American Revolution had been fought and lost in the name of parliamentary supremacy, no less an authority than William Paley both endorsed the theory and said that the original contract restrained the authority of the legislature. The original contract, he noted, was "appealed to and treated of as a reality." When appealing to it, Paley explained, Britons spoke "of laws being constitutional or unconstitutional" and thought of "laws, usages, or civil rights, as transcending the authority of the subsisting legislature, or possessing a force and sanction superior to what belong to the modern acts and edicts of the legislature."[28] Paley, although interpreting the postrevolutionary British constitution, was employing as British usage what soon would be only the American meaning of words.

ARTICLES OF THE CONTRACT

It was not only theorists such as Paley who believed that the original contract still had constitutional relevance in the governance of the mother country during the age of the American Revolution. Members of Parliament did as well. After fighting broke out in Massachusetts Bay, the ministry contracted for Hanoverian troops to assume garrison duty in some British outposts, freeing the regular army for service in North America. Members of the House of Lords protested that bringing foreign soldiers into the kingdom violated the Mutiny Act and, therefore, "the great constitutional compact entered into by the prince and people."[29]

It may be safely assumed that most constitutional scholars in Great Britain understood what was meant when members of Parliament claimed that ministerial negotiations for foreign soldiers breached the British original contract. If so, and if they thought the theory made legal sense (whether or not they agreed with the specific application of the contract to these Hanoverian troops), two lessons should be noticed. First, this is one more piece of evidence of how much British and American constitutional thought in 1776 was based on similar premises and turned on shared notions of precedents, trusts, and contracts and not power and command. Second, it is also evidence of what eighteenth-century Britons meant when they boasted that the British original contract was stronger than any other because on matters such as the constitutionality of standing armies, its terms, stipulations, and clauses were better known than were the contracts of other countries. In fact, it was pointed out, in many other nations the original contract was much less precise or had even been forgotten. "But We of this Country have been more happy," Viscount Bolingbroke had explained. "Our *original Contract* hath been recurred to often," and was well known. The articles of the colonial or second original contract were, if anything, even clearer, which did not mean there could be no disagreements about their interpretation, their relevancy to particuliar fact situations, or how they should be applied.[30]

The difficulties of interpreting the colonial original contract surfaced at the very commencement of the revolutionary controversy. If there was any provision of any original contract on which everyone agreed, it was the stipulation that should either party breach the agreement, the other contractee had the right to react. The constitutional contract in this respect was stronger than the constitutional trust, as violation of the contract could terminate the agreement. Theoretical disputes were not about whether there was a right to resist breaches of the contract by government, but how serious violations had to be to end the contract or permit armed resistance. Bolingbroke, for example, said that the right to terminate existed even against the Parliament if it adopted actions that jeopardized the constitution.[31] Some rule of that sort was universally acknowledged. Arguments were about which party was responsible for a breach and measures of culpability. In the first parliamentary debate of the American Revolution, Thomas Pitt claimed that colonial Stamp Act riots violated the original contract. "Resistance by force and violence to the civil authority being a destruction of the original compact," he charged. William Pitt disagreed. "[T]he Original Compact with the Americans was Broke, by [passage of] the Stamp Act," he told the House of Commons, concluding that Parliament's breach had given the colonists the right to resist. Perhaps this disagreement between the two Pitts also illustrates why historians have had difficulty applying the original-contract concept to the American Revolution. They were talking about different original contracts—Thomas of the British original contract and William of the colonial or second original contract.[32]

Throughout the era of the American Revolution, there was an extensive debate about the specific terms of both the original contract and the colonial original contract: how closely they reflected the British constitution,[33] how much the terms might be altered by renewals of the contract,[34] and whether the provisions of the contract, like substantive law, were to be found in immemorial custom.[35] The major portion of this constitutional literature is of no concern to us as it did not bear on the question of parliament's authority to legislate. On that issue there was, of course, little agreement, not even on whether the contract contained specific provisions dealing with legislative competence. "[C]ommon sense," Edmund Burke said, "taught me that a legislative authority not actually limited by the express terms of its foundation, or by its own subsequent acts, cannot have its powers parcelled out by argumentative distinctions, so as to enable us to say that here they can and there they cannot bind." He was speaking of the colonial original contract, not the British original contract, for he complained that there was no "record of such distinctions, by compact or otherwise, either at the successive formation of the several colonies or during the existence of any of them."[36]

Other participants in the revolutionary controversy had less difficulty than Burke "reading" the terms of the second original contract and finding clear provisions concerning the authority to legislate. American whigs, of course, thought the second original contract a good deal more informative than did Burke,[37] but then so did many of their opponents who found specific points in the contract to argue against the whigs. This bit of revolutionary history deserves much more attention than it has received, not because the issues argued are important, but because we should understand their origins and how much they owed to uncompromising lawyers' legal theory. Consider, for example, the "express reservations" discovered in the contract by Henry Goodricke and which, he said, were "acknowledgments" and "stipulations" in which the first settlers recognized parliamentary supremacy over the colonies. "The Colonists," Goodricke pointed out, "settled in a distant part of the earth, under the express avowal and claim of being *British subjects*, members of the British community; under sanction of the common protection and authority; under acknowledgment of a general subjection to the established supreme legislature; under certain charters and stipulations settled by the legal powers then existing;—which charters and stipulations not only in themselves implicitly suppose, but contain express reserve of, their remaining under the authority of the one common supreme Legislative."[38]

For the other side there were different acknowledgments and counterstipulations. A writer in London, for example, cited "the express Covenant" in the second original contract by which the emigrants limited the authority of legislation to their own assemblies. This "express Covenant" was just the opposite of Goodricke's "express reserve." On going to North America the settlers had acknowledged themselves English subjects, "but these acknowledgments have always been conditional, that *their Rights and Privileges should be preserved to them.*"

Among these *"Rights and Privileges,"* of course, was the "Power to make Laws for their better Government and Support, that is a Power of *Legislation* and *Taxation;* for a Government cannot be *supported* without Taxes, and the maintenance of these Rights, was their *Original Compact, . . .* it was the express Covenant upon which they undertook to cultivate that Wilderness."[39]

The debate about the terms of the contract, by the very nature of "evidence" deduced to prove the argument, was bound to be inconclusive. Basically, it came down to broad, sweeping propositions, that each side passed off as indisputable. Each had a basic constitutional value governing all interpretations of the contract. On the American side, that constitutional value was the overriding primacy of the doctrine of consent. By the original contract, Governor Stephen Hopkins argued, as British subjects Americans "are to be governed only agreeable to laws, to which themselves have some way consented." By the second original contract, the Reverend John Allen added, the right to consent had been reaffirmed for Americans when the king agreed "to sign, seal, and confirm, as their steward," only "such laws as the people of America shall consent to."[40]

On the imperial side the basic constitutional guide for interpreting the original contract was the fundamental right of British subjects to a government in which Parliament was supreme over the throne. It was not only a right secured under the British original contract, it was a right Parliament had contracted to preserve inviolate, or there would have been no contract. What choice, therefore, did Parliament have "in conformity with its trust," Goodricke asked, "but to compel them [Americans] to their duty and the terms of the social [i.e., original] compact? The rest of the community has a contracted right to their equal subordination, and Parliament is obliged to enforce it."[41]

It does not do to dismiss the argument as farfetched. The fact that the argument was made is more important than whether the argument was sound. Historians should be impressed by how far legal arguments could be carried. It is evidence of the seriousness with which the constitutional aspects of the debate were regarded. To say that Parliament was obliged by its trust to hold Americans to their contract was to carry contractarian reasoning about as far as it could stretch.

There is substantially more material on the second original contract than has been covered in this chapter. There are a number of unexplored questions, including the important issue of the identity of the contractee who contracted with the first settlers. Perhaps the most serious contention of fact made by the colonists was that the contract had been negotiated exclusively with the king. Parliament had not been a party. No other contractarian argument held more far-reaching implications for the authority to legislate. Then there is the counterargument that it was constitutionally immaterial that the colonial original contract was between the first settlers and James I, Charles I, or Charles II, depending on which king made the contract with which group of settlers going to which colony. As was pointed out hundreds of times during the revolutionary debate, the Crown did not have authority to exclude the supreme Parliament from the stipulations of sovereignty, loyalty, obedience, and government. "The King cannot grant away . . . the legislative power," Attorney General Charles Yorke explained to the House of Commons. "The King cannot grant away the supremacy of Parliament."[42]

What was being said was that, in the Stuart era before Parliament established its constitutional supremacy, the Crown could not contract limitations on parliamentary supremacy. It was a lawyer's argument, not a historian's argument, proving the law of yesterday by applying the law of today. Because in 1765 George III was not empowered to make an original contract granting legislative autonomy to settlers of a new colony in Upper Canada, so it followed that Charles I had not been constitutionally empowered to make such a contract with the settlers of Massachusetts Bay in 1629 even though the Glorious Revolution lay in the future and Parliament had not yet established constitutional primacy over the Crown. Modern historians have difficulty understanding such conclusions reached by this methodology of eighteenth-century common lawyers. To an eighteenth-century common lawyer it was immaterial whether the conclusion was valid as history. More relevant, it made *legal* sense, for in the timeless setting of common-law thought, the constitution of 1765 had always existed. If George III could not bind Parliament in 1765 then Charles I could not have made a contract with the first settlers of the colonies that was binding on the Parliament that sat in 1765.

These issues will have to be developed in their proper place. For present purposes, the lesson of the original contract must be that it was inconclusive on the question of the authority of Parliament to legislate for the North American colonies. Our lesson, rather, lies in the extent to which the contract was argued. Constitutional scholars in the eighteenth century took the original-contract doctrine seriously, much more seriously than have historians of the American Revolution who, when they have noticed it, have too often confused it with the social contract. We should be impressed both with the fact that the contract was extensively dissected and debated, and with why it received so much attention. It was a major point of debate because participants in the revolutionary controversy knew the dispute concerned constitutional law and because most debaters believed the original contract and the second original contract relevant to the constitution.

The lesson of the original contract may best be demonstrated by considering one of the few objections raised during the revolutionary controversy to the doctrine of the second original contract. "What are those rights which we have possessed above one hundred years, which we derived from solemn compact, which we have purchased by an unshaken allegiance, and by the profits of our trade?" a pro-American author asked, calling attention to the settlement contract and the imperial contract as well as to the second original contract. This "plea" a London magazine writer objected, was "unfair" because it treated "the difference between Great Britain and her colonies as the subject of a treaty; the colonies claiming one thing, and Great Britain offering another. The question is not what shall be granted, but what is possessed; not what the constitution of the colonists may or ought to be made, but what it is."[43] The complaint was not that the second original contract was lesser authority or that the imperial controversy was not a valid constitutional dispute. The complaint was that the second original contract should not be allowed to obscure the existing constitution by concentrating constitutional attention on how, when, and by whom the contract was negotiated. That should not have happened, for the evidence of the contract was not in the past but in the institutions and customs of government—that is, in the constitution.

CHAPTER NINE

CONSTRAINTS OF CONSTITUTIONALISM

There was a touch of irony to eighteenth-century British constitutional theory. The strongest, most popular, most cherished restraint on arbitrary power was also the least well defined. It was the concept of constitutionalism. Although everyone utilized the concept of constitutionalism—it was as much the lodestar of laity as of common lawyers—because its parameters were assumed set by obvious innate puissance, few writers bothered to analyze its elements or question its effectiveness. A relevant instance is provided by New England clergymen who, all through the eighteenth century, utilized the concept when lecturing colonial legislators on the limits of their power. God did not commission rulers or ordain constitutions, James Allen, pastor of Brookline, told Massachusetts lawmakers in 1774, stating a political given repeated over and over in "election" sermons. It was, rather, the constitution that somehow constrained authority. "And since the *power* of the *civil ruler* flows from the *constitution* he is under, the natural extent of it is limited by the maxims of doing that which is *just* and *right* to all under that *constitution.*"[1]

There were a number of theoretical premises explaining the constitutionalism of legislative restraint. One was to state a doctrine, such as taxation by consent, and say that as a working part of the constitution it limited the authority to legislate. Another was to trace the principle of constitutional restraint to an established maxim, rule, or source of authority, and say that government was restrained by popular sovereignty, the original contract, the deed of trust, or the expressed consent of the people. "[T]he Boundaries set by the People in all Constitutions are the only Limits within which any Officer can lawfully exercise Authority," the voters of New London, Connecticut, explained in 1765. Although there was wide disagreement in Great Britain about what this rule meant in pragmatic, substantive law, there was something more of a consensus in the colonies where theorists harkened back in time to the seventeenth-century constitutional jurisprudence of Sir Edward Coke and Sir John Hampden—to the "fixed constitution" limiting the king, and, therefore, the legislature, to promulgate new law. "In all free states the constitution is fixed," a colonial House of Representatives lectured the secretary of state for the colonies in 1768. "It is from thence that the legislative derives its authority; therefore it cannot change the constitution without destroying its own foundation."[2]

The outlines of seventeenth-century constitutionalism have been drawn in earlier chapters, and only one point should be reemphasized. It is to repeat that although the British of the nineteenth century would not comprehend the notion of a supreme legislature subordinate to the constitution, the theory was still championed by a vocal, but not necessarily radical minority in Great Britain during the years of the American revolutionary controversy. At its extremes the division was between the traditional or "ancient" constitutionalists, and the constitutionalists of legislative sovereignty. That division was delineated by a dialogue on the constitution between *Philodemus* and *Aristocraticus* in 1776. *Philodemus* spoke for the seventeenth-century or "American" concept of constitutionalism, a concept, he thought, that was still the norm for British constitutionalism. "[I]f the Parliament be an essential part of the Constitution," *Philodemus* asserted, "it cannot go beyond the Constitution: if it does it will not be the Parliament which the Constitution of England knows, but something else." *Aristocraticus's* reply is of interest less for rejecting the old "fixed" constitutionalism, than his grounds for doing so. It is indicative of the strength of traditional constitutional thinking that he did not anticipate the nineteenth-century constitutionalism of parliamentary supremacy, but instead relied on two of the main conceptual props of the fixed constitution: popular sovereignty and consent. Parliament, he maintained, could not go beyond the constitution because it was "a part" of the constitution. Ask "the ablest advocates . . . of America . . . if the voice of Parliament be not in law the voice of the people, the voice of the Constitution; if it do not bind persons beyond [the] sea, persons unborn, persons who never heard of the act, because it is the consent of all."[3]

If the dichotomy of the two British constitutions seems overemphasized, it should be remembered that the purpose has not been to recreate eighteenth-century political thought. It is, rather, that the dichotomy explains so much about the coming of the American Revolution, with the Americans forced to take a stand on behalf of one constitution, the British with little choice but to adhere to a newer constitution. The lesson that cannot be overemphasized is that the concept of constitutionalism in Great Britain during the 1770s was caught in the same ambiguity as were the concepts of trust, consent, and contract. If the British had already moved to the constitution of parliamentary sovereignty, they still, like *Aristocraticus* in the passage just quoted, used the language of the old constitutionalism, they still thought of constraints when in a few decades they would think only of power, policy, or command. In the age of the American Revolution they were still employing language that reads much like the vocabulary of trust or consent or contract or fundamental law, although it was saying something more general and less particular than the mechanics of why government was limited. It was harking back to an ancient tradition of the restraints of constitutionalism, the sovereignty of custom, and the rule of a law that was as close as political theory could then come to recognizing unlimited legislative command. The obvious must be repeated that, although today the vocabulary of constitutionalism is thought of as an American vocabulary, it was still the dominant vocabulary of politics in Great Britain during the closing decades of the eighteenth century. It shaped the thought of Edmund Burke, for example, when, the year after the military struggle had been lost at Yorktown, he wrote that, "Our constitution is a prescriptive constitution; it is a constitution whose sole authority is that it has existed time out of mind. . . . Your king, your lords, your judges, your juries, grand and little, all are prescriptive. . . . Prescription is the most solid of all titles, not only to property, but, which is to secure that property, to government."[4] By the next half century, no one, not even American common lawyers would speak of a citizen's "title" to government or of prescription being the "sole authority" for governmental command.

We may know that Burke's constitutionalism was archaic, but that is hindsight. We may doubt if Burke's contemporaries realized it. Other constitutional theorists used the same language, describing British government in 1769 as "mixed," as "balanced," as a government of "no arbitrary tyranny." That is another historical perspective easily overlooked: the perspective of Burke's contemporaries. Not only was the vocabulary of the constitutionalism of limited government not new—not American—what was novel to them was the vocabulary of the constitutionalism of parliamentary sovereignty; it was the theory that law was command that had the aura of innovation. The freeholders of Middlesex made that point in 1769 when they complained of "a certain Unlimited and Indefinite DISCRETIONARY POWER" that had been "introduced into every Part of the Administration of our Happy, Legal CONSTITUTION."[5]

The concept of constitutionalism as a restraint on power was not only still viable in Great Britain during the years of the American Revolution, it pervaded the way Britons conceived of government, of governmental authority, and of governmental legitimacy. They spoke not only of the British constitution or the imperial constitution, but of the constitution of institutions, such as the constitution of Parliament, which, in the language of constitutionalism, was a way of discussing limitations imposed by innate structure rather than by extrinsic restraint. "The limit therefore to the supreme legislative power is that which limits every other nature, the principle of its constitution," William Jones wrote in 1768. "That it shall preserve its form;—that it shall maintain inviolate the freedom of election:—that it shall employ the public force for the preservation of equal liberty; are the laws to which it is subject, because they are the laws of its nature. These laws it cannot trangress, without changing its character, without ceasing to be that which it is, a government by consent."[6] It is worth recalling that Jones was a common lawyer and a future imperial judge whose thoughts were shaped by the law of the eighteenth century. He did not deny that Parliament was sovereign, that its command was all powerful. His limits were inherent limits of purpose, of function, of constitutionalism.

LIMITATIONS BY BALANCE

Political theory joined with the doctrine of precedent and historical experience to give eighteenth-century constitutionalism its *raison d'être*. Responding to the basic apprehension of English history—fear of arbitrary power—eighteenth-century British political theory was wrenched by the eternal predicament that governmental power was needed because humans had to be policed, but because mere humans exercised governmental power government could not be trusted with power. The predicament was so obvious and troublesome it gave rise to thousands of hackneyed political platitudes which, by 1776, underlay what remained of British constitutionalism. "Unlimited power has generally been destructive of human happiness," the Reverend Charles Turner aphorized in a 1773 New England election sermon. "The people are not under such temptations to thwart their own interests, as absolute government is under to abuse the people."[7]

The political principle was that limitations per se, any limitations checking government power, including legislative power, were an absolute, civic good.[8] The constitutional principle was that limitations were set and enforced by *fixed*, immutable customs or rules of law. By the 1760s that second principle was more ideal than real. What constitutional limitations remained were no longer immutable rules of law but were set by *fixed* constitutional institutions—the independence of juries to determine law as well as fact, the origination of all money bills in the House of Commons, theoretical prohibitions against standing armies, equal sharing of legislative burdens, parliamentary privilege, judicial tenure *quamdiu bene se gesserint*, exclusive crown control of financial disbursements, and the accountability of executive officials to impeachment by the House of Commons with trial in the House of Lords. The centerpiece institution, the essence of British constitutionalism, and the ultimate restraint upon the authority to legislate, was the balance inherent in the tripartite division of Parliament between king, Lords, and Commons. In constitutional theory, universally accepted and revered, the three faculties of social organization limited one another: monarchy offset by aristocracy checked by democracy.

Sometimes called "the Gothic balance," the doctrine of the balanced constitution can be traced back through European and English history to the concept of a balanced monarchy, which had been a way of explaining why kings were bound by law, and had been developed over time into the theory of parliamentary government. That theory postulated a blending of the classic forms of government—monarchy, aristocracy, and democracy—joined in the legislative branches of king, Lords, and Commons.[9] The idea, William Paley explained, was that the constitution "has provided for its own preservation," and each part of the legislature "is secured in the exercise of the powers assigned to it, from the encroachment of the other parts. This security is sometimes called the *balance of the constitution;* and political equilibrium, which this phrase denotes, consists in two contrivances,—a balance of power, and a balance of interest."[10]

It should be understood that we are considering a theory of limitation on power, especially the power to legislate, which was also a theory of the preservation of liberty. "The legislature," according to the theory, "consists of three estates, which are instituted as checks upon each other, in order to secure our liberties and properties against all."[11] It was an uncompromising theory of the menace posed to human freedom by naked power and how power could be reined by dividing it, balancing the divisions, and depending on the imperatives of jealousy and fear.[12] "The equal Division of Power between the several Branches of our Legislature, is a grand Security to the Liberty of the Subject," Justice Robert R. Livingston explained to the New York House of Assembly in 1769. "For each Branch, watchful over their own Rights, are a constant Check on the Encroachments of the other two; and by this happy Balance, the Constitution is preserved."[13]

The political theory was that unchecked monarchy degenerated into tyranny, unchecked aristocracy degenerated into oligarchy, and unchecked democracy degenerated into mobocracy. The constitutional theory was that an equal balance could be maintained by guarding institutional privileges as much as by reacting to usurpations. "As each of the two Houses has a negative on the propositions made by the other," the Swiss constitutionalist J. L. De Lolme noted of British government, "there is, consequently, no danger of their encroaching on each other's rights, nor any more on those of the King, who has likewise his negative upon them both."[14]

We are concerned with the doctrine of constitutional balance only as it related to the authority of legislation. There were, it should be noted, other theories or "nonlegislative" explanations of the mechanics of "balance," including the balancing of competing "interests," whether those interests were economic interests, professional interests, geographical interests, the interests created by different forms of wealth, or by different means of acquiring wealth.[15]

The reason British constitutionalism stressed the workings of Parliament was that the major interests or powers of British life had been institutionalized into the three branches of the legislature. It may appear to us as fiction running away with wishful thinking, but balanced constitutionalism was bone and marrow of both eighteenth-century constitutional theory and eighteenth-century pragmatic politics. Of the hundreds of eighteenth-century explanations of "balance," one of special interest to us is that of Daniel Leonard, as he truly believed in the theory, becoming a loyalist and forsaking his native Massachusetts rather than lose the constitutional security of "balance." "The simple forms of government are monarchy, aristocracy and democracy, that is, where the authority of the state is vested in one, a few, or the many," Leonard explained. "A government formed upon these three principles in due proportion, is the best calculated to answer the ends of government, and to endure. Such a government is the British constitution, consisting of Kings, Lords and Commons. . . . The distributions of power are so just, and the proportions so exact, as at once to support and controul each other." Leonard was saying that he could trust the faraway, impersonal, aristocratic British Parliament in which he was not directly represented because it was "balanced." He could not trust the unbalanced democracy he feared would inevitably result should colonial whigs have their way. Leonard's theory became Charles Inglis's rule for action after the tory constitutional fear appeared to become American political reality. As the Continental Congress began to take control of the colonies and lead Americans toward war against Parliament, Inglis urged his fellow countrymen to reclaim constitutionalism by repudiating unbalanced constitutional novelty (even though local, American, and more representative than Parliament) for the proven security of balanced, constitutional restraint. "Liberty cannot exist for any time, where the supreme power of a state is not divided," Inglis argued. "Ambition, and a thirst of power, are naturally inherent in man. These will stimulate bodies of men, as well as individuals, to encroach on the rights of others. Unless there is some power to restrain those encroachments, liberty must vanish." Inglis was not saying that members of the British Parliament were more trustworthy or by inherent virtue likely to be more restrained than were American congressmen. He was stating the legal theory of balanced constitutionalism. Neither democracy nor representation was the security of liberty. Constitutionalism was, and constitutionalism was secured by restraint and restraint came from balanced constitutionalism.[16]

It is well known that eighteenth-century Britons gloried in the balanced constitution.[17] So too did the colonists, whigs just as much as tories, and they did so not one iota less than did their fellow citizens in the mother country.[18] Like Leonard and perhaps Inglis, they trusted the principle of balance to protect them on the one side from tyranny and on the other side from anarchy. And that was the rub, for the trust could be too great. It was, after all, the British constitution that was being trusted, and the British constitution was not speculative or political reasoning. It was custom, expediency, history, precedent, and practice. Not only was the trust based more on hope than on proven systems, without vigilance, the doctrine of balance could get out of whack. The constitutional security of "balance" depended on the counterpoise of power, and, as Sir William Blackstone pointed out, should power shift "we must be exposed to the inconveniences of either absolute monarchy, aristocracy, or democracy."[19]

Again it was theory, but as the theoretical benefits were enormous, so the theoretical dangers were proportionally horrendous. The end result of the loss of just one of the three branches, Blackstone predicted, could be the loss of constitutional liberty. "[T]he constitutional government of this island is so admirably tempered and compounded," he warned, "that nothing can endanger or hurt it, but destroying the equilibrium of power between one branch of the legislature and the rest. For if ever it should happen that the independence of any one of the three should be lost, or that it should become subservient to the views of either of the other two, there would soon be an end of our constitution."[20]

The question was as much whether the balanced constitution had ever existed as whether the end had come. The balance was there in theory, true enough, but had it ever been there in practice? We need not resolve that question for what concerns us are the arguments raising doubts in the minds of eighteenth-century constitutionalists, especially Americans wondering how much trust they could place in the protections of the balanced constitution.

For theorists believing the balance no longer poised, debate was not about how much the balance had been knocked out of adjustment, but which of the three estates had come to dominate the constitution. From the perspective of two centuries, we, today, can see more clearly than could eighteenth-century observers that the shift had not been to the monarchy. If the Crown had ever been a equal branch of Parliament in the eighteenth century, it no longer was by the age of the American Revolution. It no longer exercised the prerogative to veto legislation, the prerogative to prorogue Parliament, and the prerogative to discipline the House of Commons by calling new elections. For the few who grasped the significance of these changes, fear was that the constitutional balance had tilted to the Lords and Commons. If "his majesty's small remaining power of a negative shall be denied him," Christopher Keld bemoaned in 1785, "surely he will no longer have any *sovereign* power, but be reduced to the condition only of a *subject*."[21] That possibility was of vital concern to American whigs. Toward the end of the revolutionary controversy they would come to see the veto as their prime constitutional protection and could have remained in the empire only had the Crown shielded them from such parliamentary legislation as the Stamp Act and the Coercive Acts. In the history of the balanced British constitution, American whigs were close to being the last constitutionalists championing royal checks on power.

There was also the opposite perspective, a perspective that may have worried colonial whigs even more than the demise of the veto: that the Crown had accumulated more power by 1765 than at any time since the Glorious Revolution. As a result of patronage, "influence," and the ownership of "pocket boroughs," some students of the balanced constitution contended, the king and a few great lords exercised such control over the House of Commons it had lost independence.[22] Influence, or what was called "corruption" was one of the main constitutional worries among American whigs, not because it said something about the state of British morality as is often thought, but because it posed a threat to liberty. The "balanced" constitution, it was feared, might be a conspiratorial camouflage, hiding the real constitution—rule by the arbitrary power of a tiny few, accountable to no one.[23]

A third perspective was that the balance had been undermined on two sides of the constitutional triangle rather than on just one. If, as was sometimes said, the Crown had lost its legislative competence, and if influence, patronage, and corruption had compromised the independence of the Commons, the balanced constitution had been replaced by "an absolute aristocracy."[24] Rule by the House of Lords was no worse for American whigs than rule by the House of Commons or by the Crown alone. Concern was about the demise of constitutionalism rather than about which estate dominated.

There was also a school of thought, more prevalent in Great Britain than in the colonies, that the House of Commons had become too powerful. "The English government will be no more," George Rous would warn in 1784, "when the Representatives of the People, shall begin to share the Executive Authority."[25] He was predicting the emerging British constitution, the constitution of a parliamentary executive, which Americans were rebelling against not because "the people" were obtaining power, but because they perceived the command of government was becoming an arbitrary command unchecked by the balance of constitutional counterweights. Had they thought about political as well as constitutional consequences, colonial whigs might have said that the "people" represented in the House of Commons were not the "people" in the American sense of "people." King, Lords, and Commons were a small clique of British men who shared a common interest of government by patronage, corruption, and aristocracy.[26] The balance of the constitution was destroyed not because the institutions had been altered but because the interests of king, Lords, and Commons had merged into one, and no part of that interest was an American interest. True, in British constitutional theory, that factor should have been immaterial as the representation of interests did not have to be direct to be constitutional. Indeed, a strong case could be made that interests needed less direct representation than did persons, but that was theory more applicable to British interests that were unrepresented or underrepresented in Parliament than to most American interests. The latter usually shared few common values with the comparable British interest that was directly represented in Parliament.[27]

CONCEPT OF ARBITRARY

The principle of the balanced legislature was the very essence of the eighteenth-century notion of constitutionalism. It would be hackneyed to say that its jurisprudential purpose was to avoid arbitrary power, for in British legal theory avoiding arbitrary power was but another way of describing constitutionalism. The antithesis of arbitrary power was limited power, and power limited by customary restraints was constitutional power.

The fundamental legal question raised by American opposition to the constitutionality of the Declaratory Act concerned arbitrary power: did Parliament have the constitutional authority to rule the colonies by arbitrary power? For what was the claim to bind in "all cases whatsoever" in the eighteenth century but an assertion of arbitrary right? Many of the statements and arguments made by whigs about the Act can be understood only in the context of the concept of "arbitrary." Benjamin Franklin had the British ideal of constitutionalism as nonarbitrariness in mind when complaining of "the extreme meanness and folly of the attempt to establish a supreme authority in Parliament." Franklin was referring to English constitutionalism, not to some peculiar American version of British constitutionalism, when he told Irish readers "that such doctrine is incompatible with every idea of a civil constitution; . . . for this supreme authority, having no rule or law to direct its operations, or limit its power, it must necessarily become arbitrary and absolute."[28]

It would be well to think of the concept of arbitrary as it was understood in the eighteenth century. There has been a tendency by recent historians to assume that the theory of inherent restraints was then the new legalism replacing an absolutism of an earlier day. We are told that it is "generally held" that "the central ideal of modern constitutionalism is the checking and restraining of power," and that "one of its earliest and most explicit expressions" had been *Cato's Letters* published in the 1720s. Rightly or wrongly, people living in the eighteenth century had a different historical perspective. They thought constitutionalism old and arbitrariness new. Allan Ramsay traced the constitutionalism of restraint to where everyone in the eighteenth century traced it, back beyond the English to the Saxons. "[T]he quintessence, the life and soul of their constitution; and the basis of the whole fabrick of their government," he said of the Saxons, was to restrain power.[29] It should not be forgotten that during the age of the American Revolution it was still accepted legal theory that the Saxon constitution remained in force, corrupted in some details but generally unchanged.

Eighteenth-century British people, the inheritors of Saxon constitutionalism, feared arbitrary power more than any other threat to liberty. To say that "[t]here is nothing that requires more to be *watched* than power" was to state the motto of eighteenth-century constitutional theorists.[30] "Power without a Balance" was the ultimate menace,[31] and the balanced constitution was the ultimate barrier in which the Saxons, the

English, and now the British had placed their trust, justified, it was believed, by the experience of centuries, a trust in an institution that got its infrastructure from custom and its mystique from the rule of law.[32]

American constitutional theory was such a close copy of British constitutional theory it shared its weaknesses as well as its strengths, and there was a blind spot in British constitutional theory that may have left Americans less prepared to counter the challenge of parliamentary power than they might have been had their constitutionalism been more *sui generis*. Although a few commentators, such as John Locke and *Cato*, did warn that a legislature could endanger liberty, most discussion of the menace of power concentrated on royal abuse.[33] No one so much as said that the balanced constitution was structured only to limit the king. Rather, there was an assumption that if royal power was held in tight check liberty would be secure. During the eighteenth century only a few voices had been raised to suggest that legislative power might be as dangerous to liberty as the power of the throne. During the age of the American Revolution, Sir William Meredith was almost alone when he warned against the "opinion . . . that the more Power the House of Commons gains, the more is gained on the Side of the People. No opinion can be worse founded.—'Tis Protection from Power; not Power, that a free People are to covet." To forget this most basic constitutional truism, another London writer added in 1769, would be to "renounce the protection of the Law, and the security of the Constitution, and deliver over our Liberties as a prey to the chance of things and fate of times."[34] Put more concisely it would invite *arbitrary* power.

Students of the American Revolution should become acquainted with the word "arbitrary." It holds the key to much of what was said of government, power, "right," and liberty in both eighteenth-century Great Britain and eighteenth-century North America. The ostensible synonym used by twentieth-century historians of the American Revolution is "tyranny." "Taxation without representation is tyranny," colonial whigs are imagined to have exclaimed, and they are said to have feared unlimited government power because it could lead to "tyranny." Of course people in the eighteenth century spoke of "tyranny," but in legal or constitutional discussions "tyranny" was not the probative term that usually came to mind.[35] "Arbitrary" was the word most often used to measure the constitutionality of a legislative command or to test the legality of an administrative policy.[36]

When William Pitt demanded repeal of the Stamp Act on the grounds of unconstitutionality, yet asserted that the colonists should be prohibited "from manufacturing even the hob-nail of a horse-shoe," James Macpherson wondered how the prohibition on manufacturing was "less arbitrary" than the stamp tax. "I question the power, *de jure*, of the legislature to disenfranchise a number of boroughs, upon the general ground of improving the constitution," *Junius* wrote concerning the authority of Parliament to eliminate rotten boroughs. "There cannot be a doctrine more fatal to the liberty and property we are contending for, than that, which confounds the idea of a *supreme* and an *arbitrary* legislature." The Scot Thomas Tod in 1782 and the American Continental Congress in 1774 used the word "arbitrary" to summarize the revolutionary controversy. "British colonies," Tod wrote, "cannot be governed or kept in subjection in the manner of Spanish or other colonies of arbitrary powers, whose government is incompatible with the idea of British liberty." The Congress told the British people that "the legislature of Great Britain is not authorised by the constitution . . . to erect an *arbitrary form of government* in any quarter of the globe."[37]

There are two reasons why students of the American Revolution should give close study to the concept of arbitrary. First is its importance as the hinge upon which the eighteenth-century constitution once swung. Second is the historical comparative gained for understanding the differences between constitutional doctrines for arbitrary is one of the main concepts separating twentieth-century constitutional law from that of two hundred years ago. It is above all necessary to rid ourselves of the twentieth-century idea that arbitrary refers to despotism, tyranny, or cruel government. It was not power, the harshness of power, or the unreasonableness of the exercise of power that made government arbitrary. It was the possession of power unchecked.

In eighteenth-century parlance, arbitrary was a measure of the difference "between Slavery and Liberty"; between "power and right"; between "unconstitutional and constitutional." "For it is certain," Jared Eliot reminded Connecticut's lawmakers in 1738, "*That to the Constitution of every Government, Absolute Sovereignty must lodge somewhere.* So that according to this Maxim, Every Government must be Arbitrary and Despotick. The difference seems to be here; Arbitrary Despotick Government, is, When this Sovereign Power is directed by the Passions, Ignorance & Lust of that Rule. And a Legal Government, is, When this Arbitrary & Sovereign Power puts it self under Restraints, and lays it self under Limitations." It was, Viscount Bolingbroke agreed, a matter of power and not of the type and structure of government. It was immaterial if power was vested in a single monarch, in "the *principal Persons of the Community,* or in the *whole Body of the People.*" What mattered, rather, is whether power is without control. "Such Governments are Governments of *arbitrary Will,*" he concluded.[38]

Just as arbitrariness should not be confused with cruelness or terror, for it can be benevolent, mild, and materially beneficial, so it should not be confused with absoluteness. "[E]ven *absolute Power,*" John Locke pointed out, "where it is necessary, is *not Arbitrary* by being absolute, but is still limited by that reason, and confined to those ends, which required it in some Cases to be absolute," such as martial discipline which vests an army officer with power to order a trooper to die but cannot "command that Soldier to give him one penny of his Money."[39] If the officer acted according to law, his actions, even though absolute, would not be arbitrary. That distinction was all important to eighteenth-century constitutional thought. For "court whigs," Reed Browning has pointed out—and also, it should be added, for most other educated Britons and Americans—there were "but two types of government: arbitrary and lawful," or, as John Arbuthnot explained in 1733, "what is not legal is arbitrary."[40]

Arbitrary and legal was one way to state the distinction; "Arbitrary and Free" was the way John Trenchard phrased it in *Cato's Letters.* In other words, arbitrary government was the antithesis of constitutionalism. A good portion of the salient importance accorded to the concept of arbitrariness by eighteenth-century constitutionalists was that it defined constitutionalism. This point was made many times during the prerevolutionary debates, but perhaps it was most clearly delineated during the Middlesex election controversy. John Wilkes, it will be recalled, had been expelled from the House of Commons and when he was reelected, was barred from taking his seat by vote of a majority of the House. Wilkes's supporters, the *Annual Register* reported, did not dispute the Commons' power to expel Wilkes if the charge against him had been one of the customary "incapacities" "collected from the antient, uniform, and uninterrupted practice of parliament." To enforce those incapacities was not arbitrary because they "are generally known; they are enumerated by law writers of the first authority, who expressly declare all other persons eligible. . . . They are founded in good sense; analogous to the like restraints adjudged in other cases by the courts of law; and confirmed by usage. They are not occasional, but fixed: to rule and govern the question as it shall arise; not to start up on a sudden, and shift from side to side, as the caprice of the day or the fluctuation of party shall direct." The exclusion of Wilkes, by contrast, had been "the caprice of the day," an arbitrary act as it was contrary to precedent, custom, established procedure, and the rule of law.[41]

Although the mechanics of power that made the Commons arbitrary during the Middlesex controversy were unprecedented, the realization that Parliament could act arbitrarily was not entirely new. "For *Arbitrary* and *limited* power," Henry Ferne wrote in 1642, "is distinguished by the *Restraint,* which the Law or Constitution of Government casts

upon the governing power, not by the *abuse* of that power, which sometimes in the most limited Governments may break out into a licentious
arbitrarynes[s]." Ferne was a royalist, and it may be he anticipated the
time when Parliament as well as the Crown would be a concern for those
fearing arbitrary government, for he added: "If force and not Law must
tell us what Arbitrary power is, and releeve us against it in the Prince, I
fear we should too often feel it from the hand[s] of Subjects."[42] John
Shebbeare certainly meant Parliament when he complained of the doctrine of legislative supremacy: "What Power amongst Men can be more
arbitrary than that which can bind your Hands in Chains, by Laws
which it enacts, according to it's arbitrary Inclination, and levies what
Money it pleases on your Properties, unexamined, unreproved, and uncontrolled?" These words may sound like the words of American whigs,
and they were in the sense that American whigs would be saying exactly
the same, but they were written a decade before the Stamp Act crisis. In
fact, Britons did not need Americans to explain arbitrariness to them.
What separated British constitutional thought from colonial constitutional thought were those Britons unable to appreciate how a legislature
that was not acting arbitrarily when making laws for them could be
arbitrary when making laws for the colonies. The American answer
came directly out of British constitutionalism, and it was a Briton, a
member of Parliament, who first explained it to the House of Commons.
The colonists, Thomas Pownall pointed out, complained that Parliament
would be their "sovereign" without giving them any check, any "participation in the deliberation, or the will," leaving them only the obligation to obey what was commanded. "[T]hey say, that this sovereign
(however free within itself) is an absolute sovereign, an arbitrary lord,
and that their obedience and subjection, without the interposition of
their own free will, is (as to the subject so stated) absolute slavery."[43]

That argument—that direct "consent" to Parliament's command or
the check provided by direct participation in the promulgation of legislative command was necessary to make legislative command constitutional
for the colonists—seems to have been rejected by an entire school of
constitutional theorists. Or, to be more accurate, it was rejected by two
opposite schools, for there was sharp disagreement about applying the
concept of arbitrary to the authority to legislate. At one extreme were
observers who understood the legal force of command as it would be
understood in the nineteenth century, and, knowing that parliamentary
power was in fact arbitrary, could not appreciate the colonial complaint.
"To say a Power is Supream, and not Arbitrary, is not Sense," Lord
Halifax had recognized in 1750. "There is no other Fundamental, but
that *every Supream Power must be Arbitrary.*" During the prerevolu-

tionary controversy, Arthur Young said the same. "Absolute despotism must lodge somewhere, and nothing can be more unlimited in power than an act of parliament," he insisted. "[T]he legislative authority of King, Lords and Commons is as despotic over all Britons, let them live wherever they please, as that of the Grand Turk is over his own subjects." If you defined constitutional law that way, Americans were left no complaint, unless you accorded them some other right, such as direct representation or the colonial original contract.[44]

At the other extreme of constitutional theory were commentators unable to appreciate colonial whig apprehensions concerning Parliament's arbitrariness because they believed that Parliament could never become arbitrary. It did not matter how sovereign its power, the fact that power had been delegated in trust by the original contract meant that Parliament's power could not be exercised in an arbitrary manner.[45] As sometimes expressed, the theory seems flippant, but apparently not in the eighteenth century. "The British Parliament," it was said by one writer who thought he was defending the colonies from parliamentary power, "are to make *regulations* for the welfare of the Empire—they are *supreme to do justice*, but *not arbitrary to enslave*." Another writer who said Parliament was omnipotent boasted it was "impossible that this Legislature should subject either Britons or Americans to arbitrary power, because they have no such right; and therefore cannot have a power to exercise a right which has no existence."[46]

The conclusion probably reveals less about why Britons did not take more seriously American fears of Parliament, than why they failed to recognize that Parliament had acquired arbitrary power with respect to themselves. For most Britons who commented on the question, parliamentary sovereignty could not be arbitrary. Not only was parliamentary supremacy the child of that most liberating of all historical events, the Glorious Revolution, it was constrained by the balances inherent to the tripartite legislature itself. In other words, one could trust constitutionalism to be its own guarantee.

True, constitutional liberty in Great Britain was supposed to rest on much firmer foundation. The theory of constitutionalism should have made trust suspect. The ultimate right that lay behind British liberty was the right to resist. Unconstitutional legislative commands could be ignored and arbitrary legislative commands could be opposed with force.[47] With legal perceptions changing so drastically as the nation moved from the old constitution of customary restraints to the new constitution of parliamentary command, only a minority of Britons understood that Americans were no longer able to rely on the mechanics of balanced constitutionalism. Even after fighting had commenced, trust in constitutionalism remained the standard for measuring right. It was, Ambrose Serle insisted, to the rebels' "advantage, as well as [their] duty, their happiness as well as their freedom, to preserve the constitution of Britain inviolate, supreme, and absolute over all her dominions." But, of course, "by *absolute* authority" he did not mean "an *arbitrary* power, for these are widely different." Serle meant a *constitutional* power. Britain's "authority is vested in her for the good of the whole" and, therefore, could be exercised only for the good of the whole. That argument, based on the old theory that the constitution of restraint was a secure bulwark against the new constitution of sovereign discretion would no longer do Richard Price replied. If the "*supremacy* of legislation over *America*" meant anything, "it means, that the property and the legislations of the Colonies, are subject to the absolute discretion of *Great Britain*, and ought of right to be so. The nature of the thing admits of no limitations."[48]

Eighteenth-century constitutionalism may have held no assurance for American whigs by 1774. As the Bishop of St. Asaph had "intended" to warn the House of Lords, parliamentary supremacy had come to mean in the colonies something different than the inherent limitations of balanced constitutionalism. "They will complain," he wrote, "that their rights can never be ascertained; that every thing belonging to them depends upon our arbitrary will; and may think it better to run any hazard, than to submit to the violence of their mother country, in a matter in which they can see neither moderation nor end." Britons might boast of their balanced constitution, an antiadministration weekly newspaper pointed out in March, 1776, but the colonists no longer could. For them the three estates of king, Lords, and Commons had lost their balance and, now a single *unity*, had become arbitrary. "The oppressed *Americans*," *The Crisis* of London concluded, "have seen and felt how far a corrupt coalition of *three great estates*, wisely designed as checks upon each other, may form one *tyrannic mass of combination* against the liberties of their expiring country."[49] It is worth reflecting that that conclusion would be legal error if today's British constitution is not arbitrary.

CHAPTER TEN

CONSTRAINTS OF LIBERTY

Liberty was the most cherished right possessed by English-speaking people in the eighteenth century. They boasted of enjoying the best liberty known in the world and gloried in the belief that all the other peoples of Europe envied them their liberty. Liberty for the British was more than the mark of their national uniqueness. It was both an ideal to guide their governors and a standard with which to measure the constitutionality of the government itself and particular programs of the government.[1] In eighteenth-century theory, the operative principle was supposed to apply to legislation as well as to administration. Of course "supreme power can neither be defined nor limited, nor extended by argument and by assertions," Sir William Meredith told the House of Commons in 1777, contending that the cause of the American rebellion was Parliament's insistence on supremacy. "No man can deny in theory the supreme, unlimited power of the British legislature; but the execution of that power is a trust delegated by the people, and to be guided by the principles of liberty and justice."[2] Here was another of those apparent contradictions so prevalent in eighteenth-century British constitutional theory: an unlimited power limited by the concept of liberty. In fact, the concept had wider reach. Even constitutional theorists who did not think the legislature's command was supreme over the law thought liberty was one of the elements restricting power. "The Governour, Council, and House of Representatives, which compose the Assembly," Joseph Hawley wrote of colonial legislatures, explaining why they could not alter "the fundamentals" of government, "are creatures of, and derive all their power from a Constitution agreed upon and previously established, which has for its *primum mobile*, groundwork and leading principle, Liberty, civil and religious. All transactions, therefore, growing out of such a Constitution, and founded upon it, as are the acts and doings of an Assembly, must breathe the spirit of freedom, and be governed by it, as by a pole-star in the political hemisphere."[3]

In general, liberty's authority was based on what Meredith called the "trust" delegated by the people, that is, the original contract conferring jurisdiction on Parliament, or what Hawley called "a Constitution agreed upon and previously established." In that respect, the constraints of liberty were an identifiable aspect of the constraints of trust and contract discussed above.[4] There was, however, a minority theory that treated liberty as its own authority. "The rights of liberty," Capel Lofft explained, "are such as neither the violence of times, nor the power of magistrates, nor decrees or judgments, nor acts of parliament, nor the authority of the whole people, which in other things is supreme, can subvert or weaken."[5] In fact, liberty was such a restraint that even "the whole people" could not grant it away. "[R]emember," the British were told in 1767, "you have inherited the Blessing of Liberty from your Fathers, and cannot alienate that Inheritance from descending to your Sons." Translated from legal theory to positive law, that meant that legislative power is per se limited.[6]

The more accepted premise was "the trust" or grant of legislative authority by the original contract. "The trust," William Penn contended, "is, the liberty and property of the people; the limitation is, that it should not be invaded, but be inviolably preserved, according to the law of the land."[7] The contract or trust was implied from the certainty that no "man in his senses, (unless he had the temper of a slave) ever submitted his liberty, to the absolute disposal of others, under the notion of their being the sole judges of right and wrong."[8]

Although people in the eighteenth century thought of liberty as a normative concept that could be utilized when making policy choices and to set limits both on governmental power and personal license, it was not the instrumental concept most observers believed it to be. There was an inherent difficulty. Liberty might define the limits of government coercion, but how was liberty defined? There were many answers but consensus concerned the most general principles, not specific applications.

No one in the eighteenth century seems to have dissented from the idea that liberty was the opposite of arbitrariness, but that might or might not include absolute legislative command.[9] The power to restrain alone did not negate liberty; power unchecked did. "Who are a free people?," James Lovell asked in the first Boston Massacre oration. "[N]ot those who do not suffer actual oppression," he answered, "but those who have a *constitutional check upon the power* to oppress."[10] In the eighteenth century there were primarily two forms of constitutional checks securing liberty, the rule of law and the balance of institutional powers.

THE RULE OF LAW

The concept of the rule of law in Great Britain during the second half of the eighteenth century is not easily defined. Its scope and theory were narrowing from what they had been—or from what its proponents had tried to make rule of law mean—in Stuart times. Put in terms of historical-jurisprudential perspective, the definition of rule of law was changing from what it still means in twentieth-century United States to what it now means in twentieth-century Great Britain.

As an ideal, the concept of the rule of law in eighteenth-century Great Britain was a support for liberty as liberty was then defined—as a restraint on governmental power, especially on arbitrary power—and less as we would think of it, as liberating the individual. One fundamental element of liberty was the certainty of law and the certainty of law was established, in part, by the rule of law. "Free Government is the protecting the People in their Liberties by stated Rules," Thomas Gordon pointed out. "Only the Checks put upon Magistrates make Nations free," his colleague John Trenchard agreed. "[A]nd only the want of such Checks makes them Slaves."[11] In the American colonies the concept was summed up by the Connecticut clergyman, Jared Eliot. "Blessed be God. . . . We live under a Legal Government," he said, explaining that by "Legal" he meant "Limited." "It is a Corner-Stone in our Political Building, *That no mans Life, Limb, Name or Estate, shall be taken away but by his Peers and by the known Laws of the Land.*" What distinguished "Law and Freedom from Violence and Slavery," Edmund Burke added, "is, that the property vested in the Subject by a known Law—and forfeited by no delinquency defined by a known [law] could be taken away from him by any power or authority whatsoever."[12]

At its strongest, the rule of law was a general principle that government and governed alike are subject to due process. In popular expression, the concept of the rule of law defined government as "The empire of laws, and not of men,"[13] or the circumscribing of power by "some settled Rule or Order of Operation."[14] In the seventeenth century the ideal of the rule of law had obtained constitutional primacy because the power it circumscribed was monarchy.[15] "[I]t is one of the Fundamentals of Law," the prosecutor of Charles I had asserted, "That the King is not above the Law, but the Law [is] above the King."[16] Charles could be criminally charged because a prince disobeying the law was a "rebel."[17] "King Charles," an eighteenth-century writer explained, "either could not, or would not distinguish, between the executive power, which our constitution has lodged in the crown, and the supreme power, which our constitution hath lodged in the law of the land, and no where else."[18] When these words were written in 1771, it was by no means clear the theory reflected positive law in the sense that "law of the land" was fundamental or immutable. The Crown might still be subject to the rule of law, but law in this sense was what Parliament declared.[19]

Although theory was changing and it is difficult to tell just when certain principles became dominant, it seems safe to assert that in Great Britain by the age of the American Revolution the concept of the rule of law no longer included the notion of the sovereignty of law over the ruler. It was procedural only, not substantive, holding that governmental actions must conform to legislative command while that command could change at legislative will. This meant that the concept of the rule of law now restrained power from violating liberty largely by limiting the definition of liberty to the legislatively permitted. "An *English* individual," a writer who thought American resistance in 1775 was legal explained, "cannot, by the supreme authority, be deprived of liberty, unless by virtue of some law, which his representative has had a part in framing."[20] This could mean that direct representation was necessary for liberty, but that was a principle belonging to the future. For the moment it was enough that laws be both promulgated and certain for the rule of law to serve the liberty of the individual. "To assert an absolute exemption from imprisonment in all cases," Blackstone protested, "is inconsistent with every idea of law . . . : but the glory of the English law consists in clearly defining the times, the causes, and the extent, when, wherefore, and to what degree, the imprisonment of the subject may be lawful."[21]

The principle of the rule of law, therefore, may not have restrained parliamentary power so much as guided it. Certainty of procedure was perhaps its most familiar element, and meant, in John Locke's words, "to govern by *promulgated establish'd Laws*, not to be varied in particular Cases."[22] Almost as well known, although in eighteenth-century Great Britain as likely to be breached as to be honored, were the elements that punishment should not be ex post facto and property should not be taken without compensation. The most salient aspect of the rule of law in the eighteenth century, however, was one that whigs boasted was applied and which they thought of first when asked if Great Britain was ruled by the rule of law. It was the principle of equal application. "Laws, in a Free State," it was said, should be equally applied. "[T]he Peer should possess no Privilege destructive to the Commoner; the Layman obtain no Favour which is denied the Priest; nor the Necessitous excluded from the Justice which is granted to the Wealthy," or, in the words of Locke, there was but "one Rule for Rich and Poor, for the Favourite at Court, and the Country Man at Plough."[23]

INSTITUTIONAL LIBERTY

The fact that the concept of the rule of law, a barrier constraining the power of the Crown on behalf of liberty, was not extended to restrain parliamentary power, sums up much of the American Revolution's constitutional controversy. Legal theory in Britain was drawing apart from legal theory in the colonies primarily on the issue of constitutional liberty and restraint on power. The difference was summarized by a pamphlet published in Philadelphia the year of the Declaration of Independence. "No country can be called *free* which is governed by an absolute power," the pamphleteer contended; "and it matters not whether it be an absolute royal power or an absolute legislative power, as the consequences will be the same to the people."[24]

The Philadelphian was talking good American constitutional theory. It had been good seventeenth-century English constitutional theory, but was losing favor in Great Britain during the closing decades of the eighteenth century. In respect to Parliament, the concept of liberty had taken on a new meaning in the mother country that was alien to colonial whig thought. "I knew [*sic*] what liberty is," a British merchant told an American. "Is it not the representation of the whole *British* empire by *King, Lords,* and Commons?"[25] Of course it was, especially if one remembered that Parliament had been metamorphosed into liberty at the Glorious Revolution by the Act of Settlement. It was to those two seventeenth-century triumphs of English constitutionalism—the Revolution of 1688 and its political settlement—that eighteenth-century Britons traced contemporary constitutional liberty. The balances and the mixture of the tripartite Parliament had ended the ancient fear of arbitrariness. The members of the two houses—or of the House of Commons alone—had become the "Guardians of Liberty and the Laws" for all British people.[26] It did not matter who elected the members. What mattered was that they were elected according to constitutional custom and were *constitutionally* representative, which did not mean they had to represent people, but, rather, that the land and interests that they represented were land and interests entitled to representation by immemorial custom. "The spirit of our English constitutional liberty," Allan Ramsay explained, "is founded upon annual exercise of our elective rights; and not in having, a fixed representative body of men, in parliament."[27] Ramsay was saying that liberty required an extensive suffrage or, contrary to what Americans still claimed, it did not require that the power to legislate be limited. Indeed, the emerging British theory was the opposite. Liberty was maintained by the very act of parliamentary legislation. "*British* liberties are in general secured by the *acts of the British parliament.*"[28]

Because the concept was never clearly or prominently articulated, Americans may not have appreciated how deep the gulf had become. The realization that some British now defined liberty as parliamentary legislation could have staggered American constitutionalists had the fact sunk into their legal consciousness. They would never break free of the fundamentals of anti–Stuart constitutionalism in which power unrestrained was not legal. They could not see what difference it made for power to be legislative rather than monarchical. "There cannot be a more dangerous doctrine adopted in a state, than to admit that the legislative authority has a right to alter the constitution," another Philadelphian wrote in 1776. "For as the constitution limits the authority of the legislature; if the legislature can alter the constitution, they can give themselves what bounds they please."[29]

At the moment we are considering only the institution of Parliament and not the specific legislation of Parliament. Institutional perceptions played a secondary but significant role in separating Americans from Britons as they led to divergent definitions of liberty. For the British, as just noted, English constitutional history, especially the history of the Glorious Revolution, led to Parliament being equated with liberty and liberty defined as Parliament. The Americans, by contrast, were still steeped in the seventeenth-century definition that liberty was law free from arbitrariness. "It is," James Iredell told the inhabitants of Great Britain, "an obvious and sufficient answer to this extraordinary claim— of a sovereign dominion in your Parliament over us—that, if it in truth exists, we are possessed of no liberty."[30] Put more concisely, the British identified as liberty the institution that Iredell told them threatened liberty.

A growing number of constitutionalists in the mother country could no longer understand Iredell's argument. The developing perception was that as long as Parliament's institutional integrity was maintained and the functions of the three branches kept separated,[31] there would be liberty. Americans were wrong to insinuate "that no body of men, in any Empire, can exercise 'an unbounded authority over others'" without endangering liberty, James Macpherson insisted. "The great difference, between the degrees of freedom in various Governments," he contended, depended on where the "supreme and uncontroulable power" was placed. "In the British Empire it is vested, where it is most safe, in King, Lords, and Commons, under the collective appellation of the Legislature."[32]

History taught Britons they had to put their confidence in an institution that current experience, starting with the Stamp Act in 1765, was teaching Americans they could not trust. Both sides thought they had the same goals—avoidance of unrestricted, arbitrary power—and both used the same word, "limits." "The parliament has a right to make all laws within the limits of their own constitution," the colonists repeated over and over again.[33] As we shall see, the prerevolutionary debate was largely an attempt to define the limits or, as the expression went, to draw the "line" where the power of Parliament stopped and the restraints of liberty began.

The British agreed that the problem was a matter of "limits," but they no longer believed there were constitutional reasons to set parliamentary limits. The limits on Parliament's jurisdiction were inherent in the very nature or "law" of the institution itself. It was an ambivalent notion, owing something to traditional common-law ways of thinking, such as the implied restraints of the original contract,[34] and much to a reluctance by constitutionalists to think through the ramifications of parliamentary powers.

The reluctance, of course, was to face the arbitrary power of the newly sovereign Parliament. It led to some very tortured arguments about how liberty could be trusted to impose its own limitations, as, for example, Governor Thomas Pownall's contention why American liberty was safe under a sovereign Parliament. It was a central argument in Pownall's important book, one he had to make both politically persuasive and constitutionally plausible. The explanation he came up with was surprisingly unconvincing: that if the institution in which supremacy was vested was an institution of liberty, supremacy would be limited and bounded by liberty. It was, he asserted, a consequence "of the supremacy of the mother country, that all [parliamentary] statutes enacted since the establishment of Colonies and plantations, do extend to and operate within such Colonies and plantations as are specially named." This rule, Pownall hypothesized, meant parliamentary supremacy, but due to liberty, not parliamentary arbitrariness.

> [F]rom the very nature of the supremacy of a free constitution, from the essential nature of the political liberty of the constitutions of the

Colonies, this operation has its limits. In like manner, as the Supreme Being, in the moment that he creates a free-agent, does in that moment, and in that instance, necessarily create limits to his own absolute omnipotence, which *cannot act as an efficient on this free-agency:* So does *the constitution of Great Britain*, actuated by the King, in the moment that it *creates* communities, *having political liberty*, limit and bound its own supremacy; which, though in right it goes over the whole empire, cannot, in fact, in the ordinary exercise of it, do any act, within the jurisdictions of the Colonies, which supercedes or destroys that political liberty which it has created.[35]

If Pownall's theory of the constitutional safety of imperial legislation made sense to the eighteenth-century legal mind, and it may have, today it is beyond creditability. He was asking the colonists to ignore the omnipotency of Parliament because the concept of liberty, unassisted by institutional safeguards, would restrain that omnipotency.

LIMITS OF COERCION

One final constraint of liberty peculiar to the jurisprudence of eighteenth-century British constitutionalism remains to be discussed. It concerns the principle that coercive government is illegitimate government;[36] a principle left over from the old constitution of prescriptive, customary right, another doctrine that was on the decline in Great Britain, but was still strong in the colonies. A closely related principle, one we today may understand better than the notion that coercion is illegitimate, was that magistrates existed only for the good of society. This doctrine, too, was thought a restraint on power because officials who acted outside the public good converted legal authority into illegal force.[37] These two principles came together in several often-stated eighteenth-century civic maxims, also no longer understood in the twentieth century, including the aphorisms that magistrates exerting more coercion than is required for "the Welfare of the Community" are analogous to private, tortious trespassers;[38] that "[a] law, which the civil power is unable to execute, must either be in itself oppressive, or it must be such a one as affords a handle for oppression," and therefore could be treated as a civic cancer to be excised and not enforced;[39] and that "[t]he people seldom or ever assemble in any riotous or tumultuous manner unless when they are oppressed, or at least imagine they are oppressed," which meant that if the military or *posse comitatus* was employed to disperse them, the troops or the posse, not the people, could be the unlawful assembly.[40]

Coercion, the hallmark of nineteenth-century British law, was not fashionable in eighteenth-century British constitutionalism. Sir Robert Walpole was supposed to have said that, by using the sword, he could enforce the excise, but should he do so "there would be an end of the liberty of England."[41] Similarly, members of the House of Lords, protesting efforts to coerce Massachusetts into paying the tax on tea, argued that "[i]f the force proposed should have its full effect, that effect, we greatly apprehend, may not continue longer than whilst the sword is held up. To render the colonies permanently advantageous, they must be satisfied with their condition."[42] "Many indeed think of nothing but keeping them in subjection by the rules and power of government," John Mitchell agreed, "but the first thing to be considered in governing any people whatever, is, how they are to subsist under that government, without which it will be very difficult to keep them either in awe or order. A few staple commodities would govern the colonies, much better than all the laws or regulations that ever were thought of."[43]

We need not spend time puzzling over the legal theory of the illegitimacy of official, enforceable sanctions. The notion was already old-fashioned by 1776, a carryover from the customary, prescriptive, precedential constitution that in Great Britain was being replaced by the constitution of coercive command. Yet it will not do to dismiss the principle merely because we no longer comprehend it. At least it is well to realize that it was once valid constitutional law and that the constitutionalism to which it belonged was still the constitutionalism of the colonists. If nothing else, it helps to explain why all Americans, not just whigs, would be shocked by the Coercive Acts of 1774 and by London's decision to enforce the Coercive Acts with the sword.

CHAPTER ELEVEN

CONSTRAINTS OF LAW

During the eighteenth century, British constitutional theorists engaged in a lengthy debate that has generally and mistakenly been described as a debate about history. It was, in fact, a debate about law. It turned on the writings of Dr. Robert Brady, who, scoffing at the notion that the seventeenth-century English constitution was the ancient Gothic constitution brought to the country from the continent by Saxon invaders, argued that both the common law and the House of Commons owed their origins to the Normans, not to the Anglo-Saxons. Brady is usually hailed as England's first authentic constitutional historian, but his role has been misunderstood. His purpose was not to write accurate history but to propagate monarchist law. To prove as history that the House of Commons had been created by a Norman king, and was not coeval with the Crown, came very close as a matter of law to saying that the Commons existed at royal pleasure, not by prescriptive right. The eighteenth-century common lawyers who contested Brady argued against his law, not his history. We see this occurring in the one forum where lawyers addressed the public directly: charges to grand juries. Charters such as Magna Carta, Sir John Gonson told the Westminster Grand Jury in a typical charge, "were not voluntary Abatements of the King's original Power, nor Grants and Concessions of our Princes (as FILMER, BRADY, LE-

STRANGE, HICKS, LESLEY, and other Advocates for Arbitrary Power would make us believe) but Recognitions of what we had reserved unto our selves in the original Institution of our Government, and of what had always belonged to us by common Law, and most ancient Custom."[1]

The purpose of Gonson's argument has generally been misunderstood in the twentieth century, at least in the United States. Gonson was arguing for a definition of law—custom—that he equated with British liberty and was, for him and other lawyers who thought as he did, the security for preserving liberty in the future. Brady, Filmer, and the others mentioned in the grand jury charge were not friends to that liberty. They redefined law as arbitrary command—the command of the king in Brady's meaning, but by Gonson's generation it more likely meant the command of the king in Parliament. Gonson was saying that law was not command. It rested, rather, on different authority. First, the authority of the original contract—"what we had reserved unto our selves in the original Institution." Second, the authority of custom—"what had always belonged to us by common Law, and most ancient Custom." It was in this second authority that common lawyers up through the first half of the eighteenth century had always put their confidence and trust. Law, they said, was custom. Whether they also said that law was not will, pleasure, or command, is a different question, and the answer depends not only on an individual's legal philosophy, but also on the source of the will, pleasure, or command.

The authority of custom has been considered elsewhere.[2] We must limit this discussion to custom and constraints on legislative discretion. Custom was a way of using the past to establish the law of the present. It was a method of arguing law by locating the authority of law in prescriptive right—not a Burkean prescription as some historians are prone to believe,[3] but the prescription of ancient, precedential common law.

We should be on our guard as the authority of custom—or usage, as custom was also called—may easily be misunderstood. Francis Gregor described "Usage" as "the best Construction of a Law,"[4] a revealing point of view as long as we do not take that definition to mean that custom was evidence of law. Custom and usage were law's evidence in the sense of proving law but, in inveterate jurisprudence, they were much more than evidence or proof. They were law itself. Defining "Customs and Usages" for the 1726 Suffolk Grand Jury, Maurice Shelton explained that "Of this Body of our *English* Laws, the Government, and what is now call'd the Constitution, makes the principal Part; from which proceed all our other Muncipal Laws, relating to Religion, Life, Liberty, or Property. After an Use and Practice of our Laws, time out of mind, then they are taken to be the Common Law of *England*, and not before; nothing but Time imme-morial making any thing Part of our Constitution."[5]

RESTRAINTS OF CUSTOM

The authority of custom had for centuries been the infrastructure of both English common law and English constitutional law. Its reign was coming to an end by the age of the American Revolution, and by 1850 custom would be largely relegated to matters of procedure. In the 1770s it still held much theoretical importance. If not authority for law itself, it was at least evidence of law, the better and most safe mode of finding constitutional law. Today we acknowledge that custom justified and pre-served the status quo. The eighteenth century was less likely to think of the status quo than of political neutrality. By being ancient, immanent, and unmade, custom was independent of human judgment and human choice, making it not only more neutral but benign, the constitutional opposite of law by discretionary sovereign command. To the extent that it was choice, the choice was made by many generations and many minds, not by this one generation and that one mind. "A system of civil and political government," an Irish writer explained in 1783, "the funda-mental principles of which are certain immemorial usages, whose antiq-uity, if other proofs were wanting, speaks their superior wisdom; and certain memorable precedents, in which the just and virtuous struggles of our ancestors, recognized as just and virtuous by the common consent of successive generations, point out to their posterity how we too ought to act under similar circumstances."[6]

One year earlier, Edmund Burke, reaching similar conclusions, had wanted custom to be more than the guide for behavior. It should also provide the rule for law. Burke was writing out of the tradition in which custom had been the authority not just of law but of right. British liberty would surely be the loser, he knew, as the binding force of customary law was replaced by the emerging concept of law as sovereign command. After all, British security had always depended on the prescriptive sub-stance of the constitution. "Prescription is the most solid of all titles, not just to property, but, which is to secure that property, to government," Burke stated. True, it may have been a constitutional proposition that retained little viability, but that point by now is well understood. More significant was the constitutional theory of prescriptive authority and its scope, for prescription did more than secure property and government. As Burke explained, it secured law as well. "[T]his is a choice, not of one day, or one set of people, not a tumultuary and giddy choice; it is a deliberate election of ages and generations; it is a constitution made by what is ten thousand times better than choice, it is made by the peculiar circumstances, occasions, tempers, dispositions, and moral, civil and social habitudes of the people, which disclose themselves only in a long space of time."[7]

It cannot be said that had Burke made this argument in the House of Commons he would have been misunderstood. Every lawyer listening to him had been trained in prescriptive constitutionalism. Every member of Parliament had been taught that prescriptive right was the foundation both of English law and of British liberty. Moreover, Burke's legal theory was, in a limited way, still respectable in Great Britain. Certain constitutional doctrines, such as the Commons' privilege of bringing in and framing all money bills, were understood to rest entirely on the authority of custom.[8] There were even some constitutional theorists still saying that there were customary rights beyond the power of Parliament to abrogate. One such right often referred to would have kept Parliament from reforming itself. It was the right of the owners of rotten boroughs not to be deprived of their franchise. That right rested almost entirely upon prescription and its security was only as strong as prescriptive ownership. Yet many commentators said that because of it, Parliament could not constitutionally reform representation.[9]

Although the concept of customary right was still familiar enough that most English lawyers understood what Burke meant by prescription, it is likely that had he delivered these remarks in the House of Commons, some members would not have thought he was discussing law. Appeals to custom were coming to be arguments about the best way to set political policy, and less understood to be arguments of constitutional restraints. Across the Atlantic, however, colonial whigs would have read Burke to mean that custom had constitutional force. Naked command unsupported by custom or right was not constitutional. The difference has been noted before and will be again for it was one of the most basic concepts of law dividing American constitutional from British constitutional thought. Put quite simply, the authority of custom—a fading principle in eighteenth-century British jurisprudence—still dominated American constitutional legality. That is one reason why the American and British, although generally understanding one another, so often misinterpreted or did not credit what the other said.

The American theory was clear and unequivocal. The colonists stood foursquare on the prescriptive right of custom. They were, according to the articulated constitutional formula, entitled to "a full and free Enjoyment of *British* Liberty, and of our particular Rights as Colonists, long since precisely known and ascertained, by uninterrupted Practice and Usage."[10] The fact that the colonies had always legislated for themselves free of parliamentary superintendence, meant that they had a constitutional right—a right established and proven "from constant Usage"[11]— to continue free of parliamentary superintendence. Arthur Lee demonstrated both the methodology of the argument and the conclusion of law when he traced through history various precedents of the colonists taxing themselves by representative government and instances of the king or Parliament *not* taxing them. The "right of giving their own money by their own consent," he concluded, had always been claimed by the Americans and, until 1764, recognized by Parliament. The constitutional "novelty" was the British claim of parliamentary authority to tax the colonists. The conclusion of law was obvious to Lee. "[I]f the uniform claim and exercise of a right, with our [i.e., British] as uniform recognition and acquiesence for one hundred and fifty years, will not render it clear and unimpeachable, I know not by what lapse of time, or by what circumstances, the enjoyment of any privilege can be rendered sacred and secure."[12]

Lee can easily be misunderstood. He was stating neither a political plea to expediency nor an argument that tried to persuade people about policy choices by appealing to customary practice. What he said, rather, was a constitutional argument, an argument of law. Considering the postulates of eighteenth-century common-law jurisprudence, Lee did not exaggerate the predicament faced. If custom could not secure colonial rights against parliamentary manipulation then, by the premises of the constitutionalism of restraint, Americans had no rights.

There may be no stronger instance of a legal doctrine argued during the prerevolutionary controversy that was good law in America and antiquated law in London than prescriptive right as a restraint on Parliament's authority. At the very beginning of the constitutional debate, Virginia's House of Burgesses insisted on the principle when telling George III that the people of that colony were entitled to continue "in the Enjoyment of their ancient and inestimable Right of being governed by such Laws respecting their internal Polity and Taxation as are derived from their own Consent, with the Approbation of their Sovereign or his Substitute," because it was a "Right which as Men and Descendents of *Britons*, they have ever quietly possessed since first by Royal Permission and Encouragement they left the Mother Kingdom to extend its Commerce and Dominion."[13] Or, as the Burgesses stated even more strongly to the House of Lords, "they must conclude they cannot now be deprived of a Right they have so long enjoyed, and which they have never forfeited."[14] They could not be deprived of it, the New York General Assembly explained, because it was a constitutional right "gained, by uninterrupted usage," and was, therefore, "such a civil constitution as would remain secure and permanent, and be transmitted inviolate to their latest posterity."[15]

Familiar as the argument may sound, it was one of the most remarkable made by the Americans during their dispute with the mother country. It was good seventeenth-century English constitutional theory used to restrain the Stuart kings, now transposed in the eighteenth century by colonial whigs to restrain Parliament. The British could understand it. They could not accept it.

LAW OF INNOVATION

Custom, of course, was a question of fact. If Americans claimed it was their constitutional right, established by long practice and usage, that their local assemblies alone had jurisdiction to bind them by legislative command, the British, in most instances, did not challenge the principle of law. Although they no longer thought custom binding on Parliament, they respected the theory and were just as apt to counter the American claim by arguing facts rather than law. They said that the colonial whigs had not proven that they customarily enjoyed legislative autonomy or that the true facts were the opposite of what Americans claimed, that Parliament all along had legislated for the colonies. At its most extreme, the imperial case had no need to argue the law of sovereignty against the law of custom. Custom could be argued against custom. "[I]f there was no express law, or reason, founded upon any necessary inference from an express law," the lord chief justice contended in 1766, "yet the usage alone would be sufficient to support that authority: for, have not the colonies submitted ever since their first establishment to the jurisdiction of the mother-country?"[16]

Lord Mansfield was making a lawyer's argument, and the premises of his argument deserve attention. He was saying that custom was against the American claim of local legislative autonomy, or, to state the same conclusion another way, that Parliament's right to legislate was established by constitutional custom. But his grounds were not factual, they were legal. The custom existed as an inference of law, not historical fact. The conclusion—that Parliament had always legislated for the colonies—was inferred from the constitutional nature of the imperial connection and the certainty of the inference proved the customary practice. This line of argument was familiar in English constitutional history, used by supporters of royal authority in the seventeenth century and frequently by imperialists during the American controversy. The argument was deceptively easy to make and legally convincing—that customary practice could be inferred as a matter of law in support of government power. The inference, of course, was that, unless the other side proved differently, it followed from the very potential of governmental authority that that authority had been exercised.[17] It was to refute the inference that two other legal principles became pertinent to the American whig argument, the doctrine of innovation and the law of precedent.

The doctrine of innovation was one of the prime constitutional shields against arbitrary power during the seventeenth and eighteenth centuries. "Oh! Innovation is dangerous," William Pudsey had warned in his book on the English constitution,[18] and most constitutionalists continued to agree throughout the eighteenth century. "By opposing innovations, Government is preserved," the western Massachusetts lawyer, Joseph Hawley, asserted less than a week before the battle of Lexington.[19] There were two explanations. One was governmental continuity and stability. *"The opinion of right,"* William Paley pointed out, "always following the *custom,* being for the most part founded in nothing else, and lending one principal support to government, every innovation in the constitution, or, in other words, the custom of governing, diminishes the stability of government."[20] The more important explanation was the need for vigilance against encroaching power. "The *first* safety of princes and states," a pamphlet on *British Liberties* warned in 1766, "lies in avoiding all councils or designs of innovation, in antient and established forms and laws, *especially those concerning* LIBERTY, PROPERTY *and* RELIGION . . . and thereby leaving the channel of *known* and *common justice* clear and undisturbed."[21]

It was the last point, preservation of rights in hand, that made the prevention of innovation the obverse side of the security of custom. "[A] known and settled usage of governing," Paley explained, "affords the best security against the enormities of uncontrolled dominion," but "this security is weakened by every encroachment which is made without opposition, or opposed without effect."[22] The very quality of an innovation made opposition to it imperative, even to the extent of embracing a counter innovation to prevent an innovation potentially more dangerous. Balancing alternatives could be delicate, as the *New-York Journal* understood when it measured the potential innovation of American independence against the continuing innovations of parliamentary legislation.

> The British Parliament is violently usurping the powers of our colony governments, and rendering our legal Assemblies utterly useless; to prevent this, the necessity of our situation has obliged us to

depart from the common forms, and to adopt measures which would be otherwise unjustifiable; but, in this departure, we have been influenced by an ardent desire to repel innovations destructive to all good government among us, and fatal to the foundations of law, liberty, and justice: We have declared, in the most explicit terms, that we wish for nothing more, than a restoration to our ancient condition.[23]

It is difficult for us in the twentieth century to catch the urgency of the argument. Because we think of custom as static if not reactionary, we have forgotten the creative dynamicism of customary English constitutional law. Eighteenth-century whigs were always aware that today's innovation would be tomorrow's custom. Once launched, an innovation took on legal life, mutated from an aberration into a precedent. "We may introduce the innovation," John Dickinson warned against a proposed change in the Pennsylvania charter, "but we shall not be able to stop its progress. The precedent will be pernicious."[24] That was the ultimate constitutional risk. Innovation unopposed could convert the illegal into the legal and the unconstitutional into the constitutional by providing what had been illegal or unconstitutional with a legal or constitutional precedent.

CHAPTER TWELVE

PRECEDENTS OF HISTORY

The topic of precedent deserves more attention from historians of the American Revolution than it has received. It is not just the legal author-ity of precedents that should be considered, but the many types of prece-dents and the different uses of precedent in the eighteenth century. At its weakest, precedent was merely advisory. Precedent served "not to pro-mote but [to] check Innovation," Lord Mulgrave explained in 1769, "by warning" legislators "to be extremely cautious, and maturely to consider the Expediency of any Step which their Ancestors have never found it necessary to take. . . ." At its strongest, precedent was binding law, as Nathaniel Forster indicated when arguing that the expulsion of Sir Robert Walpole by the House of Commons established the right of the Commons to bar the reelection of John Wilkes. "What ever doubt then there might have been in the law before Mr. Walpole's case," Forster wrote, "there can be none now. The decision of the house upon this case is strictly in point, to prove, that expulsion creates absolute incapacity in law of being reelected."[1] The rule was even stronger if the precedent was specific legislation, especially a tax for which previously there had been no prece-dent. After the excise on cider and perry was announced in 1763, an opponent warned that "if this new extension of the Excise-laws is con-firmed, it must effectually justify and authorise every future extension of them which can be proposed, till the Excise becomes general."[2] This statement was not a political prediction. It was legal theory, an explanation of law. Two years later George Grenville asked former Attorney General Charles Yorke for an opinion on the proposed American Stamp Act. "The precedent may," Yorke replied, "be in argument extended far, to other future taxes, upon the colonies." That was one reason American whigs rioted—to keep the Act from becoming a precedent.[3]

Yorke was thinking of the strongest precedents for parliamentary jurisdiction: particuliar statutes enacted by Parliament that, as precedents, were cited to prove Parliament's authority to enact further legislation of the same or an analogous category. That type of precedent—statutory precedent—was the type most frequently cited and debated during the revolutionary controversy. It is also one of the most familiar to common law, one still practiced today, and which will be discussed in chapter 17. Other kinds of precedents were also argued during the American Revolution, precedents less well known in the twentieth century, which can be put under the heading of "precedents of history." These range from the very general to the very particular. The general consisted of broad, assumptive claims as, for example, that the colonies "never disputed" the authority of Parliament to bind them "in all cases whatsoever,"[4] or that "[t]he Supremacy of the Legislature of this country" had always been "acknowledged" by Americans.[5] The particular relied on specific statements from the past, incidents that either had happened or had not happened, and civic habits such as the fact that when the Massachusetts General Court convened in 1769 at a moment of imperial crisis, with both houses determined to demand the removal of British troops from the colony and to challenge the supremacy of Parliament, the first order of business for its members was to take the oaths "required by Act of Parliament."[6] Just taking the oath became precedent acknowledging Parliament's supremacy. "Shall we now dispute," Governor Thomas Hutchinson asked, "whether Acts of Parliament have been submitted to when we find them submitted to in Points which are of the very Essence of our Constitution?"[7]

We may not be impressed with Hutchinson's argument. Precedents from history are no longer argued as they were in the 1770s. That tactic belongs to the discipline of the customary, prescriptive, precedential eighteenth-century constitution. Historical precedents must have impressed lawyers and politicans then, however, for everyone argued them, even students of the constitution who professed to believe that Parliament was sovereign. They may have claimed that by inherent constitutional right Parliament could bind the colonies in all cases whatsoever, yet somewhat inconsistently they did not scruple to prove that authority by historical precedent. In this chapter we can do no more than look at a few examples from a very extensive debate. The purpose is to understand what was argued and why the argument was important to the prerevolutionary controversy. It would be well to keep in mind, however, that the participants were not the only observers to have taken this material and this constitutional methodology seriously. Subsequent legal scholars have as well, even using it as authority or proof when reaching conclusions about history. Such evidence persuaded the constitutional historian, Sir David Lindsay Keir, that American whigs had lost on law. "Their [constitutional] case was fatally impaired," Keir concluded, "by the undeniable fact that the authority of numerous British statutes (including some, like the Bill of Rights, which might almost be regarded as integal to their own case) had long been accepted by them as binding. Their only course was an appeal to natural justice, which removed the question from the sphere of constitutional law."[8]

FATAL PRECEDENTS

Jonathan Sewall, attorney general of Massachusetts, imperial judge of admiralty, and one of the better colonial lawyers to remain loyal to the British Crown, once explained that the constitutionality of parliamentary sovereignty over North America could be proven or disproven by historical evidence. "And from this view we shall also perceive whether the present claim of parliament is new, as many ignorantly suppose, or whether it was made, openly and expressly, before the grant of the [second Massachusetts] charter, and has ever since been uniformly exercised by them, and acknowledged by us."[9] That was the type of evidence developed and argued by both sides, evidence not just of specific legislation and recorded actions, but of attitudes both of individuals and generations about parliamentary supremacy. At first the methodology looks like history employed to prove constitutional law, but on closer examination it proves to be not history according to the historical method but that most maligned school of history, forensic history.

The technique was to cite an event, a statement, or a document, to discuss how the cited material related to an issue of constitutional law, and then to argue that material not as evidence of constitutional history but as legal authority, much like a common-law precedent. Negative evidence that something had not occurred was as authoritative as was evidence of actual historical happenings. General, sweeping suppositions were as seriously argued as were documented instances of opposition to parliamentary authority. One tactic that should be familiar today was the claim that among the first settlers of the colonies there had been an original understanding that they were independent of Parliament. The evidence was inferred from the general attitudes of some of the early elected officials in the colonies who either deliberately ignored parliamentary statutes or took active steps to oppose parliamentary supremacy.[10]

The methodology was more forensic than historical. A revealing example is provided by a report sent to Charles II by the royal commissioner, Edward Randolph, describing a visit he paid on the governor of Massachusetts in September 1676. "I told him I tooke notice of severall ships that were arrived at Boston," Randolph wrote, "contrary to your Majesties lawes for encouraging navigation, and regulating the trade of the plantations. He freely declared to me that the lawes made by your Majestie and your parliament obligeth them in nothing but what consists with the interest of that colony, that the legislative power is and abides in them solely to act and make lawes by virtue of a charter from your Majesties royall father, and . . . that your Majestie ought not to retrench their liberties, but may enlarge them if your Majestie please."[11]

By the standards of both law and history the governor's statement was questionable evidence of either the colonial understanding or the imperial constitution. It was made unofficially, at a private meeting, to a royal commissioner who was viewed as an antagonist and who was unable to obtain cooperation from the elected members of the Massachusetts government. Moreover, that official, whom no one denied was prejudiced, is the sole source of the words. Yet for eighteenth-century colonial whigs those words were, as John Adams claimed, "a positive assertion of an exemption from the authority of parliament, even in the case of the regulation of trade."[12] The governor's offhand remark, that is, was, according to Adams, direct proof of the seventeenth-century American understanding about parliamentary sovereignty, and that understanding, whigs were telling the British, should now be the rule of constitutional law. Indeed, the Massachusetts House of Representatives, when debating with Governor Thomas Hutchinson the meaning of the constitution, thought the statement would be even more authoritative if touched up a bit. To make them stronger, the House "doctored" the words that Randolph had reported to Charles II, and then, with what looks like contemptuous procacity, even "doctored" Hutchinson's version of the report. "He the (Governor) freely declared to me," the House quoted Randolph telling Charles II, "that the Laws made by your Majesty and your Parliament, obligeth them in nothing, but what consists with the Interests of that Colony, that the Legislative Power and Authority is and abides in them *solely*."[13] The source the House cited for this quotation was a *Collection* of historical papers edited by Governor Hutchinson. As quoted by Hutchinson, Randolph had reported that he was told "that the legislative power is and abides in them solely to act and make lawes by virtue of a charter from your Majesties royall father, . . . and that your Majestie ought not to retrench their liberties, but may enlarge them if your Majestie please."[14] By inserting the word "authority" for additional emphasis, and by ending the sentence at the word "solely," the Massachusetts House created the impression that the seventeenth-century governor, when talking to Randolph, claimed "legislative Power and Authority" as an inherent right, not merely as a grant by the charter as Hutchinson's original version implies.

We should not be surprised that American whigs "managed" their historical evidence. They were arguing a forensic case not writing history, and their task was to reassure the public, not convince twentieth-century historians. Both sides took liberties because both were propagating the correct constitution and knew the evidence *should* have said what they had it say. It is this technique of manipulating "history" to prove current law, a tactic that has generally been overlooked by scholars of the American Revolution, that must be our interest. It would be too lengthy and too tedious to recount the history argued—it covered a score of events, situations, and statements. The best we can hope is to sample the evidence and examine the theory of forensic history as it was practiced in the eighteenth century.

It would be best to consider the piece of evidence most frequently cited during the American Revolution controversy. Revealingly, it was, aside from the colonial charters, the earliest historical event of any significance, a fact indicating the importance that participants in the debate attached to establishing the "original understanding." Almost as revealing, it was cited near the start of the controversy—during the debate over repealing the Stamp Act—by two of the best lawyers in Parliament, Lord Chief Justice Mansfield in the House of Lords and Sir William Blackstone in the House of Commons.[15] The evidence concerned statements recorded in the Commons of 1621 during the reign of James I when Virginia was less than two decades old and Plymouth had been settled for not quite a year.

John Adams summarized the facts when he wrote for the Massachusetts House its answer to Governor Hutchinson's challenge to debate the constitution. James I, Adams explained, had declared to the Commons in 1621, "that America *was not annexed to the Realm,* and it was not fitting that Parliament should make Laws for those Countries." Adams quoted James to show the original constitutional understanding at the time of colonial settlement. A principle of constitutional law, he claimed, followed from James's ruling: "If then the Colonies were not annexed to the Realm, at the Time when their Charters were granted, they never could be afterwards, without their own special Consent, which has never since been had, or even asked. If they are not now annexed to the Realm, they are not a Part of the Kingdom, and consequently not subject to the Legislative Authority of the Kingdom."[16]

John Adams cribbed his facts from a pamphlet that Edward Bancroft had anonymously published four years earlier in London. That Bancroft was not reliable was not realized by Adams and may not have mattered as Adams was concerned with the legal conclusion, not with historical accuracy. Bancroft had described a debate in the House of Commons during April 1621 concerning the right of English subjects to fish within the territory that the Crown had granted to the Virginia Company. To clarify that right, a bill had been introduced entitled, "An act for the freer libertie of fishing and fishing voyages to be made and performed in the sea Costes and places of Newfoundland, Virginia, New-England and other the Sea Costes and partes of America."[17] In opposition to this bill, Bancroft wrote, the House of Commons "was told by the Secretary of State, from his Majesty, that *America* was not annexed to the Realm, and that it was not fitting that Parliament should make Laws for those Countries; and though the House was uncommonly sollicitous for this Bill, and often offered it for the Royal Assent, it was always refused by the Crown, for those very just and cogent Reasons."[18]

The point not to be missed is that Adams, writing for the Massachusetts House of Representatives, improved on Bancroft's account by attributing to James I words that Bancroft said were spoken by the king's secretary. It was the secretary, not the king, who did the speaking. According to a 1766 London publication which had not been available in Boston to either Adams or Governor Hutchinson,

> Mr. Secretary saith, that *Virginia, New England, Newfoundland,* and those other foreign Parts of *America,* are not yet annexed to the Crown of *England,* but are the King's as gotten by Conquest; and therefore he thinketh it worthy the Consideration of the House, whether we shall here make Laws for the Government of those Parts; for he taketh it, that in such new Plantations the King is to govern it only by his Prerogative, and as his Majesty shall think fit.[19]

The secretary's conclusion of law was disputed by at least three members of the House of Commons, but it was the secretary's words, as filtered through Bancroft's account, that provided Adams with the constitutional principle that he needed. It was, as stated by another colonial whig who also implied he was quoting James I directly, that "America was without the Realm and jurisdiction of Parliament."[20]

It tells us much about the nature of historical forensic evidence in the eighteenth century that John Adams can be said to have "won" the argument because Governor Hutchinson did not have available in Boston books that would have enabled him to answer Adams's forensic "history." Adams had used the secretary's words to prove that both the king (to whom he attributed the words) and the House of Commons understood and acted on the original understanding of the imperial constitution that the North American colonies were not within the realm of England and, therefore, not subject to the authority of Parliament. The governor might have succeeded in embarrassing Adams if he had been aware of three facts that would have been available to him had he conducted his research in Great Britain: (1) that Adams had attributed to James words actually spoken by his secretary; (2) that several members of the House of Commons had debated against the secretary, arguing that Parliament had authority to legislate for the colonies; and (3) that the House of Commons rejected James's constitutional law for it passed the bill, indicating that a majority of the members believed they could bind the colonies by legislation. Also, if Hutchinson had had a copy of William Knox's 1769 book on the imperial constitution, he could have quoted Knox's conclusion. "The majority of the commons," Knox wrote, "were so far from doubting of their jurisdiction, that they passed the bill, which occasioned the doubt, which was not only *asserting* their right, but actually *exercising* it, as far as any house of parliament can exercise any legislative jurisdiction."[21]

Although Hutchinson could have forced John Adams to better evidence had he been able to see a copy of Knox's book, it might not have made much difference. Nothing would have been settled, and this is the ultimate lesson about eighteenth-century forensic history. Using evidence that could have been available to him had he not been in a small provincial capital, Hutchinson might have raised doubts about the premises of Adams's legal conclusion; he would not have proven his own constitutional case. No matter what Hutchinson made of the fact that the House of Commons had passed the freedom of fishery bill, Adams could have countered by pointing out that it had been rejected by the Lords. He would then have argued that this rejection proved that the House of Lords agreed with the king about the original understanding, evidence at least balancing the Commons' disagreement.

In the forensic history that was used in the eighteenth century to argue the unwritten, customary constitution, one inference was as good as another. From the fact that the House of Commons had enacted the fishery bill, Hutchinson could have inferred an original understanding among a majority of the 1621 House that Parliament had legislative jurisdiction over Virginia. The fact that the Lords rejected the bill was not as strong a piece of evidence about the understanding of the members of the upper house. They could have rejected it for reasons other than doubts about their jurisdiction. But Adams would have said their rejection discredited Hutchinson's inference and whigs would have agreed. Scholars may say that these arguments are bad history or not history at all, but such complaints are irrelevant because the historical methodology was irrelevant. John Adams had not attributed the words of the king's secretary to James I because he was interested in either reconstructing or falsifying the past. He was seeking to sustain a principle of law. The secretary's statement was one piece of evidence showing what one official in 1621 said about the constitutional understanding. Adams quoted that statement, however, not because he needed historical evidence but because he wanted a common-law precedent. That is, Adams did not use the secretary's statement as evidence to prove the constitutional understanding of 1621. He used it as *authority to prove the law of 1773.*

In a political sense, Adams was successful. The secretary's statement became a precedent, made even more significant when Adams attributed it directly to James I. When Governor Hutchinson was unable to disprove the legal relevance, an argument that today can be dismissed as bad history became for Adams's whig compatriots, good but not necessarily definitive law.

ANACHRONISM OF FORENSIC HISTORY

The two factual precedents just discussed—Randolph's letter about Massachusetts attitudes and the original or 1621 understanding of the law of 1773—illustrate the use of history as precedent. They do not exhaust the topic or reveal the range of the controversy. Although everything was argued, little was conclusive. To prove that Parliament had never exercised legislative jurisdiction over the colonies or that it had been understood for 150 years that Parliament did not have jurisdiction, colonial whigs cited every *forensically* relevant historical event they could uncover: e.g., the times that the Crown asked colonial assemblies to enact specific legislation;[22] the times that colonial assemblies reenacted parliamentary statutes, making those statutes operative in the colonies;[23] the resolutions by assemblies claiming exclusive legislative jurisdiction;[24] and expressions of appreciation by the Crown or other imperial officials that colonial assemblies had enacted legislation for observing English acts of trade and navigation. Surely, American whigs asserted, had the king believed Parliament had sovereignty over the colonies he would not have asked colonial legislatures to enact laws or to reenact them. He would, rather, have censured such legislation.[25]

If we are not impressed with such arguments we should at least be impressed by how seriously they were taken in the eighteenth century. The imperial side did not dismiss them as we might expect, but argued both the facts and the relevancy of the facts. Even more telling, the imperial side cited historical instances of its own, and, expending just as much energy as did colonial whigs, tried to show that it had always been the constitutional understanding that Parliament could legislate for North America. The fact that Virginia in 1666 purchased English legal treatises "for the better conformity of the proceedings of the courts in this country, to the *Laws of England*," was said to prove that Virginia considered itself bound by English law. The fact that eighty-eight years later the Albany Congress would have submitted its plan of union to Parliament for approval had the colonies adopted the plan was cited to prove "that the constitutional authority of Parliament over them [the colonies represented at Albany] was freely acknowledged at that time." And the fact that in 1702 and in 1705 bills were brought into the Commons to abolish the charter and proprietary colonies was used to prove that some members of Parliament believed they possessed the most extreme authority—even though "[t]hese bills, it must be confessed, were not carried into laws."[26] The examples could go on and on. They would add to our knowledge of the argument but not to our understanding of its substance. All are about as equally convincing as these three. There is, however, one other instance worth considering. It shows how seriously leading lawyers took this evidence. We may be amazed, but the attorney and solicitor generals of England and the advocate general of Scotland were just as apt to argue negative evidence as were John Adams and his fellow American whigs. The following account describes the debate on the Declaratory Act. Written by a member of the Commons who was the agent in London for South Carolina, it summarizes the arguments made on the floor of the House by the law officers, claiming that the fact that certain bills that would have legislated internally for the colonies had been introduced into Parliament was proof that members of Parliament understood they had legislative jurisdiction over the colonies—even when those bills were not enacted into law. Two lessons are worth noting: how well prepared the government's lawyers were to argue historical precedents and the importance they attached to historical precedents that today would be thought irrelevant.

That in the Year 1713 a Bill was brought into Parliament for the Purpose of raising a Revenue within the Province of New York, in

Consequence of a Refusal there to levy for the Support of his Majesty's Government. . . . That in 1716 a Bill was brought in . . . for resuming Powers which had been granted in the Colony Charters: That in 1717 a Bill was brought in to take away the Charters which had been granted to the several Colonies, the Power of Parliament in any of those Cases was never questioned, that if the Parliament had the Power to take away those Charters, by Virtue of which the Colonists claim the Right and Power of imposing and levying Taxes, it cou'd not but be possessed of the Power of Taxation.[27]

Despite the great variety of the historical facts argued by both sides, they were all directed at one of two conclusions: either there was historical precedent for Parliament's legislative sovereignty over the colonies or there was not. The two opposite theories of the constitution are obvious but worth summing up because they were so important to the debate and were so often restated in the decade and a half before the Declaration of Independence. For one side, history proved a consistent, single constitutional pattern from the abortive fishery bill to the abortive Stamp Act. "The authority of parliament over the colonies was contested in the House of Commons soon after the first migrations to America," London's *Monthly Review* pointed out in 1774, referring to "the bill of free liberty of fishing" of 1621. The *Review* then cited the trade and navigation law that had been enacted during the Interregnum and which will be discussed in chapter 15. That statute, the writer asserted, had been "very little regarded any where in America, and not at all in Massachusetts Bay, until the Assembly of that colony had passed an act to enforce the observance of it," that is, had it enforced as an act of the Massachusetts General Court, not as an act of Parliament. "From this time the power of parliament being seldom and moderately exercised over America, sometimes for the manifest advantage of the colonies, and always on plausible pretences, the opposition which had formerly subsisted to it, gradually subsided, and was indeed forgotten, when the late stamp act, by the novelty of its operation, revived a dispute new to the present generation."[28]

The opposite constitutional conclusion was summarized by a ministerial writer, John Lind, in 1775. Until the Stamp Act, he argued, the colonists never denied the power of Parliament to bind them legislatively, at least they did not do so directly. "The laws past [sic] by the colonial legislatures," Lind explained, "though in some instances really repugnant to the laws of England, were not so much direct denials of that power, as modifications of the provisions made by it. They shewed a tendency which should have been carefully watched, and as carefully checked, to worm themselves out of obedience, but they did not formally disclaim it."[29]

Although we must pass over the voluminous literature and the ingenious contentions supporting these conclusions, there is one point mentioned earlier that should be elaborated if we are to understand what was being argued and why. That is the claim that these whigs and imperialists were arguing law, that they were not talking history. The distinction deserves much more attention than it has received from scholars. The tendency instead has been to repeat Frederick Madden's complaint that "Imperial and colonial politicians quoted British example and precedents only where it was useful to their case." Of course they did, and to find fault with this is to betray an ignorance of what those "politicians" were doing. It might not have been good "history" to cite only supporting evidence, but what if it is good "law" to do so? In the 1920s Charles Howard McIlwain and Robert Livingston Schuyler reargued some of the evidence that American whigs and British imperialists had argued 150 years earlier. Discussing that debate, Ian R. Christie recently concluded that "Schuyler has the better of the argument. His view is the one generally accepted by historians."[30] Christie may be correct, but what is the relevant criterion? Is it what twentieth-century historians think was the better law or what eighteenth-century lawyers understood was law? The differences are greater than some may think.

To assume, without question, that the discussion was about history runs the risk of misunderstanding the evidence. "It is not difficult to show that medieval parliaments claimed to legislate and to tax dominions," A. F. McC. Madden has written, "but are what purport to be precedents really so? What may be accepted by lawyers in advocating a case need not necessarily convince historians."[31] If we take that attitude, we run the risk of imposing our academic standards of the historical method on a forensic controversy. Of course historians have complaints, but one complaint is not that arguers of forensic history ignore the canons of history. The canons are irrelevant. It is not just a matter of selecting favorable evidence. Because law ignores time, forensic history wallows in anachronisms which for some reason scholars think prove the methodology is erroneous. "[I]t is an unsatisfactory legalism to argue that because the 'parliament' of Henry VIII had legislative authority over colonies so did the 'parliament' of George III," Harvey Wheeler has objected.[32] "Great constitutional changes lay between" the two reigns, Madden has insisted.[33] "Historians," it has been explained, "cannot overlook the gulf between a period of royal dictatorship and one of embryonic cabinet government, or between one of fundamental law and one of parliamentary omnicompetence."[34] The question should be, however, whether lawyers can do so, whether for lawyers it may be not an "unsatisfactory," but a satisfactory "legalism" to be anachronistic.

Writing on behalf of the Massachusetts House of Representatives in its constitutional debate with Governor Hutchinson, John Adams took it "to be a settled Point [of law], that the King has a constitutional Prerogative to dispose of and alienate any Part of his Territories not annexed to the Realm."[35] Criticizing Adams's statement, an administration pamphleteer wrote, "I leave it to my readers to determine whether the following proposition is not more agreeable to the fundamental principles of the British constitution: 'I take it to be a settled point, that the king, as king, has no constitutional prerogative to acquire any territories that are not annexed to the Realm.' Who would have expected to have found such zealous advocates for royal prerogative among the puritannical inhabitants of New England."[36] The pamphleteer's principle was constitutionally sound. The rule expounded by Adams on behalf of the House of Representatives was carelessly phrased as it seemed to be claiming a right belonging to the Crown in 1773 when, to make his case, Adams needed only to have proven belonged to Queen Elizabeth and the first two Stuarts, the monarchs at the time the original colonies had been settled. It was immaterial to Adams's case whether kings in the eighteenth century still possessed the same prerogative. That Adams put the argument in the present tense is indicative of how even good eighteenth-century lawyers did not take into account the fact that, over periods of time, the constitution was altered in both substance and theory.

Adams had much company. Almost every eighteenth-century practitioner of forensic history was heedless of time, imperialists as much as colonial whigs. It did not matter what the understanding had been about parliamentary supremacy at the time of colonization, supporters of imperial authority maintained, for, as Attorney General Yorke asserted, "The Crown cannot grant away the supremacy of the Parliament over any part of his dominions."[37] Yorke was speaking of James I and the time of settlement, but, like John Adams, the attorney general spoke in the present tense. "Though the King may give away by charter a right that militates against himself," James Macpherson explained, using the present tense but speaking of Elizabeth I as much as George III, "he cannot authorise, by any deed whatever, an exemption from the general laws of the state. In such a case, one of the three branches of the legislature would usurp the power of the three united; a solecism as great in polity, as it is in mathematics, to affirm, that a part is greater than the whole."[38]

The message was uncomplicated: that under the current constitution the king, George III, could not with a new colony make an understanding that it would enjoy legislative autonomy, independent of Parliament. If George III could not do so in 1770, then Elizabeth I and James I could not have done so during their reigns. Very few participants in the debate asked if the constitution of the early seventeenth century was the same as the constitution of the 1770s.[39] The method of reasoning may strike a historian as anachronistic nonsense, but it was good law and made sense to eighteenth-century constitutionalists. They could slide from the past to the present without noticing change. A revealing instance comes from a comment about a purported American claim that charter privileges were immutable privileges. "But by whom, pray, were these privileges granted? By a king, who had no power, I mean legal power, to grant you any privileges, which rendered you independent of parliament, no more than he can make a corporation in England independent of it."[40] The writer was anonymous, so we cannot learn if he was a lawyer, but the way he slipped—apparently without realizing what he was doing—from the past tense to the present tense was characteristic not just of how eighteenth-century lawyers wrote, but of how they thought about the past in relation to the present.

It is their way of thinking that deserves our attention. The aspect we should heed is not that this was a lawyer's way of thinking but that this was the forensic method of arguing historical precedents during the American revolutionary controversy. It was a method that had always been used in English constitutional litigation. We need not agree that it proved anything about history to realize that it might be useful for arguing constitutional law. The point has been made before. There is no reason why an argument that was bad history could not, at the same time, be good law. That is our lesson. For the fact that historians have not been able to take bad-history, good-law arguments seriously helps explain why some historians, unlike participants in the revolutionary controversy, have not appreciated how legal and how constitutional the argument was.

CHAPTER THIRTEEN

PRECEDENTS OF CHARTER

There is one other area of imperial constitutional law that, like precedents of history, provided the revolutionary controversy with precedents that in the twentieth century would no longer be thought legal precedents. Also involved was a branch of constitutional law that has been dealt with before,[1] though not in relation to the authority of Parliament to bind the colonies in all cases whatsoever: rights of charter.

In March 1775, as constitutional discontent was heading America toward the Declaration of Independence, Parliament enacted a statute declaring that inhabitants of New England no longer had the privilege of fishing in British territory. Several members of the House of Lords dissented on grounds of charter rights. New Englanders "are especially intitled to the fishery by their charters," the lords protested. "These charters we think (nothwithstanding the contempt with which the idea of public faith has been treated) to be of material consideration." The dissentient lords were making a restrained legal argument. They were not saying that charters were a bar to parliamentary sovereignty. They were, rather, asserting that charters vested in New Englanders the right to fish and that right had "never been declared forfeited." In other words, because the Massachusetts and New Hampshire charters had vested a property right, the question whether the Boston Tea Party and John Sullivan's raid on Fort William and Mary in Portsmouth harbor had forfeited the right was a judicial rather than a legislative issue. The British administration, therefore, should have litigated the matter by an information in the nature of *quo warranto* or by writ of *scire facias*. Without judicial process the Fishery Act was "a violation of all natural and civil right."[2]

The dissentient lords were not arguing valid law. If anything, they were suggesting a preferable procedure, one that they must have known was constitutionally dated. What interests us is that the argument was made at all. That it was is illustrative of the fact that even though colonial charters were particularized, written instruments, they were argued to support virtually every contention made by either side. Charters were *an* authority for a wide range of general principles because they were *the* authority for no specific right. Put another way, charters were so broad they could be cited to support both sides of most controversies.

The bare, single fact that the charter had been conferred was, for one side of the controversy, evidence of Parliament's reserve of supreme power. "Does not a settlement under *'the faith of charters'* imply supremacy, in the state granting these charters?" Baron Rivers asked.[3] After all, Martin Howard pointed out, when the original settlers "accepted of their charters they tacitly submitted to the terms and conditions of them," and those "charters give them no exemption from the jurisdiction of parliament."[4] But did they expressly say the colonists were subject to the jurisdiction of Parliament? Yes, a member of the House of Commons answered. The charters "not only in themselves implicitly suppose, but contain express reserve of, their [the colonists] remaining under the authority of the one common supreme Legislative."[5] American whigs, not finding in their charters the "express reserve" to which the member of Parliament referred, came to an opposite conclusion of law. "From these charters it manifestly appears to have been the Royal intention, to form these Colonies into distinct States like *Jersey, Guernsey, Isle of Man, &c.*, dependent on the Crown, but not on the Parliament of *England.*" The colonies, that is, were "exempted from the authority of Parliament" by the intention of the charter.[6]

Most references to the authority of charter were of the quality of those just quoted. Except in the matter of colonial taxation and the clause that colonial laws be not repugnant to the laws of England, there was little discussion of specific provisions or of exact phraseology. Of course words were quoted and royal grants were referred to, but when the issue in dispute was parliamentary supremacy, words were not argued as lawyers today argue a written constitution, with emphasis on the meaning of provisions and the intention of the drafters. Words were used, rather, as a peg on which to hang broad discussions of civil rights, legal principles, and constitutionality.[7] Distinctions were not even drawn between types of charters. On the question of Parliament's jurisdiction over the colonies, at least, proprietary charters were argued no differently than royal charters.[8] Indeed, it was even immaterial that one of the so-called "English" colonies, Delaware, had never been granted a royal charter. It claimed the same privileges of internal legislation and the same immunities from parliamentary supremacy claimed by colonies with royal charters. In other words, even though it did not have a royal charter, colonial whigs did not hesitate to claim for Delaware charter privileges and charter immunities.

If the generality of charter argument is unexpected, it may be that we have been conditioned to think of charters as organic acts. Colonial charters were not constitutions. They were, rather, grants of territory and rights of government conferred on proprietors or companies of adventurers. Because the privileges and immunities vested by charter generally were those of a trading company rather than a colonizing enterprise, the charters had been modeled on articles of incorporation, and had been drafted as outlines of hierarchial control rather than as blueprints for governmental action. In fact, many imperialists claimed that the corporateness of charters settled the revolutionary controversy as it meant that colonial charters had created corporations, not separate, independent governments. Colonial charters "are undoubtedly no more than those of all corporations, which impower them to make bye-laws, and raise duties for the purposes of their own police, for ever subject to the superior authority of Parliament," Soame Jenyns insisted. "And therefore they can have no more pretence to plead an exemption from this parliamentary authority, than any other corporation in England."[9]

Due to its simplicity, the "corporation" argument was very attractive to imperialists, especially to commentators like Samuel Johnson who did not understand prescriptive constitutional law. A charter, Johnson theorized, was a grant to colonizers "permitting them to settle in some distant country, and enabling them to constitute a Corporation, . . . but as a Corporation subsisting by a grant from higher authority, to the control of that authority they continue subject."[10] A better comparison for Johnson to have drawn was not between colonies and trading companies but colonies and municipal corporations in England. "There, the governor, council, and house of representatives," Allan Ramsay analogized, "are vested with the same authority, as the lord-mayor, aldermen, and common council, of the city of London. They are vested with a power, to keep the peace, to punish offenders, and to do all acts of justice, amongst themselves."[11] The constitutional situation would have been less ambiguous had those officials possessed titles that reflected their actual positions. "I wish," a critic of the colonial whig argument wrote in 1776, "that there Governors, Councils, and Assemblies, or Houses of Burgesses, had never been called by any other names or titles, than Mayors, Aldermen, and Common-Council Men; that they might have better discovered the rank they really hold in the state."[12] In any event, no matter what titles were used, the charter determined the colonies' place in constitutional law, Martin Howard explained. "[A]s corporations created by the crown, they are confined within the primitive views of their institution."[13]

In constitutional theory, the "corporation" argument owed a great deal to the fact that the concept of federalism was imperfectly understood at the time. We can see evidence of eighteenth-century unfamiliarity with federalism in an argument made by a member of the New York General Assembly opposing election of delegates to the second Continental Congress. "[T]he appointment of Delegates," he contended, "would involve us in inconsistency, be a departure from the trust reposed in us by our constituents, and plainly reduce this House to the condition of a Corporation, which only meets to enact by-laws, whilst all matters of higher importance are referred to a superiour assembly."[14] The speaker did not seem to realize that the status he feared New York might slip into if the Continental Congress became permanent was the status many imperialists said was New York's status under Parliament. His conclusion may be due to the fact that he thought of sovereignty and supremacy, not of federalism and concurrent jurisdiction.

The "corporation" analogy puzzled Governor Thomas Pownall. He found it unconvincing but was unable to explain why in his book on the administration of the colonies. "They were bodies corporate," he wrote of the colonial governments, "but certainly not corporations in the sense of such communities *within the realm*." Daniel Dulany was also somewhat uncertain, though he may have been groping toward a theory of federalism when he dismissed the "corporation" argument. "[I]t is as absurd and insensible," he concluded, "to call a Colony a common Corporation, because not an independent Kingdom, and the Powers of each to make Laws and Bye-Laws, are limited, tho' not comparable in their Extent, and the Variety of their Objects, as it would be to call Lake *Erie*, a *Duck-puddle*, because not the Atlantic Ocean." The Massachusetts House of Representatives also made the point that the legislative powers of English corporations were not comparable to the powers of colonial assemblies. "Are any of the Corporations formed within the Kingdom, vested with the Power of erecting other subordinate Corporations?" the House asked. "Of enacting and determining what Crimes shall be Capital? And constituting Courts of Common Law with all their Officers, for the hearing, trying and punishing capital Offenders with Death?" The exercise of these powers not only showed that Massachusetts "is to be considered as a Corporation in no other Light, than as every State is a Corporation," but that the jurisdiction of colonial legislatures was constitutionally equivalent to the jurisdiction of Parliament.[15]

Critics of the "corporate" analogy had no problem proving that subjects living in the colonies were not constitutionally equivalent to subjects living in municipal corporations in the mother country. "The Members of those Corporations are Resiant [sic] within the Kingdom," the Massachusetts House pointed out, "and Residence subjects them to the Authority of Parliament, in which they are also represented: Whereas the People of this Colony are not Resident within the Realm. The Charter was granted with the express Purpose to induce them to reside without the Realm; consequently they are not represented in Parliament there." Benjamin Franklin thought that representation made the constitutional difference. "If the Colonies sent, as London does, Members to Parliament," he told a London newspaper, "and their Provincial Assemblies were accidental subordinate Courts, like the Common-Council of London, and not, as at present, their whole Representation, there might be some Comparison attempted. As their Constitution is now, no two things can well be imagined more specifically different."[16]

Most imperialists drew the analogy not between the corporation of London and the colonies but between the colonies and large municipal corporations in Great Britain—Manchester would be one—that were not directly but only virtually represented in Parliament. Rejecting this analogy, Edmund Burke reasoned in terms of changing times and emerging prescriptive customary rights. Even if there had been an original understanding that the charters created "corporations," he contended, those corporations had changed over the years, growing into states. "Govern America as you govern an English Corporation which happens not to be represented in Parliament; Are Gentlemen really serious when they propose this?" Burke asked the House of Commons. Was there, he wondered, "a single Trait of Resemblence" between British municipal corporations, some citizens of which had direct representation since they voted for the two members representing the county in which the municipality was located, and colonies which, because of distance, "neither actually [n]or by a possibility" could take "part in our Government?" "[N]othing in progression can rest on its original plan," he added eleven years later still referring to the "corporation" analogy. "We may as well think of rocking a grown man in the cradle of an infant."[17]

We should ask what there was about the "corporate" analogy that generated such concern among colonial whigs and their supporters at home. It must be suspected that they did not worry that, if the charters created *pro tanto* corporations, a colony could be liable to the rule of *ultra vires* if it exceeded those set limits. The theory was too technical to put in jeopardy constitutional rights and immunities without more law.[18] What concerned American whigs, rather, were the implications that the "corporation" analogy purported for the place of their charters in constitutional law. As heirs of centuries of English constitutionalism, the colonists had inherited a way of thinking about royal "grants" such as charters which was summarized by "a London Merchant" when he told "a Noble Lord" that Americans cherished their charters, "which they look on as sacred; and make their boast of, like our magna charta of England." "Therefore any attempt to break in upon their charters," he contended, "must meet with the same reception from them, as an English ministry would find from a violation of our Magna Charta. Can you wonder than at any thing that has happened in Virginia, or any of the other provinces, by invectives against a ministry that violate their Magna Charta, and deprive them of the privileges of Englishmen?"[19]

The "London Merchant" was writing in 1765, at the very beginning of the revolutionary controversy, before American whigs had stated much of their constitutional case, yet he was right that the colonists would connect the "privileges of Englishmen" with their charters. Where their imperial opponents analogized colonial charters to English municipal corporations, Americans analogized them to Magna Carta. This way of thinking about charters helps explain why most arguments for colonial legislative autonomy based on charters were cast in broad, general terms. Americans thought of their charter rights just as common lawyers thought of the charter rights of Magna Carta. "Lawyers all know that this Charter is only declaratory of the principal Grounds of the fundamental Laws and Liberties of *England*," a 1757 *Guide* to those liberties said of Magna Carta.[20] The rights that Magna Carta enunciated "were not the grants and concessions of our Princes," an English pamphlet reprinted in Rhode Island in 1774 and attributed to Lord Chancellor Somers insisted, "but recognitions of what we have reserv'd unto ourselves in the original institution of our government, and of what had always appertain'd unto us by common law, and immemorial customs."[21]

Just as the colonists argued their charters with only the slightest reference to words, phrases, and provisions, so too Magna Carta in the eighteenth century had come to stand for much more than the acknowledgement of rights and privileges that King John had conceded to his rebellious barons. This tactic of argument can be gleaned from the constitutional law book that Jean De Lolme wrote in the 1770s, in which he contended that Magna Carta had been intended to aid the general mass of the people, not just the landholding aristocracy. De Lolme apparently saw no need to cite specific articles, offer historical evidence, or discuss "original intent." Just to mention the "Great Charter" was sufficient to remind readers that Magna Carta was a charter of individual rights.

> [W]hat extent, what caution, do we see in the provisions made by the Great Charter! All the objects for which men naturally wish to live in a state of society were settled in its various articles. The judicial authority was regulated. The person and property of the individual were secured. The safety of the merchant and stranger was provided for. The higher class of citizens gave up a number of oppressive privileges which they had long accustomed themselves to look upon as their undoubted rights. Nay, the implements of tillage of the *bondsman*, or slave, were also secured to him: and for the first time, perhaps, in the annals of the world, a civil war was terminated by making stipulations in favour of those unfortunate men to whom the avarice and lust of dominion, inherent in human nature, continued, over the greatest part of the earth, to deny the common rights of mankind.[22]

No wonder critics doubted if eighteenth-century encomiasts of Magna Carta ever read the document.[23] The literature was filled with historical nonsense such as this. When granted by King John, Magna Carta had provided none of these rights, and we may suspect that most writers who said that it had knew better. But then they knew something else as well. They knew that by the second half of the eighteenth century it was accurate constitutional theory to say Magna Carta contained "the common rights of mankind," even if none of those rights had occurred to the barons who had confronted John. No one had to read the document. What was important about Magna Carta in the eighteenth century was not what it said but what it had come to mean. Had King John died on the way to Runnymede and Magna Carta never been issued, eighteenth-century constitutionalists would have "quoted" in its stead some other official or suppositive declaration of restraints on Norman government power, the coronation oath of Henry I perhaps.

Colonial whigs simply transposed this inherited way of thinking about Magna Carta to their own charters. As Magna Carta was "a Renewal of the *Original Contract*,"[24] so, too, were the colonial charters. This fact explains why constitutional arguments that ostensibly turned on the charters were really appeals to broad, constitutional doctrines. As the charters, like Magna Carta, were "*declaratory* of the *principal* Grounds, of the *Fundamental* Laws and Liberties of *England*,"[25] so an appeal to the rights of charter could invoke all the precedents of liberty and of constitutional law.

THE REPUGNANCY OF CHARTER

We must avoid the wrong impression. It would be misleading to think that all discussions of the colonial charters were in the form of general arguments or sweeping appeals to broad constitutional principles. On rare occasions one side or the other discussed specific words and phrases in the charters to support contentions that Parliament either had or had not legislative supremacy over the colonies.[26] Even then it is indicative of the charters that only two specific provisions were of any significance. One related to the authority of taxation and is not the concern of this book.[27] The second was the "repugnancy clause" found in most charters. Conferring legislative powers on colonial governments, it provided that colonial laws should not be repugnant to the laws, statutes, and customs of England. An example, from the third charter of Virginia, provided that the colony's legislators should "have full Power and Authority, to ordain and make such Laws and Ordinances, for the Good and Welfare of the said Plantation, as to them from Time to Time, shall be thought requisite and meet: *So always*, as the same be not contrary to the Laws and Statutes of this our Realm of *England*."[28]

The imperial argument focused more on the words than on the original purpose or intent. With the repugnancy clause, imperialists contended, "the Mother Country took proper care of her own supremacy" on the one hand,[29] and the dependency of the colonies on the other,[30] for the clause meant that the Americans were "obliged by their charters to submit to the laws of England, and consequently they must all be bound by every new law that is made by our parliament for amending, explaining, or enforcing the laws of England."[31] For surely, that was what the first settlers of the colonies had contracted. By accepting the grant of a charter containing the repugnancy stipulation, the grantees had "agreed, that they and their posterity should be bound by the laws of England."[32] What did the clause "amount" to in law, James Anderson asked? "Merely to this," he answered. "That the petty legislators of these communities shall be authorised to deliberate with freedom, and to enact laws as shall seem best to them, in all such cases of the legislators of Great Britain have not thought proper to take cognizance of; but in all cases where Britain shall have thought proper to enact laws binding on the colonies, they are, by this clause, expressly prohibited from intermeddling in any sort."[33]

The clause, American whigs replied, reserved no jurisdiction to Parliament. To agree not to enact statutes that clashed "with those of England, no more subjected them [the first settlers] to the parliament of England, than their having been laid under the same restraint with regard to the laws of Scotland or any other country, would have subjected them to the parliament of Scotland, or the supreme authority of any other country."[34] The words "not repugnant to the laws," the Massachusetts House of Representatives insisted, meant "conformable to the fundamental Principles of the English Constitution."[35] After all, Jeremiah Dummer pointed out earlier in the century, "a Law may be *various* from the Laws of *England*, and yet not *repugnant* to them." Agreeing, Governor Samuel Ward of Rhode Island concluded that the clause was intended to see that the colonies did not "depart wholly from the Principles of the Laws of England," but did empower "them to make Laws differing from the Laws of England as far as the Nature & Constitution of the Place & People in America required."[36]

Adopting standard common-law strategy to retain the imperial legislature within bounds they thought constitutional, American whigs did not deny that the repugnancy clause restricted colonial legislative independence. They stressed instead limitations on the clause: its purview was limited to constitutional questions of law or procedure that they did not dispute were within the jurisdiction of either Parliament or the Crown. "[T]he constitutional Dependence of the Colonies," the New York General Assembly told the House of Commons, was "effectually secured by their total Incapacity of enacting Laws repugnant to those of *Great-Britain;* by the Royal Negative to which all their Acts are subject; and by their Constitution, which fixes in *Great-Britain* the last Resort in the Administration of Justice." In other words, the repugnancy clause complemented and guided the royal veto, and it was by the veto that it should be enforced. The constitutional theory was elaborated by the Massachusetts Council and House of Representatives. Parliament, the Council asserted, had no constitutional role even when colonial laws were repugnant to its own acts, "for the Charter reserves to his Majesty the Appointment of the Governor, whose Assent is necessary in the passing of all Orders and Laws: after which they are to be sent to England for the Royal Approbation or Dissallowance: by which double Controul effectual Care is taken to prevent the Establishment of any improper Orders or Laws whatever." "And we would add," the House voted, making the same point a bit more emphatically, "that the King in some of the Charters reserves the Right to judge of the Consonance and Similarity of their Laws with the English Constitution to himself, and not to the Parliament."[37]

Some American whigs turned the imperialist argument completely around. Not only was the repugnancy clause irrelevant to Parliament's jurisdiction over the colonies, it was constitutional evidence that they were independent of Parliament. The first settlers in the second original contract, according to this lemma, had "stipulated with the person whom they agreed should be their King" not to make laws repugnant to those of England, "from which we were then to be seperted [sic]."[38] Again it was a matter of the original understanding. "[H]owever defective their charter might be in form," the Reverend Samuel Cooke told Massachusetts lawmakers in 1770, referring to the original settlers of the colony, "the spirit and evident intention of it, appears to be then understood. . . . The reserve therein made of passing no laws contrary to those of the parent state, was then considered as a conclusive evidence of their full power, under that restriction only, to enact whatever laws they should judge conducive to their benefit."[39]

If the argument is unconvincing, it would be well to consider that it is only by degrees more unconvincing than the imperialist argument. Both sides were asking the repugnancy clause to carry too much baggage. It apparently had been copied from a provision in old English guild charters conferring power to make bylaws. That too was the function of the clause in colonial charters, although Americans insisted it conferred power to make laws, not mere corporate bylaws. It confirmed the authority to legislate: to enact new statutes as needed. Except for the limited aspects of repugnancy, it did not restrict that authority as would, for example, the Northwest Ordinance of 1787, which would limit the legislative powers of the new western territories to copying laws from the statute books of "the original States." The colonial repugnancy clause, Americans theorized, not only tolerated differences between colonial and parliamentary legislation, differences were expected. In the Connecticut charter, for example, the clause authorized the colony "to Make, Ordain, and Establish all manner of wholesome, and reasonable Laws, Statutes, Ordinances, Directions, and Instructions, not Contrary to the Laws of this realm of England."[40] Explaining the meaning, Governor Thomas Fitch and two other future loyalists, in a report adopted by the colony's Assembly, concluded that the clause granted "a full Power of Legislation," if the enacted statutes conformed "to the general Principles of the Laws of the Nation, and consequently, as when they exceed the Bounds and Limits, prescribed in the Charter, their Acts will be void, so, when they conform and regulate their Acts agreeable to the Intent and Meaning of it, their Acts may properly be said to have the Royal Approbation and Assent."[41] Although the connection was not specifically drawn, it is possible that the repugnancy clause was again being tied to the royal veto, in line with the central constitutional contention of American whigs, that the colonies were subordinate to the Crown and not to Parliament.

There remains one small point to be made. Scholars of the American Revolution should not confuse the repugnancy clause with the statute of 7 & 8 William III, legislation which some imperialists thought gave Parliament stronger claim to jurisdiction over the colonies than did the precedent of charter. 7 & 8 William provided that colonial laws "repugnant" to specified parliamentary statutes "or which are any ways repugnant to this present act, or to any other law hereafter to be made in this kingdom, so far as such law shall relate to and mention the said plantations, are illegal, null, and void."[42] "Is not this binding them *in all cases whatsoever?*" a London pamphleteer asked in 1776.[43] William Knox thought so. The statute of William "alone," he wrote, "abstracted from all other Considerations, ought surely to be a sufficient Refutation of the very singular Claim of the Colonists" to legislative autonomy.[44]

Although a connection could be made between the statute and the clause—someone described 7 & 8 William III as "no more than executive of the conditional [repugnancy] clause"[45]—the relationship was never stressed. Most imperialists citing the statute were parliamentary supremacists, and, for them, that Parliament had enacted 7 & 8 William III was enough to make the statute all the precedent needed to prove Parliament's authority over the colonies. For that reason, and also because the imperial side had much stronger precedents as will be discussed below, there was no consideration of American attitudes to the statute, whether it had been obeyed in the colonies, or whether it even had been enforced. As a result, the British did not carry the analysis beyond the assumptions of the Declaratory Act, and the statute of William III, although a persuasive precedent of Parliament's understanding in the 1690s, had little impact on the prerevolutionary debate.

THE ANACHRONISM OF CHARTER

In their search for historical evidence proving the original understanding about Parliament's jurisdiction over the colonies, American whigs made much of the fact that the early charters had been granted by James I and Charles I on their own authority.[46] The original intention, whigs claimed, was that the colonies were "to be without the Realm of *England,* and [the] Jurisdiction of its Parliament."[47] That conclusion was assumed. It could not be proven historically for there was no direct evidence, nor any evidence that anyone at the time that the charters were confirmed even thought about the colonies' constitutional relationship to

Parliament. There were inferences that could be drawn from facts, and the whigs did not hesitate to draw every inference they could. Joseph Hawley, a western Massachusetts lawyer, demonstrated the method when he drew two inferences about the original understanding of Parliament's jurisdiction. First, the grantor of the charter, Charles I, had acknowledged the Massachusetts Company's legislative powers, something he could not have done had North America been within Parliament's jurisdiction. "Does not this prove beyond a contradiction," Hawley asked, "that *Charles* the First viewed the Colonies as . . . exempt from the authority of Parliament, even in the matter of regulating Trade?" The second piece of inferential evidence was a clause exempting Massachusetts from taxation for twenty-seven years. "If he [the king] could do this for seven or twenty years, for the same reason he might for seventy or seventy times seventy," Hawley reasoned. "This proves to demonstration, either that *Charles* the First apprehended . . . that this Colony was not a part of the *British* Empire, or if it was, that it was not within the jurisdiction of Parliament."[48]

It should be repeated that although Hawley's inferences might not be persuasive history, they were a familiar, valid, accepted way of arguing constitutional law. Supporters of Parliament could answer them either by drawing counterconclusions or by contending that Hawley's inferences were irrelevant. The preferred answer was irrelevancy—it did not matter what the original intent had been, Charles I was wrong to think that the colonies were outside the realm (a contention we will return to), or he lacked authority to exempt any English territory, whether within or without the realm, from Parliament's jurisdiction. "Can the Crown of England," a pamphlet sometimes attributed to Governor Hutchinson asked, "grant a charter to any part of its subjects which *frees* them from the authority of Parliament? Are these charters of the nature of compacts between two independent powers or states?"[49] The answer was obviously "no," and it was with that conclusion that the imperialists made their strongest demur to the American whig claim to legislative autonomy—at least to that part of the claim based on precedents of charter. Richard Phelps stated the better legal doctrine when he argued, "Whatever claims then the colonies can set up, by virtue of their respective charters, they can proceed no farther than the prerogative of the crown can carry them, even suppose it exerted to its utmost extent; but no prerogative can go beyond the law, consequently no charter."[50]

The answer that the Crown lacked authority to grant charter rights exempting any citizen or national territory from parliamentary authority[51] should have conclusively settled the constitutional question, but for one flaw. That flaw was that the evidence was anachronistic, in a way

similar to the anachronisms discussed in the last chapter. Almost all critics of American claims making this argument, whether members of Parliament[52] or authors of pamphlets on the constitution,[53] assumed that
the constitutional restraints on George III had existed a century and a
half earlier, also constraining the queens and kings who granted the first
charters.

There is no need to repeat the argument. It is enough to note again that
the passage of time was irrelevant to most constitutional students. Z. T., a
colonist who answered Daniel Dulany's contention that some charters
exempted Americans from parliamentary supremacy, rejected Dulany's
law on the grounds that the king could not exempt anyone because of
Magna Carta and the Bill of Rights. Those documents vested the right of
taxation in Parliament, not in the king, Z. T. believed, or so he said. It is
not necessary to know who Z. T. was to suspect that he would not have
changed his law had he been reminded that Magna Carta had been
promulgated before there was an English Parliament and that the Bill of
Rights had been promulgated long after the original charters passed the
seals.[54]

We can never know, but it is a defensible assumption that most commentators did not take constitutional change into account, or, if they
did, they believed that it was sound constitutional law that established
rights could be abrogated by change. "The Stamp Act has indeed taxed
them," Richard Hussey told the House of Commons referring to the
Americans, "and the King by giving his consent to it has overrode and
destroyed as a limited monarch those privileges which his predecessors as
absolute monarchs had granted to them." This statement makes historical sense and we may think we know what Hussey means, but do we?
About three minutes earlier in the same speech, he had discussed the
House of Commons debate on the bill on fishery rights brought into the
Parliament of James I and had observed that the early charters "give
powers which the King alone could not give."[55] We must assume that
Hussey was saying the constitution had changed radically, and that the
change somehow altered what, except for the change, were prescriptive,
even immutable rights. The king had once been absolute and could grant
absolute immunity. But kings were no longer absolute, a constitutional
fact that, rectroactively applied, constitutionally meant that the earlier
kings had not been absolute, either. The theory is different than the
argument that, because Parliament is now absolute, there are no immutable rights since there are no rights Parliament cannot abrogate whether
those rights are customary, prescriptive rights, or rights granted by formerly absolute kings. Those were quite different doctrines, even if they
led to the same constitutional result.

Americans whigs had at least three answers to the anachronism of their opponents. First, they contended that the charters had to be interpreted in line with the royal prerogative at the time they were conferred, and not by the supremacy over the Crown that by the 1760s was vested in Parliament. The king would still possess "arbitrary" power over North America, it was said, "if the nature of our government had not changed, or our sovereigns had not divested themselves of those powers, which the common laws of the land gave them over new acquisitions."[56] This rule was more persuasive as history than as constitutional law.

Second, American whigs downplayed the creativeness of the charters. "[T]hese charters are not grants of new rights, but in confirmation of old ones," Arthur Lee asserted, and John Dickinson concurred. "[T]he royal charters were *declarations*, but not *gifts* of liberties."[57] By "declarations" of liberties, Dickinson meant prescriptive, common-law rights secured by custom from time immemorial, an authority that for most rights was persuasive only to the extent that prescriptive constitutionalism remained valid. If it was an ancient, customary, immutable right of Englishmen inherited by the British to be governed only by consent, then constitutional debate was about the meaning of "consent." If not, the issue was the degree of immunity from parliamentary legislation the colonies should enjoy as a result of having been granted charters.

The third answer was that the king, when conferring colonial charters, had been "invested with authority by the whole nation" including Parliament and had, constitutionally speaking, acted on behalf of the entire nation.[58] The grant, therefore, had been acknowledged and consented to "'really or virtually' by the Parliament"[59] at the time conferred or subsequently either by being "confirmed by Act of Parliament,"[60] or by "acquiescence."[61]

THE REVOCABILITY OF CHARTER

It is necessary to emphasize the precedent of charter. It was the law of precedent, not any inherent constitutional attribute of charters that determined the place of charter in the American revolutionary debate. By 1750, if not 1700, neither the administration in London nor constitutionalists in the colonies thought charter rights to be of any major significance in imperial constitutional law. It would not even have mattered if the charters had received the *direct* sanction of Parliament in addition to the implied sanction of acquiescence claimed by American whigs. Parliamentary sovereignty, the central constitutional issue dividing Americans from Britons, made parliamentary sanction of a charter, implied or direct, irrelevant. If Parliament was sovereign, the acquiescence of one Parliament or a series of Parliaments could not bind a subsequent Parliament from revoking or amending a charter.[62]

American whigs knew the law. They appreciated that the weakness of charter lay in the revocability of charter, and they had reason to be apprehensive. Although they did not acknowledge that their constitution was changing or could change, they knew its immutability was threatened by a newer imperial model of administration. As the eighteenth century progressed, the British imperial government paid less respect to charters as the link between London and the colonies. The reason was that the bureaucrats of empire were moving toward a constitutional theory that the colonies were governed not through the mechanism of the charters, but through instructions issued to governors. It was a menacing development. Nothing threatened the legislative autonomy and political liberty of Americans more than the possibility that their governance might depend on the whim of the cabinet, a minister, or even a mere under secretary instructing an appointed governor with binding orders that had to be followed without consulting, only informing, locally elected colonial officials. This potential constitutional change would have been even more drastic than parliamentary supremacy which, at most, meant supervision by an occasional statute. Fear of the constitutionality of instructions, and not a constitutional dependence on charters, was why the frequent rumors of plans to revoke the charters were so alarming.[63] There was a constitutional theory ready to serve as a substitute for charter rights, and it was a theory of total arbitrary rule. If the imperial government wanted a different constitution, all Parliament had to do was revoke the colonial charters and the constitutional rule for the colonies would become the ministry's instructions.

But could Parliament revoke the charters? There is no better evidence of the lingering strength of the old constitution of prescriptive right than the constitutionalists in Great Britain still insisting that a royal charter was an irrevocable grant that could not be amended, canceled, or revoked except by the common law of forfeiture.[64] Only one argument needs to be quoted. It is of interest not for the theory of irrevocability, but because in an odd way it illustrates the strange twists legal theory could take when caught in the ambivalence between the reality of the new constitution and respect for the old. Appearing in a London magazine on the eve of the American Revolution, it suggests the astonishing solution of determining the revocability of British charters by the newer constitution of parliamentary sovereignty and the revocability of colonial charters by the older constitution of restraint on legislative power.

Colonies as well as nations have for their foundation certain permanent principles unchangeable in their nature, except by their own consent. Such was the great charter of English liberty, which gave a being to our so much boasted constitution; and such are the great charters of the colonies. . . . The Parliament of England, with the consent of the King, may *lawfully* change, amend, abrogate, and new-model the constitution of England . . . because the consent of the people of England is supposed to be included in their act; but the Parliament of England cannot *lawfully* change, amend, abrogate, or new-model a constitution, founded on a separate and independent charter, in which the people residing in England have not the least or most distant concern.[65]

This remarkable blending of the two constitutions was imaginative but no more persuasive as a bar to parliamentary authority than the more frequently made argument that the colonial charters were immutable from parliamentary alteration due to the prescriptive right of both the second original contract and the migration purchase.[66] The better view was that charters were "no more sacred than other property," and were subject to revocation equally through forfeiture by judicial decree or abrogation by legislative command. The constitutional rule was executed in Great Britain when Parliament altered the charter of the East India Company, a charter some observers equated with colonial charters, especially the Massachusetts charter.[67] The amending bill was passed after a parliamentary struggle, fought largely on the premises of the old constitution of precedential, prescriptive, and contractarian rights. "We never can admit," dissentient lords protested, "that a mere speculation of political improvement can justify parliament in taking away rights, which it has expressly covenanted to preserve, especially when it has received a valuable consideration for the franchises so stipulated. Nor are grants of Parliament, under these circumstances, to be considered as gratuitious donations, resumable merely at the pleasure of the giver; but matters of binding contract, forfeitable only on such deliquency or necessity as is implied in the nature of every other bargain." In the other house, Edmund Burke also put the matter in terms of contract, though his legal theory was based on much less stringent constitutional premises. "First he thought the *Charter* ought to be held inviolable," Burke was quoted as telling the Commons. "Parliament might indeed alter any thing in the forms of religion and Government. . . . But the *faith* of Parliament is a very different thing from its Legislative *powers*. The contracts of Parliament bind Parliament as much as they do a private person. It is not above them; they are above it."[68]

These arguments, whether political or constitutional, were rejected in both houses, and opposite principles prevailed. The law of Parliament was that charters could be amended and revoked at the pleasure of Parliament. Whether a colony retained or lost a charter, the attorney general told the Commons, "is [a] mere matter of legislature power."[69] English municipal charters had in the past been seized by Parliament,[70] just as an earlier Massachusetts charter had been forfeited in an action of *scire facias* at Chancery.[71] Concisely stated, the principle of law was that "all charters granted by our Kings are subject to be revised or annihilated by the legislature whenever they operate against the general interest of the British nation."[72] Whether and when the charter operated against the general interest was a question wholly within the discretion of Parliament.

Of course American whigs did not cite the charter as a source of rights. They knew better than to depend on an authority that existed at the will and whim of the political nation.

THE PROBATIVENESS OF CHARTER

The law of the revocability of charter led directly to the Massachusetts Government Act of 1774, a parliamentary revision of the Massachusetts charter briefly mentioned in chapter 1 and which altered the colony's government to a substantial extent. That Americans understood Parliament had authority to change a colonial charter did not lessen the constitutional shock when it occurred. The American whig reaction took several forms, including civil war, but only one reaction is our concern here. It is the reaction to the actual loss of specific charter rights—such as the right to hold frequent and open town meetings and the right of the elected representatives to select the members of the governor's council. That reaction was not what it once was depicted to have been. Loss of the charter was not the constitutional concern. It was rather the awakening of a sense of constitutional insecurity that tells our story.

"If the Chartae regales or Chartered rights of the colonies can be violated and annuled by Parliament, what security can the possessors of those lands have for the estates they enjoy?" John Dickinson asked.[73] He was referring not so much to security of property as to the constitutional right of the colonists to enjoy a security in their other rights,[74] a security that was abrogated now that charter rights were at the discretion of legislative fiat.[75]

The grievance was not only that the agreement—the original contract—evidenced by the charter had been broken.[76] The colonies had

had "the most solemn faith of the Crown and Nation for their inviolable security,"[77] but now the Massachusetts Government Act had, in the words of North Carolina's Provincial Congress, diminished "that sacred confidence which ought to be placed in the Acts of Kings" and governments.[78] When American whigs protested that the Massachusetts charter "ought to be as sacred as Magna Carta,"[79] they were not thinking of the provisions of the Massachusetts charter. They were thinking of Magna Carta. They were thinking, that is, of what ten years earlier the Massachusetts General Court had called "the fundamentals of the English constitution" and what in 1778 Sir William Meredith would term "unalienable rights." "It has been said," Meredith told the House of Commons,

> that a *charter being an act of one branch of the legislature only, could never stand against the united power of all the three branches of the legislature.* But there are such things as unalienable rights; and the foundation of every unalienable right is this; when he who is competent to convey, *conveys;* and he who is competent to receive, *accepts;* such conveyance on one hand, and acceptance on the other . . . constitute a right, which, by the law and constitution of England, is *unalienable;* and, unless by consent or forfeiture, cannot be taken away.[80]

Meredith, who was speaking from the same constitutional tradition that guided American whigs, went further than most American whigs would go, when he said the legislature could not at will and pleasure nullify charters. But he made two points they also made, and which were the essence of their defense of charter: that the charter was a contract and that the charter was evidence of rights which the legislature could not abrogate. The second point needs to be developed. The word "evidence" contains the key to the American concept of charters. Colonial whigs did not think the charter was the second original contract—the contract between the Crown and the first settlers. It was, rather, evidence of the contract.

The charter, as a constitutional instrument, was important for what it represented rather than for what it contained. "[T]he American charters," counsel for the plaintiff argued in the leading judicial case on colonial rights, "are accomodated to protect the anterior rights of the colonists, and not to convey those rights, as dependent on those charters, and derivative from them."[81] That, in a nutshell, was the constitutional theory of Americans, accepted by most loyalists as well as by whigs. Like Magna Carta, the charter confirmed existing rights, and evidence was its constitutional mystique—evidence of ancient rights inherited, English rights retained, and American rights prescribed.

Not everything was general evidence. Specific clauses occasionally were argued, although not many. One, found in most charters, begged to be cited as it summarized the precise legal principle Americans drew from charters as a whole. As found in the Connecticut charter, it provided that English subjects living in the colony "shall have and enjoy all Liberties and Immunities of free and natural Subjects within any of the Dominions of Us . . . as if they and every of them were born within the realm of *England*." This proviso, which appears to be limited to guaranteeing Americans equality of rights with the English, was ingeniously expanded by both sides of the controversy. Daniel Leonard even made it a clause for parliamentary supremacy over the colonists. "If a person born in England," he reasoned, "removes to Ireland and settles there, he is then no longer represented in the British parliament, but he and his posterity are and will ever be subject to the authority of the British parliament. If he removes to Jersey, Guernsey, or any other parts of the British dominions that send no members to parliament, he will still be in the same predicament. So that the inhabitants of the American colonies do in fact enjoy all the liberties and immunities of natural-born subjects." The Massachusetts House of Representatives read the same clause and came to an opposite rule of constitutional law. Concluding that the purpose was American retention of all English rights, the House voted, "That the admitting any Authority to make Laws binding on the People of this Province in all Cases whatsoever, saving the General Court or Assembly, is inconsistent with the Spirit of our free Constitution." After all, the Pennsylvania House said, also referring to its charter, "this is the indubitable Right of all the Colonists as *Englishmen*."[82] The "Liberties and Immunities" clause was the charter in miniature, but the charter would have been the same legal instrument without the clause.

No one developed this constitutional theory more thoroughly than the Massachusetts lawyer, Joseph Hawley. "[W]e," he contended, referring to Americans in general, "were entitled to all the rights of *Englishmen*, independent of any Charters or Realms under Heaven; and surely we are not the less so for having them confirmed by compact." That original understanding took precedence over any specific charter provisions. "Supposing," Hawley asked, turning the repugnancy argument around, "that our Charter proved, and it was clearly the sense of the parties to it, that we were to be bound by *British* laws in all cases whatever; if it can be shown that such an agreement was repugnant to their first and common principle, its obligation ceases, as founded on mistake, and void from the beginning."[83]

The constitutional theory answering Hawley's thesis also relied on the doctrine of original intent. The legislative sovereignty over all the dominions was vested in Parliament because it had never been transferred to colonial assemblies, by charter or other means, Edward Thurlow told his fellow members of the House of Commons. "[N]one of the charters intended it."[84] Like the American whigs, the imperialists looked for the original intent not in charter words or provisions but in the general structure of English constitutionalism. As it would be absurd to suppose authority being conferred with the intention that it was to be independent of the conferring power, one argument concluded, "those charters, so far from furnishing . . . a plea of exemption from acts of legislature, for the inhabitants of North America, . . . place them, to all intents and purposes, legislatively among the people of Britain. . . . In effect, all powers and immunities, granted by royal prerogative, or otherwise, to any person, company, or community, imply subjection upon the face of them."[85]

There is an inescapable conclusion: the charter was largely immaterial to the British claim that Parliament could bind the colonies in all cases whatsoever. To American whigs the charter was not a grant,[86] nor was it the original contract. They did not claim, as loyalist attorney Jonathan Sewall said they claimed, that by the charter "the sole power of legislation is given for ever to our general assembly."[87] It was, rather, evidence of the original contract.[88] The whigs argued two basic constitutional facts: (1) that the colonial charter was "granted by their sovereign, and not contradicted by either house of parliament,"[89] but (2) was "an *agreement or compact* between the King and his people, to govern them by their own consent."[90] That is, Samuel Cooke told Massachusetts legislators, "the first patentees" of the colony, in what he fantasized as "their address to King Charles the second," obtained "a compact" acknowledging that they were to enjoy "full and absolute power of governing all the people of this place, by men chosen from among themselves, and according to such laws as they shall from time to time see meet to make and establish, not being repugnant to the laws of England."[91] The first colonists and their descendants paid a "valuable" consideration for this agreement which not only, in the words of Connecticut's government, added "weight and strength to the title on which the claim of the colony to the rights, immunities, and franchises therein granted and confirmed are founded," but also made the agreement binding on Parliament as well as on the parties.[92]

CHAPTER FOURTEEN

PRECEDENTS OF ANALOGY

We must give particular attention to a familiar word. It has been mentioned many times for it was used frequently on both sides of the pre-revolutionary constitutional debate by participants explaining either the authority of charter or the original understanding. The word is "realm." A great deal of constitutional law evolved around the legal concept "realm."

"All the charters of the colonies," an unknown London writer explained in 1775, confer on the colonies "privileges and legislative powers, which plainly bespeak *distinct* states." At the time of the first settlement, he added, "the lands in America wholly belonged to the executive power, and were never subject to the parliamentary, because they were never annexed to the realm." Today the principle may seem too mechanical, but in the eighteenth century some constitutional commentators thought that it might resolve very large questions of law. If, they reasoned, colonial whig legal principles were correct, and "the colonies, in their first erection, were not strictly within the realm, then [parliamentary] supremacy cannot spread itself over them in the same degree it does over us" in the mother country.[1]

From the perspective of its American context, the "realm" criterion has the appearance of being another dispute about the original understanding—at the time of the settlement of North America "no person imagined any part of that Continent to be within the Realm of *England*, which was circumscribed within certain known and established limits."[2] In fact, it was not a new legal doctrine concerned with the recent constitutional past, but ancient doctrine traceable to the distant past, to a constitution before king and Parliament, to the era of kings and councils. It had been formulated for the rule of Wales, Jersey, Guernsey, and other dominions of the Crown, and, if it did not settle questions of legislative jurisdiction, it was a test for determining whether the English common-law and administrative writs ran within the limits of those dominions.[3]

The constitutional separation of the realm from the Crown's other dominions had received significant affirmation in *Calvin's Case*, when Lord Coke ruled on the authority of Parliament over Ireland, and reached back through medieval precedent to define colonies as dominions of the king, distinct from the realm.[4] The constitutional ramifications of the "realm" doctrine were never fully developed but had great potential for arbitrary prerogative law as much as for legislative autonomy. John Palmer, chief justice of New York in the reign of James II, indicated the prerogative side of this potential when he contended, "That the Plantations are of the Dominion of the *Crown of England*, and without any regard to *Magna Charta*, may be rul'd and govern'd by such ways and methods as the Person who wears the Crown, for the good and advancement of those Settlements, shall think most proper and convenient."[5] Palmer's constitutional theory was extreme, too drastic even for the post-Restoration monarchy. Had Palmer's law prevailed, however, not only would parliamentary supremacy over the colonies never have become an issue three-quarters of a century later, but, considering James's ambitions for the royal prerogative, it would have meant the end of constitutionalism in the colonies.

In the American Revolution debate, no one spoke for Palmer's constitution. The American "realm" issue was legislative autonomy outside the realm at a time when Parliament, not the Crown, was supreme within the realm. Disagreement was not over whether the realm-non-realm distinction was valid constitutional law, but whether North America was within or beyond the realm. Of course, there were constitutionalists who thought the question of little consequence, but not John Adams who invested much effort to prove that the colonies were not within the realm of Great Britain. Besides *Calvin's Case*, Adams relied on two rules of current imperial constitutional law to support the doctrine that the colonies were beyond the realm. The first was procedural. Judicial appeals from America were not carried to the House of Lords as were appeals from England and Ireland. "[W]hich shows that the Peers of the Realm are not the Peers of America," Adams insisted. "But all such Appeals are brought before the King in [Privy] Council, which is a further Evidence that we are not within the Realm."[6] The second was a rule of construction: that the colonies were not bound by an act of Parliament unless especially "named" in the statute. "[I]f America was annexed to the realm, or a part of the kingdom," Adams argued, "every act of parliament that is made, would extend to it, named or not named. But everybody knows that every act of parliament, and every other record, constantly distinguishes between this kingdom and his Majesty's other dominions."[7]

A third evidential argument for placing the colonies beyond the realm was provided by two rules of prerogative law. One was the convention of constitutional law that newly acquired countries were governed by the Crown. The other was the eighteenth-century constitutional practice that the Crown, without Parliament, disposed of such countries, "not only," as Governor Thomas Hutchinson pointed out, "to their own subjects, but to foreign princes: particularly *Acadia* and *Nova-Scotia*, when begun to be settled by British subjects, were ceded to *France*, although France had no better claim to them than New England."[8]

A remarkable percentage of American whigs seemed persuaded that the "realm" distinction clinched their case against parliamentary supremacy. The argument they probably thought most persuasive was summed up by John Adams in the answer that he wrote to Hutchinson's constitutional theory and which was adopted by the House of Representatives as an official statement of Massachusetts whig constitutional law. If "the Colonies were not annexed to the Realm, at the Time when their Charters were granted," Adams reasoned, "they never could be afterwards, without their own special Consent, which has never since been had, or even asked. If they are not now annexed to the Realm, they are not a Part of the Kingdom, and consequently not subject to the Legislative Authority of the Kingdom."[9]

Adams's conclusion—that by common law only the realm of England had been subject to the authority of Parliament—rested on the authority of *Calvin's Case*. There was no authority, by contrast, for the principle that colonial consent was needed before North America could be incorporated into the realm, except the constitutional contract theory and some invented law fabricated by Edward Bancroft.[10] The correct constitutional rule, Governor Thomas Pownall argued, had been settled at the Restoration when Charles II "participated this sovereignty over *these his foreign dominions*, with the lords and commons; the Colonies became *in fact*, the dominions of the realm—became subjects of the kingdom.—They came, in fact; and by an actual, constitutional exercise of power; under the authority and jurisdiction of parliament."[11] Pownall was referring to the trade and navigation laws which will be discussed in chapter 15. By "permitting" Parliament to enact them, Charles reversed the constitutional policy James I had tried to impose in 1621 and "participated" Parliament in the governance of territory previously outside the realm.

Pownall's theory was somewhat forced. It was designed to get around a legal problem that, had he been asked, Lord Mansfield would have told him was not material. The Chief Justice, for whom "law" was Parliament's command, rejected every aspect of the "realm" distinction, especially Adams's equally forced argument about statutes "naming" the colonies. "No distinction ought to be taken between the authority of parliament, over parts within or without the realm," Mansfield assured the House of Lords, "but it is an established rule of construction, that no parts without the realm are bound unless named in the act. And this rule establishes the right of parliament; for unless they had a right to bind parts out of the realm, this distinction would never have been made."[12]

As he usually did, Mansfield stated the better constitutional rule. In fact, although twentieth-century scholarship has given support to the "realm" distinction,[13] it was no longer persuasive law by the age of the American Revolution. Yet colonial whigs clung tenaciously to the doctrine, perhaps because it lent such stunning credence to their ultimate constitutional position, that the colonies were united to Great Britain through the Crown and had a limited political and slight constitutional connection with Parliament. "The *British* Empire" was a group of separate societies, "subject to one King, each having a distinct legislature: such is the Realm of *Great Britain*, the Realm of *Ireland*, and each *English* Colony in *America*."[14] Of course, the parliamentary answer was that it did not matter how many realms there were and how separated they might be. If each dominion was a realm of the king, it was also a realm of Parliament, for after 1688 the king was king by election of Parliament, serving as king by authority of Parliament's sovereignty. The realms might constitutionally be separate, but only at the sufferance of Parliament.

Although the parliamentary argument did not impress John Adams, it troubled other American whig leaders, most notably John Dickinson who attempted to neutralize it by treating the "realm" theory as irrelevant or false doctrine, rejected it as a constitutional explanation for colonial legislative autonomy, and relied instead on the highest authority in American whig constitutional theory. The "realm" argument, he protested, "is built on a mere supposition, that the Colonies are thereby acknowledged to be within the Realm, and on an incantation expected to be wrought by some magick force in those words." If the debate had to turn on a word, Dickinson preferred the word "contract." "To be subordinately connected with *England* the Colonies have contracted. To be subject to the general legislative authority of that Kingdom, they never contracted."[15] Again we find the colonial argument returning to the theory of contract—as always, it was the contract.

Boundaries of the Realm

The concept of the realm had a much more important role to play in the prerevolutionary constitutional debate than merely to serve John Adams as a frail prop for using the dicta of *Calvin's Case* to establish legislative autonomy. It was the legal standard with which to identify the dominions from which American whigs drew analogies for legislative autonomy. "The Colonies are not supposed to be within the realm," Benjamin Franklin pointed out in a note written to himself; "they have assemblies of their own, which are their parliaments, and they are, in that respect, in the same situation with Ireland." What Franklin was saying was that the governance of Ireland was an analogy for the governance of North America and that this analogy was authority for North America's constitutional rights and constitutional liabilities. "[I]t was proper to include Ireland in all the debates upon American taxation," Charles James Fox explained, "in order to ascertain the parliamentary right of taxation over every part of the British dominions."[16]

The persuasiveness of analogy, like the persuasiveness of precedent, depended on facts, remoteness, relevancy, and significance.[17] Some analogies were directly on point and still unpersuasive: for example, an argument against the Quebec Bill that because Ireland, Alderney, New Hampshire, and Jamaica all had elected legislatures, Quebec could not constitutionally be denied an elected assembly. Other analogies were deceptively persuasive until examined. A few imperialists thought that because Great Britain protected the colonies from European enemies, Parliament should be allowed to enact whatever laws it pleased. "[B]ut," Joseph Priestley asked, "have we not also protected Ireland and the electorate of Hanover without pretending either to make laws for them or to tax them?"[18] Ireland looks like an obvious analogy for proving Parliament's right to bind the American colonies by internal legislation, but as material in the final section of this chapter will show, Ireland was not as analogous as it first appears. The analogousness of Hanover, by contrast, might depend on who was making the argument. If made by the British, Hanover was either a weak analogy or not an analogy at all, as the sole connection between Great Britain and Hanover was that they shared the same monarch. If the argument was being made by American whigs, that single link of a shared sovereign made Hanover an attractive analogy, as that was the only constitutional connection they acknowledged between the colonies and Great Britain.

There are two tactics characterizing analogy arguments in the eighteenth-century law that may explain why some American historians have not accorded them the attention they received from the people making them. One is that analogies were argued with little regard for their weight, and the second is that time and the passage of time was a relatively insignificant factor.

It is remarkable how weak some analogies were. One writer seeking to prove that the colonies were legislatively separated from Great Britain observed that "there is something analogous to it [separation] in the daily Practice in England; for if the same Person be Lord of two distinct Manours, he must hold a separate Court at each of them, and if the Customs of the two Manours differ, though he be Lord of both, he cannot alter those Customs, so as to make one Manour be governed by the Customs of the other." We may suspect that the writer knew the analogy was constitutionally irrelevant and used it for illustration rather than authority. Thomas Whately provided a different kind of example, a weak analogy argued as authority, which was only as persuasive as was the reader's belief in Parliament's supremacy over the colonies. Americans might be represented in their own assemblies, Whately conceded. "So are the Citizens of *London* in their Common Council. . . . [I]t is true, that the Powers vested in the Common Council of *London*, are not equal to those which the Assemblies in the Plantations enjoy; but still they are legislative Powers, to be exercised within their District, and over their Citizens; yet not exclusively of the general Superintendance of the great Council of the Nation."[19]

As was the general rule of English constitutional and common law, time was not a factor with analogies. Samuel Johnson once scoffed at the American claim to legislative autonomy independent of Parliament by observing that the colonists supposed "dominion *without authority, and subjects without subordination.*" "It supposes no such thing," one of Johnson's critics answered. "It supposes no less authority over America, than the same circumstances suppose and give authority at this instant over *Ireland*, and supposed and gave once over *Calais*, when it was part of our empire." The writer was analogizing the colonies to Ireland as it was ruled in 1775 and Calais as it had been ruled in the mid–sixteenth century. The analogies were valid to the extent that Parliament and the constitution had remained the same over two and a half centuries. "Acts of Parliament for several Hundred Years past have respected Countries, which are not strictly within the Realm," Governor Hutchinson explained to Massachusetts legislators. "You will find Acts for regulating the Affairs of Ireland, though a separate and distinct Kingdom. Wales and Calais, whilst they send no Representatives to Parliament, were subject to the like Regulation. So are Guernsey, Jersey, Alderney, &c. which send no Members [to Parliament] to this Day." He was treating as similar not just analogies from across "several" centuries, but the analogy of a conquered country with the analogy of dominions which belonged to the Crown by virtue of having once been attached to the Duchy of Normandy.[20]

Analogies of law were often argued much as were precedents of history. Analogies could be drawn between current facts and an event that had occurred in the past,[21] or between a contemporary statute and a law from another era and a quite different reign.[22] Although analogies did not have to be exact, they did have to be relevant.[23] Analogies drawn between the American colonies of the 1770s and English and British dominions outside the realm had some degree of relevancy. By contrast, analogies with no persuasiveness were those drawn between the colonies and George III's German electorate,[24] or between the colonies and such British military possessions as Bengal,[25] and, certainly, analogies of how ancient governments ruled their colonies were no authority for the eighteenth-century British constitution.[26]

THE CHANNEL ANALOGIES

There was a technique and a theory to arguing the authority of analogy in the eighteenth century. A revealing illustration of both the technique and the theory was furnished by James Wilson, the future justice of the United States Supreme Court. To "evince" as a matter of law "that the colonies are not bound by the acts of the British parliament; because they have no share in the British legislature," Wilson cited as an historical analogy a judgment from the second year of the reign of Richard III. It had been a decision rendered by "all the judges of England" meeting in the Exechequer Chamber "to consider whether the people in Ireland were bound by an act of parliament made in England." Ireland, the English judges had ruled, "has a parliament, who make laws; and our statutes do not bind them; *because they do not send knights to parliament:* but their persons are the subjects of the king, in the same manner as the inhabitants of Calais, Gascoigne, and Guienne." That judgment came from 1484, but Wilson employed it to argue law for 1774. "From this authority it follows," he concluded, slipping from the past to the present tense as was the practice of common lawyers, "that it is by no means a rule, that the authority of parliament extends to all the subjects of the crown. The inhabitants of Ireland were the subjects of the king as of his crown of England; but it is expressly resolved, in the most solemn manner, that the inhabitants of Ireland are not bound by the statutes of England. Allegiance to the king and obedience to the parliament are founded on very different principles." Finally, Wilson drew the analogy of law: "if the inhabitants of Ireland are not bound by acts of parliament made in England, *a fortiori*, the inhabitants of the American colonies are not bound by them."[27]

Neither Wilson's technique nor his analogy were unusual. In the previous century, for example, William Atwood had drawn an analogy to the governance of Cheshire in the era before the Norman Conquest to prove a point of constitutional law for 1698. "The case of the Colonies is not a new one," the Pennsylvania loyalist Joseph Galloway explained to the first Continental Congress. "It was formerly the very situation of Wales, Durham, and Chester." He was referring to a principality and two counties palatine that in the Middle Ages had not been represented in Parliament yet had been subjects of conciliar if not of parliamentary legislation. Except for the fact that they had been part of the realm, they were, therefore, an analogy to the American colonies of the 1770s. "[T]he subordination of the colonies to the supreme authority of the parliament of England (afterwards of Great Britain)," Governor Pownall agreed, stood "exactly in the same predicament with the subordination of the counties palatine, and principality of Wales; which, before they had knights and burgesses to represent them in parliament, were nevertheless bound by acts of that parliament, as far forth as the other counties of the realm were, which had knights and burgesses to represent them in that parliament."[28]

Present analogies, that is, analogies from current times, were of greater authority than past analogies, and even more relevant for the colonies when related to dominions outside rather than of the realm. The Channel Islands were in that category. "The islands of Jersey, Guernsey, Sark, and Alderney, are governed by their own laws, and not by the laws of England," a legal treatise published in 1775 explained, "because, — as Sir Matthew Hale says, 'they are not parcels of the realm of England.' Hence, according to this great lawyer, the legislative acts of Great Britain do only bind the people of the realm." An earlier legal treatise, Blackstone's *Commentaries*, had qualified the islands' legislative autonomy with the same exception that Blackstone said qualified the legislative autonomy of the colonies. The four islands, he explained, "are not bound by common acts of our parliament, unless particularly named."[29]

The Channel Islands may have been a more exact analogy for the colonies than even Ireland, the analogy most frequently cited by historians. Their trade was regulated in a manner very similar to the regulation of colonial trade, often by the same parliamentary statutes. In striking contrast to Ireland, judicial appeals lay from their courts to the king's Privy Council, the same appellate jurisdiction that entertained American appeals. Irish judgments, like English judgments, were appealed to the British House of Lords. Moreover, the islands were often described in jurisdictional terms very similar to descriptions written of the colonies by John Adams and other American whigs. Jersey, Sark, and the other islands, it was said, "though Parcel of the Dominions of the Crown, are not, or ever were, Parcel of the Realm of England. On this Account their Laws are different, being derived from the Custom of Normandy, . . . the Ordinances of our Kings, and their own Laws and Judgments, in their Royal Courts."[30]

It is not clear why the Channel analogies were not argued to better effect by the imperial side of the debate. They were, after all, a very strong analogy proving Parliament's practice of legislating for dominions outside the realm, more exact, certainly, than Ireland, the most frequently discussed analogy. Although there is no persuasive answer why they were so little cited, there are some possible reasons. First, in contrast to American whigs, defenders of parliamentary supremacy paid relatively less heed to analogies, treating other arguments, especially precedents, as stronger. Second, the Channel jurisdictions were not well known, and it is likely that many participants in the revolutionary debate were not familiar with the details of their governance. Third, the history of the islands was quite different from the history of the colonies, a factor that in the eighteenth century distracted from their persuasiveness as analogies. They were held directly by the king as an inheritance from the days when the English crown had been worn by the duke of Normandy and the islands had been Norman territory. It was a history that did not lend much support to parliamentary jurisdiction. Fourth, Parliament passed for the Channel Islands very little legislation that could be cited to demonstrate its legislative supremacy. Most statutes Parliament enacted for the islands were concerned with trade regulation, a category of legislation which the colonists acknowledged within Parliament's constitutional purview.

THE IRISH ANALOGY

The controlling analogy for Parliament's authority to bind the colonies in all cases whatsoever should have been its authority to bind Ireland in all cases whatsoever. There were some striking parallels between the legislative governance of Ireland and the colonies. As early as the sixteenth century, Sir Thomas Egerton, the future Lord Chancellor Ellesmere, anticipated some of the dicta of American whigs when he wrote that the Irish were not bound by the English Parliament "because they have a Parliament of theire owne."[31] That was just one lawyer's opinion, and, as with the colonial controversy, there were constitutional arguments supporting both sides of the question of the imperial authority to legislate for Ireland.[32]

The Irish debate, centuries older than the American debate, was remarkably similar to the American even though Irish constitutional principles were in some respects different from colonial constitutional principles. The Irish had many more judicial precedents for either side to cite, although numerous precedents did not necessarily make the law clearer. One famous Irish judgment, for example, was used by legal commentators on both sides of the American Revolution controversy, one side saying that English judges sitting in Exchequer Chamber had held that Parliament could legislate for Ireland, the other saying the judges had held that Ireland was not bound by English statutes because the Irish were not represented in the English Parliament. "I can hardly think it necessary to shew," a London pamphleteer wrote in 1776, drawing a legal analogy from the Irish decision, "that America has a Parliament, makes and alters laws, and does not send Members to our Parliament. The conclusion is unavoidable."[33]

The comparison could be taken even further. As the Irish were arguing somewhat the same constitution in the taught traditions of the same common-law methodology, the arguments about Ireland were often in the same words and used the same style of refutation as arguments about North America. *"We have not one single* Instance *of an English Act of Parliament expres[s]ly claiming this right of binding us;"* William Molyneux wrote—much as John Adams would a century later, —*"but we have several* Instances *of Irish Acts of Parliament expres[s]ly denying this Subordination."* William Atwood answered Molyneux and his answer was the same answer that later would have been given to an American whig. "As to the express claiming an Authority to do what is done, by virtue of an Authority always suppos'd; that's so far from an *Argument* against it, that it shews 'twas never call'd in question." Also answering Molyneux, John Cary writing in 1698 not only drew an early Irish analogy to the colonies, he made the same argument of necessary imperial superintendence against which Americans would be grappling three-quarters of a century later.

And because 'twas thought that the People of *Ireland* could not conveniently send Representatives to the Parliament in *Englaand* [*sic*], they were therefore authorized to hold Parliaments among themselves for the transacting such Affairs; we allow it to all our Colonies in *America*. . . . This I speak of such Laws which regard the administration of Commutative Justice regulating their own particular Affairs, or raising Taxes. But there is yet a higher kind of Law inherent in the Constitution. . . . I mean that which comprehends the Subjects of the whole Empire, and must be of Authority to ordain certain Regulations which shall be binding upon the Whole in extraordinary Cases, where the well-being of the Universality is concern'd.[34]

Nothing would be added to our knowledge of the constitutional history of the American Revolution by discussing the hundreds of other arguments which were based on Irish parallels to the American case against parliamentary sovereignty.[35] The salient point deserving emphasis, one that helps us to understand the constitutional origins of what Americans believed, is that the Irish of the 1770s were making the same case. It is a significant fact as the closeness of the two controversies demonstrates how constitutional the two were. We should expect the Irish argument to resemble the American argument if they were protesting the same constitution of legislative sovereignty, protesting, as Charles Francis Sheridan said, that if the British Parliament had authority to legislate for them, then, they, the Irish, held "their civil Freedom by no Tenure, but the Moderation of those who claim to be their sovereign Legislators."[36] The Irish constitutional complaint was the American constitutional complaint, a fact explained by Francis Dobbs, a Dublin barrister and younger brother of a London-appointed governor of North Carolina. "We complain of the British Legislature making laws to bind Ireland," he wrote Lord North. "We alledge it is without right, and we require that the legislature of Great-Britain should relinquish a claim that we say they are not entitled to." As with American whigs, the grievance was not this particular statute or that particular law, but deprivation of the constitutional right to consent to law. "[W]e are not less slaves," Dobbs concluded, "though British legislation never found it expedient to exert the power it claims."[37]

Although American whigs did not make much of the Irish analogy, historians have, especially in the twentieth century, saying that the Irish analogy supports the American constitutional case to a greater extent than participants in the controversy realized.[38] Some of the conclusions of law have been persuasive, particularly Barbara Black's thesis that the better constitutional precedent at the time of the first American settlements supported the contention that the English Parliament did not have jurisdiction beyond the realm. That precedent was *Calvin's Case.* The correct reading of Lord Coke's ruling in *Calvin's Case*, Black thinks, is that Coke held that once Ireland received the common law, the king could make new law for Ireland only with the consent of his parliament, which meant his *Irish* Parliament, not his English Parliament.[39] This interpretation of *Calvin's Case* could have provided impressive support for the American whig argument against Parliament's right to bind them in all cases whatsoever. It could have made the Irish analogy one of the fundamental elements of the colonial whig constitutional case. The problem is that no American whig, not even John Adams or James Wilson, interpreted *Calvin's Case* as saying that the king in Parliament for Ireland was the king in his Irish Parliament. If the argument was not made, it had no bearing on the American constitutional controversy, and, if it had no bearing on the constitutional controversy, what can history make of it except to wonder why the argument—if valid—was missed?

What is striking rather, is how seldom the Americans cited the Irish analogy. The point has not been statistically developed, but the impression one receives after reading the eighteenth century literature on the American and Irish questions is that British imperialists put more stock in the Irish analogy than did colonial whigs. Of course, Americans mentioned it, but infrequently.[40] British lawyers, like Chief Justice Lord Mansfield and Attorney General Charles Yorke, referred to it more often. Aware that Parliament claimed the right to legislate for Ireland's internal affairs, believing the American Declaratory Act was as constitutionally valid as the Irish Declaratory Act, they could make at least as strong a case for Ireland being an analogy proving Parliament's right to legislate for the colonies as the whigs could make a case that Ireland was an analogy proving North America's legislative autonomy.[41]

There are several explanations why American whigs did not make as much of the Irish analogy as recent historians think they should have. We should consider these explanations because some teach a great deal about why certain arguments were made or not made by the whig side of the constitutional controversy. One was that American whigs had good reason to distance themselves from the Irish analogy. Ireland was a conquered country, a constitutional category with which the colonies did not wish to be associated. The authority of conquest was the strongest of the various legal principles that vested in Parliament the power it claimed of direct legislation over Ireland. It was an authority, James Wilson argued, that had no bearing on the sovereignty of the North American colonies as the colonies had not been conquered by either England or Great Britain.[42]

There was little disagreement that Ireland was a conquered country.[43]

There was, however, a serious argument whether the mainland colonies of North America had been conquered. Except for New York, historical evidence indicated that they had been "settled" rather than "conquered." There was a good deal of doubt about the question, however, for there had been a few legal authorities who had held that the colonies had been conquered. These authorities gained instant respectability in 1765 when the first volume of Blackstone's *Commentaries* was published. Blackstone stated flatly, as if there were no other opinion, that the colonies had been conquered, in part by "driving out the natives" and in part "by treaties," indicating that he was thinking of Quebec and the Floridas, recently conquered from France and Spain.[44]

The "conquered" category was important because of a rule of constitutional law derived from the "conquered-settled" distinction. It was a rule from which Blackstone in the case of the colonies also dissented, as he held rather advanced views of the consequences of the new constitutionalism of parliamentary sovereignty. One of those consequences was his insistence that all colonies, settled as well as conquered, were equally subject to parliamentary legislation.[45] The older view, interestingly, was concisely stated by Blackstone's successor as Vinerian professor of law, not a very impressive constitutional lawyer, unfortunately, though in this case he correctly summarized the doctrine of law he was explaining. "Conquered countries are absolutely under the dominion of the conquerors," Sir Robert Chambers explained in his Oxford lectures. In a country that, in legal parlance, was "settled," "colonists are held to carry with them the laws and privileges of Englishmen," but "a conquered people" by sharp contrast "is not entitled to those advantages till they are expressly granted to them by the crown."[46] Those rights were generally granted when the common law took effect, but on the terms of the conqueror which, by the 1760s, constitutionally meant that the conquered country was under the supreme legislative jurisdiction of the British Parliament.[47]

The conquest doctrine was one of the most severe and absolutist in eighteenth-century constitutional law, one reason why all the colonies, even New York and Jamaica which, in fact, had been conquered from Europeans, strove to avoid its implications, claiming that in law they were settled not conquered countries. To avoid the label of "conquest" was one reason why American whigs and their British supporters would have made as little as possible of the Irish analogy—even if the analogy had been exact. It is also the reason that they often did the opposite, and instead of noting parallels between Ireland and the North American colonies, they noted differences separating the two dominions of George III.[48]

A second reason why American whigs did not rely on the Irish analogy as much as recent historians would have encouraged them to do is that the governance of eighteenth-century Ireland was not an analogy for the governance of the North American colonies. There were differences, arising in large part from their different histories. The colonists, as a London commentator pointed out in 1776, "were always a part of our own nation, of the same *Body* with ourselves, and under the same Laws; whereas the Irish were a distinct people and nation, before they became subject to the King of England."[49] One constitutional conclusion from this history, of course, could have been that the Irish were subjects of the king, not of Parliament, but that was not the lesson usually drawn. What was stressed instead was, that because of Ireland's peculiar history, the English had developed a system of legislating for Ireland at odds with the English legislative method—the method that in the seventeenth century had been extended from the home islands to North America.

Because of a history of "Antient Rights, Privileges, and Immunities," the governance of eighteenth-century Ireland was said to differ "totally from the Colonies, as to the several Laws and Usages by which it's present connexion with *Great Britain* is defined and ascertained."[50] The difference was especially marked by the legislative process. In Ireland, Robert Macfarlane explained with some exaggeration, "as the king's negative precedes that of the commons in passing every bill, he is an absolute monarch." The reason was a parliamentary rule, promulgated in 1495 by the famous and controversial "Poynings Law," that no bill could be introduced into either house of the Irish Parliament unless it had been approved in advance by the king and Privy Council of England and Great Britain.[51] It was because of that procedure that the legislative process of Ireland was often described as the reverse of the legislative process of Great Britain or of the colonies. Where American assemblies initiated legislation, in Ireland legislation was initiated either by the lord lieutenant and his council or the king and the British privy council. In the colonies the colonial governor and then the king acting through his privy council exercised the veto. In Ireland the veto was not an executive but a parliamentary function.[52]

The Irish difference of legislation did more than diminish the relevance of the Irish analogy. It deprived American whigs of the significance of the most important element of the Irish analogy: that over the centuries of first English and then British rule, the Westminster Parliament had enacted little internal legislation for Ireland. As the English Privy Council controlled what the Irish Parliament legislated, there had been slight need for the English Parliament to exercise jurisdiction. The colonial constitutional process was the reverse, a legal fact that took much of what was potentially analogous out of the Irish analogy. The British Privy Council could only veto American bills, it did not write legislation for American assemblies. If the mother country wanted to dictate internal legislation for the colonies, it had no alternative to the dangerous innovation of direct parliamentary promulgation.

There were other differences diminishing further the persuasiveness of the Irish analogy—differences concerning the authority to govern rather than the authority to legislate.[53] The most notable was that Ireland was a separate kingdom. The British spoke of George III as king of Ireland. They did not speak of him as king of Virginia or king of New Hampshire, although there were a few Americans who did. It may have been an insignificant difference, but it was a difference.[54]

In perspective, the Irish analogy was less a constitutional than a political consideration. Irish history and governance warned Americans why they should avoid parliamentary rule but did not furnish authority for their legislative autonomy.[55]

CHAPTER FIFTEEN

PRECEDENTS OF REGULATION

It is possible that more would have been made of the authority of analogy had participants in the debate felt the need. One reason they did not appears to be the strength of available precedents. Especially on the imperial side, there seemed little point to developing the Irish analogy when precedents of direct legislation were readily at hand to serve as more persuasive authority.

There were even precedents from the reigns before the Interregnum that could be cited to prove that the realm of England had exerted control over the dominions of the kingdom. Some of these precedents were precedents of direct legislation.[1] Although they are precedents that must be noted in a constitutional history of the authority of Parliament to legislate for the colonies, there are three reasons they need not to be given detailed consideration. First, for the earliest period, they are, as a general rule, precedents of conciliar, not legislative authority, as the "parliament" that promulgated them was still part of the medieval council of the king and had not yet developed into the legislative and judicial body known to the eighteenth century. Second, there are no precedents for the first decades of American settlement. It would be risky, however, to make much of that fact to prove anything about what today would be called "the original constitutional understanding." The period of the first settlements was a time of great constitutional flux, as demonstrated by James I's resistance to parliamentary interference with the Virginia fishery. Lack of legislative precedents from the era of the first two Stuarts may have been due to constitutional stalemate. The colonies were too thinly populated and too economically insignificant[2] to have been worth a constitutional crisis over their governance when Parliament was concerned with securing constitutional rights at home. Third, although historians in the twentieth century have found precedents from the seventeenth century of direct legal relevance for the question of parliamentary jurisdiction over the dominions outside the realm, they have not always shown that the precedents were recognized, let alone cited in the eighteenth century. What is their historical significance if they were not known in the 1760s and were not argued by participants in the revolutionary controversy? They were not part of the American whig case or the imperial answer, and, therefore, although they might tell us what could have been argued, they had no forensic bearing on the dispute.

There was little incentive for supporters of parliamentary sovereignty to search out statutory precedents before the Interregnum after Governor Thomas Pownall, in his authoritative book on imperial government, dismissed them as anachronistically irrelevant. The colonies, Pownall concluded, anticipating the American whig argument about the realm, "were dominions of the King of England; although, according to the language of those times, 'not yet annexed to the crown.' They were under the jurisdiction of the King, upon the principles of feudal sovereignty: although considered *as out of the jurisdiction of the kingdom.*' The parliament itself doubting at that time, whether it had jurisdiction to meddle with those matters, did not think proper to pass bills concerning America." It was, rather, the colonies, with "legislatures peculiar to their own separate communities," who, during those early years, legislated the precedents, proving that with the single restriction of the repugnancy clause, that they were, "in all other matters and things, free uncontrouled and compleat legislatures, in conjunction with the King or his deputy as part thereof."[3]

Had their opponents allowed them to argue on the premises of the customary constitution, American whigs might have based their precedential case just on the material in Governor Pownall's book. They could have developed much of the evidence needed to prove a prescriptive right to legislative autonomy on the facts that Pownall had conceded. Pownall, of course, thought he was describing what in the twentieth century would be called administrative law, not constitutional law. His own legal premises came from the constitution of parliamentary sovereignty for which the precedents of "legislatures peculiar to their own communities" were irrelevant. Pownall traced his precedents to the Restoration and, as noted in the last chapter, solved the "realm" problem by a transfer of sovereignty twenty-eight years before the Glorious Revolution when Charles II "participated" the Lords and Commons in the governance of the colonies. As a result of this "participation" the colonies "became connected and annexed to the state," and became subject to the authority of Parliament.[4]

It was not a serious problem for Governor Pownall that his constitutional scruples prevented him from treating as constitutional precedent any legislation enacted by the Commonwealth Parliament during the Interregnum. His constitutional theory of legislative sovereignty made precedents unnecessary for establishing authority. There were, however, imperialists who had a more traditionalist respect for precedents and may have been uncomfortable that there were no precedents of direct parliamentary legislation for the first half century of colonial rule. Lacking Pownall's scruples they looked for precedents from the Interregnum and found two. For them the first precedent of parliamentary legislation was either a Commonwealth ordinance forbidding trade with Virginia and three island colonies,[5] or the famous Navigation Ordinance of 9 October 1651.[6] Both ordinances were emphatic, uncompromising asseverations of jurisdiction. The first, intended to punish Virginia and three other colonies for royalist politics, asserted that as the colonies "were planted at the Cost, and set[t]led by the People, and by Authority of this Nation" they "are and ought to be subordinate to, and dependent upon England; and hath ever since the Planting thereof been, and ought to be subject to such Laws, Orders and Regulations as are or shall be made by the Parliament of England."[7] The second exercised unrestricted jurisdiction to regulate the foreign trade of the colonies.[8]

There were only a very few defenders of parliamentary supremacy over the colonies who treated the two Commonwealth ordinances as binding constitutional precedents settling all questions of parliamentary jurisdiction over the colonies. Daniel Leonard, for example, claimed that the ordinance of 1650 established the right that Parliament thought it was promulgating in 1766 when it passed the Declaratory Act, and Sir Egerton Leigh, the London-appointed attorney general of South Carolina, contended that the two Commonwealth precedents made it "idle to question this superintending and over-ruling power of the British Parliament, or its right to extend [law] to these remote Countries, as parcels of one great State, to which they are united."[9]

There were two reasons why the Commonwealth ordinances were not the important precedents of parliamentary legislation we otherwise would expect them to be. First, in the time-honored method of the common law, they could be distinguished away, and, second, they came from the Interregnum, a wrong time for the creation of constitutional precedents. The future presidents Thomas Jefferson and John Adams demonstrated a variation of the "distinguishing" technique when they explained away the two ordinances by arguing that they never took effect and, therefore, never became precedents. The first ordinance had been directed primarily against Virginia for remaining loyal to the House of Stuart. "This arbitrary act," Jefferson asserted, was "soon recalled" by the parliamentary rulers of England, "and by solemn treaty entered into on the 12th. day of March 1651, between the said Commonwealth by their Commissioners and the colony of Virginia by their house of Burgesses, it was expressly stipulated by the 8th. article of the said treaty that they should have 'free trade as the people of England do enjoy to all places and with all nations according to the laws of that Commonwealth.'"[10] Adams had an even easier time explaining away the Navigation Ordinance as no precedent. "This act," he wrote, "was never executed or regarded, until 17 years afterwards [after enactment], and then it was not executed as an act of parliament, but as a law of the colony, to which the king agreed."[11] In other words, the Navigation Act was one of those imperial laws with which the Massachusetts General Court played the legalistic game of reenacting on its own authority to prevent them from becoming precedents of binding parliamentary legislation and to avoid the appearance of obeying Parliament, which would have been a harmful precedent for another principle.

The other reason why the Commonwealth ordinances were not as strong precedents as they otherwise could have been can be mentioned only at a risk. It is a lawyer's reason, and historians can credit it only if they are willing to take lawyers and their values seriously. For many common lawyers, the two ordinances were precedents from a time not befitting precedents. "The argument from precedents begins unluckily for its advocates," Pennsylvania's 1774 instructions noted. It was unlucky because "[t]he first [precedent] produced against us" was the ordinance of "the Commonwealth Parliament of 1650 to 'punish' *Virginia*." "Brutal power," the instructions explained, "became an irresistible argument of boundless right. What the style of an *Aristotle* could not prove, the point of a *Cromwell's* sword sufficiently demonstrated." In constitutional language, that meant that a precedent from the unconstitutional Interregnum was not constitutional authority. It is indicative of respect for the canons of common-law methodology that imperialists tended to agree. "[N]o consequences of rights can be drawn from precedents in that period, when the two houses of parliament assumed the exercise of the sovereignty, and considered the Colonies *as their subjects*," Governor

Pownall insisted. Impressive support for this legal theory came from an imperial law officer, Anthony Stokes, a former attorney general and the wartime chief justice of Georgia, in his book on the "constitution of the British colonies." "This act," Stokes wrote of the ordinance punishing Virginia, "having been made by the Long Parliament, when the King was unjustly kept from the throne, cannot be cited as an authority; but it shews what the opinion of that Parliament was, with respect to the right of the Mother Country over the Colonies." Even William Knox, a colonial under secretary absolutely committed to parliamentary sovereignty over the colonies did not use the Virginia ordinance as a precedent. At best, he claimed, it was an evidential precedent, not a precedent of authority, or, what another imperialist, John Lind, termed "a proof" of "the opinion of those times" when the ordinance was adopted. "I do not quote this act as of force or binding upon the Colonies," Knox explained.

> I only give it as an historical fact, containing the opinion of *that parliament;* and if we believe the assertions in the preamble: "That the Colonies were *always held and deemed to be subject to all acts of parliament,*" which is a matter that must have been well known to those who made that assertion, as the first settlements were made within the memory of them, it will be full evidence, of the *opinion* which former parliaments had of their right to jurisdiction over the Colonies, though it is not a proof of the right of those who passed the act.[12]

NAVIGATION PRECEDENTS

The Virginia "punishment" ordinance was an anomaly of the prerevolutionary debate: a precedent somewhat respectable as evidence of the seventeenth-century understanding but tainted as legal authority. The Navigation Ordinance, by contrast, gained legitimate stirps and became a genuine statutory precedent when it was reenacted at the first session of Parliament following the Restoration. The Navigation ordinance might remain blemished with the stain of Cromwellism, but it had been transmuted into a constitutional precedent when it was endorsed by king, Lords, and Commons. As a result of this "constitutional" reenactment, "no doubt can remain," imperialists were able to argue of the colonies, "that the Legislature considered them as subordinate and dependent parts of the English Empire, subject to commercial regulations, and liable to be modelled and governed, in all respects, as the wisdom of Parliament should, from time to time, think proper to direct."[13]

From that time navigation precedents multiplied. On the official list sent to the last colonial governors as part of their "trade" instructions, there were at least ninety-nine statutes that had been enacted between the reigns of Charles II and George II. Many of these statutes—laws, for example, encouraging the growth of raw silk or for the making of potash—were quite different from the original Navigation Act.[14] Moreover, the bulk of the statutes could have been, and, in many cases, were ignored by people on both sides of the prerevolutionary controversy. Instead of taking into account all the statutes that had been enacted, the debate, as waged by both sides, concentrated on ten to fifteen leading precedents.

Given the rules of legal proof, it did not require many precedents to establish whether Parliament's authority to legislate was supported by constitutional precedents. John Dickinson limited his argument to seven statutes, extending from the Navigation Act of the first year of Charles II's Restoration to 1 George III, chapter 9. Thomas Jefferson also counted seven, although three of his differed from Dickinson's. For persons knowledgeable about law, it will be unsurprising that imperialists' arguments were generally confined to the same statutes. There is no need to study these precedents in detail or even to enumerate them. At times during the prerevolutionary debate, it seemed that they had been all lumped together as one, either serving imperialists as a general precedent for parliamentary jurisdiction over the colonies or cited by colonial whigs so they could then distinguish it. The purpose was either to prove, as Jonathan Sewall argued, that from the 1650s "the jurisdiction of parliament over us, was openly and explicitly claimed," or, as Dickinson concluded, "they were all intended *solely as regulations of trade*" and were not precedent for the authority to legislate.[15]

Close attention must be given to Dickinson's constitutional theory. For all American whigs and many loyalists, that theory settled the legal issue. But first there are two points to be established. One is well known and does not require documentation. It is that the various navigation and trade acts were extraordinary in their commercial scope and the range of activities they regulated. They were more than mere rules of commerce and trade. They controlled and restricted much of the economic activity of the colonies, even more in the eighteenth than in the seventeenth century, ensuring that first England and later Great Britain was the entrepôt of empire and the center of its business life. The imperial trade acts confined colonial commerce to ships owned in England, Ireland, or the colonies and manned by English, Irish, or American crews, forbade the export of "enumerated commodities" except to England, Ireland, or another colony, and forbade the import of foreign goods into a colony except through England where English customs duties were paid, with only a very few exceptions such as wine from Madeira and the Azores, Irish servants, and (for some colonies) European salt.[16] Looking at these laws from the British perspective, Edmund Burke told the House of Commons that they were "the system of a monopoly. . . . This principle of commercial monopoly runs through no less than twenty-nine Acts of parliament, from the year 1660 to the unfortunate period of 1764."[17] The American perspective was explained by the freeholders of Virginia's Fairfax County: "The *British* Parliament have claimed and exercised the power of regulating our trade and commerce, so as to restrain our importing from foreign countries such articles as they could furnish us with, of their own growth and manufacture, or exporting to foreign countries such articles and portions of our produce as *Great Britain* stood in need of, for her own consumption or manufacture."[18]

The second point to bear in mind is that these trade and navigation acts were perceived to be extremely harmful to American economic interests. Great Britain by statute maintained a monopoly over the export-import business of the colonies, the *Annual Register* pointed out. "The navigation-acts shut up their commerce with foreign countries. Their ports have been made subject to customs and regulations, which cramped and diminished their trade." Parliament, the famed Scots jurist Henry Home, Lord Kames, thought

> have acted like a stepmother to her American colonies, by prohibiting them to have any commerce but with Britain only. They must land first in Britain all their commodities, even what are not intended to be sold there; and they must take from Britain, not only its own product, but every foreign commodity that is wanted. This regulation is not only unjust but impolitic; as by it the interest of the colonies in general is sacrificed to that of a few London merchants.

The main reason was cost, Richard Glover, former member for Weymouth, poet, and student of commercial matters, pointed out. The charge of unlading and relading "was immense; and could serve no purpose whatever, except to give jobs to coopers and wharfingers."[19]

There were at least four givens generally agreed to on both sides of the Atlantic: (1) that the navigation acts imposed a severe economic burden on the Americans, not only in "useless charges," but also because the colonists were required to take inferior products and forgo the profits of markets from which they were excluded;[20] (2) that some of the provisions of the acts were capricious, benefitting no one, as for example, restrictions and duties on foreign wines, "an article which does not in the least interfere with the products of *Great Britain*, or any of its Colonies," where there were no vineyards;[21] (3) that when the regulations benefited the colonies, it was generally the older, English-settled Sugar Islands for whom economic advantages were legislated, and always at what the New York General Assembly called "a discrimination" against "the Continental colonies;"[22] and (4), even more partial, when restrictions were imposed in the interest of the mother country, they generally were not designed to promote the well-being of the nation, thus strengthening the empire, but to enrich, at American expense, individuals pursuing favored trades, manufactures, or other private enterprises.[23]

Parliament's trade statutes were a serious grievance to the colonists, as has often been shown by historians who give close attention to their private correspondence. To reconstruct the constitutional case that the whigs argued against Parliament's authority to legislate, it is necessary to concentrate not on personal communications but on the official statements and resolutions passed by whig and provincial bodies from the beginning to the end of the revolutionary controversy. At the start, several assemblies, as well as the Stamp Act Congress, complained that some of the trade duties imposed by Parliament were "extremely grievous and burthensome."[24] Toward the end of the controversy, both the first Continental Congress and the New Jersey House of Representatives complained to George III that "Commerce has been burthened with many useless and oppressive restrictions."[25] There is no need to mention every grievance voiced by the various assemblies, the high costs imposed, the arbitrary restrictions placed on commerce, or the adjectives that were used, such as "oppressive and impolitick."[26] The facts to be noted are that the colonists perceived the trade and navigation acts to be *economic* grievances, that they made the acts the subjects of official protests, and that they petitioned for reform to Parliament, not just to the king.[27] The last difference is especially important. Had the colonial assemblies thought the navigation acts unconstitutional, they would have been very cautious about acknowledging Parliament's jurisdiction by petitioning for parliamentary reform. They would have petitioned only the Crown.

On the British side of the Atlantic the grievance was not overlooked. Lord Kames termed the laws "degrading" to the colonists, putting them into a commercial situation that the duke of Richmond likened to equality with the Irish not with the British.[28] That was the minority view. Most imperial attitudes were shaped not by the burdens of the trade laws but by the complaints of the Americans. It became an imperialist's given that the constitutional grievances of the Americans were but a screen hiding the real complaint which was economic. "[T]he next attempt of the colonies would be for ridding themselves of the Navigation Act,"

Lord Mansfield had warned as early as the Stamp Act crisis. It was the objective, he said, "they had long been aiming at." It was a serious error for Mansfield to associate the repeal of the Stamp Act with the trade laws, an error he compounded by conjecturing that the American grievance was not only economic but also constitutional. "[T]hey had scarce condescended into any explanations upon the [Navigation] Act," he was reported to have warned the House of Lords, "but had directed all their objections to the principle and the power of making it."[29]

Whether Mansfield, speaking in December 1765, was referring to *constitutional* objections by the colonists against the Navigation Act prior to that date is not known. He was wrong, however, about 1765 and the subsequent years of the revolutionary controversy. Prior to the Declaration of Independence, neither the Navigation Act nor any of its companion statutes regulating colonial commerce were raised as constitutional issues. Yet most of Britain's leaders who spoke on the question, professed to believe that the Americans did not mean what they said, and that the trade laws were their basic constitutional grievance. "[I]t was not taxation, but the trade of Great-Britain, which the Americans now opposed," Sir William Meredith assured the House of Commons in 1775. "[T]he views of America are not confined to the redress of grievances, real or imaginary, but are immediately directed to the total overthrow of that great palladium of British commerce, the Act of Navigation," Lord Townshend told the upper house that same year. Even Lord North made the argument when opposing John Wilkes's motion that Parliament grant the primary American constitutional demand and repeal all statutes relating to the colonies enacted since 1763. "I fix on that period," Wilkes had explained, "because the [Continental] Congress complain of nothing prior to that era. They have never hinted at the repeal of the Navigation Act, nor any other Acts before that year." What colonial whigs said they wanted was not what they were really after, North replied. "I can assure the hon. gentleman, that he is mistaken, if he thinks a partial repeal will content America: the Navigation, and every other restrictive Act, must first give way to their unreasonable demands; and, with them, the sovereignty of this country."[30]

We need not wonder that British leaders would not take the American constitutional grievances seriously and said the complaint was really about the economics of trade regulation. Twentieth-century scholars of the Revolution have made the same assumption. But motivations are one thing and can be endlessly debated. The record is another matter, and what colonial whigs actually said and demanded deserves to be considered for they drew distinctions between kinds of grievances and were careful not to confuse constitutional grievances with political or economic grievances. Consider that record as it was explained by the duke of Richmond addressing the House of Lords several months after London had received news of the Battle of Lexington. The Navigation Act deprived the colonists of equality with Englishmen by keeping "the blessings of law and liberty" from them, Richmond pointed out. "So far, however, from the Americans deeming that as a motive inducing them to declare themselves independent states, they had not even mentioned it in the long catalogue of grievances which they enumerate as the real cause of that effect."[31]

If the regulation-of-trade story has been often missed, the fault may be due to the failure to ask the right questions because the answers were assumed. We should be asking what Richmond meant by "the long catalogue of grievances," what Wilkes intended when introducing his motion, and whether they were correct about American motives. Both men, after all, had been addressing chambers filled with colleagues who professed to believe that the Navigation grievance not only was included in "the long catalogue," but that it was "the real cause" of American discontent.

First, it should be noted that Richmond did not deny that the Navigation Act was a grievance. What he said was that, although the trade laws were grievous, they were not part of "the long catalogue." To understand that he may have meant that there were different kinds of grievances and that the trade laws were a grievance of a kind different from a constitutional grievance, we should understand that there can be a distinction between "economic," "political," and "constitutional." An economic historian has noted that "[t]he Navigation Acts were acquiesced in by the original colonists and were integral parts of the British constitution," commanding the loyalty of a large segment of the British public which could be expected to oppose American "opportunism."

> Thus, it made good political sense for George III's ministers to picture the colonists as wanting to throw off the Navigation Acts. Likewise, it made good sense for Franklin and other colonial spokesmen vehemently to deny any such desire. As contemporaries realized, therefore, the pronouncements of neither side can be equated with truth. In the end, the political import of the burden of the Navigation Acts remains ambiguous.[32]

Today's question is whether the political import can be ambiguous while the constitutional import is clearly defined. The best likelihood is that Richmond was speaking of *constitutional* grievances when saying that the Navigation Act was not listed in "the long catalogue." One could say that something was not a constitutional grievance without meaning that it was not a grievance at all. In this regard, American whigs were more careful than is generally noted. Although they might call something a grievance, if it did not raise a constitutional issue, they would treat it as a political grievance, not a constitutional grievance. They would complain that Parliament should not have enacted it into law, not that Parliament lacked authority to enact it.

On the 3d of March, 1775, the New York General Assembly took up the issue of American grievances. The motion was put that section 8 of 3 George III, chapter 22 was a grievance. Under that statute a person interposing a counterclaim in a prosecution for goods or vessels seized under the trade laws was "obliged to give Security in the Penalty of sixty Pounds, to answer and pay the Costs occasioned by such claim." The members rejected the motion. "*Resolved therefore,*" it was next voted, "That it is the opinion of this Committee [of the whole], that the sum directed in the said last mentioned Act, to be given as security by claimants of vessels, is not a grievance." Security for costs in judicial proceedings was established, customary practice. It may be that the original motion had been directed not against the practice, but against the amount, sixty pounds, a large sum. The Continental Congress the previous October had voted that the requirement of "oppressive security from a claimant of ships and goods seized," was "subversive of American rights." But economic oppression was apparently not equated with constitutional oppression by the New York legislators. The next section of the same act, section 9, vesting in the court of vice admiralty concurrent jurisdiction with "the Courts of Common Law in causes arising within the body of a County, and thereby leaving it in the power of the prosecutor to deprive the subject of a trial by Jury," was voted a grievance. Two rights were violated by section 9, and both were constitutional rights: the right to be tried by jury and the right not to be tried by the civil law of admiralty for matters occurring on land. Also voted grievances were the Declaratory Act, the Tea Act, and the Intolerable Acts, all of which were perceived by American whigs to be constitutional matters. In addition, the General Assembly voted the statute of 14 George III, chapter 88 a grievance. That act imposed duties on certain articles imported into Quebec, effectively cutting New Yorkers off from the Indian trade.[33] It is a close question whether this grievance was more economic than constitutional. New Yorkers, going back to Dutch times, had developed the Indian trade, and it had always been a major aspect of their economy. The General Assembly may have been thinking of constitutional prescription, as well as of an earlier doctrine of imperial constitutional law requiring that the trade be open to all British subjects. If not, the vote on 14 George III was a departure from the general whig practice of separating the constitutional from the economic.

The distinction that is being noted is important because colonial whigs took it seriously. There were parliamentary statutes about which, in the words of the Continental Congress, Americans "did not complain" even though they were "grievous."[34] What were these statutes and why were they treated differently from parliamentary statutes which colonial whigs not only complained about but also resisted and eventually opposed by civil war? The grievous statutes which the whigs did not make constitutional grievances were the Navigation Act and other trade laws. The distinction between them and the statutes that were constitutional grievances was a distinction of law. There may be no other aspect of the American Revolution controversy that so starkly delineates its constitutional characteristics.

THE REGULATION DISTINCTION

There are several points to be made, points that colonial whigs constantly and consistently made. The first is that colonial whigs did not object to Parliament's authority to regulate the trade of the entire British empire. Indeed, they not only accepted parliamentary regulation, they pleaded it as the consideration for the "commercial contract."

In the controversy over Parliament's authority to tax the North American colonies, the imperial side argued an "imperial contract," contending that in return for British defense, the colonists had contracted an implied obligation to pay parliamentary taxes. The American whigs answered with the commercial contract, counterclaiming that parliamentary regulation of trade with all profits being funneled into the mother country, and not direct taxation for purposes of revenue, was the consideration paid for membership in the empire.[35] Everyone who had any part in the revolutionary constitutional controversy knew the contract's terms: "the *Taxation* of the Colonies for the ordinary purposes of supply ought to be forborn;—that Britain should be satisfied with the advantage it receives from a flourishing trade, and with the free grants of the American *Assemblies*."[36]

In 1775, when it was becoming apparent that, unless new constitutional solutions were devised, the British empire would slide into civil war, Lord North proposed that in lieu of direct, internal taxation, the colonial assemblies pay requisitions. Rejecting this scheme, the Continental Congress observed, "If we are to contribute equally with other parts of the Empire let us equally with them enjoy free commerce with the whole world."[37] The Congress was not asking for free trade. It was reminding Parliament of the commercial contract.

We must pay close attention to what colonial assemblies said about Parliament's authority to regulate trade. Their phraseology was carefully crafted, and if studied with equal care it will be seen that although whig legislators raised objections to Parliament's regulation of trade, they did not raise constitutional objections. Distinctions should be made between arguments that Parliament did not possess power to promulgate a statute and that it promulgated an economically harsh, unfair, or unworkable—yet constitutional—statute. A typical instance was South Carolina's instructions to its delegates to the Continental Congress. Conceding Parliament's jurisdiction by acknowledging that reform of the law was within parliamentary discretion, the Convention told the delegates to work for repeal of acts that "lay unnecessary restraints and burthens on trade."[38] When the colonists did object to constitutional legislation that they thought too costly, too unfair, or unreasonable, they complained about the application of policy, not about Parliament's jurisdiction.[39]

Even issues such as commercial monopoly or unequal treatment between favored and less favored dominions that could have been argued as constitutional issues were complained of on trade grounds if possible. The objection voiced was to the monopoly or the unequal treatment, not to Parliament's power to regulate trade.[40] A statement written and published by the merchants of Boston in 1769 summed up the whig constitutional position.

> The merchants do not desire liberty to import any kind of goods that are prejudicial to the manufactures of Great-Britain, nor have they ever yet complain'd of their trade being confin'd to Great-Britain for such goods as are manufactured there, so long as they might be imported duty free.
>
> What the Colonists have a right to expect and hope for, is a repeal of all acts imposing duties on any kind of goods imported into the British colonies for the purpose of raising a revenue in America, as being inconsistent with their rights as free subjects—the removal of every unnecessary burden upon trade, and that it be restor'd to the same footing it was upon before the act of the 6th of George the 2d, commonly call'd the sugar-act—particularly.

The merchants of Boston who wrote this statement were typical colonial whigs. They wanted Parliament to reform its superintendence of trade, not renounce it. They asked for fairness, reasonableness, equality, and equity, not constitutional change.[41]

There were remarkably few dissents, and because they were so unusual it is worth mentioning two as illustrative of the difficulties even extreme whigs had formulating a constitutional theory opposing Parliament's jurisdiction over the regulation of imperial trade. One was by William Hicks, a Pennsylvanian, who published a pamphlet in 1768 which received wide circulation when reprinted in several newspapers. Reacting strongly against passage of the Townshend duties, Hicks admitted,

> the *necessity* of lodging in some part of the community a *restraining power*, for the regulating and limiting the trade and manufactures of each particular country or colony, in such a manner as might most effectually promote the good of the whole; and I should not obstinately object to the vesting this power in the parliament of Great-Britain, if the violent measures which have lately been carried into execution, did not afford me too much reason to believe, that every concession which might at this time be made from a *principle of necessity*, and a regard to the public utility, would be immediately considered as an acknowledgment of such a *subordination*, as is totally inconsistent with the nature of our constitution.

In other words, Hicks would have had no difficulty with Parliament's authority to regulate if the recently enacted Townshend duties had not demonstrated that the constitutional theory upon which he believed the authority rested, the rule of "necessity," contained no certain, dependable principles limiting that authority within constitutional bounds. The difficulty posed for American constitutionalists by the competing values of imperial necessity and colonial constitutional security is illustrated by Hicks's solution to the predicament. It was that the colonies should be represented in Parliament, not a full representation, but "a representation in parliament for the purposes of commerce *only*," a representation of each colony "to explain the nature of their situation, and remonstrate against any acts of oppression." If we are inclined to think the scheme utopian, Hicks also had his doubts. Limited representation "would be attended with many inconveniences," he conceded, but considering the constitutional alternative, it was preferable to "accept such a partial, disadvantageous establishment . . . than submit to such an *unnatural state of subordination*, as must continually keep alive the spirit of contention."[42]

Consideration of Hicks's solution may help explain why few whig leaders spent time defining the limits of Parliament's authority to regulate trade. American whigs gave a disproportionate amount of attention to devising a constitutional theory of *why* Parliament possessed authority, as will be discussed in chapter 16, but very little to the mechanics of restraints until the Declaration of Independence, when, referring to legislation enacted to punish New England, they alleged that one of the causes of revolution was the "cutting off our trade with all parts of the world."[43] It is possible that the only "official" restatement of the accepted constitutional doctrine was formulated by Pennsylvania counties framing issues to be addressed at the first Continental Congress. There were two problems that had to be resolved, both pertaining to Parliament's authority: "The *assumed* parliamentary power of *internal* legislation, and the power of regulating trade, as of late exercised." On the second matter, Parliament was to be told that if Great Britain would renounce all unconstitutional power, the colonies would continue to obey constitutional authority. That would mean, the Pennsylvania instructions explained, a continuation of customary constitutional practice. "From *her* alone we shall continue to receive manufactures; to *her alone* we shall continue to carry the vast multitude of enumerated articles of commerce, the exportation of which her policy has thought fit to confine to herself. With such parts of the world only as *she* has appointed us to deal, we shall continue to deal; and such commodities only as *she* has permitted us to bring from them, we shall continue to bring."[44]

Although there is much more to be said about Parliament's jurisdiction over colonial trade, there is no need to pursue further the issue of the precedents of regulation. In the Navigation Act and other laws regulating trade, the British had good, proven, convincing precedents of Parliament's legislative authority over the colonies. American whigs said they were precedents for the opposite—not for parliamentary command, but of colonial legislative autonomy. The difference lay not in a disagreement about the meaning of the statutes or their operation, but in the theory of why they were constitutional. What set the laws of trade regulation apart from the other statutes enacted by Parliament was that all colonists, whigs as well as loyalists, conceded that the laws were constitutional. The constitutional doctrine is not complicated and has been acknowledged by many historians of the American Revolution.[45] What have not received sufficient historical attention are the more difficult problems of the theoretical justification and the functional scope of that authority in eighteenth-century constitutional law.

CHAPTER SIXTEEN

AUTHORITY TO REGULATE

"It has not been made a question, that I know of, whether the parliament hath a right to make laws for the regulation of the trade of the colonies," Samuel Adams wrote in the *Boston Gazette* at the relatively late date of January, 1772. After making that observation, Adams next answered one of the questions asked in this chapter: whether, in addition to *not questioning* parliamentary authority, colonial whigs positively *acknowledged* Parliament's authority to regulate the foreign trade of the colonies. "*Power* she undoubtedly has to enforce her acts of trade," Adams said of Parliament. Historians should heed well the identity of the person who wrote these words. The messenger is more important than the message. He has often been depicted as the most militant of whigs, an advocate for independence, not a constitutionalist willing to concede Britain its customary due. Yet on this issue of trade regulation, a potential area of contention that some scholars surmise must have been a *real* cause of the American Revolution, Adams did not make an issue of Parliament's "right to make laws for the regulation of the trade of the colonies."[1] He accepted that jurisdiction. Like all other American whigs, he said that Parliament's authority to regulate the trade of the colonies was a constitutional authority.

The unanimity of American whig acceptance of Parliament's authority to regulate trade helps make the case for saying that the Revolution was a constitutional conflict. After all, trade regulation, as Albert B. Southwick has pointed out, was a power every colonial whig knew could have "proved more onerous than a hundred Stamp Acts. This is something to remember by those who hold that the Revolution was ignited by grievances basically and principally economic, and who believe that the political theories advanced were merely so much specious rationalization designed to conceal the 'real' motivations of the struggle."[2]

There is a side issue, a myth of the American Revolution that is worth reconsidering in terms of the fact that colonial whigs said Parliament had constitutional authority to regulate their trade. It is the fantastic assumption that colonial whigs found their "legal" principles in natural law, that the British constitution was not their guide, but wanting independence they excogitated from the "laws" of nature a case to fit their needs. Surely, if the Americans had any grounds for appropriating natural law it would have been on the authority-to-trade issue. Just as if the colonial motivations had been nationalism, the strongest argument would have been natural law—that the colonies had come to age, that they were large enough, mature enough, and rich enough for independence—so, if freedom of trade had motivated them, and had they believed that natural law could be authority for constitutional innovation, they would have claimed that free trade was one of the natural "rights of mankind." After all, if any legislative program was "unnatural," it was the British Navigation Act, which not only defied economic laws but also prevented Americans from doing business with people that today would be called their natural trading partners. The natural-law claim, to be sure, was asserted late in the contest,[3] but it was drowned out by the overwhelming chorus of American acquiescence to Parliament's authority.

Just what jurisdiction did American whigs concede to Parliament's authority? The question deserves closer examination than it has received in most studies of the Revolution. A good start at finding the answer are two statements of a single colonial legislature: the New York General Assembly. The first statement was made *before* passage of the Stamp Act, the legislation that began the constitutional crisis, and the second was made after passage of the Coercive Acts, the legislation making civil war inevitable. "The Authority of the Parliament of *Great-Britain,* to model the Trade of the whole Empire, so as to subserve the Interest of her own, we are ready to recognize in the most extensive and positive Terms," the Assembly assured the House of Commons in October, 1764. "But a Freedom to drive all Kinds of Traffick in a Subordination to, and not inconsistent with, the *British* Trade; and an Exemption from all Duties in such a Course of Commerce, is humbly claimed by the Colonies, as the most essential of all the Rights to which they are intitled, as Colonists from, and connected, in the common Bond of Liberty, with the uninslaved Sons of *Great-Britain*." To be certain that they were not misunderstood, that they meant Parliament had unqualified authority over trade and the right not to be taxed by "duties" did not qualify that authority, the New York legislators formulated and adopted as policy what may have been the most comprehensive explanation of the meaning of that authority in practical terms. The details are too involved to be summarized here, but "to assign one instance, instead of many, the Colonies cannot, would not ask for a Licence to import woolen Manufactures from *France;* or to go into the most lucrative Branches of Commerce, in the least Degree incompatible with the Trade and Interest of *Great-Britain.*"[4] In other words, Britain's authority over colonial trade should serve not just the mother country's imperial and defensive interests, but her commercial interest as well.

Eleven years later, in the month before the Battle of Lexington, a time when the drums of war were beating to the eastward, the same General Assembly resolved, "that his Majesty, and the Parliament of Great Britain, have a right to regulate the trade of the colonies, and to lay duties on articles that are imported directly into this colony from any foreign country or plantation, which may interfere with the products or manufacturers of Great Britain, or any other parts of his Majesty's dominions."[5] Although it should be noted that this resolution was carelessly worded, as it referred to the "right" of Parliament at a time when it was official American whig policy to speak not of parliamentary "right" but of colonial "acquiescence," the basic constitutional doctrine stated by the New York General Assembly in 1775 was the same constitutional doctrine it had stated in 1764, before the Stamp Act crisis. This fact was emphasized twenty-two days later when the same General Assembly summed up the constitutional principles, not only as they then stood, but as American whigs claimed they had always stood, and—so they also claimed—as they hoped they would continue to stand for the future.

> [W]e acknowledge the parliament of Great-Britain [is] necessarily entitled to a supreme direction and government over the whole empire, for a wise, powerful, and lasting preservation of the great bond of union and safety among all the branches. Their authority to regulate the trade of the colonies so as to make it subservient to the interest of the mother-country, and to prevent its being injurious to the other parts of his Majesty's dominions, has ever been fully recognized; but an exemption from duties on all articles of commerce which we import from Great-Britain, Ireland, and the British plantations, or on commodities which do not interfere with their prod-

ucts or manufactures, we can justly claim; and always expect that our commerce will be charged with no other, than a necessary regard to the trade and interest of Great-Britain and her colonies evidently demands.[6]

A fact deserving close consideration is that the assemblies of the other colonies—Virginia and New Hampshire just to cite two[7]—said the same as did New York's. Little would be learned by repeating all the language that was used, but there is one word, "superintending," that is worth special notice. The drafters of petitions and resolutions in Massachusetts tended to stress Parliament's "superintending" function. "The superintending authority of his Majesty's high Court of Parliament over the whole Empire, in all cases which can consist with the fundamental rights of the constitution, was never questioned in this province, nor, . . . in any other," the House of Representatives assured Lord Camden.[8] By contrast, some of the other colonial legislators stressed the purpose, rather than the function of trade regulation. Saying that they did not wish for independence, Rhode Island's legislators explained that, "They are also sensible of the necessity of a supreme legislature over the whole empire, who, from the nature of things, must have the power of regulating the commerce of all the parts in such a manner as best to promote the general good of the whole community; and this power, they confess, is in the Parliament of Great Britain."[9]

There was one element of "this power" of Parliament that Americans watched closely to see that it was not employed for a purpose other than the regulation of trade. It has been exhaustively discussed before[10] but must be mentioned briefly here as it is vital to understanding how eighteenth-century constitutionalists formulated principles that we have since learned to call "federalism." It was the distinction between imposing customs duties for the purposes of regulating trade and for purposes of raising revenue.

American whigs never quarreled with the constitutional proposition that Parliament's authority to regulate trade included the authority to impose duties on imports or exports. Those duties, however, were constitutional only for regulating commerce, they were unconstitutional if imposed for purposes of taxation.[11] "Resolved," whigs of a Virginia county voted, "we apprehend there is a clear Distinction between Regulations of Trade and Taxation, and in no Degree admit the latter under the colourable Denomination of the former, well knowing that the Nature of Things is not alterable by the Change of Terms."[12]

Although the constitutional distinction was well understood at the time,[13] it has been occasionally misrepresented in more recent literature.

A British historian, purporting to explain the "constitutional struggle" between the colonies and London, commented that the insistence by a colonial legislature that Great Britain had no right to raise a revenue in North America "was the denial absolute of the right of the Crown to levy duties on trade."[14] This statement is simply untrue. It misrepresents both the intention of American whigs and the eighteenth-century constitutional understanding. The correct interpretation could be stated from several perspectives. It was, according to the Connecticut Assembly, a distinction between "preventing the Subject from acquiring Property" and "taking it from him, after it is legally become his own," or, as Governor George Johnstone defined it when addressing the House of Commons, the Americans "admit you have the power of limiting the means by which they may acquire property, but they deny you the power of disposing of this property, after it is so acquired."[15] The regulation-revenue distinction, Arthur Lee told British readers, was a "line . . . drawn between the superintending sovereignty of the parent state, and the constitutional liberty of her Colonies."[16]

The line was of substantive constitutional importance to American whigs, and it was surprisingly clear. Few colonial commentators, whether loyalist or whig, had any difficulty either locating it or describing precisely where it lay. "That the Parliament may make Laws for regulating the Trade of the Colonies has been granted," the Virginia legislature explained to the House of Lords. "[S]ometimes Duties have been imposed to restrain the Commerce of one part of the Empire, that was likely to prove injurious to another, and by this means the general Welfare of the whole may have been Promoted." But a tax imposed "not with the most distant view to the Interests of Commerce, but merely to raise a Revenue . . . your Memorialists conceive to be a Tax internal to all Intents and Purposes." The New York General Assembly thought the distinction so definite that it could be used by Parliament as a standard to restrain itself within constitutional bounds. "[T]he Parliament," the General Assembly told the House of Commons at a time when the Stamp Act was barely a rumor, "will charge our Commerce with no other Duties, than a necessary Regard to the particular Trade of *Great-Britain*, evidently demands; but leave it to the legislative Power of the Colony, to impose all other Burthens upon it's own People, which the publick Exigences may require." The New York lawmakers' constitutional theory could be misinterpreted if not fully quoted. There was no difference, they said, whether parliamentary impositions were "internal Taxes, or Duties paid," that is internal or external taxes if the purpose was to raise a revenue rather than regulate trade. "[W]hat avails it to any People, by which of them they are improverished?" Almost as if to stop future historians from twisting this last question into an economic argument, the General Assembly stressed that its import was constitutional. "[W]e carry all to her Hive, and consume the Returns," it explained, referring to Great Britain, "and we are content with any constitutional Regulation that inriches her, though it improvishes ourselves."[17]

THEORY OF REGULATION

Many Britons and most imperialists saw ambiguity where American whigs saw clarity. Some thought the distinction between internal legislation and legislation regulating imperial trade had been concocted by American whigs to elude the provisions of the Stamp Act.[18] In fact, the distinction had been argued as imperial constitutional law in the last decade of the seventeenth century, if not earlier. William Petyt's contention in 1690 that, "The *Parliament* of *England* cannot bind *Ireland*, as to their Lands, as they have a *Parliament* there: but they may bind them, as to Things transitory, as the shipping of Wool, or Merchandize, to the intent to carry it to another Place beyond the Sea," was, in constitutional substance, the same argument American whigs would be making eighty-five years later.[19] Even so, there were imperialists who doubted if the distinction could exist either in fact[20] or at law. "[T]o me it appears a flat and positive Contradiction to acknowledge '*the British Parliament to be* [the] *supreme legislative power over the whole British Empire*' (of which We are a Part) and in the same breath to deny the power of that very Parliament over us," Governor James Wright told the Georgia Commons House of Assembly raising the point of law. To try to govern by such a distinction, Richard Hussey added, "would make the measure of obedience so precarious and uncertain that the abolition of this right would soon be followed by that of every other," because, Earl Gower explained, "it being in vain to talk of rights which cannot be maintained but at the option of those who are to submit to their operation."[21]

The unusual attraction that the doctrine of sovereignty held for British constitutional theorists during the last half of the eighteenth century gave the imperialist argument persuasive strength. Again the fundamental notion was that there could be no gradations of authority. The colonists, of course, rejecting the full implications of the emerging sovereignty doctrine, answered the argument that if Parliament could regulate trade it also could legislate in all cases whatsoever, by denying that one authority followed from the other. The Assembly of Jamaica did so when telling the king that even though Jamaicans allowed "our fellow subjects of England, and Great Britain," to make "regulations of trade" for them, "we did not thereby confer on them a power of legislating for us."[22] The difficulty for colonial whigs was to formulate that constitutional position within the context of their opponents' jurisprudence.

The constitutional issue was delineated by John Dickinson in his response to an argument by the Barbados Committee of Correspondence. The Committee had contended that it was inconsistent to acknowledge Parliament's supremacy to regulate trade and yet deny the constitutionality of the Stamp Act. "Do you maintain, that because the parliament may legally make *some* laws to bind us, it therefore may legally make *any* laws to bind us?" Dickinson asked. "Do you assert, that where power is constitutionally vested in particular persons for certain purposes, the same obedience is due to the commands of those persons, when they exceed the limits of that power, as when they are restrained within them?"[23] The problem with answering these questions is that we know very little about what English lawyers and British political theorists in the 1760s thought about federalism. This fact may be unexpected if we recall it was a time when restraint on power was still the fundamental value defining constitutionalism. That restraint, however, was not thought of in terms of federal levels of government but of limitations on authority or of balances within the sovereign authority itself. That may be the reason why Daniel Dulany explained how Parliament could exercise some supreme power without being all powerful by drawing an analogy to the Crown rather than thinking of a division of jurisdiction between Parliament and the colonial assemblies. The king, Dulany pointed out, could secure the safety of the kingdom in emergencies by exercising absolute power, "and this Power is not specifically annexed to the Monarchy by any express Law; it necessarily results from the End and Nature of Government, but who would infer from this, that the King, in every Instance, or upon every Occasion, can, upon the Principles of the Constitution, exercise this supreme Power?"[24]

Another difficulty was that the concept of federalism had not yet been developed as a constitutional doctrine or, at best, was only vaguely understood in America during those years of controversy with Great Britain. When federalism was alluded to, it was not necessarily a federalism based on geographical jurisdictions, although John Adams came somewhat close to discovering the idea when he contended that there was "a line fairly drawn between the rights of Britain and the rights of the colonies, viz. the banks of the ocean, or low water mark." In the next sentence, however, he showed he was thinking of something quite different from federalism when he said the "line of division" he had in mind was the "line of division between common law and civil, or maritime law." The concept of federalism that was developing as part of the pre-

revolutionary controversy was also not the federalism of concurrent jurisdiction that eventually became the hallmark of American constitutionalism. It may be that the eighteenth-century notion of sovereignty got in
the way. "I agree," John Adams wrote, "that 'two supreme and independent authorities cannot exist in the same state,' any more than two supream beings in one universe. And therefore I contend, that our provincial legislatures are the only supream authorities in our colonies."[25] Legal
formalism of this sort left little opening for concurrent jurisdiction.

The concept of federalism that may have been within the contempla-
tion of American whigs, though they do not seem to have used the term
or to have thought of federalism as an apparatus of government, was a
federalism of function. Drafting Pennsylvania's instructions, Dickinson,
as he had several years earlier when replying to Barbados, used an analogy to the Crown to explain the notion. "It seems," he wrote, "as if the
power of regulation might not inaptly be compared to the prerogative of
making peace, war, treaties, or alliances whereby 'the whole Nation are
bound against their consent;' and yet the prerogative by no means implies a Supreme Legislature." Also explaining "what is to be understood
by *acts for regulating of trade*," another Philadelphian contended, "We
acknowledge the King of Great Britain for our Sovereign . . . but *cannot—must not* allow *any kind of authority in his Parliament;* and if *that*
Parliament would but attend to the true constitutional interest of the
empire, they would cease to claim it." This odd argument may have
resulted from the difficulty people had thinking in terms of federalism,
but the theory seems clear enough. From our perspective the writer did
not mean that Parliament could not be allowed "*any kind of authority.*"
He was speaking in terms of eighteenth-century concepts of sovereignty.
What he meant in today's concepts was that, should Parliament attend
only to matters within its sphere of imperial affairs, it would not claim
unconstitutional jurisdiction in colonial affairs.[26]

Among American whigs, Richard Bland seems to have come the closest
to formulating a theory for Parliament's authority to regulate trade in
terms of federalism—as federalism would later be understood. "In every
Instance, therefore, of our EXTERNAL Government, we are and must be
subject to the authority of the British Parliament, but in no others,"
Bland contended. "As all power, therefore, is excluded from the Colony
of withdrawing its Dependence from the Mother Kingdom, so is all
Power over the Colony excluded from the Mother Kingdom but such as
respects its EXTERNAL Government." On the other side of the Atlantic,
Edmund Burke may have been the member of Parliament who came
closest to theorizing the authority to regulate trade in terms of a federalism of functions. "The Parliament of Great Britain," Burke explained,

"sits at the head of her extensive empire in two capacities: one as the local legislature of this island . . . ; the other . . . is what I call her *imperial character*, in which, . . . she superintends all the several inferior legislatures, and guides and controls them all. . . . She is never to intrude into the place of the others, whilst they are equal to the common ends of their institution. But . . . her powers must be boundless." Both Bland's and Burke's solutions to the division of authority belonged to the eighteenth century and are evidence that the day of a federalist imagination was just beginning. Burke agreed with Bland that there should be divisions but approached the center from the opposite theoretical end. Where Bland vested "all power" over internal affairs in the colonial assemblies, Burke vested "boundless" power in Parliament, though he was thinking of the old constitutional boundlessness—a boundlessness restrained within bounds from which it should "never intrude." Thomas Whately had a more imperialist formulation: divide power in fact but not in theory. "Local Purposes may indeed be provided for by local Powers," Whately wrote on behalf of Grenville's administration during the Stamp Act crisis, "but general Provisions can only be made by a Council that has general Authority; that Authority [is] vested by indefeasable right in Parliament over all the subjects of *Great-Britain*, wheresoever resident in the *British* Dominions."[27]

Whately was answering a question different from the "how" of federalism. He was saying "why" Parliament had authority to regulate trade, and his answer, as an imperialist and a follower of George Grenville, was that trade regulation was one of the "cases" over which the sovereign Parliament had jurisdiction "in all cases whatsoever." Most imperialists answered the "why" the same way, even some who believed the sovereign Parliament did *not* have authority to tax the colonists without their consent or should not have the authority to legislate for the internal affairs of the colonies.[28] Although we are not accustomed to thinking of the problem in such terms, that theory was one extreme. It was rejected by all American whigs and by many legal theorists in Great Britain who still thought to some degree in terms of the old constitutional restraints. They had explanations other than sovereignty why Parliament possessed authority to regulate colonial trade. It is worth considering some of them in brief outline, not only because of the light they throw on this, one of the most pivotal issues of the American Revolution, but also because these various explanations of why Parliament possessed constitutional power to regulate colonial trade further illustrate the imprecision of eighteenth-century constitutional law.

One theory was based on the founding of the colonies and their subsequent constitutional attitudes. "These colonies were evidently founded in subservience to the commerce of Great Britain," Edmund Burke explained. "From this principle, the whole system of our laws concerning them became a system of restriction." Calling the system a hard, costly "condition" of "servitude," Burke asked why Americans had borne it for so many years. "Because," he explained, finding as might be expected his answer in custom, "men do bear the inevitable constitution of their original nature with all its infirmities. The Act of Navigation attended the colonies from their infancy, grew with their growth, and strengthened with their strength. They were confirmed in obedience to it, even more by usage than by law." *Junius Americanus* seems to have had a similar theory in mind when telling *Junius* that Parliament's authority to regulate trade "has been *long exercised, and as long acquiesced in.* Whatever then can be the full rights of the colonies, it is here that, according to the old rule of law, it may be said, *modus & conventio vincunt legem*, agreement alters right."29

A related theory located the right of regulation not in the founding of the colonies but in their constitutional connection to Great Britain. "Such an authority [to regulate trade]," John Dickinson reasoned, "is essential to the relation between a mother country and her colonies. . . . We are but parts of a *whole;* and therefore there must exist a power somewhere to preside, and preserve the connection in due order." That power had to be the "power of regulation" as it "was the only band that could have held us together." As it existed for that limited purpose, it was a limited power, "legally vested in parliament, not as a supreme legislature over the colonies, but as the supreme legislature and full representative of the parent state, and the only judge between her and her children in commercial interests."30

Surprisingly, considering that this was the eighteenth century, contractarian theories for Parliament's regulatory authority had little support. There was, of course, the all-important commercial contract, but colonial whigs thought of it as a bar to parliamentary taxation, not authority for parliamentary regulation.31 The earl of Abingdon appears to have been the theorist who took most seriously the possibility that Parliament's authority over trade depended on Great Britain's "contract" to protect the colonies. Freedom in trade, along with life, liberty, and property, he believed, was one of the four "fundamental Rights of the English Constitution." As it was inalienable, the colonists had not the constitutional right to surrender it. What they had done rather, and this act was constitutional, was exchange it for security. The mother country received regulation of trade and the colonies received British military protection. "Right for Power, Contribution for Protection," Abingdon explained, "and if Protection ceased, (or was withdrawn, as has been the

Case [he was speaking in 1780]) Contribution ceased likewise; and the Right reverted (as it has done) to its native Source."[32]

A more favored explanation for Parliament's authority to regulate colonial trade, at least until 1774, was derived from what Governor Stephen Hopkins termed "the nature of their [Parliament's] authority and the necessity of the thing." The "nature" did not refer to Parliament's inherent strength but to colonial weakness. As regulation was for "the *general good* of the *whole*," Jasper Mauduit contended, it was a function that could be performed only "by the *Legislative Authority* of the Mother-Country, even though they [*sic*] may, in their nature, appear to be local." The colonies, in terms of the empire, were certainly "local," and imperial trade regulation "cannot be done, by the *limitted Powers* of their *particular* Assemblies." Besides, as Gouverneur Morris suggested, if trade was to be regulated it had to be left to Parliament alone. "If *Great Britain*, if *Ireland*, if *America*, if all of them are to make laws of trade, there must be a collision of these different authorities, and then who is to decide the *vis major*?"[33]

The justification of natural right should not be confused with Morris's justification of necessity, even though the two were close in theory. Although actually saying the opposite from Morris, Samuel Seabury, the loyalist, seemed to be echoing Morris when he argued that "all parts of the British empire must be subject to the *British parliament*, for otherwise the trade of the *whole* cannot be regulated."[34] Necessity explained why there had to be an authority to regulate in the first place. "The inherent supremacy of the state in regulating and protecting the navigation and commerce of all her subjects," the earl of Chatham told the House of Lords, "is necessary for the mutual benefit and preservation of every part, to constitute and preserve the prosperous arrangement of the whole empire."[35] A surprising number of American whigs acknowledged the same necessity: "It being indispensably necessary for preserving the Dependence of the Colonies on their Mother Country, that all their European Trade shou[l]d be confined to her," Dickinson had assured Chatham twelve years earlier; Parliament's regulation of trade was "indissolubly connected with the Principle of Self-Preservation," New York's General Assembly told the House of Commons. Americans did not even complain that the mother country channeled the colonial trade exclusively to herself because "such a regulation . . . is natural and absolutely necessary for the security of *Great-Britain* herself," Christopher Gadsden wrote in the *South Carolina Gazette*.[36]

The justification of necessity explaining Parliament's jurisdiction over the external trade of the colonies had attractions for the British and the Americans. For the British, the strong point was that if the colonists admitted the necessity they came close to admitting there was no alternative to parliamentary regulations and that the practical benefits of regulation were worth whatever constitutional costs were incurred. For American whigs, the rule of necessity limited the power to the need for its exercise and implied that the authority was more political than constitutional. It conferred "a token of superiority, but not an absolute one," an anonymous Briton pointed out in 1775. That token, he thought, "seems happily effected by the act of navigation . . . : yet this we should observe *is not a matter of* [constitutional] *right*, but of *political necessity*."[37]

DEFINING THE AUTHORITY

The theory explaining Parliament's jurisdiction to regulate colonial trade required more precision of definition than any other issue dividing American whigs from imperialists in the 1770s. Unlike so much of eighteenth-century constitutional law, it could not be left ambiguous. After the constitutional crisis thrust the issue of Parliament's supremacy upon them, it was no longer possible for the colonists to permit the authority to be explained by changing circumstances, to suffer, as a New York pamphlet said in 1765, "the Expediency of the Measure [regulation], to prevent their examining into it's Legality." The theory of regulation just simply could not remain indeterminate as it had been before 1766. Passage of the Declaratory Act required its reformulation to take into account Parliament's claim to legislate in all cases whatsoever. "The difficulty," James Duane told his fellow delegates to the first Continental Congress, "is to establish a Principle upon which we can submit this Authority to Parliament without the Danger of a hurtful Precedent their pleading a Right *to bind us in all Cases* whatsoever." Before doubting whether the issue was of real constitutional significance, consider that had the "difficulty" been resolved and had the colonies not rebelled, the resolution of the question would have been the most important constitutional event of the eighteenth century.[38]

The caution with which colonial whigs approached the issue is indicative of how seriously it was regarded. No other resolutions were worded with more care than were legislative and congressional explanations of Parliament's constitutional authority to regulate colonial trade. Such restraint was exercised that some formulations were watered down to the point where today they seem relatively meaningless. One example may illustrate the difficulty whigs encountered. It is the solution drafted by the inhabitants of Middlesex County, Virginia, just before the first Continental Congress convened. "[W]e acknowledge a constitutional dependence on the Parliament," they noted, "conceiving it not incompatible with the condition of Colonists to submit to commercial regulations in consequence of the protection that is given to our trade by the superintendence of the mother country." The Middlesex voters undoubtedly had been puzzled how best to explain Parliament's constitutional role. They could not say Parliament had a "right," and apparently did not know how to say it had jurisdiction that was less than a right. Their solution was to ignore the problem by falling back on loose words and indeterminate expressions—"constitutional dependence," "incompatible with the condition," "submit to commercial regulations." If we were able to question the Middlesex voters, they probably could not have explained precisely what they had meant when saying that "protection" was "given" by "superintendence."[39]

The problem was one of constitutional theory, not of commercial practice. It could not be solved by saying that intraempire and foreign trade could be regulated by Parliament, but not intracolonial trade. The challenge was not to set limits on the meaning of "trade," but to set limits on the constitutionality of legislation. Needed was a jurisprudential theory explaining two rules of imperial constitutional law. First, why Parliament had jurisdiction over the regulation of colonial trade, and yet did not possess authority to tax Americans for purposes of revenue or to bind them in all other cases whatever. Second, why the statutes that Parliament had enacted to regulate the trade of the colonies were precedents only for the authority to regulate imperial trade and were not precedents for Parliament's right to pass legislation binding the colonies in matters unrelated to the regulation of trade.

There were surprisingly few answers. One, the concept of custom, was advanced by Edmund Burke and Thomas Hutchinson. Custom had the merit of being an established, easily understood constitutional principle, as Duane demonstrated when asking what imperial law would have been had there not been a century and a half of custom of parliamentary regulation of trade. "Had Great Britain till this late day taken no measures to secure the Commerce of the Colonies," he surmised, "but left them free to pursue their own Interest and Inclinations I shou[l]d not hesitate to pronounce that all Restraints by Authority of Parliament would now be unauthoritative and oppressive."[40] We should be impressed with that statement as Duane was a colonial whig who said that, due to law, Britain had the constitutional power to regulate trade, yet, even he would not rest that power on custom. Custom might tell eighteenth-century constitutionalists that the right could not be denied, but if they sought inherent limitations on that right American whigs needed further theory explaining why Parliament had authority to regulate colonial trade. Custom had been demonstrated to be a risky justification for parliamentary law when Parliament, itself, had cited duties collected as an incident of trade as precedent for the right to promulgate the Townshend duties, which had as their purpose not the regulation of trade but the raising of revenue.

We have already considered some aspects of another of the possible authorities of regulation which colonial whigs could not accept: necessity. Probably the strongest American argument that Parliament possessed jurisdiction to regulate trade due to necessity was written by John Adams. "We had considered ourselves as connected with Great-Britain, but we never thought parliament the supreme legislature over us," he explained, discussing the American constitutional understanding before the imperial crisis had begun in 1764. "We never generally supposed it to have any authority over us, but from necessity, and that necessity we thought confined to the regulation of trade, and to such matters as concern'd all the colonies together."[41] Although Adams's argument is clear, it is difficult to know what to make of it when we note that Adams published the article in which it appeared several months after he had joined a majority of delegates to the Continental Congress in rejecting necessity as the doctrine that explained the constitutionality of Parliament's authority to regulate colonial trade. Indeed, it would be fair to accuse Adams of recklessness were it not for the fact he was not drafting a congressional resolution or instructions for a town meeting. He was writing anonymously and may have felt that the risk of misunderstanding was not serious. As much as any of his fellow whigs, Adams knew that necessity was too broad a justification for Parliament's authority to regulate colonial trade. Almost any internal legislation enacted in response to an emergency or as part of a war effort could be defended as necessary and would be constitutional if necessity were the constitutional criterion. Generally, when necessity was mentioned, it was couched in reservations conceding a much more attenuated jurisdiction than Adams's words implied.[42]

The challenge for American whigs, as Adams well understood, was to explain how Parliament's authority to regulate their trade was constitutional and yet not an exception to or a violation of their right to be bound only by laws to which they had given constitutional consent. Their challenge was to devise a formula of indirect consent—not virtual consent, but an indirect consent, either expressed or implied, arising from their free, voluntary will. The voters in Virginia's York County were moving toward such a theory when they instructed that colony's delegates to the first Continental Congress to acknowledge the legality of parliamentary regulation of colonial trade, "and that this right of supremacy be deemed or expressed a resignation of our own voluntary act, flowing from a just sense of the protection we have hitherto received from *Great-Britain.*"[43] The Connecticut Assembly thought the solution should say something about "freely yielding to the British Parliament the regulation of our external commerce," a formulation that also occurred to John Adams who believed an acceptable legal principle could be traced back to the seventeenth-century practice in Virginia and Massachusetts of reenacting Parliament's statutes to give them legality in each colony. "Thus it appears," he explained, "that by the voluntary act of the colonies, their free cheerful consent, it [Parliament] should be allowed the power of regulating trade." Adams professed to think that the execution of the practice a few times by just two jurisdictions had established the "general sense of the colonies" that otherwise illegal acts of Parliament could be made constitutional by American legislative adoption.[44]

What disagreement existed was not over the need for colonial consent, but the nature and the form of that consent. For Adams, "our implied consent," proven "by long usage and uninterrupted acquiescence," was sufficient. "America," he asserted, "has all along consented, still consents, and ever will consent, that parliament being the most powerful legislature in the dominions, should regulate the trade of the dominions. This is founding the authority of parliament to regulate our trade, upon *compact* and *consent* of the colonies, not upon any principle of common or statute law, not upon any original principle of the English constitution. . . ."[45] This theory, which reflected the majority American view, made express consent unnecessary. There was a minority view that sought the additional security—perhaps as much economic security as constitutional security—of explicit, formal consent. This proposal took several forms, ranging from giving consent to each parliamentary regulatory statute—"for the Legislature of each Colony to confirm, by their own acts, all such laws of trade as are to be executed within their respective jurisdictions"—to the famous blanket consent voted by the Jamaica Assembly. The Jamaicans were both telling Parliament the limits of its jurisdiction and giving constitutional consent to the acts of trade, when they voted, "that we freely consent to the operation of such acts of the British Parliament, as are limited to the regulation of our external commerce only, and the sole object of which, is the mutual advantage of Great Britain and her colonies."[46]

The Jamaica formula was not followed elsewhere for it solved only the problem of being bound without consent. The consent that Jamaica gave was to whatever Parliament had previously done, without guaranteeing the constitutional future. After all, the limits Jamaica set were not recognized by Parliament. None of the mainland colonies followed Jamaica's lead, although a committee of Pennsylvania counties which was instructing legislators proposed a plan that would have both guaranteed the future and solved the problem of consent. The Pennsylvania instructions wanted the Continental Congress to demand that Parliament repeal all the statutes to which the colonies objected on constitutional grounds. If that were done the colonies in return should "engage their obedience to the acts of parliament, commonly called the Acts of *Navigation*, and to every other act of parliament declared to have force at this time in these colonies . . . and to confirm such statutes by acts of the several assemblies." The confirmation would have been similar to Jamaica's direct consent except that the Pennsylvanians did not contemplate adopting whatever Parliament had enacted. They were willing that Great Britain continue her monopoly of both trade and manufactures, reaping a disproportionate share of the economic profits, but they did want some "adjustments," the details of which, for our purposes, are unimportant. "[W]e are of opinion," they concluded, "that by making some few amendments, the commerce of the colonies might be settled on a firm establishment, advantageous to Great Britain and them [the colonies], requiring, and subject to, no future alterations, without mutual consent." That last stipulation—"mutual consent," meaning direct consent of colonial assemblies—was the most radical proposal made by any whig group concerning the authority of Parliament to regulate trade. Asking far more than the Continental Congress would ask, it would have drastically changed the imperial constitution by placing colonial assemblies on an equality with Parliament.[47]

John Dickinson wrote these instructions, but it is difficult to believe he could have formulated the requirement of "mutual consent." What we may have in this case is one of those rare occasions when the constitutionalists lost control to a more extremist group among the whigs. This supposition is supported by the fact that the instructions contained a second stipulation that has the appearance of having been forced on Dickinson. It was a provision asking that Americans be made "secure in our lives, liberties, properties, and an equitable share of commerce." What constituted an "equitable share" was a question that might somehow have been resolved, but there was no feasible method for the colonies to give "mutual consent" unless the British government sanctioned the constitutionality of the Continental Congress, an event constitutionally as well as politically impossible in 1774. Congress, do not forget, represented only some of Britain's many colonies. If the idea was that the assemblies would individually give consent, the mechanics would have proved difficult considering the number of Caribbean islands with legislatures and the potential number of dependencies that might be carved out of the Indian subcontinent. The task would have become impossible if each colony had a veto or if regulations favorable to the sugar colonies had to be approved by the mainland colonies.[48] It is a striking fact, seldom noted, that the constitutional demands adopted by the Continental Congress and by the whig colonial assemblies required no changes in the existing imperial constitution.

The Pennsylvania counties referred to their plan as a "compact." It has been noted that none of the serious explanations for Parliament's authority to regulate were contractarian, but it was not intended to suggest that the concept was not in the air. As we have just seen, John Adams used the same word although his *implied* contract was already in existence and would not have needed negotiation. Surely we should not be surprised that some participants in the constitutional controversy spoke in terms of contract.[49] We should expect it. Contract was the concept that probably came first to the minds of eighteenth-century constitutionalists when resolving issues of the source or extent of governmental authority. It is that conditioned way of thinking that makes the trade regulation debate unusual. It was unusual because the words "contract" and "compact" were so seldom used. The fact can be illustrated by considering one of the few times the concept was mentioned—by James Duane when he argued at the first Continental Congress that "the Regulation of Trade may be yielded to Parliament upon the footing of a Compact."[50] What is significant is that the suggestion was not followed. The Congress did not pursue the contract solution, and that it did not take the most obvious, the "easy" solution is one more indication of the importance that American whigs attached to formulating a constitutionally viable justification for Parliament's authority to regulate the trade of the colonies. The occasion on which Duane spoke is even more significant. For it was at the first Continental Congress that American whigs had to take a stand and could no longer avoid telling Parliament the measure of its jurisdiction over the regulation of trade. That it was James Duane who mentioned "compact" to the Congress is also significant as he is generally depicted by historians as one of the "conservative" members of the Congress, who, along with Joseph Galloway and John Dickinson, insisted that the Congress had to acknowledge Parliament's constitutional authority to regulate the commerce of the empire.[51] That he used the term "compact" may indicate that he thought in traditional legal concepts, but whether he or the other delegates to the first Continental Congress were "conservative" in the sense meant by twentieth-century historians is a question that bears reexamination.

To understand the constitutional issue as it was debated at the first Continental Congress, it is only necessary to consider the arguments of the three "conservative" members who are said to have wanted Congress to concede to Parliament the right of trade regulation. The constitutional theory of the majority "nonconservatives" need not be scrutinized as closely. The final resolution of the whig debate tells the story of what they wanted to accomplish.

Ironically, the most extreme of the "conservatives," the only loyalist among them, Joseph Galloway, did not think of himself as representing a conservative point of view. He professed to believe, rather, that he was in the the mainstream of colonial whig constitutional theory. Galloway claimed that middle position when telling his fellow delegates to Congress that "Every gentleman here thinks the Parliament ought to have the power over trade, because Britain protects it and us. Why then will we not declare it?" The answer, he claimed with only partial accuracy, was whig fear that Parliament "will take advantage of such declaration to tax us, and will also reason from this acknowledgement to further power over us." Galloway thought the fear groundless, stating a reason which colonial whigs appreciated: colonial acknowledgment of the jurisdiction would have constituted a contract restraining Parliament within constitutional limits. "We shall not be bound further then we acknowledge it."[52] That may have been the extreme "conservative" solution to the question why Parliament had a right to regulate trade, but if it implied that Americans would have a constitutional role in the determination of what "bound" them, it was a solution Lord North and his colleagues in the ministry would have found neither conservative nor acceptable.

Dickinson, the second "conservative," is more difficult to summarize. He wrote and spoke a great deal on the topic of Parliament's authority to regulate trade, but what he said must be interpreted with caution. We should not, for example, attribute to him the extreme whiggish views of the Pennsylvania instructions which have been extensively quoted. True, he drafted them and they are often cited as his words, but he was speaking for a constituency and what he wrote had to satisfy the majority of those voting for the instructions, not himself alone. In an essay that may have been written at the time he was working on the instructions, Dickinson described Parliament's "power of regulation" as "the only band that could have held us together; formed on one of these 'original contracts,'—which only can be a foundation of just authority." It would seem that he, along with all his fellow whigs, rejected any theory that would have located the authority to regulate trade in parliamentary sovereignty. Seeking a solution that gave Parliament its customary jurisdiction without acknowledging its sovereignty over the colonies, Dickinson explained that "power" was "legally vested in parliament, not as a supreme legislature over these colonies, but as the supreme legislature and full *representative* of the parent state, and the only judge between her and her children in commercial interests." It was a lawyer's crafted distinction that avoided the doctrines of sovereignty and necessity, and, although also avoiding precise definition, did not compromise the principle Dickinson strove to save.[53]

A year later, several months after the first Continental Congress had enunciated the colonies' final understanding on the matter, Dickinson became so apprehensive of the potential consequences the colonies might suffer from the Revolutionary War that he urged the second Congress to concede "the Power of Parliament to regulate our Intercourse with Foreigners—exclusive of every Idea of Taxation." In the notes Dickinson wrote for the speech he would deliver on the subject to Congress, he did not use the word "sovereignty" but spoke of "the Right of Regulation" and relied primarily on the "commercial contract" to define the constitutional foundation of Parliament's "right" to regulate colonial trade. "It is both just & politic to acknowledge it," he contended. It was "just" because the colonies had been settled "under the protection" of England and continued to look to Great Britain for protection. "This is the Ground America has always stood upon. Our Mother Country has not only exercised this Power without Objection from our very Infancy—but it has been expressly recognized by every Colony, the Constitution, & by the [Stamp Act] Congress of 1765." Either in his speech Dickinson gave more away to Great Britain than he did in his notes, or he was misunderstood, for his contemporaries reacted as if he had advocated Parliamentary sovereignty. A week earlier, Silas Deane had described Dickinson as "very timid," and complained that he "is for giving up intirely the Regulating of Trade, argues smoothly but Sophistically on the Subject and gives rather disgust."[54]

Dickinson had not been in Congress the previous September when the issue was resolved by the majority and there may have been resentment that he reopened a matter that Deane thought closed. Still, it seems too strong to say he was "for giving up intirely the Regulating of Trade," or to conclude, as a recent historian has, that Dickinson advocated "an unequivocal acknowledgment of Parliament's right to regulate imperial trade."[55] Dickinson wanted to acknowledge the jurisdiction. Most whigs did. It is possible that he also wanted to acknowledge the right. But it takes a very subjective reading of the available evidence to support the notion that he wanted to acknowledge a sovereign right in Parliament. If Dickinson would have drawn the line short of sovereignty, he was only by degrees more "timid" than his colleagues. His difficulty was that he sought a more middle ground for an issue of constitutional law that had no center.

James Duane, the third "conservative," participated in the decision when the Congress resolved the question why Parliament had jurisdiction over colonial trade, and he spoke at some length to the issue. "I think," John Adams quotes him as saying, "Justice requires that we should expressly ceed to Parliament the Right of regulating Trade." That statement is about as strong a concession as could be made, but we may wonder if it correctly reflects what Duane said. We have his notes for the speech he intended to give on the subject and he took the problem of regulation so seriously that he wrote and rewrote that part of the talk at least four times. He apparently did so to clarify his argument. The constitutional principle remained unchanged in the various versions. Duane made two points of law. First, he reiterated the familiar legal theory explaining how Parliament's authority was derived from contract.

> *Some* of the Colonies have been planted since the navigation Act passed in the reign of King Charles the Second which expressly asserts claims and reserves for the people of England the Commercial Advantages we have enumerated. In such Colonies therefore this Statute is part of the Law of the Land. *Others* have adopted or extended it by positive Law. All have submitted to and acquiesced in its Authority for more than a Century. By all therefore the Regulation of Trade may be yielded to Parliament upon the footing of a Compact, reasonable in itself, & essential to the well-being of the whole Empire, as a Commercial People.

Second, Duane explained the constitutional doctrine that followed from the implied contract, which, it will be noted, was implied not from parliamentary legislation but from American acceptance, either through subsequent settlement or legislative adoption. It was a theory, therefore, of parliamentary jurisdiction derived from American "acknowledgment."

> That from the Spirit of this Compact, & the Necessity of a Supreme controuling Power in this Respect, & for the Protection which we have enjoyed & still derive from Great Britain we cheerfully acknowledge that it belongs only to Parliament to direct & superintend the Trade of all his Majesty's Dominions And that this Authority exercised bona fide for the Purposes of securing the Commercial Advantages of the whole Empire to Great Britain with a Just Regard to the Interests of its respective Members ought not to be drawn into Question.[56]

It is not clear if Duane delivered this speech although it is safe to assume that he gave some version of it. A month later he again brought up in Congress the "right of regulating trade," saying, among other arguments, that, "It is agreed on all hands that there must be some supreme controlling power over our trade, and that this can only rest with Parliament." He also made a statement that greatly disturbed John Adams. "Mr. Duane has had his Heart sett upon asserting . . . the Authority of Parliament to regulate the Trade of the Colonies," Adams complained. "He is for grounding it on Compact, Acquiescence, Necessity, Protection, not merely on our Consent."[57]

The debate in Congress must have turned on some very fine legal points if Adams could draw a distinction between "compact" and "acquiescence," as Duane used those terms, and the concept of "consent." "Necessity" and "protection" were admittedly risky grounds for the colonies to concede, but in Duane's presentation they were used primarily to explain both the framing of the contract and why there had been willingness to "acknowledge" the jurisdiction.

Certainly Duane went further than other American whigs were willing to go when he undertook to reenforce his notion of "Compact" with "the Necessity of a Supreme controuling Power." And, of course, his notion that custom could be proven by showing acceptance of parliamentary statutes made Adams uneasy, even though Duane meant a colonial acceptance that was voluntary, perhaps even democratic. But his formulation of the constitutional basis for Parliament's authority to regulate trade—"we cheerfully acknowledge that it belongs only to Parliament"—does not differ substantially from the resolution adopted the next day by the Continental Congress and generally credited to John Adams. That resolution became part of Proposition Four of the Declaration of Rights of 14 October 1774. As far as American whigs were concerned, Proposition Four resolved the only outstanding constitutional question concerning the authority of Parliament to regulate imperial trade. That question had never been whether Parliament could regulate trade, but why.

> [F]rom the necessity of the case, and a regard to the mutual interests of both countries, we cheerfully consent to the operation of such acts of the British parliament, as are bona fide, restrained to the regulation of our external commerce, for the purpose of securing the commercial advantages of the whole empire to the mother country, and the commercial benefits of its respective members, excluding every idea of taxation internal or external, for raising a revenue on the subjects in America without their consent.

The main difference between this acknowledgment and those of the "conservatives" such as Duane, is that Parliament's jurisdiction was limited to "our external commerce." In the future the imperial legislature would not have jurisdiction over intercolonial or intracolonial trade, a restriction that the British must have thought a drastic constitutional innovation, but the whigs professed to believe had always been the constitutional rule.[58]

The expression that the Congress settled on to define Parliament's jurisdiction—"we cheerfully consent"—was not formulated for the occasion or new to the debate. "Cheerfully" was a familiar adverb in the constitutional vocabulary used to explain the colonies' connection with Parliament. A governor of Rhode Island had employed it as early as 1765 when explaining the duty of Americans to obey parliamentary "acts, laws, orders, and regulations" governing "general matters," and three years later another Rhode Island governor, writing on behalf of the General Assembly, assured George III that "we cheerfully and readily submit" whenever Parliament exercised constitutional authority.[59]

The word "consent" may have been chosen for its legal connotations associated with representation, taxation, and contract. A related term, one that possibly was used even more frequently to define Parliament's authority to legislate for the colonies, was "acquiesce." An address to Philadelphia merchants issued in April, 1768, said that Americans' ancestors had "tacitly acquiesced in the superintending authority of the parliament,"[60] and a month later Virginia's House of Burgesses assured other colonial legislatures that Virginians "cheerfully acquiesce in the Authority of Parliament to make laws for preserving a necessary dependence, and for regulating the trade of the Colonies."[61] "Acquiesce" seems to have been a favored word in Virginia. The Fairfax Resolves, for which George Washington voted, said that the colonies had "allways chearfully acquiesced in" parliamentary trade regulation,[62] and Virginia's instructions to the Continental Congress had pointed out that "we have long acquiesced in their Acts of Navigation."[63]

It was, of course, the principle and not the wording that mattered. The issue, remember, had not been whether Parliament possessed jurisdiction to regulate imperial trade, but the constitutional authority for that jurisdiction. Once Congress resolved the American answer there was a deep division between British constitutional law and colonial whig constitutional theory. The British said the authority, even if never exercised, was inherent. Americans whigs said it was delegated. The difference, a summary of the revolutionary controversy, was placed in constitutional context by Henry Seymour Conway's plan for peace with the colonies. Conway introduced a bill that, if enacted, would have promulgated the constitutional proposition that the colonies possessed autonomous legislative authority over their own affairs, "the Legislature of

Great Britain reserving only to itself" certain authority including "the due regulation of the trade." Conway undoubtedly thought that he was codifying colonial whig constitutional theory, but in fact he was proceeding from British constitutional premises. Under his formulation, Parliament possessed the inherent sovereignty and it, the sovereign, did the delegating, in this case "reserving" a part of its sovereignty. American whigs, knowing that what one sovereign Parliament delegated, another sovereign Parliament could reclaim, insisted that the act of delegating or of "cheerfully consenting" inherently belonged to the colonies. It was a posture the whigs had to defend, a fact explaining why so many Americans were upset when the New York General Assembly, a month before the battle of Lexington, broke ranks and spoke to Parliament directly rather than through the Continental Congress. "[W]e acknowledge the Parliament of Great Britain [is] necessarily entitled to a supreme direction and government over the whole empire," the Assembly assured the House of Commons, adding that Parliament had "authority to regulate the trade of the colonies, so as to make it subservient to the interest of the mother country." The New Yorkers, to be conciliatory, skirted dangerously close to the concept of parliamentary sovereignty.[64]

We must keep in mind that American whigs argued the fine distinction between James Duane's "cheerfully acknowledge" and John Adams's "cheerfully consent" because they wished to remain in the British empire. They could remain in the empire if Parliament regulated their trade by the authority of their cheerful consent. They could do so with only great difficulty if Parliament regulated their trade by the authority of inherent sovereignty. "Zealous on our part for an indissoluble union with the parent-state," New York's Committee of Correspondence told the mayor, alderman, and Common Council of London less than a month after the battle of Lexington, "studious to promote the glory and happiness of the empire, impressed with a just sense of the necessity of a controuling authority to regulate and harmonize the discordant commercial interests of its various parts, we chearfully submit to a regulation of commerce, by the legislature of the parent-state, excluding, in its nature, every idea of taxation." The Londoners had not needed to receive this message. They understood the constitutional issue at stake. Twenty-four days earlier they had pleaded the American constitutional cause with their king. "Subordinate in commerce, under which the colonies have always chearfully acquiesced, is, they conceive, all that this country ought in justice to require," the London officials petitioned George III, indicating that the words "cheerfully acquiesced" were as easily British constitutional words as American constitutional words.[65]

The king did not answer petitions, but even if he had he could not have answered these petitioners to their satisfaction for none of the rulers of eighteenth-century Great Britain could accept the constitutionality of rule by the chaos of colonial acquiescence in place of the stability of imperial command. But then, whatever answer he had concocted would not have mattered. Across the sea in Massachusetts Bay, the church bells of Middlesex county were summoning New England farmers to civil war. They would be fighting for their constitutional rights—the right to tax by consent and the right to be free of arbitrary government. They would not be fighting for freedom of trade.

CHAPTER SEVENTEEN

PRECEDENTS OF LEGISLATION

There was more going on than meets the eye. It does not do to dismiss the New York General Assembly as a loose cannon on the whig revolutionary deck, defying the other colonies and addressing the British directly rather than through the Continental Congress. If we look again at what the New York legislators said, we may learn something further of how much American whig thought was shaped in the common-law tradition, as well as learn something of American whig legal strategy. After reciting the colony's "principal grievances," the General Assembly, in its petition to the House of Lords, rephrased the theory of Parliament's constitutional authority of trade regulation that it previously had stated to the House of Commons.

> [W]e shall always cheerfully submit to the CONSTITUTIONAL exercise of the supreme regulating power, lodged in the King, Lords and Commons of Great Britain; and to all acts calculated for the general weal of the empire, and the due regulation of the trade and commerce thereof.
>
> We conceive this power includes a right to lay duties upon all articles imported directly into the colonies, from any foreign country or plantation, which may interfere with products or manufactur-

ers of Great Britain, or any other part of his Majesty's dominions; but that it is essential to freedom, and the undoubted rights of our constituents, that NO TAXES be imposed on them but with THEIR CONSENT, given personally or by their lawful representatives.[1]

What interests us is the tactic of legal argumentation adopted by the General Assembly. It was a tactic that American whigs, hoping to control the premises of the debate, had been employing since 1765. The procedure resembled the common-law plea in confession and avoidance, of admitting the truth of an allegation but asserting other matters calculated to avoid the legal consequences. Colonial whigs were "confessing" that Parliament possessed authority to regulate their trade but "avoiding" another constitutional authority that otherwise would have followed from the statutory precedents enacted by Parliament exercising its authority to regulate trade. It was a vital plea, because, except for the doctrine of sovereignty, there was no legal principle more damaging to the American claim of a constitutional right to legislative autonomy than the authority of statutory precedent.

As discussed in the companion volume, *The Authority to Tax*, colonial whigs were remarkably successful in separating the constitutional authority to tax from the constitutional authority to legislate. They found it much more difficult to separate constitutional authority of trade regulation from constitutional authority to legislate in all cases whatsoever. Many participants on the imperial side of the controversy paid no heed to the distinction. Their practice was to cite regulatory precedents as well as internal-legislation precedents to prove parliamentary authority to legislate in all cases whatsoever, and to cite nonregulatory as well as regulatory precedents to prove parliamentary authority to regulate trade. Sir William Blackstone, for example, claimed the military Quartering Act and the White Pine Act were statutory precedents proving Parliament's authority to tax the colonies for purposes of revenue, William Knox and Charles Mellish cited an act for the suppression of piracy to prove by statutory precedent Parliament's authority of general superintendence, and John Shebbeare used three laws—one encouraging silk manufacturing, another making debts owed to British residents provable in colonial courts on oaths taken in Great Britain, and a naturalization statute—as precedents for Parliament's jurisdiction over internal legislation. "All these are unanswerable proofs of their being and acknowledging themselves subject to the British parliament," Shebbeare concluded, referring to colonial acceptance of the constitutionality of the three statutes.[2]

The amount of time imperial propagandists invested in substantiating precedents of Parliament's jurisdiction to legislate for the colonies is simply amazing. Those actively engaged on the British side of the dispute attached much more significance to this law than would be realized by reading histories of the American Revolution written in the twentieth century. Again we find the imperial side unable or unwilling to rely on the authority of sovereignty alone. Instead of saying that Parliament was sovereign and resting their case on the Blackstonian constitution, most imperial commentators argued precedents of legislation much as if the prescriptive, precedential constitution was the only constitution. Some, even those compiling long lists of precedents, relied wholly on precedents of regulation,[3] but the more common tactic was to lump together precedents of every type, perhaps on the premise that the more precedents cited, the stronger the legal authority.[4]

It is somewhat of a puzzle just why imperialists, especially writers and speakers retained to promote the imperial government's side, depended on statutory precedents to prove what Charles Jenkinson called Great Britain's "right to regulate the internal concerns of America." At best, enacted and enforced statutes were authority under the old constitution of prescriptive, customary rights. They were much less significant, perhaps they were even irrelevant, under the constitution of sovereign command. At best, under that constitution they were evidence of law, not law's authority. It could be contended that just to discuss these precedents is to write the constitutional history of the American Revolution along colonial whig perimeters. But how do we account for the fact that imperialists, including ministerial hacks who obtained income writing political tracts on behalf of the administration, made as much of these precedents as did their opponents? There are only two plausible explanations. One is that the imperialists thought their case so strong that they might as well argue the law of the old constitution and persuade the colonial whigs that their own case was wrong. If so, it must mean they believed American whigs sincere about the constitution, and (not motivated by economics, nationalism, religious values, or any of the other suggested nonconstitutional causes that have intrigued historians) that they could be dissuaded by sound constitutional arguments. If not, then perhaps these imperialists agreed with the colonial whigs that the customary constitution—the constitution that sometimes has been depicted as an American invention—was the constitution in dispute. When reading this chapter, a good deal can be learned by just heeding how much of the precedential evidence comes from arguments defending the imperial side of the debate. There are in addition four other points worth keeping in mind. First is that by today's standards there are surprisingly few statutory precedents. That fact is true, despite Edmund Burke's famous boast that, when he entered public life, he "could not open the statute book without seeing the actual exercise of" "an unlimited legislative power over the colonies" "in all cases whatsoever." As Frederic William Maitland observed, there was little legislation in the eighteenth century. Changes in "the general rules of laws," for example were effected at common law, not by Parliament, and although the statute book was "bulky," that bulk consisted of private acts or public acts of a "petty local character."[5]

Second, we should not look for some of the "precedents" listed in twentieth-century histories of the American Revolution for many were not legal precedents. As a precedent for parliamentary supremacy over North America, for instance, Lawrence Henry Gipson cited 4 George I, chapter 11, section 5, setting rules for the indenture of minors for service in the colonies.[6] That statute, however, was limited to policing the procedures for making legal contracts in London. Its intention was to protect minors in Great Britain, not regulate indentured service in the colonies, and it is not a precedent for parliamentary supremacy beyond the realm.

Third, even stauch imperialists did not claim as precedents of legislation the general statutes of *English* law that colonial courts held applicable to local American conditions, and, therefore, in force in one or more colonies. The constitutionality of these acts in the colonies depended on colonial adoption, not parliamentary supremacy.

Fourth, because of both the whig doctrine of the legality of trade regulation and the willingness of most imperialists to argue the customary, precedential constitution, it is almost predetermined for constitutional historians to arrange statutory precedents of parliamentary supremacy into three categories: precedents of trade regulation, precedents of statutes that supported parliamentary laws of trade regulation or which to some extent were related to imperial commerce or imperial superintendence, and precedents of internal legislation that had nothing to do with trade regulation or imperial superintendence.

The distinctions between these categories of statutory precedents are clear in theory, yet there are risks to organizing the evidence in this manner. Because of the whig constitutional doctrine that trade regulatory legislation was a different kind of constitutional precedent than was legislation of internal governance, American whigs thought differently about that legislation than did imperialists. To use whig categories, therefore, runs the risk of implying that whig legal thought reflected the sounder theory of constitutional law. An example of the problem is the Revenue of Customs Act of 1763. It extended the British Hovering Act of 1718 to the colonies, vesting in customs officials authority to seize vessels of under fifty tons, found hovering off the coast, "laden with customable or prohibited goods," and unable to provide an explanation to overcome the suspicion of smuggling.[7] Just to ask how to categorize this act— whether an act regulating trade and not a precedent of legislation for internal governance as the Americans claimed, or an act policing colonial affairs as London claimed—suggests that the colonial whig distinction was constitutionally valid.

There is a second difficulty of categorization illustrated by the Revenue of Customs Act. This difficulty is caused by the demand of American whigs that the constitutional conflict over the authority to legislate be resolved by restoring the governance of the empire to what it had been before 1763. A key stipulation was the repeal of all statutes to which they objected as unconstitutional and which had been enacted after 1762. From their constitutional perspective, but decidedly not from the imperial constitutional perspective, only objectionable acts passed before 1763 were precedents of legislation. Acts passed after 1762 were constitutional grievances, not precedents for Parliament's authority to legislate. It was the American whig contention, therefore, that the Revenue of Customs Act, although a precedent for the authority to regulate trade, could not be a precedent for the authority to legislate internally, and that for purposes of the authority to legislate, it was in a different category from pre-1763 statutes such as the Sugar Act of 1733.[8] Americans had accepted the enforcement provisions of the Sugar Act and had acquiesced in its operation. The British could not make that claim concerning the Revenue of Customs Act.

A different problem of evaluation occurs when both sides cited the same statute to support opposite constitutional conclusions. As precedents proving Parliament's omnipotence over the colonies, Attorney General Charles Yorke depended on two statutes of George II for naturalizing foreign Protestants domiciled in British territory for seven years. "We have communicated naturalisation," Yorke asserted, "which the greatest writers think one of the highest acts of sovereignty," proof, he thought, that Parliament routinely legislated for the internal governance of the colonies. Governor Stephen Hopkins of Rhode Island, by contrast, cited the naturalization statutes to prove that Americans enjoyed the same civil rights as their fellow subjects resident in Great Britain and, therefore, should be free of internal parliamentary legislation. The naturalization statutes, he pointed out, provided that once naturalized, new citizens were "deemed, adjudged, and taken to be His Majesty's natural-born subjects of the kingdom of Great Britain to all intents, constructions, and purposes, as if they, and every one of them, had been or were born within the same." "No reasonable man," Hopkins concluded, "will here suppose the Parliament intended by these acts to put foreigners who had been in the colonies only seven years in a better condition than those who had been born in them or had removed from Britain thither, but only to put these foreigners on an equality with them; and to do this, they are obliged to give them all the rights of natural-born subjects of Great Britain."[9]

It was a mistake for whigs like Governor Hopkins to stress how the naturalization acts affected individual rights, William Knox answered. Think instead, he urged, of how they effected the internal governance of the colonies. As a result of the first, 13 George II, foreign-born residents, who, but for the act, would have been aliens, "have not only voted in the election of members of the several Colony assemblies, but have been elected into those assemblies and sat therein, in consequence of and by authority of this act." Surely, Knox reasoned, 13 George II had such an impact on colonial internal affairs it was precedent for Parliament's authority to bind the colonies in all cases whatsoever.[10]

A fact to consider is that even had the British agreed with American whigs that statutes of trade regulation were constitutional precedents of a different kind from statutes of internal legislation, the distinction between the two categories was not as clear as we in the twentieth century might suppose. There was no institution available to settle fine points of interpretation, such as the evolving meaning of "trade regulation," in the manner that the United States Supreme Court settles the evolving meaning of "commerce among the several States" in the "Commerce Clause" of the Constitution. It is not even clear if the whig leadership was agreed that there was a constitutional distinction between statutes regulating trade and statutes of general imperial superintendence. On a few occasions, not many, colonial whigs appeared to say that parliamentary legislation of imperial supervision, such as statutes governing the British military in the colonies, was constitutional. To the extent that any such statutes were constitutional, then, at least by American whig premises, Parliament's constitutional jurisdiction to bind the colonies would be that much broader than merely the authority to regulate trade.

Unless we adopt the American whig perspective, and agree that precedents of parliamentary statutes binding the colonies legislatively were not always precedents for the authority to legislate, it is difficult to differentiate between statutes. For those imperialists who defined law from the perspective of sovereign absolutism, every statute was a precedent—although, of course, merely an evidential precedent, and not a precedent of authority, since under the constitution of sovereign command, precedents were irrelevant as authority. But if the historian is no more willing to assume law from the British side than from the colonial side, there is no solution other than to discuss the issue of precedents as it was discussed by participants in the revolutionary controversy, even those precedents that American whigs distinguished in rather peculiar ways.[11] Particularly unusual was a body of statutes that were not directly regulation of trade but which were so closely related that they could easily be accommodated under the category of constitutional regulation of trade. These covered such activities as bounties encouraging production in the colonies of products needed in Great Britain and an act that set the value of foreign coins circulating in the colonies.[12] Less easily pegged were statutes applying to North America the law in force in Britain for the disposal of shipwrecked vessels. On the one hand they have the aspect of internal legislation, determining property rights in the colonies. On the other hand, they established uniform rules throughout the empire in a significant commercial area.[13]

A yet different category of legislation consists of those statutes which, in their main operation, were indisputably regulation but contained provisions altering internal laws of the colonies. The Act of William III, extending to revenue officers in North America the powers possessed by officers of the customs in England, directly legislated police laws for North America. Activities by customs agents that previously might have been criminal in certain colonies were, by parliamentary statute, made legal, and a seizure of suspected contraband goods that could have been a civil trespass redressable at common law was made legally privileged. "Does not this place their legislatures under the direction of the British parliament?" John Shebbeare asked of the colonies.[14] Moreover, almost any trade statute, just by providing penalties and forfeitures, made law that the colonial judiciary had to apply. If a customs informer was authorized by Parliament to bring an action in any court, not just in Vice-Admiralty, the jurisdiction of common law was changed. So too were the local rules of "probable cause" and of the relevancy of evidence.[15]

These pieces of legislation can be called statutes of quasi regulation. Their legislative purpose was regulatory, yet they intruded into the internal governance of the colonies and were as "direct" in their effect as were any parliamentary statutes intended for governance and not for trade regulation or imperial superintendence. An example was Parliament's command that, for the convenience of customs informers and to encourage people to report trade violations, colonial common-law courts were to hear admiralty matters. American whigs claimed that if the statute containing that command was a precedent, it was a precedent limited to trade regulation. Imperialists disagreed. For them it was a precedent for Parliament's jurisdiction to legislate in all cases whatsoever. William Knox described the 1696 "Act for preventing Frauds, and regulating

Abuses in the Plantation Trade" as "remarkable for the exercise of parliamentary jurisdiction in the Colonies, not only over the individuals and their effects, but over their courts of justice, and even over *their assemblies* also." Another commentator thought that that statute, along with five others enacted by Parliament, were "the fullest exercise of Sovereign Authority and Parliamentary Interposition with respect to the Plantations, that the wit or ingenuity of man could possibly devise, or the circumstances and situations of both Countries demand or require."[16] Parliament in those six statutes had commanded everything one could have expected it to command. They were, therefore, binding, uncontrovertible precedents for Parliament's authority to legislate—but were they authority to legislate in all cases whatsoever?

PRECEDENTS OF QUASI LEGISLATION

The conclusion should be clear. Individual statutes were sometimes ambivalent and therefore difficult to identify as either trade regulation or internal legislation. When enacting a law, the administration might begin with the intent of regulating imperial trade, yet, in the process of drafting the bill, a clause could be inserted that assumed the authority of Parliament to bind the colonies in all cases whatsoever. An often-cited instance occurred in a 1700 statute, 11 & 12 William III, chapter 7, entitled "An Act for the more effectual suppression of piracy." It dealt with piracy on the high seas, not just in the colonies, but there had been concern in Parliament either about colonial collusion with pirates or about colonial cooperation with imperial officials. To correct the problem, section 15 provided, "that if any of the governors in the said plantations, or any person or persons in authority there shall refuse to yield obedience to this act, such refusal is hereby declared to be a forfeiture of all and every the charters granted for the government or propriety of such plantation." These words, imperialists insisted, gave them a precedent for much more than trade regulation. "It cannot be denied, that this clause is conceived in as absolute terms of authority as is possible to be devised," it was said. "The submission the colonies paid to this law is the strongest confirmation of the high sense they had of the authority of parliament over them." The last sentence overstated the case being made. There is no evidence of colonial submission. Section 15 does not appear to have been enforced. Even so, although this section was not quite "confirmation of the high sense" the colonies had of Parliament's authority, it is striking evidence of the sense that the Parliament of 1700 had of its own authority. The problem of categorizing legislation is further illustrated by another statute regulating colonial governors. Also enacted in 1700, it was entitled "An Act to Punish Governors of Plantations in this Kingdom, for Crimes committed by them in the Plantations." This law provided that colonial governors "guilty of oppressing any of his Majesty's subjects beyond the seas, within their respective governments or commands, or [who] shall be guilty of any other crime or offense, contrary to the laws of this realm," should be liable to trial "in his Majesty's Court of *King's Bench* here in *England*." As governors were appointed by London, the legislation could be considered as a detail of imperial, not of colonial, governance, a matter, that is, of general not internal superintendence. The law was, however, internal colonial legislation in one respect. It vested in King's Bench authority to deprive colonial courts of jurisdiction not only over these "general" crimes, but also over violations of laws "in force within" a colony, that is, local colonial criminal legislation. King's Bench, therefore, could preempt jurisdiction over prosecution of an offense that was a crime only in the colony where the defendant served as governor and which was not "contrary to the Laws of this Realm," that is, not a crime by English law.[17]

Keep in mind that we are not considering the interpretation of statutes, but whether certain statutes were precedents for the authority of Parliament to bind the colonies in all cases whatsoever or precedents only for the authority of Parliament to regulate colonial trade. Legal commentators might agree on the interpretation of a law, yet disagree whether it was precedent for broad or narrow legislative powers, a point demonstrated by the Mutiny Act governing the conduct and discipline of the British Army in North America, a law that will be examined in some detail below, in relation to the statute suspending the New York General Assembly. In general, control of the military, although unrelated to trade, appears to be an activity that was readily analogized to commercial regulation as part of the superintendence of the empire. Jonathan Sewall, however, argued that the Mutiny Act was a precedent for internal legislation, because, under its provisions and despite the protests of colonial assemblies, not just troops sent over from Great Britain, but also men recruited in North America, were made subject to the British articles of war. Daniel Dulany, by contrast, argued that even this section of the Mutiny Act was not precedent for internal legislation. Pointing out that all American wars were continent-wide affairs, that troops employed in a unified service were subject to the same discipline, and that statutes passed by colonial assemblies had no effect beyond the borders of each jurisdiction, he concluded that the Mutiny Act was precedent for imperial superintendence, not for internal legislation. "[I]t was," Dulany pointed out, "indispensibly necessary that this Discipline should be established by *Act of Parliament*."[18]

Even Dulany would have had to admit that Parliament intruded into colonial internal affairs with other pieces of military legislation. One defined a crime, gave jurisdiction to local courts, and set the fine at £20 when army officers, without a warrant from a colonial justice of the peace, broke into private houses searching for deserters. The precedent was not only that the entry could have been criminal trepass under local law except for the legislation, but also that Parliament was authorizing colonial magistrates to issue warrants superseding provincial law. Colonial judicial process was also interfered with by another proviso of the same statute making volunteer military recruits immune from court actions unless criminal, or, if civil, for a debt of over £10. That meant an American sued in a colonial court for assault and battery could avoid liability, at least for a time, by joining the British regulars. Finally, the statute changed the substantive law of a colony by authorizing officers to enlist indentured servants, "any Law, custom or Usage to the contrary in any wise notwithstanding," although there were provisions for the master to protest and seek compensation.[19]

There was also legislation—at least five pieces—dealing with the navy which lay somewhere in the area of quasi regulation and had enough features to be cited as precedential authority supporting either side: by the colonial as limited precedent for American acquiescence to Parliament's authority to regulate trade, and by the imperial as precedent for the much broader authority of internal legislation. In general, these statutes had been enacted to protect trees that either could grow into masts for the king's ships or which provided the pitch and tar of naval stores. The most famous of these precedents prohibited cutting white pines on any land "not theretofore granted to any private Person" or "not growing within any Township, or the bound lines or limits thereof."[20] To protect trees needed for the Royal Navy, Parliament made it a crime for any person "to cut, fell, or destroy any Pitch, Pine Trees, or Tar Trees, not being within any Fence or actual enclosure," or to set fire "to any Woods or Forest, in which there are any Pitch, Pine Trees, or Tar Trees, prepared for the making of Pitch or Tar, without first giving notice" to the owner of the prepared trees. Any of these actions might not have been criminal but for Parliament's mandate, a fact, a commentator argued, making the Act of 3 & 4 Anne a precedent that "strongly supports the authority of parliament."[21]

There was even a more authoritative piece of legislation supporting or supplementing the naval statutes. That act, the Act of Anne, had vested

jurisdiction in colonial courts. An act of George I transferred that jurisdiction to a court of admiralty, shifted the burden of proof onto the
defendant, defined the judicial process, and set the penalty to be imposed, "any former Law, Usage or Custom to the contrary notwithstanding." All in all, the act of George I was not only a claim to broad legislative authority to reform the judicial procedures of the colonies, it was a
sweeping assertion by Parliament of discretionary right to alter constitutional practice and to do so for no other reason than to strengthen imperial rule. That was why jurisdiction was transferred from common law to
admiralty, for, as Thomas Whately said, the admiralty would be "more
proper Judges in Crown-Causes than Magistrates elected by the People."
He should have explained that the admiralty judge rendered decisions on
questions that at common law were decided by juries—and which American whigs said could not be taken away from juries without violating the
constitutional rights of colonial defendants. Some whigs also professed to
be worried about impartiality. "[I]t may happen," *Junius Americanus*
warned, "that an information laid against a man for cutting a white
pine-tree, though in fact, in his own land, will bring it to a determination before the Judge Admiral, and make him arbiter of the subject's
property of this particular description."[22] Even if the worst never occurred, any New Englander charged by the authorities with cutting proscribed pines was in trouble not because of colonial law but because
Parliament had changed the jurisdiction of both local American courts
and the imperial admiralty courts, and, to that extent, the White Pine
Acts were either precedents for internal legislation or precedents proving
only that the imperial government was responsible for the well being of
the Royal Navy.

There is a risk that this material could become repetitious. Although
every piece of evidence does not need attention, there are similar statutes
that bear close scrutiny for, although they reenforce the same historical
conclusion, their role in the revolutionary controversy has been overlooked to a degree that is not justified. The problem is not that historians
have misunderstood the importance of these statutes, but that they have
preferred to remove this evidence from the legal context in which it was
debated in the 1770s, and interpret it instead from economic, social,
religious, or nationalistic premises. An example of this reinterpretation is
provided by the 1732 "Act for the more easy Recovery of Debts in his
Majesty's Plantations and Colonies in America." Historians have discussed this statute in economic terms. Contemporaries, by contrast, were
concerned with its constitutional aspects. "The continuance of our trade
to the Colonies depends on the laws of England having authority there,"
a commentator on parliamentary supremacy in 1775 wrote of the "Re-

covery of Debts" Act. "Their operation binds the commerce of the Colonies to this country, and gives security to the property sent thither. Give up the authority of Parliament," he warned, and there would not only be "an end of your trade," but "a total loss of your property."[23]

The writer was saying that the "Recovery of Debts" Act was a precedent of trade regulation and that as a precedent it was limited to trade regulation. But the limitation is not as certain as he would have made it. Two of the law's sections contained remarkably extensive alterations of colonial civil procedure giving the statute strong claims to being a precedent for parliamentary legislation in all cases whatsoever. The preamble declared that because British merchants trading in the colonies encountered "great Difficulties" proving and recovering debts, it was necessary for Parliament to "retrieve" the "Credit formerly given by the trading Subjects of *Great Britain*" to Americans. "From this preamble alone," John Lind concluded, "the subordinate legislatures in America must have been apprised by these inconveniences, and had either refused, or at least neglected to provide an adequate remedy." There was, however, "more positive proof" than the preamble. "The bill was brought in, in consequence of repeated petitions from the merchants of England. They set forth, that by the *laws* then in force in the plantations, the British subjects had none, or at least but a precarious remedy for the recovery of their just debts." The act provided that affidavits taken in Great Britain according to specified procedures were to be received in American courts to prove debts and "allowed to be of the same force and effect, as if the person or persons making the same upon oath . . . had appeared and sworn . . . *vive voce* in open court." Again, although directly concerned with the regulation of imperial commerce, this statute was a precedent for altering the adjective law in the local courts of most of the colonies.[24]

In a second section of the same act, Parliament went even further, altering not just internal procedural practice, but colonial substantive, statutory law. The section superseded American legislation designed to protect local debtors from British creditors by shielding certain property from execution on recovery of debt. Parliament provided that

> the houses, lands, negroes, and other hereditaments and real estates, situate or being within any of the said plantations belonging to any person indebted, shall be liable to and chargeable with all just debts . . . owing by any such person to his Majesty, or any of his subjects . . . in like manner as real estates are by the law of *England* liable to the satisfaction of debts due by bond . . . and shall be subject to the like remedies, proceedings and process in any court of law or equity, in any of the said plantations.

Here was a parliamentary precedent, altering not only the jurisdiction of colonial courts, but also the process that they followed, the evidence they received, and the substantive law they applied.[25] "And what gives this act a higher air of importance, than any other," William Knox pointed out, "is, that it was passed upon the petition of the English merchants trading to the Colonies, who complained, 'that in Virginia and Jamaica, a privilege was claimed to exempt their houses, lands, and tenements, and their negroes also from being extended for debt; and the Lords of Trade represented, that the *assemblies* of those Colonies, could never be induced to divest themselves of these privileges by *any act of their own.*'" These facts, Knox concluded, made the statute just about as strong a precedent as it was possible to find. "What the Colony assemblies therefore had refused to do, parliament of its own authority did."[26]

It could be expected that the imperialist Knox would have thought the "Recovery of Debts" Act precedent for proving parliamentary legislative supremacy over the colonies. What historians might not have expected is that Daniel Dulany, a man American whigs believed their opponent and who admitted that the statute had been enacted only "after repeated requisitions [to American assemblies] to provide a remedy in the colonies in which the grievance was most sensibly felt had been disregarded," argued that it was a trade regulation precedent, nothing more. "This was, without doubt," Dulany contended, "a subject upon which the superintendence of the mother country might be justly exercised, it being relative to her trade and navigation . . . and the preservation of her superiority and the subordination of the colonies are secured, and therefore is comprehended in the distinction." Thomas Jefferson, whose legal arguments were generally more extreme than most colonial whigs, tried to distinguish the statute as unequal legislation. "American lands are made subject to the demands of British creditors," he noted, "while their [i.e., British] own lands were still continued unanswerable for their debts; from which one of these conclusions must necessarily follow, either that justice is not the same thing in America as in Britain, or else that the British parliament pay less regard to it here than there."[27]

Jefferson's equal treatment argument was irrelevant to the issue of what weight should be accorded to the "Recovery of Debts" Act as precedent for parliamentary supremacy. But the principle of equality did have an application to the act that went unnoticed during the debate over whether it was a precedent. Parliament had not limited the benefits of the act to British creditors. It had made American lands and slaves answerable for debts owed "any" of the king's subjects, implying that American creditors could have taken advantage of the act. If that was the intent—and if the law ever operated to recover debts owed by one colonist to another, a fact that is unknown but which seems most doubtful—the Act was an even stronger precedent for Parliament's legislative jurisdiction over the colonies than imperialists contended. All in all, it must be concluded that John Lind, not Dulany or Jefferson, argued the better law when he pointed out that the "Recovery of Debts" Act exercised "two of the highest acts of internal legislation. In one and the same law it alters the *nature* of evidence in their courts of common law; and it alters the nature of their estates, by treating real estates as chattels."[28]

Dulany either believed there should have been three categories of precedents—precedents of internal legislation, precedents of trade regulation, and precedents of general imperial superintendence—or that the trade regulation category should include statutes of general superintendence. One that he put into the superintendence category was the English Post Office Act of 9 Anne, a statute he thought would otherwise have been the strongest precedent London had for claiming constitutional authority to bind the colonies with legislation in all cases whatsoever. Certainly it was important for, as discussed in the companion volume *The Authority to Tax*, it was unquestionably the strongest precedent for Parliament's authority to tax the colonies for the purposes of raising revenue.[29] The Post Office Act, Dulany observed, came "the nearest to the Subject of any Regulation" binding the colonies internally than did any other statute of Parliament. It was near but not near enough. And the reason it did not come quite near enough to be a controlling precedent was that it was much nearer to the authority of imperial superintendence than to the authority to legislate. "For the same Reason that an Act of Parliament was necessary to secure the Discipline of the Provincial Troops, acting in Conjunction with the *British* Forces during the late War, the Authority of Parliament might be proper for the general Establishment of a regular Post-Office." The "Reason" was that "the Laws of each Colony, are in their Operation confined within the Limits of each," and could not enforce "a general Observance" throughout North America, something only an act of Parliament could accomplish. As a result, the Post Office Act "may be referred to the general Superintending Authority of the Mother-Country, the Power of the Provincial Legislatures being too stinted to reach it."[30]

Had the criterion been general superintendence, Dulany would have had a good case. If there was to be an imperial post office, it was not necessary but certainly preferable to control it from the center. Yet, just as strong a justification could be made on the authority to regulate trade—the imperial post office was needed for imperial commerce. The problem was that to maintain an adequate, efficient postal service, London had to do more than create an organization and set the rates of postage.[31] It had to legislate the governance of the system in ways affecting the internal affairs of the colonies.[32] For one thing, the imperial Post Office Act altered colonial criminal law by providing the death penalty for postal agents destroying or stealing from the mails.[33] It also imposed penalties on ferrymen refusing to transport letter carriers free of charge, and directed the prosecution of anyone delivering letters for a fee, including sailors and masters of common carriers, even if they did not charge a fee.[34]

There was sharp disagreement in the eighteenth century about what to make of the postal monopoly and its criminal sanctions. Even American whigs saw the precedent in different ways. Moses Mather thought the monopoly created by the Post Office Act less a precedent than did Dulany, not for reasons of the purpose of the legislation or of the legislative intent of the enacting Parliament, but for reasons of fact. The law was clear enough, he acknowledged, but the colonists had not obeyed it, and for that reason—because it had not commanded American obedience—it was not a precedent. "[I]t is well known, that this part of the act was daily violated," he said, referring to the prohibition on ordinary citizens carrying letters, "yet no person was ever prosecuted: Which shews that the post-office in America was not such, as the parliament had enacted; but such as the universal consent and practice of the people there had made it; and also, how little deference is paid to acts of parliament in America." Taking a somewhat different perspective, *Brutus* labeled the same aspect of the Post Office Act an "instance of oppression." Establishment by Parliament in the colonies of a monopoly that alone had the right to carry mail was "seizing, in effect, the private property of individuals here who had engaged in that business. By that act, all letters coming from Great Britain, or otherwise circulating through these colonies, are liable to be seized by the post-master appointed to that office, and subjected to a tax to be paid before the delivery of them." The act was, therefore, more than oppressive, and there was more to be concluded from it than Mather's example of a lack of colonial consent to parliamentary legislation. It was a precedent for Parliament's authority to legislate in all cases whatsoever. "[S]urely, my friends," *Brutus* warned his fellow Americans, "you cannot be but sensible, that if, as in this instance, the *British parliament* have a right to make a law to seize your effects, and keep them from you, until you pay a tax to redeem them, you must be in a wretched condition, whenever parliament shall think it proper to extend this authority to things which may more essentially and more immediately affect all ranks and degrees of people in these colonies."[35]

Brutus intended to explain why Americans should not obey the Post Office Act but he was really telling why the act was a precedent for binding the colonies in all cases whatsoever. Certainly his unintended argument was more persuasive than Mather's contention that Americans had consented to the act, oppressive or not. Colonial whigs may not have acknowledged that the Post Office Act was binding precedent but they knew it was as dangerous to their constitutional legislative autonomy as any other law enacted by Parliament. Long before *Brutus* made his argument, they had taken steps against the Post Office precedent. To put the imperial post office out of business, they had set up a post office of their own, which, as can be expected, they called a "constitutional" post office. They were, to be sure, primarily interested in destroying the Act of Anne as the leading precedent for internal taxation for purposes of revenue,[36] but they also had the secondary objective of depriving the British of their "dangerous usurpation . . . the boasted precedent of all the innovations with which an abandoned Administration have presumed to vex the Colonies."[37]

The creation of a new "continental" postal service meant nothing to imperial constitutional theory, despite American whig hopes it would "put an entire stop to their [British] placing any further unconstitutional burdens upon us."[38] For imperialists the post office precedent was so well established that even had Parliament, for the express purpose of quieting American apprehensions, repealed the Act of Anne, the precedent would have remained. To the extent that the Post Office Act could not be distinguished away as a precedent limited to the regulation of trade or a precedent limited to the general authority of imperial superintendence, it was a precedent for Parliament's legislative jurisdiction over the internal governance of the colonies.

There is another area of quasi-regulation legislation furnishing precedents of Parliament's authority to legislate for the internal governance of the colonies. Perhaps it was the precedent of direct legislation best known at the time: restrictions upon colonial bills of credit and upon other forms of paper money. Although these instances of legislation have enchanted historians looking for the economic causes of the American Revolution, from the perspective of constitutional history there is uncertainty how to treat them. Imperial superintendence of commercial credit and money in the colonies belongs more in a book dealing with London's executive authority to govern rather than its authority to legislate. British policy regulating paper money and civil liability for private debts was much more the result of ministerial instructions to colonial governors and of Privy Council disallowance of colonial legislation than of promulgation by Parliament.[39] It does not really matter, however, that there was little direct parliamentary legislation. One statute on point was all that was needed to make a precedent for a particular area of law, and one precedent was all that Charles Jenkinson needed to claim that, on the basis of "an Act for regulating" the "paper currency" of the colonies, "and from their submission to that, . . . they ought to submit to every act of English legislative."[40]

Jenkinson meant a statute such as the Act of 14 George II. Intended to outlaw the popular land-bank scheme of paper money in Massachusetts, 14 George II had a legislative history making it doubly relevant as a precedent supporting Parliament's supremacy over the colonies—its passage had been solicited by the minority political faction in the colony. After failing to destroy the land bank in the General Court, the fiscal conservatives of Massachusetts had appealed to Parliament to intervene, a fact that could have added weight to 14 George II as a precedent of parliamentary supremacy had imperialists thought it worth arguing. For, after all, it was evidence of Massachusetts citizens living in the colonies, not imperial officials in London, asking Parliament to override a provincial statute they disliked and to legislate directly for the colony's internal affairs. The statute also mixed aspects of internal with regulatory legislation, as it created civil causes of action and imposed penalties that could be enforced in colonial courts.[41] Everyone seems to have agreed that 14 George II was a precedent of quasi regulation enacted by Parliament to protect the commercial interests of Great Britain by curbing the monetary experiments of a colony. It was disputed, however, whether it was also a precedent of direct internal legislation.

If Jenkinson was right and a single precedent was enough, 14 George II may not have mattered. There was a better, more relevant precedent of legal-tender regulation. It was the "Act to regulate and restrain Paper Bills of Credit" in New England. Like the Act of 14 George II against the Massachusetts land bank, its legislative history has been noticed by historians, especially from the economic perspective, because it was a compromise, prohibiting future issues of legal-tender paper in the four New England colonies, but not requiring that bills then in circulation be retired before their due date. The financial evil that the act sought to correct was that colonial "bills of credit have, for many years past, been depreciating in their value, by means whereof all debts of late years have been paid and satisfied with a much less value than was contracted for," a situation causing instability in imperial trade. If one considered only that purpose, the precedential category of the act would have to be trade regulation or imperial superintendence. If, however, one considered the mechanics for executing the act, the precedential category is more clearly internal legislation. The act was a direct injunction on the New England assemblies, prohibiting them from creating "any paper bills or bills of credit" and prohibiting potential "relief" legislation by requiring that private debts, including those owed to fellow Americans, be paid "according to the terms of such loans respectively, and the true intent and meaning thereof."[42]

The act had a second bit of interesting legislative history: when first proposed in the 1730s its reception was so mixed that later it would be claimed as a precedent by constitutionalists on both sides of the American Revolution dispute. Arguing that it was a precedent for Parliament's authority to legislate internally for North America, John Lind, an administration pamphleteer, contended that Richard Partridge, the agent for at least two colonies, when opposing passage, had not raised constitutional objections. "Did he call in question the right of parliament to make this regulation?" Lind asked. "Was it on any pretended exemption from parliamentary authority that he grounded his objections to the bill? No such thing. All he ventured to do was to apply himself to the equity of parliament, by insinuating that the provisions of the bill were contrary to the privileges of the colony."[43]

Lind was off the mark. It was true that, when petitioning as agent for Pennsylvania, Partridge had raised economic and not constitutional objections to the bill restricting New England bills of credit. But when petitioning on behalf of Rhode Island, one of the New England colonies directly affected by the proposed legislation, he had raised legal considerations. The bill, he had charged, "would effect the said [Rhode Island] charter, and some of the most valuable privileges thereby granted to the inhabitants of the said colony." He was referring, of course, to the privileges of local legislation contained in the charter—"to make or repeal such laws and statutes as to them should seem meet, for the good and welfare of the said company, and for the government of their lands, and of the people that should inhabit the same"—which would have been abrogated to some degree if the bill were enacted.[44]

It is surprising that Lind missed the argument. From the imperial perspective, it could have strengthened his side of the controversy to show that in the 1740s, colonial agents had protested the constitutionality of the bill against bills of credit and, that despite these objections, Parliament had gone ahead and enacted it. Of course, from the opposite perspective, the argument could have been made that this evidence showed that, long before 1765, Americans had been on guard against the constitutional dangers of parliamentary legislation. The argument was by no means as strong in law as was a direct precedent, but for what it was worth, it strengthened the American whig case, at least to the extent of showing that that case was an established one, and not one concocted to meet the challenge of the new brand of legislation Parliament had begun to promulgate with the Stamp Act. The petition submitted to the same Parliament by Eliakim Palmer provides supporting evidence for that argument. Also directed against the bill to restrict bills of credit in New England—but on behalf of Connecticut, another New England colony—it protested even more emphatically than did Partridge the invasion of colonial legislative autonomy. The bill if enacted, Palmer warned, could be "destructive of all the rights, privileges, and powers, of government granted to the said colony by their charter." The petition then made a constitutional claim that, except for placing emphasis on the charter as a "grant" of rights, almost word for word anticipated the arguments of colonial whigs a quarter of a century later.

> [T]hat it is the inestimable privilege of this colony, confirmed by the royal charter, granted to their predecessors to be governed by laws of their own making; a privilege the present inhabitants are intituled to by their birthrights, and which their ancestors purchased at the hazard of their lives and fortunes, to the great benefit and advantage of their mother country, and of which they hope they shall never be deprived by a British legislature: and therefore praying, that as their charter has invested the governor and company of Connecticut with the full powers of government, and as they have never yet abused any of the privileges granted by their charter, and as the most valuable of them, should this bill pass into law, will be irretrievably torn from them, in violation of the security and sanction of the charter.[45]

The wording may have been more cautiously respectful than it would have been if drafted in 1775, but the constitutional principle was the same.

In April 1764, the "Act to regulate and restrain Paper Bills of Credit" received additional strength as a precedent supporting Parliament's authority to legislate in all cases whatsoever. It was expanded from restricting the law-making powers of only four New England colonies, to restricting lawmaking in all the mainland colonies. The change was promulgated by the so-called Currency Act, permitting bills then in circulation to continue as legal tender but mandating that their term not be extended. Colonies were required to retire existing bills on the expiration date previously set by local statute and were prohibited from issuing new paper in any form. The statute also acted internally on the colonies, especially Connecticut and Rhode Island where governors were elected from among the resident population, as it imposed on any governor violating its provisions a fine of £1000, dismissal from office, and lifetime exclusion from positions of public trust.[46]

Historians have disagreed about how colonial whigs reacted to the

Currency Act. Jack P. Greene and Richard M. Jellison find that all of the colonies except Delaware thought the statute "a major grievance" but do not say what type of grievance. Robert M. Weir concludes that for North Carolina the grievance was not constitutional. "Not once in the record of the eleven years between passage of the Currency Act and the downfall of royal authority," he notes, "did the colonists question Parliament's right to pass the law, but they repeatedly questioned the wisdom of its application to North Carolina." That nonconstitutional argument sums up the general colonial response. Only a few whigs like Governor Stephen Hopkins put currency matters in the category of trade regulation and said that the regulation of money was constitutional legislation.[47] Most colonial commentators avoided the issue of constitutionality, but the need for legal tender was so severe, the economic grievance so great,[48] and the petitions for relief so pronounced,[49] that for once categories became blurred and colonial objections to the wisdom of Parliament's policy could be read as questioning Parliament's authority.[50]

Because of the nature of the grievance, obedience or disobedience does not tell us as much as we would like to know about whether colonial assemblies thought the Currency Act unconstitutional or just bad or unequal economic policy. Some relevant facts that bear examination in a study of the authority of Great Britain to govern the colonies, rather than the authority of Parliament to legislate, are that several North American legislatures believed the situation desperate enough to keep old issues in circulation despite Parliament's direct unambiguous command, and that North Carolina even suspended collection of taxes that had been voted to finance the retirement of its paper money.[51] Perhaps most revealing of constitutional attitudes was the tendency of assemblies after 1765 to protest the Currency Act not to Parliament but to their governors, to the Board of Trade, and to the ministry, all as representatives of the Crown. There was an apparent reluctance to acknowledge Parliament's right of jurisdiction by addressing either house for legislative relief.[52] There was never a denial of the constitutional right of London to control the issuance of colonial paper money by the governor's veto of bills or by royal disallowance of colonial legislation.

By the fall of 1774 and the first Continental Congress, the constitutional situation had deteriorated enough for the whigs to draft comprehensive lists of grievances. The Currency Act was one of seven statutes of Parliament that the Congress voted "subversive of American rights."[53] That statement defined the official position of all the colonies except for the New York General Assembly when, in March 1775, it restated colonial grievances. The terms in which the General Assembly framed its complaint about the Currency Act are striking and deserve more attention from students of the American Revolution than they have received. "We likewise think," the New York legislators told George III, "the act prohibiting the legislature of this colony from passing any law for the emission of *paper currency*, to be a legal tender therein, is disadvantageous to the growth and commerce thereof; an abridgement of your Majesty's prerogative (in the preservation of which we are deeply interested) and a violation of our legislative rights. . . ."[54]

It is risky to evaluate how much the New York petition reflected American whig constitutional thought. As previously noted, the New York General Assembly was the only legislature to speak to London directly on matters that the Continental Congress had taken under its jurisdiction. After 1774, other assemblies simply voted concurrence with Congress and did not address Parliament on their own authority. It may be that the New York legislators expressed ideas endorsed only by themselves, but that is unlikely for their constitutional argument, especially their remarkable statement that they were "deeply interested" in the "preservation" of the king's "prerogative," was well within mainstream American whig constitutional thought. They were saying that the regulation of paper money was a matter properly within the orbit of imperial superintendence, but as part of the Crown's authority to govern rather than Parliament's authority to legislate. It was the prerogative, exercised through the governor's veto and the Privy Council's power of disallowance, that alone had constitutional right to enforce imperial policy governing legal tender. In a remonstrance to the House of Commons, the New York Assembly concluded a long complaint against the Currency Act on economic grounds by adding, "nor can we avoid remonstrating against this act, as an abridgement of the royal prerogative, and a violation of our legislative rights."[55]

The Currency Act was a grievance and following passage of the Intolerable Acts, it became a constitutional grievance, a usurpation by Parliament of authority properly belonging to the Crown. The complaint was constitutional. Economic grievances were serious but not the issue at bar. Moreover, if we take into account the general constitutional theory of American whigs and the role they assigned the Crown in the governance of the empire, the conclusion must be that the New York General Assembly more accurately expressed the American whig constitutional grievance against the Currency Act than did the Continental Congress which settled for the ambiguous complaint that the statute was "subversive of American rights."

Precedents of Internal Legislation

There is a final category of precedents of internal legislation enacted before 1763. These are the precedents directly on point, of Parliament making law for the internal governance of the colonies, the strongest precedents for establishing Parliament's constitutional right. Again it is important to draw distinctions, for not all the precedents relied on by imperialists are of equal weight, at least not by American whig constitutional premises. John Shebbeare, for example, cited the statute of 7 & 8 William III as a clear precedent for parliamentary supremacy. "The right of the supreme legislature, in the reign of William the Third," he wrote, "to inhibit the colonists the selling of their lands, but to the English subjects, without the consent of King and council, essentially affected their internal government." "Is not this act alone," Shebbeare asked, "that interferes so conspicuously in their *internal* concerns and properties, and its being unopposed by them, a demonstration of their being subject to the legislature of *Great Britain?*" In fact, the precedent is nowhere as strong as Shebbeare would have it. For one thing, it is part of a statute entitled "An Act for preventing Frauds, and regulating Abuses in the Plantation Trade," the preamble of which states that the purpose of the law is "for the better securing and regulating the Plantation Trade," evidence that the Parliament enacting 7 & 8 William III thought it was dealing with a problem of trade regulation. Moreover, the section in question is much narrower than most imperialists acknowledged. John Lind, a ministerial writer, described it as a prohibition on "the colonists from alienating their lands in favour of other than natural born subjects."[56] The act provided that "all Persons . . . claiming any Right or Propriety in any Islands or Tracts of Land upon the Continent of *America*, by Charter or Letters Patents, shall not at any Time hereafter aliene, sell or dispose of any of the said Islands, Tracts of Land or Proprieties, other than to the natural-born Subjects of *England*, *Ireland*, Dominion of *Wales*, and Town of *Berwick* upon *Tweed*, without the Licence and Consent of His Majesty." It would seem that the statute applied to grantees of proprietorships holding directly of the king, tenants-in-chief such as William Penn. It is not a surprising area of imperial concern as such property owners were quite likely to convey very large tracts of land, grants that could include privileges of local government.[57]

There was no need for imperialists to make as much as they did of 7 & 8 William III. There were other statutes, at least three others, that were stronger precedents for Parliament's authority to bind the colonies by internal legislation. One was the Hat Act of 1732 forbidding the export of beaver hats from any colony, even to a second colony or to any other destination within the empire. The legislation, enacted for the benefit of British hatters, was a blatant instance of home favoritism. The act, its preamble stated, was "for the better encouraging the making Hats in Great Britain."

> Whereas the Art and Mystery of making Hats in Great Britain hath arrived to great Perfection, and considerable Quantities of Hats manufactured in this Kingdom have heretofore been exported to his Majesty's Plantations or Colonies in America, who have been wholly supplied with Hats from Great Britain; and whereas great Quantities of Hats have of late Years been made, and the said Manufacture is daily increasing in the British Plantations in America, and is from thence exported to foreign Markets, which were heretofore supplied from Great Britain, and the Hat-makers in the said Plantations take many Apprentices for very small Terms, to the Discouragement of the said Trade, and debasing the said Manufacture: Wherefore for preventing the said ill Practices for the future, and for promoting and encouraging the Trade of making Hats in Great Britain. . . .

As the *Gentleman's Magazine* explained, "the hatters of England prevailed so far as to obtain an act in their own favour, restraining that manufacture in America, in order to oblige the Americans to send their beaver to England to be manufactured, and purchase back the hats loaded with the expense of manufacturing, and the charges of a double transportation."[58]

With the Hat Act, Parliament asserted its most complete jurisdiction over a commercial aspect of internal colonial affairs. In addition to prohibiting exportation of hats among the colonies or to any other place, the statute attempted to discourage manufacture even for the domestic trade of a single colony by making it difficult for a local hatter to do business. No colonist was permitted to manufacture "any Felt or Hat of or with any Wool or Stuff whatsoever, unless he shall have first served as an Apprentice in the Trade or Art of Felt-making during the Space of seven Years at the least." Even then, a hatter was to have at any time no more than two apprentices who could not serve terms of less than seven years.[59]

The Hat Act was admittedly harsh and was often complained of,[60] facts lending it strength as a precedent. From the imperial perspective the Hat Act may well have been the leading precedent of Parliament's jurisdiction to legislate internally for the colonies. "This act," the author of *The Supremacy of the British Legislature over the Colonies* contended, "is the more striking, as it shows that parliament exerted their authority in the internal regulations of the provinces in America; and the ready submission of the Americans to this act, notwithstanding its severity, is an acknowledgment of the right of parliament so to do."[61] Colonial whigs would have disputed the last point, but its importance to the precedent is questionable.

The second strong precedent of internal legislation was the Iron Act. It was similar to the Hat Act, giving a monopoly to British manufacturers. "[A] few Nailmakers, and still a smaller body of Steelmakers (perhaps there are not half a dozen of these in England)," Benjamin Franklin complained, "prevailed totally to forbid by an Act of Parliament the erecting of slitting mills or steel furnaces in America, that the Americans may be obliged to take all the nails for their buildings, and steel for their tools, from these artificers, under the same disadvantages."[62]

At the session of Parliament for 1736 and 1737, ironmasters and workers from several English localities had complained that American forges and slitting mills were manufacturing iron into nails, axes, and other wares "to the great decay and prejudice of the iron-trade in this kingdom."[63] "[T]hat Pig and Bar Iron made in his Majesty's Colonies may be further manufactured in this Kingdom, Be it further enacted," Parliament responded, "That . . . no mill or other engine for slitting or rolling of iron or any plateing-forge to work with a tilt hammer, or any furnace for making steel" could henceforth be erected in the colonies.[64] Again the force of the precedent was strengthened by the economic harshness and unequal favoritism of the law. "This," a "Bystander" told the *Gentleman's Magazine* of the Iron Act, "sacrificed all America to five or six persons in England, engaged in this manufacture, who are so far from being able to supply the [British] market, that considerable quantities are yearly imported from Germany."[65]

Constitutional consistency must be credited however. Enacted before 1763, the Iron Act, like the Hat Act and a third strong precedent, the Woolen Act[66] which was so closely related it does not need separate discussion, were not among the constitutional grievances that the first Continental Congress demanded be repealed. Nor were they mentioned in the Declaration of Independence. Compiling a list of six major economic statutes that he termed "wantonly oppressive," Arthur Lee cited the restrictions on iron and steel as the first and fourth, the restrictions on hatters as the third, and the restrictions on wool as the fifth. Even though economically oppressive, they were all constitutional statutes, and Lee thought them significant, not as instances of economic oppression, but as proof that Americans would obey Parliament's constitutional commands.[67]

For Lee, even these acts of unquestionable direct *internal* legislation were precedents of constitutional regulation, not precedents for Parliament's authority to bind the colonies in all cases whatsoever. For defenders of parliamentary supremacy, by contrast, all the statutes mentioning the colonies that Parliament had promulgated since at least the Restoration, were proof of Parliament's constitutional jurisdiction. "The truth is," *Benevolus* told the *London Chronicle*, "that all acts of the British legislature, expres[s]ly extended to the colonies, have ever been received there as laws, and executed in their courts, the right of parliament to make them, being never yet contested, acts to raise money upon the colonies by internal taxes only and alone excepted."[68] Massachusetts Attorney General Jonathan Sewall thought the list of precedents for binding the colonies internally so convincing that he had only to recount them to prove the case for Parliament's supremacy over all of British North America.

> [T]he trade of hatters, and the manufacture of iron, by slitting mills, has been regulated and restrained—wool prohibited from being water-born—the post-office erected—the rates of coin established—the cutting of pine trees prohibited—lands made liable to the payment of debts—the statute of wills extended to the colonies—the paper current [*sic*] restrained—indent[ur]ed servants impowered to inlist—troops raised here made subject to the articles of war—acts of assembly made void—and in divers other instances has this supreme right of parliament been exercised and acquiesced in, continually, without interruption, from the usurpation of Oliver Cromwell to the reign of George the third.

"These acts and ordinances, incontestibly prove," John Roebuck summed up, "that the legislative power, during every king's reign, and the Lords and Commons during the Interregnum, from the first granting of the charters to his present majesty's reign, have uniformly exercised a supreme authority over all the colonies." Or to put it in sarcastic terms as John Lind did when referring to Massachusetts Bay, "the power of parliament to regulate the internal rights of the colony was not only not contested, but cheerfully acquiesced in."[69]

CONCLUSION

The constitutional debate came down to British precedents against American distinctions. The Pennsylvania lawyer John Dickinson studied the very same statutes that were precedents of governance legislation to Massachusetts lawyer Jonathan Sewall and spotted no precedents. "I have looked over *every statute* relating to these colonies, from their first settlement to this time," Dickinson concluded, "and I find every one of them founded on this principle, till the *Stamp-Act* administration. *All before*, are calculated to regulate trade, and preserve or promote a mutually beneficial intercourse between the several constituent parts of the empire."[70] That was the "mainstream" American whig perspective of the legislative precedents: to neutralize as many as they could under the category of "regulation," complain of others as economic—not constitutional—grievances,[71] and distinguish those that were indisputably constitutional on some ground other than Parliament's sovereign power—at the very least, because of colonial acquiescence. True there were exceptions, most notably Thomas Jefferson, but at the Continental Congress better lawyers than Jefferson spoke for the majority of whig leaders voting on the issue.[72]

Colonial whigs, whether or not good lawyers, had to explain why Parliament had been able to create any precedents at all. Why, if statutes were unconstitutional in 1775, had their unconstitutionality not always been claimed? Why had American whigs not protested as loudly at the time of passage as they did after the revolutionary controversy erupted? Several answers were given: when the important precedents were enacted—the Navigation and Post Office Acts, to name two—the colonies had been young[73] and reluctant to quarrel with the mother country[74] over matters that were not economically worthwhile,[75] because, whether regulation or not, the statutes "were for the most part evaded."[76] "This I deny," John Adams wrote of the British claim that there were precedents for direct parliamentary legislation binding the colonies internally.

> So far otherwise, that the hatter's act was never regarded; the act to destroy the [Massachusetts] Land Bank Scheme raised a greater ferment in this province than the Stamp-Act did, which was appeased only by passing province laws directly in opposition to it. The act against slitting-mills and tilt-hammers never was executed here. As to the postage, it was so useful a regulation, so few persons paid it, and they found such a benefit by it, that little opposition was made to it: yet every man who thought about it, call'd it an usurpation.[77]

If the American whigs' argument changed, so did their perception of the future once it was realized what it would mean to spend that future under a sovereign British Parliament. "[A] party has lately arisen in England," Philadelphia merchants were warned as early as 1768, "who, under colour of the superintending authority of parliament, are labouring to erect a new sovereignty over the colonies, with a power inconsistent with liberty or freedom."[78] When James Macpherson argued that because of the many statutory precedents Parliament's authority over the colonies "is warrantable by constant usage and uninterrupted practice," the *Monthly Review* answered that that usage and practice had been measurably different from laws Parliament had enacted in the 1770s. "[T]he power formerly assumed by Parliament over the Colonies was exerted in mild, lenient, and beneficial acts; and the people of America, did not, at those early periods, think even these exertions of parliamentary authority justifiable, so long as they were unrepresented in Parliament."[79] In Virginia, Thomson Mason had previously made the same point in much stronger terms. "[I]f you submit to the laws already made," he warned Americans, "you will soon have others, equally arbitrary imposed upon you, for restraining your manufactures." He then compiled an incredible list of legislative horrors colonists could expect if Americans "submitted" to legislation that could be cited as precedents of internal legislation and, by default, conceded to Parliament jurisdiction to bind them by arbitrary command in all cases whatsoever.[80]

It was this altered perception of the future that changed the interpretation American whigs had of the constitutional past. The fact that the colonists had "not opposed the operation of these precedents" did not prove that Parliament had possessed the authority to enact them, New Yorkers were told a half year after the battle of Lexington. "[F]or the bare submission to power unconstitutionally exercised, does no wise confer right to those who thus exercise it, any more than it confers right to a robber, who by force obtains a submission from those he despoils." It is immaterial that this argument was not good law. By the time it was made the debate had moved beyond law to civil war. The final, popular, though unofficial American perception was not that, in the 1760s, the British Parliament had begun to introduce unconstitutional laws, but that British precedents of internal legislation had been unconstitutional all along.[81]

CHAPTER EIGHTEEN

LEGISLATION OF SUPREMACY

Thomson Mason summed up American whig constitutional strategy when telling his fellow colonists that one way to oppose parliamentary sovereignty was not to admit the authority of imperial laws that could become precedents for that sovereignty. On the other side of the contro versy, imperial constitutional strategy sought to enact and to enforce parliamentary statutes in support of Parliament's claim to sovereignty over the colonies. This chapter considers that legislation, which was jurisprudentially different from the precedents of legislation discussed in the previous chapter as it was enacted after repeal of the Stamp Act, when American whigs were on guard against assertions of parliamentary supremacy and the British administration was on guard against any erosion of the mother country's legislative authority.

Parliamentary imperialists passed four statutes or resolutions that were designed to strengthen Britain's claim to legislative supremacy. These four were the Act of 7 George III suspending the legislative authority of the New York General Assembly, resolutions to enforce the Act of 32 Henry VIII authorizing trials within the realm for treason committed outside the realm, the Townshend Acts which included the tea tax, and the Tea Act. Certain aspects of this legislation related to taxation and have been discussed elsewhere.[1] That discussion did not exhaust the con-

stitutional matters in dispute. Just as legislation requiring colonial billeting of British soldiers raised constitutional issues of taking American
money without the consent of the billets' owner or of the owner's representative, so statutes placing a duty on imported tea, quartering troops
in taverns, and suspending the authority of an assembly raised constitutional issues of freedom, equality, the legality of standing armies,[2] and,
most significantly, parliamentary supremacy. The point that deserves
emphasis is that these issues were not accidents. They were the deliberate
result of a carefully devised imperial legal strategy. In fact, from one
perspective, the law to suspend the New York General Assembly and the
Tea Act were potentially the most constitutionally gravid statutes enacted by Parliament during the revolutionary controversy. They were
intended to assert legislative supremacy. The New York law, Sir William
Blackstone noted with satisfaction, was designed to carry "into effect"
the "authority" of the Declaratory Act,[3] and the Tea Act, when considered as legislating Parliament's supremacy, was nothing more or less than
the Declaratory Act executed.

Had American whigs no strategy of constitutional avoidance, Parliament would not have had to enact the statute suspending the authority of
the New York General Assembly. It was because colonial whigs, avoiding
precedents of parliamentary supremacy, tried to keep the Mutiny Act
from being a precedent of internal legislation, that Parliament, to force
compliance and to obtain the precedent, suspended the New York General Assembly. American whigs, in turn, had to devise a strategy permitting both compliance with Parliament's demands and avoidance of
precedent.

The section of the Mutiny Act precipitating suspension of the New York
legislature directed colonial assemblies to supply any troops London
might station within their jurisdiction "with Sundry necessaries," as the
governor of Pennsylvania put it. All costs were "at the Expense of the
Province," the imperial government not "paying anything for the same."[4]
Besides raising the constitutional issue of billeting soldiers that had long
been controversial in the mother country as well as in the colonies,[5] this
provision of the imperial Mutiny Act legislated parliamentary supremacy and colonial legislative subordination. Indeed, it placed in constitutional jeopardy what the Massachusetts House of Representatives called
"the very Nature of a free Constitution." After all, that House was commanded by the Mutiny Act to spend specific amounts of money raised by
taxing the citizens of the colony, but given no discretion as to how the
funds were to be spent. "[I]f we are not *free* and independent Judges we
can no longer be *free* Representatives, nor our Constituents *free* subjects," the House contended. "[M]uch less can we be *free* Judges, if we

are but blindly to give as much of our own and of our Constituents Substance, as may be commanded, or thought fit to be expended, by those we know not."[6] That was the flip side of parliamentary supremacy, American legislative subordination.

Few other questions gave colonial assemblies as much difficulty. The sums involved were so small they were not worth contention, but the constitutional principle was teeming with peril. It is true that even after the Stamp Act crisis some assemblies voted the funds requisitioned by their governors, either because they had requested that British troops be sent to their jurisdiction or because they were not troubled by the constitutional implications.[7] Others, not wanting a constitutional confrontation with London, yet determined to avoid what Georgia's Commons House of Assembly called "founding a precedent,"[8] provided funds in a manner that, although meeting the requisition, did not comply with the Mutiny Act. In some cases they voted stipends for the troops instead of furnishing the specific supplies requested, even specifying precise amounts to be paid the officers and men as individuals,[9] or they provided only part of the money required,[10] or only some of the supplies, deliberately omitting items enumerated in the Mutiny Act,[11] or they did not mention the Mutiny Act or the provisions specified in the act, creating a record of supplying the troops but not—at least on the record—of complying with Parliament's command. The strategy turned on small technical points, allowing American whigs—as Parliament[12] and royal governors[13] complained—to claim that the assemblies had not, as a matter of law, obeyed the Mutiny Act.

The British administration tolerated evasions until, due to circumstances of local politics, its patience was broken by the New York General Assembly. In reply to Governor Henry Moore's request that they furnish troops passing through the colony with the items required by the Mutiny Act, New York's legislators voted funds for some of the enumerated supplies—bedding, firewood, candles, and kitchen utensils—but not for others—salt, vinegar, cider, beer.[14] The House gave the excuse that these things were not provided in some other parts of the empire,[15] but it was well understood in London that the members of the Assembly were "shewing their power to grant only what they should suppose proper,"[16] that they wanted the grant to "appear a voluntary act of their own, and not done in obedience to an act of parliament, which they thought contrary to right"[17] and a breach of the "sacred trust" they owed their constituents.[18]

Although the bill was signed by Governor Moore, he told London what had happened and it did not take much debate for the House of Commons to conclude that New York was guilty "of a direct denial of the authority of Parliament."[19] The Crown vetoed the New York bill[20] and the earl of Shelburne instructed Moore, "That as it is the indispensable duty of his subjects in America, to obey the acts of the legislature of Great Britain, the King both expects and requires a due and cheerful obedience" of the Mutiny Act.[21] When the New York legislators failed to comply, Parliament for the first time was confronted with an overt official defiance of its claim to constitutional supremacy over the colonies.

New York Suspending Act

It may be that New York's obstinacy angered members of Parliament more than any other American action prior to the Boston Tea Party. William Samuel Johnson reported to Connecticut that "all who spoke [in the Commons] being agreed (except Mr. Beckford, whom nobody would mind) that it was become absolutely necessary to do something to assert and support the sovereignty of this country and the dignity of Parliament."[22] Although the former governor of Massachusetts, Thomas Pownall, warned the House that "any resolutions ordering Assemblies to do an act would be vain and fruitless,"[23] what William Pitt called "a torrent of indignation" proved to be "irresistible."[24] Various punishments were proposed—to close New York's harbors, quarter troops in private homes, authorize the governor to draw upon the colonial treasury for military supplies, and impose a direct port duty on goods entering the province— but all schemes were overridden by Charles Townshend's plea that Great Britain not accept penalties in lieu of obedience.[25] Constitutional supremacy was at stake, not taxation or procurement. What was needed, he insisted, were "some steps . . . showing the Americans that this country would not tamely suffer her sovereignty to be wrested out of her hands." The way to get obedience, Townshend claimed, was "a law to prevent the Governor, Council or Assembly of New York from passing any Act till they had complied with the Act of Parliament," that is, to suspend the authority of the New York General Assembly until it acknowledged the supremacy of Parliament by obeying the Mutiny Act.[26]

The two houses of Parliament agreed, although it is not clear whether the statute enacted was as demanding as Townshend had wanted. It suspended the legislative authority of the New York General Assembly "until provision shall have been made by the said assembly of *New York* for furnishing his Majesty's Troops within the said province with all such necessaries as are required by the said acts of parliament."[27] These words could mean that the legislature had to vote the "necessaries" and that money granted the military sufficient to purchase the "necessaries," without directly furnishing the "necessaries," would not lift the suspension. The suspending statute, however, did not say that the General Assembly had to furnish specific monies for each item enumerated in the Mutiny Act, nor did it require, as some members thought it did, that New York's legislators either acknowledge the supremacy of Parliament or admit they were acting in obedience to the Mutiny Act.[28]

Even those thinking the Suspending Act too lenient, and there were many in London,[29] thought it significant legislation that might promulgate parliamentary supremacy throughout the empire. The House of Commons accompanied its passage with a series of resolutions accusing the New York General Assembly of "direct Disobedience of the authority of the Legislature of *Great Britain*" and restating elements of the Declaratory Act in terms of parliamentary supremacy.[30] The Mutiny Act itself was almost of no consequence. Some observers even supposed that, should New York obey the Suspending Act, "the Mutiny Act will probably be suffered to expire silently by its own limitation, and be no more revived."[31] The law was simply not worth the effort if enforcement meant yearly battles with colonial assemblies uneasy with its implications of parliamentary supremacy. Nor was New York of much significance. Legislative supremacy over all the colonies, not one province, was the issue,[32] a fact underscored by the Suspending Act itself. It was constitutionally unprecedented, even revolutionary, for Parliament to instruct a colonial governor. To direct a governor to disallow legislation or to adjourn an assembly was a traditional Crown function. It was prerogative power, not legislative power.[33] "It was not *necessary* that this suspension should be caused by an act of parliament," John Dickinson argued, pleading better law than did the drafters of the Suspending Act. "The crown might have restrained the governor of *New-York*, even from calling the assembly together, by its prerogative in the royal governments." It was a drastic departure from constitutional practice that Dickinson blamed on New York's defiance of Parliament. "This gives the suspension a consequence vastly more affecting," he wrote in his *Letters from a Farmer.* "It is a parliamentary assertion of the *supreme authority* of the *British* legislature over the colonies. . . ."[34] He meant all the colonies.

Before the Suspending Act went into operation, the New York General Assembly informed Governor Henry Moore—or so Moore reported to London—that funds would be voted to furnish the British troops stationed in the colony with the necessaries "prescribed by the Act of Parliament."[35] That, at least, was how Moore understood the message. He soon learned his mistake. The bill he received met only one of the objections that had been raised to the previous act. It "made an appropriation of such a sum as was thought necessary to furnish all the articles" enumerated in the Mutiny Act. "[N]o particular mention was made" of these articles, however, "nor of the money being raised in consequence of the Act of Parliament, there being only a bare recital of the Sum ordered to be paid into the hands of General Gage for the use of His Majesty's Troops quartered here." Moore was so chagrined that he "resolved not to pass the Bill in the Present Form." Circumstances forced him "to change my resolution," for some of the troops were preparing to leave the colony and their officers "had not received the least Provision by virtue of the Billeting [Mutiny] act and of course would have been great sufferers if they could not before their departure have been furnished with the money." The military must have put a good deal of pressure on Moore, for, disobeying his instructions, he signed the legislation and passed the constitutional controversy back to London.[36]

The British administration faced a difficult political decision. Although the General Assembly had voted all the money required by law, it had not acknowledged the supremacy of Parliament. "I do not see," George Grenville observed, "how the Conduct of the Assembly of New York in giving a sum of money to the Crown but refusing to take the least Notice of the mutiny act can be called a Submission to that Law or represented as a Discouragement to the popular opinions of America not being bound by our Laws."[37]

There was a technical problem confronting those like Grenville who wanted Parliament to reject New York's "acquiesence" and enforce the Suspending Act.[38] That act had not specifically called for "a Submission," so, technically, New York's noncompliance could be winked at and called compliance. The question was submitted by the Board of Trade to the law officers, and the attorney and solicitor generals took the road of narrow construction, considering only the Suspending Act and ignoring the terms of the Mutiny Act. As "the only Object" of the Suspending Act, they ruled, was "fully accomplished by the Supply of the Money which is admitted to be competent to the Service, The Mode of applying it, and the Specification of the Articles made no part of the Condition, the Performance of which was to restore the Legislature of the Colony to their former Activity."[39]

It is important to understand that to say the New York General Assembly avoided acknowledging supremacy, yet satisfied the Act by giving the ministry something to "wink" at, is not the same as saying that the Assembly did not vigorously oppose the Mutiny Act. The Assembly, in fact, opposed the Act and did so on the only two grounds that were constitutionally significant: by ignoring Parliament's assertion of supremacy and by not acknowledging Parliament's supremacy. A different question is why the colonial assemblies did not refuse to pay any money and use noncompliance with the Mutiny Act to protest Britain's stationing standing armies in their midst. The answer is that the grievance against a standing army involved the Crown's authority to govern, not Parliament's authority to legislate. Colonial whigs, like other British constitutionalists, treated control of the military as a prerogative not a parliamentary power. Their quarrel with the standing army was not that the Crown lacked authority to station troops in the colonies but that the Crown did not interpret the Bill of Rights as requiring consent of the local assembly for the army to be legally in a colony. The Mutiny Act, promulgated by Parliament for the support of troops after the Crown had sent them to a colony, was not a statute determining where they would be stationed and did not, in a constitutional sense, raise the issue of a standing army. Therefore, it would not have been the proper vehicle for challenging the constitutionality of sending soldiers to New York without the consent of the General Assembly.

The ministry may accurately be described as having "winked" because it was overlooking technical noncompliance. It was not overlooking noncompliance. The prescribed amount of money had been voted, complying with the Mutiny Act. It was the New York Suspending Act, not the Mutiny Act, that was complied with only technically, not complied with in spirit. It was also the New York Suspending Act, not the Mutiny Act, that had been intended to promulgate supremacy. Faced with New York's technical compliance, the administration had to make a decision. We know that the decision it made was strongly opposed, and it may have been a close decision, but that is doubtful. The ruling that New York had satisfied the Suspending Act was political, not constitutional. It was evident that New York, if pressed again, would keep coming up with technical compliances. It was politically wise, and not constitutionally risky, to drop such a potentially dangerous quarrel with a single colony when the main question in the controversy, Parliament's supremacy, was better fought on the issue of the constitutionality of the Townshend duties or the tea tax. The Townshend taxes involved all the colonies; noncompliance could not be hidden behind a technicality. All in all, the New York Suspending Act was not solid ground on which to push American whigs to civil war.

It is, however, true that many students of the American Revolution say that the controversies over quartering British troops had little to do with parliamentary supremacy, that they were economic disputes precipitated by colonial assemblies seeking imperial concessions in exchange for supplying the troops.[40] Whatever merit that contention has, the most salient fact about the dispute is that it was dominated by constitutional maneuvering—by the development of technical defenses and the strategy of avoidance. It may be that Great Britain succeeded in obtaining "necessaries" for its armed forces from most assemblies that were requisitioned, but money had not been the matter in controversy—at least, not in "constitutional" controversy. The constitutional necessity to deny London a precedent of obedience to Parliament's command was why American legislatures did not give governors precisely what was asked, or, as Dickinson noted, "in complying with the act relating to the troops, [every colony on the continent] cautiously avoided the mention of that act, lest their conduct should be attributed to its supposed obligation."[41]

As the money was paid, the constitutional maneuvering around the New York Suspending Act may be seen—as some historians have seen it—as a victory for Parliament, or, at best, a "compromise."[42] It would be difficult to prove that this was the view of people who participated in the debate. Just two years after the administration dropped the dispute, Robert Macfarlane, a London newspaper editor and an acute observer of the contemporary scene, lamented that "[t]he suspending act is no longer in force, while the resolutions of the assembly which gave birth to it, have had their full effect." Edmund Burke, New York's agent, agreed. The Suspending Act had been a failure, he told the House of Commons. "[I]nstead of producing a submission from that Assembly, on which the dignity of government was to be established, it produced resolutions in that Assembly, against both the dignity and authority of this government. The Quartering Bill, which this suspending Act was meant to enforce, was never submitted to. . . . [T]he Act of Parliament is now no longer in force, but the [New York] resolutions are, and have had their effect."[43]

The resolutions to which Macfarlane and Burke referred had been passed by the New York General Assembly a year after Governor Moore accepted the bill providing money for the "necessaries." To the extent that assembly resolutions could save constitutional rights, those resolutions sought to save the right to legislative autonomy. For the record, they also unequivocally denied both the doctrine of parliamentary supremacy and the constitutionality of the Suspending Act. In one the New York lawmakers voted

> that this colony lawfully and constitutionally has and enjoys an
> internal legislature of its own, in which the crown, and the people of
> this colony, are constitutionally represented; and that the power and
> authority of the said legislature, cannot lawfully or constitutionally
> be suspended, abridged, abrogated or annulled by any power, au-

thority or prerogative whatsoever, the prerogative of the crown or-
dinarily exercised for prorogations and dissolutions only excepted.[44]

Historians may resist the conclusion, but that resolution contains the
main legacy of the New York Suspending Act. Exactly the opposite of
what the ministry had intended, it was continual and unqualified colonial defiance of the doctrine of parliamentary supremacy. American
assemblies went right on ignoring the Mutiny Act, not only by refusing to
acknowledge obedience when they did vote funds for the troops, but by
insisting on the primacy of their own legislative prerogatives.[45] It is no
exaggeration to suggest that the chief effect of the Suspending Act in the
coming of the American Revolution was not as a precedent for Parliament's supremacy over North America, but as a constitutional grievance
"dangerous to the rights of his Majesty's subjects in this Colony," as the
New York General Assembly expressed it just a month before the battle of
Lexington.[46] The Suspending Act and the Mutiny Act, the General Assembly told George III, "were unconstitutional, and tended to destroy
that confidence which we had always reposed in the mother country."[47]

ACT OF 35 HENRY VIII

At the time that the New York controversy dominated the attention of
Parliament, the colonial secretary, the earl of Shelburne, was asking cabinet colleagues whether they should consider drafting a statute making it
high treason for Americans to disobey an act of Parliament. Offenders,
he supposed, could be tried "either *within the Colonies* or *sent over to
Great Britain.*"[48]

The thought of trying Americans for treason within the realm of England may have been in the air at the time. Two years after Shelburne
floated his idea, the two houses of Parliament, troubled by disturbances
in Massachusetts Bay over the Townshend legislation and the seizure of
John Hancock's sloop *Liberty*,[49] urged George III "to proceed in the most
speedy and effectual manner for bringing to condign punishment the
chief authors and instigators of the late disorders." They asked the king to
obtain evidence so the government could prosecute "within this realm"
offenses committed in Massachusetts "pursuant to the provisions of the
statute of the 35th year of the reign of king Henry VIII, in case your
majesty shall, upon receiving the said information, see sufficient ground
for such a proceeding."[50]

The Act of 35 Henry VIII, promulgated over two hundred years be-

fore, provided that "all . . . treasons, misprisons of treasons, or conceal-
ments of treasons" committed "out of this realm of *England*" were cognizable in England as if committed "within the same shire where they
shall be so enquired of, heard and determined."[51] A few days before
addressing the king, both houses of Parliament had voted the Act of
Henry VIII applicable to the American colonies.[52] It was a drastic assertion of legislative supremacy, for although it had not enacted a new statute, Parliament was saying that committing treason, not reporting a
known act of treason, or concealment of treason were all crimes which,
when committed in North America and competently cognizable by a
court of the colony in which they were committed, could by the authority of Parliament's supremacy, first promulgated in 1543, result in the
removal for trial to the former Kingdom of England, divesting colonial
courts and juries of jurisdiction. By resurrecting the Act of 35 Henry
VIII, Parliament asserted perhaps its strongest claim to supremacy up to
that date—except for the Declaratory Act.

There was something constitutionally unsavory about the law of 35
Henry VIII. Criminal trials were supposed to be at the venue, not thousands of miles away. Yet—and this may be surprising—precedents, since
at least Tudor times, indicated that trial away from the vicinage was
constitutional. Irishmen accused of committing treason in Ireland had
been tried in England since at least the reign of Elizabeth I.[53] More
recently Parliament had passed legislation authorizing trial in the nearest English county of murders and felonies perpetrated in parts of Wales,
and under a law enacted in the reign of George II, high treason committed in the Scottish Highlands might be tried in other Scots counties or in
England.[54] There were even exceptions to the rule of trial at the venue in
England itself. Smugglers were brought to London when it was thought
they could not be convicted by a jury in a smuggling county.[55] There
was, in fact, precedent for trying in England people accused of raising
rebellion in the colonies of Carolina and Antigua. Captain William Kidd
was only one of several colonial pirates tried at Old Bailey and, most
important of all, New Englanders had sent Governor Edmund Andros as
a prisoner to London following the Glorious Revolution.[56]

American whigs and British legalists could make a stronger factual
than constitutional case against the Act of Henry. It was certainly easier
to depict the jurisdiction as both unreasonable and oppressive than as a
violation of constitutional precedent. "[H]ow truly deplorable," North
Carolina's House of Assembly complained to the king, "must be the case
of a wretched American, who, having incurred the displeasure of any
one in power, is dragged from his native home, and his dearest domestick
connections, thrown into a prison, not to await his tryal before a Court,

Jury or Judges, from a knowledge of whom he is encouraged to hope for speedy Justice, but to exchange his imprisonment in his own country, for fetters among strangers. . . ."[57] Edmund Burke claimed that trial of an American in England for a crime committed in the colonies was tantamount to condemning a defendant unheard. "A person," he explained, "is brought hither in the dungeon of a ship's hold, thence he is vomited into a dungeon on land, loaded with irons, unfurnished with money, unsupported by friends, three thousand miles from all means of calling upon or confronting evidence, where no one local circumstance that tends to detect perjury can possibly be judged of—such a person may be executed according to form, but he can never be tried according to justice."[58] The administration answered that although transporting defendants to London for trial might be to condemn unheard, indictment in America was to acquit without trial.[59]

In point of constitutional law, American whigs, despite the precedents, could make a strong legal case against 35 Henry VIII. First, trial at the venue was a sacrosanct principle, fundamental to English common law. Second, the law of Henry had been promulgated before any of the colonies were founded and, therefore, could not have been intended to apply to them. And, third, it had been enacted during the "bloody" reign of Henry VIII, a time when, William Dowdeswell reminded the Commons, "Parliament was compliant, not perhaps through corruption, but through fear." It was, Frederick Montagu said, making a point against the Act of Henry, "the worst reign that ever disgraced our annals."[60] Each of these arguments was made in the Commons, where the motion was offered that "the Vote for sending for such Persons as may have been guilty of Treasons or Misprison of Treason upon the Act of Hen. 8 was . . . an unconstitutional Measure."[61] The motion, of course, was rejected, but had its proponents looked hard enough they could have found authority in eighteenth-century legal literature saying trial away from the venue was unconstitutional.[62] "Eminent" lawyers are reported to have argued that trials on the other side of the Atlantic would violate Magna Carta, as it could mean accusation without indictment[63]— but the country's leading lawyer, Lord Chief Justice Mansfield, had no constitutional doubts. He earlier had suggested "that the Authors of the Riots and seditious Pieces in America, should be sent for to England and tried for Treason," a quite drastic step if he meant to treat verbal opposition to parliamentary taxation as treason.[64]

Members of Parliament may have regretted they had ever learned of the law of Henry. Many people in London believed that the administration had never intended to execute the act, that the resolutions activating 35 Henry VIII had been passed *in terrorem*, partly to "make the people of Boston tremble," but mainly as "Prevention rather than Punishment, and in Order that the Subject in America might Authoritatively know the Extent of the executive Power of Great Britain."[65] If so, the imperial government paid a fearsome price for making a moot constitutional point. The American reaction was remarkable for its swiftness, its spontaneity, and its unity of constitutional sentiment. Colony after colony protested with both unrestrained anger and similar wordings,[66] asserting with almost one voice that Parliament's threat to apply the Act of 35 Henry VIII to the North American colonies was "highly derogatory of the Rights of British Subjects,"[67] or, as South Carolina put it, "oppressive and illegal, and highly derogatory of the rights of British subjects."[68] Both the Virginia and North Carolina legislatures were dissolved for protesting Parliament's vote on the law of Henry.[69] The governor of North Carolina was keenly disappointed as he had been anticipating no controversies at that session, and Lord Hillsborough lamented a turn of events so unexpected that the "Colony of North Carolina whose Conduct has hitherto been so decent & moderate, and distinguished by its respect for the supreme Legislature of the British Empire, should have been induced by the ill example of its neighbours to adopt and concur in Measures and Resolves so unbecoming and unwarrantable."[70]

Much like the New York Suspending Act, 35 Henry VIII, intended to legislate Parliament's supremacy over the colonies, had the opposite effect. If we consider the assembly and town-meeting resolutions passed in reaction, it may not exaggerate to suggest that the statute of Henry more than any other issue except for taxation and the Coercive Acts forced Americans to think about the implications of legislative sovereignty. Some of the most extreme and clearly worded statements about the right of the colonies to be legislatively autonomous of Parliament were drafted to protest the Act of Henry.[71] Compelled by the British to confront the issue of supremacy, some American legislators, with obvious reluctance, felt it necessary to claim exclusive criminal jurisdiction. The Act of 35 Henry VIII, South Carolina's Commons House of Assembly bluntly stated, could not extend to the colonies "where there is sufficient provision by the laws of the land, for the impartial trial of all such persons as are charged with" treason, misprison of treason, or concealment of treason.[72] No matter what Parliament had intended, 35 Henry VIII was universally condemned in the colonies, with most assemblies agreeing, at least by implication, with the representatives of Delaware and North Carolina that the act was both "unconstitutional and illegal."[73]

Although the Act of 35 Henry VIII contributed little substance to the constitutional debate leading to the American Revolution, it became a serious grievance helping to drive Americans to rebellion.[74] The grievance was compounded by two related assertions of supremacy that not only failed to strengthen Parliament's claims of authority but further irritated American constitutional sensibilities. The first was a statute—the Dockyards Act—providing that sabotage of naval dockyards, or royal arsenals, magazines, or ropeyards, "in any place out of this realm, may be indicted and tried . . . in any shire or county within this realm . . . as if such offence had been committed within the said shire or county." This legislation precipitated a new round of colonial protests—protests which became widely circulated restatements of rights to trial at the vicinage and of the constitutional grievance against internal parliamentary rule.[75] The second related claim to supremacy was the appointment of a royal commission to investigate the burning of the revenue ship *Gaspee* in Rhode Island. It was, in fact, the only overt step taken by London to apply the Act of 35 Henry. There was no realistic chance that anyone would be charged, arrested, and transported for trial in Great Britain. Another miscalculation by the ministry, the *Gaspee* affair only served to revive the constitutional grievance and to allow American whigs to restate their constitutional case.[76]

The evidence could be taken further. An argument can be made that the controversy over the statute of 35 Henry VIII was more than an American grievance, that it helped to condition colonial whigs to resist British authority. "Agre[e]able to the Constitution of the Colonies," the town of Boston instructed its representatives in 1770, the *Gaspee* commission should "be held in the same contempt and detestation, with a *Banditti of Slave Makers on the Coast of Africa.*" Four years later, this kind of talk had found a place in the highest circles of whig leadership. John Adams proposed to the Continental Congress that the arrest of an American by authority of either the Act of Henry or the Dockyards Act "ought to be considered, as a Declaration of War and a Commencement of Hostilities against all the Colonies and that Reprisals ought to be made in all the Colonies, and held as Hostages for the Security of the Person or Persons so arrested." Congress may not have gone quite as far as Adams suggested it go. It sanctioned both resistance and reprisal but did not mention Adams's rather odd idea about hostages. "*Resolved,* THAT the seizing or attempting to seize any person in America, in order to transport such person beyond the sea for trial of offenses, committed within the body of a county in America, being against law, will justify and ought to be met with resistance and reprisal."[77]

Congress's surprisingly bellicose resolution was so uncharacteristic of the colonial whigs in 1774, it provides a minor puzzle regarding the coming of the Revolution. From the historical perspective, the Act of Henry was not a very significant grievance, certainly not compared to the loss of trial by jury, restrictions on colonial trade, the stationing of a standing army in some seaports, or the extension of the vice-admiralty jurisdiction. Yet American whigs seem to have voiced more official objections to trial beyond the seas than to any other imperial legislation except parliamentary taxation for the purpose of revenue, and parliamentary abrogation of governmental autonomy in Massachusetts Bay. Perhaps the Act of Henry posed an issue readily understood, about which it was relatively easy to draft resolutions that would arouse political support. From what whigs said, however, they reacted so strongly to the Act of Henry and to the Dockyards Act not because they thought they would be enforced, but because the resurrection of 35 Henry VIII summed up their worst fears of parliamentary supremacy.

TOWNSHEND ACTS

The Townshend Acts are at the heart of the revolutionary controversy, yet, due to their diverse nature, discussion is always piecemeal. There were aspects of the acts that concerned Parliament's authority to tax, other aspects that related to London's authority to govern the colonies, and only a portion had to so with the topic of this book, Parliament's authority to legislate. The authority to tax has been dealt with elsewhere, and the authority to govern must be deferred to another study.[78] Here we are limited to the authority to legislate, an issue to which the Townshend Acts contributed mainly by attempting to create a precedent supporting Parliament's authority to bind the colonies with internal legislation.

We are concerned with only one of Charles Townshend's acts, a tax for the purpose of raising revenue placed on four products—glass, paper, paints, and teas—exported from Great Britain and imported into the colonies. The legislative objective was constitutional, not financial. The money was not to relieve British taxpayers—the purpose of the Stamp Act—but to secure tighter control of colonial governance by making local judicial and executive officials dependent on the Crown for their salaries.[79] Whatever money was raised, Townshend told the Commons as reported by a member who was South Carolina's agent, would enable the king "to establish salaries that might be better suited to support the dignity of the respective Officers, and . . . to be no longer dependent upon the pleasure of any Assembly."[80]

Making colonial officials dependent on the Crown could mean making them independent of the elected assemblies or could, as Governor Thomas Pownall told the Commons, "render their Assemblies useless." Pownall's words seem an exaggeration today, but they reflected what many political leaders, parliamentarians as well as colonial whigs, then were saying. The Townshend salary provision "takes away and renders useless entirely their [Americans'] Assembly," Richard Pennant, member for Liverpool, argued. "It changes in effect their constitution. It takes from them that power which we are right to look at so secured. The disposing of our own money. And at the same time it certainly affects their liberty, because liberty [and property] are so intimately connected. You cannot take away the one without taking away the other. It appears to me the principle of it to be pretty Parliamentary."[81]

More was going on than we are usually told. Parliamentary supremacy threatened the colonies with external legislation governing their internal affairs, which is certainly true, but that is only part of the story. Parliamentary supremacy also threatened to end colonial autonomy or to codify permanent colonial legislative subordination, that is, to introduce what has been called "a Stuart-like denial of legislative rights."[82] "[B]y raising a revenue for the support of the civil government, you destroy the utility of the Assemblies," Pownall told the Commons. "[I]t operates as a revocation of the rights and privileges of the legislatures of those colonies, as they have been permitted hitherto to enjoy them." John Dickinson explained what Pownall meant when he wondered to what shadows would American legislators be reduced. "The men whose deliberations heretofore had an influence on every matter relating to the *liberty* and *happiness* of themselves and their constituents," he pointed out, "will *now* find their deliberations of no more consequence, than those of *constables*. They may *perhaps* be allowed to make laws *for the yoking of hogs*, or *the pounding of stray cattle*. Their influence will hardly be permitted to extend *so high*, as the *keeping roads in repair*, as *that business* may more properly be executed by those who receive the public cash."[83]

As a matter of eighteenth-century constitutionalism,[84] parliamentary supremacy was not the only issue raised by the salary provision of the Townshend Acts. There was also the rule of law, especially rule by customary constitutional law. When Parliament enacted duties with the intent to pay the salaries of certain officials, it was knowingly voting that sovereign power could disregard 150 years of constitutional custom, colonial legislative privilege, and traditional civil rights; in effect, it was discarding the rule of law. That was what the voters of New Shoreham, Rhode Island, meant when they asserted that "the express purpose" of Townshend was "to introduce arbitrary government and slavery," and what the Connecticut Assembly meant when it charged that the "manner in and by which" the Act had been "made most undeniably deprives the Colonists of their essential rights as Englishmen, [and] may strip them of all that is good and valuable in life." The reason, the Assembly explained, was that if the Townshend Acts were constitutional, the "power that makes laws for us, the power that takes our property from us, that rules us, that judges us, that defends us, is entirely independent on us for appointment. . . . Bare, naked power is an awful thing, and very unamiable to a people that have been used to be free."[85]

Due to concerted, organized, and effective American opposition both to the Townshend Acts and to their execution, British imperialists were unable to give due weight to the colonial whig fear for the rule of law. Colonial opposition seemed so overt and menacing it diverted attention to the single issue of parliamentary supremacy. The earl of Hillsborough made that point when telling the Lords, one colonial agent reported, that the issue at bar was legislative sovereignty:

> that Parliament must now give up its authority over the Colonies, or they be brought to effectual submission to its laws; that he thought their Lordships would see it absolutely necessary to stand firm, and not recede an ace; that for his part he could not entertain a thought of repealing the late [Townshend] acts, and hoped nobody would even move it, or so much as wish for it; that it was not the amount of the duties . . . that was complained of, but the principle upon which the laws were founded, the supremacy and legislative authority of Parliament, — a principle essential to the existence of the empire.[86]

It had happened before and it would again. The administration's own constitutional maneuverings now forced its hand and severely limited its choices. It had enacted the Townshend laws in part as legislation of supremacy, to assert, defend, and execute Parliament's claim to sovereignty over the North American colonies. Lord Hillsborough, the cabinet officer responsible for the colonies, might, as he said, wish Townshend had never been enacted, but once American whigs resisted, not on economic grounds such as costs, but on the constitutional grounds that Parliament did not possess authority to tax them for purposes of revenue and did not possess authority to use that revenue to support colonial officials, the administration found itself in a legal trap. After the constitutional nature of the resistance was appreciated in London, the secretary-at-war reported to the governor of Massachusetts that the cabinet had unanimously concluded "not to repeal Mr. Townshend's Acts till the Colonies have submitted thoroughly to them." Four months later, when Governor Pownall moved repeal, the ministry was united in opposition.

They argued, Connecticut's agent wrote his governor, summing up the debate in Parliament,

> that it was in vain to think of retaining any connection with the Colonies but upon the sure ground of their clear subordination to Parliament, and submission to its laws; . . . they thought it absolutely necessary to assert and maintain their supremacy over them; that that supremacy was denied, and their authority disputed, and while this was the case, it was not, in their opinion, a time to make concessions to them; . . . that to submit to them was to give up Parliament and all its authority into the hands of the Americans.[87]

The constitutional doctrine guiding the ministry could be called "unpurposed precedent," "bastard precedent," or "surreptitious precedent." It was the legal principle—or supposition—that repeal of legislation to quiet constitutional objections against the legislation was, in constitutional effect, an adoption of those objections; that is, to have repealed the Stamp Act in 1766 without qualifying repeal with the Declaratory Act would have provided American whigs with a surreptitious precedent of Parliament admitting that it was unconstitutional to tax the colonies for purposes of revenue. By the same principle, outright repeal of the Townshend duties, without some qualification, such as claiming they were "anti-commercial" or retaining one duty as a token of supremacy, could have become a precedent supporting the constitutional pretensions of American whigs to internal legislative autonomy.[88]

The dynamics of constitutional advocacy did more than put British imperialists into a legal bind. The dynamics narrowed the forensic argument by thrusting the issue of parliamentary supremacy more and more to the front until it became the single point in dispute. It was at this stage of the controversy, when the ministry was seeking a way to escape the Townshend predicament, that the vocabulary of "the right" first crept into the debate, introducing a phraseology that by 1775 would, by narrowing the constitutional argument to a mere legalism, make political compromise more difficult.[89]

The ministry was largely responsible for narrowing the vocabulary when it adopted the strategy of legislating supremacy. "The substance of the whole [Townshend] Act," Edmund Burke would remind the Commons, "was to draw the recognition of America of our right."[90] If that was not the "substance" or intent of the act at the time of passage, it was soon adopted by the administration. Once the grounds of colonial opposition became apparent, Lord Hillsborough cautioned Connecticut's agent to rely on different principles. "Had they petitioned on the ground of inexpediency only," he said of Connecticut's Assembly, "they would have succeeded; but while you call in question the right, we cannot hear you."[91] About two months later, Hillsborough met with all the agents, telling them that the way to get repeal was to drop "the point of right,"[92] "that if they would *waive* the point of right, and petition for a repeal of the duties as *burdensome and grievous*, Administration were disposed to come into it."[93] A few days afterward, Hillsborough explained to the Lords that the Declaratory Act should "have established the right," but that the colonies "had gone on ever since to deny the right, and to call in question the authority of Parliament upon every occasion."[94] In response the agents employed the same vocabulary, telling Hillsborough that "they could not leave out the point of right, consistent with their present instructions."[95]

Over the next three months the agents held several consultations debating what course to adopt. The ministry, William Samuel Johnson reported, encouraged them to think "that, if they are *very quiet* and *quite silent upon the right*, and will *humbly ask it as a favor, perhaps* the offensive acts shall be repealed *next winter.*" This suggestion was apparently enough for some agents to consider petitioning on "the ground of inexpediency only," omitting any mention of "the right." The majority, however, fearful that the American side would create a surreptitious precedent supporting parliamentary supremacy, vetoed the suggestion. "[I]t was objected," one agent explained, "that silence upon so essential a point might perhaps be construed a consent to waive, at least, if not to give up, the right, and would be dangerous; that all the petitions, remonstrances, &c. from America, having uniformly denied the right, it was not fit for the Agents to take upon themselves to waive it, nor ought they to be even silent upon it." Also, there was concern that failure to mention the right might "be made use of by Administration as a ground of declaration that the Colonies had, by their Agents, in effect receded from their claim of exemption from Parliamentary taxation as of right."[96]

The constitutional controversy over supremacy was in danger of becoming mired in the concept of right. There were only two solutions: one side could surrender the right, or one side could back away from conflict, saving its claim to right by avoiding a surreptitious precedent.

TEA TAX

Exercising constitutional caution, the ministry broke the impasse. Just as American whigs had refused to give Parliament the precedent it wanted of obedience to the Townshend legislation, Parliament refused to give the whigs the precedent they wanted, repeal of the Townshend duties. When the motion was made in the Commons to repeal all the duties, the debate turned almost exclusively on the issue of parliamentary supremacy.[97] For many members of Parliament, perhaps even for most, revenue had become at best a secondary consideration.

The idea is difficult to accept, but it seems likely that Lord North believed American whigs were more opposed to the Townshend taxes than to the Townshend claim to the right. When, however, he told colonial agents the ministry planned to repeal the duties on three of the four items taxed by the Townshend law, keeping only the impost on tea, they replied "that this will signify nothing,"[98] indicating that they understood the colonists were primarily concerned about the constitutional principle. Upset as they may have been with the continued tax on tea, the agents were even more troubled with North's two-part constitutional strategy. First—a point he strongly stressed on the floor of the House of Commons—North insisted that the three duties were being repealed on the expediency grounds that they were "anti-commercial," that is, that it had been economically unsound to put import duties on three items— glass, paper, and paints—manufactured in Great Britain because the government should be encouraging their export, not burdening their export with taxes. Second, North told the Commons, "the preamble to the act and the duty on tea must be retained, as a mark of the supremacy of Parliament, and an efficient declaration of their right to govern the Colonies."[99]

We must pay attention to North's words. He was not ambiguous. He told the Commons precisely what its legislative intent would be when it retained the Tea Tax. The preamble to which he referred—the preamble of the Townshend Acts—contained the claim to supremacy by stating its purpose, to provide for "the support of the civil government" in the colonies. It had to be saved, North explained, because colonial whigs had stated their constitutional objections against the Townshend legislation too clearly and too often. They had not, North complained, expressed "much dislike to the [Townshend] duty, but a great dislike to the preamble." Colonial whigs, he warned, demanded that all four duties be repealed, "as if Britain had negatively resigned her right," for which reason, he insisted, "I cannot consent to give up [the tea impost], whilst there is no solid reason assigned," by which he meant, without the "anti-commercial" excuse.[100] In other words, Parliament was not to give the Americans a surreptitious precedent.

More intent on saving the empire than on saving the right, Governor Pownall wanted all four duties repealed. There could be no surreptitious precedent while the Declaratory Act remained on the statute books, he argued. The right was as fully reserved by that act as it could be, and total repeal of Townshend would not diminish its force.[101] "Let the matter of right rest upon the declaratory law, and say no more about it," Pownall urged. "Do nothing which may bring into discussion *questions of right*, which must become *mere articles of faith.*" Lord North disputed Pownall's law. The Declaratory Act alone was not enough to preserve the right. He would have preferred, North explained, to have repealed all four Townshend duties, "if it could have been done without giving up that absolute right." But comprehensive repeal would be a surreptitious precedent since the Americans "totally denied the power of *Great Britain* to tax them." It was, therefore, "more absolutely necessary to compel the observance of the laws to vindicate our undoubted rights."[102]

North was in command. Parliament supported his version of the constitution, voting to preserve what the marquis of Rockingham called "the invidious right." "[T]he tea duty," Rockingham would complain, "was left as a pepper-corn, merely for the sake of contest with America, as the Ministry had likewise avowed."[103]

Rockingham oversimplified the issue. There was much more at stake in keeping the claim to right than continuing the constitutional controversy with the colonies. Lord North had not been devious. He had told the House of Commons why the duty on tea must not be repealed, and everyone understood the intent of the Tea Tax, especially colonial whigs. The tax was "retained upon tea," Virginia's House of Burgesses knew, "for the avowed purpose of establishing a precedent against us."[104]

There had been two closely related objectives for retaining the Tea Tax. One, of course, was to save the right of taxation. Some members of Parliament still nourished the hope of raising an American revenue, and there was even thought that, if the tea impost was collected, it could then be extended to other "commercial" products when the constitutional controversy quieted down.[105] "While the duty on tea continues," Maryland's Deputy Governor Robert Eden explained, "the general view is that it will stand as a precedent for laying duties in America on some future occasion."[106]

The more significant objective was to legislate the right to supremacy. Recently it has been suggested that retention of the tax was a "symbol," a "symbolic gesture" that had "symbolic significance."[107] If that is the belief of twentieth-century historians, it is inaccurate. In the eighteenth century, legal precedent was not a symbol or a reservation of power. It was authority.[108] The tea duty, Edmund Burke told the Commons, was "kept only to support the preamble of the Bill which is the offensive part." Burke meant "support" in the sense of legal or constitutional authority. That was why, in the debate on repeal, Governor Pownall had said that Parliament was "keeping this preamble, in order to the maintaining your claim, and this paltry duty, in order to the exercise of your right of taxing the *Americans*." The preamble, as he put it, was retained, "as a yoke upon the neck of the *Americans*," a metaphor he used at least once more in the speech. "That by thus continuing the duty on tea, you preserve the preamble of the Act, you still keep the yoke about the neck of the *Americans*."[109]

The case against the word "symbol" deserves to be understood. It is neither a matter of legal semantics nor that the connotations to "symbol" may be too weak to convey the constitutional substance of "precedent." By retaining the Tea Tax, Parliament intended to maintain not a symbol of the right to supremacy, but the right itself.

The legal importance the eighteenth century attached even to a surreptitious precedent may be gleaned from arguments made by members of the House of Commons who were worried that the dominant precedent would be repeal of the three Townshend duties, not retention of the tax on tea. "I still retain my own private opinion, that it [repeal] was sacrificing the essential rights of this country as far as that [Townshend] Act went," Welbore Ellis told the Commons in 1774, talking of supremacy and not of the authority to tax. "The principle goes against the supreme power of this country," Lord George Germain agreed. The Americans would not have continued their boycott and staged the Boston Tea Party had "this Act not been repealed." Repeal of three duties, not retention of one, had been the precedent. "[T]he colonies look upon it [repeal] as a desertion of our rights."[110]

The constitutional argument that repeal of the Townshend taxes compromised Parliament's claim to legislative supremacy over the colonies is unpersuasive. Yet it should be taken seriously enough that it is not misinterpreted. The legal theory that retention of the tax on tea would save Parliament's supremacy was sound, but like all law its application could be made imprecise by differing arguments of facts and by individual variations of emphasis and degree. The difficulty with North's legal position was not the doctrine that retention of one duty saved the claims of supremacy made by the Townshend Acts. There was still the threshold question, the one American whigs had originally raised, whether the Townshend duty that was being saved had been constitutional.

TEA ACT

Of the five statutes asserting parliamentary supremacy that are discussed in this chapter, the Tea Act of 1773 was the one least directly concerned with legislating supremacy. It was, however, the most memorable as the events which it precipitated drove Parliament to enact another series of laws that quickly raised the claim of supremacy to such a level America could no longer maneuver around the issue and Great Britain could no longer retreat from it.

Constitutional strategy was not the overt purpose of the Tea Act. Finances were—the finances of the East India Company.[111] "[T]he East India Company have now actually in their warehouse very near seventeen million pounds of tea, which the Company report near three years' consumption," Lord North explained in the House of Commons. "It must be obvious to everybody to what a great loss the East India Company keep it in their warehouses."[112] To reduce inventory, North proposed allowing "the company to export such part of the tea at present in their warehouses to British America, as they should think proper, duty-free." He meant "duty free" in Great Britain, not in the colonies. There would still be a tax of three pence a pound to be paid before the tea was landed in America. Previously the tax had totaled a shilling a pound. His plan, North admitted, would lessen "the revenue of the customs; yet he proposed it with a view to give the company all possible assistance."[113]

Some members of Parliament warned North that he had to remove the entire duty or the Americans would still refuse to accept the tea.[114] North replied that the bill had a second purpose: to finance the preamble of the Townshend Acts. "I am unwilling to give up that duty upon America upon which the [colonial salaries] are charged," he explained. "If the East India Company will export tea to America, they will very much increase that duty, and consequently very much facilitate carrying on government in that part."[115] North was saying that the constitutional issue had not changed, that the Tea Act was to a degree a piece of supremacy legislation much as the Townshend Acts had been. For American whigs, therefore, the impost on tea was as constitutionally offensive as a single tax as it had been as part of the Townshend package.

Members of Parliament may have been surprised by colonial reaction. "Whoever can sell the cheapest, the Americans will buy," Charles Jenkinson had predicted. "Teas may be exported cheap enough to find a market in America, and preserve the duty," North had agreed. "You will have your market and your revenue."[116] After all, as Charles Wolfran Cornwall would remind the Commons after American whigs had begun to use violence against the Tea Act, "The consumer of a pound of tea before that Act took place, paid 12d. By this Act he pays only 3d." Surely it was obvious that this "3d duty can never be the bone of contention, especially when it is consumed 9d per lb. cheaper than formerly."[117] North claimed he had "thought it not possible the Americans could complain" of the Act, that "it was impossible for him to foretell the Americans would resist at being able to drink their tea at nine-pence in the pound cheaper." "If they deemed this a grievance," he lamented, "they were ready to make any thing a grievance."[118]

It may be wondered what North meant. He understood the constitutional issue. As every member of Parliament knew, North's legislative purpose for enacting the Tea Act had been both to save and to force the constitutional issue. Edmund Burke is but one example. Speaking on the very day that war broke out across the Atlantic at Lexington and Concord, he reminded the ministry that "the 3d duty" may have been "given up as a tax of revenue," but it had been retained "for a tax of litigation and quarrell. The 3d is not the object; it's the principle that the Americans could not submit to; they would be slaves if they did."[119] After all, as Charles James Fox told the Commons that same day, "[a] tax can only be laid for three purposes; the first for a commercial regulation, the second for a revenue, and the third for asserting your right."[120]

In one sentence Fox had summed up the constitutional aspects of the Tea Act controversy. North had said that he intended the Tea Act for the second and third purposes. Maybe he really thought the Americans would be pleased to save nine pence in a pound of tea—to the extent that their grievance concerned the amount of tax—but surely he expected them to react, as they had before, to his saving of the right. Moreover, North had legislated a new grievance, for the Tea Act authorized the East India Company to restrict sale of tea in the colonies to consignees chosen by the British. Monopolies had been a constitutional issue since the reign of Elizabeth I, as North must have known.[121]

No longer having to clothe their strategy in legalisms, American whigs stated exactly why they had to react to the Tea Act, and their reasons were the same as Burke's: because, in the words of the Providence town meeting, the Tea Act had "a direct tendency to render Assemblies useless, and to introduce arbitrary government and slavery."[122] We think of the whig reaction—the Boston Tea Party—as a change in whig strategy, from the policy of avoiding acknowledgment of Parliament's right or of avoiding assertion of the colonial claim of right to legislative autonomy, to direct confrontation and violence. In point of constitutional fact, however, American whigs tried to continue the practice of avoidance. They were dealing with a statute, however, containing provisions that, under certain circumstances, made confrontation unavoidable.

We cannot be certain, but the best reading of the evidence is that the whig leadership—even in Boston—hoped to repeat the legal tactics that had worked successfully during the Stamp Act crisis. As in 1765 when whig crowds took to colonial streets to prevent implementation of the stamp tax, denying the British a precedent for the authority to tax for purposes of revenue,[123] so in 1774 crowds in Boston and all other colonial seaports except Charleston, South Carolina, prevented tea from even staying aboard ships at anchor for more than twenty days. By implication if not explicitly, that time limit had been set by parliamentary legislation. Once a ship carrying tea arrived in a colonial port, that tea was imported and had to be entered at the customs house as a dutied product. After twenty days, if the tea was not unladed and the provisions of law met, the tea was seized, sold, and the proceeds applied to satisfy the duty. Either directly or indirectly, once a ship was in harbor, London would obtain a precedent of colonial payment of the tax on tea.[124] Moreover, once in a harbor, a ship bearing tea could not depart without a clearance from the customs house, a pass from the naval officer, or (at least in the case of Boston) a pass from the governor.[125] To further complicate the situation, there were people in Boston, including Governor Hutchinson and the whig selectmen, who interpreted seventeenth-century statutes as providing that no tea once exported from England could be reentered there on pain of confiscation.[126]

Why Parliament mandated these restrictions is unclear. Although unlikely, it is not impossible that the ministry was trying to obtain the precedent for taxation that had eluded London when the Stamp Act and the Townshend duties were repealed. The whigs still could have avoided the precedent without overt, direct disobedience had the first tea ship, *Dartmouth*, remained outside the legal limits of the harbor as it was warned to do by both the town meeting and Governor Thomas Hutchinson. That was how the problem was solved in most other ports. The pilots anchored the ships outside the harbors of New York and Philadelphia, and the whigs in those towns did not have to throw tea overboard. Boston whigs apparently formed the same plan but had to abandon it when *Dartmouth* made an entry, perhaps because her owner hoped to earn freight on the remainder of the cargo, which he would have lost had the ship not come in.

After the whig crowd prevented the owner from unlading, he applied to Hutchinson for a pass which was refused. *Dartmouth* could neither unlade nor leave port. Both sides of the constitutional controversy, imperial governor and colonial town meeting, seemed to be trapped by parliamentary law. On 17 December 1773, after *Dartmouth* had been in harbor for twenty days, the tea would, by law, be entered at the customs house and, even if none were sold, London would have its precedent because the duty would be credited on entry. That was why Boston's whigs staged their Tea Party on the night of the sixteenth. The law, and perhaps Thomas Hutchinson, had left them no other way to avoid the precedent. Hutchinson admitted that their objective had been avoidance, not destruction, when he wrote his predecessor, Francis Bernard, that Boston whigs, after they "had tried every method they could think of to force the tea back to England, and all in vain, they left what they call their lawful assembly . . . and reassembled at Giffin's Wharf, and in two or three hours destroyed three hundred and forty chests."[127] The source of that statement is very important. For Hutchinson is admitting that the Bostonians wanted to avoid the Tea Party, that the whigs changed their legal tactics because all their options of avoidance had been blocked by the circumscriptive rules of imperial legislation.

Of course, it can be said, as scholars have often said, that law was not a factor in the Boston Tea Party, that the whig leadership felt it was time to take the conflict to violence and the arrival of the tea was a handy excuse for starting civil war.[128] After all, the Americans could have let the tea be landed, refused as before to buy it, and have said that the duty entered was not precedent for a colonial tax because it had been paid by consignees of the East India Company or paid by proimperialists at the public sale conducted by the customs house. True, the British would have claimed the precedent, saying that what mattered was that the tax had been paid by Americans, but, at best, it would have been a tarnished precedent.

From the narrow perspective of law, the argument could also be made that the Tea Party was not necessary. Had the tea been entered as dutied goods, the constitutional position of the colonists in relation to Parliament would not have been altered. But even if one accepted that legal conclusion, it would not prove that whigs had abandoned the constitutional defense of their claims and that they were using the tea as a means to raise the physical level of the conflict. The better explanation is that American whigs, like the parliamentary opposition in London, had come to the conclusion that, with the Tea Act, the administration had pushed its program of legislating supremacy so far that any possible acquiescence, even a badly tarnished precedent, had to be avoided.

The constitutional impasse had been outlined by Burke at the opening of Parliament following news from the colonies that American merchants, responding to repeal of the three Townshend duties, had ended agreements not to import British products except tea and other dutiable goods. The administration had been congratulating itself that "the American controversy is now at an end." Not so, Burke warned.

> [T]he Ministry had no reason to plume themselves so much as they did upon the concessions of the Americans, since they had receded only in exact proportion as Parliament had done, and both upon commercial principles; one had taken off duties, the other extended the liberty of imports. Parliament retained the duty upon tea as a

test of their right to tax, and America forbid the importation of it, in direct denial of that right; so they were but pretty nearly where they were at first.[129]

The constitutional embolism was not so much a matter of stalemate as of checkmate. Parliament had passed the Tea Act of 1773 partly, as William Dowdeswell said in the Commons, "as a test to America." It was a constitutional test that colonial whigs had to check or risk the pleading of a precedent for Parliament's legislative supremacy. The predicament was that once a step had been taken, a precedent was created and the law was changed. With passage of the Tea Act, the controversy had been pushed to a point that Parliament had to respond to the Boston Tea Party or jeopardize the claim—legislative supremacy over the colonies—that it had been trying to make with the Tea Act. Charles Wolfran Cornwall was applying that rule when he told the Commons, "America does not meet you on the mode of taxation, but upon the question of right." Parliament had to respond or diminish the right.[130]

When members of the House of Commons met to consider the Boston Tea Party, the opposition asked whether the Tea Act, promulgated largely to preserve the right to supremacy, was a proper issue with which to force the colonies to admit the right. It was, Edmund Burke charged with a wonderful choice of scornful words, *"a preambulary tax*. It is indeed a tax of sophistry, a tax of pendantry, a tax of disputation, a tax of war and rebellion, a tax for anything but benefit to the imposers, or satisfaction to the subject." From that point of view, the Tea Act was not solid constitutional ground on which to risk armed conflict with the colonists. "Why keep up this duty?" Thomas Townshend, Jr., asked. "Merely to show you ought to keep up the subject of contest," he answered. "The Stamp Act might have been worth preserving, but this is an unproducing tax and nothing but a matter of contest."[131]

General John Burgoyne, who soon would be posted to the army at Boston, seeing the issue from the opposite vantage point, argued that precisely because the Tea Act had been promulgated for contest it could not be repealed. "I am sure the tax is not the grievance but the power of laying it," he told the House. Burgoyne meant that the colonists meeting Parliament's contest by refusing to obey the act, made it imperative for Parliament to defend its claim to the power. Once the Tea Act had been passed as a test, it had to be supported as a test. "If we repeal this [Act], they [colonial whigs] will next say we have no power in any case to make laws to bind them," George Rice said, stating what would be the majority view. "I wish for no new tax, but that which remains must not be given up." "Can you give up the tax, without [giving up] the constitution?" Lord George Germain asked, summing up the predicament into which Parliament had gotten itself with the Tea Act.[132]

The issue in controversy was less complicated than may be thought. "We are risking the loss of America," Charles James Fox warned, "not for future taxation, but for the sake of the Tea Act." The constitutional principle at stake was not the authority to tax but legislative sovereignty over the colonies.[133]

CHAPTER NINETEEN

CONCLUSION

There are factors both striking and puzzling about Parliament's risking the loss of America by enacting legislation of supremacy. It is striking that Parliament deliberately forced the very constitutional issue that colonial whig leaders were studiously striving to avoid. Puzzling, however, is what the members of the British ministry and the imperial legislature had in mind. Possibly they hoped that the constitutional crisis would dissipate once the authority to legislate for colonial internal affairs in all cases whatsoever was irrevocably asserted to be part of Parliament's sovereign power. Confronted with the reality of the new constitution of absolute legislative command that must be obeyed, the Americans would realize that the old constitution of customary, prescriptive rights was no longer extant. Or possibly they thought the controversy had dragged on long enough, that it was time to proclaim the new constitution, and should the colonies resist, the pain of constitutional adjustment would be only temporary since Great Britain possessed sufficient military might to make the Americans obey.

There is a third possibility. The British administration may have appreciated that the colonies would resist with force Parliament's exercise of the authority to legislate in all cases whatsoever and could have been aware that, if there were armed conflict, the Americans might prevail. Yet the British may have concluded they had no choice but to risk civil war if they believed that their interpretation of the constitution had to be defended. After all, the dispute was about legislative supremacy, and when eighteenth-century British constitutionalists thought of supremacy, they did not think of legislative supremacy over the colonies but of parliamentary supremacy over the king. The American doctrine of customary, prescriptive legislative autonomy, making colonial assemblies independent of Parliament in all matters except trade regulation and the general superintendence of the empire, contained peril for the future of British constitutional liberty.

The colonies, it should be understood, were telling the British much more than that they were not subject to Parliament's legislative supremacy in all cases whatsoever. They were saying that their constitutional connection to the mother country was with the Crown. It was a constitutional doctrine frightening to eighteenth-century British constitutionalists ever on guard against any growth of independent royal authority. American wealth and the American population constitutionally autonomous from Parliament, yet in allegiance to the king, held the potential threat of unbalancing the balanced British constitution.

It is easier to speculate about possibilities than to discuss resolutions. The controversy between Great Britain and her American colonies could not have been constitutionally resolved. It could have been terminated by one side or the other backing down on certain issues, or by both sides agreeing to disagree. But such solutions became more and more difficult as Parliament pursued its program of legislating supremacy. America's quarrel, after all, was with Parliament's claim to the authority of binding the colonies in all cases whatsoever. Under the British constitution, there was no institution in which that constitutional question could be settled except in the two houses of the supreme, sovereign Parliament. That is the reason why the extensive constitutional debates discussed in the preceding chapters remain historically indeterminable. They can still be debated in the twentieth century because, in the eighteenth century, they were resolved only on the battlefield of Yorktown. They were resolved, that is, outside the apparatus of British constitutional law.

The constitutional rule was stated by Lord North in a speech to the House of Commons. "Parliament themselves," he said, "are the only persons to judge of the propriety of their measures."[1] That rule created a constitutional predicament for American whigs, as Governor George Johnstone explained when reminding the Commons that for a person to be a judge of his own cause violated natural law. "Yet such is the precise situation in which we contend we ought to be placed, respecting the Americans, and for the denial of which we are ready to condemn our fellow-subjects to all the tortures enacted by the laws of treason."[2]

The constitutional predicament colonial whigs faced was that the British constitution made Parliament the sole judge of its authority to legislate. The solution to this predicament favored by most Americans who expressed their thoughts was to return to the old constitution and balance the sovereignty of Parliament with the prerogative of the king— to make George III the imperial arbiter of constitutional disputes between Parliament and the colonial assemblies.[3] It was a whig solution both revealing and historically surprising. It is revealing as it graphically demonstrates just how committed colonial leaders were to the Crown as an active, autonomous element in the tripartite balanced constitution. It is surprising because the course of subsequent history in the nineteenth century would lead us to expect that the Americans would have preferred the common-law courts as the dernier constitutional judge—the twelve judges of England, for example,[4] or perhaps a combination of some English judges sitting with jurists from other sections of the empire.[5] Following the Revolution, Americans had to remedy what they perceived as the fatal flaw in the British constitution—no final, neutral institution, independent of politics, with authority to hold the legislature to the rule of law. They would continue to separate the concept of the rule of law from legislative command and entrust its guardianship to a judiciary appointed for life and not removable by the political process. The British, of course, went the opposite way in the nineteenth century and entrusted the rule of law to the will of the legislative majority.

The ambiguities and irresolvable nature of the eighteenth-century British constitution need not trouble us. These are ambiguities and irresolvable questions of law, not of history. History is clear enough. We know what arguments were made. It is law that lets us down because law can offer no definitive answer as to which arguments a final, nonpolitical judge would have found most persuasive.

History can be faulted for a different kind of defect, however, at least a theory of history that once was influential in the United States. There was a time when some historians of the "progressive school"—or what, in the present context, might also be labelled the "anti-ideological school" of history—wrapped their accounts of Parliament's claim of legislative sovereignty around a supposed fact and a historical theme, both of which tended to muddle the story and misinform their readers. The supposed fact was that the American case against parliamentary supremacy was "inconsistent." The historical theme was that inconsistencies in the American case proved that colonial whigs were not sincere when they said their reason for opposing Parliament's authority to legislate was to defend constitutional principles. The argument may no longer be espoused, and the question whether the American case was "inconsistent" may no longer interest historians, yet it is worth looking back to the "progressive historians." Their charge of colonial whig inconsistency provides a revealing perspective from which to summarize both the debate over the authority to legislate and the American strategy of constitutional avoidance.

How, these historians asked, could the whigs have been sincerely defending constitutional rights when the constitutional case they expounded was inherently inconsistent and their constitutional demands changed literally "from day to day"?[6] It is interesting that all of the "inconsistencies" perceived by these historians had also been marked by eighteenth-century defenders of Parliament's supremacy: that American legal theory shifted from constitutional law, to natural law, to the rights of man, and "back again;"[7] that colonial whigs "enlarged" the revolutionary controversy from opposition only to internal taxation to demands for independence from Parliament;[8] and that they claimed rights under the British constitution yet rejected dependence under Parliament which that constitution made supreme—positions so inconsistent that they could not have been sincerely asserted.[9] The most important charge, the one "progressive historians" found especially convincing, was that American whigs had been constitutional hypocrites, that either they "shifted and advanced the ground of their claim of rights"[10] as the British government reacted to their provocations,[11] or no sooner did they win one concession from the British than they stated a new demand.[12] William Knox, imperial under secretary, used taxation to document the last contention. "When the repeal of the stamp-act was their object, a distinction was set up between internal and external taxes; they pretended not to dispute the right of parliament to impose external taxes, or port duties upon the Colonies," Knox explained. "[B]ut when parliament seemed to adopt the distinction, and waiving for the present the exercise of its right to impose internal taxes, imposed certain [Townshend] duties on merchandizes imported into the Colonies, . . . the distinction between internal and external taxes is rejected by the colony advocates, and a new one devised between taxes for *the regulation of trade*, and taxes for the *purpose of revenue*."[13]

It is necessary to understand Knox's intention. Writing part of the British constitutional answer to the American case, he was attempting to disparage the law of the other side. His argument is an example of what Edmund S. Morgan has labelled "a Tory libel that has too readily been accepted by modern historians."[14] As Professor Morgan pointed out, historians such as Lawrence H. Gipson have "tended to accept the Tory analysis" of the American constitutional defense against parliamentary supremacy.[15] "In objecting to Parliamentary taxation, the Americans talked much about constitutional principles; but the sincerity of their attachment to those principles, Professor Gipson suggests, may be questioned, especially in the light of their shifting from one argument to another as the situation altered."[16] To refute the historical conclusion, Morgan wrote the best concise summary of the evidence upon which it was based:

> [T]he colonists did not really mean what they said. What they wanted was to avoid being taxed, and they had improvised one set of high-sounding principles after another to block the efforts of the British Parliament, to make them pay. When Parliament passed the Stamp Act, imposing a duty on legal and other documents, the colonists invented a distinction between external taxes, which were allowable, and internal taxes, which were not. When Parliament obliged them by repealing the Stamp Act and giving them some external taxes in the Townshend duties, they decided that Parliament could tax only for the regulation of trade, not for revenue. When Parliament repealed most of the Townshend duties, but then passed the Coercive Acts to punish Massachusetts for the Boston Tea Party, the colonists decided that Parliament had no authority over them at all, that their only connection with England lay in their loyalty to the king. And they finally repudiated that too in the Declaration of Independence.[17]

It should puzzle us why these shifting principles and doctrines have been said to prove that the American revolutionary controversy was not constitutional. The best explanation seems to be that some twentieth-century scholars have peculiar notions about law and assume that constitutional arguments should proceed to a conclusion by "logical" reasoning rather than legal reasoning. "Of all arguments, a constitutional one requires logic and consistency," Carl N. Degler has suggested, "if it can be shown that an argument used in one place is forgotten in another, then suspicion grows that the constitutional objection is simply a cover for a deeper and more self-interested objection." We may understand why Degler wrote what he did, yet wonder if his conclusion is quite what he intended. As he was addressing historians, it is possible that he was referring to a special kind of suspicion—a historian's suspicion, perhaps. Certainly, it is not a lawyer's suspicion. Lawyers are not troubled if a constitutional argument used in one place is forgotten in the next, unless, of course, they catch an opponent doing the forgetting. Professor Degler's argument is, however, useful for illustrating why the American whig constitutional case against Parliament's authority to legislate for the colonies in all cases whatsoever has been so often dismissed as not constitutional. When commenting on historians who had "pointed out that the American pamphleteers shifted their constitutional ground as British actions changed in response to colonial objections, Degler drew from them the conclusion that "[s]uch a procedure certainly belied the colonists' concern for constitutional scruples."[18] Or, as Bernard Bailyn explained the same conclusion, "There was no logic or law behind such gyrations."[19] This perception of illogic or inconsistency caused the "progressive historians" to ask the wrong question.

Edmund S. Morgan phrased the question that the "progressive historians" asked: "If the American colonists were sincere, we say, why did they not state at the outset exactly what they believed and then stick to it without faltering?"[20] The question is best understood by again comparing professions, for this is a historian's question, not a lawyer's question. Indeed, in the fact that it is not a lawyer's question can be found its answer. For the answer is not one of those that have been suggested: that the colonial whigs were merely human[21] or that they were motivated by "the desire not to give offense, to show good will and common sense by conceding something in order to retain the rest."[22] The better explanation is that if the American constitutional case was sincere, it would have been argued by the premises of constitutional advocacy. And that is just how it was argued, for had the whigs been eighteenth-century common lawyers, thinking as eighteenth-century common lawyers thought, they would have argued their case exactly as they did argue it. They would have argued it, in fact, very much as the historians whom Morgan criticizes—Lawrence H. Gipson, Carl Becker, and Randolph Greenfield Adams—accused them of arguing it when those historians concluded that whatever strategy the whigs followed, it was not a strategy of constitutional law.

Take the charge levelled in Morgan's rephrased question: that had American whigs in 1774 been sincere that Parliament could not constitutionally bind them by internal legislation not related to the regulation of trade, they would have pleaded that defense at the very start of the controversy, during the Stamp Act crisis. Of course, American whigs could have opposed the Stamp Act by raising the ultimate issue of the authority of Parliament to legislate for them in all cases whatsoever. Had they done so, they might have met some twentieth-century test for "logic" or "consistency," but they would not have been competent eighteenth-century lawyers. The constitutional issue in 1765 was neither Parliament's authority to legislate nor its authority to impose taxes incidental to the regulation of trade. The issue was the constitutionality of a tax innovation, of the abrogation of precedents with which Americans had long associated constitutional security, which was why the whigs used the adjective "internal." In the context of eighteenth-century constitutional advocacy, to call the stamp tax "internal" was to focus on the legal contention that the tax was an innovation that departed from long-standing constitutional precedent. It supplemented, therefore, the related grievance that the Stamp Act was taxation without consent. Whigs were not claiming that the tax was illegal, but that as taxation without consent it was unconstitutional and, as internal taxation of the colonies, it was constitutionally unprecedented.

The word "internal" has been responsible for a misunderstanding that could have been avoided had the forensic context been given due weight. The idea has been that when American whigs called internal taxation unconstitutional they were saying that the opposite type of taxation— "external"—was constitutional. That conclusion is a major eisegesis of the debate. To plead the unconstitutionality of a specific action was not in the eighteenth century, as it is not today, to concede the constitutionality of an apparent opposite.

It is a relevant question whether those who have charged that the American whig constitutional case was not "consistent" took common-law methodology into account. Contrary to the assumption made by Professor Degler, a trial or appellate advocate does not seek the widest possible ground on which to stand. As was previously explained,[23] the forensic advocate takes a position that is both narrow enough to defend successfully and broad enough to win the point at bar. Put another way, lawyers and other constitutionalists involved in a constitutional controversy, are not theorists, philosophers, or historians. They are advocates. They are not concerned with developing constitutional consistency as their task is winning the case in controversy. They will not adopt an argument they know is "right" but has been rejected by or is likely to antagonize the tribunal of judgment. Whig lawyers in 1765 might or might not have agreed with Professor Gipson that potentially the ultimate issue between the colonies and the mother country was parliamentary sovereignty. But, unlike Gipson, they were disputing a point of law and politics, the constitutionality of the Stamp Act, and their case had to be won in Parliament. If those lawyers wanted the colonies to remain legislatively autonomous parts of the British empire—and the people writing resolutions against the Stamp Act[24] sought to return constitutional affairs to what they had been before the Act—it was not relevant to tell Parliament it was neither supreme nor sovereign. Far better strategy was to do what they did do, concentrate on the fact that any tax on the colonies for the purpose of revenue was unprecedented legislation and the fact that the Stamp Act itself violated one of the most fundamental doctrines of English and British constitutional law, that consent of the taxed was required for taxation to be constitutional. These were the probative issues, the two points American lawyers would have concentrated on had they been able to challenge the constitutionality of the Stamp Act in a supreme imperial court with power of judicial review.

The Declaratory Act was the first occasion when American whigs were confronted with what would be the ultimate constitutional issue of the revolutionary controversy, Parliament's claim of authority to bind the colonies in all cases whatsoever. Scholars puzzling over why the colonists did not protest the Declaratory Act as they had protested the Stamp Act, and perhaps not as certain as Becker and Gipson that it is evidence of American insincerity, have suggested that the whigs may have "misunderstood" or "disregarded" the act and, as a result, made a mistake in not protesting its passage. But as was discussed in chapter 3,[25] Americans did not react to the Declaratory Act as they had reacted to the Stamp Act because there was no legal or constitutional grievance against which to react. There was no enforcement of the Declaratory Act to prevent. The act was a declaration of constitutional principle, not the promulgation of a legislative program. It made an abstract statement—that Parliament had authority to bind the colonies in all cases whatsoever—and did not go beyond constitutional theory to the constitutionally concrete.

Perhaps the "progressive historians" of the school of Adams and Becker were misled as much by looking in the wrong direction as by asking the wrong questions. Their attention focused on American inconsistencies when American consistencies would have told a more revealing story. Overlooked, as a result, was how consistently colonial whigs maintained their strategy of avoidance, of staying joinder or "maturity" of issue, in hopes that the ultimate question of sovereignty would not be reached. Two further instances of their avoidance strategy—besides their responses to the Declaratory Act and to the Townshend legislation[26]—were set in motion by Parliament's joint resolution urging George III to activate the statute of 35 Henry VIII[27] and the act to suspend the New York General Assembly.[28] Both were manifestations of internal legislation that colonial whigs held unconstitutional, but, it should be recalled, both were argued in a manner to protect the legal rights for which whigs contended without directly disputing the supremacy of Parliament.

Consider the resolution first. Colonial assemblies strongly and frequently protested it but always on theoretical legal grounds of inapplicability or on abstract constitutional grounds. Indeed, protests were so constitutionally circumspect that some assemblies even made the unusual and questionable argument that transportation "beyond the Sea, to be tried, is highly derogatory to the Rights of *British* Subjects"[29]— unusual because Americans almost never claimed British rights, they claimed English rights, and questionable because trial at the venue was not a British right. It was a basic English right that in certain circumstances had been denied to Scots, Welsh, and Irish. The whigs never had to raise their protest against 35 Henry VIII above the theoretical, however, because it was not enforced in the colonies, in part because whig defensive measures prevented enforcement, as when the *Gaspee* enquiry was frustrated or when British officials were intimidated by the knowledge that arresting Americans for trial beyond the venue made them liable to tort actions or criminal charges before whig juries in local colonial courts.

An even clearer campaign of avoiding the ultimate constitutional issue was directed against the legislation discussed in chapter 18: the Mutiny Act commanding American assemblies to provide fuel and other specified provisions for British troops stationed in a colony. One does not have to be an eighteenth-century lawyer to recognize that the tactics of the colonial legislatures—giving London some response that the ministry could tolerate as less than disobedience, yet not quite compliance and certainly not the precedent that Parliament sought—were the tactics of constitutional avoidance. Certainly this was the legal strategy adopted by New York whigs after Parliament retaliated by suspending that colony's General Assembly until it conformed to Parliament's command and furnished all items specified in the Mutiny Act. For the first time in the revolutionary controversy, American whigs were potentially faced with the naked issue of executed parliamentary sovereignty. Had they wished national independence or economic autonomy, they could have joined the issue by challenging the authority of Parliament to order a colonial government to enact specified legislation. But if they wanted what they said they wanted, only their customary constitutional privileges, they would have avoided a confrontation, just as they had with the Stamp Act, the Declaratory Act, and the Townshend duties. That was the strategy adopted by the New York General Assembly at a moment when military circumstances were such that imperial representatives had to take noncompliance as compliance. The whig constitutional objective, after all, had not been to avoid paying the troops. It had been to avoid giving the British a precedent of parliamentary sovereignty, and technically they succeeded. We may find the solution contrived and unconvincing, but there were sound legal reasons why it was appealing to lawyers and other constitutionalists who were trying to remain within the constitutional system.

It would be difficult to exaggerate the importance to colonial whigs of the strategy of avoiding constitutional precedent or the extent to which they put the strategy into practice. It was to avoid precedents that crowds took over colonial streets in 1765 to prevent implementation of the stamp tax, denying the British a precedent for the authority to tax for purposes of raising revenue.[30] And it was to avoid even the appearance of precedents that colonial assemblies forbade their London agents to ask for repeal of the Townshend duties on grounds of inexpediency even though Lord Hillsborough seemed to assure them that if they would plead inexpediency the taxes would be repealed. A petition that Parliament had enacted inexpedient legislation was not constitutionally harmless. A later minister might say that the petitioning colony had implied Parliament's authority to legislate. For the same reason crowds in Boston and all other seaports except Charleston, South Carolina, prevented tea from staying aboard ships at anchor for more than twenty days. The ministry, after all, gave every indication that it was seeking precedents. Instead, it got the Boston Tea Party.[31]

In one respect, it can be said that the constitutional strategy of avoiding precedents led to the very civil war that it had been designed to prevent. For the need to avoid precedents made the Boston Tea Party constitutionally advisable, and the Boston Tea Party, in turn, led to the Coercive Acts that punished Boston by closing its harbor to commerce,[32] altered by legislative fiat the charter government of Massachusetts Bay,[33] provided the option of trial outside the venue for British officials accused of capital crimes in Massachusetts, reversing, in a sense, the procedure of 35 Henry VIII,[34] and extended imperial authority to quarter troops.[35] Each of these statutes was direct, internal legislation, and, except for the last, each changed in substantive ways the constitutional rights and constitutional security of the American colonists. From the point of view of whig lawyers and their strategy of avoidance, the Coercive Acts so substantively changed the constitutional controversy that constitutional resistance became unavoidable.

Americans for the first time were confronted by the ultimate constitutional issue of executed parliamentary sovereignty; confronted, that is, by an exercise of legislative authority that could not be ignored, distinguished away, or neutralized by partial compliance. The resolutions of a Rhode Island town meeting tell us what whigs all up and down the Atlantic coast were saying: "That the act of the British Parliament, claiming the right to make laws binding upon the colonies, in all cases whatsoever, is inconsistent with the natural, constitutional and charter rights and privileges of the inhabitants of this colony."[36] That colonial whigs finally stated the Declaratory Act as the grievance does not mean that they had changed their constitutional stand; that they were inconsistent. Now, after eight years, the Declaratory Act had become the constitutional grievance in law as well as in symbol because, if we think about them as law, the Coercive Acts were the Declaratory Act executed.

There remained one more development or "change" in the American whig constitutional case. It took place between the denial of parliamentary sovereignty made unavoidable by the Coercive Acts and the promulgation of the Declaration of Independence. It was the emergence of the doctrine that the colonists owed their sole allegiance to the Crown, that Parliament had no constitutional role in the governance of North America except for the regulation of trade and superintendence of the empire. Again, because this doctrine generally had been "avoided" until British assertions of parliamentary sovereignty made its defense unavoidable, it gives a first impression of being another inconsistency proving whig insincerity.[37] From the perspective of constitutional advocacy, however, an eighteenth-century lawyer would have thought of it as always having been potentially stated, a doctrine so alarming to British constitutional sensibilities that forensic strategy mandated that it remain dormant unless the dynamics of the imperial constitutional initiative thrust it so forward it could be avoided no longer.

The conclusion may be understated. It is not necessary to contend that the motivations of colonial whigs were solely constitutional. All that is claimed is that their constitutional strategies were consistently forensic. The purpose behind the strategies is a question quite separate from whether the strategies were dictated by legal considerations. Nor is it denied that there are different perspectives from which to evaluate events. Even if we insist on remaining "progressive historians" or economic determinists, however, we should not forget that eighteenth-century lawyers argued as they were trained to argue, like eighteenth-century lawyers, and that in the eighteenth century it was usual for political arguments to cite precedent, draw analogy, and appeal to doctrine, a methodology that in the twentieth century is more likely to be confined to appellate advocacy. If we view the constitutional controversy from that perspective, the perspective of forensic advocacy and the common-law mind, we should understand why the once disparaged "inconsistencies" in the American whig case have been reassessed in our own times. Indeed, the "inconsistency" of the changes in argument that once were cited as proof that the colonial case could not have been constitutional, turns out to be convincing evidence of how very constitutional the whig case actually was. Of course, the legal strategy pursued by the imperial side of the controversy was also constitutionally consistent. Tragically for the old British empire, however, it was not a strategy of constitutional avoidance. It was, rather, a strategy of sovereign command, a British adoption of the principle of legislative sovereignty and a British abrogation of the English constitutional principle that Americans cherished above all others, the rule of law.

ACKNOWLEDGMENTS
SHORT TITLES
NOTES
INDEX

ACKNOWLEDGMENTS

Research for this study was supported by a fellowship from the John Simon Guggenheim Memorial Foundation and by a Huntington Library–National Endowment for the Humanities Fellowship. Leave from teaching responsibilities at New York University School of Law was provided by the Filomen D'Agostino Greenberg and Max E. Greenberg Faculty Research Fund at the School of Law, and by John Sexton, dean of the School of Law. The manuscript was written amid the beauty and scholarship of the Huntington Library where Mary Wright furnished the eighteenth-century pamphlets, Doris Smedes located the reference books, Gordon Bakken provided the conversation, and Martin Ridge herded the coyotes. The final version in some inexplicable fashion may have benefited from being partly read by that premier band of American legal historians, the members of the New York University School of Law Colloquium in Legal History: John Wertheimer, Peter Hoffer, Jack R. Pole, Martin Flaherty, Robert J. Kaczorowski, Eben Moglen, and William E. Nelson. As with the other volumes in this Revolution-era series, the index was prepared by Carol B. Pearson of Alhamabra, California, and the Huntington Library. A serious error might have appeared in the text except that Richard B. Bernstein pointed out that it was Franklin Pierce and not Levi Woodbury who argued, "We fought the American Revolution to have actual representation, not virtual representation. What we need now is virtual legislation, not actual legislation. It would save us more money than the Stamp Act would have saved the British." Barbara Wilcie Kern discovered that Pierce made this argument during a speech to the New Hampshire House of Representatives when the General Court was debating whether to place a memorial commemorating the revolutionary engagement at Websterbridge.

New York University School of Law

SHORT TITLES

Abercromby, "De Jure"
> James Abercromby, "Do Jure et Gubernatione Coloniarum, or An Inquiry into the Nature and the Rights of the Colonies, Ancient, and Modern." ca. 1780. HM 518, Huntington Library, San Marino, Calif.

Abingdon, *Dedication*
> Willoughby Bertie, earl of Abingdon, *Dedication to the Collective Body of the People of England, in which the Source of our present Political Distractions are pointed out, and a Plan proposed for their Remedy and Redress.* Oxford, England, 1780.

Abingdon, "Speech on Right"
> "Lord Abingdon's Speech on Introducing his Bill for a Declaration of Right over every Part of the British Dependencies," reprinted in Flood, *Declaratory Act*, pp. 34–38.

Abingdon, *Thoughts on Burke's Letter*
> Willoughby Bertie, earl of Abingdon, *Thoughts on the Letter of Edmund Burke, Esq; to the Sheriffs of Bristol, on the Affairs of America.* 6th ed. Oxford, England [1777].

Account of Stamp Act Congress
> *Authentic Account of the Proceedings of the Congress held at New-York, in MDCCLXV, On the Subject of the American Stamp Act.* N.i., 1767.

Acherley, *Britannic Constitution*
Roger Acherley, *The Britannic Constitution: or, the Fundamental Form of Government in Britain.* 2d ed. London, 1741.

Acts and Ordinances
Acts and Ordinances of the Interregnum, 1642–1660. Edited by C. H. Firth and R. S. Rait. 3 vols. London, 1911.

Acts of the Privy Council
Acts of the Privy Council of England. Colonial Series. Vol. IV. A.D. 1745–1766. Vol. V. A.D. 1766–1783. Edited by James Munro. 1911, 1912.

Adams, "Novanglus"
John Adams, "Novanglus," reprinted in *The American Colonial Crisis: The Daniel Leonard–John Adams Letters to the Press 1774–1775.* Edited by Bernard Mason. New York, 1972, pp. 99–266.

Adams, *Works*
The Works of John Adams, Second President of the United States. Edited by Charles Francis Adams. 10 vols. Boston, 1850–56.

Adams, *Writings*
The Writings of Samuel Adams. Edited by Harry Alonzo Cushing. 4 vols. New York, 1904–8.

Addresses and Petitions of Common Council
Addresses, Remonstrances, and Petitions; Commencing the 24th of June, 1769, Presented to the King and Parliament, from the Court of Common Council, and the Livery in Common Hall assembled, with his Majesty's Answers: Likewise the Speech to the King, made by the late Mr. Alderman Beckford, When Lord Mayor of the City of London. London, [1778].

Addresses of the Common Council
Addresses Presented from the Court of Common Council to the King, On his Majesty's Accession to the Throne, and on various other Occasions, and his Answers. Resolutions of the Court . . . Instructions at different Times to the Representatives of the City in Parliament. Petitions to Parliament for different Purposes. . . . Agreed to between the 23d October, 1760, and the 12th October, 1770. London, [1770].

Allen, *American Crisis*
William Allen, *The American Crisis: A Letter, Addressed by Permission to the Earl Gower, Lord President of the Council, &c. &c. &c. On the present alarming Disturbances in the Colonies.* London, 1774.

[Allen,] *American Alarm*
[John Allen,] *The American Alarm, or the Bostonian Plea, For the Rights, and Liberties, of the People. Humbly Addressed to the King and Council, and to the Constitutional Sons of Liberty, in America.* Boston, 1773.

[Allen,] *Beauties of Liberty*
[John Allen,] *An Oration, Upon the Beauties of Liberty, or the Essential Rights of the Americans. Delivered At the Second Baptist Church in Boston, Upon the last Annual Thanksgiving.* 3d ed. New London, Conn., 1773.

Allen, *Magistracy an Institution*
James Allen, *Magistracy an Institution of Christ upon the Throne. A Sermon preached in the Audience of His Excellency William Shirley, Esq; the Honourable His Majesty's Council and House of Representatives of the Province of the Massachusetts-Bay in New-England, on the Day of Election of Councellors for said Province.* Boston, 1744.

[Allen,] "To the Governor"
[John Allen,] "To his Excellency the Governor of the Province of the Massachusetts-Bay," printed in [Allen,] *American Alarm.*

[Allen,] "To the King"
[John Allen,] "To the King's most excellent Majesty," printed in [Allen,] *American Alarm.*

American Archives
American Archives, Fourth Series. Containing a Documentary History of the English Colonies in North America From the King's Message to Parliament, of March 7, 1774, to the Declaration of Independence by the United States. Vols. 1 and 2. Washington, D.C., 1837.

American Gazette
The American Gazette. Being a Collection of all the Authentic Addresses, Memorials, Letters, &c. Which relate to the Present Disputes Between Great Britain and her Colonies. Containing also Many Original Papers Never Before Published. London, 1768.

Ammerman, *Common Cause*
David Ammerman, *In the Common Cause: American Response to the Coercive Acts of 1774.* Charlottesville, Va., 1974.

[Anderson,] *Free Thoughts*
[James Anderson,] *Free Thoughts on the American Contest.* Edinburgh, 1776.

Anderson, *Interest of Britain*
James Anderson, *The Interest of Great-Britain with Respect to her American Colonies Considered.* London, 1782.

Andrews, *Settlements*
Charles M. Andrews, *Our Earliest Colonial Settlements: Their Diversities of Origin and Later Characteristics.* Ithaca, N.Y., 1933.

Andrews, "Western Phase"
> Charles M. Andrews, "Anglo-French Commercial Rivalry, 1700–1750: The Western Phase, II." *American Historical Review* 20 (1915): 761–80.

Anglo-American Political Relations
> *Anglo-American Political Relations. 1675–1775.* Edited by Alison Gilbert Olson and Richard Maxwell Brown. New Brunswick, N.J., 1970.

Annual Register 1765
> *The Annual Register, or a View of the History, Politics, and Literature For the Year 1765.* 4th ed. London, 1784.

Annual Register 1766
> *The Annual Register, or a View of the History, Politics, and Literature, For the Year 1766.* 4th ed. London, 1785.

Annual Register 1767
> *The Annual Register, or a View of the History, Politics, and Literature for the Year 1767.* 4th ed. London, 1786.

Annual Register 1768
> *The Annual Register, or a View of the History, Politics, and Literature, For the Year 1768.* 4th ed. London, 1786.

Annual Register 1769
> *The Annual Register, or a View of the History, Politics, and Literature, For the Year 1769.* 4th ed. London, 1786.

Annual Register 1774
> *The Annual Register, or a View of the History, Politics, and Literature, for the Year 1774.* London, 1810.

Annual Register 1972
> *The Annual Register: World Events in 1972.* Edited by Ivison Macadam. London, 1973.

Anon., *Abuse of Power*
> Anonymous, *On the Abuse of Unrestrained Power. An Historical Essay.* London, 1778.

Anon., *Address to Mansfield*
> Anonymous, *An Address to the Right Honourable L[or]d M[an]sf[iel]d; in which the Measures of Government, Respecting America, are Considered in a New Light: With a View to His Lordship's Interposition Therein.* London, 1775.

Anon., *Address to Middlesex Freeholders*
> Anonymous, *An Address to the Freeholders of Middlesex, Assembled at Free Masons Tavern, in Great Queen Street, Upon Monday the 20th of December 1779, Being the Day Appointed for a Meeting of the Free-*

holders, For the Purpose of Establishing Meetings to Maintain and Support the Freedom of Election. 3d ed. London, [1779].

Anon., *Address to People of Britain*
Anonymous, *An Address to the People of Great-Britain in General, the Members of Parliament, and the Leading Gentlemen of Opposition in Particular, on the Present Crisis of American Politics.* Bristol, England, 1776.

Anon., *Ancient and Modern Constitution*
Anonymous, *The Ancient and Modern Constitution of Government Stated and Compared. And also Some Remarks on the Controversy Concerning the Dependence of Members of Parliament on the Crown.* London, 1734.

Anon., *Animadversions on Discourse*
Anonymous, *Animadversions on a Discourse Entituled, God's Way of Disposing of Kingdoms.* London, 1691.

Anon., *Answer to Burke*
Anonymous, *An Answer to the Letter of Edmund Burke, Esq., One of the Representatives of the City of Bristol, to the Sheriffs of that City.* London, 1777.

Anon., *Answer to Sheridan*
Anonymous, *Answer to a Pamphlet, Written by C. F. Sheridan, Esq; Entitled, A Review of the Three Great National Questions, Relative to a Declaration of Right, Poyning's Law, and the Mutiny Bill. Part the First, Declaration of Right.* Dublin, 1782.

Anon., *Appeal to Reason and Justice*
Anonymous, *An Appeal to Reason and Justice in Behalf of the British Constitution, and the Subjects of the British Empire. In which the present Important Contest with the Revolted Colonies is impartially considered, the Inconsistency of Modern Patriotism is demonstrated, the Supremacy of Parliament is asserted on Revolution Principles, and American Independence is proved to be a manifest Violation of the Rights of British Subjects.* London, 1778.

Anon., *Application of Political Rules*
Anonymous, *An Application of some General Political Rules, to the Present State of Great-Britain, Ireland and America. In a Letter to the Right Honourable Earl Temple.* London, 1766.

Anon., *Arguments in Support of Supremacy*
Anonymous, *A Brief Extract, or Summary of Important Arguments Advanced by Some Late Distinguished Writers, in Support of the Supremacy of the British Legislature, and their Right to Tax the Americans, Addressed to the Freemen and Liverymen of London, And Recommended to the serious Perusal of every Candid and Dispassionate Man.* London, 1775.

Anon., *Arguments to Prove*
Anonymous, *Arguments to Prove the Interposition of the People to be Constitutional and Strictly Legal: In which the Necessity of a more Equal Representation of the People in Parliament is also Proved: and a Simple, Unobjectionable Mode of Equalizing the Representation is Suggested.* Dublin, 1783.

Anon., *British Liberties*
Anonymous, *British Liberties, or the Free-born Subject's Inheritance; Containing the Laws that form the Basis of those Liberties, with Observations thereon; also an Introductory Essay on Political Liberty and a Comprehensive View of the Constitution of Great Britain.* London, 1766.

Anon., *Characters of Parties*
Anonymous, *Characters of Parties in the British Government.* London, 1782.

Anon., *Civil Liberty Asserted*
Anonymous, *Civil Liberty Asserted, and the Rights of the Subject Defended, Against the Anarchial Principles of the Reverend Dr. Price.* London, 1776.

Anon., *Colonising*
Anonymous, *Colonising, or a Plain Investigation of that Subject; with a Legislative, Political and Commercial View of Our Colonies.* London, 1774.

Anon., *Common Sense Conferences*
Anonymous, *Common Sense: in Nine Conferences, Between a British Merchant and a Candid Merchant of America, in their private capacities as friends; tracing the several causes of the present contests between the mother country and her American subjects; the fallacy of their prepossessions; and the ingratitude and danger of them; the reciprocal benefits of the national friendship; and the moral obligations of individuals which enforce it.* London, 1775.

Anon., *Conciliatory Address to the People*
Anonymous, *Conciliatory Address to the People of Great Britain and of the Colonies, on the Present Important Crisis.* London, 1775.

Anon., *Considerations on Information*
Anonymous, *Considerations on Proceedings by Information and Attachment. Addressed to the Members of the House of Commons. By a Barrister at Law.* 2d ed. London, 1768.

Anon., *Considerations on National Independence*
Anonymous, *Considerations on National Independence, Suggested by Mr. Pitt's Speeches on the Irish Union. Addressed to the People of Great Britain and Ireland. By a Member of the Honourable Society of Lincoln's Inn.* London, n.d.

Anon., *Considerations Upon Rights of Colonists*
Anonymous, *Considerations Upon the Rights of the Colonists to the Privileges of British Subjects, Introduc'd by a brief Review of the Rise and Progress of English Liberty, and concluded with some Remarks upon our present Alarming Situation.* New York, 1766.

Anon., *Considerations Upon the Act*
Anonymous, *Considerations Upon the Act of Parliament Whereby a Duty is laid of six Pence Sterling per Gallon on Molasses, and five Shillings per Hundred on Sugar of foreign Growth, imported into any of the British Colonies. Shewing, some of the many Inconveniencies necessarily resulting from the operation of the said Act, not only to those Colonies, but also to the British Sugar-Islands, and finally to Great-Britain.* Boston, 1764.

Anon., *Constitution*
Anonymous, *The Constitution, or a Full Answer to Mr. Edmund Burke's Anti-Constitutional Plan of Reform.* London, 1781.

Anon., *Constitution with Address*
Anonymous, *The Constitution. With an Address to a Great Man.* 2d ed. London, 1757.

Anon., *Constitutional Right*
Anonymous, *The Constitutional Right of the Legislature of Great Britain, to Tax the British Colonies in America, Impartially Stated.* London, 1768.

Anon., *Critical Review of Liberties*
Anonymous, *A Critical Review of the Liberties of British Subjects. With a Comparative View of the Proceedings of the H[ous]e of C[ommon]s of I[relan]d, against an unfortunate Exile of that Country; who, in contending for the Rights and Liberties of the Publick, lost his own. By a Gentleman of the Middle-Temple.* 2d ed. London, 1750.

Anon., *Cursory Remarks on Price*
Anonymous [Jonathan Watson,] *Cursory Remarks on Dr. Price's Observations on the Nature of Civil Liberty in a Letter to a Friend.* London, 1776.

Anon., *Defence of English History*
Anonymous, *A Defence of English History, Against the Misrepresentations of M. de Rapin Thoyras, in his History of England, Now Publishing Weekly.* London, 1734.

Anon., *Defence of Magna Charta*
Anonymous, *A History and Defence of Magna Charta.* Dublin, 1769.

Anon., *Defence of Resolutions*
Anonymous, *A Defence of the Resolutions and Address of the American Congress, in Reply to Taxation no Tyranny.* London, [1775].

Anon., *Dialogue on Principles*
> Anonymous, *A Dialogue on the Principles of the Constitution and Legal Liberty, compared with Despotism; applied to the American Question; and the Probable Events of the War, with Observations on some important Law Authorities.* London, 1776.

Anon., *Dialogue on the Constitution*
> Anonymous, *A Dialogue on the Principles of the Constitution and Legal Liberty, Compared with Despotism; Applied to the American Question; and the Probable Events of the War, with Observations on some important Law Authorities.* London, 1776.

Anon., *Dialogue on the State*
> Anonymous, *A Dialogue on the Actual State of Parliament.* London, 1783.

Anon., *Discourse on Constitution*
> Anonymous [William Stevens], *A Discourse on the English Constitution; Extracted from a Late Eminent Writer, and Applicable to the Present times.* London, 1776.

Anon., *Easie Method*
> Anonymous, *An Easie Method for Satisfaction Concerning the Late Revolution & Settlement: With a Particular Respect to Two Treatises of Dr. Sherlock's; viz. The Case of Resistance, and the Case of Allegiance.* London, 1691.

Anon., *Essay on the Constitution*
> Anonymous, *An Essay on the Constitution of England.* London, 1765.

Anon., *Essay on the Right*
> Anonymous, *An Essay on the Right of Every Man in a Free State to Speak and Write Freely, in order to Defend the Public Rights, and Promote the Public Welfare; and on Various Great Occasions for the Present Use of It.* London, 1772.

Anon., *Evidence of Common and Statute Laws*
> Anonymous, *The Evidence of the Common and Statute Laws of the Realm; Usage, Records, History, with the Greatest and Best Authorities Down to the 3d of George the IIId, in Proof of the Rights of Britons Throughout the British Empire. Addressed to the People.* London, 1775.

Anon., *Examination of the Rights*
> Anonymous, *An Examination of the Rights of the Colonies, Upon Principles of Law.* London, 1766.

Anon., *Experience preferable to Theory*
> Anonymous, *Experience preferable to Theory. An Answer to Dr. Price's Observations on the Nature of Civil Liberty, and the Justice and Policy of the War with America.* London, 1776.

Anon., *Fair Trial*
Anonymous, *A Fair Trial of the Important Question, or the Rights of Election Asserted; Against the Doctrine of Incapacity by Expulsion, or by Resolution: Upon True Constitutional Principles, the Real Law of Parliament, the Common Right of the Subject, and the Determinations of the House of Commons.* London, 1769.

Anon., *Fatal Consequences*
Anonymous, *The Fatal Consequences of the Want of System In the Conduct of Public Affairs.* London, 1757.

Anon., *First Letter to Grafton*
Anonymous, *A First Letter to the Duke of Grafton.* London, 1770.

Anon., *Four Letters*
Anonymous, *Four Letters on Interesting Subjects.* Philadelphia, 1776.

Anon., *Fundamentall Lawes*
Anonymous, *Touching the Fundamentall Lawes, or Politique Constitution of this Kingdome, the Kings Negative Voice, and the Power of Parliaments.* London, 1643.

Anon., *General View of the Company*
Anonymous, *A General View of the East-India Company, Written in January, 1769. To which are Added, Some Observations on the Present State of their Affairs.* London, 1772.

Anon., *Importance of British Dominion*
Anonymous, *The Importance of the British Dominion in India, Compared with that in America.* London, 1770.

Anon., *Inquiry into the Nature*
Anonymous, *An Inquiry into the Nature and Causes of the Present Disputes Between the British Colonies in America and their Mother-Country; and their reciprocal Claims and just Rights impartially examined, and fairly stated.* London, 1769 [*sic* 1768].

Anon., *Judgment of Whole Kingdoms*
Anonymous [generally attributed to Lord Somers or to Daniel Defoe,], *The Judgment of Whole Kingdoms and Nations, Concerning the Rights, Power, and Prerogative of Kings, and the Rights, Privileges, & Properties of the People.* 12th ed. Newport, R.I., 1774.

Anon., *Justice and Necessity of Taxing*
Anonymous, *The Justice and Necessity of Taxing the American Colonies, Demonstrated. Together with a Vindication of the Authority of Parliament.* London, 1766.

Anon., *Justice and Policy*
> Anonymous, *Justice and Policy. An Essay on the Increasing Growth and Enormities of our Great Cities*. London, 1773.

Anon., *Late Occurences*
> Anonymous, *The Late Occurences in North America, and Policy of Great Britain, Considered*. London, 1766.

Anon., *Legality of Impressing Seamen*
> Anonymous, *An Essay on the Legality of Impressing Seamen*. London, 1777.

Anon., *Letter*
> Anonymous, *A Letter to the People of Pennsylvania*, reprinted in Bailyn, *Pamphlets*, pp. 257–72.

Anon., *Letter to a Member*
> Anonymous, *A Letter to a Member of Parliament on the Present Unhappy Dispute between Great-Britain and her Colonies. Wherein the Supremacy of the Former is Asserted and Proved; and the Necessity of Compelling the Latter to Pay Due Obedience to the Sovereign State, is Enforced, upon Principles of Sound Policy, Reason, and Justice*. London, 1774.

Anon., *Letter to Doctor Tucker*
> Anonymous, *A Letter to Doctor Tucker on his Proposal of a Separation Between Great Britain and her American Colonies*. London, 1774.

Anon., *Letter to Hillsborough*
> Anonymous, *A Letter to the Right Honourable the Earl of Hillsborough, on the Present Situation of Affairs in America*. Boston, 1769.

Anon., *Letter to Rev. Cooper*
> Anonymous, *A Letter to the Rev. Dr. Cooper, on the Origin of Civil Government; in Answer to his Sermon, Preached before the University of Oxford, on the Day appointed by Proclamation for a General Fast*. London, 1777.

Anon., *Letter to the Essay Author*
> Anonymous, *A Letter to the Author of an Essay on the Middlesex Election: In which his Objections to the Power of Expulsion are considered: And the Nature of Representation in Parliament examined*. London, 1770.

Anon., *Liberty in Two Parts*
> Anonymous, *Liberty in Two Parts*. London, 1754.

Anon., *Licentiousness Unmask'd*
> Anonymous, *Licentiousness Unmask'd; or Liberty Explained*. London, n.d.

Anon., *Magna Charta Opposed to Privilege*
> Anonymous, *Magna Charta, Opposed to Assumed Privilege: Being a com-*

plete View of the late Interesting Disputes between the House of Commons and the Magistrates of London. London, 1771.

Anon., *Middle Temple Letter to Dublin*

Anonymous, *A Letter from a Gentleman of the Middle Temple, to his Friend in Dublin, Relative to the Present Crisis of Affairs in the Kingdom.* Dublin, 1780.

Anon., *Moderation Unmasked*

Anonymous, *Moderation Unmasked; or, the Conduct of the Majority Impartially Considered. By the Author of a Scheme for a Constitutional Association.* Dublin, 1780.

Anon., *National Mirror*

Anonymous, *The National Mirror. Being a Series of Essays on the Most Important Concerns: But Particularly those of the East-India Company.* London, 1771.

Anon., *New Political Catechism*

Anonymous, *A New Political Catechism for the Present Times. Very proper to be Learned by every British Subject, Before He he brought to be Confirm'd by a Minister of State. To which is added Machiavel's Ghost: A Satire.* 2d ed. London, 1790.

Anon., *Plain Question*

Anonymous, *The Plain Question Upon the Present Dispute with our American Colonies.* 4th ed. London, 1776.

Anon., *Plain Reasons for New-Modelling*

Anonymous, *Plain Reasons for New-Modelling Poynings' Law, in such a Manner as to assert the Ancient Rights of the Two Houses of Parliament, Without Entrenching on the King's Prerogative.* Dublin, 1780.

Anon., *Plain State*

Anonymous, *A Plain State of the Argument Between Great-Britain and Her Colonies.* London, 1775.

Anon., *Plan of Reconciliation with America*

Anonymous, *A Plan of Reconciliation with America; Consistent with the Dignity and Interests of Both Countries. Humbly inscribed to the King.* London, 1782.

Anon., *Plan to Reconcile*

Anonymous, *A Plan to Reconcile Great Britain & her Colonies, and Preserve the Dependency of America.* London, 1774.

Anon., *Policy of the Laws*

Anonymous, *An Inquiry into the Policy of the Laws, Affecting the Popish Inhabitants of Ireland, Preceded by a Short Political Analysis of the History and Constitution of Ireland, In which the Rights of Colonists and*

Planters are briefly mentioned . . . with some Hints respecting America. Dublin, 1775.

Anon., *Political Balance*
Anonymous, *The Political Balance. In which the Principles and Conduct of the Two Parties are weighed.* London, 1765.

Anon., *Political Disquisitions*
Anonymous, *Political Disquisitions Proper for Public Consideration in the Present State of Affairs. In a Letter to a Noble Duke.* London, 1763.

Anon., *Power and Grandeur*
Anonymous, *The Power and Grandeur of Great-Britain, Founded on the Liberty of the Colonies, and The Mischiefs attending the Taxing them by Act of Parliament Demonstrated.* New York, 1768.

Anon., *Present Crisis*
Anonymous, *The Present Crisis, With Respect to America, Considered.* London, 1775.

Anon., *Protest of a Private Person*
Anonymous [Granville Sharp], *An Address to the People of England: Being the Protest of a Private Person Against every Suspension of Law that is liable to injure or endanger Personal Security.* London, 1778.

Anon., *Reasons Against*
Anonymous, *Reasons Against the Renewal of the Sugar Act, As it will be prejudicial to the Trade, Not Only Of the Northern Colonies, but to that of Great-Britain Also.* Boston, 1764.

Anon., *Reflections on the Contest*
Anonymous, *Reflections on the American Contest: In which the Consequence of a Forced Submission, and the Means of a Lasting Reconciliation are pointed out, Communicated by Letter to a Member of Parliament, Some Time Since, and now Addressed to Edmund Burke, Esq. By A. M.* London, 1776.

Anon., *Reflexions on Representation*
Anonymous, *Reflexions on Representation in Parliament: Being an Attempt to shew the Equity and Practicability, not only of establishing a more equal Representation throughout Great Britain, but also of admitting the Americans to a Share in the Legislature.* London, 1766.

Anon., *Remarks on Conduct*
Anonymous, *Remarks on the Conduct of Opposition with Regard to America; Shewing their Inconsistency, by a Short Review of their own Measures.* London, 1777.

Anon., *Remarks on the New Essay*
Anonymous [John Gray], *Remarks on the New Essay of the Pen[n]sylva-*

nian Farmer; and on the Resolves and Instructions Prefixed to that Essay; By the Author of the Right of the British Legislature Vindicated. London, 1775.

Anon., *Resistance No Rebellion*
Anonymous, *Resistance No Rebellion: In Answer to Doctor Johnson's Taxation no Tyranny.* London, 1775.

Anon., *Review of Present Administration*
Anonymous, *A Review of the Present Administration.* London, 1774.

Anon., *Rights of Parliament*
Anonymous, *The Rights of Parliament Vindicated, On Occasion of the late Stamp-Act. In which is exposed the Conduct of the American Colonists. Addressed to all the People of Great Britain.* London, 1766.

Anon., *Rights of People to Petition*
Anonymous, *The Rights of the People to Petition, and the Reasonableness of complying with such Petitions: In a Letter to a Leading Great Man.* New ed. London, 1769.

Anon., *Second Answer to Wesley*
Anonymous [W. D.], *A Second Answer to Mr. John Wesley. Being a Supplement to the Letter of Americanus, In which the Idea of Supreme Power, and the Nature of Royal Charters, are briefly considered.* London, 1775.

Anon., *Sequel to Essay*
Anonymous, *Sequel to an Essay on the Origin and Progress of Government.* London, 1783.

Anon., *Serious and Impartial Observations*
Anonymous, *Serious and Impartial Observations on the Blessings of Liberty and Peace. Addressed to Persons of all Parties. Inviting them also to enter into that Grand ASSOCIATION, which is able to secure the Safety and Happiness of the British Empire.* London, 1776.

Anon., *Serious Considerations*
Anonymous, *Serious Considerations on a Late Very Important Decision of the House of Commons.* London, 1769.

Anon., *Short Appeal to the People*
Anonymous, *A Short Appeal to the People of Great-Britain; Upon the Unavoidable Necessity of the Present War With our Disaffected Colonies.* 2d ed. London, 1776.

Anon., *Some Fugitive Thoughts*
Anonymous, *Some Fugitive Thoughts on a Letter Signed Freeman, addressed to the Deputies, assembled at the High Court of Congress in Philadelphia.* South Carolina, 1774.

Anon., *Speech Never Intended*
> Anonymous, *A Speech Never Intended to be Spoken, In Answer to a Speech Intended to have been Spoken on the Bill for Altering the Charter of the Colony of Massachuset's Bay. Dedicated to the Right Reverend the Lord Bishop of St. A———.* London, 1774.

Anon, *Standing Army in Colonies*
> Anonymous, *No Standing Army in the British Colonies, or an Address to the Inhabitants of the Colony of New-York Against Unlawful Standing Armies.* New York, 1775.

Anon., *Supremacy of Legislature*
> Anonymous, *The Supremacy of the British Legislature over the Colonies, Candidly Discussed.* London, 1775.

Anon., *"Taxation no Tyranny" Considered*
> Anonymous, *The Pamphlet, Entitled, "Taxation no Tyranny," Candidly Considered, and It's Arguments, and Pernicious Doctrines, Exposed and Refuted.* London, [1775].

Anon., *Taxation, Tyranny*
> Anonymous, *Taxation, Tyranny. Addressed to Samuel Johnson, L.L.D.* London, 1775.

Anon., *Thoughts on the Constitution*
> Anonymous, *Some Thoughts on the Constitution; Particularly with respect to the Power of making Peace and War: The Use of Prerogative: The Rights of the People, &c.* London, 1748.

Anon., *Three Letters*
> Anonymous, *Three Letters to a Member of Parliament, On the Subject of the Present Dispute With Our American Colonies.* London, 1775.

Anon., *To Freeholders of New York* (1768)
> Anonymous, *To the Freeholders and Freemen of the City and County of New-York. This Vindication, of the Professors of the Law, in Answer to the Remarks on the 17 Queries, is humbly submitted by a sincere Friend to the Cause of Liberty, and this Colony.* [New York, 1768.]

Anon., *To the Princess of Wales*
> Anonymous, *Letter to Her R[oya]l H[ighnes]s the P[rinces]s D[o]w[a]g[e]r of W[ales] on the Approaching Peace. With a few Words concerning the Right Honourable the Earl of B[ute], and the General Talk of the World.* 3d ed. London, 1762.

Anon., *Tyranny Unmasked*
> Anonymous, *Tyranny Unmasked. An Answer to a Late Pamphlet, Entitled Taxation no Tyranny.* London, 1775.

Anon., *View of North*
Anonymous, *A View of the History of Great-Britain, During the Administration of Lord North, to the Second Session of the Fifteenth Parliament.* London, 1782.

Anon., *Vindication of the Livery*
Anonymous, *Vindication of the Petition of the Livery of the City of London, to his Majesty, as to the Charge upon the Ministry of raising a Revenue in our Colonies.* N.p., 1769.

Anon., *With Respect to America*
Anonymous, *Reflections on Government, With Respect to America. To which is Added, Carmen Latinum.* London, 1766.

"Another Origin of Judicial Review"
John Phillip Reid, "Another Origin of Judicial Review: The Constitutional Crisis of 1776 and the Need for a Dernier Judge," *New York University Law Review* 64 (1989): 963–89.

Arbuthnot, *Freeholder's Catechism*
[John] Arbuthnot, *The Freeholder's Political Catechism. Written by Dr. Arbuthnot.* [London,] 1769.

Atkyns, *Enquiry into Power*
Sir Robert Atkyns, *An Enquiry into the Power of Dispensing with Penal Statutes.* London, 1689.

Atwood, *Dependency of Ireland*
W[illiam] Atwood, *The History, and Reasons, of the Dependency of Ireland Upon the Imperial Crown of the Kingdom of England. Rectifying Mr. Molineux's State of the Case of Ireland's being bound by Acts of Parliament in England.* London, 1698.

[Auckland,] *Considerations Submitted*
[William Eden, Baron Auckland,] *Considerations Submitted to the People of Ireland, on their Present Condition with Regard to Trade and Constitution.* 2d ed. Dublin, 1781.

Authority of Rights
John Phillip Reid, *Constitutional History of the American Revolution: The Authority of Rights.* Madison, Wis., 1986.

Authority to Tax
John Phillip Reid, *Constitutional History of the American Revolution: The Authority to Tax.* Madison, Wis., 1987.

[Baillie,] *Appendix to a Letter*
[Hugh Baillie,] *An Appendix to a Letter to Dr. Shebbeare. To which are added, Some Observations on a Pamphlet, Entitled, Taxation no Tyranny;*

In which the Sophistry of that Author's Reasoning is Detected. London, 1775.

Baillie, *Letter to Shebear*
Hugh Baillie, *A Letter to Dr. Shebear: Containing a Refutation of his Arguments Concerning the Boston and Quebec Acts of Parliament: and his Aspersions upon the Memory of King William, and the Protestant Dissenters.* London, 1775.

Bailyn, *Ideological Origins*
Bernard Bailyn, *The Ideological Origins of the American Revolution.* Cambridge, Mass., 1967.

Bailyn, *Ordeal*
Bernard Bailyn, *The Ordeal of Thomas Hutchinson.* Cambridge, Mass., 1974.

Bailyn, *Pamphlets*
Pamphlets of the American Revolution, 1750–1776. Vol. 1. Edited by Bernard Bailyn. Cambridge, Mass., 1965.

Baldwin, *New England Clergy*
Alice M. Baldwin, *The New England Clergy and the American Revolution.* New York, 1958.

Ball, *Power of Kings*
William Ball, *The Power of King's Discussed; or, an Examen of the Fundamental Constitution of the Free-born People of England, in Answer to several Tenets of Mr. David Jenkins* (1649), reprinted in *Somers' Tracts,* 5:132–39.

[Bancroft,] *Remarks*
[Edward Bancroft,] *Remarks on the Review of the Controversy Between Great Britain and her Colonies. In which the Errors of its Author are exposed, and the Claims of the Colonies vindicated, Upon the Evidence of Historical Facts and authentic Records.* London, 1769.

Barker, *Essays*
Ernest Barker, *Essays on Government.* Oxford, England, 1945.

Barker, "Natural Law"
Sir Ernest Barker, "Natural Law and the American Revolution," in Sir Ernest Barker, *Traditions of Civility: Eight Essays.* Cambridge, England, 1948, pp. 263–355.

[Barrington,] *Revolution Principles*
[John Shute Barrington, First Viscount Barrington,] *The Revolution and Anti-Revolution Principles Stated and Compar'd, the Constitution Explain'd and Vindicated, And the Justice and Necessity of Excluding the*

Pretender, Maintain'd against the Book Entituled, Hereditary Right of the Crown of England Asserted. 3d ed. London, 1714.

[Barwis,] *Three Dialogues*
[Jackson Barwis,] *Three Dialogues Concerning Liberty.* London, 1776.

Becker, *Declaration*
Carl Becker, *The Declaration of Independence: A Study in the History of Political Ideas.* New York, 1958.

Becker, *Political Parties*
Carl Becker, *The History of Political Parties in the Province of New York, 1760-1776.* Madison, Wis., 1909.

Bellot, *William Knox*
Leland J. Bellot, *William Knox: The Life & Thought of an Eighteenth-Century Imperialist.* Austin, Tex., 1977.

Beloff, *Debate*
Max Beloff, "Introduction," in *The Debate on the American Revolution 1761-1783.* Edited by Max Beloff. 2d ed. London, 1960.

Bentham, *Comment on Commentaries*
Jeremy Bentham, *A Comment on the Commentaries*, reprinted in Bentham, *Principles of Legislation*, pp. 1-389.

Bentham, *Fragment on Government*
Jeremy Bentham, *A Fragment on Government* (1776), reprinted in Bentham, *Principles of Legislation*, pp. 391-551.

Bentham, *Principles of Legislation*
Jeremy Bentham, *The Collected Works of Jeremy Bentham: Principles of Legislation;—A Comment on the Commentaries and a Fragment on Government.* Edited by J. H. Burns and H.L.A. Hart. London, 1977.

Bernard & Barrington, *Correspondence*
The Barrington-Bernard Correspondence. Edited by Edward Channing and Archibald Cary Coolidge. Cambridge, Mass., 1912.

Black, "Constitution of Empire"
Barbara Aronstein Black, "The Constitution of Empire: The Case for the Colonists," *University of Pennsylvania Law Review* 124 (1976): 1157-1211.

Blackall, *Subjects Duty*
Offspring Blackall, *The Subjects Duty. A Sermon Preach'd at the Parish Church of St. Dunstan in the West, On Thursday, March the 8th, 1704/5.* London, 1705.

Blackstone, *Analysis of the Laws*
William Blackstone, *An Analysis of the Laws of England.* 6th ed. Oxford, England, 1771.

Blackstone, *Commentaries*
William Blackstone, *Commentaries on the Laws of England.* 4 vols. Oxford, England, 1765–69.

Blackstone, *Tracts*
William Blackstone, *Tracts Chiefly Relating to the Antiquities and Laws of England.* 3d ed. Oxford, England, 1771.

Bland, *An Inquiry*
Richard Bland, *An Inquiry into the Rights of the British Colonies, Intended as an Answer to the Regulations lately made concerning the Colonies, and the Taxes imposed upon them considered.* Williamsburg, Va., 1766.

[Bland,] *Colonel Dismounted*
[Richard Bland,] *The Colonel Dismounted: Or the Rector Vindicated. In a Letter addressed to His Reverence: Containing A Dissertation Upon the Constitution of the Colony.* Williamsburg, Va., 1764.

[Bolingbroke,] *Dissertation*
[Henry Saint John, Viscount Bolingbroke,] *A Dissertation Upon Parties; In Several Letters to Caleb D'Anvers, Esq.* 3d ed. London, 1735.

Bolingbroke, *Political Writings*
Viscount Bolingbroke, *Political Writings.* Edited by Isaac Kramnick. New York, 1970.

[Bollan,] *Freedom of Speech*
[William Bollan,] *The Freedom of Speech and Writing upon Public Affairs, Considered.* London, 1766.

Boston Chronicle
The Boston Chronicle. (Weekly newspaper).

Boston Evening-Post
The Boston Evening-Post. (Weekly newspaper).

Boston Gazette
The Boston Gazette and Country Journal. (Weekly newspaper).

Boston Merchants, *Observations*
Observations on Several Acts of Parliament, Passed In the 4th, 6th, and 7th Years of his present Majesty's Reign: and also, on The Conduct of the Officers of the Customs, since Those Acts were passed, and the Board of Commissioners appointed to Reside in America. Published by the Merchants of Boston. Boston, 1769.

Boston News-Letter
The Massachusetts Gazette and Boston News-Letter, also sometimes *The Massachusetts Gazette and the Boston News-Letter,* or *The Boston News-Letter.* (Weekly newspaper.)

Boston Post-Boy
　　The Boston Post-Boy & Advertiser. (Weekly newspaper.)

Boston Town Records
　　A *Report of the Record Commissioners of the City of Boston, Containing the Boston Town Records, 1758 to 1769.* 16th Report. Boston, 1886. *A Report of the Record Commissioners of the City of Boston, Containing the Boston Town Records, 1770 Through 1777.* 18th Report. Boston, 1887. (Listed by the Library of Congress in library catalogues as: BOSTON. *Registry dept.* "Records relating to the early history of Boston.")

[Boucher,] *Letter from a Virginian*
　　[Jonathan Boucher,] A *Letter From A Virginian to the Members of the Congress to be held at Philadelphia, on the first of September, 1774.* London, 1774.

Bowdoin Papers
　　The Bowdoin and Temple Papers. Collections of the Massachusetts Historical Society. 6th series, vol. 9. Boston, 1897.

Bracton, *Laws and Customs*
　　Henry de Bracton, *On the Laws and Customs of England.* Translated and Edited by Samuel E. Thorne. 5 vols. Cambridge, Mass., 1968–.

Brand, *Defence of Reeves*
　　John Brand, A *Defence of the Pamphlet Ascribed to John Reeves, Esq. and Entitled "Thoughts on the English Government."* London, 1796.

Brewer, "English Radicalism"
　　John Brewer, "English Radicalism in the Age of George III," in *Three British Revolutions,* pp. 323–67.

Brewer, *Party Ideology*
　　John Brewer, *Party Ideology and Popular Politics at the Accession of George III.* Cambridge, England, 1976.

Brewer, "Wilkites and the Law"
　　John Brewer, "The Wilkites and the Law, 1763–74: A Study of Radical Notions of Governance," in *An Ungovernable People: The English and Their Law in the Seventeenth and Eighteenth Centuries.* Edited by John Brewer and John Styles. New Brunswick, N.J., 1980, pp. 128–71.

Bridenbaugh, *Cities*
　　Carl Bridenbaugh, *Cities in Revolt: Urban Life in America, 1743–1776.* London, 1955.

Briefs of Revolution
　　The Briefs of the American Revolution: Constitutional Arguments Between Thomas Hutchinson, Governor of Massachusetts Bay, and James

Bowdoin for the Council and John Adams for the House of Representatives. Edited by John Phillip Reid. New York, 1981.

British Liberties
British Liberties, or the Free-Born Subject's Inheritance: Containing the Laws that form the Basis of those Liberties with Observations thereon; also an Introductory Essay on Political Liberty and a Comprehensive View of the Constitution of Great Britain. London, 1766.

[Brooke,] *Liberty and Common Sense*
[Henry Brooke,] *Liberty and Common-Sense to the People of Ireland, Greeting.* London, 1760.

Brown, *Becker on History*
E. Brown, *Carl Becker on History and the American Revolution.* East Lansing, Mich., 1970.

Brown, "Violence"
Richard Maxwell Brown, "Violence and the American Revolution," in *Essays on the American Revolution.* Edited by Stephen G. Kurtz and James H. Hutson. Chapel Hill, N.C., 1973, pp. 81–120.

Browning, *Court Whigs*
Reed Browning, *Political and Constitutional Ideas of the Court Whigs.* Baton Rouge, La., 1982.

Burgh, *Political Disquisitions*
J. Burgh, *Political Disquisitions; or, An Enquiry into public Errors, Defects, and Abuses. Illustrated by, and established upon Facts and Remarks, extracted from a Variety of Authors, Ancient and Modern.* 3 vols. Philadelphia, 1775.

Burgoyne, "Letter to Lee"
"A Copy of General Burgoyne's Answer, (dated July 8, 1775) to General Lee's Letter of June 7, 1775," in *Letters of Major General Lee, to the Right Honourable Earl Percy, and Major General John Burgoyne. With the Answers.* New York, 1775.

Burke on American Revolution
Edmund Burke on the American Revolution: Selected Speeches and Letters. Edited by Elliot Robert Barkan. New York, 1966.

Burke, *Letter to Sheriffs*
Edmund Burke, A Letter from Edmund Burke, Esq; One of the Representatives in Parliament for the City of Bristol, to John Farr and John Harris, Esqrs. Sheriffs of that City, on the Affairs of America. 3d ed. London, 1777.

[Burke,] *Observations on Late State*
[Edmund Burke,] *Observations on a Late State of the Nation.* 4th ed. London, 1769.

Burke, *Speech on American Taxation*
   Speech of Edmund Burke, Esq. on American Taxation, April 19, 1774. 3d. ed. New York, 1775.

Burke, "Speech on American Taxation"
   Edmund Burke, "Speech on American Taxation, House of Commons, 19 April 1774," in *The Debate on the American Revolution 1761-1783.* Edited by Max Beloff. 2d ed. London, 1960, pp. 135-50.

Burke Writings
   The Writings and Speeches of Edmund Burke. Volume II Party, Parliament, and the American Crisis. Edited by Paul Langford. Oxford, England, 1981.

Burlamaqui, *Natural Law*
   J. J. Burlamaqui, *The Principles of Natural Law. In which the true Systems of Morality and Civil Government are established; and the different Sentiments of Grotius, Hobbes, Puffendorf, Barbeyrac, Locke, Clark, and Hutchinson, occasionally considered.* London, 1748.

Burlamaqui, *Politic Law*
   J. J. Burlamaqui, *The Principles of Politic Law: Being a Sequel to the Principles of Natural Law.* London, 1752.

Bushman, *King and People*
   Richard L. Bushman, *King and People in Provincial Massachusetts.* Chapel Hill, N.C., 1985.

Butler, *Sermon*
   John Butler, Bishop of Oxford, *A Sermon Preached Before the House of Lords, at the Abby Church, Westminster, on Friday, February 27, 1778; Being the Day appointed by His Majesty's Royal Proclamation, to be observed as a Day of Solemn Fasting and Humiliation.* London, 1778.

Butler, *Sermon Preached in Dublin*
   Samuel Butler, *A Sermon Preached in the Parish Church of St. Michan's Dublin, On Friday the 13th Day of December, 1776, Being the Day appointed by His Majesty for holding a General Fast and Humiliation throughout this Kingdom.* Dublin, [1776].

Campbell, *Political Survey*
   John Campbell, *A Political Survey of Britain: Being a Series of Reflections on the Situation, Lands, Inhabitants, Revenues, Colonies, and Commerce of this Island. Intended to Shew that we have not as yet approached near the Summit of Improvement, but that it will afford Employment to many Generations before they push to their utmost Extent the natural Advantages of Great Britain. In Two Volumes.* London, 1774.

Candidus, *Two Letters*
   Mystagogus Candidus, *Two Letters: viz. I. A Letter to the Earl of Abing-*

*don, in which his Grace of York's Notions of Civil Liberty are examined by
Liberalis; published in the London Evening Post, November 6th, 1777. II.
Vera Icon; or a Vindication of his Grace of York's Sermon, preached on
February 21st, 1777.* London, 1777.

Canning, *Letter to Hillsborough*
George Canning, *A Letter to the Right Honourable Wills Earl of Hills-
borough, on the Connection Between Great Britain and her American
Colonies.* London, 1768.

Caplan, "Ninth Amendment"
Russell L. Caplan, "The History and Meaning of the Ninth Amendment,"
Virginia Law Review 69 (1983): 223–68.

Carlyle, *Justice and Necessity*
Alexander Carlyle, *The Justice and Necessity of the War with our American Colonies Examined. A Sermon Preached at Inveresk, December 12,
1776, Being the Fast-Day Appointed by the King, on account of the American Rebellion.* Edinburgh, 1777.

Carlyle, *Political Liberty*
A. J. Carlyle, *Political Liberty: A History of the Conception in the Middle
Ages and Modern Times.* Oxford, England, 1941.

Carpenter, *Development of Thought*
William Seal Carpenter, *The Development of American Political
Thought.* Princeton, N.J., 1930.

Cartwright, *Appeal on Constitution*
John Cartwright, *An Appeal on the Subject of the English Constitution.*
Boston, England [1797].

Cartwright, *Constitution Produced*
John Cartwright, *The English Constitution Produced and Illustrated.*
London, 1823.

Cartwright, *Legislative Rights*
John Cartwright, *The Legislative Rights of the Commonalty Vindicated;
or, Take Your Choice! Representation and Respect: Imposition and Contempt: Annual Parliaments and Liberty: Long Parliaments and Slavery.* 2d
ed. London, 1777.

Cartwright, *Letter to Abingdon*
John Cartwright, *A Letter to the Earl of Abingdon: Discussing a Position
Relative to a Fundamental Right of the Constitution: Contained in his
Lordship's Thoughts on the Letter of Edmund Burke, Esq. to the Sheriffs
of Bristol.* London, 1778.

[Cary,] *Answer to Molyneux*
[John Cary,] *An Answer to Mr. Molyneux His Case of Ireland's being bound*

by Acts of Parliament in England, Stated: and His Dangerous Notion of Ireland's being under no Subordination to the Parliamentary Authority of England Refuted; By Reasoning from his own Arguments and Authorities. London, 1698.

[Carysfort,] *Serious Address*
> [Carysfort, John Joshua Proby, 1st earl of,] *A Serious Address to the Electors of Great-Britain, on the Subject of Short Parliaments and an Equal Representation.* London, 1782.

Carysfort, *Thoughts on Constitution*
> Lord Carysfort [John Joshua Proby, 1st earl of,] *Thoughts on the Constitution, with a View to the Proposed Reform in the Representation of the People, and Duration of Parliaments.* London, 1783.

Cato's Letters
> *Cato's Letters: or, Essays on Liberty, Civil and Religious, And other Important Subjects. In Four Volumes.* 6th ed. London, 1755.

"Cato's Letters"
> John Trenchard and Thomas Gordon, "Cato's Letters," reprinted in *The English Libertarian Heritage From the Writings of John Trenchard and Thomas Gordon in The Independent Whig and Cato's Letters.* Edited by David L. Jacobson. Indianapolis, 1965.

Celebrated Speeches of Flood
> *The Celebrated Speeches of Colonel Henry Flood, on the Repeal of the Declaratory Act of the 6th George 1st. As Delivered in the House of Commons of Ireland, On the 11th and 14th of June 1782. Also, the Speech of Lord Abingdon, In the English House of Peers the 5th of July 1782, on Introducing his Bill for a Declaration of Right over every Part of the British Dependencies.* Dublin, [1782].

Chaffin, "Declaratory Act"
> Robert J. Chaffin, "The Declaratory Act of 1766: A Reappraisal," *The Historian* 37 (1974): 5–25.

[Chalmers,] *Answer from Bristol to Burke*
> [George Chalmers,] *An Answer from the Electors of Bristol to the Letter of Edmund Burke, Esq. on teh* [sic] *Affairs of America.* London, 1777.

[Chalmers,] *Beauties*
> [George Chalmers,] *The Beauties of Fox, North, and Burke, Selected from their Speeches, from the Passing of the Quebec Act, in the Year 1774, Down to the Present Time.* London, 1784.

[Chalmers,] *Plain Truth*
> [James Chalmers,] *Plain Truth; Addressed to the Inhabitants of America, Containing, Remarks on a Late Pamphlet, entitled Common Sense. Wherein are shewn, that the Scheme of Independence is Ruinous,*

Delusive, and Impractical: That were the Author's Asseverations, Respecting the Power of America, as Real as Nugatory; Reconcilation on liberal Principles with Great Britain, would be exalted Policy: And that circumstanced as we are, Permanent Liberty, and True Happiness, can only be obtained by Reconciliation with that Kingdom. Philadelphia, 1776.

[Chalmers,] *Second Thoughts*
> [George Chalmers,] *Second Thoughts: or, Observations upon Lord Abingdon's Thoughts on the Letter of Edmund Burke, Esq. to the Sheriffs of Bristol.* London, 1777.

Chambers, *Lectures*
> Sir Robert Chambers, *A Course of Lectures on the English Law: Delivered at the University of Oxford 1767-1773.* Edited by Thomas M. Curley. 2 vols. Madison, Wis., 1986.

"Charles Garth's Letter"
> Letter from Charles Garth to Ringgold, Murdoch, and Tilghman, 5 March 1766, in Morgan, *Prologue*, pp. 148-54.

Chatham, *Genuine Abstracts*
> *Genuine Abstracts from Two Speechs of the Late Earl of Chatham: And his Reply to the Earl of Suffolk.* London, 1779.

Chatham, *Speech 20 May*
> *Lord Chatham's Speech in the House of Lords on Friday the 20th of May 1777.* (One-page broadside, Huntington Library Rare Book #87304).

Chauncy, *Civil Magistrates*
> Charles Chauncy, *Civil Magistrates must be just, ruling in the Fear of God. A Sermon Preached before His Excellency William Shirley, Esq; the Honourable His Majesty's Council, and House of Representatives, of the Province of the Massachusetts-Bay in N. England; May 27, 1747. Being the Anniversary for the Election of His Majesty's Council for said Province.* Boston, 1747.

Christie, *Crisis*
> I. R. Christie, *Crisis of Empire: Great Britain and the American Colonies 1754-1783.* London, 1966.

Christie, "Quest for the Revolution"
> Ian R. Christie, "The Historians' Quest for the American Revolution," in *Statesmen, Scholars and Merchants: Essays in Eighteenth-Century History presented to Dame Lucy Sutherland.* Edited by Anne Whiteman, J. S. Bromley, and P. G. M. Dickson. Oxford, England, 1973, pp. 181-201.

Christie & Labaree, *Empire*
> Ian R. Christie and Benjamin W. Labaree, *Empire or Independence 1760-1776: A British-American Dialogue on the Coming of the American Revolution.* New York, 1976.

[Claridge,] *Defence of Government*
    [Richard Claridge,] A *Defence of the Present Government under King William & Queen Mary. Shewing the Miseries of England under the Arbitrary Reign of the Late King James II.* London, 1689.

Clark, *British Opinion*
    Dora Mae Clark, *British Opinion and the American Revolution.* New Haven, Conn., 1930.

Cobban, "Kings, Courts and Parliaments"
    Alfred Cobban, "Kings, Courts and Parliaments from 1660 to the French Revolution," in *The Eighteenth Century: Europe in the Age of the Enlightment.* Edited by Alfred Cobban. London, 1969, pp. 11–40.

Colbourn, *Lamp of Experience*
    H. Trevor Colbourn, *The Lamp of Experience: Whig History and the Intellectual Origins of the American Revolution.* Chapel Hill, N.C., 1965.

Colden, *Letters and Papers*
    The Letters and Papers of Cadwallader Colden: Volume VII 1765–1775. Collections of the New-York Historical Society for the Year 1923. Vol. 56. New York, 1923.

Colden Papers
    The Colden Letter Books, Vol. II, 1765–1775. Collections of the New-York Historical Society for the Year 1877. Vol. 10. New York, 1878.

Coleman, *McKean*
    John MacDonald Coleman, *Thomas McKean: Forgotten Leader of the Revolution.* Rockaway, N.J., 1975.

Collection on Salaries
    A Collection of the Proceedings of the Great and General Court or Assembly of His Majesty's Province of the Massachusetts-Bay, in New England; Containing several Instructions from the Crown, to the Council and Assembly of that Province, for fixing a Salary on the Governour, and their Determination thereon. Boston, 1729.

Commager, *Documents*
    Documents of American History. Edited by Henry Steele Commager. New York, 1934.

Commemoration Ceremony
    Commemoration Ceremony in Honor of the Two Hundredth Anniversary of the First Continental Congress in the United States House of Representatives. House Document No. 93–413, 93d Congress, 2d Session. Washington, D.C., 1975.

Commons Debates 1621
   Commons Debates 1621. Edited by Wallace Notestein, Frances Helen Relf, and Hartley Simpson. 7 vols. New Haven, Conn., 1935.

Concept of Liberty
   John Phillip Reid, *The Concept of Liberty in the Age of the American Revolution*. Chicago, 1988.

Concept of Representation
   John Phillip Reid, *The Concept of Representation in the Age of the American Revolution*. Chicago, 1989.

Conkin, *Truths*
   Paul K. Conkin, *Self-Evident Truths: Being a Discourse on the Origins & Developments of the First Principles of American Government—Popular Sovereignty, Natural Rights, and Balance & Separation of Powers*. Bloomington, Ind., 1974.

Conway, *Peace Speech*
   Henry Seymour Conway, *The Speech of General Conway, Member of Parliament for Saint Edmondsbury, on moving in the House of Commons, (On the 5th of May, 1780)*. London, 1781.

Cook, *King Charls his Case*
   John Cook, *King Charl[e]s his Case: Or an Appeal to all Rational Men, Concerning his Tryal at the High Court of Justice. Being for the most part that which was intended to have been delivered at the Bar, if the King had Pleaded to the Charge, and put himself upon a fair Tryal*. London, 1649.

Cooke, *Election Sermon*
   Samuel Cooke, *A Sermon Preached at Cambridge, in the Audience of his Honor Thomas Hutchinson, Esq; Lieutenant-Governor and Commander in Chief; The Honorable His Majesty's Council, and the Honorable House of Representatives, of the Province of the Massachusetts-Bay in New-England, May 30th, 1770. Being the Anniversary for the Election of His Majesty's Council for the Said Province*. Boston, 1770.

Cooper, *The Crisis*
   Samuel Cooper, *The Crisis. Or, a Full Defence of the Colonies. In which it is incontestibly proved that the British Constitution has been flagrantly violated in the late Stamp Act, and rendered indisputably evident, that the Mother Country cannot lay any arbitrary Tax upon the Americans, without destroying the essence of her own liberties*. London, 1766.

Correspondence George III
   The Correspondence of King George the Third From 1760 to December 1783. Vol. I 1760–1767. Vol. II 1768–June 1773. Vol. III July 1773–December 1777. Vol. IV 1778–1779. Edited by Sir John Fortescue. London, 1927–28.

Corwin, "Book Review"
Edward S. Corwin, "Book Review," *American Historical Review* 29 (1924): 775–78 (reviewing Charles Howard McIlwain, *The American Revolution: A Constitutional Interpretation* [1923]).

Costin & Watson, *Documents*
W. C. Costin and J. Steven Watson, *The Law and Working of the Constitution: Documents 1660–1914*. Vol. 1. London, 1952.

Countryman, *Revolution*
Edward Countryman, *The American Revolution*. New York, 1985.

Craftsman
The Craftsman. Vol. 1. London, 1737.

Cragg, *Freedom and Authority*
Gerald R. Cragg, *Freedom and Authority: A Study of English Thought in the Seventeenth Century*. Philadelphia, 1975.

Crane, "Franklin and Stamp Act"
Verner W. Crane, "Benjamin Franklin and the Stamp Act," *Publications of the Colonial Society of Massachusetts* 32 (1934): 56–77.

Crisis
The Crisis. (Weekly newspaper "Printed and published for the Authors by T. W. Shaw," London, 20 January 1775 to 6 October 1776).

Critical Review
The Critical Review: Or Annals of Literature by a Society of Gentlemen. (Monthly magazine, London).

De Beer, "Locke and English Liberalism"
Esmond S. De Beer, "Locke and English Liberalism: The *Second Treatise of Government* in Its Contemporary Setting," in *John Locke: Problems and Perspectives: A Collection of New Essays*. Edited by John W. Yolton. Cambridge, England, 1969, pp. 34–44.

"Declaratory Debates"
"Debates on the Declaratory Act and the Repeal of the Stamp Act, 1766," *American Historical Review* 17 (1912): 563–86.

Degler, "Preface 3"
Carl N. Degler, "Preface 3," in *Pivotal Interpretations of American History*. Edited by Carl N. Degler. Vol. 1. New York, 1966.

Delaware House Minutes (1765–70)
Votes and Proceedings of the House of Representatives of the Government of the Counties of New Castle, Kent and Sussex, upon Delaware. At Sessions held at New Castle in the Years 1765–1766–1767–1768–1769–1770. Dover, Del., 1931.

De Lolme, *Constitution*
> J. L. De Lolme, *The Constitution of England, or an Account of the English Government*. London, 1775.

De Lolme, *Constitution: New Edition*
> J. L. De Lolme, *The Constitution of England; or, an Account of the English Government; in which it is Compared Both with the Republican Form of Government, and the Other Monarchies in Europe*. New ed. London, 1807.

Demophilus, *Genuine Principles*
> Demophilus, *The Genuine Principles of the Ancient Saxon, or English Constitution, Carefully collected from the best Authorities; With some Observations, on their peculiar fitness, for the United Colonies in general, and Pennsylvania in particular*. Philadelphia, 1776.

Denison, *Westerly*
> Frederic Denison, *Westerly and Its Witnesses*. Providence, R.I., 1878.

De Pinto, *Letters on Troubles*
> M. De Pinto, *Letters on the American Troubles; Translated From the French*. London, 1776.

Dickinson, "Debate on Sovereignty"
> H. T. Dickinson, "The Eighteenth-Century Debate on the Sovereignty of Parliament," in *Transactions of the Royal Historical Society*. 5th series, 26 (1976): 189–210.

Dickinson, "Letter to Inhabitants"
> John Dickinson, "Letter to the Inhabitants of the British Colonies," reprinted from the *Pennsylvania Journal* of May and June 1774, in Dickinson, *Writings*, pp. 469–501.

Dickinson, *Letters*
> John Dickinson, *Letters from a Farmer in Pennsylvania, to the Inhabitants of the British Colonies* (1768), reprinted in Dickinson, *Writings*, pp. 305–406.

Dickinson, *Liberty and Property*
> H. T. Dickinson, *Liberty and Property: Political Ideology in Eighteenth-Century Britain*. London, 1977.

[Dickinson,] *New Essay*
> [John Dickinson,] *A New Essay [By the Pennsylvania Farmer] on the Constitutional Power of Great-Britain over the Colonies in America; with the Resolves of the Committee For the Province of Pennsylvania, and their Instructions to their Representatives in Assembly*. London, 1774.

Dickinson, "Non-Importation"
> John Dickinson, "An Address Read at a Meeting of Merchants to Consider

Non-Importation, April 25, 1768," reprinted in Dickinson, *Writings*, pp. 411–17.

Dickinson, *Reply to Galloway*
John Dickinson, *A Reply to a Piece Called the Speech of Joseph Galloway, Esquire*. Philadelphia, 1764.

Dickinson, *Speech*
John Dickinson, *A Speech Delivered in the House of Assembly of the Province of Pennsylvania, May 24th, 1764* (1764), reprinted in Dickinson, *Writings*, pp. 9–49.

Dickinson, *Speech Delivered*
John Dickinson, *A Speech Delivered in the House of Assembly of the Province of Pennsylvania, May 24th, 1764*. 2d ed. Philadelphia, 1764.

Dickinson, *Writings*
The Writings of John Dickinson: Political Writings 1764–1774. Edited by Paul Leicester Ford. Philadelphia, 1895.

D'Innocenzo & Turner, "New York Newspapers Part 2"
Michael D'Innocenzo and John J. Turner, Jr., "The Role of New York Newspapers in the Stamp Act Crisis, 1764–66, Part 2," *New-York Historical Society Quarterly* 51 (1967): 345–65.

Dobbs, *Letter to North*
Francis Dobbs, *A Letter to the Right Honourable Lord North, on his Propositions in Favour of Ireland*. Dublin, 1780.

Documents of New Hampshire
Documents and Records Relating to the Province of New-Hampshire, From 1764 to 1776; Including the whole Administration of Gov. John Wentworth; the Events immediately preceding the Revolutionary War; the Losses at the Battle of Bunker Hill, and the Record of all Proceedings till the end of our Provincial History. Volume VII. Provincial Papers. Edited by Nathaniel Bouton. Nashua, N.H., 1873.

Donoughue, *British Politics*
Bernard Donoughue, *British Politics and the American Revolution: The Path to War, 1773–75*. London, 1964.

[Downer,] *Discourse in Providence*
[Silas Downer,] *A Discourse, Delivered in Providence, in the Colony of Rhode-Island, upon the 25th Day of July, 1768. At the Dedication of the Tree of Liberty, From the Summer House in the Tree*. Providence, 1768.

[Downley,] *Sentiments*
[———Downley,] *The Sentiments of an English Freeholder, on the Late Decision of the Middlesex Election*. London, 1769.

[Draper,] *Thoughts of a Traveller*
[Sir William Draper,] *The Thoughts of a Traveller Upon our American Disputes*. London, 1774.

[Drayton et al.,] *The Letters*
[William Henry Drayton, William Wragg, Christopher Gadsden, and John Mackenzie,] *The Letters of Freeman, &c*. London, 1771.

[Dulany,] *Considerations*
[Daniel Dulany,] *Considerations on the Propriety of Imposing Taxes in the British Colonies, For the Purpose of raising a Revenue, by Act of Parliament* (1765), reprinted in Bailyn, *Pamphlets*, pp. 608–58.

[Dulany,] *Considerations on the Propriety*
[Daniel Dulany,] *Considerations on the Propriety of Imposing Taxes in the British Colonies, For the Purpose of raising a Revenue, by Act of Parliament*. 2d ed. Annapolis, Md., 1765.

Dulany, *English Laws*
Daniel Dulany, Sr., *The Right of the Inhabitants of Maryland to the Benefit of the English Laws* (1728), reprinted in Johns Hopkins University Studies in Historical and Political Science. Edited by J. M. Vincent, J. H. Hollander, and W. W. Willoughby. 21st series, nos. 11–12. Baltimore, Md., 1903.

Dummer, *Defence*
Jer[emiah] Dummer, *A Defence of the New-England Charters*. London, 1721.

Dunn, *Puritans and Yankees*
Richard S. Dunn, *Puritans and Yankees: The Winthrop Dynasty of New England 1630–1717*. Princeton, N.J., 1962.

[Dyson,] *Case of Middlesex*
[Jeremiah Dyson,] *The Case of the Late Election for the County of Middlesex, Considered on the Principles of the Constitution, and the Authorities of Law*. London, 1769.

[Eardley-Wilmot,] *Short Defence*
[John Eardley-Wilmot,] *A Short Defence of the Opposition; in Answer to a Pamphlet Intitled "A Short History of the Opposition."* London, 1778.

Eccleshall, *Order and Reason*
Robert Eccleshall, *Order and Reason in Politics: Theories of Absolute and Limited Monarchy in Early Modern England*. New York, 1978.

Edgar, *Colonial Governor*
Lady Edgar, *A Colonial Governor in Maryland: Horatio Sharpe and His Times 1753–1773*. London, 1912.

Egerton, *Discourse*
  A Discourse upon the Exposicion & Understandinge of Statutes With Sir Thomas Egerton's Additions. Edited by Samuel E. Thorne. San Marino, Cal., 1942.

Egmont Diary
  Manuscripts of the Earl of Egmont: Diary of Viscount Percival Afterwards First Earl of Egmont. Vol. I. 1730–1733. Historical Manuscripts Commission Reports. London, 1920.

Eliot, *Give Cesar His Due*
  Jared Eliot, *Give Cesar his Due. Or, the Obligation that Subjects are under to their Civil Rulers, As was shewed in a Sermon Preach'd before the General Assembly of the Colony of Connecticut at Hartford, May the 11th, 1738. The Day for the Election of the Honourable the Governour, the Deputy-Governour, and the Worshipful Assistants.* New London, Conn., 1738.

Eliot, "Letters"
  "Letters From Andrew Eliot to Thomas Hollis," *Collections of the Massachusetts Historical Society*, 4 (1858): 398–461.

Ellys, *Tracts on Liberty*
  Anthony Ellys, *Tracts on the Liberty, Spiritual and Temporal, of Protestants in England. Addressed to J. N. Esq; at Aix-la-Chapelle. Part II. [Of the Temporal Liberty of Subjects in England.]* London, 1765.

[Erskine,] *Reflections on the Rise*
  [John Erskine,] *Reflections on the Rise, Progress, and Probable Consequences, of the Present Contentions with the Colonies. By a Freeholder.* Edinburgh, 1776.

Estwick, *Letter to Tucker*
  Samuel Estwick, *A Letter to the Reverend Josiah Tucker, D. D. Dean of Glocester, in Answer to His Humble Address and Earnest Appeal, &c. with a Postscript, in which the present War against America is shewn to be the Effect, not of the Causes assigned by Him and Others, But of a Fixed Plan of Administration Founded in System.* London, 1776.

[Evans,] *Letter to John Wesley*
  [Caleb Evans,] *A Letter to the Rev. Mr. John Wesley, Occasioned by his Calm Address to the American Colonies.* London, 1775.

Evans, *Reply to Fletcher*
  Caleb Evans, *A Reply to the Rev. Mr. Fletcher's Vindication of Mr. Wesley's Calm Address to Our American Colonies.* Bristol, England, [1776].

Examination of Franklin
  The Examination of Doctor Benjamin Franklin, before an August Assembly, relating to the Repeal of the Stamp-Act, &c. Philadelphia, [1776].

F. B., *Causes of Distraction*
F. B., *The Causes of the Present Distractions in America Explained: In Two Letters to a Merchant in London*. London, 1774.

Fenning, *Dictionary*
D[aniel] Fenning, *The Royal English Dictionary: or, a Treasury of the English Language*. London, 1761.

[Ferguson,] *Brief Justification*
[R. Ferguson,] *A Brief Justification of the Prince of Orange's Descent into England, and of the Kingdoms Late Recourse to Arms*. London, 1689.

[Ferguson,] *Remarks on a Pamphlet*
[Adam Ferguson,] *Remarks on a Pamphlet lately Published by Dr. Price, Intitled, Observations on the Nature of Civil Liberty, the Principles of Government, and the Justice and Policy of the War with America, &c. In a Letter from a Gentleman in the Country to a Member of Parliament*. London, 1776.

Ferne, *Conscience Satisfied*
H[enry] Ferne, *Conscience Satisfied. That there is no Warrant for the Arms now Taken up by Subjects*. Oxford, England, 1643.

Filmer, *Anarchy of Mixed Monarchy*
Robert Filmer, *The Anarchy of a Limited or Mixed Monarchy or A succinct Examination of the Fundamentals of Monarchy, both in this and other Kingdoms, as well about the Right of Power in Kings, as of the Originall or Naturall Liberty of the People* (1648), reprinted in Filmer, *Patriarcha*, pp. 275–313.

Filmer, *Necessity of Absolute Power*
Robert Filmer, *The Necessity of the Absolute Power of all Kings: And in particular of the King of England by John Bodin a Protestant according to the Church of Geneva* (1648), reprinted in Filmer, *Patriarcha*, pp. 315–26.

Filmer, *Observations upon Aristotle*
Robert Filmer, *Observations Upon Aristotles Politiques Touching Forms of Government Together with Directions for Obedience to Governours in dangerous and doubtfull Times* (1652), reprinted in Filmer, *Patriarcha*, pp. 185–229.

Filmer, *Patriarcha*
Patriarcha and Other Political Works of Sir Robert Filmer. Edited by Peter Laslett. Oxford, England, 1949.

Fiske, *Importance of Righteousness*
Nathan Fiske, *The Importance of Righteousness to the Happiness, and the Tendency of Oppression to the Misery of a People; illustrated in two Discourses Delivered at Brookfield, July 4. 1774*. Boston, 1774.

[Fitch et al.,] *Reasons Why*
[Thomas Fitch, Jared Ingersoll, Ebenezer Silliman, and George Wyllys,] *Reasons Why the British Colonies, in America, Should not be Charged with Internal Taxes, by Authority of Parliament; Humbly offered, For Consideration, In Behalf of the Colony of Connecticut.* New Haven, Conn., 1764.

[Fitch,] *Some Reasons*
[Thomas Fitch,] *Some Reasons That Influence the Governor to Take, and the Councillors to Administer the Oath, Required by the Act of Parliament; commonly called the Stamp-Act.* Hartford, Conn., 1766.

Flaherty, "Empire Strikes Back"
Martin Stephen Flaherty, "The Empire Strikes Back: *Annesley* v. *Sherlock* and the Triumph of Imperial Parliamentary Supremacy," *Columbia Law Review* 87 (1987): 593–622.

Fletcher, *Vindication of Wesley*
John Fletcher, *A Vindication of the Rev. Mr. Wesley's "Calm Address to our American Colonies:" In Some Letters to Mr. Caleb Evans.* London, [1776].

Flood, *Declaratory Act*
Henry Flood, *The Celebrated Speeches of Colonel Henry Flood, on the Repeal of the Declaratory Act of the 6th George 1st.* Dublin, [1782].

Foner, *Labor and Revolution*
Philip S. Foner, *Labor and the American Revolution.* Westport, Conn., 1976.

[Forster,] *Answer to the Question Stated*
[Nathaniel Forster,] *An Answer to a Pamphlet Entitled, "The Question Stated, Whether the Freeholders of Middlesex forfeited their Right by Voting for Mr. Wilkes at the last Election? In a Letter from a Member of Parliament to one of his Constituents."* London, 1769.

Foster, *Short Essay*
Dan Foster, *A Short Essay on Civil Government, the Substance of Six Sermons, Preached in Windsor, Second Society, October 1774.* Hartford, Conn., 1775.

[Fowle,] *Appendix to Eclipse*
[Daniel Fowle,] *An Appendix to the late Total Eclipse of Liberty.* Boston, 1756.

Fox, *Speeches*
The Speeches of the Right Honourable Charles James Fox, in the House of Commons. Vols. 1 and 2. London, 1815.

Frank, "Sketch of an Influence"
Jerome Frank, "A Sketch of an Influence," in *Interpretations of Modern Legal Philosophies: Essays in Honor of Roscoe Pound*. Edited by Paul Sayre. New York, 1947, pp. 189–261.

Franklin, *Address to Ireland*
Benjamin Franklin, *An address to the Good People of Ireland, on behalf of America, October 4th, 1778*. Edited by Paul Leicester Ford. Brooklyn, N.Y., 1891.

Franklin, *Writings*
The Writings of Benjamin Franklin. Vol. 5. Edited by Albert Henry Smyth. New York, 1906.

Franklin-Jackson Letters
Letters and Papers of Benjamin Franklin and Richard Jackson 1753–1785. Edited by Carl Van Doren. Memoirs of the American Philosophical Society, vol. 24. Philadelphia, 1947.

Franklin's Letters to the Press
Benjamin Franklin's Letters to the Press, 1758–1775. Edited by Verner W. Crane. Chapel Hill, N.C., 1950.

Free, *Speech of John Free*
John Free, *The Speech of Dr. John Free, Containing A concise and clear Account of the English Constitution, both Old and New: And of the Rise and Progress of the modern Part of that Assembly, which we now call the Parliament*. London, 1753.

Freeman Letters
The Letters of Freeman, Etc. Essays on the Nonimportation Movement in South Carolina Collected by William Henry Drayton. Edited by Robert M. Weir. Columbia, S.C., 1977.

Gage, *Papers*
Military Papers of General Gage. Ann Arbor, Mich. Clements Library, University of Michigan.

[Galloway,] *Candid Examination*
[Joseph Galloway,] *A Candid Examination of the Mutual Claims of Great-Britain, and the Colonies: With a Plan of Accommodation, on Constitutional Principles*. New York, 1775.

[Galloway,] *Historical Reflections*
[Joseph Galloway,] *Historical and Political Reflections on the Rise and Progress of the American Rebellion*. London, 1780.

[Galloway,] *Political Reflections*
[Joseph Galloway,] *Political Reflections on the Late Colonial Governments: In which their original Constitutional Defects are pointed out, and*

shown to have naturally produced the Rebellion, which has unfortunately terminated in the Dismemberment of the British Empire. London, 1783.

[Galloway,] *Reply to an Address*
[John Galloway,] *A Reply to an Address to the Author of a Pamphlet, entitled, "A Candid Examination of the Mutual Claims of Great Britain and her Colonies," &c.* New York, 1775.

[Galloway,] *True and Impartial State*
[Joseph Galloway,] *A True and Impartial State of the Province of Pennsylvania.* Philadelphia, 1759.

"Garth Correspondence"
"Correspondence of Charles Garth," [Part 1] *South Carolina Historical and Genealogical Magazine* 28 (1927): 79–93; [Part 2] 28 (1927): 226–35; [Part 3] 29 (1928): 41–48; [Part 4] 29 (1928): 115–32; [Part 5] 29 (1928): 212–30; [Part 6] 29 (1928): 295–305; [Part 7] 30 (1929): 27–49; [Part 8] 30 (1929): 105–16; [Part 9] 30 (1929): 168–84; [Part 10] 30 (1929): 215–35; [Part 11] 31 (1930): 46–62; [Part 12] 31 (1930): 124–53; [Part 13] 31 (1930): 228–55; [Part 14] 31 (1930): 283–91; [Part 15] 33 (1932): 117–39; [Part 16] 33 (1932): 228–44; [Part 17] 33 (1932): 262–80.

Gazette & News-Letter
See *Massachusetts Gazette and Boston News-Letter.*

Gazette & Post-Boy
The *Massachusetts Gazette and Boston Post-Boy and the Advertiser.*

Gentleman's Magazine
The *Gentleman's Magazine and Historical Chronicle.* (Monthly magazine, London.)

Georgia Commons House Journal
The *Colonial Records of the State of Georgia. Volume XIV. Journal of the Commons House of Assembly January 17, 1763, to December 24, 1768, Inclusive. Volume XV. Journal of the Commons House of Assembly October 30, 1769, to June 16, 1782, Inclusive.* Atlanta, Ga., 1907.

Georgia Revolutionary Records
The *Revolutionary Records of the State of Georgia.* 3 vols. Compiled by Allen D. Candler. Atlanta, Ga., 1908.

Georgia Upper House Journal
The *Colonial Records of the State of Georgia. Volume XVII. Journal of the Upper House of Assembly January 17, 1763, to March 12, 1774, Inclusive.* Atlanta, Ga., 1908.

Gerardi, "King's College Controversy"
Donald F. M. Gerardi, "The King's College Controversy 1753–1756 and

the Ideological Roots of Toryism in New York," *Perspectives in American History* 11 (1977–78): 147–96.

Gibbes, *Documentary History*
R. W. Gibbes, *Documentary History of the American Revolution, Consisting of Letters and Papers Relating to the Contest for Liberty, Chiefly in South Carolina 1764–1776.* New York, 1855.

Gipson, *British Empire*
Lawrence Henry Gipson, *The British Empire Before the American Revolution.* 15 vols. Revised ed. New York, 1958–70.

Gipson, "Debate on Repeal"
Lawrence Henry Gipson, "The Great Debate in the Committee of the Whole House of Commons on the Stamp Act, 1766, as Reported by Nathaniel Ryder," *Pennsylvania Magazine of History and Biography* 86 (1962): 10–41.

Glorious Revolution.
The Glorious Revolution in America: Documents on the Colonial Crisis of 1689. Edited by Michael G. Hall, Lawrence H. Leder, and Michael G. Kammen. Chapel Hill, N. C., 1964.

[Glover,] *Considerations*
[Richard Glover,] *Considerations on the Attorney-General's Proposition for a Bill for the Establishment of Peace with America.* London, 1782.

Goebel, "Matrix of Empire"
Julius Goebel, "The Matrix of Empire," in Smith, *Appeals*, pp. xiii–lxi.

Gonson, *Charges*
Sir John Gonson's Five Charges to Several Grand Juries. . . . 4th ed. London, n.d.

Goodhart, *Law of the Land*
Arthur L. Goodhart, *Law of the Land.* Charlottesville, Va., 1966.

[Goodricke,] *Observations*
[Henry Goodricke,] *Observations on Dr. Price's Theory and Principles of Civil Liberty and Government, Preceded by a Letter to a Friend, on the Pretensions of the American Colonies, in respect of Right and Equity.* York, England, 1776.

Gordon, *Discourse Preached*
William Gordon, *A Discourse Preached December 15th 1774. Being the Day Recommended by the Provincial Congress; And Afterwards at the Boston Lecture.* Boston, 1775.

Gordon, *History*
William Gordon, *The History of the Rise, Progress, and Establishment of*

the Independence of the United States of America. 3d American ed. Vol. 1. New York, 1801.

Gough, *Fundamental Law*
> J. W. Gough, *Fundamental Law in English Constitutional History*. Oxford, England, 1955.

Gray, *Doctor Price's Notions*
> John Gray, *Doctor Price's Notions of the Nature of Civil Liberty, Shewn to be Contradictory to Reason and Scripture*. London, 1777.

[Gray,] *Right of the Legislature*
> [John Gray,] *The Right of the British Legislature to Tax the American Colonies Vindicated; and the Means of Asserting that Right Proposed*. 2d ed. London, 1775.

Greene, *Peripheries and Center*
> Jack P. Greene, *Peripheries and Center: Constitutional Development in the Extended Polities of the British Empire and the United States, 1607–1788*. Athens, Ga., 1986.

Greene, "Perspective of Law"
> Jack P. Greene, "From the Perspective of Law: Context and Legitimacy in the Origins of the American Revolution," *South Atlantic Quarterly* 85 (1986): 56–77.

Greene, *Quest*
> Jack P. Greene, *The Quest for Power: The Lower Houses of Assembly in the Southern Royal Colonies, 1689–1776*. Norton Library ed. New York, 1972.

Greene, "Virginia"
> Jack P. Greene, "Society, Ideology, and Politics: An Analysis of the Political Culture of Mid-Eighteenth-Century Virginia," in *Society, Freedom, and Conscience: The American Revolution in Virginia, Massachusetts, and New York*. Edited by Richard M. Jellison. New York, 1976, pp. 14–76.

Greene & Jellison, "Currency Act"
> Jack P. Greene and Richard M. Jellison, "The Currency Act of 1764 in Imperial-Colonial Relations, 1764–1776," *William and Mary Quarterly* 18 (1961): 485–518.

Gregor, "Preface"
> Francis Gregor, "The Preface" to Sir John Fortescue, *De Lauibus Legum Angliae*. New ed. London, 1775.

Grenville Letterbooks
> Letterbooks of George Grenville. ST 7, Huntington Library, San Marino, Calif.

Grenville Papers
> *The Grenville Papers: Being the Correspondence of Richard Grenville Earl Temple, K. G., and the Right Hon: George Grenville, their Friends and Contemporaries.* 4 vols. Edited by William James Smith. London, 1852–53.

[Grenville,] *Speech on Wilkes*
> [George Grenville,] *The Speech of a Right Honourable Gentleman, on the Motion for Expelling Mr. Wilkes, Friday, February 3, 1769.* London, 1769.

Grey, "Unwritten Constitution"
> Thomas C. Grey, "Origins of the Unwritten Constitution: Fundamental Law in American Revolutionary Thought," *Stanford Law Review* 30 (1978): 843–93.

Guide to Rights
> *A Guide to the Knowledge of the Rights and Privileges of Englishmen.* London, 1757.

Gunn, "Influence"
> J. A. W. Gunn, "Influence, Parties and the Constitution: Changing Attitudes, 1783–1832," *Historical Journal* 17 (1974): 301–28.

Hale, *Jurisprudence*
> Lord Justice [Matthew] Hale, *The Jurisprudence of the Lords House, or Parliament, Considered According to Antient Records.* London, 1796.

Halifax, *Charles II*
> George Savile, Marquis of Halifax, *A Character of Charles the Second: And Political, Moral and Miscellaneous Thoughts and Reflections.* London, 1750.

Hall, *Apology for Freedom*
> Robert Hall, *An Apology for the Freedom of the Press, and for General Liberty.* London, 1793.

Hall, *Edward Randolph*
> Michael Garibaldi Hall, *Edward Randolph and the American Colonies 1676–1703.* Chapel Hill, N.C., 1960.

Hamilton, *Farmer Refuted*
> Alexander Hamilton, *The Farmer Refuted: or A more impartial and comprehensive View of the Dispute between Great-Britain and the Colonies, Intended as a Further Vindication of the Congress* (1775), reprinted in *The Papers of Alexander Hamilton. Vol. 1.* Edited by Harold C. Syrett. New York, 1961, pp. 81–165.

[Hampson,] *Reflections on the Present State*
> [Rev. J. Hampson,] *Reflections on the Present State of the American War.* London, 1776.

Harper, "Mercantilism and the Revolution"
Lawrence A. Harper, "Mercantilism and the American Revolution," reprinted in *Causes and Consequences of the American Revolution.* Edited by Esmond Wright. Chicago, 1966, pp. 155–72.

Hart, "Bentham and America"
H. L. A. Hart, "Bentham and the United States of America," *Journal of Law and Economics* 19 (1976): 547–67.

Hay, "Criminal Prosecution in England"
Douglas Hay, "The Criminal Prosecution in England and its Historians," *Modern Law Review* 47 (1984): 1–29.

Headlam, "Constitutional Struggle"
Cecil Headlam, "The Constitutional Struggle With the American Colonies, 1765–1776," in *The Cambridge History of the British Empire. Vol. 1, The Old Empire From the Beginnings to 1783.* Edited by J. Holland Rose, A. P. Newton, and E. A. Benians. Cambridge, England, 1929, pp. 646–84.

[Heath,] *Case of Devon Excise*
[B. Heath,] *The Case of the County of Devon, With Respect to the Consequences of the New Excise Duty on Cyder and Perry. Published by the Direction of the Committee appointed at the General Meeting of that County to superintend the Application for the Repeal of that Duty.* London, 1763.

Hey, *Observations on Civil Liberty*
Richard Hey, *Observations on the Nature of Civil Liberty, and the Principles of Government.* London, 1776.

Hibernian Magazine
The Hibernian Magazine or Compendium of Entertaining Knowledge Containing The greatest Variety of the most Curious & useful Subjects in every Branch of Polite Literature. (Monthly magazine, Dublin.)

[Hickes,] *Jovian*
[George Hickes,] *Jovian. Or, An Answer to Julian the Apostate.* London, 1683.

[Hicks,] *Nature of Parliamentary Power*
[William Hicks,] *The Nature and Extent of Parliamentary Power Considered; In some Remarks upon Mr. Pitt's Speech in the House of Commons, previous to the Repeal of the Stamp-Act: With an Introduction, Applicable to the present Situation of the Colonies.* Philadelphia, 1768.

Hinkhouse, *Preliminaries*
Fred Junkin Hinkhouse, *The Preliminaries of the American Revolution as Seen in the English Press 1763–1775.* New York, 1926.

Hitchcock, *Sermon Preached before Gage*
> Gad Hitchcock, *A Sermon Preached Before his Excellency Thomas Gage, Esq; Governor: The Honorable His Majesty's Council, and the Honorable House of Representatives, of the Province of the Massachusetts-Bay in New-England, May 25th, 1774. Being the Anniversary of the Election of his Majesty's Council for said Province.* Boston, 1774.

Hoadly, *Works*
> *The Works of Benjamin Hoadly, D.D. Successively Bishop of Bangor, Hereford, Salisbury, and Winchester.* 3 vols. London, 1773.

Hobbes, *Elements of Law*
> Thomas Hobbes, *The Elements of Law Natural and Politic.* Edited by Ferdinand Tonnies. 2d ed. New York, 1969.

Holliday, *Life of Mansfield*
> John Holliday, *The Life of William Late Earl of Mansfield.* London, 1797.

[Hollis,] *True Sentiments*
> [Thomas Hollis,] *The True Sentiments of America: Contained in a Collection of Letters Sent from the House of Representatives of the Province of Massachusetts Bay to Several Persons of High Rank in this Kingdom.* London, 1768.

Home Office Papers (1766–69)
> *Calendar of Home Office Papers of the Reign of George III. 1766–1769, Preserved in Her Majesty's Public Record Office.* Edited by Joseph Redington. London, 1879.

Hooker, *Laws of Ecclesiastical Polity*
> Richard Hooker, *Of the Laws of Ecclesiastical Polity,* reprinted in *The Works of that Learned and Judicious Divine Mr. Richard Hooker With an Account of His Life and Death by Isaac Walton.* Edited by John Keble. 7th ed. New York, 1970.

Hope, *Letters*
> John Hope, *Letters on Certain Proceedings in Parliament, During the Sessions of the Years 1769 and 1770.* London, 1772.

[Hopkins,] *Grievances of the Colonies*
> [Stephen Hopkins,] *The Grievances of the American Colonies Candidly Examined.* London, 1766.

Hopkins, *Rights*
> Stephen Hopkins, *The Rights of Colonies Examined* (1765), reprinted in Bailyn, *Pamphlets,* pp. 507–22.

Hotoman, *Franco-Gallia*
> Francis Hotoman, *Franco-Gallia: Or, an Account of the Ancient Free*

State of France, and Most other Parts of Europe, before the Loss of their Liberties. Translated by Robert, Viscount Molesworth. London, 1711.

Howard, *Artillery-Election Sermon*
Simeon Howard, *A Sermon Preached to the Ancient and Honorable Artillery-Company, in Boston, New-England, June 7th, 1773. Being the Anniversary of their Election of Officers.* Boston, 1773.

[Howard,] *Defence of the Letter*
[Martin Howard,] *A Defence of the Letter from a Gentleman at Halifax, to His Friend in Rhode-Island.* Newport, R.I., 1765.

[Howard,] *Halifax Letter*
[Martin Howard, Jr.,] *A Letter from a Gentleman at Halifax to his Friend in Rhode-Island, Containing Remarks Upon a Pamphlet, Entitled, The Rights of the Colonies Examined* (1765), reprinted in Bailyn, *Pamphlets,* pp. 532–44.

Howard, *Road from Runnymede*
A. E. Dick Howard, *The Road from Runnymede: Magna Carta and Constitutionalism in America.* Charlottesville, Va., 1968.

[Howard,] *Some Questions Upon the Legislative*
[Gorges Edmond Howard,] *Some Questions Upon the Legislative Constitution of Ireland, proposed to the several Pamphleteers and other Writers against the Late Prorogation.* Dublin, 1770.

Hume, *Essays*
David Hume, *Essays and Treatises on Several Subjects.* New ed., 4 vols. London, 1765.

Humphreys, "Shelburne and Policy"
R. A. Humphreys, "Lord Shelburne and British Colonial Policy, 1766–1768," *English Historical Review* 50 (1935): 257–77.

[Hurd,] *Moral and Political Dialogues*
[Richard Hurd,] *Moral and Political Dialogues Between Divers Eminent Persons of the Past and Present Age; with Critical and Explanatory Notes.* 2d ed. London, 1760.

[Hutchinson,] *Collection of Papers*
[Thomas Hutchinson,] *A Collection of Original Papers Relative to the History of the Colony of Massachusetts-Bay.* Boston, 1769.

Hutchinson, "Dialogue"
Thomas Hutchinson, "A Dialogue Between an American and a European Englishman," edited by Bernard Bailyn, *Perspectives in American History* 9 (1975): 369–410.

Hutchinson, *Massachusetts-Bay*
Thomas Hutchinson, *The History of the Colony and Province of Mas-*

sachusetts-Bay. Edited by Lawrence Shaw Mayo. 3 vols. Cambridge, Mass., 1936.

[Hutchinson,] *Strictures Upon the Declaration*
[Thomas Hutchinson,] *Strictures Upon the Declaration of the Congress at Philadelphia; In a Letter to a Noble Lord, &c.* London, 1776.

"In Accordance with Usage"
John Phillip Reid, "In Accordance with Usage: The Authority of Custom, the Stamp Act Debate, and the Coming of the American Revolution," *Fordham Law Review* 45 (1976): 335–68.

"In a Defensive Rage"
John Phillip Reid, "In a Defensive Rage: The Uses of the Mob, the Justification in Law, and the Coming of the American Revolution," *New York University Law Review* 49 (1974): 1043–91.

In a Defiant Stance
John Phillip Reid, *In a Defiant Stance: The Conditions of Law in Massachusetts Bay, the Irish Comparison, and the Coming of the American Revolution.* University Park, Pa., 1977.

In a Rebellious Spirit
John Phillip Reid, *In a Rebellious Spirit: The Argument of Facts, the Liberty Riot, and the Coming of the American Revolution.* University Park, Pa., 1979.

In Defiance of the Law
John Phillip Reid, *In Defiance of the Law: The Standing-Army Controversy, the Two Constitutions, and the Coming of the American Revolution.* Chapel Hill, N.C., 1981.

"In Legitimate Stirps"
John Phillip Reid, "In Legitimate Stirps: The Concept of 'Arbitrary,' the Supremacy of Parliament, and the Coming of the American Revolution," *Hofstra Law Review* 5 (1977): 459–99.

"In Our Contracted Sphere"
John Phillip Reid, "'In Our Contracted Sphere:' The Constitutional Contract, the Stamp Act Crisis, and the Coming of the American Revolution," *Columbia Law Review* 76 (1976): 21–47.

Independent Reflector
The Independent Reflector or Weekly Essays on Sundry Important Subjects More Particularly adapted to the Province of New-York By William Livingston and Others. Edited by Milton M. Klein. Cambridge, Mass., 1963.

"Ingersoll Correspondence"
"A Selection from the Correspondence and Miscellaneous Papers of Jared

Ingersoll," Edited by Franklin B. Dexter, *Papers of the New Haven Colony Historical Society* 9 (1918): 201–472.

[Inglis,] *Letters of Papinian*
[Charles Inglis,] *Letters of Papinian: In which the Conduct, present State, and Prospects of the American Congress are Examined.* London, 1779.

[Inglis,] *True Interest*
[Charles Inglis,] *The True Interest of America Impartially Stated, in Certain Strictures on a Pamphlet Intitled Common Sense.* 2d ed. Philadelphia, 1776.

Interesting Letters
A New and Impartial Collection of Interesting Letters from the Public Papers; Many of them Written by Persons of Eminence. Vol. 2. London, 1767.

"In the First Line of Defense"
John Phillip Reid, "In the First Line of Defense: The Colonial Charters, the Stamp Act Debate and the Coming of the American Revolution," *New York University Law Review* 51 (1976): 177–215.

"In the Taught Tradition"
John Phillip Reid, "In the Taught Tradition: The Meaning of Law in Massachusetts-Bay Two Hundred Years Ago," *Suffolk University Law Review* 14 (1980): 931–74.

"Irrelevance of the Declaration"
John Phillip Reid, "The Irrelevance of the Declaration," in *Law in the American Revolution and the Revolution in the Law: A Collection of Review Essays on American Legal History.* Edited by Hendrik Hartog. New York, 1981, pp. 46–89.

Jackson, *Grounds of Government*
John Jackson, *The Grounds of Civil and Ecclesiastical Government Briefly Consider'd.* 2d ed. London, 1718.

[Jacob,] *Laws of Liberty*
[Giles Jacob,] *The Laws of Liberty and Property: Or, A Concise Treatise of all the Laws, Statutes and Ordinances, made for the Benefit and Protection of the Subjects of England.* 2d ed. London, 1734.

Jefferson, *Summary View*
Thomas Jefferson, *A Summary View of the Rights of British America Set Forth in some Resolutions Intended For the Inspection of the Present Delegates of the People of Virginia Now in Convention* (1774), reprinted in *Papers of Jefferson* 1:121–35.

Jenkinson Papers
> *The Jenkinson Papers 1760–1766.* Edited by Ninetta S. Jucker. London, 1949.

Jensen, *Documents*
> *English Historical Documents: American Colonial Documents to 1776.* Edited by Merrill Jensen. Vol. 9. New York, 1955.

Jenyns, "Observations"
> Soame Jenyns, "The Objections to the Taxation of Our American Colonies by the Legislature of Great Britain, briefly consider'd," reprinted in *The Debate on the American Revolution 1761–1783.* Edited by Max Beloff. 2d ed. London, 1960.

Jezierski, "Parliament or People"
> John V. Jezierski, "Parliament or People: James Wilson and Blackstone on the Nature and Location of Sovereignty," *Journal of the History of Ideas* 32 (1971): 95–106.

Johnson, *Notes on Pastoral*
> Samuel Johnson, *Notes Upon the Phoenix Edition of the Pastoral Letter. Part I.* London, 1694.

[Johnson,] *Political Tracts*
> [Samuel Johnson,] *Political Tracts. Containing, The False Alarm. Falkland's Islands. The Patriot; and Taxation no Tyranny.* London, 1776.

Johnson, *Remarks on Sherlock*
> Samuel Johnson, *Remarks Upon Dr. Sherlock's Book, Intituled the Case of Resistance of the Supreme Powers Stated and Resolved, according to the Doctrine of the Holy Scriptures.* London, 1689.

[Johnson,] *Some Important Observations*
> [Stephen Johnson,] *Some Important Observations, Occasioned by, and adapted to, the Publick Fast, Ordered by Authority, December 18th,* A.D. *1765.* Newport, R.I., 1766.

Johnstone, "Speech of November, 1775"
> William [*sic* George] Johnstone, "Governor Johnstone's Speech to the House of Commons, November, 1775," reprinted in *The American Revolution: The Anglo-American Relation, 1763–1794.* Edited by Charles R. Ritcheson. Reading, Mass., 1969, pp. 85–91.

[Jones,] *Constitutional Criterion*
> [William Jones,] *The Constitutional Criterion: By a Member of the University of Cambridge.* London, 1768.

Journal of Burgesses
> *Journals of the House of Burgesses of Virginia [Vol. 10] 1761–1765, [Vol. 11] 1766–1769, [Vol. 12] 1770–1772, [Vol. 13] 1773–1776 Including the*

records of the Committee of Correspondence. Edited by John Pendleton Kennedy. Richmond, Va., 1905, 1906, 1907.

Journal of New York Assembly (1766–76)
Journal of the Votes and Proceedings of the General Assembly of the Colony of New-York, From 1766 to 1776 Inclusive. Reprinted in pursuance of a joint resolution of the Legislature of the State of New-York, passed 30 April, 1820. Albany, N.Y., 1820.

Journal of the First Congress
Journal of the Proceedings of the Congress, Held at Philadelphia, September 5, 1774. Philadelphia, 1774.

Journal of the House
Journal of the Honorable House of Representatives of His Majesty's Province of the Massachusetts-Bay in New-England, Begun and held at Harvard College in Cambridge, in the County of Middlesex, on Wednesday the Twenty-seventh Day of May, Annoque Domini, 1772. Boston, 1772.

Journals of Congress
Journals of the Continental Congress 1774–1789. Edited by Worthington Chauncey Ford et al. 34 vols. Washington, D.C., 1904–37.

Judson, *Crisis*
Margaret Atwood Judson, *The Crisis of the Constitution: An Essay in Constitutional and Political Thought in England 1603–1645.* New Brunswick, N.J., 1949.

"Junius," *Junius*
["Junius,"] *Junius.* 2 vols. London, [1772].

[Kames,] *History of Man*
[Henry Home, Lord Kames,] *Sketches of the History of Man. In Two Volumes.* Edinburgh, 1774.

Kammen, *Empire and Interest*
Michael Kammen, *Empire and Interest: The American Colonies and the Politics of Mercantilism.* Philadelphia, 1970.

Kammen, "Meaning of Colonization"
Michael Kammen, "The Meaning of Colonization in American Revolutionary Thought," *Journal of History of Ideas* 31 (1970): 337–58.

Keir, *Constitutional History*
Sir David Lindsay Keir, *The Constitutional History of Modern Britain Since 1845.* 8th ed. Princeton, N.J., 1966.

Keith, *Papers and Tracts*
Sir William Keith, *A Collection of Papers and other Tracts, Written occasionally on Various Subjects.* London, 1740.

[Keld,] *Polity of England*
[Christopher Keld,] *An Essay on the Polity of England*. London, 1785.

Kemp, "Parliamentary Sovereignty"
Betty Kemp, "Parliamentary Sovereignty," *London Review of Books* 5, no. 4 (18 January 1984): pp. 12–14.

Kenyon, *Revolution Principles*
J. P. Kenyon, *Revolution Principles: The Politics of Party 1689–1720*. Cambridge, England, 1977.

Kettner, *American Citizenship*
James H. Kettner, *The Development of American Citizenship, 1608–1870*. Chapel Hill, N.C., 1978.

King, *English Constitution*
Edward King, *An Essay on the English Constitution and Government*. London, 1767.

Kliger, *Goths*
Samuel Kliger, *The Goths in England: A Study in Seventeenth and Eighteenth Century Thought*. Cambridge, Mass., 1952.

Knollenberg, "Adams and Tea Party"
Bernhard Knollenberg, "Did Samuel Adams provoke the Boston Tea Party and the Clash at Lexington?" *Proceedings of the American Antiquarian Society* 70 (1960): 494–503.

Knollenberg, *Growth of Revolution*
Bernhard Knollenberg, *Growth of the American Revolution 1766–1775*. New York, 1975.

Knollenberg, *Origin*
Bernhard Knollenberg, *Origin of the American Revolution. 1759–1766*. Revised ed. New York, 1965.

[Knox,] *Claim of the Colonies*
[William Knox,] *The Claim of the Colonies to an Exemption from Internal Taxes Imposed By Authority of Parliament, Examined: In a Letter from a Gentleman in London, to his Friend in America*. London, 1765.

[Knox,] *Controversy*
[William Knox,] *The Controversy Between Great Britain and her Colonies Reviewed; The Several Pleas of the Colonies, In Support of their Right to all the Liberties and Privileges of British Subjects, and to Exemption from the Legislative Authority of Parliament, Stated and Considered; and the Nature of their Connection with, and Dependence on, Great Britain, Shewn, Upon the Evidence of Historical Facts and Authentic Records*. London, 1769.

[Knox,] *Controversy* (Dublin Edition)
[William Knox,] *The Controversy Between Great Britain and her Colonies Reviewed; The Several Pleas of the Colonies, In Support of their Right to all the Liberties and Privileges of British Subjects, and to Exemption from the Legislative Authority of Parliament, Stated and Considered; and The Nature of their Connection with, and Dependence on, Great Britain, Shewn, Upon the Evidence of Historical Facts and Authentic Records.* Dublin, 1769.

[Knox,] *Justice and Policy*
[William Knox,] *The Justice and Policy of the Late Act of Parliament, for Making more Effectual Provision for the Government of the Province of Quebec, Asserted and Proved, and the Conduct of Administration Respecting that Province, Stated and Vindicated.* London, 1774.

[Knox,] *Letter to a Member*
[William Knox,] *A Letter to a Member of Parliament, Wherein the Power of the British Legislature, And the Case of the Colonists, Are briefly and impartially considered.* London, 1765.

[Knox,] *Present State*
[William Knox,] *The Present State of the Nation: Particularly with respect to its Trade, Finances, &c. &c. Addressed to the King and both Houses of Parliament.* London, 1769.

Koebner, *Empire*
Richard Koebner, *Empire.* New York, 1961.

Kramnick, *Bolingbroke's Circle*
Isaac Kramnick, *Bolingbroke and His Circle: The Politics of Nostalgia in the Age of Walpole.* Cambridge, Mass., 1968.

Kramnick, "Introduction to Writings"
Isaac Kramnick, "Introduction" to Bolingbroke, *Political Writings.*

"L.," Letter to G[renville]
"L.," *A Letter to G. G. Stiff in Opinions, always in the wrong.* London, 1767.

Labaree, *Royal Instructions*
Leonard Woods Labaree, *Royal Instructions to British Colonial Governors 1670-1776.* 2 vols. New York, 1935; reprint, 1967.

Labaree, *Tea Party*
Benjamin Woods Labaree, *The Boston Tea Party.* New York, 1964.

Lamprecht, "Introduction"
Sterling P. Lamprecht, "Introduction" to Thomas Hobbes, *De Cive or the Citizen.* Edited by Sterling P. Lamprecht. New York, 1947.

Langford, "Old Whigs"
Paul Langford, "Old Whigs, Old Tories, and the American Revolution,"
Journal of Imperial and Commonwealth History 8 (1980): 106–30.

Langford, *Rockingham Administration*
P. Langford, *The First Rockingham Administration 1765–1766.* Oxford,
1973.

Larkin, *Property in Eighteenth Century*
Paschal Larkin, *Property in the Eighteenth Century with Special Reference to England and Locke.* Dublin and Cork, 1930.

Laslett, "Introduction and Notes"
Peter Laslett, "Introduction [and footnotes]," to John Locke, *Two Treatises of Government.* 2d ed. Edited by Peter Laslett. Cambridge, England, 1967.

Lawson, "George Grenville"
Philip Lawson, "George Grenville and America: The Years of Opposition,
1765 to 1770," *William and Mary Quarterly* 37 (1980): 561–76.

Lawson, *Politica Sacra*
George Lawson, *Politica Sacra & Civilis: Or, a Model of Civil and Ecclesiastical Government.* 2d ed. London, 1689.

Leder, *Liberty*
Lawrence H. Leder, *Liberty and Authority: Early American Political
Ideology 1689–1763.* Chicago, 1968.

Lee, *Appeal to Justice*
[Arthur] Lee, *An Appeal to the Justice and Interests of the People of Great
Britain, in the Present Dispute with America.* London, 1774.

[Lee,] *Junius Americanus*
[Arthur Lee,] *The Political Detection; or, the Treachery and Tyranny of
Administration, both at Home and Abroad; Displayed in a Series of Let-
ters, signed Junius Americanus.* London, 1770.

Lee, *Richard Henry Lee*
Richard Henry Lee, *Memoir of the Life of Richard Henry Lee, and His
Correspondence with the Most Distinguished Men in America and
Europe, Illustrative of their Characters, and of the Events of the American
Revolution.* 2 vols. Philadelphia, 1825.

[Lee,] *Second Appeal*
[Arthur Lee,] *A Second Appeal to the Justice and Interests of the People,
on the Measures Respecting America. By the Author of the First.* London,
1775.

[Lee,] *Speech Intended*
   [Arthur Lee,] *A Speech, Intended to have been Delivered in the House of Commons, in Support of the Petition from the General Congress at Philadelphia.* London, 1775.

Leigh, *Considerations*
   Sir Egerton Leigh, *Considerations on Certain Political Transactions of the Province of South Carolina* (1774), reprinted in *The Nature of Colony Constitutions: Two Pamphlets on the Wilkes Fund Controversy in South Carolina by Sir Egerton Leigh and Arthur Lee.* Edited by Jack P. Greene. Columbia, S.C., 1970, pp. 63–123.

Leonard, "Massachusettensis"
   Daniel Leonard, "Massachusettensis Letters," reprinted in *The American Colonial Crisis: The Daniel Leonard–John Adams Letters to the Press 1774–1775.* Edited by Bernard Mason. New York, 1972.

Leslie, "Gaspee Affair"
   William R. Leslie, "The Gaspee Affair: A Study of its Constitutional Significance," *Mississippi Valley Historical Review* 39 (1952): 233–56.

Letters of Charles Carroll
   Unpublished Letters of Charles Carroll of Carrollton, and of his Father, Charles Carroll of Doughoregan. Edited by Thomas Meagher Field. New York, 1902.

Letters of Delegates to Congress
   Letters of Delegates to Congress: 1774–1789. 12 vols. Edited by Paul H. Smith. Washington, D.C., 1976–1985.

"Letters of Dennys De Berdt"
   "Letters of Dennys De Berdt, 1757–1770," *Publications of the Colonial Society of Massachusetts* 13 (1911): 293–461.

Lieberman, *Province of Legislation*
   David Lieberman, *The Province of Legislation Determined: Legal Theory in Eighteenth-Century Britain.* Cambridge, England, 1989.

[Lind,] *Englishman's Answer*
   [John Lind,] *An Englishman's Answer, To the Address From the Delegates, To the People of Great-Britain, In a Letter to the Several Colonies which were Represented in the Late Continental Congress.* New York, 1775.

[Lind,] *Thirteenth Parliament*
   [John Lind,] *Remarks on the Principal Acts of the Thirteenth Parliament of Great Britain. Vol. I. Containing Remarks on the Acts relating to the Colonies. With a Plan of Reconciliation.* London, 1775.

[Littleton,] *Groans of Plantations*
   [Edward Littleton,] *The Groans of the Plantations: or a True Account of*

their Grievous and Extreme Sufferings by the Heavy Impositions upon Sugar, and other Hardships. Relating more particularly to the Island of Barbados. London, 1689.

Livingston, *Address to the House*
The Address of Mr. Justice Livingston, to the House of Assembly, In Support of his Right to a Seat. New York, [1769].

[Lloyd,] *Conduct Examined*
[Charles Lloyd,] *The Conduct of the Late Ministry Examined; From July, 1765, to March, 1766.* London, 1767.

[Lloyd,] *Examination of the Principles*
[Charles Lloyd,] *An Examination of the Principles and Boasted Disinterestedness of a Late Right Honourable Gentleman. In a Letter from an Old Man of Business, to a Noble Lord.* London, 1766.

Locke, *Two Treatises*
John Locke, *Two Treatises of Government: A Critical Edition with an Introduction and Apparatus Criticus.* 2d ed. Edited by Peter Laslett. Cambridge, England, 1967.

Lockwood, *Connecticut Election Sermon*
Samuel Lockwood, *Civil Rulers an Ordinance of God, for Good to Mankind. A Sermon, Preached Before the General Assembly, of the Colony of Connecticut, at Hartford; On the Day of their Anniversary Election, May 12th, 1774.* New London, Conn., 1774.

Lockwood, *Worth and Excellence*
James Lockwood, *The Worth and Excellence of Civil Freedom and Liberty illustrated, and a Public Spirit and the Love of our Country recommended. A Sermon Delivered before the General Assembly of the Colony of Connecticut, at Hartford, on the Day of the Anniversary Election. May 10th, 1759.* New London, Conn., 1759.

Lofft, *Observations on Wesley's Address*
Capel Lofft, *Observations on Mr. Wesley's Second Calm Address, and Incidently on other Writings upon the American Question. Together with Thoughts on Toleration, and on the Point how Far the Conscience of the Subject is Concerned in a War; Remarks on Constitution in General, and that of England in Particular; on the Nature of Colonial Government, and a Recommendation of a Plan of Peace.* London, 1777.

Lofft, *Summary of Treatise*
Capel Lofft, *A Summary of Treatise by Major Cartwright, entitled the People's Barrier Against Undue Influence: or the Commons' House of Parliament According to the Constitution.* [London,] 1780.

London Evening Post
(Newspaper, London.)

London Journal
(Weekly newspaper, London.)

London Magazine
The London Magazine or Gentleman's Monthly Intelligencer. (Monthly magazine, London.)

"Lords Debate on Declaratory Act"
"Debate on the Conway Resolutions. House of Lords, 10 February 1766," in *The Debate on the American Revolution.* 2d ed. Edited by Max Beloff. London, 1960, pp. 106–18.

Lounsbury, *British Fishery*
Ralph Greenlee Lounsbury, *The British Fishery at New Foundland, 1634–1763.* New Haven, Conn., 1934.

Lovejoy, *Rhode Island Politics*
David S. Lovejoy, *Rhode Island Politics and the American Revolution 1760–1776.* Providence, R.I., 1958.

Lovell, *An Oration*
James Lovell, *An Oration Delivered April 2d, 1771. At the Request of the Inhabitants of the Town of Boston; to Commemorate the bloody Tragedy of the Fifth of March, 1770.* Boston, 1771.

Lowth, *Durham Assize Sermon*
Robert Lowth, *A Sermon Preached Before the Honourable and Right Reverend Richard, Lord Bishop of Durham, the Honourable Henry Bathurst, One of the Justices of the Court of Common Pleas, and the Honourable Sir Joseph Yates, One of the Justices of the Court of King's Bench; at the Assizes Holden at Durham, August 15, 1764.* 2d ed. Newcastle, England, 1764.

Lucas, "Burke's Doctrine of Prescription"
Paul Lucas, "On Edmund Burke's Doctrine of Prescription: Or, an Appeal from the New to the Old Lawyers," *The Historical Journal* 11 (1968): 35–63.

Lucas, "To the Lord Lieutenant"
Charles Lucas, "To his Excellency George Lord Viscount Townshend, Lord Lieutenant General and General Governor of Ireland," preface to the reprint of [John Lodge,] *The Usage of Holding Parliaments and of Preparing and Passing Bills of Supply, in Ireland, Stated from Record.* London, 1770.

[Macfarlane,] *George Third*
[Robert Macfarlane,] *The History of the Reign of George the Third, King of Great-Britain, &c. to the Conclusion of the Session of Parliament Ending in May 1770.* London, 1770.

[Macfarlane,] *Second Ten Years*
    [Robert Macfarlane,] *The History of the Second Ten Years of the Reign of George the Third, King of Great-Britain, &c.* London, 1782.

[Macpherson,] *Retrospective View*
    [James Macpherson,] *A Retrospective View of the Causes of the Difference Between Great Britain and her Colonies in America: And a Consideration of Some Probable Consequences of the Dismemberment of the Empire.* N.p., [1782].

[Macpherson,] *Rights of Great Britain*
    [James Macpherson,] *The Rights of Great Britain Asserted against the Claims of America: Being an Answer to the Declaration of the General Congress.* 6th ed. London, 1776.

Madden, "Origins"
    Frederick Madden, "Some Origins and Purposes in the Formation of British Colonial Government," in *Essays in Imperial Government Presented to Margery Perham.* Edited by Kenneth Robinson and Frederick Madden. Oxford, England, 1963.

Madden, "Relevance of Experience"
    A. F. McC. Madden, "1066, 1776 and All That: The Relevance of English Medieval Experience of 'Empire' to Later Imperial Constitutional Issues," in *Perspectives of Empire: Essays Presented to Gerald S. Graham.* Edited by John E. Flint and Glyndwr Williams. New York, 1973.

Maier, *Old Revolutionaries*
    Pauline Maier, *The Old Revolutionaries: Political Lives in the Age of Samuel Adams.* New York, 1980.

Maitland, *Constitutional History*
    F. W. Maitland, *The Constitutional History of England: A Course of Lectures Delivered.* Cambridge, England, 1908.

Manning, "Puritanism and Democracy"
    Brian Manning, "Puritanism and Democracy, 1640–1642," in *Puritans and Revolutionaries: Essays in Seventeenth-Century History Presented to Christopher Hill.* Edited by Donald Pennington and Keith Thomas. Oxford, England, 1978, pp. 139–160.

[Mantell,] *Short Treatise of the Lawes*
    [Walter Mantell,] *A Short Treatise of the Lawes of England: With the jurisdiction of the High Court of Parliament, With the Liberties and Freedomes of the Subjects.* London, 1644.

[Marat,] *Chains of Slavery*
    [J. P. Marat,] *The Chains of Slavery. A Work Wherein the Clandestine and Villainous Attempts of Princes to Ruin Liberty are Pointed Out, and the Dreadful Scenes of Despotism Disclosed. To which is prefixed, An Address*

to the Electors of Great Britain in order to draw their timely Attention to the Choice of proper Representatives in the next Parliament. London, 1774.

Markham, *Sermon Preached*
William Markham, Archbishop of York, *A Sermon Preached before the Incorporated Society for the Propagation of the Gospel in Foreign Parts, at their Anniversary Meeting, in the Parish Church of St. Mary-le-Bow, on Friday, February 21, 1777.* London, 1777.

Marshall, "Empire and Authority"
P. J. Marshall, "Empire and Authority in the later Eighteenth Century," *Journal of Imperial and Commonwealth History* 15 (1987): 105–22.

Martin, "Long and Short"
Thomas S. Martin, "The Long and the Short of It: A Newspaper Exchange on the Massachusetts Charters, 1772," *William and Mary Quarterly* 43 (1986): 99–110.

Maryland Archives
Archives of Maryland. Vol. 7. Baltimore, 1889.

Maryland Votes and Proceedings (1766)
Votes and Proceedings of the Lower House of Assembly of the Province of Maryland. November Session, 1766. Being the Fourth Session of this Assembly. Annapolis, Md., n.d.

Maryland Votes and Proceedings (1769)
Votes and Proceedings of the Lower House of Assembly of the Province of Maryland. November Session, 1769. Being the Second Session of this Assembly. Annapolis, Md., [1770].

Massachusetts Gazette
The Massachusetts Gazette. (Weekly newspaper, Boston.)

Massachusetts Gazette and Boston News-Letter
The Massachusetts Gazette and Boston News-Letter. (Weekly newspaper. An alternative title sometimes used for the *Boston News-Letter* and located in the same files and on the same microfilm with that newspaper.)

Massachusetts House Journal (1765)
Journal of the Honourable House of Representatives, of His Majesty's Province of the Massachusetts-Bay, in New-England, Begun and held at Boston, in the County of Suffolk, on Wednesday the Twenty-ninth Day of May, Annoque Domini, 1765. Boston, [1765–1766].

Massachusetts House Journal (1769)
Journal of the Honourable House of Representatives of His Majesty's Province of the Massachusetts-Bay, in New-England, Begun and held at

Boston, in the County of Suffolk, on Wednesday the Thirty-first Day of May, Annoque Domini, 1769. Boston, 1769.

Massacre Orations

Orations Delivered at the Request of the Inhabitants of the Town of Boston, to Commemorate the Evening of the Fifth of March, 1770; When a Number of Citizens were Killed by a Party of British Troops, Quartered Among them, in a Time of Peace. Boston, [1785].

[Mather,] *America's Appeal*

[Moses Mather,] *America's Appeal to the Impartial World. Wherein the Rights of the Americans, as Men, British Subjects, and as Colonists; the Equity of the Demand, and of the Manner in which it is made upon them by Great-Britain, are stated and considered. And, the Opposition made by the Colonies to Acts of Parliament, their resorting to Arms in their necessary Defence, against the Military Armaments, employed to enforce them, Vindicated.* Hartford, Conn., 1775.

Mauduit, *Legislative Authority*

Jasper Mauduit, *The Legislative Authority of the British Parliament, with respect to North America, and the Privileges of the Assemblies there, briefly Considered.* London, 1766.

Mauduit Letters

Jasper Mauduit: Agent in London for the Province of the Massachusetts Bay 1762–1765. Boston, 1918.

[Mauduit,] *Letters of Hutchinson*

[Israel Mauduit,] *The Letters of Governor Hutchinson, and Lieut. Governor Oliver, &c. Printed at Boston. And Remarks thereon. With the Assembly's Address, and the Proceedings Of the Lords Committee of Council. Together with the Substance of Mr. Wedderburn's Speech relating to those Letters. And the Report of the Lords Committee to his Majesty in Council.* 2d ed. London, 1774.

Mauduit, *Short View*

Israel Mauduit, *A Short View of the History of the Colony of Massachusetts Bay, With Respect to their Charters and Constitution.* 3d ed. London, 1774.

Mayhew, *Snare Broken*

Jonathan Mayhew, *The Snare broken. A Thanksgiving-Discourse, Preached At the Desire of the West Church in Boston, N.E. Friday May 23, 1766, Occasioned by the Repeal of the Stamp-Act.* Boston, 1766.

Maynwaring, *First Sermon*

Roger Maynwaring, *Religion and Alegiance: In Two Sermons Preached before the Kings Majestie: The one on the fourth of July, Anno 1627. At*

Oatlands. The other on the 29. of July the same yeere, at Alderton. London, 1627.

McAdam, *Johnson and Law*
E. L. McAdam, *Dr. Johnson and the English Law.* Syracuse, N.Y., 1951.

McIlwain, *Constitutionalism*
Charles Howard McIlwain, *Constitutionalism: Ancient and Modern.* Ithaca, N.Y., 1940.

McIlwain, *Revolution*
Charles Howard McIlwain, *The American Revolution: A Constitutional Interpretation.* Ithaca, N.Y., 1958.

McIlwain, "Transfer of the Charter"
Charles H. McIlwain, "The Transfer of the Charter to New England, and its Significance in American Constitutional History," *Proceedings Massachusetts Historical Society* 63 (1929–30): 53–64.

Memoirs of William Smith
Historical Memoirs from 16 March 1763 to 9 July 1776 of William Smith Historian of the Province of New York; Member of the Governor's Council, and Last Chief Justice of that Province Under the Crown; Chief Justice of Quebec. In Two Volumes. Edited by William H. W. Sabine. New York, 1956.

[Meredith,] *Question Stated*
[Sir William Meredith,] *The Question Stated, Whether the Freeholders of Middlesex lost their Right, by voting for Mr. Wilkes at the last Election?* London, [1769].

[Meredith,] *Remarks on Taxation*
[Sir William Meredith,] *Historical Remarks on the Taxation of Free States, in a Series of Letters to a Friend.* London, 1778.

Middlekauff, *Glorious Cause*
Robert Middlekauff, *The Glorious Cause: The American Revolution 1763–1789.* New York, 1982.

[Mitchell,] *Present State*
[John Mitchell,] *The Present State of Great Britain and North America, with Regard to Agriculture, Population, Trade and Manufactures, impartially considered.* London, 1767.

Monthly Review
The Monthly Review; or, Literary Journal: by Several Hands. (Monthly magazine, London.)

Moore, *Taxing Colonies*
Maurice Moore, *The Justice and Policy of Taxing the American Colonies, in Great-Britain, considered* (1765), reprinted in *Not a Conquered People:*

Two Carolinians View Parliamentary Taxation. Edited by William S. Price, Jr. Raleigh, N.C., 1975, pp. 35–48.

Morgan, *American Revolution*
Edmund S. Morgan, *The American Revolution: A Review of Changing Interpretations.* New York, 1958.

Morgan, *Birth*
Edmund S. Morgan, *The Birth of the Republic, 1763–89.* Chicago, 1956.

Morgan, *Challenge*
Edmund S. Morgan, *The Challenge of the American Revolution.* New York, 1976.

Morgan, "Colonial Ideas"
Edmund S. Morgan, "Colonial Ideas of Parliamentary Power 1764–1766," *William and Mary Quarterly* 5 (1948): 311–41.

Morgan, *Justice Johnson*
Donald G. Morgan, *Justice William Johnson The First Dissenter: The Career and Constitutional Philosophy of a Jeffersonian Judge.* Columbia, S.C., 1954.

Morgan, "Parliamentary Power"
Edmund S. Morgan, "Colonial Ideas of Parliamentary Power, 1764–1766," in *Pivotal Interpretations of American History.* Vol. 1. Edited by Carl N. Degler. New York, 1966, pp. 40–73.

Morgan, *Prologue*
Prologue to Revolution: Sources and Documents on the Stamp Act Crisis, 1764–1766. Edited by Edmund S. Morgan. Chapel Hill, N.C., 1959.

Morris, "Legal Profession in America"
Richard B. Morris, "The Legal Profession in America on the Eve of the Revolution," in *Political Separation and Legal Continuity.* Edited by Harry W. Jones. Chicago, 1976, pp. 3–34.

Mulford, *Speech to New York Assembly*
Samuel Mulford's Speech to the Assembly at New-York, April the Second, 1714. [New York, 1714.]

[Mulgrave,] *Letter from a Member*
[Mulgrave, C. J. Phipps, Lord,] *A Letter from a Member of Parliament to One of his Constituents, on the Late Proceedings of the House of Commons in the Middlesex Elections.* London, 1769.

Mullett, "English Imperial Thinking"
Charles F. Mullett, "English Imperial Thinking, 1764–1783," 45 *Political Science Quarterly* 548–79 (1930).

Mullett, *Fundamental Law*
>Charles F. Mullett, *Fundamental Law and the American Revolution 1760–1776*. New York, 1933.

Murdin, *Three Sermons*
>Cornelius Murdin, *Three Sermons, Entitled I. Liberty when Used as a Cloke of Maliciousness, the Worst of Evils. II. The Evil of Rebellion, as Applicable to American Conduct, Considered. III. Great Britain Oppressing America, a Groundless Charge. Preached on the three preceding Fast Days, appointed to be observed on Account of the American Rebellion; In the Parish Churches of Twyford and Ouzlebury, Hampshire.* Southampton, England, [1779].

Namier, *Age of Revolution*
>L. B. Namier, *England in the Age of the American Revolution*. London, 1930.

New Jersey Votes and Proceedings (1768)
>*Votes and Proceedings of the General Assembly of the Province of New-Jersey. At a Session of the General Assembly, began at Perth-Amboy, April 12, 1768, and continued till the 10th of May following.* Woodbridge, N.J., 1768.

New Jersey Votes and Proceedings (1769)
>*Votes and Proceedings of the General Assembly of the Province of New-Jersey. At a Session of General Assembly, began at Burlington, October 10, 1769, and continued till the 6th Day of December following.* Woodbridge, N.J., 1769.

New Jersey Votes and Proceedings (September 1770)
>*Votes and Proceedings of the General Assembly of New-Jersey. At a Session, began at Perth-Amboy, September 26, 1770, and continued till the 27th of October following.* Burlington, N.J., 1770.

New Jersey Votes and Proceedings (1771)
>*Votes and Proceedings of the General Assembly of the Colony of New-Jersey. At a Sesson began at Burlington, Wednesday, April 17, 1771, and continued till [the 2d day of December following].* Burlington, N.J., 1771.

New Jersey Votes and Proceedings (January 1775)
>*Votes and Proceedings of the General Assembly of the Colony of New-Jersey. At a Session began at Perth-Amboy, Wednesday January 11, 1775, and continued until the 12th Day of February following.* Burlington, N.J., 1775.

New York Colonial Documents
>*Documents Relative to the Colonial History of the State of New-York; Procured in Holland, England, and France.* Edited by E. B. O'Callaghan. Vol. 7. Albany, N.Y., 1856.

New York Journal of Votes
Journal of the Votes and Proceedings of the General Assembly of the Colony of New-York. Began the 8th Day of November, 1743; and Ended the 23d of December, 1765. Vol. II. Published by Order of the General Assembly. New York, 1766.

Newton, "Great Emigration"
A. P. Newton, "The Great Emigration, 1618–1648," in *The Cambridge History of the British Empire: Volume I, the Old Empire From the Beginnings to 1783*. Edited by J. Holland Rose, A. P. Newton, and E. A. Benians. Cambridge, England, 1929, pp. 136–82.

Nicholas, *Present State of Virginia*
Robert Carter Nicholas, *Considerations on the Present State of Virginia Examined* (1774), reprinted in *Revolutionary Virginia*. 1:259–85

[Nicholas,] *Proceedings of 1620–21*
[Edward Nicholas,] *Proceedings and Debates of the House of Commons, in 1620 and 1621*. 2 vols. Oxford, England, 1766.

North Carolina Colonial Records
The Colonial Records of North Carolina, Published Under the Supervision of the Trustees of the Public Libraries, By Order of the General Assembly. Vols. 6, 7, 8, 9, and 10. Edited by William L. Saunders, Raleigh, N.C., 1888, 1890.

Norton, "Loyalist Critique"
Mary Beth Norton, "The Loyalist Critique of the Revolution," in *The Development of a Revolutionary Mentality*. First Library of Congress Symposia on the American Revolution. Washington, D.C., 1972, pp. 127–48.

[Oldfield,] *History of the Boroughs*
[T. H. B. Oldfield,] *An Entire and Complete History, Political and Personal, of the Boroughs of Great Britain; to which is Prefixed, an Original Sketch of Constitutional Rights, from the Earliest Period Until the Present Time; and the Principles of our Ancient Representation Traced from the Most Authentic Records, Supported by Undeniable Testimonies, and Illustrated by a Variety of Notes and References, Collected from the Most Respectable, Legal, Political, and Historical Authorities*. 3 vols. London, 1792.

Onuf, "Introduction"
Peter S. Onuf, "Introduction" to *Maryland and the Empire, 1773: The Antilon–First Citizen Letters*. Edited by Peter S. Onuf. Baltimore, 1974, pp. 3–39.

Onuf, "Toward Federalism"
> Peter Onuf, "Toward Federalism: Virginia, Congress, and the Western Lands," *William and Mary Quarterly* 34 (1977): 353–74.

Osgood, "American Revolution"
> Herbert L. Osgood, "The American Revolution," reprinted in *Causes and Consequences of the American Revolution*. Edited by Esmond Wright. Chicago, 1966, pp. 65–77.

[Otis,] *Considerations*
> [James Otis,] *Considerations On Behalf of the Colonists. In a Letter to a Noble Lord.* 2d ed. London, 1765.

Otis, *Rights*
> James Otis, *The Rights of the British Colonies Asserted and Proved* (1764), reprinted in Bailyn, *Pamphlets*, pp. 419–82.

[Paine,] *Common Sense*
> [Thomas Paine,] *Common Sense; Addressed to the Inhabitants of America, on the following interesting Subjects.* New ed. Philadelphia, [1776].

Paine, *Letter to Raynal*
> Thomas Paine, *A Letter Addressed to the Abbe Raynal on the Affairs of North-America.* London, 1782.

Paley, *Essay Upon the Constitution*
> W. Paley, *An Essay Upon the British Constitution: Being the Seventh Chapter of the Sixth Book of the Principles of Moral and Political Philosophy.* London, 1792.

Paley, *Principles of Philosophy*
> William Paley, *The Principles of Moral and Political Philosophy.* London, 1785.

Palmer, *Impartial Account*
> John Palmer, *An Impartial Account of the State of New England: Or, the Late Government there, Vindicated. In Answer to the Declaration Which the Faction Set Forth, when they Over-turned that Government* (1690), reprinted in *The Andros Tracts*. Prince Society Publications, vol. 5. Boston, 1868, pp. 23–62.

Papers of Franklin
> *The Papers of Benjamin Franklin.* Edited by William B. Willcox. 27 vols. New Haven, Conn., 1959–88.

Papers of Iredell
> *The Papers of James Iredell: Volume I. 1767–1777.* Edited by Don Higginbotham. Raleigh, N.C., 1976.

Papers of Jefferson
> *The Papers of Thomas Jefferson.* Edited by Julian P. Boyd. 20 vols. Princeton, N.J., 1950–82.

Papers of John Adams.
> *Papers of John Adams.* Vol. 1. Edited by Robert J. Taylor, et al. Cambridge, Mass., 1977.

[Parker,] *Observations upon some Answers*
> [Henry Parker,] *Observations upon some of his Majesties late Answers and Expresses.* [London, 1642.]

Parliamentary History
> *The Parliamentary History of England, From the Earliest Period to the Year 1803.* 36 vols. London, 1806–20.

Parmenter, *Pelham*
> C. O. Parmenter, *History of Pelham, Mass., From 1736 to 1898, Including the Early History of Prescott.* Amherst, Mass., 1898.

Patten, *Discourse at Hallifax*
> William Patten, *A Discourse Delivered at Hallifax in the County of Plymouth, July 24th 1766. On the Day of Thanks-giving to Almighty* GOD, *throughout the Province of the Massachusetts-Bay in New England, for the* REPEAL *of the* STAMP-ACT. Boston, 1766.

Peach, *Richard Price*
> Bernard Peach, *Richard Price and the Ethical Foundations of the American Revolution.* Durham, N.C., 1979.

Pease, *Leveller*
> Theodore Calvin Pease, *The Leveller Movement: A Study in the History and Political Theory of the English Great Civil War.* Washington, D.C., 1916.

Peckard, *Nature and Extent of Liberty*
> Peter Peckard, *The Nature and Extent of Civil and Religious Liberty. A Sermon Preached before the University of Cambridge, November the 5th, 1783.* Cambridge, England, 1783.

Pemberton, *Divine Original*
> Ebenezer Pemberton, *The Divine Original and Dignity of Government Asserted; and an Advantageous Prospect of the Rulers Mortality Recommended. A Sermon Preached before His Excellency the Governour, the Honourable Council, and Assembly of the Province of the Massachusetts-Bay in New-England, May 31, 1710. The Day for the Election of Her Majesties Council there.* Boston, 1710.

Pennsylvania Archives
> *Pennsylvania Archives: Eighth Series [Votes and Proceedings of the House of Representatives.]* 8 vols. [Harrisburg, Pa.,] 1931–35.

Pennsylvania Council
> *Minutes of the Provincial Council of Pennsylvania, From the Organization to the Termination of the Proprietary Governor. Vol. IX. Containing the Proceedings of Council From October 15th, 1762, to 17th of October, 1771, Both Days Included. Vol. X. Containing the Proceedings of Council From October 18th, 1771, to 27th of September, 1775, Both Days Included; Together with Minutes of the Council of Safety From June 30th, 1775, to November 12th, 1776, Both Days Included.* Harrisburg, Pa., 1852.

Perry, *Connecticut Election Sermon*
> Joseph Perry, *A Sermon Preached before the General Assembly of the Colony of Connecticut, at Hartford, on the Day of their Anniversary Election, May 11, 1775.* Hartford, Conn., 1775.

Perry, *Dictionary*
> William Perry, *The Royal Standard English Dictionary.* First American ed. Worcester, Mass., 1783.

Perspectives on Revolution
> *Perspectives on the American Revolution: A Bicentennial Contribution.* Edited by George G. Suggs. Carbondale, Ill., 1977.

Petition of Middlesex to King, 24 May 1769
> *A Petition of the Freeholders of the County of Middlesex, Presented to his Majesty, the 24th of May, 1769.* London, [1769].

Petyt, *Lex Parliamentaria*
> G[eorge] P[etyt], *Lex Parliamentaria: or, a Treatise of the Law and Custom of the Parliaments of England.* London, 1690.

[Phelps,] *Rights of the Colonies*
> [Richard Phelps,] *The Rights of the Colonies, And the Extent of the Legislative Authority of Great-Britain, Briefly Stated and Considered.* London, 1769.

Plowden, *Rights of Englishmen*
> Francis Plowden, *Jura Anglorum. The Rights of Englishmen.* Dublin, 1792.

Pocock, *Politics*
> J. G. A. Pocock, *Politics, Language and Time: Essays on Political Thought and History.* New York, 1971.

Pole, *Gift*
> J. R. Pole, *The Gift of Government: Political Responsibility From the English Restoration to American Independence.* Athens, Ga., 1983.

Pole, *Legislative Power*
> J. R. Pole, *The Seventeenth Century: The Sources of Legislative Power.* Jamestown Essays on Representation. Charlottesville, Va., 1969.

Pole, *Pursuit of Equality*
J. R. Pole, *The Pursuit of Equality in American History*. Berkeley, Calif., 1978.

Political Register
The Political Register; and Impartial Review of New Books. (Monthly magazine, London.)

Pollock, "Sovereignty in English Law"
Frederick Pollock, "Sovereignty in English Law," *Harvard Law Review* 8 (1894): 243–51.

Potter, *Liberty We Seek*
Janice Potter, *The Liberty We Seek: Loyalist Ideology in Colonial New York and Massachusetts*. Cambridge, Mass., 1983.

[Power,] *Comparative State*
[Richard Power,] *A Comparative State of the Two Rejected Money Bills, in 1692 and 1769. With Some Observations on Poynings Act, and the Explanatory Statute of Philip and Mary*. Dublin, 1770.

Pownall, *Administration*
Thomas Pownall, *The Administration of the Colonies. Wherein their Rights and Constitution are Discussed and Stated*. 4th ed. London, 1768.

Pownall, *Administration Fifth Edition*
Thomas Pownall, *The Administration of the British Colonies. The Fifth Edition. Wherein their Rights and Constitution are discussed and stated*. 2 vols. London, 1774.

[Pownall,] *Considerations*
[Thomas Pownall,] *Considerations on the Points lately brought into Question as to the Parliament's Right of Taxing the Colonies, And of the Measures necessary to be taken at this Crisis. Being an Appendix, Section III, to the Administration of the Colonies*. London, 1766.

Prall, *Agitation*
Stuart E. Prall, *The Agitation for Law Reform During the Puritan Revolution 1640–1660*. The Hague, 1966.

[Prescott,] *Calm Consideration*
[Benjamin Prescott,] *A Free and Calm Consideration of the Unhappy Misunderstandings and Debates, which have of late Years arisen, and yet subsist, Between the Parliament of Great-Britain, and these American Colonies. Contained in Eight Letters, Six whereof, Directed to a Gentleman of Distinction in England, Formerly printed in the Essex Gazette. The other Two, directed to a Friend*. Salem, Mass., 1774.

Price, "Introduction to Two Tracts"
Richard Price, "Introduction," to Price, *Two Tracts*.

Price, *Nature of Civil Liberty*
    Richard Price, *Observations on the Nature of Civil Liberty, the Principles of Government, and the Justice and Policy of the War with America.* London, 1776.

Price, *Two Tracts*
    Richard Price, *Two Tracts on Civil Liberty, the War with America, and the Debts and Finances of the Kingdom: with a General Introduction and Supplement.* London, 1778.

Price, *Two Tracts: Tract One*
    Richard Price, *Observations on the Nature of Civil Liberty, the Principles of Government, and the Justice and Policy of the War with America.* 8th ed. London, 1778, reprinted in Price, *Two Tracts*, pp. 1–112.

[Priestley,] *Address to Dissenters*
    [Joseph Priestley,] *An Address to Protestant Dissenters of all Denominations, on the Approaching Election of Members of Parliament, With Respect to the State of Public Liberty in General, and of American Affairs in Particular.* Philadelphia, 1774.

Priestley, *First Principles*
    Joseph Priestley, *An Essay on the First Principles of Government, and on the Nature of Political, Civil, and Religious Liberty, Including Remarks on Dr. Brown's Code of Education.* London, 1768.

[Priestley,] *Present State of Liberty*
    [Joseph Priestley,] *The Present State of Liberty in Great Britain and Her Colonies.* London, 1769.

Prior Documents
    A Collection of Interesting, Authentic Papers, Relative to the Dispute Between Great Britain and America; Shewing the Causes and Progress of that Misunderstanding, From 1764 to 1775. London, 1777.

Privy Council Copies
    Copies of papers and letters transmitted to the Council re: the Riots which have lately happened in America in opposition to the Stamp Act . . . [and] copies of all orders etc. issued from the Council Office thereupon. HM 1947, Huntington Library, San Marino, Calif.

Proceedings and Debates
    Proceedings and Debates of the British Parliaments Respecting North America 1754–1783. Edited by R. C. Simmons and P. D. G. Thomas. 6 vols. White Plains, N.Y., 1982–87.

Proceedings and Debates of Parliaments
    Proceedings and Debates of the British Parliaments respecting North America. Edited by Leo Francis Stock. 5 vols. Washington, D.C., 1924–41.

Protests of Lords
A Complete Collection of the Protests of the Lords with Historical Intro-
ductions. Edited by James E. Thorold Rogers. 3 vols. Oxford, England, 1875.

Protests of Lords of Ireland
A Collection of the Protests of the Lords of Ireland, From 1634 to 1771.
Dublin, 1772.

Protests of the Peers
A Complete Collection of all the Protests of the Peers in Parliament,
entered on their Journals, Since the Year 1774, on the Great Questions of
the Cause and Issue of the War Between Great-Britain and America, &c.
to the Present Time. London, 1782.

Providence Gazette
The Providence Gazette and Country Journal. (Weekly newspaper, Providence, R.I.)

Public Records of Connecticut
The Public Records of the Colony of Connecticut. Edited by Charles J.
Hoadly and J. H. Trumbull. Vols. 12–15. Hartford, Conn., 1881–90.

Pudsey, *Constitution and Laws*
William P[udse]y, The Constitution and Laws of England Consider'd.
London, 1701.

Pulteney, *Effects of the Bill*
William Pulteney, The Effects to be Expected from the East India Bill,
Upon the Constitution of Great Britain, if passed into a Law. 4th ed.
London, 1784.

Pulteney, *Plan of Reunion*
William Pulteney, Plan of Re-Union Between Great Britain and Her Colonies. London, 1778.

Pym, *Speech of Summing Up*
John Pym, The Speech or Declaration of John Pym, Esquire: After the
Recapitulation or summing up the Charge of High-Treason, Against
Thomas, Earle of Strafford, 12 April, 1641. London, 1641.

Quincy, *Observations with Thoughts*
Josiah Quincy, Jr., Observations on the Act of Parliament Commonly
Called the Boston Port-Bill; with Thoughts on Civil Society and Standing
Armies (1774), reprinted in Memoir of the Life of Josiah Quincy Jun. of
Massachusetts: By his Son, Josiah Quincy. Boston, 1825, pp. 355–469.

Rakove, *Beginnings*
Jack N. Rakove, The Beginnings of National Politics: An Interpretative
History of the Continental Congress. Baltimore, 1979.

Rakove, "Decision for Independence"
Jack N. Rakove, "The Decision for American Independence: A Reconstruction," *Perspectives in American History* 10 (1976): 217–75.

[Ramsay,] *Historical Essay*
[Allan Ramsay,] *An Historical Essay on the English Constitution: Or, An impartial Inquiry into the Elective Power of the People, from the first Establishment of the Saxons in this Kingdom. Wherein the Right of Parliament, to Tax our distant Provinces, is explained, and justified, upon such constitutional Principles as will afford an equal Security to the Colonists, as to their Brethren at Home.* London, 1771.

[Ramsay,] *Thoughts on Nature of Government*
[Allan Ramsay,] *Thoughts on the Origin and Nature of Government. Occasioned by the late Disputes between Great Britain and her American Colonies. Written in the Year 1766.* London, 1769.

Ramsay, *History*
David Ramsay, *The History of the American Revolution.* Vol. 1. New English ed. London, 1793.

[Rawson,] *Revolution in New England*
[Edward Rawson,] *The Revolution in New England Justified, And the People there Vindicated From the Aspersions cast upon them by Mr. John Palmer, In his Pretended Answer to the Declaration, Published by the Inhabitants of Boston, and the Country adjacent, on the day when they secured their late Oppressors, who acted by an Illegal and Arbitrary Commission from the Late King JAMES.* Boston, 1691.

[Raynal,] *Sentiments*
[Guillaume Thomas F. Raynal,] *The Sentiments of a Foreigner on the Disputes of Great-Britain with America. Translated from the French.* Philadelphia, 1775.

[Reeves,] *Thoughts, Second Letter*
[John Reeves,] *Thoughts on the English Government. Addressed to the Quiet Good Sense of the People of England. In a Series of Letters. Letter the Second.* London, 1799.

"Regulus," *Defence of the Resolutions*
"Regulus," *A Defence of the Resolutions and Address of the American Congress, in Reply to Taxation no Tyranny. By the Author of Regulus. To which are added, General Remarks on the Leading Principles of that Work as Published in The London Evening Post on the 2d and 4th of May; and a Short Chain of Deductions From One Clear Position of Common Sense and Experience.* London, [1775].

Reid, "Economic Burden"
Joseph D. Reid, Jr., "Economic Burden: Spark to the American Revolution," *Journal of Economic History* 38 (1978): 81–100.

Remembrancer for 1776: Part II
The Remembrancer; or, Impartial Repository of Public Events: Part II. For the Year 1776. London, 1776.

Report of Lords on Massachusetts
The Report of the Lords Committees, Appointed by the House of Lords to Enquire into the several Proceedings in the Colony of Massachuset's Bay, in Opposition to the Sovereignty of His Majesty, in His Parliament of Great Britain, over that Province; and also what hath passed in this House relative thereto, from the First Day of January, 1764. London, 1774.

Revolution Documents
Documents of the American Revolution 1770–1783. Edited by K. G. Davies. Vols. 1 to 16. Dublin, 1972–81.

Revolutionary Virginia
Revolutionary Virginia The Road to Independence—Volume I: Forming Thunderclouds and the First Convention, 1763–1774. A Documentary Record. Compiled by William J. Van Schreeven, edited by Robert L. Scribner. *Volume II: The Committees and the Second Convention, 1773–1775. A Documentary Record.* Compiled by William J. Van Schreeven and Robert L. Scribner. *Volume III: The Breaking Storm and the Third Convention, 1775. A Documentary Record.* Compiled and edited by Robert L. Scribner and Brent Tarter. *Volume IV: The Committee of Safety and the Balance of Forces, 1775. A Documentary Record.* Compiled and edited by Robert L. Scribner and Brent Tarter. *Volume V: The Clash of Arms and the Fourth Convention, 1775–1776. A Documentary Record.* Compiled and edited by Robert L. Scribner and Brent Tarter. *Volume VI: The Time for Decision, 1776. A Documentary Record.* Compiled and edited by Robert L. Scribner and Brent Tarter. [Charlottesville, Va.,] 1973–79.

Rhode Island Colony Records
Records of the Colony of Rhode Island and Providence Plantations in New England. Edited by John Russell Bartlett. 10 vols. Providence, R.I., 1856–65.

Rhode Island Correspondence
The Correspondence of the Colonial Governors of Rhode Island 1723–1775. Edited by Gertrude Selwyn Kimball. Vol. 2. Boston, 1903.

Ritcheson, *British Politics*
Charles R. Ritcheson, *British Politics and the American Revolution.* Norman, Okla., 1954.

[Rivers,] *Letters*
[George Pitt, Baron Rivers of Stratfieldsaye,] *Letters to a Young*

Nobleman, upon Various Subjects, Particularly on Government and Civil Liberty. London, 1784.

Robbins, *Commonwealthmen*
Caroline Robbins, *The Eighteenth-Century Commonwealthmen: Studies in the Transmission, Development and Circumstance of English Liberal Thought from the Restoration of Charles II until the War with the Thirteen Colonies.* Cambridge, Mass., 1959.

Robson, *American Revolution*
Eric Robson, *The American Revolution in its Political and Military Aspects 1763–1783.* New York, 1966.

Roebuck, *Enquiry Whether the Guilt*
John Roebuck, *An Enquiry Whether the Guilt of the Present Civil War in America, Ought to be Imputed to Great Britain or America.* New ed. London, 1776.

Rogers, *Empire and Liberty*
Alan Rogers, *Empire and Liberty: American Resistance to British Authority 1755–1763.* Berkeley, Calif., 1974.

[Rokeby,] *Further Examination*
[Matthew Robinson-Morris, Second Baron Rokeby,] *A Further Examination of our Present American Measures and of the Reasons and the Principles on which they are founded.* Bath, England, 1776.

Rossiter, *Political Thought*
Clinton Rossiter, *The Political Thought of the American Revolution.* New York, 1963.

Rossiter, *Six Characters*
Clinton Rossiter, *Six Characters in Search of a Republic: Studies in the Political Thought of the American Colonies.* New York, 1964.

[Rous,] *Claim of the Commons*
[George Rous,] *The Claim of the House of Commons, to a Negative on the Appointment of Ministers by the Crown, Examined and Confuted.* London, 1784.

Royle & Walvin, *English Radicals*
Edward Royle and James Walvin, *English Radicals and Reformers 1760–1848.* Brighton, England, 1982.

Rushworth, *Historical Collections: Third Part*
John Rushworth, *Historical Collections: The Third Part; in Two Volumes.* Vol. 1. London, 1692.

Russell, *Parliaments and Politics*
Conrad Russell, *Parliaments and English Politics 1621–1629.* Oxford, England, 1979.

Rusticus, *Good of Community*
Rusticus, *The Good of the Community Impartially Considered, in a Letter to a Merchant in Boston; In Answer to one Received Respecting the Excise-Bill.* Boston, 1754.

Rutherforth, *Natural Law*
T. Rutherforth, *Institutes of Natural Law Being the substance of a Course of Lectures on Grotius de Jure Belli et Pacis Read in S. Johns College Cambridge.* 2 vols. Cambridge, England, 1754, 1756.

Ryder, "Parliamentary Diaries"
"Parliamentary Diaries of Nathaniel Ryder, 1764–7," edited by P.D.G. Thomas. *Camden Miscellany Vol. XXIII.* Camden Society, 4th Series, vol. 7. London, [1969], pp. 229–351.

Ryerson, *Revolution Begun*
Richard Alan Ryerson, *The Revolution is Now Begun: The Radical Committees of Philadelphia, 1765–1776.* Philadelphia, 1978.

St. Patrick's Anti-Stamp Chronicle
St. Patrick's Anti-Stamp Chronicle: Or, Independent Magazine, of News, Politics, and Literary Entertainment. Dublin.

Schlesinger, "Revolution Reconsidered"
Arthur Meier Schlesinger, "The American Revolution Reconsidered," *Political Science Quarterly* 34 (1919): 61–78.

Schutz, *Thomas Pownall*
John A. Schutz, *Thomas Pownall British Defender of American Liberty: A Study of Anglo-American Relations in the Eighteenth Century.* Glendale, Calif., 1951.

Schuyler, "Britannic Question"
Robert Livingston Schuyler, "The Britannic Question and the American Revolution," *Political Science Quarterly* 38 (1923): 104–14.

Schuyler, *Empire*
Robert Livingston Schuyler, *Parliament and the British Empire: Some Constitutional Controversies Concerning Imperial Legislative Jurisdiction.* New York, 1929.

Scots Magazine
The Scots Magazine. (Monthly magazine, Edinburgh.)

[Seabury,] *View of the Controversy*
[Samuel Seabury,] *A View of the Controversy Between Great-Britain and her Colonies: Including a Mode of Determining their present Disputes, Finally and Effectually; and of Preventing all Future Contentions. In a Letter, to the Author of a Full Vindication of the Measures of the Congress, from the Calumnies of their Enemies.* New York, 1774.

[Serle,] *Americans against Liberty*
[Ambrose Serle,] *Americans against Liberty: or, an Essay on the Nature and Principles of True Freedom, Shewing that the Design and Conduct of the Americans tend only to Tyranny and Slavery.* 3d ed. London, 1776.

[Sewall,] *Americans Roused*
[Jonathan Sewall,] *The Americans Roused, in a Cure for the Spleen.* New York, [1775].

Shebbeare, *An Answer*
John Shebbeare, *An Answer to the Queries Contained in a Letter to Dr. Shebbeare, printed in the Public Ledger, August 10 . . .* London, [1775].

Shebbeare, *Essay on National Society*
J. Shebbeare, *An Essay on the Origin, Progress and Establishment of National Society; in which the Principles of Government, the Definitions of physical, moral, civil, and religious Liberty, contained in Dr. Price's Observations, &c. are fairly examined and fully refuted; Together with a Justification of the Legislature, in reducing America to Obedience by Force.* London, 1776.

[Shebbeare,] *Second Letter*
[John Shebbeare,] *A Second Letter to the People of England on Foreign Subsidies, Subsidiary Armies, and Their Consequences to this Nation.* 3d ed. London, 1756.

[Shebbeare,] *Seventh Letter*
[John Shebbeare,] *A Seventh Letter to the People of England. A Defence of the Prerogative Royal, As it was exerted in His Majesty's Proclamation For the Prohibiting the Exportation of Corn. In which it is Proved That this Authority ever has been, is, and must be essential to the constitution, and inseperable from the Rights and Liberties of the Subject.* London, 1767.

Shelburne Abstracts
Abstracts of Colonial Dispatches to the Earl of Shelburne. *Shelburne Papers,* vols. 51 and 52. Clements Library, Ann Arbor, Mich.

Shelton, *Charge to Suffolk Grand Jury*
Maurice Shelton, *A Charge Given to the Grand-Jury, at the General Quarter-Sessions of the Peace, Holden at St. Edmunds-Bury for the Liberty thereof; In the County of Suffolk: On the 11th of October, An. Dom. 1725.* London, 1726.

Sheps, "English Republicanism"
Arthur Sheps, "The American Revolution and the Transformation of English Republicanism," *Historical Reflections* 2 (1975): 3–28.

[Sheridan,] *Observations on the Doctrine*
[Charles Francis Sheridan,] *Observations on the Doctrine laid down by Sir William Blackstone, Respecting the extent of the Power of the British*

Parliament, Particularly with relation to Ireland. In a letter to Sir William Blackstone, with a Postcript Addressed to Lord North. Dublin, 1779.

[Sheridan,] *Review of Three Questions*
[Charles Francis Sheridan,] *A Review of the Three Great National Questions Relative to a Declaration of Right, Poynings' Law, and the Mutiny Bill.* Dublin, 1781.

Sherlock, *Case of Resistance*
William Sherlock, *The Case of Resistance of the Supreme Powers Stated and Resolved, According to the Doctrine of the Holy Scriptures.* London, 1684.

[Shipley,] *Intended Speech*
[Jonathan Shipley,] *A Speech Intended to have been Spoken on the Bill for Altering the Charters of the Colony of Massachusett's Bay.* 2d ed. London, 1774.

Shirley, *Richard Hooker*
F. J. Shirley, *Richard Hooker and Contemporary Political Ideas.* London, 1949.

[Short,] *Rights*
[John Short,] *The Rights and Principles of an Englishman Considered and Asserted, on a Review of the late Motion at the Hotel, for a County Meeting in Devonshire.* Exeter, England, 1780.

Shute, *Election Sermon*
Daniel Shute, *A Sermon Preached before his Excellency Francis Bernard, Esq.; Governor, his Honor Thomas Hutchinson, Esq; Lieutenant-Governor, the Honourable His Majesty's Council, and the Honourable House of Representatives, of the Province of the Massachusetts-Bay in New-England, May 25th. 1768.* Boston, 1768.

Shy, "Thomas Pownall"
John Shy, "Thomas Pownall, Henry Ellis, and the Spectrum of Possibilities, 1763–1775," in *Anglo-American Political Relations*, pp. 155–86.

Sidney, *Discourses Concerning Government*
Algernon Sidney, *Discourses Concerning Government*, reprinted in *Works of Algernon Sydney.* New ed. London, 1772, pp. 1–542.

Sisson, "Idea of Revolution"
Daniel Sisson, "The Idea of Revolution in the Declaration of Independence and the Constitution," in *Constitutional Government in America: Essays and Proceedings from Southwestern University Law Review's First West Coast Conference on Constitutional Law.* Edited by Ronald K. L. Collins. Durham, N.C., 1980.

Smith, *Appeals*
> Joseph H. Smith, *Appeals to the Privy Council from the American Planta-tions.* New York, 1950.

Smith, *Writs of Assistance*
> M. H. Smith, *The Writs of Assistance Case.* Berkeley, Calif., 1978.

Somers' Tracts
> *A Collection of Scarce and Valuable Tracts, on the Most Interesting and Entertaining Subjects: But Chiefly such as Relate to the History and Con-stitution of these Kingdoms. Selected from an Infinite Number in Print and Manuscript, in the Royal, Cotton, Sion, and other Public, as well as Private, Libraries; Particularly that of the Late Lord Somers.* Edited by Walter Scott. Vols. 4 and 5. London, 1809–15.

Sosin, "Imperial Regulation"
> Jack M. Sosin, "Imperial Regulation of Colonial Paper Money, 1764–1773," *Pennsylvania Magazine of History and Biography* 88 (1964): 174–98.

South-Carolina Gazette
> (Weekly newspaper, Charles Town, S.C.)

Southwick, "Molasses Act"
> Albert B. Southwick, "The Molassess Act—Source of Precedents," *William and Mary Quarterly* 8 (1951): 389–405.

Speech upon the Scaffold
> King Charls [*sic*] *His Speech Made upon the Scaffold at Whitehall-Gate, Immediately before his Execution, On Tuesday the 30 of Jan. 1648. With a Relation of the maner of his going to Execution.* London, 1649.

Speeches
> *Speeches of the Governors of Massachusetts From 1765 to 1775; And the Answers of the House of Representatives to the Same; with their Resolu-tions and Addresses for that Period.* Boston, 1818.

Speeches in the Last Session
> *The Speeches in the Last Session of the present Parliament, Delivered by several of the Principal Advocates in the House of Commons, in Favour of the Rights of America.* New York, 1775.

Speeches of John Wilkes in Parliament
> *The Speeches of John Wilkes, One of the Knights of the Shire for the County of Middlesex, In the Parliament appointed to meet at Westminster the 29th day of November 1774, to the Prorogation the 6th Day of June 1777.* 2 vols. London, 1777.

Spelman, "Certain Considerations"
> Sir John Spelman, "Certain Considerations upon the Duties both of Prince and People" (1642), reprinted in *Somers' Tracts,* 4:316–30.

[Squire,] *Historical Essay on Ballance*
> [Samuel Squire,] *An Historical Essay Upon the Ballance of Civil Power in England, From its first Conquest by the Anglo-Saxons, to the Time of the Revolution; in which is introduced a new Dissertation upon Parties: With a proper Dedication to the Freeholders and Burgesses of Great Britain.* London, 1748.

"Stamp Act Debates"
> "Debates on the Declaratory Act and the Repeal of the Stamp Act, 1766," *American Historical Review* 17 (1912): 563–86.

Stanlis, "British Views"
> Peter J. Stanlis, "British Views of the American Revolution: A Conflict over Rights of Sovereignty," *Early American Literature* 11 (1976): 191–201.

State Trials
> *A Complete Collection of State Trials and Proceedings for High Treason and Other Crimes and Misdemeanors From the Earliest Period to the Year 1783, With Notes and Other Illustrations.* Compiled by T. B. Howell. 34 vols. London, 1816–28.

Stearns, *View of the Controversy*
> William Stearns, *A View of the Controversy subsisting between Great-Britain and the American Colonies. A Sermon, Preached at a Fast, in Marlborough in Massachusetts-Bay. On Thursday May 11, 1775. Agreeable to a Recommendation of the Provincial Congress.* Watertown, Mass., 1775.

[Steuart,] *Jus Populi*
> [Sir James Steuart,] *Jus Populi Vindicatum, or the Peoples Right, to defend themselves and their Covenanted Religion, vindicated.* N.p., 1669.

Stevens, *Election Sermon*
> Benjamin Stevens, *A Sermon Preached at Boston, Before the Great and General Court or Assembly of the Province of the Massachusetts Bay in New England, May 27, 1761. Being the Day appointed by Royal Charter for the Election of his Majesty's Council for said Province.* Boston, 1761.

[Stevens,] *Revolution Vindicated*
> [William Stevens,] *The Revolution Vindicated, and Constitutional Liberty Asserted. In Answer to the Reverend Dr. Watson's Accession Sermon, Preached before the University of Cambridge, on October 25th, 1776.* Cambridge, England, 1777.

[Stevens,] *Strictures on a Sermon*
> [William Stevens,] *Strictures on a Sermon, Entitled, the Principles of the Revolution vindicated; Preached before the University of Cambridge, on Wednesday, May 29th, 1776, by Richard Watson, D.D. F.R.S. Regius Professor of Divinity in that University. In a Letter to a Friend.* 2d ed. Cambridge, England, 1777.

[Stillingfleet,] *Discourse*
[Edward Stillingfleet,] *A Discourse Concerning the Unreasonableness of a New Separation, on account of the Oaths. With an Answer to the History of Passive Obedience so far as it relates to Them.* London, 1689.

Stokes, *View of Constitution*
Anthony Stokes, *A View of the Constitution of the British Colonies, in North-America and the West Indies, at the Time the Civil War broke out on the Continent of America.* London, 1783.

Stone, "Results of Revolutions"
Lawrence Stone, "The Results of the English Revolutions of the Seventeenth Century," in *Three British Revolutions.* Edited by J. G. A. Pocock. Princeton, N.J., 1980, pp. 23–108.

Story, *Commentaries*
Joseph Story, *Commentaries on the Constitution of the United States: with a Preliminary Review of the Constitutional History of the Colonies and States before the Adoption of the Constitution.* 3 vols. Boston and Cambridge, Mass., 1833.

Straka, "Sixteen Eighty-Eight"
Gerald M. Straka, "Sixteen Eighty-eight as the Year One: Eighteenth-Century Attitudes Towards the Glorious Revolution," *Studies in Eighteenth-Century Culture* 1 (1971): 143–67.

Symonds, *Remarks Upon Essay*
John Symonds, *Remarks Upon an Essay, Intituled The History of the Colonization of the Free States of Antiquity, Applied to the Present Contest Between Great Britain and her American Colonies.* London, 1778.

Tate, "Social Contract in America"
Thad W. Tate, "The Social Contract in America, 1774–1787: Revolutionary Theory as a Conservative Instrument," *William and Mary Quarterly* 22 (1965): 375–91.

Tetlow, *Impartial Letter*
Richard-John Tetlow, *An Impartial Letter, Relating to the Unhappy Dissentions now subsisting betwixt Old-England and America.* York, England, 1776.

The Crisis
The Crisis. (Newspaper "Printed and published for the Authors by T. W. Shaw," London, 20 January 1775 to 6 October 1776.)

They Preached Liberty
They Preached Liberty: With an Introductory Essay and Biographical Sketches by Franklin P. Cole. Indianapolis, ca. 1980.

Thomas, "British Imperial Policy"
    Robert Paul Thomas, "A Quantitative Approach to the Study of the Effects
    of British Imperial Policy upon Colonial Welfare: Some Preliminary Find-
    ings," *Journal of Economic History* 25 (1965): 615–38.

Thomas, *British Politics*
    P. D. G. Thomas, *British Politics and the Stamp Act Crisis: The First Phase
    of the American Revolution, 1763–1767.* Oxford, England, 1975.

Thomas, "Effects of Imperial Policy"
    Robert Paul Thomas, "The Effects of British Imperial Policy upon Colo-
    nial Welfare," reprinted in *The American Revolution: The Critical Issues.*
    Edited by Robert F. Berkhofer, Jr. Boston, 1971, pp. 128–46.

Thomas, "George III"
    P. D. G. Thomas, "George III and the American Revolution," *History* 70
    (1985): 16–31.

Thomas, *Lord North*
    Peter D. G. Thomas, *Lord North.* London, 1976.

Thomas, *Townshend Duties*
    Peter D. G. Thomas, *The Townshend Duties Crisis: The Second Phase of
    the American Revolution, 1767–1773.* Oxford, England, 1987.

Thompson, *Whigs and Hunters*
    E. P. Thompson, *Whigs and Hunters: The Origin of the Black Act.* New
    York, 1975.

Thomson, *Constitutional History*
    Mark A. Thomson, *A Constitutional History of England 1642 to 1801.*
    London, 1938.

Thorpe, *Charters*
    Francis Newton Thorpe, *The Federal and State Constitutions: Colonial
    Charters, and other Organic Laws of the States, Territories, and Colonies
    now or heretofore forming The United States of America.* 7 vols. Wash-
    ington, D.C., 1909.

Tierney, *Religion, Law, and Growth*
    Brian Tierney, *Religion, Law, and the Growth of Constitutional Thought
    1150–1650.* Cambridge, England, 1982.

[Tod,] *Consolatory Thoughts*
    [Thomas Tod,] *Consolatory Thoughts on American Independence; Shew-
    ing the great Advantages that will arise from it to the Manufactures, the Agri-
    culture, and commercial Interest of Britain and Ireland.* Edinburgh, 1782.

Toohey, *Liberty and Empire*
    Robert E. Toohey, *Liberty and Empire: British Radical Solutions to the
    American Problem 1774–1776.* Lexington, Ky., 1978.

Trade & Plantations (1765–67)
> *Journal of the Commissioners for Trade and Plantations from January 1764 to December 1767 Preserved in the Public Record Office.* London, 1936.

Trevelyan, *Revolution Condensation*
> George Otto Trevelyan, *The American Revolution.* Edited by Richard B. Morris. London, 1964.

Trumbull, *Discourse at New Haven*
> Benjamin Trumbull, *Discourse, Delivered at the Anniversary Meeting of the Freemen of the Town of New-Haven, April 12, 1773.* New Haven, Conn., 1773.

Trumbull Papers
> *The Trumbull Papers.* Collections of the Massachusetts Historical Society. 5th series, vol. 9. Boston, 1885.

Tryal of Sacheverell
> *The Tryal of Dr. Henry Sacheverell, before the House of Peers, For High Crimes and Misdemeanors; Upon an Impeachment by the Knights, Citizens and Burgesses in Parliament Assembled, in the Name of themselves, and of all the Commons of Great Britain: Begun in Westminster Hall the 27th Day of February, 1709/10; and from thence continu'd by several Adjournments until the 23d Day of March following.* London, 1710.

Tuck, *Natural Rights Theories*
> Richard Tuck, *Natural Rights Theories: Their Origin and Development.* Cambridge, England, 1979.

Tucker, *Election Sermon*
> John Tucker, *A Sermon Preached at Cambridge, Before his Excellency Thomas Hutchinson, Esq; Governor: His Honor Andrew Oliver, Esq; Lieutenant-Governor, the Honorable His Majesty's Council, and the Honorable House of Representatives, of the Province of the Massachusetts-Bay in New England, May 29th, 1771. Being the Anniversary for the Election of His Majesty's Council for said Province.* Boston, 1771.

Tucker, *Four Letters to Shelburne*
> [Josiah Tucker,] *Four Letters on Important National Subjects, Addressed to the Right Honourable the Earl of Shelburne, His Majesty's First Lord Commissioner of the Treasury.* 2d ed. London, 1773 [*sic* 1783].

[Tucker,] *Four Tracts*
> [Josiah Tucker,] *Four Tracts, Together with Two Sermons, on Political and Commercial Subjects.* Glocester, England, 1774.

Tucker, *Letter to Burke*
> Josiah Tucker, *A Letter to Edmund Burke, Esq; Member of Parliament for the City of Bristol, and Agent for the Colony of New York, &c. In Answer*

to His Printed Speech, Said to be Spoken in the House of Commons on the Twenty-Second of March, 1775. 2d ed. Gloucester, England, 1775.

Tucker, *Tract Five*
Josiah Tucker, *Tract V. The Respective Pleas and Arguments of the Mother Country, and of the Colonies, Distinctly Set Forth; and the Impossibility of a Compromise of Differences, or a Mutual Concession of Rights, Plainly Demonstrated. With a Prefatory Epistle to the Plenipotentiaries of the late Congress at Philadelphia.* London, 1775.

Tucker, *True Interest of Britain*
Jos[iah] Tucker, *The True Interest of Britain Set Forth in Regard to the Colonies; and the only means of Living in Peace and Harmony with Them.* Philadelphia, 1776.

Tucker & Hendrickson, *Fall*
Robert W. Tucker and David C. Hendrickson, *The Fall of the First British Empire: Origins of the War of American Independence.* Baltimore, 1982.

Turner, *Election Sermon*
Charles Turner, *A Sermon Preached Before His Excellency Thomas Hutchinson, Esq; Governor: The Honorable His Majesty's Council, and the Honorable House of Representatives, of the Province of the Massachusetts-Bay in New-England, May 26th, 1773. Being the Anniversary of the Election of His Majesty's Council for said Province.* Boston, 1773.

Twysden, *Certaine Considerations*
Sir Roger Twysden, *Certaine Considerations Upon the Government of England.* Camden Society, Vol. 45. London, 1849.

Valentine, *Lord North*
Alan Valentine, *Lord North.* 2 vols. Norman, Okla., 1967.

Virginia Gazette
Rival Newspapers published in Williamsburg, Virginia, and identified by their owners or printers: "Dixon and Hunter" (John Dixon and William Hunter), "Pinckney" (John Pinckney), "Purdie and Dixon" (Alexander Purdie and John Dixon), "Purdie" (Alexander Purdie), and "Rind" (William Rind or Clementina Rind).

Wagner, "Judicial Review"
D. O. Wagner, "Some Antecedents of the American Doctrine of Judicial Review," *Political Science Quarterly* 40 (1925): 561–93.

Walpole, *Memoirs*
Horace Walpole, *Memoirs of the Reign of King George the Third First Published by Sir Denis Le Marchant Bart, and now Re-Edited by G. F. Russell Barker.* 4 vols. New York, 1894.

Walsh, *Appeal from the Judgments*
Robert Walsh, Jr., *An Appeal from the Judgments of Great Britain Respecting the United States of America. Part First, Containing an Historical Outline of their Merits and Wrongs as Colonies; and Strictures upon the Calumnies of the British Writers.* 2d ed. Philadelphia, 1819.

Warrington, *Works*
Henry Booth, earl of Warrington, *The Works of the Right Honourable Henry late L[ord] Delamer, and Earl Warrington.* London, 1694.

Washburn, "Preface"
Charles G. Washburn, "Preface" and notes, in *Mauduit Letters*, pp. xvii-xxxvii.

Waters, *Otis Family*
John J. Waters, Jr., *The Otis Family in Provincial and Revolutionary Massachusetts.* Chapel Hill, N.C., 1968.

[Watson,] *Answer to Disquisition*
[Richard Watson,] *An Answer to the Disquisition on Government and Civil Liberty; in a Letter to the Author of Disquisitions on Several Subjects.* London, 1782.

Watson, *Principles of the Revolution*
Richard Watson, *The Principles of the Revolution vindicated in a Sermon Preached Before the University of Cambridge, on Wednesday, May 29, 1776.* Cambridge, England, 1776.

Wedgwood, "Trial of Charles I"
C. V. Wedgwood, "The Trial of Charles I," in *The English Civil War and After.* Edited by R. H. Perry. Berkeley, Calif., pp. 41-58.

Weir, "Currency Act"
Robert M. Weir, "North Carolina's Reaction to the Currency Act of 1764," *North Carolina Historical Review* 40 (1963): 183-99.

Weir, *Most Important Epocha*
Robert M. Weir, *"A Most Important Epocha": The Coming of the Revolution in South Carolina.* Columbia, S.C., 1970.

[Wells,] *Political Reflections*
[Richard Wells,] *A Few Political Reflections Submitted to the Consideration of the British Colonies, by a Citizen of Philadelphia.* Philadelphia, 1774.

Wesley, *Calm Address*
John Wesley, *A Calm Address to our American Colonies.* London, 1775.

West, *Election Sermon*
Samuel West, *A Sermon Preached Before the Honorable Council, and the Honorable House of Representatives of the Colony of the Massachusetts-Bay, in New-England, May 29th, 1776. Being the Anniversary for the*

Election of the Honorable Council for the Colony (Boston, 1776), reprinted in *The Pulpit of the American Revolution or, the Political Sermons of the Period of 1776.* Edited by John Wingate Thornton, 2d ed. Boston, 1876, pp. 259–322.

Weston, "Theory of Mixed Monarchy"
Corinne Comstock Weston, "The Theory of Mixed Monarchy under Charles I and After," *English Historical Review* 75 (1960): 426–43.

[Whately,] *Considerations on Trade*
[Thomas Whately,] *Considerations on the Trade and Finances of this Kingdom, and on the Measures of Administration, with Respect to those great National Objects since the Conclusion of the Peace.* 3d ed. London, 1769.

[Whately,] *Regulations Lately Made*
[Thomas Whately,] *The Regulations Lately Made Concerning the Colonies, and the Taxes Imposed Upon Them, Considered.* London, 1765.

Wheeler, "Calvin's Case"
Harvey Wheeler, "Calvin's Case (1608) and the McIlwain-Schuyler Debate," *American Historical Review* 61 (1956): 587–97.

[Wheelock,] *Reflections*
[Matthew Wheelock,] *Reflections Moral and Political on Great Britain and her Colonies.* London, 1770.

[Whitby,] *Historical Account*
[Daniel Whitby,] *An Historical Account of Some Things Relating to the Nature of the English Government, and the Conceptions which our Forefathers had of it.* London, 1690.

[Whitelocke,] *Concerning Impositions*
[Sir James Whitelocke,] *The Rights of the People Concerning Impositions, Stated in a learned Argument; With a Remonstrance presented to the Kings most excellent Majesty, by the Honorable House of Commons, in the Parliament, An. Dom. 1610. Annoq; Regis Jac. 7.* London, 1658.

Whitney, *Transgression*
Peter Whitney, *The Transgression of a Land punished by a multitude of Rulers: Considered in Two Discourses, Delivered July 14, 1774, Being voluntarily observed in most of the religious Assemblies throughout the Province of Massachusetts-Bay, as a Day of Fasting and Prayer, On Account of the Dark Aspect of our Public Affairs.* Boston, 1774.

Wickwire, *Subministers*
Franklin B. Wickwire, *British Subministers and Colonial America 1763–1783.* Princeton, N.J., 1966.

Wilkes, *Letter to Grenville*
[John Wilkes,] *A Letter to the Right Honourable George Grenville, Occa-*

sioned By his Publication of the Speech he made in the House of Commons on the Motion for expelling Mr. Wilkes, Friday, February 3, 1769. To which is added, a Letter on the Public Conduct of Mr. Wilkes. London, 1769.

[Williams,] *Letters on Liberty*
[David Williams,] *Letters on Political Liberty. Addressed to a Member of the English House of Commons, on his being Chosen into the Committee of an Associating County.* London, 1782.

Williamson, "Imperial Policy"
J. A. Williamson, "The Beginnings of an Imperial Policy, 1649–1660," in *The Cambridge History of the British Empire: Volume I, The Old Empire From the Beginnings to 1783.* Edited by J. Holland Rose, A. P. Newton, and E. A. Benians. Cambridge, England, 1929, pp. 207–38.

[Williamson,] *Plea of the Colonies*
[Hugh Williamson,] *The Plea of the Colonies On the Charges brought against them by Lord Mansfield, and Others, in a letter to His Lordship.* Philadelphia, 1777.

Wills, *Inventing America*
Garry Wills, *Inventing America: Jefferson's Declaration of Independence.* Garden City, N.Y., 1978.

Wilson, *Considerations*
James Wilson, *Considerations on the Nature and Extent of the Legislative Authority of the British Parliament* (1774), reprinted in *The Works of James Wilson.* Vol. 2. Edited by Robert Green McCloskey. Cambridge, Mass., 1967, pp. 721–46.

Wilson, "Speech of 1775"
James Wilson, "Speech Delivered in the Convention for the Province of Pennsylvania," in *The Works of James Wilson.* Vol. 2. Edited by Robert Green McCloskey. Cambridge, Mass., 1967, pp. 747–58.

Wolin, "Hume and Conservatism"
Sheldon S. Wolin, "Hume and Conservatism," in *Hume: A Re-Evaluation.* Edited by Donald W. Livingston and James T. King. New York, 1976, pp. 239–56.

Wood, *Creation*
Gordon S. Wood, *The Creation of the American Republic 1776–1787.* Chapel Hill, N.C., 1969.

[Wood,] *Institute of the Law*
[Thomas Wood,] *A New Institute of the Imperial or Civil Law. With Notes, Shewing in some Principal Cases, amongest other Observations, How the Canon Law, the Laws of England, and the Laws and Customs of other Nations differ from it. In Four Books.* London, 1704.

Wooddeson, *Brief Vindication*
Richard Wooddeson, *A Brief Vindication of the Rights of the British Legis-lature; in Answer to Some Positions Advanced in a Pamphlet, Intitled, "Thoughts on the English Government, Letter the Second, Addressed to the quiet good Sense of the People of England."* London, 1799.

Wooddeson, *Jurisprudence*
Richard Wooddeson, *Elements of Jurisprudence Treated of in the Prelimi-nary Part of a Course of Lectures on the Laws of England.* Dublin, 1792.

Works of Algernon Sydney
The Works of Algernon Sydney: A New Edition. London, 1772.

Wright, *Fabric of Freedom*
Esmond Wright, *Fabric of Freedom, 1763–1800.* New York, 1961.

Wright, "Two Countries"
Esmond Wright, "Men with Two Countries," in *The Development of a Revolutionary Mentality.* First Library of Congress Symposium on the American Revolution. Washington, D.C., 1972, pp. 151–57.

Wynne, *Eunomus*
Edward Wynne, *Eunomus: or, Dialogues Concerning the Law and Consti-tution of England. With an Essay on Dialogue.* 2d ed. 4 vols. London, 1785.

Yale, "Hobbes and Hale"
D. E. C. Yale, "Hobbes and Hale on Law, Legislation and the Sovereign," *Cambridge Law Journal* 31 (1972): 121–56.

Young, *Example of France*
Arthur Young, *The Example of France A Warning to Britain.* 4th ed. London, 1794.

[Young,] *Political Essays*
[Arthur Young,] *Political Essays Concerning the Present State of the British Empire.* London, 1772.

Zaller, *Parliament of 1621*
Robert Zaller, *The Parliament of 1621: A Study in Constitutional Conflict.* Berkeley, Calif., 1971.

Zemsky, *River Gods*
Robert Zemsky, *Merchants, Farmers, and River Gods: An Essay on Eigh-teenth-Century American Politics.* Boston, 1971.

NOTES

INTRODUCTION

1 *Authority to Tax*, pp. 247–59.
2 *Authority of Rights*, pp. 196–98.
3 Caplan, "Ninth Amendment," p. 230.
4 For the original contract and its variations, see *Authority of Rights*, pp. 132–58. For the colonial original contract and its variations, see *Authority to Tax*, pp. 53–84. Also, see "In Our Contracted Sphere," pp. 21–47.
5 "Irrelevance of the Declaration," pp. 47–69 (for the irrelevance of John Locke to the American case, see pp. 69–80); *Authority to Tax*, pp. 53–60; *Authority of Rights*, pp. 87–95.
6 Bailyn, *Ordeal*, p. 377. See also Becker, *Declaration*, pp. 102–3. Of course, there were those in the eighteenth century who were dogmatic about sovereignty. Thomas, *British Politics*, p. 195 (quoting Lord Lyttleton).
7 Grey, "Unwritten Constitution," pp. 866–67.
8 Thomson, *Constitutional History*, p. 397; Schlesinger, "Revolution Reconsidered," p. 77.
9 McIlwain, *Revolution*, pp. 196–98; Robert Livingstone Schuyler, "Book Review," *Political Science Quarterly* 39 (1924): 151. Similarly, see Schuyler, *Empire*, p. 1.

10 "Schuyler's evidence is legally unanswerable." Madden, "Relevance of Experience," p. 23.

11 Black, "Constitution of Empire," pp. 1160–74; Flaherty, "Empire Strikes Back."

12 Schuyler argued a second proof from acquiescence. "[I]f an American Congress were to take legal steps resulting in American statehood for Newfoundland, would an acceptance by Newfoundland amount to an admission on her part that American statutes had traditionally applied to her? Obviously not, though it was a roughly similar type of proof that Professor Schuyler sometimes relied on." Wheeler, "Calvin's Case," pp. 591–92.

13 Middlekauff, *Glorious Cause*, p. 120. See similarly Wood, *Creation*, p. 352. Also, there were many contemporaries who understood or professed to believe that colonial whigs denied only Parliament's power to tax, not its authority to legislate. E.g., *Boston Post-Boy*, 22 June 1767, p. 1, col. 3 (reprinting Benevolus, *London Chronicle*, 11 April 1767); Anon., *Inquiry into the Nature*, pp. 28–30; Anon., *Supremacy of Legislature*, p. 12.

14 *Authority to Tax*, pp. 85–96.

15 Virginia Resolves, 30 May 1765, Rhode Island Resolves, September 1765, Pennsylvania Resolves, 21 September 1765, Connecticut Resolves, 25 October 1765, Massachusetts Resolves, 29 October 1765, South Carolina Resolves, 29 November 1765, New Jersey Resolves, 30 November 1765, New York Resolves, 18 December 1765, Maryland Resolves, 28 September 1765, Morgan, *Prologue*, pp. 48, 50–51, 51, 55, 57, 58, 60, 61, 53; Maryland Resolves, 17 December 1765, *Boston Post-Boy*, 30 December 1765, p. 3, col. 1.

16 Declarations of Stamp Act Congress, October 1765, Morgan, *Prologue*, pp. 62–63. In the Memorial to the House of Lords the Congress acknowledged "a due Subordination to that August Body the *British* Parliament," and in the Petition to the House of Commons said that "their Subordination to the Parliament, is universally acknowledged." Ibid., pp. 65, 68.

17 [Knox,] *Controversy*, p. 29.

18 Weir, *Most Important Epocha*, p. 19. See also Letter from the Committee of the South Carolina Commons House to Charles Garth, 4 September 1764, Gibbes, *Documentary History*, pp. 2–3.

19 Instructions of 26 May 1766 and of 17 June 1768, *Boston Town Records* 16:183, 258; Answer of the Massachusetts House to Governor Francis Bernard, 24 October 1765, *Boston News-Letter*, 31 October 1765, p. 1, col. 2. See also Address from the Massachusetts House to the King, n.d., *Boston Post-Boy*, 8 December 1766, p. 3, col. 1; Petition from the Representatives of the Counties Upon Delaware to the King, 27 October 1768, *Gentleman's Magazine* 39 (1769): 28.

20 [Knox,] *Controversy*, p. 28; Declaration of both Houses to Charles I, 9 March 1641/42, Rushworth, *Historical Collections: Third Part* 1:531.

21 Countryman, *Revolution*, p. 68; Morgan, "Colonial Ideas," p. 324. A similar word that has misled nonlegal scholars is "superintendence": "Because the Parliament may, when the relation between Great Britain and her

colonies calls for an exertion of her superintendence, bind the colonies by statute, therefore a Parliamentary interposition in every other instance is justifiable, is an inference that may be denied." Dulany, *Considerations*, reprinted in Bailyn, *Pamphlets*, p. 620. See also Petition from Virginia to House of Lords, 16 April 1768, *Revolutionary Virginia* 1:57; Letter from Massachusetts House to Henry Seymour Conway, 13 February 1768, *Boston Post-Boy*, 28 March 1768, p. 2, col. 2.

22 Mayhew, *Snare Broken*, pp. 25–26; [Bancroft,] *Remarks*, p. 5. Of course, colonial tories said the whigs claimed too much. E.g., Anon., *To Freeholders of New York* (1768), p. 2. There were pamphleteers who flatly denied all aspects of parliamentary authority over the colonies. [Downer,] *Discourse in Providence*, pp. 6–7; Greene, *Quest*, p. 371; Toohey, *Liberty and Empire*, p. 150; Wagner, "Judicial Review," p. 575; Lovejoy, *Rhode Island Politics*, p. 126.

23 Stanlis, "British Views," p. 191 (quoting Governor Francis Bernard); Wagner, "Judicial Review," p. 571 n. 1 (quoting Lieutenant Governor Thomas Hutchinson).

24 Extract of a letter from London, 8 February 1765, *South-Carolina Gazette*, 20 April 1765, p. 3, col. 2; Langford, *Rockingham Administration*, pp. 153, 149 (quoting a letter from Governor John Wentworth to D. Rindge, 29 November 1765); *Boston News-Letter*, 4 April 1765, p. 3, col. 2; *Boston Evening-Post*, 25 November 1765, p. 1, col. 1; *Boston Post-Boy*, 3 March 1766, p. 1, col. 1.

25 Headlam, "Constitutional Struggle," p. 654; Report of Committee of the Privy Council, 3 October 1765, *Privy Council Copies*, p. 28. See also *Report of Lords on Massachusetts*, p. 2; Letter from Agent Jasper Mauduit to Secretary Andrew Oliver, 7 April 1764, *Mauduit Letters*, p. 147 n. 1.

26 Speech of Governor Francis Bernard to Council and House, 25 September 1765, and Answer of the House to Governor Francis Bernard, 23 October 1765, *Speeches*, pp. 40, 45; Resolutions of the Assembly, Minutes of 8 March 1775, *Journal of New York Assembly* (1766–76), p. 63.

27 *In a Defiant Stance*, pp. 7–84. A related legal history topic pertaining to the Mutiny Act was the legal restrictions placed on the police functions of the British army. It is an important and too little understood aspect of the Revolution that due to both local colonial and parliamentary law the military could not, without a request from local officials, be used to police crowds in British North America. *In Defiance of the Law*, pp. 172–228.

28 Christie, "Quest for the Revolution," pp. 197–99; *Authority to Tax*, pp. 242–46.

29 Knollenberg, *Origin*, p. 156.

30 These subjects are discussed in *Authority to Tax*.

31 See *Authority of Rights*.

CHAPTER ONE: CULTURE OF CONSTITUTIONALISM

1 Thompson, *Whigs and Hunters*, p. 266.

2 "One strongly-held belief was that private prosecution was an essential constitutional safeguard against possible executive tyranny, a belief which
served to preserve in England the right of prosecution relatively unim-
paired into the twentieth century." Hay, "Criminal Prosecution in England," p. 10.

3 Anon., *First Letter to Grafton*, p. 36.

4 Speech of Edmund Burke, Commons Debates, 31 January 1770, *Burke Writings* 2:235. See also [Downley,] *Sentiments*, p. 8.

5 [Macfarlane,] *George Third*, pp. 315–16 (quoting Middlesex Petition to the
King, 1769).

6 Suggs, "Introduction," to *Perspectives on Revolution*, p. 2.

7 Wolin, "Hume and Conservatism," p. 253; Dover Resolves, 10 January 1774,
Boston Evening-Post, 31 January 1774, p. 1, col. 3; Statement of Samuel
Kemp, 12 September 1775, *Revolutionary Virginia* 4:102.

8 "Authority of migration": *Authority of Rights*, pp. 114–23; "migration purchase": ibid., pp. 124–31; purchase as ownership: ibid., pp. 96–113;
equality: ibid., pp. 82–86. For the legalism of "slavery," see *Concept of
Liberty*, pp. 38–54.

9 Evans, *Reply to Fletcher*, pp. 35–36.

10 *Authority to Tax*, pp. 16–24.

11 Anon., *First Letter to Grafton*, pp. 33, 35; Pulteney, *Plan of Reunion*, p. 44;
Hope, *Letters*, pp. 54–55.

12 Speech of George Grenville, Commons Debates, 15 April 1769, *Parliamentary History* 16:587–88. For a contemporary discussion of the precedents,
see Anon., *Serious Considerations*, pp. 13–29. For an excellent summary
of the debates, showing how legal the arguments were, see *Annual Register
1769*, pp. 68*–73*. The summary concludes by observing, "These arguments were supported by a long train of precedents, shewing the usage of
the house in a number of cases." Ibid., p. 73*.

13 [Grenville,] *Speech on Wilkes*, p. 38; [Downley,] *Sentiments*, pp. 22–23. See
also Speech of Edmund Burke, Commons Debates, 15 April 1769, *Burke
Writings* 2:229; [Macfarlane,] *George Third*, p. 365; Anon., *Serious Considerations*, p. 6.

14 Motion of William Dowdeswell, 25 January 1770, *Parliamentary History*
16:786; [Downley,] *Sentiments*, p. 10.

15 Speech of Sir William Blackstone, Commons Debates, 31 January 1770,
Parliamentary History 16:802; Anon., *First Letter to Grafton*, pp. 35–36.

16 [Grenville,] *Speech on Wilkes*, pp. 12, 29–30 (see also pp. 19, 30–31);
[Downley,] *Sentiments*, p. 36 (see also p. 8); Protest of the Lords, 31 January 1770, *Parliamentary History* 16:821. See also Speech of Thomas
Townshend, Commons Debates, 25 January 1770, *Parliamentary History*
16:789–90; Speech of John Wilkes, Commons Debates, 29 April 1777,
Parliamentary History 19:193–97; [Wilkes,] *Letter to Grenville*,
pp. 28–29; [Macfarlane,] *George Third*, pp. 306–8, 367.

17 Thomas, *Lord North*, pp. 75–76.

18 Boston Committee of Correspondence to the Newport Committee of Correspondence, May 1774, *Rhode Island Colony Records* 7:291; Connecticut

Resolutions, June 1774, *Revolutionary Virginia* 2:116. Also, see Petition of Several Natives of North America to the House of Commons, 2 May 1774, *Proceedings and Debates* 4:115, 327; Petition from Natives of America to the King, 19 May 1774, *American Archives* 1:96.

19 Speech of William Dowdeswell, Commons Debates, 28 April 1774, *Proceedings and Debates* 4:317.

20 *Annual Register 1972*, p. 4

21 *Annual Register 1774*, p. [71]. For a different evaluation of the law, see Chambers, *Lectures* 1:287.

22 Speech of Sir George Savile, Commons Debates, 22 April 1774, *Proceedings and Debates* 4:274.

23 Speech of George Byng, Commons Debates, 2 May 1774, ibid., p. 379; Speech of Lord John Cavendish, Commons Debates, 14 March 1774, ibid., p. 77; Speech of William Dowdeswell, Commons Debates, 28 April 1774, ibid., p. 313; Speech of John St. John, Commons Debates, 2 May 1774, ibid., p. 352. For a common lawyer's discussion of the law, see Tetlow, *Impartial Letter*, pp. 4–5.

24 Speech of Edmund Burke, Commons Debates, 25 March 1774, *Proceedings and Debates* 4:136; Speech of Sir George Yonge, Commons Debates, 22 April 1774, ibid., p. 276. Similarly, see Speech of William Dowdeswell, Commons Debates, 14 March 1774, ibid., p. 76; Speech of Thomas De Grey, Commons Debates, 6 May 1774, ibid., p. 403.

25 Speech of Sir George Savile, Commons Debates, 29 April 1774, ibid., p. 317. Similarly, see Speeches of Sir George Savile, Commons Debates, 22 April 1774, 28 April 1774, 2 May 1774, 4 May 1774, ibid., pp. 274–75, 311–12, 374, 383.

26 Speeches of Henry Seymour Conway and Sir George Savile, 22 April 1774, ibid., pp. 275, 274.

27 Protest of 11 May 1774, *Protests of the Peers*, pp. 2–3. For somewhat related arguments, see Address from the Continental Congress to the People of Great Britain, 21 October 1774, *Journals of Congress* 1:87; Speech of Lord Chatham, Lords Debates, 20 January 1775, *Parliamentary History* 18:150–51; Trumbull, *Discourse at New Haven*, p. 24.

28 Speech of Lord North, Commons Debates, 14 March 1774, *Proceedings and Debates* 4:78. Like most of the debates on American affairs at the time, this debate was widely printed in Great Britain and Ireland. E.g., *London Evening Post*, 15–17 March 1774; *London Magazine* 43 (1774): 168; *Hibernian Magazine* 4 (1774): 304; *Annual Register 1774*, p. [63]. Other members also cited other precedents to support other points of law. E.g., Speech of Lord Clare, Commons Debates, 28 April 1774, *Proceedings and Debates* 4:309 (debate on Massachusetts Government Bill).

29 E.g., Speech of William Dowdeswell, Commons Debates, 14 March 1774, *Proceedings and Debates* 4:80–81.

30 Petition of Several Natives of North America to the House of Commons, 25 March 1774, ibid., p. 115; [Macfarlane,] *Second Ten Years*, p. 139; Anon., *View of North*, p. 131 footnote.

31 See chart, *London Magazine* 43 (1774): 187; Baillie, *Letter to Shebear,*

pp. 23–24; [Baillie,] *Some Observations on a Pamphlet*, p. 25; Petition of
Several Natives of North America to the House of Commons, 25 March
1774, *Proceedings and Debates* 4:115–16; [Macfarlane,] *Second Ten Years*,
p. 139; Anon., *"Taxation no Tyranny" Considered*, p. 81–82.

32 *Annual Register 1774*, p. [67]; Speech of Rose Fuller, Commons Debates, 23
   March 1774, *Proceedings and Debates* 4:89.

33 Speech of Lord North, Commons Debates, 23 March 1774, *Proceedings and
   Debates* 4:92.

34 Protest of the Lords, 11 May 1774, ibid., pp. 417–18 (first and third dissents);
   Annual Register 1774, p. [71].

35 [Eardley-Wilmot,] *Short Defence*, p. 10 (quoting argument of William
   Dowdeswell in Commons debates); Address, Remonstrance, and Petition
   of the City of London, *The Crisis*, 15 April 1775, p. 89. For the administration's answer on the law, see Speeches of Lord North, Commons Debates,
   14 March 1774, 23 March 1774, and 25 March 1774, *Proceedings and
   Debates* 4:58–59, 108, 132; Speeches of Grey Cooper and Welbore Ellis,
   Commons Debates, 25 March 1774, ibid., pp. 127, 135, 136; Anon., *View
   of North*, p. 132.

36 Speeches of William Dowdeswell and Edmund Burke, Commons Debates,
   25 March 1774, *Proceedings and Debates* 4:135, 140. The administration
   replied that it was Boston's actions and leadership that incited New York
   and Philadelphia. Speech of Lord North, Commons Debates, 14 March
   1774, ibid., p. 59.

37 Speech of John Sawbridge, Commons Debates, 25 March 1774, ibid., p. 142.
   For the administration's answer, see Speech of Lord North, Commons
   Debates, 25 March 1774, ibid., p. 143.

38 Speech of George Johnstone, Commons Debates, 25 March 1774, *American
   Archives* 1:54; *London Gazetteer*, 7 April 1774, reprinted in *American
   Archives* 1:244; Extract of a Letter from Boston in a Philadelphia news-
   paper, 6 June 1774, reprinted in *American Archives* 1:389; "An American,"
   Boston, 20 June 1774, ibid., pp. 434–35; "To the Inhabitants of . . . South-
   Carolina," 4 July 1774, ibid., p. 509.

39 Speech of John Sawbridge, Commons Debates, 14 March 1774, *Proceedings
   and Debates* 4:66, 76. For the administration's answer, see Speech of Lord
   North, Commons Debates, 14 March 1774, ibid., pp. 58–59; [Lind,] *Thirteenth Parliament*, pp. 379–92.

40 Speeches of William Dowdeswell and Edmund Burke, Commons Debates,
   25 March 1774, *Proceedings and Debates* 4:120, 135, 136, 141. For the
   administration's reply, see Speech of Lord North, Commons Debates, 14
   March 1774, ibid., pp. 56, 57–58, 60–61; Speech of Rose Fuller, Commons
   Debates, 23 March 1774, ibid., p. 107; Speeches of Welbore Ellis and Grey
   Cooper, Commons Debates, 25 March 1774, ibid., pp. 135–36, 142.

41 Speech of George Byng, Commons Debates, 23 March 1774, ibid., p. 110
   ("You are not punishing the Bostonians; you are punishing the English
   merchants . . ."); Speech of Edmund Burke, Commons Debates, 25
   March 1774, ibid., 136 ("This punishment does not appear as the act of a

sovereign but as an enemy. It's a renunciation of our authority . . .");
Speech of Lord Chatham, Lords Debates, 26 May 1774, ibid., p. 439. For
the Administration's answer, see Speeches of Lord North, Commons
Debates, 14 March 1774 and 23 March 1774, ibid., pp. 75, 92; *Annual
Register 1774*, p. [63].

42 Protest of the Lords, 11 May 1774, *Proceedings and Debates* 4:417.

43 Ibid., p. 419.

44 Letter from Arthur Lee to Richard Henry Lee, 18 March 1774, *American
Archives* 1:229. See also, Petition of the New York Assembly to the King, 24
March 1775, ibid., p. 1315; Connecticut Resolutions, June 1774, *Revolu-
tionary Virginia* 2:116.

45 Petition of Several Natives of North America to the House of Commons, 25
March 1774, *American Archives* 1:47. This petition was widely reprinted.
See, e.g., *Hibernian Magazine* 4 (1774): 182; *Annual Register 1774*,
p. [66]; [Macfarlane,] *Second Ten Years*, p. 138.

46 Resolves of the General Assembly, June 1774, *Rhode Island Colony Records*
7:246; Georgia Resolves, 10 August 1774, *Georgia Revolutionary Records*
1:16; Address to the People of Great Britain, 21 October 1774, *Journals of
Congress* 1:87. Also, see Address of the Massachusetts Provincial Congress
to the People, 9 February 1775, *American Archives* 1:1333; Perry, *Connecticut Election Sermon*, p. 7.

Chapter Two: Passage of the Declaratory Act

1 Langford, *Rockingham Administration*, p. 143 (quoting letter from Lord
Rockingham to Charles Yorke, 25 January 1766); Speech of Lord Rockingham, Lords Debates, 18 May 1774, *Proceedings and Debates* 4:434;
Speech of Lord Beauchamp, Commons Debates, 10 December 1777, *Parliamentary History* 19:576-77; [Burke,] *Observations on Late State*,
pp. 121-22; *London Magazine* 45 (1776): 411; Knollenberg, *Growth of
Revolution*, p. 24 (quoting Lord Mansfield); Thomas, *British Politics*,
p. 245.

2 [Draper,] *Thoughts of a Traveller*, p. 13. It should be noted that some American whigs thought Parliament should do the opposite: repeal the Stamp
Act while implying a saving of the right, thus avoiding the precedent and
acknowledging that Great Britain "has no Right to tax the Colonies."
Letter from John Dickinson to William Pitt, 21 December 1765, Morgan,
Prologue, p. 121. Oddly, it would seem that to the twentieth-century
historical mind, expediency could itself be a precedent. Thus the combination of passage of the Declaratory Act with the repeal of the Stamp Act has
been described as setting "a precedent for expediency." Clark, *British
Opinion*, p. 242.

3 *Authority to Tax*, pp. 204-7; Address of Governor Francis Bernard to the
Council and House, 25 September 1765, *Speeches*, p. 40; Anon., *Consid-
erations Upon Rights of Colonists*, p. 11; Abingdon, *Thoughts on Burke's
Letter*, p. 49.

4 Langford, *Rockingham Administration*, pp. 174–97. Langford concludes that "[i]t is no coincidence that the British Parliament came nearer than ever after to a genuinely conciliatory attitude at a time of severe economic unrest. Ten years later the situation was very different." Ibid., p. 189. That may be, but it is also true that ten years later the constitutional situation was entirely different. The excuse of expediency would then be of no avail.

5 [Hicks,] *Nature of Parliamentary Power*, p. iii.

6 Langford, *Rockingham Administration*, p. 174; Speech of Sir William Blackstone, Commons Debates, 24 February 1766, and Letter from R. Palmer to R. Cust, 24 February 1766, *Proceedings and Debates* 2:299, 301; Dissentient Lords, *Boston Evening-Post* (Supplement), 9 June 1766, p. 2, col. 1.

7 Speech of William Dowdeswell, Commons Debates, 4 March 1766, Ryder, "Parliamentary Diaries," p. 317; Langford, *Rockingham Administration*, pp. 127, 131, 132, 143, 151–52.

8 Christie & Labaree, *Empire*, p. 73. See also Ritcheson, *British Politics*, pp. 51, 55–56; Letter from R. Palmer to R. Cust, 21 February 1766, *Proceedings and Debates* 2:289.

9 Letter to Samuel White, 15 February 1766, "Letters of Dennys De Berdt," p. 312; Speech of George Onslow, Commons Debates, 4 December 1777, *Parliamentary History* 19:547; "Indulgence": Anon., *Remarks on Conduct*, pp. 10–11. See also "Charles Garth's Letter," p. 149; Letter from London Merchants to New York Merchants, 28 February 1766, *South-Carolina Gazette*, 16 June 1766, p. 2, col. 3; Thomas, *British Politics*, pp. 248, 174; Langford, *Rockingham Administration*, pp. 151, 174.

10 Speech of Lord Beauchamp, Commons Debates, 10 December 1777, *Parliamentary History* 19:576–77; Langford, *Rockingham Administration*, pp. 174–75.

11 6 George III, cap. 12; Speech of Governor Thomas Pownall, *Gentleman's Magazine* 39 (1769): 570; Speech of Lord Beauchamp, Commons Debates, 10 December 1777, *Parliamentary History* 19:576; Chaffin, "Declaratory Act," p. 7; Franklin, *Address to Ireland*, p. 15. For Declaratory Resolves, see Resolutions of the House of Lords, 10 February 1766, and Resolutions of the House of Commons, 24 February 1766, 15 May 1767, *Proceedings and Debates* 2:178, 293, 477; "Proposed Resolutions Preceding the Declaratory Act," Morgan, *Prologue*, pp. 141–42.

12 Speech of Hans Stanley, Commons Debates, 3 February 1766, "Declaratory Debates," pp. 565–66.

13 Speech of Charles Yorke, ibid., pp. 566–67.

14 *Authority to Tax*, pp. 17, 19–20.

15 Speech of Charles Yorke, Commons Debates, 3 February 1766, *Proceedings and Debates* 2:146, and "Declaratory Debates," p. 567. For the inconclusiveness of charters, see *Authority of Rights*, pp. 159–68; "In the First Line of Defense," pp. 194–215.

16 Speech of Charles Yorke, Commons Debates, 3 February 1766, *Proceedings and Debates* 2:139.

17 Speech of William Beckford, Commons Debates, 3 February 1766, ibid., p. 147, and "Declaratory Debates," p. 568.
18 Speech of Robert Nugent, Commons Debates, 3 February 1766, *Proceedings and Debates* 2:147.
19 Speech of Henry Seymour Conway, Commons Debates, 3 February 1766, "Declaratory Debates," p. 568.
20 Speech of Sir William Blackstone, Commons Debates, 3 February 1766, ibid., pp. 568–69, and *Proceedings and Debates* 2:140.
21 Speech of Thomas Pitt, Commons Debates, 3 February 1766, *Proceedings and Debates* 2:148.
22 Speech of Richard Hussey, 3 February 1766, ibid., pp. 141–42, 148–49, and "Declaratory Debates," pp. 569–70.
23 Speech of Alexander Wedderburn, 3 February 1766, *Proceedings and Debates* 2:142–43, 149, and "Declaratory Debates," pp. 570–71.
24 Speech of Edmund Burke, 3 February 1766, *Proceedings and Debates* 2:143, 149, and "Declaratory Debates," p. 571; *Briefs of Revolution*, pp. 62–66, 136–40.
25 Speech of Isaac Barré, 3 February 1766, *Proceedings and Debates* 2:144, and "Declaratory Debates," p. 571.
26 Speech of William Dowdeswell, 3 February 1766, "Declaratory Debates," pp. 571–72.
27 Speech of George Grenville, 3 February 1766, ibid., p. 572, and *Proceedings and Debates* 2:149, 145.
28 Speech of William Pitt, 3 February 1766, "Declaratory Debates," pp. 572–73, and *Proceedings and Debates* 2:150. For power and right, see "In the Taught Tradition," pp. 947–61.
29 Speech of Sir Fletcher Norton, Commons Debates, 3 February 1766, "Declaratory Debates," pp. 573–74.
30 Hardwicke's Reports, 11 March 1766, *Proceedings and Debates* 2:342 (reporting Speech of Lord Mansfield, Lords Debates, 11 March 1766); Hardwicke's Reports, 10 March 1766, ibid., p. 329 (reporting Speech of the Duke of Newcastle, Lords Debates, 10 March 1766).

CHAPTER THREE: SCOPE OF THE DECLARATORY ACT

1 Speech of Lord Beauchamp, Commons Debates, 10 December 1777, *Parliamentary History* 19:576; Speeches of Lord Halifax and Lord Lyttelton, Lords Debates, 11 March 1766, "Declaratory Debates," pp. 581, 584. See also Chaffin, "Declaratory Act," p. 11 (quoting Lord Rockingham in 1768); Speech of Lord Rockingham, Lords Debates, 20 January 1775, *Parliamentary History* 18:167; Speech of William Dowdeswell, Commons Debates, 3 February 1766, Ryder, "Parliamentary Diaries," p. 275; Letter from Edmund Burke to Richard Champion, 19 March 1776, *Burke on American Revolution*, p. xxi.
2 There was, first of all, the issue whether the right existed independently of its

exercise by virtue of sovereignty, or whether, if custom as much as command determined constitutionality, an unexercised right was not a right. There was the additional argument, that the right had been exercised in other legislation. Knox believed the statute 7 & 8 William III, cap. 22 did away with all legal objections to parliamentary colonial legislation when it enacted: "That all Laws, Bye-Laws, Usages and Customs which shall be in Practice in any of the Plantations, repugnant to any Law made *or to be made in this Kingdom relative to the said Plantations*, shall be void and of none Effect." That clause, Knox wrote, "ought surely to be a sufficient Refutation of the very singular Claim of the Colonists." [Knox,] *Letter to a Member*, p. 17. Lawrence Gipson agreed, but in fact the statute was by no means clear and can be distinguished, especially if legislative history is admissible. Knollenberg, *Growth of Revolution*, p. 206.

3 An exception is Edmund Burke. Unfortunately, he drew the right "from the Nature of a supreme power, from the existing powers from the usual Course of the British constitution, and even from the original Compacts of these Colonies." Burke may have tossed in the last authority as extra but unnecessary support for the first two. If he meant the original compacts were necessary to establish the right, that assertion was inconsistent with the authority of "the Nature of a supreme power." Speech of Edmund Burke, 3 February 1766, *Burke Writings* 2:48.

4 Letter from R. Palmer to R. Cust, 7 March 1766, Letter from Charlemont to H. Flood, 7 March 1766, Letter from Lord Hardwicke to Charles Yorke, 7 March 1766, *Proceedings and Debates* 2:321, 320, 318.

5 "Charles Garth's Letter," p. 148 (for the best summary of the arguments made by the law officers, see ibid., pp. 151–53); Speech of Sir William Meredith, Commons Debates, 10 February 1775, *Gentleman's Magazine* 45 (1775): 260. See also Speech of Governor George Johnstone, Commons Debates, 27 February 1775, *Gentleman's Magazine* 45 (1775): 613.

6 Pownall, *Administration*, pp. 129–30; Speech of Lord Beauchamp, Commons Debates, 10 December 1777, *Parliamentary History* 19:576–77. Pownall was elected to Parliament in 1767, the year after passage of the Declaratory Act.

7 Speech of Richard Rigby, Commons Debates, 16 December 1774, *Parliamentary History* 18:64. Like the American Act, the Irish Act was called "Oppressive on the People of this Country." Anon., *Moderation Unmasked*, p. 10 footnote. The Irish Declaratory Act was 6 George I, cap. 5.

8 Letter III from Philadelphia, *Boston Evening-Post*, 4 July 1774, p. 1, col. 1; "To the Inhabitants of the British Colonies in America," from a Philadelphia newspaper of 8 June 1774, and "To P. P. Author of the Letters to the Inhabitants of the British Colonies in America," June 1774, *American Archives* 1:395, 396. See also Demophoon, *Political Register* 7 (1770): 155; Chaffin, "Declaratory Act," p. 9.

9 Morgan, *Birth*, p. 31; Morgan, "Parliamentary Power," p. 60. For Pitt's

dichotomy between legislation and taxation, see *Authority to Tax*, pp. 85–96.

10 Speech of Isaac Barré, Commons Debates, 3 February 1766, "Declaratory Debates," p. 571, and *Proceedings and Debates* 2:144; Speech of Robert Nugent, Commons Debates, 3 February 1766, *Proceedings and Debates* 2:139. For the constitutional context of Barré's motion, see text of n. 25, chap. 2.

11 Speeches of William Pitt and George Grenville, Commons Debates, 7 February 1766, Ryder, "Parliamentary Diaries," pp. 287, 288. See also Thomas, *British Politics*, pp. 199, 240.

12 Thomas, *British Politics*, p. 199; Morgan, "Parliamentary Power," p. 60. See also Speech of William Dowdeswell, Commons Debates, 25 March 1774, *Proceedings and Debates* 4:119; Chaffin, "Declaratory Act," p. 16. A year later Thomas Whately observed that those who had denied Parliament's right to tax the colonies during the Stamp Act debates had changed their stands now "that the Declaratory Act has put an end to the question, and determined the law." Letter from Thomas Whately to John Temple, 2 May 1767, *Bowdoin Papers*, p. 83.

13 Speech of John Wilkes, Commons Debates, 10 December 1777, *Parliamentary History* 19:571; [Burke,] *Observations on Late State*, p. 122; Chaffin, "Declaratory Act," p. 11. Grenville ridiculed the Declaratory Act for embodying the notion that Parliament had the right to tax, but should not exercise it. Lawson, "George Grenville," p. 562.

14 *London Magazine* 35 (1766): 611–12; [Lloyd,] *Examination of the Principles*, p. 8; Speech of Richard Rigby, Commons Debates, 25 April 1774, *Proceedings and Debates* 4:280; [Williamson,] *Plea of the Colonies*, p. 6; Morgan, "Colonial Ideas," p. 330; Morgan, *Challenge*, p. 28 n. 59.

15 Petition of New York General Assembly to the King, 25 March 1775, *Journal of New York Assembly* (1766–76), p. 110; Speech of Lord Camden, Lords Debates, 3 February 1766, *Proceedings and Debates* 2:128; Speech of Lord Camden, Lords Debates, 10 February 1766, "Lords Debate on Declaratory Act," pp. 111–12; Speech of Lord Chatham, Lords Debates, 20 January 1775, *Parliamentary History* 18:156–57; Speech of John Wilkes, Commons Debates, 10 December 1777, *Parliamentary History* 19:564; Letter from W. S. Johnson to W. Pitkin, 15 December 1768, *Proceedings and Debates* 3:48; Anon., *Sequel to Essay*, p. 11.

16 The most confusing interpretation belonged to Arthur Lee. He agreed that Parliament, in the Declaratory Act, intended to maintain the right of colonial taxation, "yet, in my opinion, it does not conclude to the right of taxing America." "Junius Americanus," *Boston Evening-Post*, 4 May 1772, p. 1, col. 1; *Political Register* 9 (1771): 323.

17 Christie, *Crisis*, p. 63; *Boston Chronicle*, 19 June 1769, p. 193, col. 2. See also, Headlam, "Constitutional Struggle," pp. 660–61.

18 Speech of William Burke, Commons Debates, 19 April 1769, *Proceedings and Debates* 3:150; Donoughue, *British Politics*, p. 132; Toohey, *Liberty and Empire*, p. 122.

19 Anon., *Experience preferable to Theory*, p. 56; *South-Carolina Gazette*, 9 June 1766, p. 1, cols. 1-2; *Massachusetts Gazette and Boston News-Letter*, 22 May 1766, p. 1, cols. 1-2; *Boston Evening-Post*, 28 April 1766, p. 4, col. 1 and 26 May 1766, p. 2, col. 2; Letter from Governor William Pitkin to Secretary Henry Seymour Conway, 4 August 1766, *Prior Documents*, pp. 109-10; Letter from Thomas Bradshaw to Charles Jenkinson, 24 June 1766, *Jenkinson Papers*, p. 413.

20 Morgan, "Parliamentary Power," pp. 61-62; Morgan, *Justice Johnson*, p. 4; Leder, *Liberty*, p. 145; Beloff, *Debate*, p. 31; Morris, "Legal Profession in America," pp. 23-24.

21 Langford, *Rockingham Administration*, p. 197; Morgan, "Colonial Ideas," p. 329.

22 "To P. P. Author of the Letters to the Inhabitants of the British Colonies in America," (June 1774), *American Archives* 1:395. See also Letter from George Mason to Committee of London Merchants, 6 June 1766, Morgan, *Prologue*, p. 159.

23 Cartwright, *Letter to Abingdon*, p. 17 footnote. Knox wrote of Parliament unwisely giving up the stamp tax "without requiring an acknowledgement from the colonies of its supremacy." [Knox,] *Present State*, p. 46.

24 Report from Charles Garth to South Carolina, *Proceedings and Debates* 2:468 (reporting event of 13 May 1767).

25 Clark, *British Opinion*, p. 198 (quoting Maurice Morgann); Speech of Charles James Fox, Commons Debates, 10 December 1777, *Parliamentary History* 19:584; Ritcheson, *British Politics*, p. 66. "The *Brutum fulmen* that preceded the repeal does not in ye least damp our Joy.—It will not hurt us much to resolve or pass an Act that ye Parliament has a right to tax America, if they never put it in practice." Letter from Charles Carroll of Carrollton to Daniel Barrington, 29 May 1766, *Letters of Charles Carroll*, p. 121.

26 Speech of Thomas Pownall, Commons Debates, 8 February 1769, *Proceedings and Debates* 3:110. See also Speech of Thomas Pownall, Commons Debates, 19 April 1769, ibid., p. 149. Contrary, see Speech of Alexander Wedderburn, Commons Debates, 3 February 1766, Ryder, "Parliamentary Diaries," p. 272.

27 Speech of Henry Flood, Irish Commons, 14 June 1782, *Celebrated Speeches of Flood*, p. 26; [Galloway,] *Historical Reflections*, p. 14.

28 Testimony of Benjamin Franklin, House of Commons, 13 February 1766, Ryder, "Parliamentary Diaries," p. 300; *Examination of Franklin*, p. 7; Nicholas, *Present State of Virginia*, p. 263; Morgan, *Challenge*, p. 28. For the theory that "the peaceable Possession of the Estate" should satisfy Ireland, that "we need not contend for the Title Deeds," see [Sheridan,] *Review of Three Questions* p. 51. Contrary, see Anon., *Answer to Sheridan*, p. 12.

29 King of France: Anon., *Characters of Parties*, p. 71; Jerusalem: Ammerman, *Common Cause*, p. 67.

30 Letter from Charles Carroll of Carrollton to Daniel Barrington, 17 March

1765, *Letters of Charles Carroll*, p. 110; Estwick, *Letter to Tucker*, p. 113 footnote; Dickinson, *Letters*, p. 359; [Lloyd,] *Conduct Examined*, p. 158; Speech of George Grenville, Commons Debates, 24 February 1766, Ryder, "Parliamentary Diaries," p. 315; [Williamson,] *Plea of the Colonies*, p. 6. See also Ramsay, *History*, p. 74; Pownall, *Administration*, p. 164 footnote; Headlam, "Constitutional Struggle," p. 661; Wright, *Freedom*, p. 58.

31 *South-Carolina Gazette*, 10 November 1766, p. 1, col. 2; *Boston Evening-Post*, 7 March 1768, p. 4, col. 1. See also Letter from Thomas Cushing to Arthur Lee, October 1773, *Collections Massachusetts Historical Society* 4 (1858): 362; D'Innocenzo & Turner, "New York Newspapers Part 2," p. 364. (quoting *New York Post-Boy*, 18 September 1766); Foner, *Labor and Revolution*, p. 75. For a comparable Irish attitude, see Anon., *Answer to Sheridan*, pp. 13–14.

32 *Gentleman's Magazine* 36 (1766): 616 (reprinting "British American" from colonial newspapers); Speech of Charles James Fox, Commons Debates, 15 May 1775, Fox, *Speeches* 1:42; *Gentleman's Magazine* 39 (1769): 570 (reprinting Pownall's speech urging repeal of the Townshend duties).

33 Massachusetts Resolves, 3 March 1773, *Journal of the House*, p. 281. See also Letter from Massachusetts Subcommittee to Virginia Committee of Correspondence, 21 October 1773, *Revolutionary Virginia* 2:46. For the constitutional issue of the Townshend duties, see *Authority to Tax*, pp. 217–22. The Massachusetts House voted the resolutions the day after its "Rejoinder" in which, for the first time, it was forced to confront parliamentary sovereignty. *Briefs of Revolution*, pp. 125–43.

34 Price, *Nature of Civil Liberty*, p. 35; Paine, *Letter to Raynal*, p. 4.

35 "To P. P. Author of the Letters to the Inhabitants of the British Colonies in America," (June 1774), *American Archives* 1:396. Similarly, see Stearns, *View of the Controversy*, p. 19.

36 Memorial from New York General Assembly to the House of Lords, 25 March 1775, *American Archives* 1:1316. See also Petition of New York General Assembly to the King, 24 March 1775, ibid., p. 1314.

37 Petition from Jamaica to the King, 28 December 1774, *Revolutionary Virginia* 2:365; Instructions of Deputies from Pennsylvania Counties to Representatives, 21 July 1774, *London Magazine* 43 (1774): 585; Price, *Nature of Civil Liberty*, p. 34. John Dickinson drafted the Pennsylvania instructions. [Dickinson,] *New Essay*, p. 13.

38 Memorial from New York General Assembly to the House of Lords, 25 March 1775, *Journal of New York Assembly* (1766–76), p. 113. See also Speech of John Wilkes, Commons Debates, 10 December 1777, *Parliamentary History* 19:564, 569–70; "Brutus," *Virginia Gazette*, 14 July 1775, reprinted in *Revolutionary Virginia* 3:129; John Dickinson's Draft Address to the Inhabitants of America, January 1776, *Letters of Delegates to Congress* 3:139; [Joseph Hawley,] "To Inhabitants," 9 March 1775, *American Archives* 2:100; J. J. Zubly, "An Address to Lord Dartmouth," *Hibernian Magazine* 5 (1775): 811; Paine, *Letter to Raynal*, p. 5.

39 Representation and Remonstrance of New York to the House of Commons,

1775, *Hibernian Magazine* 5 (1775): 359; Memorial of New York to the House of Lords, 25 March 1775, *American Archives* 1:1317. See also Resolutions of Dinwiddie County, Virginia, 15 July 1774 and Petition of the New Jersey Assembly to the King, 13 February 1775, *American Archives* 1:552, 1133.

40 Speech of John Wilkes, Commons Debates, 10 December 1777, *Parliamentary History* 19:565–66; Speech of Lord Rockingham, Lords Debates, 20 January 1775, *Parliamentary History* 18:167. Ambrose Serle, however, claimed the first Congress made more of the Declaratory Act as a grievance than any other statute. [Serle,] *Americans against Liberty*, p. 33. For what was said, see Address to the People of Great Britain, 21 October 1774, *Commemoration Ceremony*, pp. 106–12.

41 Declaration of the Congress, 6 July 1775, *Papers of Jefferson* 1:215; Anon., *Address to People of Britain*, p. 56. See also [Williamson,] *Plea of the Colonies*, p. 6.

42 [Williamson,] *Plea of the Colonies*, pp. 4–5 (quoting Mansfield).

43 Charles Town, South Carolina, Resolves, July 1774, *Hibernian Magazine* 4 (1774): 609; "Instructions by the Virginia Convention to Delegates in Congress," August 1774, *Papers of Jefferson* 1:141; Resolutions of the Pennsylvania Provincial Meeting, 15 July 1774, *Gentleman's Magazine* 44 (1774): 438, 439; New Jersey Resolutions, 21 July 1774, *American Archives* 1:624.

44 Speech of John Wilkes, Commons Debates, 10 December 1777, *Parliamentary History* 19:566.

45 Speech of Edmund Burke, Commons Debates, 16 November 1775, *Burke on American Revolution*, p. 132; Chaffin, "Declaratory Act," p. 18.

46 E.g., Commons Debates, 7 December 1768, *Proceedings and Debates* 3:32; Valentine, *Lord North* 1:175.

47 Letter from Charles Garth to South Carolina Commons House Committee, 12 March 1767, "Garth Correspondence" 5:218. See also same to same, 10 December 1768, "Garth Correspondence" 10:234.

48 Cartwright, *Legislative Rights*, p. 109 footnote.

49 F. B., *Causes of Distractions*, p. 4; Instructions to Pennsylvania Representatives, 15 July 1774, *American Archives* 1:566. See also Adams, *Writings* 1:286 (reprinting an article in *Boston Gazette*, 9 January 1769); [Hicks,] *Nature of Parliamentary Power*, pp. 10–11.

50 Christie, *Crisis*, p. 66; Goodhart, *Law of the Land*, p. 60.

51 Speech of William Beckford, Commons Debates, 7 December 1768, *Proceedings and Debates* 3:32; Speech of Lord Abingdon, Lords Debates, 7 December 1778, *Parliamentary History* 20:14; Speech of Henry Seymour Conway, 20 November 1775, *Gentleman's Magazine* 46 (1776):101. See also Anon., *Defence of Resolutions*, p. 29.

52 Pownall, *Administration Fifth Edition* 1:iii; Pownall, *Administration Fifth Edition* 2:41. Perhaps the most remarkable discussion of the Act written by a commentator who was lost somewhere between the two constitutions, is the following:

[H]aving received the Sanction of PARLIAMENTARY AUTHORITY, is to be considered as the Act of the legislative Body of this Kingdom; an Opposition to it can be no longer maintained, in consistence with the Allegiance due to that Authority. Upon this State of the Case, however the AMERICANS may be justified in resisting an Authority, which according to the general Opinion in that Country was *unconstitutionally* exerted; yet Members of the British Community, who have a CONSTITUTIONAL STANDARD set up for them to judge by this Affair, can no longer countenance such Resistance, upon any Principle of *sound* Policy, or *true* Patriotism.

Anon., *Address to People of Britain*, p. 33.
53 Speech of Governor Thomas Pownall, Commons Debates, 5 March 1770, *Proceedings and Debates* 3:230.
54 Speech of Lord George Germain, Commons Debates, 26 January 1775, *London Magazine* 44 (1775): 337. Also, see Speech of John Burgoyne, Commons Debates, 19 April 1774, *Proceedings and Debates* 4:193; Speech of John Burgoyne, Commons Debates, 27 February 1775, *Gentleman's Magazine* 45 (1775): 612; Burgoyne, "Letter to Lee," p. 2.
55 Anon., *Remarks on Conduct*, p. 10.

CHAPTER FOUR: THE LOGIC OF SUPREMACY

1 Schutz, *Thomas Pownall*, p. 220.
2 Of sovereignty, Judge Sir Robert Atkyns said in 1689: " . . . tho' now frequently used in our humble Addresses to the King, or in our reverend mention of him, yet we find it very rarely, if ever, used in our ancient Acts of Parliament, or in our Law Books." Atkyns, *Enquiry into Power*, p. 41.
3 [Whitelocke,] *Concerning Impositions*, p. 9. See also Prall, *Agitation*, p. 14; Cragg, *Freedom and Authority*, pp. 84–85.
4 Hobbes, *Elements of Law*, part 2, chap. 1, sec. 13, and part 2, chap. 8, sec. 6; Filmer, *Necessity of Absolute Power*, p. 317; Locke, *Two Treatises*, book 1, sec. 129; Eccleshall, *Order and Reason*, p. 100; Judson, *Crisis*, p. 236; Lamprecht, "Introduction," p. xxviii; Dickinson, "Debate on Sovereignty," p. 191; Bailyn, *Pamphlets*, pp. 116–17; Wood, *Creation*, pp. 346–47.
5 Both arbitrary sovereignty and nonresistance had English supporters before the eighteenth century. [Hickes,] *Jovian*, pp. 200–202; Sherlock, *Case of Resistance*, pp. 110–11; Anon., *Easie Method*, p. 9.
6 Fenning, *Dictionary*; Perry, *Dictionary*; *Scots Magazine* 25 (1763): 700 (quoting George Berkeley, "Passive Obedience"). For standard definitions, see Burlamaqui, *Politic Law*, p. 44; Burlamaqui, *Natural Law*, p. 80; [Phelps,] *Rights of the Colonies*, pp. 3–4; Anon., *Essay on the Constitution*, pp. 9–10.
7 Speech of Lord Northington, Lords Debates, 10 February 1766, *Parliamentary History* 16:170; McIlwain, *Constitutionalism*, p. 7.

8 Anon., *Discourse on Constitution*, p. 11; Pollock, "Sovereignty in English
   Law," p. 249 (quoting Blackstone, *Commentaries* 1:49). Fewer theorists
   attempted to outline the actions of sovereignty. One that did said: "The
   acts incident to sovereignty are principally these. To frame and reform the
   internal polity; whether general and supreme, or partial and subordinate:
   to regulate the administration of justice: and to demand from the individual members of the state contributions from their private property, for
   the support and maintenance of the whole community." [Hampson,]
   Reflections on the Present State, pp. 24–25.
9 Hart, "Bentham and America," p. 551; [Johnson,] *Political Tracts*, pp. 195–
   96. See also Kemp, "Parliamentary Sovereignty," p. 12 (quoting Johnson);
   McAdam, *Johnson and Law*, pp. 189–90; Blackall, *Subjects Duty*, p. 9;
   Hobbes, *Elements of Law*, part 1, chap. 19, sec. 10; *London Magazine* 9
   (1740): 2.
10 Wooddeson, *Jurisprudence*, p. 71; Wooddeson, *Brief Vindication*, p. 3.
11 Eliot, *Give Cesar his Due*, p. 14. See also [Knox,] *Letter to a Member*, p. 5;
   Pownall, *Administration*, p. 130; Bailyn, *Pamphlets*, p. 117.
12 Anon., *Thoughts on the Constitution*, p. 6. See also Plowden, *Rights of
   Englishmen*, p. 149; Speech of Mr. Phipps, 3 March 1709/10, *Tryal of
   Sacheverell*, p. 142; Filmer, *Necessity of Absolute Power*, p. 320; Lawson,
   Politica Sacra, pp. 66–67; Sisson, "Idea of Revolution," p. 411 (quoting
   Lord Chancellor Northington).
13 Bolingbroke, "The Freeholder's Political Catechism," *Gazette & Post-Boy*, 27
   February 1775, p. 2, col. 1. See also Arbuthnot, *Freeholder's Catechism*,
   p. 6; [Bollan,] *Freedom of Speech*, p. 141.
14 Blackstone, *Commentaries* 1:46, 52, 46. See also Anon., *Letter to the Essay
   Author*, p. 6; Anon., *Arguments in Support of Supremacy*, p. 13. "There is
   no position more firmly established, in the conduct of mankind, Than that
   there must be in every state a supreme legislative authority, universal in its
   extent, over every member." [Galloway,] *Candid Examination*, p. 4.
15 Blackstone, *Tracts*, p. 15; Blackstone, *Analysis of the Laws*, p. 3.
16 [Jacob,] *Laws of Liberty*, p. 110. For Blackstone's more famous, longer
   description, see Blackstone, *Commentaries* 1:156. The roots of Jacob's
   description went back at least to 1644. [Mantell,] *Short Treatise of the
   Lawes*, pp. 12–13. It was also traced to Coke. *Political Register* 8 (1771):
   193. See also Maitland, *Constitutional History*, p. 255; Bailyn, *Pamphlets*,
   p. 118.
17 Anon., *Arguments in Support of Supremacy*, p. 14.
18 Speech of Thomas Pownall, 12 April 1769, *Parliamentary History* 16:612.
19 [Knox,] *Controversy*, p. 72 (quoting Locke); [Serle,] *Americans against Liberty*, pp. 34–35 (quoting Locke); Anon., *Arguments in Support of Supremacy*, p. 13; Locke, *Two Treatises*, book 2, sec. 134.
20 *Boston Evening-Post*, 9 September 1765, p. 2, col. 1 (reprinting *Connecticut*
   [New London] *Gazette*, 30 August 1765); Anon., *Appeal to Reason and
   Justice*, p. 94.
21 Anon., *Dialogue on the Constitution*, p. 8; Bentham, *Comment on Com-*

mentaries, p. 56. "[A]fter the publication in 1756 of Blackstone's influential *An Analysis of the Laws of England*, the doctrine of the unlimited legislative authority of the King in Parliament seems to have become generally, though by no means universally, accepted in Great Britain, but not in the colonies." Knollenberg, *Growth of Revolution*, p. 206.

22 Anon., *Appeal to Reason and Justice*, pp. 86–87. See also ibid., p. 4; Speech of Charles Yorke, Commons Debates, 3 February 1766, Ryder, "Parliamentary Diaries," p. 264; Book Review, *Scots Magazine* 38 (1776): 707; [Knox,] *Controversy*, p. 155; Letter from J. P. S. L. H., 3 June 1774, *Scots Magazine* 36 (1774): 283; Letter from Alexander Elmsly to Samuel Johnston, 22 December 1774, *North Carolina Colonial Records* 9:1093.

23 Anon., *Some Fugitive Thoughts*, pp. 15–16; Anon., *Appeal to Reason and Justice*, p. 5; Leonard, "Massachusettensis," p. 34.

24 Anon., *Appeal to Reason and Justice*, pp. 27, 85.

25 Ibid., p. 5; Advice and concurrence: [Phelps,] *Rights of the Colonies*, pp. 17–18; Anon., *Short Appeal to the People*, p. 22; enabling acts: [Knox,] *Controversy*, p. 137. See also Corwin, "Book Review," p. 777.

26 *Briefs of Revolution*, p. 162 (quoting Charles Inglis).

27 Hamilton, *Farmer Refuted*, pp. 90–91. For the second original contract, see *Authority of Rights*, pp. 139–45; *Authority to Tax*, pp. 53–64. It is also discussed below, in chapter 8. John Dickinson avoided the Glorious Revolution predicament by saying William III was king before the act of Parliament made him so. Mullett, *Fundamental Law*, p. 144. "But they say, they *recognized* his majesty's title before many people in England had done it. That is, they *obey'd* an act of parliament before it was *obey'd* by many people in England." [Knox,] *Controversy* (Dublin Edition), pp. 137–38. Knox claimed the Revolution settled the question. See reply of Daniel Dulany, Jr. Dulany, *Considerations*, pp. 635–36.

28 Reference is to the governor's history of the colony. See Hutchinson, *Massachusetts Bay* 1:328.

29 Adams, "Rejoinder of the House," *Briefs of Revolution*, pp. 139–40; Adams, "Novanglus," p. 208. But note argument from Virginia legislature: "The supreme Authority of Parliament, not only over all the *British* Dominions, but also over the Crown, was rendered manifest at this memorable Period [Glorious Revolution]; and the Subjection of the Colonies to Parliament cannot be more strongly featured than in that Resolve of the Assembly of *Virginia*, which unanimously agreed, That if 'the Parliament had constituted the Prince of *Orange* King, *we, who are subject to Parliament, must acknowledge him likewise.*'" Anon., *Some Fugitive Thoughts*, p. 15.

30 Governor Pownall made sense when he suggested that the Revolution ended the likelihood the colonies would be governed by the Privy Council. The ending of executive rule meant imperial control had to be legislative. Again, American whigs would have raised the defense of no consent. Pownall, *Administration*, p. 64.

31 After all, as many theorists as claimed that the Revolution changed some aspect of the constitution, asserted that the constitution remained exactly

as it had before the Revolution. All that had changed was the legal status of a few members of the House of Stuart. Cartwright, *Appeal on Constitution*, pp. 31-32; Brand, *Defence of Reeves*, pp. 62-63. "In eighteenth-century America neither rationalist whig nor high church tory denied the values of the Glorious Revolution or the evils of the Civil War. But each side accused its opponents of subverting the constitution that had developed in the aftermath of these events." Gerardi, "King's College Controversy," p. 179.

32 "[I]n my opinion it were better to have had no revolution, and to have continued our old race of tyrants, than to see a septennial parliament established under any family whatever." Speech of John Sawbridge, Commons Debates, 26 January 1773, *London Magazine* 42 (1773): 373. Writing on the justice of the American War, a 1776 pamphleteer concluded: "I am sorry for the Revolution, and sorry that Magna Charta, or the Bill of Rights, ever passed, if our war against them be a just one." Anon., *Dialogue on the Constitution*, p. 30.

33 Anon., *Letter*, p. 267; [Knox,] *Justice and Policy*, pp. 63-64; [Hutchinson,] *Strictures Upon the Declaration*, p. 18. But for the argument that it was the Americans who were inconsistent, see *Gentleman's Magazine* 36 (1766): 628; Anon., *Review of Present Administration*, p. 31.

34 A point understood in 1765 at the very beginning of the controversy. "[W]e think any American pays a very indifferent compliment to the protestant establishment, if he endeavours to shelter himself, by a prerogative charter, against an act of parliament. We are not sure whether such a plea does not aim at the very vitals of the constitution, as established at the Revolution." *Critical Review* 19 (1765): 226.

35 [Dickinson,] *New Essay*, pp. 84 (discussing Knox), 93.

36 Eliot, *Give Cesar his Due*, p. 14; Anon., *Second Answer to Wesley*, p. 15.

37 Address of Governor Francis Bernard to General Court, 30 May 1765, *Massachusetts House Journal* (1765), p. 11; [Wheelock,] *Reflections*, p. 52. See also Anon., *Political Balance*, p. 42; Pulteney, *Plan of Reunion*, p. 172; Bellot, *William Knox*, pp. 96-97.

38 Speech of Thomas Pownall, Commons Debates, 19 April 1769, *Proceedings and Debates* 3:154; Speech of Charles Yorke, Commons Debates, 3 February 1766, *Proceedings and Debates* 2:137, 139. See also "Charles Garth's Letter," p. 153 (discussing arguments of the law officers); Speech of Lord Mansfield, Lords Debates, 3 February 1766, *Proceedings and Debates* 2:130; Address of Governor James Wright to Georgia Commons House of Assembly, 24 December 1768, *Massachusetts Gazette*, 13 February 1769, p. 2, col. 1.

39 Speech of William Augustus Montagu, Commons Debates, 23 March 1774, *Proceedings and Debates* 4:95; [Serle,] *Americans against Liberty*, p. 16; Wright, "Two Countries," p. 153 (quoting Isaac Hunt on two hearts); Bailyn, *Pamphlets*, pp. 133-34; Wood, *Creation*, pp. 351-52.

40 Leigh, *Considerations*, p. 117; Anon., *Letter to a Member*, p. 22; Clark, *British Opinion*, p. 259 (quoting Anon., *Civil Liberty Asserted*). See also [Ramsay,] *Historical Essay*, pp. 190-91.

41 Pulteney, *Plan of Reunion*, pp. 29–30.

42 Anon., *Letter to the Essay Author*, p. 16; Richard Jackson's Arguments on American Taxation, 1765, *Franklin-Jackson Letters*, p. 194. See also Pulteney, *Plan of Reunion*, p. 152 footnote.

43 *Boston Chronicle*, 10 April 1769, p. 115, col. 1; [Seabury,] *View of the Controversy*, p. 9.

44 Anon., *Inquiry into the Nature*, pp. 19–20. See also Speech of Lord Mansfield, Lords Debates, 10 February 1766, *Parliamentary History* 16: 176; Anon., *Remarks on the New Essay*, p. 7; Wood, *Creation*, pp. 349–51.

45 [Whately,] *Regulations Lately Made*, p. 40.

46 [Bollan,] *Freedom of Speech*, p. 141; Anon., *Inquiry into the Nature*, p. 20; [Seabury,] *View of the Controversy*, pp. 10, 16; Pulteney, *Plan of Reunion*, p. 29.

47 [Galloway,] *Candid Examination*, p. 6. See also [Mather,] *America's Appeal*, p. 46; Hobbes, *Elements of Law*, part 2, chap. 8, sec. 7; Filmer, *Observations upon Aristotle*, pp. 228–29.

48 *Gazette & Post-Boy*, 9 May 1774, p. 1, col. 1 (reprinting London *Public Advertiser*, 13 February 1774).

49 [Galloway,] *Political Reflections*, p. 3; [Galloway,] *Candid Examination*, pp. 10, 17; [Boucher,] *Letter from a Virginian*, pp. 19–23; [Seabury,] *View of the Controversy*, p. 9; [Howard,] *Halifax Letter*, pp. 536–37. See also Wilson, *Considerations*, p. 723; Jezierski, "Parliament or People," p. 96.

50 [Galloway,] *Historical Reflections*, pp. 75–76; [Macpherson,] *Rights of Great Britain*, p. 50.

51 For John Adams's summary, see Adams, "Novanglus," pp. 127–28.

52 Memorial from New York General Assembly to House of Lords, 25 March 1775, *American Archives* 1:1316.

53 The doctrine of parliamentary supremacy, it was said, would "reduce their [American] liberties to a level with the colonies of France and Spain." "Governor Johnstone's Speech upon Lord Barrington's Motion," *Speeches in the Last Session*, p. 3.

CHAPTER FIVE: LIMITS OF SUPREMACY

1 Middlekauff, *Glorious Cause*, p. 122.

2 This point was made before. Unfortunately, too often scholars tend to assume without investigation that the doctrine was new. Compare Cobban, "Kings, Courts and Parliaments," p. 40 to Kemp, "Parliamentary Sovereignty," p. 13.

3 Jezierski, "Parliament or People," p. 96.

4 *South-Carolina Gazette*, 4 April 1768, p. 2, col. 1 (reprinting *Pennsylvania Journal*). See also *American Archives* 1:488 (reprinting Boston newspaper, 27 June 1774); "A Letter from a Tradesman in Newport, to his Friend in Providence," *Providence Gazette*, 23 February 1765, p. 3, col. 3.

5 Baldwin, *New England Clergy*, p. 42 n.33. There were various theories explaining why the Assembly or General Court was limited. Frequently it was the original contract, but there were others: "There are certain

boundaries, beyond which, submission cannot be justly required, nor is therefore due. These limits are marked out, and fixt, by the known, established, and fundamental laws of the state. These laws being consented to by the governing power, confine, as well as direct its operation and influence, and are the connecting band between authority and obedience." Tucker, *Election Sermon*, pp. 29–30.

6 Shute, *Election Sermon*, p. 25; "Freeman, in the New York Gazette," *Boston Post-Boy*, 2 December 1765, p. 2, col. 1.

7 Not coherent and inconsistent: Rossiter, *Six Characters*, pp. 202–3; [Lee,] *Second Appeal*, p. 72 (quoting Hutchinson). Again, the point is that the limits were imposed not by a principle of federalism, but by constitutional precedent and custom. Thus a writer said Americans did not object to Parliament exercising power where it had always exercised it, over "the dominion of the seas, to external taxation [this is an error], or to the imposing of duties on merchandize imported or exported, and to the absolute regulation thereby of trade and commerce for the good of the whole." Anon., *Conciliatory Address to the People*, p. 18.

8 Greene, "Perspective of Law," p. 71; opposition: Onuf, "Introduction," pp. 7–8. And, of course, it is wrong to say that the theory was a new one, developed by the opposition or radicals in defense of American rights. Sheps, "English Republicanism," p. 12.

9 Abingdon, *Dedication*, p. xxx; Anon., *Address to Mansfield*, p. 17. The word "supremacy" was "not a mysterious and indescribible claim like that of the Pope, but only a synonymous term denoting the quality of its power." Anon., *Three Letters*, p. 5.

10 Abingdon, *Thoughts on Burke's Letter*, pp. 12–13, xxxv. Abingdon took the words from Bolingbroke—or from Locke, whom Bolingbroke cited. [Bolingbroke,] *Dissertation*, p. 210.

11 Candidus, *Two Letters*, p. 8.

12 Kemp, "Parliamentary Sovereignty," p. 12 (quoting Abingdon); [Mulgrave,] *Letter from a Member*, p. 7; McAdam, *Johnson and Law*, p. 189 (quoting Johnson). See also Abingdon, *Thoughts on Burke's Letter*, p. liv; Potter, *Liberty We Seek*, p. 104 (quoting Blackstone); Anon., *Civil Liberty Asserted*, p. 59.

13 [Goodricke,] *Observations*, pp. 43–44 footnote; "Junius," *Junius* 1:v–vi. See also Anon., *Remarks on the New Essay*, p. 36; Anon., *General View of the Company*, p. 38; Anon., *Defence of Resolutions*, pp. 21–28; Priestley, *First Principles*, pp. 42–43.

14 "Junius," *Junius* 1:vi; [Rokeby,] *Further Examination*, pp. 81, 79. See also *London Magazine* 43 (1774): 537–38; Free, *Speech of John Free*, pp. 11–12; Lofft, *Observations on Wesley's Address*, p. 31; Brewer, "English Radicalism", pp. 341–42.

15 Gordon, *Discourse Preached*, p. 7; Howard, *Road from Runnymede*, p. 184–85 (quoting Gordon, 15 December 1774).

16 For defenses of the doctrine made in Parliament, see Speech of the duke of R[ic]h[mon]d, Lords Debates, 30 May 1777, *Gentleman's Magazine* 47

(1777): 605; Speech of Lord Camden, Lords Debates, 16 March 1775, *Proceedings and Debates* 5:543; Speech of Temple Luttrell, Commons Debates, 27 February 1775, *London Magazine* 44 (1775): 559; Speech of George Johnstone, Commons Debates, 18 December 1772, *London Magazine* 42 (1773): 223.

17 Anon., *Second Answer to Wesley*, p. 16; Anon., *Supremacy of Legislature*, p. 2; Hart, "Bentham and America," p. 552. But see Anon., *Letter to Doctor Tucker*, pp. 6–10.

18 Estwick, *Letter to Tucker*, p. 85; [Jones,] *Constitutional Criterion*, p. 14; Gregor, "Preface," p. xxxviii. For a nonlawyer endorsing the doctrine of limits in a law textbook, see Rutherforth, *Natural Law* 2:92–93. In the previous century, when a lawyer argued that there could be no limits on power and that it was "absurd" to say "a Government can be mixed or limited," Judge and later Chief Baron Atkyns protested that the limited government was a doctrine concurred with by "all the ancient Authors in our profession of the Common Law, who being learned and so ancient, are therefore the most Competent Witnesses of our *English* Constitution." Atkyns, *Enquiry into Power*, p. 8.

19 [Sheridan,] *Observations on Doctrine*, pp. 61–62. See also Pownall, *Administration Fifth Edition* 2:61–62; Speech of Edmund Burke, Commons Debates, 22 March 1775, *Burke on American Revolution*, p. 114; Benjamin Franklin, *Public Advertiser* (London), 11 January 1770, reprinted in *Franklin's Letters to the Press*, p. 174. But see argument attributed to Thomas Hutchinson, *Boston Evening-Post*, 5 April 1773, p. 1, col. 1; Keith, *Papers and Tracts*, p. 175.

20 See quotation from Bentham's *Comment on Commentaries* in chap. 4, p. 68.

21 Anon., *Defence of Resolutions*, pp. 78, 84–85 (reprinting *London Evening Post*). See also Anon., *Tyranny Unmasked*, p. 50.

22 Warrington, *Works*, p. 646. For distinction of "right" and "power," see "In the Taught Tradition", pp. 947–72.

23 [Chalmers,] *Second Thoughts*, p. 63; *London Journal* (#739), 25 August 1733, p. 1, col. 2. See also Young, *Example of France*, p. 83; Anon., *Reflexions on Representation*, p. 45; Blackall, *Subjects Duty*, p. 15.

24 *Craftsman* 13, no. 441, 14 December 1734, p. 122 (citing John Locke); Letter from the Massachusetts House to Henry Seymour Conway, 13 February 1768, *Boston Gazette*, 28 March 1768, p. 1, col. 1; Message from the Massachusetts House to Lords Commissioners of the Treasury, 17 February 1768, Adams, *Writings* 1:196; Answer from the Massachusetts House to Governor Francis Bernard, 23 October 1765, *Speeches*, p. 45. See also Letter from the Massachusetts House to Dennys de Berdt, 12 January 1768, Adams, *Writings* 1:135; *South-Carolina Gazette* (Supplement), 26 August 1765, p. 1, col. 3 (reprinting *Connecticut Gazette*); Abingdon, *Dedication*, pp. xxxiv–xxxvi (quoting Bolingbroke); Cartwright, *Constitution Produced*, pp. 87, 263; Lawson, *Politica Sacra*, pp. 162–63; Yale, "Hobbes and Hale," p. 147; Kemp, "Parliamentary Sovereignty," p. 13.

CHAPTER SIX: CONSTRAINTS OF TRUST

1 Speech of John Wilkes, Commons Debates, 10 December 1777, *Parliamentary History* 19:569, 570.

2 *Rusticus Americanus* in *Boston Evening-Post*, 18 July 1774, p. 2, col. 3; [Stevens,] *Strictures on a Sermon*, p. 32; Cartwright, *Constitution Produced*, p. 264 (see also p. 18); Toohey, *Liberty and Empire*, p. 55 (quoting Sharp).

3 Abingdon, *Dedication*, p. lxiv.

4 Peckard, *Nature and Extent of Liberty*, p. 3 footnote; Abingdon, *Dedication*, p. xxxiii. See also Speech of Charles Yorke, Commons Debates, 3 February 1766, *Proceedings and Debates* 2:137; [Rivers,] *Letters*, p. 67; [Canning,] *Letter to Hillsborough*, pp. 25–26; Lieberman, *Province of Legislation*, p. 16.

5 [Ferguson,] *Remarks on a Pamphlet*, p. 40.

6 [Rivers,] *Letters*, pp. 66–67; Anon., *Tyranny Unmasked*, p. 51.

7 Anon., *Fair Trial*, p. 122. See also Cartwright, *Appeal on Constitution*, pp. 23–24; Cartwright, *Constitution Produced*, pp. 29–30.

8 [Goodricke,] *Observations*, p. 44 footnote.

9 Anon., *Conciliatory Address to the People*, p. 7; [Goodricke,] *Observations*, p. 43 footnote.

10 Price, *Nature of Civil Liberty*, p. 15. An American expressed the theory as "the tenure of this delegated power." Citizen to Pennsylvania Farmer, *South-Carolina Gazette*, 18 January 1768, p. 1, col. 4.

11 [Downley,] *Sentiments*, p. 52. A sophisticated variation of the theory held that those who "chuse" the "trustees," the electors of the House of Commons, themselves were trustees, for the "right of election is a trust reposed in them by the constitution, that is, by the people." Anon., *Letter to the Essay Author*, p. 14.

12 Indeed, an extension of the theory placed the fiduciary duty on the Lords and Crown rather than on the Commons, as "there were three Estates, whereof two delegated by the People in Trust, the third reserved to themselves." Anon., *Liberty in Two Parts*, p. 82. For arguments that the monarchy was held in trust for the people, see Lofft, *Observations on Wesley's Address*, pp. 35–36; Anon., *British Liberties*, p. lvii (quoting John Locke).

13 Anon., *Cursory Remarks on Price*, p. 12; [Meredith,] *Question Stated*, p. 63; [Downley,] *Sentiments*, p. 52. See also [Marat,] *Chains of Slavery*, p. 198.

14 *St. Patrick's Anti-Stamp Chronicle* 2 (1774): 54 (questioning Parliament's authority to enact the Quebec Bill). See also Locke, *Two Treatises*, book 2, sec. 141; Dickinson, *Liberty and Property*, pp. 216–17 (quoting John Wilkes); Brewer, "Wilkites and the Law," pp. 132–33 (quoting a protagonist in a 1774 parliamentary election).

15 Speech of Lord Camden, Lords Debates, 16 March 1775, *Proceedings and Debates* 5:543. It is possible that earlier in the century some American legislators thought that their trust had been delegated by the Crown. "Seeing we have the Priviledge to be an Assembly, granted by Her Majesty,

let us not Betray the Trust reposed in us." Mulford, *Speech to New York Assembly*, p. 7.

16 Subordinate and limited: Price, *Two Tracts: Tract One*, p. 15; Price, *Nature of Civil Liberty*, p. 15; Limited by its nature: [Goodricke,] *Observations*, p. 37; Preserve constitution: Cartwright, *Appeal on Constitution*, p. 23. See also Evans, *Reply to Fletcher*, pp. 72–73n.; [Marat,] *Chains of Slavery*, p. 201; Ball, *Power of Kings*, p. 139. But see the suggestion that the trust could have been used as much as a moral argument as a legal argument. Gough, *Fundamental Law*, pp. 181–82.

17 [Goodricke,] *Observations*, p. 40. Goodricke further commented:

> Government is a general discretionary trust of command over the actions, concerns, property, and strength of those, who belong to the community, for the purposes of the civil union. . . . The nature of things admits of and necessarily implies palpable limitations, viz.— the *ends* of the *trust*,—the *laws* of *reason* and *nature*. The Colonies are judges, and so are we and every people on the face of the earth, in all cases, when oppressed by a tyrannical exertion of authority; nor does this destroy or impair at all the authoritative exertions of the supreme Power within the limits of its trust; and beyond those limits it has, properly speaking, no existence.

Ibid., p. 41. For arguments made in Parliament that the trust excluded arbitrary power, see Speech of John Wilkes, Commons Debates, 10 December 1777, *Parliamentary History* 19:570; *London Magazine* 43 (1774): 538 (quoting Sir Edward Deering in the Commons, 1641).

18 Anon., *Evidence of Common and Statute Laws*, p. 5. See also Locke, *Two Treatises*, part 2, secs. 221–22; [Joseph Hawley,] "To the Inhabitants," 13 April 1775, *American Archives* 2:333–34 (quoting John Locke); Price, "Introduction to Two Tracts," p. v footnote; Instructions to Jasper Mauduit from the Massachusetts House of Representatives, 1762, *Mauduit Letters*, p. 40; [Goodricke,] *Observations*, p. 43 footnote.

19 [Ramsay,] *Historical Essay*, pp. 145–46. See also [Brooke,] *Liberty and Common Sense*, p. 5; Cartwright, *Appeal on Constitution*, p. 24.

20 Anon., *Evidence of Common and Statute Laws*, p. 5. See also Anon., *British Liberties*, p. lvii (quoting John Locke); Laslett, "Introduction and Notes," p. 114. "But if they [the people's representatives] break their Trust, by thwarting the general Intent of the People, (for the Trust of every of them goes to the whole People, and not to any Part only) or by introducing Innovations in the Constitution, to the Injury of their Liberties or Properties, such Acts in the Representatives must in their Nature be necessarily void. Because those can't be the Acts of the People, which are against their Consent, or Usurpations on their original inherent Power." Anon., *Liberty in Two Parts*, pp. 77–78.

21 Anon., *Experience preferable to Theory*, p. 101.

22 Argument of Richard Jackson (1765), *Franklin-Jackson Letters*, pp. 194–95.

23 Bailyn, *Pamphlets*, p. 417 (see also p. 547); Bellot, *William Knox*, p. 66 (quoting Knox); Speech of Charles Yorke, Commons Debates, 3 February 1766, Ryder, "Parliamentary Diaries," p. 264; Letter from "Philanthropos," *Boston Chronicle*, 12 December 1768, p. 470, col. 1. An American tory wrote: "the freedom and happiness of every British subject depends not upon his share in elections but upon the sense and virtue of the British Parliament." Howard, *Halifax Letter*, p. 538.

24 Letter from Lord Shelburne to Governor Francis Bernard, 13 September 1766, and Address from Governor Francis Bernard to General Court, 30 May 1765, *Speeches*, pp. 99, 35.

25 Grey, "Unwritten Constitution," p. 873 (quoting Governor Fitch); [Stephen Hopkins,] "An Essay on the Trade of the Northern Colonies," *Providence Gazette*, 21 January 1764, p. 2, cols. 1–2. James Otis's arguments for trusting Parliament are probably the most famous of those of American whigs. Smith, *Writs of Assistance*, pp. 481–82; Bailyn, *Pamphlets*, pp. 415–17. For an extreme statement of the theory that the unrepresented can trust Parliament, a plea that Irish Protestants do so, see [Sheridan,] *Review of Three Questions*, p. 51.

26 Hopkins, *Rights*, pp. 516–17; Weir, *Most Important Epocha*, p. 32 (quoting a *Resolutionist*, 1770). See also Letter from Charles Carroll of Carrollton to William Graves, 12 August 1766, *Letters of Charles Carroll*, p. 128.

27 James Iredell, "To the Inhabitants of Great Britain," *Papers of Iredell* 1:259; Letter from Andrew Eliot to Thomas Hollis, 10 July 1769, Eliot, "Letters," p. 442; Wilson, *Considerations*, p. 724. See also Grey, "Unwritten Constitution," p. 887.

28 *Boston Post-Boy*, 9 September 1765, p. 1, col. 3 (quoting *Cato* in "*Connecticut Gazette*").

29 Dickinson, *Letters*, p. 350. "Certainly the *British* Parliament will not do what they think an unjust act: but I cannot persuade myself that *they* will think it unjust to place us on the same footing with themselves." Dickinson, *Speech*, p. 40. See also *Boston Post-Boy*, 2 December 1765, p. 2, col. 1 (reprinting *Freeman* in *New York Gazette*); Instructions of Newburyport, 21 October 1765, *Boston Post-Boy*, 4 November 1765, p. 1, col. 2.

30 Gregor, "Preface," pp. xxxviii–xxxix.

31 A pamphleteer stated the theory as follows:

> The representatives of the people can therefore never be supposed lawfully to consent to any thing destructive of their rights and privileges. But if under a government hostile to all principles of truth, virtue, and freedom, they should betray their trust, and sell both themselves and the nation, it is evident that the compact between the representative and represented bodies would be null and void; and the legislature being imperfect by this traitorous defection and revolt of the Commons from the people, it is clear to demonstration, that no resolutions or acts of parliament in that mutilated state, could be valid or binding upon the nation by any principle of law or justice.

Anon., *Defence of Resolutions*, pp. 85–86 (reprinting *London Evening Post*).

32 Anon., *Remarks on the New Essay*, p. 9. "A celebrated foreign politician" was quoted as saying: "The laws do not indicate, with proper perspicuity and explicitness how far the rights of each of the three legislative powers extend: There are three things in England, without any known limits; the King's prerogative; the liberties of the people; & the privileges of the Parliament." *Boston Evening-Post*, 30 April 1770, p. 1, col. 3 (quoting a London newspaper).

33 Anon., *Experience preferable to Theory*, p. 38; Abingdon, *Dedication*, p. xxviii.

34 *Boston Evening-Post*, 9 September 1765, p. 2, col. 1 (reprinting *Connecticut* [New London] *Gazette*, 30 August 1765); [Chalmers,] *Second Thoughts*, p. 57; Fletcher, *Vindication of Wesley*, p. 8; Anon., *Tyranny Unmasked*, p. 48; Jackson, *Grounds of Government*, p. 7.

35 Cartwright, *Appeal on Constitution*, p. 23. See also Wagner, "Judicial Review," p. 581 (quoting *Boston Gazette*, 19 October 1767); Speech of John Wilkes, Commons Debates, 10 December 1777, *Parliamentary History* 19:570; Message from Massachusetts House to Governor Francis Bernard, *Boston Post-Boy*, 28 October 1765, p. 1, col. 2; Sheridan, *Observations on the Doctrine*, p. 10; Lawson, *Politica Sacra*, pp. 162–63.

36 *London Journal* (#726), 26 May 1733, p. 1, col. 2; Address to New York, 2 June 1775, *American Archives* 2:882; Anon., *Tyranny Unmasked*, pp. 47–48; [Oldfield,] *History of the Boroughs* 1:13.

37 Wilson, *Considerations*, p. 723; [Macfarlane,] *Second Ten Years*, pp. 146–47 (quoting dissenting lords protest against Massachusetts Government Act); Pownall, *Administration Fifth Edition* 2:43–44; Anon., *Letter to the Essay Author*, p. 7; Anon., *British Liberties*, pp. lvi–lvii (quoting John Locke).

38 Speech of John Wilkes, Commons Debates, 10 December 1777, *Parliamentary History* 19:569–70; Price, *Nature of Civil Liberty*, p. 15; Anon., *Evidence of Common and Statute Laws*, pp. 1–2.

39 Speech of Temple Luttrell, Commons Debates, 27 February 1775, *Proceedings and Debates* 5:470; Locke, *Two Treatises*, book2, sec. 141 (see also secs. 134, 135, 121–22).

40 [Williams,] *Letters on Liberty*, pp. 76–77; [Carysfort,] *Serious Address*, pp. 29–30; Letter from *Junius* to John Wilkes, 7 September 1771, *Speeches of John Wilkes in Parliament*, 1:99 footnote.

41 Speech of John Wilkes, Commons Debates, 10 December 1777, *Parliamentary History* 19:570; Abingdon, *Thoughts on Burke's Letter*, p. 17.

42 Parliament could not "enact any thing against the divine law" or "take away any man's private property without making him a compensation." Speech of Lord Camden, Lords Debates, 3 February 1766, *Proceedings and Debates* 2:127.

43 Otis listed six powers Parliament could not execute. The third was: "No legislative, supreme or subordinate, has a right to make itself arbitrary." Otis, *Rights*, p. 446.

44 [Jones,] *Constitutional Criterion*, pp. 12–13. See also [Keld,] *Polity of En-*

gland, p. 511; Anon., *Defence of Resolutions*, p. 21; [Bolingbroke,] *Dissertation*, p. 210.

CHAPTER SEVEN: CONSTRAINTS OF CONSENT

1 As stated by American assemblies, the doctrine was that the people of the colonies "are entitled to life, liberty, and property, and they never have ceded to any sovereign power whatever a right to dispose of either without their consent." Resolves of the Georgia Commons House of Assembly, January 1775, *American Archives* 1:1156; " . . . that no Man can be justly taxed by, or bound in Conscience to obey, any Law to which he has not given his Consent in Person, or by his Representative." Resolves of Massachusetts House, *Boston Post-Boy*, 3 July 1769, p. 1, col. 1 (reaffirming resolves of 1765).

2 [Anderson,] *Free Thoughts*, p. 16, col. 1; Tucker, *Four Letters to Shelburne*, p. 55; [Ramsay,] *Thoughts on Nature of Government*, pp. 31–48; Fletcher, *Vindication of Wesley*, pp. 37–38; *Interesting Letters*, p. 122; Anon., *Defence of English History*, p. 66.

3 "Since they [English laws and customs] have been approved by the consent of those who use them and confirmed by the oath of kings, they cannot be changed without the common consent of all those by whose counsel and consent they were promulgated." Bracton, *Laws and Customs* 2:21.

4 Locke, *Two Treatises*, book 2, sec. 212; [Joseph Hawley,] "To the Inhabitants," 30 March 1775, *American Archives* 2:248 (quoting Locke); Carlyle, *Political Liberty*, pp. 136–39.

5 Anon., *Animadversions on Discourse*, p. 4 (attributing to Hooker the principle that consent is "absolutely necessary for the making of Laws"); [Claridge,] *Defence of Government*, p. 2 (quoting Hooker); Pole, *Pursuit of Equality*, p. 44 (quoting John Lilburne); Pole, *Legislative Power*, p. 9 (quoting Philip Hunton); De Beer, "Locke and English Liberalism," p. 39 (quoting Edward Chamberlayne); Manning, "Puritanism and Democracy," p. 143 (quoting Goodwin and Nye); Tierney, *Religion, Law, and Growth*, p. 99 (discussing George Lawson).

6 Filmer, *Observations upon Aristotle*, p. 225; Filmer, *Anarchy of Mixed Monarchy*, pp. 284, 286; "His Majesties Reasons against the . . . High Court of Justice (22 January 1648)," *Somers' Tracts* 5:213; *Speech upon the Scaffold*, pp. 9–10; Maynwaring, *First Sermon*, p. 13.

7 Lord Bolingbroke, "The Freeholders Political Catechism," *London Magazine* 43 (1774): 478. See also Arbuthnot, *Freeholder's Catechism*, p. 3; *London Journal* (#727), 2 June 1733, p. 1, col. 1 (Robert Walpole's newspaper); Barrington, *Revolution Principles*, pp. 5–6, 9.

8 *Political Register* 2 (1768): 97 (reprinting *Boston Gazette*, 24 August 1767). See also Greene, "Virginia," pp. 62–63 (quoting Richard Bland).

9 Letter from John Adams to James Sullivan, 26 May 1776, Adams, *Works* 9:375; Johnson, *Notes on Pastoral*, p. 30; Trenchard, Letter of 8 June 1723, *Cato's Letters* 4:231.

10 Trenchard, Letter of 8 June 1723, *Cato's Letters* 4:231; Lockwood, *Connecticut Election Sermon*, p. 7; Fiske, *Importance of Righteousness*, p. 31.

11 E.g., *Guide to Rights*, p. 2; Mullett, *Fundamental Law*, p. 59 (quoting William Molyneux saying that English rights were founded on being governed by laws made by "representatives in parliament").

12 Anon., *Inquiry into the Nature*, p. 21.

13 See *Concept of Representation*, pp. 11–30. It should be emphasized that many scholars in the eighteenth century associated the doctrine of consent with English common law. In 1760, for example, the Bishop of Worcester traced the doctrine through the common law, from Glanvil, Bracton, Fleta, Thornton, and Fortescue, to Coke and Selden. [Hurd,] *Moral and Political Dialogues*, pp. 310–11.

14 Wooddeson, *Jurisprudence*, p. 35.

15 Anon., *Evidence of Common and Statute Laws*, pp. 2–4. The Act, as printed in *Statutes at Large*, 1763, provided:

> . . . for where this your Grace's realm recognizing no superior under God, but only your Grace, hath been and is free from subjection to any man's laws, but only to such as have been devised, made and obtained within this realm, for the wealth of the same, or to such other as by sufference of your Grace and your progenitors, the people of this your realm have taken at their free liberty, by their own consent to be used amongst them, and have bound themselves by long use and custom to the observance of the same, not as to the observance of laws of any foreign prince, potentate or prelate, but as to the customed and ancient laws of this realm, originally established as laws of the same, by the said sufferance, consents and custom, and none otherwise.

25 Henry VIII, cap. 21.

16 *Authority to Tax*, pp. 105–21, 135–46.

17 *Authority of Rights*, pp. 114–31.

18 Letter from Virginia House of Burgesses to North Carolina House of Assembly, 9 May 1768, *North Carolina Colonial Records* 7:747

19 Dulany, *Considerations*, p. 633.

20 Ibid.

21 Becker, *Declaration*, pp. 116–17 (quoting Jefferson, *Summary View*). Jefferson's theory, which was an extension of an old argument of Saxon laws being carried from the Continent to Britannia and English laws carried as rights to Ireland in the sixteenth century, is sometimes discussed as a Jeffersonian invention. Wills, *Inventing America*, p. 84. Contemporary British commentary, by contrast, saw nothing original in Jefferson's thesis. Book Review, *Monthly Review* 51 (1774): 393; Book Review, *London Magazine* 43 (1774): 645–46; *Critical Review* 38 (1774): 423. For a recent appraisal, see Kammen, "The Meaning of Colonization," pp. 349–50. It

should be appreciated, however, that Kammen does not understand the legal nature of the arguments discussed.

22 Governor Hutchinson thought he was caricaturing the migration thesis when in fact he summed it up rather accurately: "The authority of Parliament over the Colonists ceased upon their leaving the Kingdom," he said of the authority of migration. "Every degree of subjection is therefore voluntary, and ought to continue no longer than the authority shall be for the public good." [Hutchinson,] *Strictures Upon the Declaration*, p. 6. "A common assumption, which would evolve into a central point of revolutionary theory, was that the colonists upon leaving England had 'totally disclaim[ed] all *subordination* to and dependence upon the two inferior estates of their mother country'." Bailyn, *Pamphlets*, p. 49 n. 18 (quoting William Hicks).

23 [Draper,] *Thoughts of a Traveller*, p 22.

24 [Phelps,] *Rights of the Colonies*, p. 13.

25 *Authority of Rights*, pp. 65–81.

26 [Hampson,] *Reflections on the Present State*, p. 26 footnote (Hampson was 16 at the time and probably was not the author of this work. The views expressed, however, do reflect those of his mentor, John Wesley); *Boston Post-Boy*, 12 August 1765, p. 1, col. 3 (reprinting *New-York Gazette*); *Boston Evening-Post*, 5 June 1769, p. 4, col. 3.

27 [Draper,] *Thoughts of a Traveller*, p. 23 (this part of Draper's argument was republished, *Scots Magazine* 36 (1774): 593); Wesley, *Calm Address*, p. 11.

28 [Phelps,] *Rights of the Colonies*, pp. 13–14; [Draper,] *Thoughts of a Traveller*, pp. 24–25. It was a conclusion that seemed self-evident. "[N]othing is more certain, or better known, than that necessity has been the cause of almost every emigration that has happened, and that the beginnings of most American properties were remarkably slender." Anon., *Application of Political Rules*, p. 75. Ironically, Thomas Hutchinson was cited by contemporaries for evidence that Massachusetts had been settled by "persons of rank and good circumstances." *Critical Review* 21 (1766): 35.

29 Anon., *Licentiousness Unmask'd*, p. 42. The emigrant "willingly, and voluntarily reliquishes the exercise of his elective power, in favour of something more substantial; and can never, constitutionally, so long as he continues there, exercise that right, in the election of any member, to serve in the parliament." [Ramsay,] *Historical Essay*, p. 195.

30 Anon., *Resistence no Rebellion*, p. 28; [Ramsay,] *Historical Essay*, p. 196; [Johnson,] *Political Tracts*, p. 213.

31 Book Review, *Monthly Review* 52 (1775): 259. Expectation was another ground for claiming the right to legislative autonomy. In a variation of the "settlement contract," the Massachusetts General Court asserted: "If the first settlers of the colonies had not imagined that they were as secure in the enjoyment of this right as of their titles to their lands, in all probability they would never have left England, and no one colony could have been settled." Letter from the General Court to Agent Mauduit, [1764,]

Speeches, p. 24. For the "settlement contract," see, *Authority to Tax*, pp. 60–64.

32 [Evans,] *Letter to John Wesley*, p. 14. Evans was answering Wesley who had plagiarized Johnson. "True, *it is no longer possible*, that they should vote for Members of the British Parliament; consequently *no longer possible* they should be *represented* in the British Parliament, and therefore *no longer possible*—that the British Parliament should dispose of their property *without their consent.*" Ibid. Similarly, see Anon., *Tyranny Unmasked*, p. 71.

33 Anon., *"Taxation no Tyranny" Considered*, pp. 3–4.

34 Letter from Joseph Galloway to Samuel Verplanck, 30 December 1774, *Letters of Delegates to Congress* 1:288–89. See also Knollenberg, *Origin*, pp. 172–73 (quoting letter from Richard Henry Lee).

35 [Lind,] *Englishman's Answer*, p. 6; Anon., *Letter to Member*, p. 13.

36 [Lind,] *Thirteenth Parliament*, p. 49; [Ramsay,] *Historical Essay*, pp. 179–80.

37 Anon., *Present Crisis*, pp. 12–13. See also [Knox,] *Letter to a Member*, pp. 19–20; Anon., *Speech Never Intended*, pp. 14–15.

38 *American Archives* 1:338.

39 "[W]e contend, that in all *just* governments, the people have delegated to their governors the particuliar degree of trust with which they are invested, have limited the extent of the controul to which they are to be subjected." [Watson,] *Answer to Disquisition*, p. 19.

40 Brown, "Violence," p. 103. See also Onuf, "Toward Federalism," p. 361; Carpenter, *Development of Thought*, pp. 34–36.

41 Anon., *Characters of Parties*, p. 40.

42 There were some in Britain like Samuel Johnson who would express royalist sentiments for the sake of shock effect, but very few vested sovereignty in the Crown or claimed the king was above the "law." More common were constitutionalists who disputed "the *sovereign Will* of the people" and attributed sovereignty to some other source. [Reeves,] *Thoughts, Second Letter*, p. 163; [Stevens,] *Revolution Vindicated*, pp. 3–15; Tucker, *Tract Five*, p. 12; Anon., *Political Disquisition*, p. 43. One has to go back to the Stuarts or the Exclusion Crisis to find strong statements supporting "divine right" in kings. See Dickinson, *Liberty and Property*, p. 20; Filmer, *Patriarcha*, p. 53. Three weeks before ordering that Charles I stand trial, the House of Commons proclaimed that, "The people under God are the source of all just power." Wedgwood, "Trial of Charles I," p. 41. The legal explanation given in the seventeenth century was: "If there was a People before there was a King, as no doubt there was, then will it be a difficult undertaking to prove that Kings have a just right to Arbitrary Power." Grand Jury Charge, Warrington, *Works*, p. 388.

43 Foster, *Short Essay*, p. 5; Hitchcock, *Sermon Preached before Gage*, p. 19. For statements of the doctrine before the age of the American Revolution, see *Craftsman* 13, no. 441, 14 December 1734, pp. 122–23 (Bolingbroke's

newspaper); Barrington, *Revolution Principles*, p. 5; *Works of Algernon Sydney*, p. 25 (chief justice commenting on Sidney); [Fowle,] *Appendix to Eclipse*, pp. 22–23. For the doctrine stated by a barrister as a "Revolution Principle," see Anon., *Considerations on National Independence*, pp. 64, 72.

44 See explanations by clergymen on both sides of the Atlantic. John Wesley, "Some Observations on Liberty," reprinted in Peach, *Richard Price*, p. 250; *They Preached Liberty*, p. 75 (reprinting John Tucker, 1771); [Evans,] *Letter to John Wesley*, p. 10; Price, "Sermon at Hackney," reprinted in Peach, *Richard Price*, p. 277; Stevens, *Election Sermon*, p. 54.

45 Anon., *With Respect to America*, p. 11; Anon., *Power and Grandeur*, p. 9. For a "mainstream" constitutional argument, see Speech of Lord North (December 1770), *Gentleman's Magazine* 41 (1771): 292.

46 Hall, *Apology for Freedom*, p. 9. See also [Watson,] *Answer to Disquisition*, pp. 16–17.

47 Burgh, *Political Disquisitions* 3: 278; [Rokeby,] *Further Examination*, p. 100; [Barwis,] *Three Dialogues Concerning Liberty*, pp. 81–82; Locke, *Two Treatises*, book 2, sec. 149.

48 [Priestley,] *Present State of Liberty*, p. 11; Foster, *Short Essay*, p. 5; Sidney, *Discourses Concerning Government*, p. 267. The king derived his power from the people and had to act in the people's interest. Carysfort, *Thoughts on Constitution*, p. 50; [Steuart,] *Jus Populi*, p. 96.

49 *Craftsman* 11, no. 368, 21 June 1733, p. 95; West, *Election Sermon*, p. 275. See also Speech of John Wilkes, Commons Debates, 21 March 1776, *Speeches of John Wilkes in Parliament* 1:107; [Short,] *Rights*, p. 10; Anon., *Critical Review of Liberties*, pp. 11–12. Of course, it also followed that the people could not delegate "a Power of injuring themselves." [Shebbeare,] *Second Letter*, p. 8.

50 Eliot, *Give Cesar His Due*, p. 38. See also Watson, *Principles of the Revolution*, p. 12; Lockwood, *Connecticut Election Sermon*, pp. 15–17; [Allen,] "To the King," p. 1 (quoting Bishop Gilbert Burnet).

51 [Squire,] *Historical Essay on Ballance*, p. 64. See also Anon., *Second Answer to Wesley*, p. 16; Evans, *Reply to Fletcher*, p. 71; *Gentleman's Magazine* 38 (1768): 505; Burgh, *Political Disquisitions* 1:3–4.

52 Estwick, *Letter to Tucker*, p. 84. See also Anon., *Evidence of Common and Statute Laws*, p. 13.

53 Clark, *British Opinion*, p. 189 (quoting Hey, *Observations on Civil Liberty*, pp. 51, 52, 62).

54 Gray, *Doctor Price's Notions*, p. 43. It should be stressed that Gray's main premise, that "Parliament had no right to alter fundamental law without the acquiesence of the people" was staple constitutional doctrine in the eighteenth century. Thus two years earlier, the Massachusetts whig lawyer, Joseph Hawley, wrote: "The authority of General Courts do not extend to the alteration of the fundamentals of Governments, much less to their subversion. This can be done only by the express voice of the whole people

at large. The Governour, Council, and House of Representatives, which compose the Assembly, are creatures of, and derive all their power from a Constitution agreed upon and previously established." "To Inhabitants," 9 March 1775, *American Archives* 2:96–97. The difference, of course, was that Gray's legal fiction permitted constitutional theory to bridge the differences between seventeenth-century immutable fundamental law and nineteenth-century parliamentary sovereignty. Hawley's premise, if anything, became even more valid under the American written constitutions which in fact, and not just legal fiction, could be said to have been "agreed upon and previously established."

CHAPTER EIGHT: CONSTRAINTS OF CONTRACT

1 Hume, *Essays* 2:287–88; Hey, *Observations on Civil Liberty*, p. 46; Anon., *Letter to Rev. Cooper*, pp. 15–16; Rutherforth, *Natural Law* 2:220. Late into the nineteenth century, United States Supreme Court Justice Joseph Story associated the contract with consent. Story, *Commentaries*, book 3, chap. 3, sec. 325, at 1:293. A similar connection was made by continental jurists. The Swiss law writer Jean Jacques Burlamaqui contended that "sovereignty derives its origin from a covenant founded on a free consent between the king and his subjects." Burlamaqui, *Politic Law*, p. 112. At the beginning of the American Revolution controversy, Governor Hopkins noted that the British constitution "will be confessed by all to be founded by compact and established by consent of the people." Hopkins, *Rights*, p. 507.

2 Bushman, *King and People*, p. 122 (quoting Bernard); Norton, "Loyalist Critique," p. 133 (quoting Smith); "Proceedings of the Freeholders in Chowan County," 22 August 1774, *North Carolina Colonial Records* 9:1037.

3 Speech of Lord Lyttelton, Lords Debates, 3 February 1766, *Proceedings and Debates* 2:126. Lyttelton said Great Britain, but as he was referring to the original settlers of North America, he had to have meant the laws of England.

4 Anon., *Letter to a Member*, pp. 13–14 (quoting Vattel).

5 Anon., *Serious and Impartial Observations*, p. 34.

6 Anon., *Inquiry Into the Nature*, p. 50.

7 Adams, "Novanglus," p. 246. For a brief survey of the historical background of the colonial argument, see "In Our Contracted Sphere," pp. 22–28. Some of the historical literature of the American Revolution, especially when discussing the ideas of individuals such as Thomas Jefferson, tend to treat the theory as original and do not indicate that Jefferson, Richard Bland, and others, were writing out of a very rich European constitutional background. See Conkin, *Truths*, p. 36; Rossiter, *Six Characters*, pp. 185–86. Contrary, see Tate, "Social Contract in America," p. 377.

8 For the distinction between the two contracts, see Acherley, *Britannic Constitution*, pp. 102, 108–62; [Barwis,] *Three Dialogues*, pp. 78, 65 (re-

printed in *Monthly Review* 55 [1776]: 263); *Authority of Rights*, pp. 133–34; *Authority to Tax*, pp. 55–60; Shirley, *Richard Hooker*, p. 210; Wright, *American Interpretation*, p. 55. For a different description of the two contracts, see Paley, *Principles of Philosophy*, pp. 414–15. For an American discussion before the period of the American Revolution, see [Fowle,] *Appendix to Eclipse*, p. 4.

9 For a compounding of the two contracts, see [Dickinson,] *New Essay*, pp. 10–11. For the argument of an original contract with a social contract, see Kramnick, *Bolingbroke's Circle*, pp. 98–110.

10 This statement was staple English constitutional theory. See "In Our Contracted Sphere," pp. 22–23. For a serious discussion of the original contract with the king, published in London the year of the Declaration of Independence, see [Barwis,] *Three Dialogues*, pp. 65–87.

11 In 1690, immediately after the Glorious Revolution, a clergyman noted the various occasions when William I granted the ancient laws and swore to rule by law, and called "these things" the contract. "Now all these things put together seem plainly to conclude an *Original Compact* or Establishment of Laws, by which the *Kings* of *England* were to govern, and the *Kingdom* to be governed." [Whitby,] *Historical Account*, p. 4.

12 [Hawley,] "To Inhabitants," 2 March 1775, *American Archives* 2:24.

13 Anon., *Critical Review of Liberties*, p. 97 (quoting Charles Lucas); "Humble Representation of the Lords Spiritual and Temporal," 17 October 1719, *Protest of Lords of Ireland*, pp. 40–41. "The terms upon which Ireland became an accession to the crown of England, were a compleat participation of the privileges of Englishmen, and as the most valuable of these the boasted constitution of parliament." Anon., *Plain Reasons for New-Modelling*, p. 9.

14 For taxation, see *Authority to Tax*, pp. 53–64; for rights, see *Authority of Rights*, pp. 132–58.

15 "Some Thoughts on the Constitution," Philadelphia, 12 June 1775, *American Archives* 2:963; Lovell, *An Oration*, p. 14; Resolves of Pembroke, 28 December 1772, *Boston Evening-Post*, 11 January 1773, p. 2, col. 2.

16 For the reality of the contract, see *Authority of Rights*, pp. 146–55. Of course, there were eighteenth-century constitutional students who denied the reality and insisted it was nonsensical. Anon., *Experience preferable to Theory*, p. 16.

17 "[T]here is, there must be, an implied contract, for there never yet was an express one." Letter from Gouverneur Morris to Mr. Penn, 20 May 1774, *American Archives* 1:343 (speaking of the social contract as well as the original contract).

18 "Instructions from the Committee to the Representatives in Assembly met," July 1774, [Dickinson,] *New Essay*, p. 10 footnote.

19 [Ferguson,] *Remarks on a Phamphlet*, p. 21.

20 Anon., *Plain Question*, pp. 13–14; Pownall, *Administration*, pp. 119–20. For uncertainty regarding the right of migration, see *Authority of Rights*, pp. 119–20.

21 Blackstone, *Commentaries* 1:230; [Claridge,] *Defence of Government*, p. 2. Lord Abingdon said that *"Contract* is that *Bargain* of the People with the *executive Power* concerning their *different* Rights." Abingdon, *Thoughts on Burke's Letter*, p. 25. See also Hotoman, *Franco-Gallia*, p. 71; Shirley, *Richard Hooker*, p. 136.

22 Book Review, *Monthly Review* 55 (1776): 263 (paraphrasing [Barwis,] *Three Dialogues*, pp. 78, 83). See also for a Scots lawyer, [Steuart,] *Jus Populi*, p. 96. For colonial explanations of the theory, see Patten, *Discourse at Hallifax*, p. 10; Baldwin, *New England Clergy*, p. 39 n. 28 (quoting Joseph Moss, *Connecticut Election Sermon* [1715]).

23 Hoadly, *Works* 2:256.

24 "Some Thoughts on the Constitution," Philadelphia, 12 June 1775, *American Archives* 2:962; Anon., *New Political Catechism*, p. 6; [Hawley,] "To the Inhabitants," 13 April 1775, *American Archives* 2:334. "Must Great-Britain submit to enter into discussions of this kind [about contributions in lieu of taxes] with her refractory Colonies? Must she humble herself to receive as bounty, what she can compel as a right? . . . To this I answer; that wherever there is a compact, it can be no degradation to examine strictly into the terms of that compact." *Gentleman's Magazine* 45 (1775): 544.

25 [Ferguson,] *Brief Justification*, pp. 7–8. Also, see Rutherforth, *Natural Law* 2:387, 631; James Iredell, "To His Majesty," February 1777, *Papers of Iredell* 1:436; [Ramsay,] *Thoughts on Nature of Government*, p. 10.

26 Tucker, *Election Sermon*, p. 14; Estwick, *Letter to Tucker*, p. 83. See also Fiske, *Importance of Righteousness*, p. 31. For perhaps the fullest expression of the contract theory in the age of the American Revolution, see Pownall, *Administration*, p. 50.

27 Turner, *Election Sermon*, p. 16.

28 Paley, *Principles of Philosophy*, pp. 417–18. For a fuller quotation from Paley's argument, see *Authority of Rights*, pp. 136–37. For the argument in 1781 that the contract was immutable and higher than Parliament's law, see Anon., *Constitution*, pp. 41–42.

29 "Parliamentary History," *London Magazine* 45 (1776): 64.

30 [Bolingbroke,] *Dissertation*, p. 155. For knowledge of the colonial contract terms, see *Authority of Rights*, p. 141.

31 "[W]ho hath the *Right*, and the *Means*, to resist the *supreme, legislative Power;* I answer, the *whole Nation* hath the *Right.* . . . An Attempt of this Kind would break the Bargain between the *King* and the *Nation*, between the *representative* and *collective Body of the People*, and would dissolve the *Constitution.*" [Bolingbroke,] *Dissertation*, p. 210; Straka, "Sixteen Eighty-Eight," p. 154. See also Letter X, 20 December 1768, Anon., *National Mirror*, p. 61; Anon., *Defence of Resolutions*, p. 85 (reprinting *London Evening Post*, 2 and 4 May 1776); Pym, *Speech of Summing Up*, p. 16; Anon., *Fundamental Lawes*, p. 12; Kenyon, *Revolution Principles*, pp. 134–35 (quoting speech of Lechmere in impeachment of Sacheverell). For the American interpretation, see Perry, *Connecticut Election Sermon*, p. 23; Leder, *Liberty*, p. 82. If the government's breach was not drastic,

but an assumption of powers not authorized by the contract, the remedy was not to obey. Tucker, *Election Sermon*, p. 18.

32 Speech of Thomas Pitt, Commons Debates, 3 February 1766, *Proceedings and Debates* 2:141; Letter from Henry Seymour Conway to George III, 27 January 1766, ibid., p. 112 (quoting William Pitt); Ritcheson, *British Politics*, p. 57.

33 In fact, some theorists defined the contract as the constitution: "Our constitution, properly so called, I define to be the original treaties which, at divers epochs, have been entered into, ratified, and confirmed, by and between the people of England, and some other person or state, . . . the several articles of which treaties are immutable and indefeasible laws, in contradistinction to acts of parliament, which are alterable and repealable at pleasure." Anon., *Constitution*, pp. 41–42. See also *Craftsman* 13, no. 437, 16 November 1734, p. 71.

34 As suggested by the quotation in note 33 above, there could be changes or renewals in the original contract (also see Tucker, *Election Sermon*, p. 31). Roger Acherley summed up Magna Carta as "a Renewal of the *Original Contract*." Colbourn, *Lamp of Experience*, p. 37. Joseph Galloway described the oaths of allegiance sworn by foreigners when naturalized as "no more than renewals of the original covenant." [Galloway,] *Candid Examination*, p. 17. Because of the British constitution, however, Richard Hussey was wrong when he asserted: "If an Act of Parliament had said the colonists should not be taxed, this would have been their Magna Carta, and an attempt to tax them in general would have been a violation of the original compact." Speech of Richard Hussey, Commons Debates, 3 February 1766, *Proceedings and Debates* 2:141.

35 Rutherforth, *Natural Law* 2:631; Book Review, *Monthly Review* 70 (1784): 170 (quoting Richard Wooddeson); Hale, *Jurisprudence*, p. 4.

36 Edmund Burke, "Letter to the Sheriffs," reprinted in Peach, *Richard Price*, p. 271.

37 In one respect, everyone agreed that the second original contract was reasonably clear. That was the part of the contract made up of the proclamation contract. *Authority of Rights*, pp. 153–58. It was argued in the issue of the authority to legislate primarily with regard to the Quebec Bill. E.g., Argument of Mr. Mansfield, House of Commons, 31 May 1774, *Proceedings and Debates* 4:498.

38 [Goodricke,] *Observations*, p. 13. Similiarly see Anon., *Plain Question*, p. 16.

39 "A Short View of the ancient and present State of our American Colonies," *Remembrancer for 1776: Part II*, p. 11.

40 [Hopkins,] *Grievances of the Colonies*, p. 6; [Allen,] *Beauties of Liberty*, p. 8. See also Patten, *Discourse at Hallifax*, p. 13.

41 [Goodricke,] *Observations*, p. 33.

42 Speech of Charles Yorke, Commons Debates, 3 February 1766, *Proceedings and Debates* 2:146.

43 Book Review, *Gentleman's Magazine* 39 (1769): 97. For the settlement contract and the imperial contract, see *Authority to Tax*, pp. 60–74.

CHAPTER NINE: CONSTRAINTS OF CONSTITUTIONALISM

1 Allen, *Magistracy an Institution*, p. 26. See also Pemberton, *Divine Original*, pp. 25–26 (1710 election sermon); Lockwood, *Worth and Excellence*, p. 10 (1759 election sermon). And see Baldwin, *New England Clergy*, p. 18 (quoting Jonathan Mayhew's discussion of the limitations on God's rule).

2 New London Resolves, 10 December 1765, *Boston Post-Boy*, 16 December 1765, p. 3, col. 2 (also reprinted in Jensen, *Documents*, pp. 670–71); Letter from the Massachusetts House to the earl of Shelburne, 15 January 1768, in [Hollis,] *True Sentiments*, p. 14. See also letter from the Massachusetts House to Henry Seymour Conway, 13 February 1768, *Boston Gazette*, 28 March 1768, p. 1, col. 1; *Boston Gazette*, 10 May 1756, p. 1, col. 1.

3 Anon., *Dialogue on Principles*, p. 10. See also Kemp, "Parliamentary Sovereignty," p. 12 (quoting the earl of Abingdon); Cartwright, *Appeal on Constitution*, p. 27

4 Pocock, *Politics*, p. 226 (quoting a Commons speech Burke did not deliver).

5 Brewer, *Party Ideology*, pp. 243–44 (quoting *Freeholder's Magazine* [1769]); *Petition of Middlesex to King, 24 May 1769*, p. 4. See also Anon., *Critical Review of Liberties*, pp. 13–14.

6 [Jones,] *Constitutional Criterion*, p. 14.

7 Turner, *Election Sermon*, p. 17 (reprinted in *They Preached Liberty*, p. 89). For the day of fasting and prayer against the Coercive Acts, a Massachusetts clergyman preached: "Power is too intoxicating, and liable to abuse. As great a blessing as government is, like all other blessings, it may become a scourge, a curse, a severe punishment to a people." Whitney, *Transgression*, pp. 21–22 (see also pp. 6–7, 13–14). "Unlimited Power is so wild and monstrous a Thing, that however natural it be to desire it, it is as natural to oppose it; nor ought it to be trusted with any mortal Man, be his Intentions ever so upright." Trenchard, Letter of 9 February 1722, *Cato's Letters* 4:81. See also Trenchard, Letter of 6 January 1721, *Cato's Letters* 2:230; Stone, "Results of Revolutions," p. 33 (quoting J.G.A. Pocock).

8 *The Crisis*, 3 August 1776, pp. 509–10; Memorial from New York General Assembly to House of Lords, 25 March 1775, *American Archives* 1:1316; *American Archives* 2:2. A related reason for legislative limitations was said to be social stability. "[T]o ensure stability to the constitution of a state, it is indispensably necessary to restrain the legislative authority." De Lolme, *Constitution: New Edition*, p. 219.

9 Kliger, *Goths*, pp. 203–4; Pease, *Leveller*, p. 10; Spelman, "Certain Considerations," p. 327; Charles I, Answer to the Nineteen Propositions, June 1642, Rushworth, *Historical Collections: Third Part* 1:731; Hotoman, *Franco-Gallia*, pp. 65–67; Tierney, *Religion, Law, and Growth*, p. 80;

Corinne Comstock Weston, "The Theory of Mixed Monarchy Under Charles I and After," *English Historical Review* 75 (1960): 426–27.

10 Paley, *Principles of Philosophy*, p. 478. The theory should not be confused with the "separation of powers" doctrine which was known in English political theory but was not of such significance. Hobbes, *Elements of Law*, part 2, chap. 1, sec. 15.

11 "Analysis of the British Constitution," *Political Register* 5 (1769):72. On liberty see also Book Review, *Monthly Review* 46 (1772):580; Anon., *British Liberties*, p. xix; *Craftsman* 13, no. 437, 16 November 1734, p. 75; Anon., *Ancient and Modern Constitution*, pp. 6–7. The doctrine of separation of powers was also understood to be a doctrine of limitations and liberty. [Williams,] *Letters on Liberty*, pp. 8–9.

12 "It is good policy to presume that great powers *will be abused*, where-ever they may be placed. The excellence of our constitution is, that there is a check on every power existing in it: and the probability of its continuance depends upon constantly maintaining those checks in their full effect and vigour. This cannot be done, unless there is a *constant* jealousy, and apprehension of abuse." [Downley,] *Sentiments*, p. 52.

13 Livingston, *Address to the House*, p. 4. See also Anon., *Political Balance*, p. 29; Leder, *Liberty*, pp. 93–94.

14 De Lolme, *Constitution*, p. 42. See also, Bailyn, *Pamphlets*, pp. 47, 170–71; Dickinson, *Liberty and Property*, pp. 142–59; Robbins, *Commonwealthmen*, p. 83.

15 Browning, *Court Whigs*, p. 160. "By the *balance of interest*, which accompanies and gives efficacy to the *balance of power*, is meant this, that the respective interests of the three estates of the empire are so disposed and adjusted, that whichever of the three shall attempt any encroachment, the other two will unite in resisting it." Paley, *Principles of Philosophy*, pp. 480–81. See also Paley, *Essay Upon the Constitution*, p. 22; Protest of 7 May 1800, *Protests of Lords* 2:337. For a discussion of the interests balanced resembling the checks and balances of legislative, executive, and judicial, see Otis, *Rights*, p. 455. Although not as well defined as we might expect, the concept of balanced interests was understood to be a necessary ingredient for the constitutional preservation of liberty. In 1779 an Irish barrister wrote: "The fact is, that in order to preserve the freedom of a people, such is the necessity of controlling the power of government, no matter in what hands such power may be placed, that the great object of a free constitution is, that by its own particular construction, by the opposition of interests between the constituent parts of it, the legislature shall be made to control itself, and by that means render the exercise of a defensive power on the part of the people unnecessary." Sheridan, *Observations on the Doctrine*, pp. 59–60.

16 Leonard, "Massachusettensis," p. 33; [Inglis,] *Letters of Papinian*, pp. 74–75. See also [Serle,] *Americans against Liberty*, pp. 24–25. For a discussion of the "balance" theory of Loyalist Thomas Hutchinson, see Bailyn, *Ordeal*, pp. 199–201.

17 For a sampling of praise of the theory, see "Constitutional Observations," *London Magazine* 45 (1776):140; Pulteney, *Effects of the Bill*, pp. 32–33; Anon., *Defence of Magna Charta*, p. 135; Anon., *Considerations on Information*, p. 19; Lowth, *Durham Assize Sermon*, p. 10; Anon., *Critical Review of Liberties*, p. 14; *London Journal*, no. 796, 28 September 1734, p. 1, col. 1; Barrington, *Revolution and Anti-Revolution Principles*, p. 49.

18 For a sampling of American praise over the eighteenth century, see Wood, *Creation*, p. 198 (discussing John Adams); *Independent Reflector*, 12 July 1753, p. 288; Chauncy, *Civil Magistrates*, p. 15; Eliot, *Give Cesar His Due*, p. 32; Bushman, *King and People*, p. 126 (quoting Massachusetts House, 1728).

19 Blackstone, *Commentaries* 1:51.

20 Ibid., pp. 51–52. See also Letter from *North Briton*, No. CXXXV, *London Magazine* 34 (1765):101.

21 [Keld,] *Polity of England*, p. 325.

22 Bentham, *Fragment on Government*, p. 464; *Concept of Representation*, pp. 110–18. There is, however, historical opinion that the constitutional balance existed up until 1783 between Crown and Commons. Gunn, "Influence," p. 306.

23 Cooke, *Election Sermon*, p. 17.

24 "The British American, No. VI," Williamsburg, 7 July 1774, *American Archives* 1:521; Anon., *Application of Political Rules*, p. 66.

25 [Rous,] *Claim of the Commons*, p. 5 (quoting De Lolme). See also [Squire,] *Historical Essay on Ballance*, p. vii; Anon., *Dialogue on the State*, pp. 23–24. Oddly, the argument that the Crown and Lords were dependent on the Commons was even made about the servile Irish House of Commons. Anon., *Arguments to Prove*, p. 21.

26 "Constitutional Observations," *London Magazine* 45 (1776):142. See also *Craftsman* 12, no. 395, 26 January 1733/34, p. 107; [Bolingbroke,] *Dissertation*, p. 208; Kramnick, "Introduction to Writings," p. xxii–xxiii.

27 *Concept of Representation*, pp. 45–48.

28 Franklin, *Address to Ireland*, pp. 7–8.

29 Kramnick, *Bolingbroke's Circle*, p. 250; [Ramsay,] *Historical Essay*, pp. 6–7.

30 Price, *Two Tracts: Tract One*, p. 18. In 1771 the Massachusetts House voted that "A Power without a Check is subversive of all Freedom." Middlekauff, *Glorious Cause*, p. 207. In 1778 a London pamphlet protested a statute suspending the benefit of laws for American rebels, and warned of the "danger of an *unlimited* power, against which all true Englishmen ought to be ever upon their guard." Anon., *Protest of a Private Person*, pp. 5–6.

31 *Cato's Letters*, 1:xxviii. Another eighteenth-century statement on the dangers of unrestrained power warned:

> The desire of power . . . is natural to man. It is the motive to his best and to his worst actions. . . . Yet, although this love of power be so general, when it is possessed beyond a certain degree and measure, it is almost constantly fatal to interest, virtue, and felicity. It inflames

the most criminal and destructive passions, it corrupts the most humane and gentle natures. What, indeed, [is] so adverse to moderation, to humanity, to equal justice, as the dangerous and stimulating consciousness of being above all account or controul.

Anon., *Abuse of Power*, pp. 7-8.

32 [Galloway,] *Candid Examination*, p. 39; Address to Lord Mayor Brass Crosby from the Inhabitants of the Ward of Lime-Street, 25 April 1771, Anon., *Magna Charta Opposed to Privilege*, p. 162; Chauncy, *Civil Magistrates*, p. 15 (reprinted in Baldwin, *New England Clergy*, p. 43); Eliot, *Give Cesar his Due*, p. 32; Trenchard, Letter of 28 January 1720, *Cato's Letters* 1:91-92; Sidney, *Discourses Concerning Government*, p. 492; Brewer, *Party Ideology*, p. 243; Kramnick, *Bolingbroke's Circle*, p. 250-51.

33 Locke: Anon., *Vindication of the Livery*, p. 6; Cato: Kramnick, *Bolingbroke's Circle*, p. 251. As late as 1790 a writer would describe Britain's government of restraint in terms of restraints on the king only. Anon., *New Political Catechism*, pp. 7-8.

34 [Meredith,] *Question Stated*, p. 63; Anon., *Fair Trial*, p. 226. See also Argument of Serjeant Glynn, Court of Common Pleas, 22 April 1771, Anon., *Magna Charta Opposed to Privilege*, pp. 137-38; Shelton, *Charge to Suffolk Grand Jury*, p. 14. In the previous century Henry Parker, the parliamentary lawyer, contended: " . . . and there can be nothing said against the Arbitrary supremacy of Parliaments, &c. But farre more upon better grounds, may be said against the Arbitrary supremacy of the King." [Parker,] *Observations upon some Answers*, p. 36.

35 When Governor Thomas Hutchinson in his great constitutional debate with the Massachusetts General Court in 1773 postulated an imperialist's concept of parliamentary supremacy, *Xenopeon* protested that the governor conceded to Parliament power that "is *absolute, arbitrary*, and *despotic.*" *Xenopeon's* words were common usage and may have been synonyms. Yet, even though "absolute," "despotic," and "tyranny" were useful and frequently employed, the probative concept in eighteenth-century constitutional discussions was "arbitrary." *Boston Evening-Post*, 15 March 1773, p. 2, col. 3. For the debate of 1773, see *Briefs of Revolution*, especially pp. 17-23.

36 For lengthy discussions of the concept of arbitrary in the age of the American Revolution, see "In Legitimate Stirps"; *Concept of Liberty*, pp. 55-59.

37 [James Macpherson,] "Rights of Great Britain", *Scots Magazine* 38 (1776):31 (quoting Pitt); "Junius," *Junius* 2:353; [Tod,] *Consolatory Thoughts*, p. 3; Letter from the Continental Congress to the British People, 5 September 1774, *London Magazine* 43 (1774):628.

38 Eliot, *Give Cesar His Due*, p. 36 footnote; [Bolingbroke,] *Dissertation*, p. 159. See also Bolingbroke, *Political Writings*, p. 54; Anon., *Essay on the Right*, p. 37 (quoting Montesquieu: "every government where the power is immoderately exerted is a despotic state"); Tucker, *Election Sermon*, p. 19

(quoting Locke: "Tyranny is the exercise of power beyond right, which no body can have a right to"); Lawson, *Politica Sacra*, p. 138.

39 Locke, *Two Treatises*, book 2, sec. 139. See also Anon., *British Liberties*, pp. liv–lv (quoting Locke).

40 Browning, *Court Whigs*, p. 196; Arbuthnot, *Freeholder's Catechism*, p. 9. See also Pemberton, *Divine Original*, p. 25 (Massachusetts election sermon quoting Bishop Gilbert Burnet).

41 John Trenchard, Letter of 6 January 1721, "Cato's Letters," pp. 119–20; *Annual Register 1769*, pp. 68*–69*. See also Lowth, *Durham Assize Sermon*, p. 9.

42 H[enry] Ferne, *Conscience Satisfied. That there is no Warrant for the Armes now taken up by Subjects* (Oxford, 1643), p. 46. See also Judson, *Crisis*, p. 389.

43 [Shebbeare,] *Second Letter*, pp. 10–11; Speech of the Governor Thomas Pownall, Commons Debates, 15 May 1767, *Proceedings and Debates*, 2:484.

44 Halifax, *Charles II*, p. 76; [Young,] *Political Essays*, p. 39. See also, Browning, *Court Whigs*, p. 196 (quoting William Arnall); Gough, *Fundamental Law*, pp. 117–18; Pease, *Leveller*, p. 27 (discussing Henry Parker); Pole, *Gift*, p. 100 (discussing Henry Parker).

45 "Junius," *Junius* 1:iv–v; [Otis,] *Considerations*, p. 36, McIlwain, *Revolution*, p. 156 (discussing James Otis); [Stillingfleet,] *Discourse*, p. 7; Burlamaqui, *Politic Law*, pp. 156–157. Locke put the argument more on institutional grounds, saying that the legislative "is *not*, nor can possibly be absolutely *Arbitrary* over the Lives and Fortunes of the People. For it being but the joynt power of every Member of the Society given up to that Person, or Assembly, which is Legislator, it can be no more than those persons had in a State of Nature before they enter'd into Society, and gave up to the Community." Locke, *Two Treatises*, book 2, sec. 135.

46 Anon., *"Taxation no Tyranny" Considered*, p. 50; Anon., *Civil Liberty Asserted*, p. 87. "This *Freedom* from Absolute, Arbitrary Power, is so necessary to, and closely joyned with a Man's Preservation, that he cannot part with it, but by what he forfeits his Preservation and Life together." Locke, *Two Treatises*, book 2, sec. 23.

47 It was a standard platitude of eighteenth-century British constitutionalism that "No obedience is due to arbitrary, unconstitutional edicts, calculated to enslave a free people." [Johnson,] *Some Important Observations*, p. 21. See also King, *English Constitution*, p. 52; Abingdon, *Dedication*, p. xxxi; Locke, *Two Treatises*, book 2, sec. 149. Contrary, see Sherlock, *Case of Resistance*, pp. 109–10.

48 [Serle,] *Americans Against Liberty*, pp. 27–28; Price, *Two Tracts: Tract One*, p. 35.

49 [Shipley,] *Intended Speech*, p. 26; *The Crisis*, 2 March 1776, p. 379.

CHAPTER TEN: CONSTRAINTS OF LIBERTY

1 The meaning and operation of eighteenth-century liberty has been discussed elsewhere. See *Concept of Liberty.*

2 Speech of Sir William Meredith, Commons Debates, 10 December 1777, *Parliamentary History* 19:588.

3 [Joseph Hawley,] "To the Inhabitants of the Massachusetts-Bay," 9 March 1775, *American Archives* 2:96–97.

4 Chapters 6 and 7. The theory could also be stated in natural-law terms. Sheridan, *Observations on the Doctrine,* p. 33.

5 Lofft, *Summary of Treatise,* p. 2. In another publication, Lofft used the word "sovereign" rather than "supreme," saying that the authority of the whole people "in other cases is *sovereign.*" Lofft, *Observations on Wesley's Address,* p. 32.

6 [Shebbeare,] *Seventh Letter,* p. 8.

7 Dickinson, *Reply to Galloway,* p. 30 footnote (quoting William Penn).

8 Patten, *Discourse at Hallifax,* p. 18.

9 But see James Iredell, "To the Inhabitants of Great Britain," *Papers of Iredell* 1:256; Anon., *Constitution with Address,* pp. 23–24.

10 James Lovell's Oration (1771), *Massacre Orations,* p. 11. Similarily, see Anon., *Address to Middlesex Freeholders,* p. 4 footnote.

11 Gordon, Letter of 20 January 1721, "Cato's Letters" p. 131. Trenchard, Letter of 9 February 1722, "Cato's Letters," p. 256.

12 Eliot, *Give Cesar his Due,* p. 36; Speech of Edmund Burke, Commons Debates, 26 May 1767, *Burke Writings* 2:65. See also Otis, *Rights,* p. 446; Sidney, *Discourses Concerning Government,* p. 462.

13 [Inglis,] *True Interest,* p. 12.

14 Anon., *Fatal Consequences,* p. 2. See also Murdin, *Three Sermons,* p. 6; Fiske, *Importance of Righteousness,* p. 31.

15 And also in the sixteenth century. Hooker, *Laws of Ecclesiastical Polity,* book 8, chap. 2, sec. 12 and book 8, chap. 8, sec. 9.

16 Cook, *King Charls his Case,* p. 6. See also Johnson, *Notes on Pastoral,* pp. 30–31, 57; Johnson, *Remarks on Sherlock,* pp. 3–4; Twysden, *Certain Considerations,* p. 17; Tuck, *Natural Rights Theories,* p. 149 (quoting John Lilburne). Contrary, see Sherlock, *Case of Resistance,* pp. 196–97.

17 *Boston Evening-Post,* 25 March 1771, p. 2, col. 1. See also *New York Evening-Post,* 7 December 1747, reprinted in *Boston Evening-Post,* 28 December 1747, p. 1, col. 2.

18 [Ramsay,] *Historical Essay,* p. 80.

19 [Phelps,] *Rights of the Colonies,* p. 6; Anon., *Defence of Resolutions,* pp. 20–21.

20 Anon., *Resistance no Rebellion,* p. 14.

21 Blackstone, *Commentaries* 3:133.

22 Locke, *Two Treatises,* book 2, sec. 142 (see also sec. 137).

23 [Shebbeare,] *Second Letter,* p. 17; Locke, *Two Treatises,* book 2, sec. 142. Another aspect of the rule of law was protection of legal rights. "[T]he very Essence of Government consists in making and executing Stated Rules, for

the determining of all Civil Differences, and in doing all other Acts that tend to secure the Subjects, against all Enemies Foreign and Domestick, in the quiet Possession of their Legal Rights." Barrington, *Revolution and Anti-Revolution Principles*, p. 15.

24 Anon., *Four Letters*, p. 19; Sisson, "Idea of Revolution," p. 411.

25 Anon., *Common Sense Conferences*, p. 7.

26 Anon., *Rights of People to Petition*, p. 32. For House of Commons, see "The North Briton, No. 135," *Scots Magazine* 27 (1765): 116. For the House of Lords, see Memorial from the Council and Burgesses of Virginia to the House of Lords, 18 December 1764, *Journal of Burgesses* 10:302.

27 [Ramsay,] *Historical Essay*, p. 115.

28 Anon., *Common Sense Conferences*, p. 12.

29 Demophilus, *Genuine Principles*, p. 35.

30 James Iredell, "To the Inhabitants of Great Britain," (September 1774), *Papers of Iredell* 1:253. See also J. J. Zubly, To Lord Dartmouth, 3 September 1775, *London Magazine* 45 (1776): 36.

31 One clear threat to liberty was the precedent of the Long Parliament when all power had been usurped by one branch. It could happen again. "[T]he truth is, that if the legislative assemblies, or either of them, should ever acquire a share of the executive authority, and so become, as it were, *partners* in power with the Crown, farewel[l] liberty!" [Keld,] *Polity of England*, p. 313.

32 [Macpherson,] *Rights of Great Britain*, p. 3.

33 Answer from the House of Representatives to Governor Francis Bernard, 24 October 1765, *Boston News-Letter*, 31 October 1765, p. 1, col. 2.

34 See the theory of David Hume, which resembles the limitations implied by the original contract. Anon., *Legality of Impressing Seamen*, pp. 119–20 (quoting Hume). See also Charge to Tower of London Grand Jury, 16 July 1728, Gonson, *Charges*, pp. 73–74.

35 Pownall, *Administration Fifth Edition*, pp. 48–49.

36 This ambivalent aspect of the two constitutions is detailed elsewhere with relation to the use of the military to suppress civilian riots. *In Defiance of the Law*, pp. 107–29.

37 Trenchard, Letter of 30 December 1721, *Cato's Letters* 2: 214; Sidney, *Discourses Concerning Government*, p. 348.

38 *Independent Reflector*, 23 August 1753, p. 332.

39 Speech of Lord Carteret, Lords Debates, 9 March 1738, *Parliamentary History* 10:489; "In a Defensive Rage," pp. 1050–52.

40 Burgh, *Political Disquisitions* 3:243; *In Defiance of the Law*, p. 229.

41 [Meredith,] *Remarks on Taxation*, p. 81 (quoting Walpole).

42 Protest of 11 May 1774, *Protests of the Peers*, p. 10.

43 [Mitchell,] *Present State*, p. 131.

CHAPTER ELEVEN: CONSTRAINTS OF LAW

1 Charge of 9 October 1728, Gonson, *Charges*, p. 107.

2 *Authority to Tax*, pp. 181–86; *Authority of Rights*, pp. 67–73; "In Accordance with Usage," pp. 344–55.

3 Browning, *Court Whigs*, p. 157. But see Lucas, "Burke's Doctrine of Prescription," p. 59.

4 Gregor, "Preface," p. xlix.

5 Shelton, *Charge to Suffolk Grand Jury*, p. 21.

6 Anon., *Arguments to Prove*, pp. 7–8.

7 Pocock, *Politics*, p. 226 (quoting Burke). This statement is more fully quoted at p. 128.

8 [Dyson,] *Case of Middlesex*, p. 41; [Lind,] *Thirteenth Parliament*, p. 21 footnote. See also page 22 where Lind defines the constitution as "that assemblage of institutions and customs which compose the general system, according to which the several powers in the state are distributed."

9 *Monthly Review* 50 (1774): 451 (quoting Wynne, *Eunomus*); Speech of Governor George Johnstone, Commons Debates, 16 December 1774, *American Archives* 1:1481. In 1766 it was said of rotten boroughs: " . . . strangers stand amazed at, and every one must confess needs a remedy. Though most think it hard to find one, because the constitution of the legislative being the original and supreme act of the society, antecedent to all postive laws, in it; and depending wholly on the people, no inferior power can alter it. And therefore the people, when the legislative is once constituted, having in such a government as we have been speaking of, no power to act as long as the government stands; this inconvenience is thought incapable of remedy." Anon., *British Liberties*, p. xxiii.

10 Providence Instructions, 13 August 1765, *Boston Post-Boy*, 19 August 1765, p. 3, col. 1.

11 Resolves of Caroline County, 14 July 1774, *Revolutionary Virginia* 1:115. See also Hinkhouse, *Preliminaries*, p. 99 (quoting *London Chronicle*, 12 November 1768).

12 Lee, *Appeal to Justice*, p. 30.

13 Petition to the King, 18 December 1764, *Journal of Burgesses* 10:302. See also Resolves of 30 May 1765, ibid., p. 360; Resolutions of Chesterfield County Virginia, 14 July 1774, *American Archives* 1:537.

14 Memorial of the Council and Burgesses to the House of Lords, 18 December 1764, *Revolutionary Virginia* 1:12.

15 Petition to the King, 31 December 1768, entered on the journal 7 April 1769, *Journal of New York Assembly* (1766–77), p. 12. See also Representation of the New York General Assembly to the House of Commons, 25 March 1775, *Scots Magazine* 37 (1775): 235; Petition of the Pennsylvania House to the House of Commons, 22 September 1768, *Pennsylvania Archives* 7:6275–76.

16 Speech of Lord Mansfield, Lords Debates, 3 February 1766, Holliday, *Life of Mansfield*, pp. 244–45.

17 "But, if there had been no exercise of this right of the legislature [to tax the colonies], prior to our own days, the right must have remained entire,

because it is essential to government, founded in justice and equity, and in the law of nature and nations." Carlyle, *Justice and Necessity*, p. 10.

18 Pudsey, *Constitution and Laws*, p. 201.

19 [Hawley,] "To the Inhabitants of Massachusetts-Bay," 13 April 1775, *American Archives* 2:332.

20 Paley, *Principles of Philosophy*, p. 411.

21 Anon., *British Liberties*, p. lx. For an American adoption of this argument, see *Boston Evening-Post*, 19 August 1765, p. 2, col. 2.

22 Paley, *Principles of Philosophy*, p. 426. See also Howard, *Artillery-Election Sermon*, p. 5.

23 *New-York Journal* quoted in Rossiter, *Political Thought*, p. 43.

24 Dickinson, *Speech Delivered*, p. 28. See similarly, Resolution of the Massachusetts House, 7 September 1728, *Collection on Salaries*, p. 64.

CHAPTER TWELVE: PRECEDENTS OF HISTORY

1 [Mulgrave,] *Letter from a Member*, p. 21; [Forster,] *Answer to the Question Stated*, p. 34.

2 [Heath,] *Case of Devon Excise*, p. 31 (see also p. 3). See also Petition to the House of Commons, 15 November 1763, *Addresses of the Common Council*, p. 54. For the relationship of the excise controversy to the American Revolution debate, see *Authority to Tax*, pp. 277–78.

3 Wickwire, *Subministers*, p. 191 (quoting Yorke). For avoidance of the Stamp Act precedent, see *Authority to Tax*, pp. 132–34.

4 [Macpherson,] *Rights of Great Britain*, p. 32. See also [Pownall,] *Considerations*, pp. 3–5; Speech of Lord Mansfield, Lords Debates, 10 February 1766, "Lords Debate on Declaratory Act," pp. 117–18.

5 Butler, *Sermon*, p. 9. See also [Galloway,] *Historical Reflections*, p. 103; Leonard, "Massachusettensis," p. 47.

6 *Boston Gazette*, 5 June 1769, p. 1, col. 1.

7 Replication of the Governor, 16 February 1773, *Briefs of Revolution*, p. 99.

8 Keir, *Constitutional History*, p. 363.

9 [Sewall,] *Americans Roused*, p. 12.

10 Adams, "Novanglus," pp. 203–4; "Some Thoughts on the Constitution," 12 June 1775, *American Archives* 2:963; Walsh, *Appeal from the Judgments*, p. 59. For this evidence evaluated by historians, see McIlwain, "Transfer of the Charter," p. 56; Schuyler, "Britannic Question," p. 110; Newton, "Great Emigration," p. 179; Andrews, *Settlements*, p. 76; Mullett, *Fundamental Law*, p. 67.

11 Report from Edward Randolph, 20 September 1676, *Glorious Revolution in America*, p. 19.

12 Adams, "Novanglus," p. 205. For the statement treated by historians, see Dunn, *Puritans and Yankees*, pp. 214–15; Hall, *Edward Randolph*, pp. 24–25.

13 Answer of the House, 26 January 1773, *Briefs of Revolution*, p. 67.

14 "Copy of a Paper endorsed Mr. E. R.'s Narrative Sept. 20th and Octo. 12th 1676," [Hutchinson,] *Collection of Papers*, p. 506.

15 Speech of Lord Mansfield, Lords Debates, 10 February 1766, *Parliamentary History* 16:176; Speech of Sir William Blackstone, Commons Debates, 3 February 1766, *Proceedings and Debates* 2:148. See also Speech of Richard Hussey, Commons Debates, 3 February 1766, Ryder, "Parliamentary Diaries," p. 269.

16 Answer of the House, 26 January 1773, *Briefs of Revolution*, p. 59.

17 *Commons Debates 1621* 7:202–4.

18 [Bancroft,] *Remarks*, pp. 23–24.

19 Speech of Sir George Calvert, Commons Debates, 25 April 1621, [Nicholas,] *Proceedings of 1620–21* 1:318–19. Reprinted in *Briefs of Revolution*, p. 107. Another contemporary printing that neither Adams nor Hutchinson seem to have had available is [Knox,] *Controversy*, Appendix, pp. i–xviii. In the twentieth century other manuscript reports of the debate have been published. See Debate of 25 April 1621, *Commons Debates 1621* 2:321, 3:82, 4:256, 5:98–99. These are also reprinted in *Briefs of Revolution*, pp. 107–10.

20 A Letter Supposed written by Edmund Burke to Lord North and published in Colonial Newspapers, May 19, 1774, *American Archives* 1:338. John Adams and Edward Bancroft attributed these words to Charles I, also refusing assent to a fishing bill. Answer of the House, 26 January 1773, *Briefs of Revolution*, p. 58; [Bancroft,] *Remarks*, p. 24. Bancroft undoubtedly fabricated that precedent. Like Adams, he cited no authority. What is known is that Charles I vetoed no bill on freedom of fishing as none was enacted. Lounsbury, *British Fishery*, p. 51; *Papers of John Adams* 1:330 n.2.

21 [Knox,] *Controversy*, pp. 147–48. See for similar contemporary conclusions, [Lind,] *Thirteenth Parliament*, pp. 181–82; Anon., *Some Fugitive Thoughts*, pp. 6–7. But contrary, see Pownall, *Administration Fifth Edition*, pp. 122–23. For the fishery bill discussed by recent historians, see Russell, *Parliaments and Politics*, p. 94; Lounsbury, *British Fishery*, p. 50; Robert Zaller, *The Parliament of 1621: A Study in Constitutional Conflict* (Berkeley, Calif., 1971), p. 102.

22 Message from the House of Burgesses to Governor Lord Dunmore, 10 June 1775, *American Archives* 2:1200; Remonstrance from Virginia Council and Burgesses to House of Commons, *Boston Post-Boy*, 25 March 1765, p. 1, col. 3; Answer of the Massachusetts House, 26 January 1773, *Briefs of Revolution*, pp. 59–60; Anon., *Standing Army in Colonies*, p. 6.

23 Answer of the Massachusetts House, 23 January 1773 and Rejoinder of the House, 2 March 1773, *Briefs of Revolution*, pp. 66, 138–39; Adams, "Novanglus," pp. 205–6; "Some Thoughts on the Constitution . . . ," 12 June 1775, *American Archives* 2:963–64.

24 "Introductory Remarks by the Editor," *Speeches*, p. 4 footnote (quoting 1692 Massachusetts act); Brown, *Becker on History*, pp. 118–19 (quoting 1661 Massachusetts resolution); Robson, *American Revolution*, p. 11 (1707 Pennsylvania resolution).

25 Adams, "Novanglus," p. 206; Bland, *An Inquiry*, p. 24.

26 Virginia: [Knox,] *Controversy*, p. 182; Albany Plan: Anon., *Experience preferable to Theory*, pp. 51–52; 1702: "Rights of G. Britain asserted," *Scots Magazine* 38 (1776): 67.

27 "Charles Garth's Letter," p. 151.

28 "Book Review," *Monthly Review* 51 (1774): 390–91.

29 [Lind,] *Thirteenth Parliament*, pp. 235–36. See also Answer of the House, 26 January 1773, *Briefs of Revolution*, p. 63.

30 Madden, "Origins," p. 2; Christie, *Crisis*, p. 13 footnote.

31 Madden, "Relevance of Experience," p. 23.

32 Wheeler, "Calvin's Case," pp. 596–97.

33 Madden, "Origins," p. 13.

34 Madden, "Relevance of Experience," p. 24.

35 Answer of the House, 26 January 1773, *Briefs of Revolution*, pp. 55–56.

36 [Gray,] *Right of the Legislature*, p. 36.

37 Speech of Charles Yorke, Commons Debates, 3 February 1766, Ryder, "Parliamentary Diaries," p. 265. See similarily [Knox,] *Controversy* (Dublin Edition), pp. 71–72; Anon., *Present Crisis*, pp. 14–15; Anon., *Letter to Member*, p. 16; Anon., *Rights of Parliament*, pp. 20–24.

38 [James Macpherson,] "The Rights of Great Britain," *Scots Magazine* 38 (1776): 29. See similarly speech of Richard Hussey, Common Debates, 1766, "Stamp Act Debates," pp. 569–70; [Knox,] *Letter to a Member*, p. 12; [Knox,] *Claim of the Colonies*, p. 8; [Canning,] *Letter to Hillsborough*, p. 38; Speech of Lord Lyttleton, "Lords Debate on Declaratory Act," p. 109; Anon., *Middle Temple Letter to Dublin*, p. 31; [Cary,] *Answer to Molyneux*, pp. 41–42. For an American imperialist making the argument, see Howard, *Halifax Letter*, p. 536.

39 Which does not mean that some constitutional observers were not aware of change. One who was not a lawyer said: "When America was first settled the whole right to conquest, discovery, and division of lands was in the King; it was in his power to grant them to any body, and on any condition. This power he used in America, in all cases without and in some against the consent of parliament. . . . " Speech of Sir Cecil Wray, Commons Debates, 6 April 1778, *Parliamentary History* 19:1011. For the king's prerogative at the time referred to by Wray, see Judson, *Crisis*, pp. 23–34. See also Anon., *Letter to Hillsborough*, pp. 4–5.

40 Anon., *Justice and Necessity of Taxing*, p. 30.

CHAPTER THIRTEEN: PRECEDENTS OF CHARTER

1 *Authority to Tax*, pp. 97–104; "In the First Line of Defense," pp. 177–215.

2 Protest of 21 March 1775, *Protests of the Peers*, p. 34.

3 [Rivers,] *Letters*, p. 137. See also address of Governor Hutchinson, 6 January 1773, *Briefs of Revolution*, p. 15; [Galloway,] *Candid Examination*, p. 20.

4 Howard, *Halifax Letter*, p. 535; [Howard,] *Defense of the Letter*, p. 13. See also [Seabury,] *View of the Controversy*, p. 14.

5 Goodricke, *Observations*, p. 13.

6 A Letter Supposed written by Edmund Burke to Lord North published in Colonial Newspapers, 19 May 1774, *American Archives* 1:338. See also Instructions of Ipswich, 21 October 1765, *Boston Post-Boy*, 4 November 1765, p. 2, col. 2.

7 Compare, e.g., Answer of the House, 26 January 1773, *Briefs of Revolution*, p. 63, to Leonard, "Massachusettensis," pp. 42-43.

8 It was possible to draw constitutional distinctions on behalf of the "charter" colonies of Rhode Island and Connecticut, but on the matter of the authority of Parliament these distinctions were not important. Interesting (because drawn by leading loyalists) examples are, [Galloway,] *Historical Reflections*, pp. 43-45; Letter from Jared Ingersoll to Governor Thomas Fitch, 11 February 1765, "Ingersoll Correspondence," p. 307, and Morgan, *Prologue*, p. 30.

9 Jenyns, "Observations," p. 80. See also [Galloway,] *Reply to an Address*, pp. 26-27; [Knox,] *Controversy* (Dublin Edition), pp. 156-64.

10 Johnson, *Political Tracts*, pp. 196-97. See also "Extract of a Letter from London," *Gazette & News-Letter* (Supplement), 10 April 1766, p. 2, col. 1; Anon., *Speech Never Intended*, p. 32; Leonard, "Massachusettensis," p. 47.

11 [Ramsay,] *Historical Essay*, p. 185. For a discussion of charters in eighteenth-century British constitutional law, see Barker, *Essays*, pp. 151-52.

12 Anon., *Cursory Remarks on Price*, p. 5. For a similar argument by a colonial governor, see Keith, *Papers and Tracts*, p. 175.

13 Howard, *Halifax Letter*, p. 535. See also Wynne, *Eunomus* 3:308.

14 Speech of Mr. Brush, New York Assembly Debates, 23 February 1775, *American Archives* 1:1292.

15 Pownall, *Administration*, p. 56; [Dulany,] *Considerations on the Propriety*, p. 14; Answer of the House, 26 January 1773, *Briefs of Revolution*, p. 64. See also Otis, *Rights*, p. 468.

16 Answer of the House, 26 January 1773, *Briefs of Revolution*, p. 64; London *Public Advertiser*, 11 January 1770, *Franklin's Letters to the Press*, p. 175.

17 Speech of Edmund Burke, Commons Debates, 3 February 1766, *Burke Writings* 2:49; Burke, *Letter to Sheriffs*, p. 59. See also Greene, *Peripheries and Center*, p. 48.

18 Although Blackstone and Mansfield are said to have contended that the rule *ultra vires* was sufficient law. Barker, "Natural Law," p. 288.

19 Second Letter from a London Merchant to a Noble Lord, *Gazette & News-Letter*, 2 January 1766, p. 1, col. 3.

20 *Guide to Rights*, p. 8.

21 Anon., *Judgment of Whole Kingdoms*, p. 20.

22 De Lolme, *Constitution: New Edition*, pp. 336-37 (see also pp. 27-28).

23 Anon., *Essay on the Constitution*, p. 11.

24 Colbourn, *Lamp of Experience*, p. 37 (quoting Roger Acherley).

25 *Boston Gazette*, 10 May 1756, p. 1, col. 1.

26 A minor illustration is the habendum clause, used to show that as a result of

the grant the colonies were "dependent" on the Crown, a point colonial whigs never disputed. E.g., "Bob Short," *Gazette & News-Letter,* 19 March 1772, p. 1, col. 2; Martin, "Long and Short," p. 109.

27 See *Authority to Tax,* pp. 98–101.

28 "The Third Charter of Virginia—1611–12," Thorpe, *Charters* 7:3806.

29 Anon., *Plain Question,* p. 15. See also [Prescott,] *Calm Consideration,* p. 8; *Boston Gazette,* 10 May 1756, p. 1, col. 2.

30 "Bob Short," *Gazette & News-Letter,* 19 March 1772, p. 1, col. 2; Mauduit, *Letters of Hutchinson,* p. 61; Anon., *Plain Question,* p. 16.

31 "The History of the Last Session," *London Magazine* 36 (1767): 61.

32 *London Magazine* 35 (1766): 565.

33 [Anderson,] *Free Thoughts,* p. 38, col. 2. See also Pownall, *Administration,* p. 120.

34 *Annual Register 1765,* p. [35].

35 Answer of the House, 26 January 1773, *Briefs of Revolution,* p. 69. See also ibid., p. 57; Anon., *Tyranny Unmasked,* p. 46.

36 Dummer, *Defence,* pp. 55–56; "Samuel Ward's Notes for a Speech in [Continental] Congress," 12 October 1774, *Letters of Delegates to Congress* 1:186. See also [Mather,] *America's Appeal,* p. 37.

37 Petition of New York Assembly to the Commons, 31 December 1768, *Boston Post-Boy,* 8 May 1769, p. 2, col. 1; Answer of the Massachusetts Council, 25 January 1773, and Answer of the House, 26 January 1773, *Briefs of Revolution,* pp. 39, 58.

38 Martin, "Long and Short," p. 109. A whig, disputing Governor Hutchinson's interpretation of the clause, offered an argument also based on the original contract. "Was not this, Sir, a mutual compact between England and America . . . ? Though America was by this charter, or agreement, to make no laws repugnant to the law of England. —Was not England bound (and did not our predecessors understand it so) by the same honour, to make no laws repugnant to the laws, and rights of America?" [Allen,] "To the Governor," p. 5.

39 Cooke, *Election Sermon,* p. 32. The argument was carried further by a leading loyalist. Coupling the Pennsylvania charter's repugnancy clause with a clause providing that English laws remain in force "until the said laws shall *be altered*" by the colony, he contended that Parliament was made subordinate to Pennsylvania's Assembly. "[W]hile the charter prohibits a discordancy between the laws of the inferior society and of the superior, it fully authorizes it, and that legislature which ought to be *inferior and subordinate,* is impowered to annul the acts of that which is *supreme.*" [Galloway,] *Political Reflections,* pp. 123–24.

40 "Northwest Ordinance," Commager, *Documents,* p. 129, col. 1; "Charter of Connecticut—1662," Thorpe, *Charters* 1:533. For a discussion of the commercial origins and the interpretation of the repugnancy clause, see Madden, "Relevance of Experience," p. 21.

41 [Fitch et al.,] *Reasons Why,* p. 13.

42 7 & 8 William III, cap. 22, sec. 9.

43 Anon., *Plain Question*, p. 12.

44 [Knox,] *Letter to a Member*, p. 17. See also [Knox,] *Controversy*, pp. 13–14; Replication of Governor Hutchinson, 16 February 1773 and Rejoinder of the House, 2 March 1773, *Briefs of Revolution*, pp. 95–96, 136–37; Roebuck, *Enquiry Whether the Guilt*, pp. 12–13.

45 Letter from Æquus, 16 January 1766, *London Magazine* 35 (1766): 33.

46 *South-Carolina Gazette*, 27 July 1767, p. 1, col. 1 (quoting "Benevolus" in *London Chronicle*).

47 [Bancroft,] *Remarks*, p. 37. See also Anon., *Tyranny Unmasked*, p. 46.

48 [Hawley,] "To the Inhabitants," 2 March 1775, *American Archives* 2:23, 22.

49 Anon., *Experience preferable to Theory*, p. 40.

50 [Phelps,] *Rights of the Colonies*, p. 10. See also [Tucker,] *Four Tracts*, pp. 96–97; Anon., *Appeal to Reason and Justice*, p. 56; "Vindex Partriae," *Interesting Letters*, pp. 132–33; [Lind,] *Thirteenth Parliament*, pp. 45–49.

51 [Macpherson,] *Rights of Great Britain*, p. 10; [Shebbeare,] *An Answer*, p. 57; Anon., *Review of Present Administration*, pp. 30–31.

52 E.g., Speech of the Archbishop of York, Lords Debates, 30 May 1777, *Parliamentary History* 19:348; Speeches of Charles Yorke and Richard Hussey, Commons Debates, 3 February 1766, Ryder, "Parliamentary Diaries," pp. 265, 269–70; [Pownall,] *Considerations*, p. 12; Markham, *Sermon Preached*, p. 22.

53 [Galloway,] *Political Reflections*, pp. 87–91; Anon., *Supremacy of Legislature*, pp. 11–12; Allen, *American Crisis*, p. 25; Letter IV, 26 December 1768, Anon., *National Mirror*, pp. 28–29; Anon., *Review of Present Administration*, p. 30; De Pinto, *Letters on Troubles*, p. 8.

54 "Z. T.," *Boston Evening-Post*, 3 July 1769, p. 4, col. 1. Similarly see Anon., *Plain State*, pp. 3–8 (argument that parliamentary supremacy was established by election of William and Mary, but earlier kings violated that supremacy when they issued colonial charters); "Book Review," *Critical Review* 31 (1771): 318 (arguing that privileges granted to London in the charter of Edward III could not limit Parliament).

55 Speech of Richard Hussey, Commons Debates, 3 February 1766, Ryder, "Parliamentary Diaries," pp. 270, 269.

56 Anon., *Late Occurences*, p. 35 (see also pp. 1–2). See also Dickinson, "Letter to Inhabitants," p. 485; "A Short View of the History," *Critical Review*, 27 (1769):64.

57 [Arthur Lee,] "Monitor V," *Virginia Gazette* (Rind), 24 March 1768, p. 1, col. 1; [John Dickinson,] Address to Barbadoes, *South-Carolina Gazette*, 4 August 1766, p. 1, col. 3.

58 *Boston Evening-Post* (Supplement), 8 March 1773, p. 1, col. 1 (reprinting *New York Journal*).

59 Instructions of Weymouth, n.d., *Boston Evening-Post*, 21 October 1765, p. 2, col. 2.

60 Answer of the Council, 25 January 1773, *Briefs of Revolution*, p. 37.

61 Price, *Nature of Civil Liberty*, p. 40. See also Anon., *Defence of Resolutions*,

p. 30. Contrary, see [Boucher,] *Letter from a Virginian*, p. 18 (arguing that Parliament had not legislated for the colonies because they had not been significant enough to warrant attention).

62 [Anderson,] *Free Thoughts*, p. 38, col. 1.

63 Entry for 28 July 1732, *Egmont Diary* 1:288; Washburn, "Preface," p. xix; Letter from John Sherwood to Governor Joseph Wanton, 13 August 1774, *Rhode Island Correspondence*, p. 438.

64 Speech of Alderman John Sawbridge in Defence of the Lord Mayor of London, *Hibernian Magazine* 1 (1771): 125; [Baillie,] *Appendix to a Letter*, p. 34 (argument of irrevocability by an admiralty judge); [Prescott,] *Calm Consideration;* "Regulus," *Defence of the Resolutions*, p. 30; Mullett, "English Imperial Thinking," p. 554 (discussing arguments of Gervase Bushe); Letter from Thomas Hutchinson to Richard Jackson, 23 July 1764, Knollenberg, *Origin*, p. 175. For the contention of a future United States Supreme Court Justice, see Wilson, "Speech of 1775," pp. 754–55.

65 "Causes of the present Discontent and Commotion in America," *Gentleman's Magazine* 44 (1774): 515–16. See also [Priestley,] *Present State of Liberty*, p. 28.

66 Anon., *Late Occurences*, p. 2. For the second original contract, see *Authority to Tax*, pp. 53–64; for the migration purchase, see *Authority of Rights*, pp. 124–31.

67 Anon., *Experience preferable to Theory*, pp. 74–75.

68 "The Lords' Protest against Passing the East-India Regulation Bill," *Gentleman's Magazine* 43 (1773): 264; Speech of Edmund Burke, Commons Debates, 13 April 1772, *Burke Writings* 2:372. See also Protests of 23 December 1772 and 10 June 1773, *Protests of Lords* 2:130, 135; Letter from the Committee of the East India Company to London Common Council, 27 May 1773, *Boston Evening-Post*, 9 August 1773, p. 2, col. 1; Petition of the Lord Mayor. *et al.* to the House of Commons, 28 May 1773, *London Magazine* 43 (1774): 417. Contrary, see Anon., *Review of Present Administration*, pp. 20–30; Marshall, "Empire and Authority," pp. 113–14, 118.

69 Speech of Attorney General Thurlow, Commons Debates, 2 May 1774, *American Archives* 1:90. See also Anon., *Plain State*, pp. 3–19

70 *Critical Review* 19 (1765): 226. And many English charters, including the charter of London, were forfeitable by process of *quo warranto.* Dummer, *Defence*, p. 3; Costin & Watson, *Documents*, p. 254; Shy, "Thomas Pownall," p. 180 (quoting Burke).

71 Speech of the Bishop of Peterborough, Lords Debates, 6 February 1775, *Gentleman's Magazine* 45 (1775): 155; Adams, "Novanglus," pp. 262–63; Keir, *Constitutional History*, p. 349; Barker, "Natural Law," p. 288. For some discussion, see "In the First Line of Defense," pp. 199–204.

72 "Royal charters subject to review," *Scots Magazine* 36 (1774): 120. See also Letter IX in answer to the Farmer's Letter, *Boston Evening-Post*, 29 May 1769, p. 4, col. 2.

73 Dickinson, "Letter to Inhabitants," p. 487.

74 *Authority of Rights*, pp. 34–38.

75 An argument understood and supported in Great Britain. Remonstrance to the King, 5 April 1775, *Addresses and Petitions of Common Council*, p. 82; Bill for Conciliation with the Colonies, 5 May 1780, Conway, *Peace Speech*, p. 47.

76 Georgia Committee to Virginia Committee, 10 August 1774, *Revolutionary Virginia* 2:158; Letter from Benjamin Franklin to Governor William Franklin, 22 March 1775, *Papers of Franklin* 21:560.

77 "A Brief Examination of *American* Grievances; being the heads of a Speech at the General Meeting at *Lewestown*, on *Delaware*, July 28, 1774," *American Archives* 1:658.

78 Resolves of the First Provincial Congress, 27 August 1774, *North Carolina Colonial Records* 9:1045.

79 "Y," "To 'Z' of New-Jersey," 5 January 1775, *American Archives* 1:1096. For a similar reaction in 1691 to the loss of the first Massachusetts charter, see [Rawson,] *Revolution in New England*, p. 43.

80 Letter from the Massachusetts General Court to Agent Mauduit, November 1764, *Speeches*, p. 24; Speech of Sir William Meredith, Commons Debates, 23 February 1778, *Gentleman's Magazine* 48 (1778): 616.

81 Argument of Mr. Alleyne, Campbell v. Hall, *State Trials* 20:239, 273 (K.B., 1774).

82 Charter of Connecticut—1662, Thorpe, *Charters* 1:533; Leonard, "Massachusettensis," p. 43; Massachusetts Resolution of 3 March 1773, *Journal of the House*, p. 281; Instructions of the House of Representations to Richard Jackson, 22 September 1764, *Pennsylvania Archives* 7:5643. See also [Thomas Fitch et al.,] *Reasons Why* (1764), reprinted in Bailyn, *Pamphlets*, pp. 389–90; Anon., *Taxation, Tyranny*, pp. 42–43.

83 [Hawley,] "To the Inhabitants," 6 April 1775 and 9 March 1775, *American Archives* 2:295, 95. See also ibid., 2 March 1775, and 6 April 1775, pp. 23, 290–91.

84 Speech of Edward Thurlow, Commons Debates, 26 May 1774, *Proceedings and Debates* 4: 458–59.

85 Anon., *Colonising*, p. 9. See also Anon., *Civil Liberty Asserted*, p. 92; [Sewall,] *Americans Roused*, pp. 11–14.

86 On the authority of the Crown to govern (rather than the authority to legislate), the whigs reversed the historical perspective and viewed the charter as a grant from the original settlers to the king. [Joseph Hawley,] "To the Inhabitants," 30 March 1775, *American Archives* 2:247; Second Letter from a London Merchant to a Noble Lord, *Gazette & News-Letter*, 2 January 1766, p. 1, col. 3.

87 [Sewall,] *Americans Roused*, p. 12. See also Instructions of 5 May 1773, *Boston Town Records* 18:132; Anon., *Second Answer to Wesley*, p. 10. For the theory in the seventeenth century, see Message from Maryland House to Lord Baltimore, 23 August 1681, *Maryland Archives* 7:125.

88 Resolves of Westerly, Rhode Island, 2 February 1774, Denison, *Westerly*, p. 111; Letter to Lord Dartmouth, September 1765, "Letters of Dennys De Berdt," p. 437.

89 *Gentleman's Magazine* 36 (1766): 613; "British American," *Boston Post-Boy*, 11 August 1766, p. 1, col. 3.

90 Anon., *Second Answer to Wesley*, p. 10.

91 Cooke, *Election Sermon*, pp. 33–34.

92 [Thomas Fitch et al.], *Reasons Why* (1764), reprinted in Bailyn, *Pamphlets*, p. 399. See also Patten, *Discourse at Hallifax*, pp. 13–15; [Goodricke,] *Observations*, p. 22.

CHAPTER FOURTEEN: PRECEDENTS OF ANALOGY

1 Anon., *Tyranny Unmasked*, pp. 46–47.

2 Letter published in colonial newspapers, May 1774, *American Archives* 1:338.

3 Adams, "Novanglus," pp. 227–31; Smith, *Appeals*, pp. 10–12. Despite Schuyler, few of the precedents of the pre-American English dominions were precedents of legislation. Black, "Constitution of Empire," pp. 1158–72.

4 Calvin's Case, 7 *Coke's Reports* 107, 77 *English Reports* pp. 378–411 (K.B., 1607); Black, "Constitution of Empire," pp. 1179–81; Smith, *Appeals*, pp. 466–69; Goebel, "Matrix of Empire," pp. xxiv, lx–lxi.

5 Palmer, *Impartial Account*, p. 40.

6 Answer of the House, 26 January 1773, *Briefs of Revolution*, p. 64.

7 Adams, "Novanglus," p. 217. See also Stokes, *View of Constitution*, pp. 13–14.

8 Gordon, *History*, p. 125 (quoting Hutchinson). See also Anon., *Tyranny Unmasked*, pp. 44–45. But see Replication of Governor Hutchinson, 16 February 1773, *Briefs of Revolution*, p. 88.

9 Answer of the House, 26 January 1773, *Briefs of Revolution*, p. 59.

10 [Bancroft,] *Remarks*, p. 25. Others besides Bancroft and Adams thought consent was needed. See, e.g., Letter from Benjamin Franklin to Thomas Cushing, 24 December 1770, Franklin, *Writings* 5:284.

11 Pownall, *Administration Fifth Edition*, 1: 142.

12 Speech of Lord Mansfield, Lords Debates, 10 February 1766, *Parliamentary History* 16:173. See also Pownall, *Administration*, p. 131; Anon., *Some Fugitive Thoughts*, p. 6. The argument also was made, of course, that if the colonies were outside the realm, the colonists were not British subjects and "can have no title to such privileges and immunities as the people of England derive under acts of parliament, nor to any other of those rights which are peculiar to British subjects within the realm." [Knox,] *Controversy*, pp. 6–7.

13 Black, "Constitution of Empire."

14 "Some Thoughts on the Constitution," Philadelphia, 12 June 1775, *American Archives* 2:962–63. See also [Mather,] *America's Appeal*, p. 30.

15 Instructions to Pennsylvania Representatives, 15 July 1774, *American Archives* 1:583.

16 Crane, "Franklin and Stamp Act," p. 72; Speech of Charles James Fox, Commons Debates, 16 December 1774, *Parliamentary History* 18:64.

17 For related discussion, see *Authority to Tax*, pp. 147–57, 160.

18 [Priestley,] *Address to Dissenters*, p. 19.

19 "A Short View of the ancient and present State of our American Colonies," *Remembrancer for 1776: Part II*, p. 11 footnote; [Whately,] *Regulations* reprinted in Morgan, *Prologue*, p. 21.

20 Anon., *Tyranny Unmasked*, pp. 38–39 (quoting Johnson); Replication of Governor Hutchinson, 16 February 1773, *Briefs of Revolution*, pp. 94–95.

21 See for example the report on the House of Lords debate, 3 February 1766, in which analogies were drawn between the law to be applied to the Stamp Act riots in Massachusetts and the law that was applied to riots earlier in the century that occurred in Glasgow and Edinburgh. Letter from H. Hamersley to Governor Horatio Sharpe, *Proceedings and Debates* 2:570–71.

22 As for example the frequent analogies drawn between the ship-money tax of Charles I and Parliament's taxation of the colonies. "That [ship money] was money raised, not by an English legislature, . . . but it was raised by the [Crown]. The principles are exactly the same. If they are to have their money given away, it is pretty much the same whether by one man or body of men. I do not see how any man who condemns the principle of ship money cannot condemn the principle [of the Townshend duties]." Speech of Richard Pennant, Commons Debates, 19 April 1774, *Proceedings and Debates* 4:181. See also *Authority to Tax*, pp. 25–27, 117–18.

23 "Were the American Colonies ever looked upon as independent states, surrendered to Britain by compact, or gained by conquest? If not, how can arguments drawn from such instances apply to them?" [Rivers,] *Letters*, p. 134.

24 Gray, *Doctor Price's Notions*, p. 53.

25 The analogy would be valid only if "Britain was possessed of an absolute and unlimited power over both . . . and it is plain that Britain hath no such power over America." Anon., *Importance of British Dominion*, p. 8.

26 Symonds, *Remarks Upon Essay*, pp. 3–52.

27 Wilson, *Considerations*, pp. 735–37.

28 Atwood, *Dependency of Ireland*, pp. 60–61; [Galloway,] *Historical Reflections*, p. 78; Pownall, *Administration Fifth Edition* 2:7. See also *Authority to Tax*, pp. 19–20, 150–53; Schuyler, *Empire*, pp. 9–10 (see also discussion of legislation binding Calais, pp. 11–12).

29 Anon., *Evidence of Common and Statute Laws*, p. 25; Blackstone, *Commentaries* 1:104. There was also the Isle of Man, but it was incorporated into the realm during the prerevolutionary controversy. Dulany, *English Laws*, p. 20; Blackstone, *Commentaries* 1:102; *Authority to Tax*, pp. 148, 154.

30 Campbell, *Political Survey* 1:520–21. For colonial judicial appeals, see Petitions of the New York General Assembly to the House of Lords and to the House of Commons, 11 December 1765, *New York Journal of Votes*, pp. 797, 801; Petition from the Assembly of Jamaica to the King, 28 December 1774, *Revolutionary Virginia* 2:364; "Book Review," *Gentleman's Magazine* 35 (1765): 578.

31 Egerton, *Discourse*, pp. 110–11. A century later, George Petyt said the same, but said Parliament could regulate the foreign trade of Ireland, also anticipating an American whig argument. Petyt, *Lex Parliamentaria*, p. 32.

32 Wheeler, "Calvin's Case," pp. 593–96; Bailyn, *Pamphlets*, p. 723 n. 38.

33 Anon., *Dialogue on Principles*, p. 77. The author admitted the case was interpreted differently: " . . . whereas it has been said that the meaning was, that *Ireland* should not be bound unless named." Ibid., p. 76. For the interpretation of an American whig, see Wilson, *Considerations*, p. 735–37. For support see Black, "Constitution of Empire," pp. 1178–79. For a contrary interpretation, see Madden, "Origins," pp. 12–13. See also, for discussion of Yearbook cases of similiar holdings, Anon., *Middle Temple Letter to Dublin*, p. 35.

34 Atwood, *Dependency of Ireland*, p. 191 (also quoting Molyneux); [Cary,] *Answer to Molyneux*, pp. 71–72.

35 Even the Irish Declaratory Act (see chap. 3, pp. 49–51) did not settle the question of supremacy as is sometimes supposed. Irish opposition remained, as is seen by the argument of Irish lords that, although the Irish Crown was annexed to the Crown of Great Britain, "yet this Kingdom being of itself a distinct Dominion, and no Part of the Kingdom of *England*, none can determine concerning the Affairs thereof, unless authorized thereto by the known Laws and Custom of this Kingdom, or by the express Consent of the King." "Humble Representation of the Lords," 17 October 1719, *Protests of Lords of Ireland*, p. 42.

36 [Sheridan,] *Review of Three Questions*, p. 15 (see also p. 28). It was even argued that the Irish Declaratory Act of 6 George I was not valid because Parliament went beyond its powers when enacting it and "violated the constitution of England." Anon., *Middle Temple Letter to Dublin*, pp. 20–31. On the imperial side, also, the same constitutional arguments were made against Ireland as against the colonies. See, e.g., Speech of Richard Rigby, Commons Debates, 16 December 1774, *Parliamentary History* 18:64.

37 Dobbs, *Letter to North*, pp. 6, 10. See also [Auckland,] *Considerations Submitted*, p. 45; *Celebrated Speeches of Flood*, p. 11. The Irish were more likely than the Americans to complain of trade regulation grievances on constitutional-law grounds. "If you thank the British Parliament, I said, for the enlargement of your foreign trade, you admit she can restrain it: if you admit she can restrain it, you admit her legislative authority; that is, you gain little in *commerce*, and you lose everything in *constitution*." Speech of 11 June 1782, Irish Commons, Flood, *Declaratory Act*, p. 13. See also Anon., *Policy of the Laws*, p. 123.

38 Greene, *Peripheries and Center*, pp. 61–62, 98; McIlwain, *Revolution*, pp. 32–53; Grey, "Unwritten Constitution," pp. 887–88. See also Bailyn, *Pamphlets*, p. 723 n. 38. But see Madden, "Relevance of Experience," pp. 16–18; Madden, "Origins," pp. 11–12.

39 Black, "Constitution of Empire," pp. 1179–98; [Flaherty,] "Empire Strikes Back," pp. 593–96; Greene, "Perspective of Law," pp. 67–69. See also

Wheeler, "Calvin's Case," p. 594. Contrary, see Schuyler, *Empire*, p. 238 n. 64.

40 Franklin, of course, referred to it when he wrote for an Irish audience. Franklin, *Address to Ireland*, pp. 14–15. Also William Molyneux's 1698 treatise *The Case of Ireland* was reprinted in part to support the whig constitutional case. *Boston Gazette*, 24 August 1767, p. 1, cols. 1–3.

41 Speech of Lord Mansfield, Lords Debates, 10 February 1766, *Parliamentary History* 16:177; Speech of Charles Yorke, Commons Debates, 3 February 1766, Ryder, "Parliamentary Diaries," p. 264. See also "William Pym" in *London General Evening Post*, 20 August 1765, reprinted in Morgan, *Prologue*, p. 98; Anon., *Examination of the Rights*, pp. 24–25. On 10 May 1776, a motion was made in the English Commons for putting the Americans on the same constitutional footing as the Irish. [Chalmers,] *Beauties*, p. 8.

42 Wilson, *Considerations*, pp. 739–41. See also Blackstone, *Commentaries* 1:99; Kettner, *American Citizenship*, p. 137 n. 15.

43 Chambers, *Lectures* 1:282; [Governor Hopkins,] Letter to the Editor, *Providence Gazette* (Postscript), 8 April 1765, p. 1, col. 3.

44 Blackstone, *Commentaries* 1:105; [Flaherty,] "Empire Strikes Back," p. 600 n. 45.

45 Blackstone, *Commentaries* 1:105.

46 Chambers, *Lectures* 1:282, 285.

47 Argument for the plaintiff, Campbell v. Hall, 20 *State Trials* 239, 289–90 (K.B., 1774); Blackstone, *Commentaries* 1:101; Speeches of Edward Thurlow and Sergeant John Glynn, Commons Debates, 26 May 1774, *Proceedings and Debates* 4:455, 464; Letter from Hugh Hamersley to Governor Horatio Sharpe, *Proceedings and Debates* 2:569 (reporting speech by Lord Mansfield, 3 February 1766).

48 Wilson, *Considerations*, pp. 738–40; *Proceedings and Debates* 2:8 (quoting Horace Walpole's report of debate between Beckford and Townshend). But see argument reversed, that "Ireland is not to be compared with [conquered] Virginia." Anon., *Policy of the Laws*, pp. 125–26.

49 Anon., *Serious and Impartial Observations*, pp. 32–33. For an argument that the peoples of Ireland, America, and Britain were constitutionally equal, see Speech of Alderman Frederick Bull, Commons Debates, 18 November 1777, *Parliamentary History* 19:427.

50 Anon., *Examination of the Rights*, p. 26.

51 [Macfarlane,] *George Third*, p. 392 (see also p. 390). See also Lucas, "To the Lord Lieutenant," p. 9. By the age of the American Revolution, it was Irish parliamentary practice to raise questions initially in the two houses by discussing "what they call *heads of a bill*, which the lord-lieutenant is desired afterwards to transmit to the king, who selects out of them what clauses he thinks proper, or sets the whole aside; and is not expected to give, at any time, a precise answer to them." De Lolme, *Constitution: New Edition*, p. 236 footnote. For a 1770 defense of Poynings Law as constitutional, see [Power,] *Comparative State*. There had been some thought to

applying Poynings Law to the colonies. Goebel, "Matrix of Empire," p. lviii.

52 Lucas, "To the Lord Lieutenant," p. 9; [Howard,] *Some Questions Upon the Legislative*, p. 7.

53 Judicial appeals from the colonies lay to the privy council (which for Ireland originated legislative bills). For Ireland, appeals lay to the House of Lords. Wilson, *Considerations*, p. 737. Ireland, like England, was subject to a different admiralty jurisdiction than that of the colonies. *Boston Gazette*, 9 January 1769, p. 2, col. 2.

54 For an argument that all these constitutional differences "proved insignificant," see [Flaherty,] "Empire Strikes Back," p. 600.

55 For the depth of the feeling that this warning aroused, see Letter from Town of Pelham to Boston Committee of Correspondence, 16 November 1773, Parmenter, *Pelham*, p. 125; Letter from the Town of Colrain to Boston Committee of Correspondence, 31 January 1774, Bushman, *King and People*, p. 205.

CHAPTER FIFTEEN: PRECEDENTS OF REGULATION

1 Black, "Constitution of Empire," pp. 1163–64; Schuyler, *Empire*, pp. 8–25.

2 [Knox,] *Controversy* (Dublin Edition), pp. 155–56.

3 Pownall, *Administration*, pp. 138–39.

4 Ibid., p. 139.

5 "An Act for forbidding Trade with the Barbadoes, Virginia, Bermuda, and Antego," *Acts and Ordinaces* 2:425–26. For imperialist arguments, see [Sewall,] *Americans Roused*, p. 12; [Macpherson,] *Retrospective View*, pp. 4–5; Roebuck, *Enquiry Whether the Guilt*, p. 9.

6 "An Act for increase of Shipping, and Encouragement of the Navigation of this Nation," *Acts and Ordinances* 2:559–62.

7 "An Act . . . ," *Acts and Ordinances* 2:425; Stokes, *View of Constitution*, pp. 4–5; Williamson, "Imperial Policy," pp. 215–16.

8 Mauduit, *Short View*, p. 41; Dunn, *Puritans and Yankees*, p. 99.

9 Leonard, "Massachusettensis," p. 66; Leigh, *Considerations*, p. 117. See also [Lind,] *Thirteenth Parliament*, pp. 188–89.

10 Jefferson, *Summary View*, pp. 123–24. Similarly, see A Letter Supposed Written by Edmund Burke . . . , May 1774, *American Archives* 1:339.

11 Adams, "Novanglus," p. 207. Adams's discussion refers to the act of 1660, which was the royalist reenactment of the Commonwealth's ordinance. "An act for encouraging and increasing of shipping and navigation." 12 Charles II, cap. 18.

12 [Dickinson,] "Instructions . . . ," 15 July 1774, *American Archives* 1:586; Pownall, *Administration Fifth Edition* 1:ix; Stokes, *View of Constitution*, p. 5; [Lind,] *Thirteenth Parliament*, p. 191; [Knox,] *Controversy* (Dublin Edition), pp. 154–55. See also Roebuck, *Enquiry Whether the Guilt*, pp. 9–10; Speech of George Dempster, Commons Debates, 6 May 1774, *Proceedings and Debates* 4:399. For a whig statement, see Untitled Paper,

June 1776, *Papers of Iredell* 1:390 footnote. A related principle was that "precedents of unconstitutional power" were not binding. Anon., *Fair Trial*, p. 219; "An Anti-Despot," Address to New York, [2 June 1775], *American Archives* 2:883.

13 12 Charles II, cap. 18; Anon., *Letter to a Member*, pp. 18–19.

14 Labaree, *Royal Instructions* 2:752–60.

15 Dickinson, *Letters*, pp. 315 footnote (for Dickinson's theory, see pp. 312–15); Jefferson, *Summary View*, p. 124; [Sewall,] *Americans Roused*, pp. 13–14.

16 Thomas, "British Imperial Policy," pp. 619–20; Keir, *Constitutional History*, p. 348; Knollenberg, *Origin*, p. 157; Kammen, *Empire and Interest*, p. 23; [Knox,] *Controversy*, pp. 164–66.

17 Speech of Edmund Burke, Commons Debates, 19 April 1774, *Proceedings and Debates* 4:209. See also Speech of Barlow Trecothick, Commons Debates, 7 December 1768, *Proceedings and Debates* 3:35; [Macfarlane,] *George Third*, pp. 249–50; Roebuck, *Enquiry Whether the Guilt*, pp. 11–12.

18 Fairfax Resolutions, 18 July 1774, *American Archives* 1:598. See also Jefferson, *Summary View*, p. 124; Ramsay, *History*, p. 42.

19 *Annual Register 1766*, p. [42]; [Kames,] *History of Man* 1:504 footnote; [Glover,] *Considerations*, p. 28. See also [Lind,] *Thirteenth Parliament*, p. 251; Jefferson, *Summary View*, p. 124; Anon., *Justice and Policy*, p. 57; [Macfarlane,] *George Third*, pp. 249–50; Thomas, "Effects of Imperial Policy," pp. 132–33.

20 [Raynal,] *Sentiments*, p. 7; Christopher Gadsden, "Letter to Mr. Timothy," *Freeman Letters*, p. 62; Moore, *Taxing Colonies*, p. 43. See also Thomas, "Effects of Imperial Policy," pp. 140, 195 (but see p. 146); Harper, "Mercantilism and the Revolution," p. 157.

21 Memorial from the New York General Assembly to the House of Lords, 25 March 1775, *American Archives* 1:1317; [Wells,] *Political Reflections*, p. 28.

22 Resolutions of New York General Assembly, 3 March 1775, *American Archives* 1:1300; Representation from New York General Assembly to the House of Commons, *Gentleman's Magazine* 45 (1775): 248; Namier, *Age of Revolution*, p. 277 (quoting Boston Merchants in "Statement of the Trade and Fisheries of Massachusetts," 1764); Letter from John Dickinson to William Pitt, 21 December 1765, Morgan, *Prologue*, p. 122; Anon., *Considerations Upon the Act*, pp. 10–12, 16–17; Anon., *Reasons Against*, pp. 5, 7. See also Andrews, "Western Phrase," p. 769 n. 24.

23 "F. S.," to the *London Chronicle*, *Scots Magazine* 30 (1768): 28; Anon., *To the Princess of Wales*, p. 30; Ritcheson, *British Politics*, p. 101 n. 40. See also Jefferson, *Summary View*, p. 124.

24 Memorial of the Stamp Act Congress to House of Lords, 22 October 1765, *Account of Stamp Act Congress*, p. 17; Declarations of the Stamp Act Congress, and New York Resolves, 18 December 1765, Morgan, *Prologue*, pp. 63, 62.

25 Petition to the King, 26 October 1774, *Journal of the First Congress*, p. 136; Petition of the House of Representatives to the King, 13 February 1775, *New Jersey Votes and Proceedings* (January 1775), p. 59. Similarly see Letter from the New York Committee of Correspondence to the Mayor, Aldermen, and Common Council of London, 5 May 1775, *Scots Magazine* 37 (1775): 399; Pomfret (Connecticut) Resolves, 25 December 1765, *Gazette & News-Letter*, 9 January 1766, p. 1, col. 2.

26 Message from the Lower House of Assembly to Governor Horatio Sharpe, 6 December 1766, *Maryland Votes and Proceedings* (1766), p. 150; South Carolina Resolves, 29 November 1765, Morgan, *Prologue*, p. 59; Letter from Governor William Pitkin to Earl of Hillsborough, 10 June 1768, *Public Records of Connecticut* 13:84 (writing on behalf of the Assembly); Petition of New York General Assembly to the King, 24 March 1775, *American Archives* 1:1315 (saying "oppressive and impolitick"); Representation from New York General Assembly to the House of Commons, *Gentleman's Magazine* 45 (1775): 248. See also Dickinson, "Non-Importation," pp. 412–13 (listing the "most grievous" of the restrictions on trade); [Drayton et al.,] *The Letters*, pp. 37–38. The complaint was old. See [Littleton,] *Groans of Plantations*, pp. 4–5 (Barbadoes, 1689).

27 "Proceedings in the Session of Parliament 1766–67," *Scots Magazine* 30 (1768): 516 (reporting on a petition of New York merchants); Instructions of Pennsylvania Provincial Congress to Deputies to Continental Congress, 15 July 1774, *London Magazine* 43 (1774): 586; Morgan, "Colonial Ideas," p. 317 (quoting Rhode Island Petition to the King, 29 November 1764) See also "British American," *Gentleman's Magazine* 36 (1766): 613; Rusticus, *Good of Community*, p. 27 (Massachusetts, 1754).

28 *London Magazine* 43 (1774): 543 (quoting Lord Kames); [Kames,] *History of Man* 1:504 footnote; Speech of the Duke of Richmond, Lords Debates, 31 October 1776, *Scots Magazine* 38 (1776): 572; "F. S." to *London Chronicle*, January, 1768, *Scots Magazine* 30 (1768): 27; *Letter from F. B.*, 27 August 1774, *Scots Magazine* 36 (1774): 417; Anon., *Plan of Reconciliation with America*, p. 46.

29 Letter from H. Hamerley to Governor Horatio Sharpe, *Proceedings and Debates* 2:565 (reporting Mansfield speech of 17 December 1765).

30 Speech of Sir George Meredith, *London Magazine* 44 (1775): 447; Speech of Lord Townshend, Lords Debates, 20 January 1775, *Parliamentary History* 18:166; Speeches of John Wilkes and Lord North, Commons Debates, 10 December 1777, *Parliamentary History* 19:572, 577. See also Clark, *British Opinion*, p. 225 (quoting Lord Lyttleton); Anderson, *Interest of Britain*, appendix, p. 5; [Anderson,] *Free Thoughts*, p. 2, col. 2.

31 Speech of the Duke of Richmond, Lords Debates, 31 October 1776, *Scots Magazine* 38 (1776): 572 and *Hibernian Magazine* 6 (1776): 763.

32 Reid, "Economic Burden," p. 90.

33 Resolutions of New York General Assembly, 3 March 1775, *American Archives* 1:1298–1300; Declarations and Resolves, 14 October 1774, *Journals of Congress* 1:71–72 (It is not clear from the resolution which statute

Congress found objectionable. Some printed versions of the resolution cite 8 George III, cap. 22, which did not require a bond). For the jury right and the admiralty grievance, see *Authority of Rights*, pp. 47–59, 177–83.

34 Letter from the Continental Congress to People of Great Britain, 5 September 1774, *London Magazine* 43 (1774): 629.

35 *Authority to Tax*, pp. 65–84; Franklin, *Address to Ireland*, pp. 15–17; Lee, *Appeal to Justice*, p. 26.

36 Anon., *Serious and Impartial Observations*, p. 19.

37 Koebner, *Empire*, p. 217. For North's scheme, see *Authority to Tax*, pp. 250–53.

38 Resolves of the South Carolina Convention, 8 July 1774, *American Archives* 1:526; Jack P. Greene, "Introduction" to *Commemoration Ceremony*, p. 41.

39 Minutes of 3 March 1775, *Journal of New York Assembly* (1766–76), p. 54; Letter from Virginia House of Burgesses to Pennsylvania House of Representatives, 9 May 1768, *Pennsylvania Archives* 7:6191; Lovejoy, *Rhode Island Politics*, pp. 33, 40–41; Anon., *Reasons Against*; Anon., *Considerations Upon the Act*; Benjamin Franklin's Plan for a Durable Union, January 1775, *American Archives* 2:184.

40 *Memoirs of William Smith* 1:30; Bland, *An Inquiry*, p. 23; Anon., *Plan to Reconcile*, p. 3.

41 Boston Merchants, *Observations*, p. 20.

42 [Hicks,] *Nature of Parliamentary Power*, pp. xii, xiv; *South-Carolina Gazette*, 4 April 1768, p. 1, col. 4. See also Wagner, "Judicial Review," p. 575.

43 *Papers of Jefferson* 1:356, 418, 425. The authority to regulate may have been challenged in the Resolutions of Albemarle County, Virginia, 26 July 1774, *American Archives* 1:638. There is little evidence Americans thought trade restrictions a cause for the war. But see *Virginia Gazette*, 12 April 1776, discussed in *Revolutionary Virginia* 6:282; Rakove, *Beginnings*, p. 36 (quoting Thomas Mason); Ammerman, *Common Cause*, pp. 3–4.

44 Instructions of the Pennsylvania Congress, 15 July 1774, *London Magazine* 43 (1774): 586–87. Another Pennsylvania solution, offered by James Wilson, was to make the authority to regulate part of the prerogative. Rakove, *Beginnings*, p. 36.

45 Morgan, *Challenge*, p. 23; Morgan, "Colonial Ideas," pp. 325–26.

CHAPTER SIXTEEN: AUTHORITY TO REGULATE

1 *Boston Gazette*, 27 January 1772, reprinted in Adams, *Writings* 2:323.

2 Southwick, "Molasses Act," p. 399.

3 Jefferson, *Summary View*, p. 123; [Paine,] *Common Sense*, p. 39. Adam Smith referred to the resolutions on colonial trade as "a manifest violation of the most sacred rights of mankind." Larkin, *Property in Eighteenth Century*, p. 144.

4 New York Petition to Commons, 18 October 1764, Morgan, *Prologue*, pp. 11–12.

5 Minutes of 3 March 1775, *Journal of New York Assembly* (1766–76), pp. 53, 56.

6 Representation and Remonstrance of New York General Assembly to the House of Commons, 25 March 1775, *Gentleman's Magazine* 45 (1775): 248. The leading magazines in the two other capitals also thought this Representation important enough to print. *Scots Magazine* 37 (1775): 236; *Hibernian Magazine* 5 (1775): 359–350*.

7 Petitions of the Council and Burgesses to the House of Lords and to the House of Commons, 14 April 1768, *Journal of Burgesses* 11:167, 169; Message from Burgesses to Massachusetts House of Representatives, 9 May 1768, *American Gazette*, p. 19; Petition of New Hampshire House of Representatives to the King, 29 October 1768, *Documents of New Hampshire*, p. 249.

8 Letter from Massachusetts House to Lord Camden, 29 January 1768, *Boston Post-Boy*, 4 April 1768, p. 1, col. 2. See also Letter from Massachusetts House to Henry Seymour Conway, 13 February 1768, *Boston Post-Boy*, 28 March 1768, p. 2, col. 1; Petition of Massachusetts House to the King, 20 January 1768, *Speeches*, p. 123; Letter from James Otis et al., 20 December 1765 and Instructions of Boston, May 1764, Adams, *Writings* 1:67, 5; Instructions of Boston, 17 June 1768, Adams, *Works* 3:502.

9 Letter from Governor Josiah Lyndon to Lord Hillsborough, 17 September 1768, *Rhode Island Colony Records* 6:562. For a similar argument by an earlier Rhode Island governor, see Hopkins, *Rights*, pp. 512–13.

10 *Authority to Tax*, pp. 44–52.

11 *Papers of Iredell* 1:333, 375–76; *Boston Gazette*, 20 January 1772 and 27 January 1772, reprinted in Adams, *Writings* 2:313–26.

12 Resolutions of Middlesex County, July 1774, *Revolutionary Virginia* 1.143–44. See also Petition of the Stamp Act Congress to the House of Commons, 23 October 1765, Morgan, *Prologue*, p. 68.

13 Speech of Isaac Barré, Commons Debates, 3 February 1766, Ryder, "Parliamentary Diaries," p. 274; [Draper,] *Thoughts of a Traveller*, p. 14; Ramsay, *History*, p. 48.

14 Headlam, "Constitutional Struggle," p. 671 (see also p. 665). See similarly Christie, *Crisis*, p. 14. Of course, there were contemporaries who denied the *constitutionality* of the distinction. *Boston News-Letter* (Supplement), 11 April 1765, p. 1, col. 2.

15 [Fitch et al.,] *Reasons Why*, p. 19; Johnstone, "Speech of November, 1775," pp. 86–87. See also Hopkins, *Rights*, p. 521 (governor of Rhode Island); Otis, *Rights*, pp. 467–68 (discussing the Sugar Act of 1733).

16 To the People of England, 24 January 1770, [Lee,] *Junius Americanus*, p. 71.

17 Petition of Virginia "General Assembly" to the House of Lords, 16 April 1768, *Revolutionary Virginia* 1:58; Petition of the New York General Assembly to the House of Commons, 18 October 1764, Morgan, *Prologue*, p. 12. For the most influential discussion of the distinction, see Dickinson, *Letters*, pp. 332, 349; Bailyn, *Pamphlets*, p. 128.

18 Anon., *Examination of the Rights*, p. 29; Anon., *Constitutional Right*, pp. 31–32.

19 Petyt, *Lex Parliamentaria*, p. 32.

20 "But how the Commercial Benefits of the *whole* Empire can be *secured* to the *Mother Country* and at the Same Time to its *American Members*, I think will puzzle a Causist to determine." Letter from Joseph Galloway to Samuel Verplanck, 30 December 1774, *Letters of Delegates to Congress* 1:284.

21 Speech of Governor James Wright to the Commons House of Assembly, 24 December 1768, *Georgia Commons House Journal* 14:657; Speech of Richard Hussey, Commons Debates, 3 February 1766, *Proceedings and Debates* 2:141; Speech of Earl Gower, Lords Debates, 30 May 1777, *Parliamentary History* 19:321. See also [Burke,] *Observations on Late State*, p. 122; Roebuck, *Enquiry Whether the Guilt*, p. 50; Williamson, "Imperial Policy," p. 216. For doubts of law expressed by the American whig side, see "The British American, No. VII," 14 July 1774, *American Archives* 1:541; [Hicks,] *Nature of Parliamentary Power*, p. 28.

22 Petition from the Assembly of Jamaica to the King, 28 December 1774, *Revolutionary Virginia* 2:364; *Gentleman's Magazine* 45 (1775): 618 footnote. Discussed in Schuyler, *Empire*, pp. 135–36.

23 [Dickinson,] "An Address to the Committee of Correspondence in Barbados," *South-Carolina Gazette*, 4 August 1766, p. 1, col. 3.

24 [Dulany,] *Considerations on the Propriety*, p. 16.

25 Adams, "Novanglus," p. 199.

26 [Dickinson,] Instructions of the Pennsylvania Representatives, 15 July 1774, *American Archives* 1:592 (quoting Blackstone, *Commentaries*); [Wells,] *Political Reflections*, p. 17. See also Cooper, *The Crisis*, p. 28.

27 Bland, *Colonel Dismounted*, p. 22; Speech of Edmund Burke, Commons Debates, 19 April 1774, *Burke on American Revolution*, pp. 66–67; [Whately,] *Regulations Lately Made*, p. 40.

28 "L.," *Letter to G[renville]*, p. 39; Abingdon, "Speech on Right," p. 38; "To the Author of the *Centinel*," *American Gazette*, p. 46.

29 [Burke,] *Observations on Late State*, p. 117; Speech of Edmund Burke, Commons Debates, 19 April 1774, *Burke on American Revolution*, p. 41; *Junius Americanus*, "To *Junius*," *Political Register* 9 (1771): 324.

30 Dickinson, *Letters*, p. 312; [Dickinson,] Instructions of the Pennsylvania Representatives, 15 July 1774, *American Archives* 1:592; Rakove, *Beginnings*, p. 37 (quoting Dickinson, *Essay . . . .* [1774]). Dickinson also seems to have conceptualized the authority by analogy to international or transnational law. Trade was outside the nation and once had been regulated by the Crown without participation by Parliament. "When an universal empire is established, and not till then, can regulations of trade properly be called acts of supreme legislature." [Dickinson,] *New Essay*, p. 113.

31 *Authority to Tax*, pp. 75–84.

32 Abingdon, *Thoughts on Burke's Letter*, p. vi; Abingdon, *Dedication*, p. vii. See also [Erskine,] *Reflections on the Rise*, p. 15; [Lee,] *Speech Intended*, p. 55; Ramsay, *History*, p. 48. For rejection of the "protection" theory, see "Samuel Ward's Notes for a Speech in Congress," 12 October 1774, *Letters of Delegates to Congress* 1:186–87.

33 Hopkins, *Rights*, p. 512; Mauduit, *Legislative Authority*, pp. 8, 13; Letter from Governeur Morris to Mr. Penn, 20 May 1774, *American Archives*

1:343. See also [Dulany,] *Considerations on the Propriety*, p. 34; Chronus, *Gazette & Post-Boy*, 13 January 1772, p. 4, col. 1.

34 [Seabury,] *View of the Controversy*, p. 15. See also [Fitch et al.,] *Reasons Why*, p. 18; [Hawley,] "To the Inhabitants," 13 April 1775, *American Archives* 2:330–31; Anon., *Reflections on the Contest*, p. 22; Letter of 9 June 1768, *American Gazette*, p. 66.

35 Speech of Lord Chatham, Lords Debates, 20 November 1777, Chatham, *Genuine Abstracts*, p. 44. See also Cooper, *The Crisis*, p. 28; Anon., *Political Balance*, pp. 42–43; [Macfarlane,] *George Third*, p. 243 (summarizing the American argument).

36 Letter from John Dickinson to Willim Pitt, 21 December 1765, Morgan, *Prologue*, p. 121; New York Petition to the House of Commons, 18 October 1764, ibid., p. 11; Gadsden, "Letter to Mr. Timothy," *Freeman Letters*, p. 62. See also Instructions of Boston, 17 June 1768, *Political Register* 3 (1768): 79; *Boston Chronicle*, 20 June 1768, p. 254, col. 1.

37 Anon., *Second Answer to Wesley*, p. 15.

38 Anon., *Considerations Upon Rights of Colonists*, p. 11; "James Duane's Propositions," 7–22 September 1774, *Letters of Delegates to Congress* 1: 38. See also "Instructions," July 1774, [Dickinson,] *New Essay*, p. 17.

39 Middlesex Resolutions, 15 July 1774, *American Archives* 1: 551. See, similarly, Address of the House of Assembly of the Counties upon Delaware, 27 October 1768, *Delaware House Minutes* (1765–70), p. 167.

40 Burke, "Speech on American Taxation," p. 146 (see also pp. 136, 138–39, 142–43); Hutchinson, "Dialogue," pp. 375–76; "James Duane's Speech to the Committee on Rights," 8 September 1774, *Letters of Delegates to Congress* 1: 53.

41 Adams, "Novanglus," p. 141.

42 For an excellent example, see Resolutions of Fairfax County, Virginia, 18 July 1774, *American Archives* 1: 598. See also Untitled Paper, June 1776, *Papers of Iredell*, p. 375. Necessity is mentioned in private correspondence. Letter from Governeur Morris to Mr. Penn, 20 May 1774, *American Archives* 1: 343; Letter from Benjamin Franklin to Lord Kames, April 1767, Crane, "Franklin and Stamp Act," p. 75.

43 York County Resolutions, 18 July 1774, *American Archives* 1: 596. For an explanation of the theory, see Philo-Americae to Phil-Britannia, *Boston Post-Boy*, 5 December 1768, p. 1, col. 1.

44 "An Act for regulating and ordering the Troops that are or may be raised for the Defence of this Colony," May 1775, *Public Records of Connecticut* 15: 21; Adams, "Novanglus," pp. 206, 140.

45 Adams, "Novanglus," pp. 207, 193. See also ibid., p. 122; Greene, *Peripheries and Center*, p. 135.

46 "Some Thoughts on the Constitution," Philadelphia, 12 June 1775, *American Archives* 2:964; Petition from the Jamaica Assembly to the King, 28 December 1774, *Revolutionary Virginia* 2:365.

47 Instructions of Pennsylvania, 15 July 1774, *London Magazine* 43 (1774): 586–87.

48 Ibid.

49 See, e.g., "Proposed Vindication and Offer to Parliament, Drawn up in a Committee of Congress," 25 June 1775, *American Archives* 2:1083 ("willing to enter into a covenant with *Britain*, that she shall fully possess, enjoy, and exercise that right for a hundred years to come"); Abingdon, *Dedication*, p. viii; [Dickinson,] *New Essay*, p. 123; Benjamin Franklin's Vindication, [June–July? 1775], *Letters of Delegates to Congress* 1:565.

50 Duane also turned to "contract" to resolve the controversy over rights. *Authority of Rights*, pp. 229–31.

51 Ammerman, *Common Cause*, pp. 55–56; Jack P. Greene, "Introduction" to *Commemoration Ceremony*, p. 45; Rakove, *Beginnings*, p. 73.

52 Speech of Joseph Galloway, First Continental Congress, 28 September 1774, *Commemoration Ceremony*, p. 95.

53 [Dickinson,] *New Essay*, pp. 123, 110.

54 "John Dickinson's Notes for a Speech in Congress," 23–25 May 1775, *Letters of Delegates to Congress* 1: 378–79 (see also pp. 386–87); Silas Deane's Diary, 16 May 1775, ibid., p. 352.

55 Rakove, *Beginnings*, p. 73.

56 John Adams, "Notes of Debates," 28 September 1774, *Letters of Delegates to Congress* 1:111; "James Duane's Propositions Before the Committee on Rights," 7–22 September 1774, ibid., pp. 39, 41.

57 "James Duane's Notes for a Speech in Congress," 13 October 1774, ibid., pp. 189, 190; "John Adam's Diary," 13 October 1774, ibid., p. 189.

58 Declaration of Rights, 14 October 1774, *Journal of the First Congress*, p. 61. It is wrong to say, "The delegates had carefully avoided any reference to Parliament's right to regulate trade." The right was one of consent. Ammerman, *Common Cause*, p. 61.

59 Hopkins, *Rights*, pp. 512–13 ("cheerfully to obey and patiently to submit"); Letter from Governor Josias Lyndon to the King, 16 September 1768, *Rhode Island Colony Records* 6:560. See also Cooke, *Election Sermon*, p. 45 ("cheerfully submit to regulations of trade, productive of the common interest").

60 Address, 25 April 1768, *Scots Magazine* 30 (1768): 524. For Dickinson's denial that he was the author, see *Gentleman's Magazine* 39 (1769): 343.

61 Letter from Virginia House to New Hampshire House, 9 May 1768, *Documents of New Hampshire*, pp. 250–51. For criticism of the expression, see Address of Governor James Wright to Georgia's Commons House of Assembly, 24 December 1768, *Massachusetts Gazette*, 13 February 1769, p. 2, col. 1.

62 Resolves of Fairfax County, 18 July 1774, *Revolutionary Virginia* 1:128. It has been suggested that this formulation was the inspiration for Congress's wording. Rakove, *Beginnings*, p. 36.

63 Instructions for Deputies to the Continental Congress, 6 August 1774, *Revolutionary Virginia* 1:237. Similar language was used in Great Britain. For example, see Speech of Mr. Cruger, Commons Debates, 16 December 1774, *American Archives* 1:1483 ("the Colonies tacitly acquiesced"); Anon., *Letter to Hillsborough*, p. 15 ("tacitly submitted to the superintending authority").

64 General Conway's Bill for Conciliation with the Colonies, 5 May 1780, Conway, *Peace Speech*, p. 49; Representation and Remonstrance of New York General Assembly to the House of Commons, 25 March 1775, *Journal of New York Assembly* (1766–76), p. 116 (see also Memorial to the Lords, same date, p. 114).

65 Letter from the New York Committee of Correspondence to the Mayor, Aldermen, and Common Council of London, 5 May 1775, *Scots Magazine* 37 (1775): 400; Address, Remonstrance, and Petition of the Lord Mayor, Aldermen, and Livery of London to the King, 11 April 1775, *London Magazine* 44 (1775): 209.

CHAPTER SEVENTEEN: PRECEDENTS OF LEGISLATION

1 New York Memorial to the House of Lords, 25 March 1775, *Journal of New York Assembly* (1766–76), p. 114. For an early statement of the principle, less carefully worded, by a colonial governor, see Hopkins, *Rights*, pp. 512–13.

2 Speech of William Blackstone, Commons Debates, 3 February 1766, Gipson, "Debate on Repeal," p. 17; [Knox,] *Controversy*, p. 175; Speech of Charles Mellish, Commons Debates, 27 October 1775, *Proceedings and Debates* 6:131; Shebbeare, *Essay on National Society*, p. 99. See also Whately, *Regulations Lately Made*, reprinted in Morgan, *Prologue*, p. 19. Some historians have done the same, treating trade-regulations statutes as if they were precedents for every kind of legislation. Keir, *Constitutional History*, pp. 352–53; Osgood, "American Revolution," pp. 70–71.

3 Stokes, *View of Constitution*, pp. 32–41; "Rights of G. Britain asserted," *Scots Magazine* 38 (1776): 66.

4 [Macpherson,] *Rights of Great Britain*, pp. 30–40, 101–2; [Lind,] *Thirteenth Parliament*, pp. 208–9, 224–25; [Knox,] *Controversy*, pp. 175–77; [Whately,] *Regulations Lately Made*, pp. 104–7 (list of customs duties); Pownall, *Administration*, pp. 126–28; Tucker, *True Interest of Britain*, pp. 5–10; Speech of Charles Mellish, Commons Debates, 27 October 1775, *Proceedings and Debates* 6: 131; Shebbeare, *Essay on National Society*, p. 99; Roebuck, *Enquiry whether the Guilt*, pp. 13–14; Anon., *Plain Question*, p. 10. For an especially impressive collection of all precedents, see letter dated 28 November 1768, from Boston to London, *Boston Chronicle*, 1 May 1769, p. 138, col. 2. Some historians have also indiscriminately compounded precedents, as they should if they disagree with the colonial constitutional theory that regulation was a special category. Gipson, *British Empire* 3: 274–75; Schuyler, *Empire*, pp. 11–25.

5 Speech of Charles Jenkinson, Commons Debates, 26 January 1775, *Proceedings and Debates* 5:311; Edmund Burke, "Letter to the Sheriffs," reprinted in Peach, *Richard Price*, p. 271; Maitland, *Constitutional History*, pp. 382–83; Gough, *Fundamental Law*, p. 24 (discussing Maitland).

6 Gipson, *British Empire* 3: 275.

7 Act of 1763: 3 George III, cap. 22, sec. 9.

8 Sugar Act: 6 George II, cap. 13, sec. 4.

9 Gipson, "Debate on Repeal," p. 16 (quoting Yorke in Commons Debates, 3 February 1766); Hopkins, *Rights*, p. 511. For other interpretations of the statutes as evidence of Americans' right to equality with Britons, see "A British American," *Gentleman's Magazine* 36 (1766): 613; Massachusetts Instructions to Jasper Mauduit, *Mauduit Letters*, pp. 41–42; Letter from Æqqus, 16 January 1766, *London Magazine* 35 (1766): 33; Letter from Samuel Adams to John Smith, 19 December 1765, Adams, *Writings* 1: 45–46.

10 [Knox,] *Controversy*, p. 177. The acts were: 13 George II, cap. 7; 20 George II, cap. 44.

11 8 George I, cap. 15, sec. 24 (Fur Act). Some statutes of enumeration were, 25 Charles II, cap. 7; 10 & 11 William III, cap. 10; 3 & 4 Anne, cap. 5; 4 George II, cap. 15. Again, it should be recalled that the American distinction did not take into consideration the harshness of a statute or its economic burdens. The Act of 8 George I, requiring that all furs exported from the colonies be imported directly into Great Britain and prohibiting colonial fur merchants from seeking markets elsewhere, was economically unreasonable, yet, as a regulation of trade, was unquestionably legal under the American whig constitutional theory. The uneconomical costs and the partiality of the statute were irrelevant to the question of constitutionality. Just as constitutional were all the statutes enumerating products that had been landed in Britain and most of the other acts of Parliament that are accorded much importance in histories of the American Revolution.

12 21 George II, cap. 30 (bounties); 6 Anne, cap. 30 (foreign coins).

13 Report of the Attorney and Solicitor Generals to the Board of Trade, 25 June 1767, Colden, *Letters and Papers*, pp. 121–22 (ruling that 12 Anne, cap. 18 and 4 George I, cap. 12 apply to the colonies).

14 7 & 8 William III, cap. 22, sec. 6; Shebbeare, *Essay on National Society*, p. 99.

15 Phileirene, "My Worthy Friends," *Gazette & News-Letter*, 30 March 1775, p. 1, col. 2 (discussing 7 & 8 William III, cap. 22, sec. 7 and 24 George II, cap. 51).

16 [Knox,] *Controversy*, p. 172 (referring to 7 & 8 William, cap. 22); Anon., *Letter to a Member*, p. 20 (referring to the Act of William; 3 & 4 Anne, cap. 5; 8 Anne, cap. 13; 5 George II, cap. 7; 13 George II, cap. 4).

17 Anon., *Supremacy of Legislature*, pp. 25–26. Oaths: 11 & 12 William III, cap. 12.

18 [Sewall,] *Americans Roused*, p. 14; [Dulany,] *Considerations on the Propriety*, p. 39. For an extreme claim of colonial legislative autonomy with regard to the military, see Quincy, *Observations with Thoughts*, p. 450 footnote.

19 29 George II, cap. 35, sec. 9 (house entering), sec. 3 (volunteers not subject to process), sec. 2 (indentured servants). It was wrongly claimed that the statute dissolved indentures by discharging servants from all obligations. Pownall, *Administration*, p. 126. See also *Scots Magazine* 38 (1776): 68.

20 2 George II, cap. 35, sec. 2; 8 George I, cap. 12, sec. 5. It was claimed that the statutes prohibited cutting pitch and tar trees on private lands when not enclosed. [Knox,] *Controversy* (Dublin Edition), pp. 175–76. See also [Lind,] *Thirteenth Parliament*, p. 211.

21 3 & 4 Anne, cap. 10, secs. 6 and 7; Anon., *Supremacy of Legislature*, p. 26.

22 8 George I, cap. 12, sec. 5; [Whately,] *Considerations on Trade*, p. 227; "Junius Americanus," *Boston Evening-Post*, 28 January 1771, p. 1, col. 2. For a broad interpretation of the acts, see Richard Jackson's opinion of 5 June 1771, *Revolution Documents* 3:110.

23 5 George II, cap. 7; Anon., *Arguments in Support of Supremacy*, p. 47.

24 5 George II, cap. 7, sec. 1; [Lind,] *Thirteenth Parliament*, pp. 215–16. See also Stokes, *View of Constitution*, pp. 372–374; Pownall, *Administration*, p. 126.

25 5 George II, cap. 7, sec. 4. See also Pownall, *Administration*, p. 126; Stokes, *View of Constitution*, p. 373; [Knox,] *Controversy*, p. 14; [Knox,] *Claim of the Colonies*, pp. 11–12; Anon., *Supremacy of Legislature*, p. 28; Anon., *Plain Question*, p. 9.

26 [Knox,] *Controversy* (Dublin Edition), pp. 178–79. "What the provincial legislatures would not, or at least did not do, parliament did for them." [Lind,] *Thirteenth Parliament*, p. 217. See also Tucker, *Letter to Burke*, p. 30.

27 Dulany, *Considerations*, p. 641; Jefferson, *Summary View*, p. 125.

28 [Lind,] *Thirteenth Parliament*, pp. 214–15.

29 *Authority to Tax*, pp. 171–80.

30 [Dulany,] *Considerations on the Propriety*, pp. 39–40 (discussing 9 Anne, cap. 10).

31 See, e.g., *Boston Evening-Post,* 5 August 1765, p. 2, col. 1, 9 September 1765, p. 1, cols. 2–3, 7 October 1765, p. 4, col. 1.

32 Roebuck, *Enquiry Whether the Guilt*, p. 13; [Knox,] *Controversy* (Dublin Edition), p. 176; Butler, *Sermon Preached in Dublin*, pp. 6–7.

33 *Boston Evening-Post*, 5 August 1765, p. 2, col. 1.

34 *Boston Evening-Post*, 30 July 1764, p. 2, cols. 1–3.

35 [Mather,] *America's Appeal*, pp. 42–43; "Brutus," An Address to a Virginia County, 14 July 1775, *Revolutionary Virginia* 3:127.

36 *Authority to Tax*, pp. 174–78.

37 Boston newspaper, 17 March 1774, *American Archives* 1:501 footnote.

38 "Extract of a Letter from a Gentleman at New-York to his Friend in Boston, Dated February 28, 1774," *American Archives* 1:500 footnote. The letter writer referred to "the Post Office establishment, upon which every other unconstitutional Act has been grounded, as our tame submission to it has been constantly urged, by the enemies of our country, as a precedent against us." Ibid.

39 See, e.g., [Galloway,] *True and Impartial State*, pp. 67–68 (instructions to colonial governors concerning proscribed legislation); Pole, *Gift*, pp. 75–76 (veto of South Carolina issuance of paper money); Sosin, "Imperial Regulation," pp. 174–96.

40 Speech of Charles Jenkinson, Commons Debates, 26 January 1775, *Proceedings and Debates* 5:311. See also [Whately,] *Regulations Lately Made*, pp. 41–43.

41 14 George II, cap. 37 (extending 6 George I, cap. 18 to all the colonies, not just to Massachusetts); Pole, *Gift*, pp. 74–75; Zemsky, *River Gods*, p. 129; *Proceedings and Debates of Parliaments* 5:100 n. 100; Bridenbaugh, *Cities*, pp. 90–92.

42 24 George II, cap. 53. See also Walsh, *Appeal from the Judgments*, p. 174; Tucker, *Letter to Burke*, p. 30; Anon., *Plain Question*, p. 10. For a historical perspective, see Weir, "Currency Act," p. 183.

43 [Lind,] *Thirteenth Parliament*, p. 237.

44 Petition of Richard Partridge, Agent for Pennsylvania, to the House of Commons, 15 March 1748/49, *Proceedings and Debates of Parliaments* 5:306–7; Petition of Richard Partridge, Agent for Rhode Island, to the House of Commons, 1 April 1751, ibid., p. 474; Petition same to same, 15 March 1748/49, ibid. p. 307.

45 Petition of Eliakim Palmer, Agent for Connecticut, to the House of Commons, 15 March 1748/49, ibid., pp. 305–6 (Palmer, in the second quotation, was also protesting a provision of the bill "to enforce his Majesty's orders and instructions throughout all the British colonies and plantations in America"). The agent for Massachusetts also petitioned on behalf of "the special powers and privileges they enjoy by their charter" and "all the liberties they hold in common with other British subjects." Petition of William Bollan, Agent for Massachusetts, to the House of Commons, 6 April 1749, ibid., p. 318. The Agent for New York, like Pennsylvania not affected by the bill restricting bills of credit, objected to that part of the bill entirely on economic grounds, but he objected to the part on the enforcement of ministerial instructions on constitutional grounds. Petitions of Robert Charles, Agent for New York, to the House of Commons, 22 May 1751 and 7 April 1749, ibid., pp. 506–7, 320.

46 4 George III, cap. 34; *Boston Evening-Post*, 23 July 1764, p. 1, col. 1; *London Magazine* 34 (1765): 280; Weir, "Currency Act," p. 183; Greene, *Quest*, p. 388; Namier, *Age of Revolution*, p. 293; Sosin, "Imperial Regulation," p. 185.

47 Greene & Jellison, "Currency Act," p. 517; Weir, "Currency Act," p. 198; Lovejoy, *Rhode Island Politics*, p. 73 (quoting Hopkins). See also Tucker & Hendrickson, *Fall*, p. 116.

48 Tucker & Hendrickson, *Fall*, p. 115; Weir, "Currency Act," pp. 188–92.

49 Address from the House of Assembly to Governor Josiah Martin, 22 November 1771, *North Carolina Colonial Records* 9:142; Message from the House of Assembly to Governor William Tryon, 12 December 1768, *North Carolina Colonial Records* 7:931; Address of the Assembly to the House of Commons, 14 January 1766, *Pennsylvania Archives* 7:5824–27; Letter from the South Carolina Commons House of Assembly to Agent Charles Garth, 4 September 1764, Gibbes, *Documentary History*, pp. 1–2; Petition from the General Assembly to the House of Lords, 18

October 1764, *New York Journal of Votes*, p. 775; Greene, *Quest*, pp. 391-92.

50 It has been said that historians "singled out" these protests "as illustrative of constitutional conflict" when, if looked at from the proper perspective, "it appears that the economic content of the contested rulings has a more believable claim to be the prime reason for colonists' opposition." Unfortunately, the author cites no sources identifying the historians to whom he refers, and research has not uncovered any. Reid, "Economic Burden," p. 94.

51 Greene & Jellison, "Currency Act," p. 517.

52 Parliament did provide relief in 1773 by permitting certificates, notes, bills, or debentures to be legal tender at colonial treasuries for duties and taxes. As this paper could be redeemed at the treasuries, it was expected to circulate at face value. 13 George III, cap. 57; Weir, "Currency Act," p. 197; Sosin, "Imperial Regulation," p. 198.

53 Declaration and Resolves, 14 October 1774, *Journals of Congress* 1:71-72.

54 Petition of General Assembly to the King, 25 March 1775, *Journal of New York Assembly* (1766-76), p. 111.

55 Representation from the New York General Assembly to the House of Commons, 25 March 1775, *Gentleman's Magazine* 45 (1775): 248. This document was widely circulated in Great Britain. See *Hibernian Magazine* 5 (1775): 350; *Scots Magazine* 37 (1775): 236. In the companion petition to the Lords, the General Assembly did not raise the right of prerogative, but instead remonstrated against the grievance of "laying an unreasonable restraint upon us, with respect to the emission of a *Paper Currency* to be a legal tender within the Colony." Memorial from the New York General Assembly to the House of Lords, 25 March 1775, *American Archives* 1:1317. In the long, preliminary list of grievances voted by the legislators, the Currency Act was stated as an economic grievance, although it was noted that the statute "prohibits the legislature of the colony from passing any law for the emission of a paper currency. . . . " The injunction was not stated as a constitutional grievance. The grievance was the inability to obtain relief. Minutes for 3 March 1775, *Journal of New York Assembly* (1766-76), p. 54.

56 Shebbeare, *Essay on National Society*, pp. 146, 99; [Lind,] *Thirteenth Parliament*, p. 208.

57 7 & 8 William III, cap. 22, sec. 16; Abercromby, *De Jure*, pp. 53-54.

58 5 George II, cap. 22; "An authentic Account of the Rise of the present Ill-Humour in America," *Gentleman's Magazine* 44 (1774): 415.

59 5 George II, cap. 22, sec. 7. Section 8 forbade hiring "any black or negro". The act is discussed by [Knox,] *Controversy*, p. 177; [Lind,] *Thirteenth Parliament*, p. 218; Anon., Plain Question, pp. 9-10.

60 E.g., Christopher Gadsden in *Freeman Letters*, p. 99. The only complaint in Great Britain seems to have been that hats of *British manufacture* also could not be exported from one colony to another. Minutes of 26 February 1765, *Trade & Plantations* (1765-67), p. 152.

61 Anon., *Supremacy of Legislature*, p. 27.
62 "Causes of the American Discontents before 1768," printed in the *London Chronicle*, *Papers of Franklin* 15:10–11. This article was widely reprinted, e.g., *Scots Magazine* 30:27–28 and 36:418.
63 *Proceedings and Debates of Parliaments* 4:xiii.
64 23 George II, cap. 29, sec. 9. See also 30 George II, cap. 16; Anon., *Plain Question*, p. 10.
65 *Gentleman's Magazine* 45 (1775): 476. This argument was copied from an earlier "address" mistakenly attributed to John Dickinson. *Scots Magazine* 30 (1768): 524; *Gentleman's Magazine* 38 (1768): 419. Also, see "An authentic Account of the Rise of the present Ill-Humour in America," *Gentleman's Magazine* 44 (1774): 415; Price, *Two Tracts: Tract One*, pp. 67–68.
66 10 & 11 William III, cap. 10. "They are prohibited from carrying wool, or any kind of woolen goods made in one colony, to another. A single fleece of wool, or a dozen of home-made hose, carried from one colony to another, is not only forefeited, but subjects the vessel if conveyed by water, or the waggon or horses, if by land, to a seizure, and the owner to a heavy fine." Lee, *Appeal to Justice*, p. 27. Another act of Parliament that has not been discussed as a precedent of legislation because it was not cited as a precedent and, as a grievance, was considered more a governance than a legislative matter, is the statute for the transportation of criminals to the colonies. 4 George I, cap. 11. See Kettner, *American Citizenship*, p. 110.
67 Lee, *Appeal to Justice*, pp. 26–27.
68 *South-Carolina Gazette*, 27 July 1767, p. 1, col. 3 (reprinting *Benevolus*). For instances of the "precedent" argument made in Parliament, see Speech of Charles Mellish, Commons Debates, 27 October 1775, *Proceedings and Debates* 6:130–31; Speech of Lord Mansfield, Lords Debates, 7 February 1775, *Proceedings and Debates* 5:388; Speech of Charles Yorke, Commons Debates, 3 February 1766, Ryder, "Parliamentary Diaries," p. 264; Speech of Jeremiah Dyson, Commons Debates, 15 February 1765, *Proceedings and Debates* 2:27.
69 [Sewall,] *Americans Roused*, p. 14; Roebuck, *Enquiry Whether the Guilt*, p. 15; [Lind,] *Thirteenth Parliament*, p. 236. See also Johnson, *Political Tracts*, p. 204; Anon., *Supremacy of Legislature*, p. 30; Anon., *Arguments in Support of Supremacy*, pp. 24–25; Anon., *Plain Question*, pp. 9–10; Christie, *Crisis*, pp. 12–13.
70 Dickinson, *Letters*, pp. 312–13. See also Philadelphia Merchants Address, 25 April 1768, *Gentleman's Magazine* 38 (1768): 419 (wrongly attributed to Dickinson); Abingdon, *Thoughts on Burke's Letter*, pp. 43–44.
71 Letter from a Merchant in Philadelphia to London, 19 June 1765, *Scots Magazine* 27 (1765): 438; *Gazette & Post-Boy*, 28 February 1774, p. 2, col. 3 (from the *Newport Mercury*); *London Magazine* 35 (1766): 228. It was in private correspondence that the whigs were more likely the describe legislation such as the Iron Act as a "liberty" issue. See, e.g., Letter from

Charles Carroll of Carrollton to Edmund Jennings, 9 March 1767, *Letters of Charles Carroll*, pp. 139–40.

72 Jefferson, *Summary View*, pp. 124–25. See similarly, [Prescott,] *Calm Consideration*, p. 23;[Wells,] *Political Reflections*, p. 6.

73 Letter from John Dickinson to William Pitt, 21 December 1765, Morgan, *Prologue*, p. 120.

74 *Report of Lords on Massachusetts*, p. 29 (paraphrasing Massachusetts House of Representatives).

75 "Brutus," An Address to a Virginia County, 14 July 1775, *Revolutionary Virginia* 3:127.

76 Ramsay, *History*, p. 43. On this point, see Christie & Labaree, *Empire*, p. 12. A related argument was that the Americans did a great deal of manufacturing. "The Interest of the Merchants and Manufacturers of Great Britain . . . ," *Hibernian Magazine* 5 (1775): 45.

77 Adams, "Novanglus," p. 141.

78 Address to Philadelphia Merchants Meeting, 25 April 1768, *Gentleman's Magazine* 38 (1768): 419.

79 "Book Review," *Monthly Review* 54 (1776): 146.

80 [Thomson Mason,] "British American," 21 July 1774, reprinted in *Revolutionary Virginia* 1:190.

81 "To the Inhabitants of New-York," 6 October 1774, *American Archives* 1:825.

CHAPTER EIGHTEEN: LEGISLATION OF SUPREMACY

1 *Authority to Tax*, pp. 29–32, 217–33.

2 Representation of the Freeholders of Prince William County, 4 April 1768, *Journal of Burgesses* 11:148; Morgan, *Birth*, p. 45; *In Defiance of the Law*, pp. 45–47, 78–92, 156–77.

3 Frank, "Sketch of an Influence," p. 196 (quoting Blackstone).

4 Message from Governor John Penn to the Assembly, 10 September 1766, *Pennsylvania Council* 9:323–24.

5 Great Britain: Ellys, *Tracts on Liberty* 2:77–80; colonies: Rogers, *Empire and Liberty*, p. 77. Billeting also could be very expensive on individuals (*Scots Magazine* 27 [1765]: 216) and raised very difficult constitutional questions concerning taxation, consent, and equality. Message from Massachusetts House of Representatives to Governor Francis Bernard, February 1767, *Scots Magazine* 29 (1767): 276; Petition of Freeholders of Westmoreland County, Minutes of 2 April 1768, *Journal of Burgesses* 11:146; Letter from William Samuel Johnson to Governor William Pitkin, 15 March 1769, *Proceedings and Debates* 3:137; Letter from Secretary at War Barrington to Secretary of State Conway, 6 February 1766, *Home Office Papers* (1766–69), p 12; [Knox,] *Controversy* (Dublin Edition), pp. 53–54. Blackstone cited the billeting clause as a precedent for internal taxation (Gipson, "Debate on Repeal," p. 17 n. 17), but Franklin dismissed it as an "imposition" that was "not properly taxes." Morgan, *Prologue*, p. 146.

6 Answer from House to Governor Francis Bernard, 15 July 1769, *Massachusetts House Journal* (1769), pp. 81–82. Also, see Petition of Council and Burgesses to House of Lords, 14 April 1766, *Journal of Burgesses* 11:168. To imperialists, the American whig argument was "repugnant to every idea of sovereignty." [Knox,] *Controversy* (Dublin Edition), p. 54.

7 Message from the Assembly to Governor John Penn, 12 September 1766, *Pennsylvania Council* 9:324; *Gentleman's Magazine* 37 (1767): 89; *Scots Magazine* 29 (1767): 104, 277; *Scots Magazine* 30 (1768): 74; Ryerson, *Revolution Begun*, p. 20. Also, see Address from the Upper House to Governor James Wright, 28 October 1767, *Georgia Upper House Journal*, p. 383.

8 Address from Commons House to Governor James Wright, 18 February 1767, *Georgia Commons House Journal* 14:441.

9 Address from Commons House to Governor James Wright, 26 March 1767, ibid., p. 475.

10 Speech of Charles Townshend, Commons Debates, 13 May 1767, *Proceedings and Debates* 2:463–64 (referring to New Jersey for which see below note 12).

11 *Scots Magazine* 30 (1768): 74.

12 Reporting on the debate in the House of Commons, 13 May 1767, Charles Garth wrote:

> With respect to New Jersey, in their Act of Assembly for providing for the King's troops they had omitted to enumerate the several articles mentioned in the Mutiny Act, and had limited the sum given for this service, but as under the words "other necessaries," and upon the Governor's representation, the material articles required in the Act might in all probability be furnished and with which the King's troops were perfectly satisfied, it should seem rather too slight a ground to found any severe proceeding against that colony, in which the Committee concurred, but not without some animadversion for a behaviour that in its tendency seemed to be a question of the authority of Parliament.

Proceedings and Debates 2:469.

13 Letter from Governor James Wright to the earl of Shelburne, 26 May 1767, *Shelburne Abstracts*, vol. 52. Wright instructed the Georgia House to end technical evasions, "that his Majesty expects and requires that you will render an exact and Complete obedience in all respects what ever to the Terms of the Meeting [*sic*] Act." Message from Governor James Wright to the Commons House, 27 October 1767, *Georgia Commons House Journal* 14:479. Also, see Answer from Governor James Wright to Commons House, 30 October 1767, *Georgia Commons House Journal* 14:486. In London, it was originally understood that Georgia refused to comply. Letter from William Samuel Johnson to Governor William Pitkin, 9 June 1767, *Trumbull Papers*, p. 237.

14 *Scots Magazine* 30 (1768): 74; Coleman, *McKean*, p. 83.

15 *Scots Magazine* 30 (1768): 74; Becker, *Political Parties*, p. 54.

16 *Scots Magazine* 30 (1768): 74.

17 Letter from F. B., 27 August 1774, *Scots Magazine* 36 (1774): 416.

18 Address from New York General Assembly to Governor Henry Moore, *Gentleman's Magazine* 37 (1767): 89.

19 Charles Garth's report of the debate of 13 May 1767, *Proceedings and Debates* 2:469. For background explaining the extent of New York's disobedience as discussed in the Commons, see Garth's report. For evidence that the background dispute was constitutional, not economic, see Minutes of 13 December 1765, *New York Journal of Votes*, p. 803; Letter from Secretary at War Barrington to Secretary of State Conway, 6 February 1766, and Letter from Lord Shelburne to General Thomas Gage, 13 September 1766, *Home Office Papers* (1766-69), pp. 12, 79.

20 Becker, *Political Parties*, p. 55.

21 Letter from Lord Shelburne to Governor Henry Moore, 9 August 1766, *Scots Magazine* 29 (1767): 102; *Gentleman's Magazine* 37 (1767): 89.

22 Letter from William Samuel Johnson to Governor William Pitkin, 16 May 1767, *Trumbull Papers*, p. 233. The depth of the anger was attested to by William Pitt who wrote, New York's "disobedience to the mutiny Act will justly create a great ferment here, open a fair field to the arraigners of America, and leave no room to any to say a word in their defence. . . . The torrent of indignation will be irresistable, and they will draw upon their heads national resentment by their ingratitude, and ruin, I fear, upon the whole state, by the consequences." Knollenberg, *Growth of Revolution*, p. 39. But see Ritcheson, *British Politics*, p. 86 (quoting the earl of Shelburne to Pitt).

23 Letter from J. West to Duke of Newcastle, 15 May 1767, *Proceedings and Debates* 2:477.

24 Knollenberg, *Growth of Revolution*, p. 39 (see note 22 above for full quotation).

25 Walpole, *Memoirs* III: 23-24. For the various schemes, see Letter from Charles Garth to South Carolina Committee, 17 May 1767, "Garth Correspondence" 5:225-26; Letter from J. West to Lord Hardwicke, 13 May 1767, and Charles Garth's report, 13 May 1767, *Proceedings and Debates* 2:468-70; Ritcheson, *British Politics*, p. 90; Lawson, "George Grenville," p. 566; Humphreys, "Shelburne and Policy," pp. 269-70. For the extraordinarily harsh proposal by the secretary of state in charge of colonial affairs, see Ritcheson, *British Politics*, pp. 90-91. Others proposed that American legislators and other officials take an oath to uphold the Declaratory Act. Speech of George Grenville, Commons Debates, 13 May 1767, *Proceedings and Debates* 2:471-72; Chaffin, "Declaratory Act," pp. 19-20.

26 Speech of Charles Townshend, Commons Debates, 13 May 1767, Ryder, "Parliamentary Diaries," p. 344.

27 7 George III, cap. 59. The statute refers to "Acts" because, although not

mentioned in the debates, it accused New York of violating 6 George III, cap. 13, as well as the Mutiny Act, 5 George III, cap. 33.

28 Although the preamble of the Suspending Act accused the New York "House of Representatives" of "direct disobedience of the Authority of the British Legislature," of refusing to vote supplies "in the Manner required by the said Act," and of providing firewood and other supplies "inconsistent with the Provisions, and in Opposition to the Directions, of the said Act of Parliament," the body of the statute did not specify that these particulars be remedied.

29 *Annual Register 1767*, p. [48]; [Macfarlane,] *George Third*, p. 260; [Macfarlane,] *Second Ten Years*, p. x.

30 "*Resolved*, That the King's Majesty, by and with the Advice and Consent of the Lords Spiritual and Temporal, and Commons of *Great Britain*, in Parliament assembled, had, hath, and of Right ought to have full Power and Authority to make Laws and Statutes, of sufficient Force and Validity to bind the Colonies and People of *America*, Subjects of the Crown of *Great Britain*, in all Cases whatsoever." Resolutions of 15 May 1767, House of Commons, *Proceedings and Debates* 2:474.

31 Letter from William Samuel Johnson to Governor William Pitkin, 16 May 1767, *Trumbull Papers*, p. 232.

32 *Annual Register 1767*, p. [48]; [Macfarlane,] *George Third*, p. 260.

33 "Lord *George Sackville* objected" that it was "superfluous to do by a *law*, what the King could do by his prerogative alone." Letter from J. Harris to Lord Hardwicke, 13 May 1767, *Proceedings and Debates* 2:468.

34 Dickinson, *Letters*, p. 310.

35 Letter from Governor Henry Moore to Lord Shelburne, 10 June 1767, *New York Colonial Documents* 7:942. On reading the Assembly's address to Moore, Shelburne also concluded that the legislators had "declared their intention of making that Provision for the Troops which is prescribed by the Mutiny act." Letter from Lord Shelburne to Governor Henry Moore, 18 July 1767, ibid., p. 945.

36 Letter from Governor Henry Moore to Lord Shelburne, 21 August 1767, ibid., pp. 948–49.

37 Letter from George Grenville to Thomas Whately, 13 April 1768, *Grenville Letterbooks*; Thomas, *Townshend Duties*, p. 80; Lawson, "George Grenville," p. 566.

38 See, e.g., "Measures Proposed by Lord Hillsborough to the Cabinet," 15 February 1769, *Correspondence George III* 2:83; Letter from William Samuel Johnson to Governor William Pitkin, 13 July 1767, *Trumbull Papers*, p. 241.

39 Minutes for 12 August 1768, *Acts of the Privy Council*, p. 139.

40 Maier, *Old Revolutionaries*, pp. 74–75; Potter, *Liberty We Seek*, p. 77; Becker, *Political Parties*, pp. 78–82; Sosin, "Imperial Regulation," pp. 191–96.

41 Dickinson, *Letters*, p. 309.

42 Ritcheson, *British Politics*, p. 113.

43 Speech of Edmund Burke, 9 May 1770, *Proceedings and Debates* 3:324; [Macfarlane,] *George Third*, p. 399.

44 Resolves of 31 December 1768, *Journal of New York Assembly* (1766–76), p. 70.

45 E.g., New Jersey: Message from Governor William Franklin to the General Assembly, 18 April 1768 and Message from the General Assembly to Governor William Franklin, 5 May 1768, *New Jersey Votes and Proceedings* (1768), pp. 9, 31; Message from Governor William Franklin to the General Assembly, 25 October 1770 and Order of 28 October 1770, *New Jersey Votes and Proceedings* (September 1770), pp. 46–47, 49; Message from Governor William Franklin to the Council and General Assembly, 18 April 1771, Address from the General Assembly to Governor William Franklin, 20 April 1771, Messages from Governor William Franklin to the General Assembly, 23 April 1771 and 29 April 1771, and Resolution of 31 May 1771, *New Jersey Votes and Proceedings* (1771), pp. 4, 9, 16, 32, 36, 38.

46 Resolutions of New York General Assembly, 3 March 1775, *American Archives* 1:1299. Also, see Representation and Remonstrance from New York General Assembly to the House of Commons, 25 March 1775, *Scots Magazine* 37 (1775): 236.

47 Petition of the New York General Assembly to the King, 24 March 1775, *American Archives* 1:1314–15. This grievance was the tenth listed. Earlier, Delaware's representatives had cited the Suspending Act as their first grievance. Address from the House of Assembly of the Counties upon Delaware to the King, 27 October 1768, *Delaware House Minutes* (1765–70), p. 167. Also, see [Hicks,] *Nature of Parliamentary Power*, p. v.

48 Humphreys, "Shelburne and Policy," p. 270.

49 *In a Rebellious Spirit*, pp. 86–126.

50 Address of the House of Parliament, 13 February 1769, *Annual Register 1769*, p. [227].

51 "An act for the trial of treasons comit[t]ed out of the King's dominions." 35 Henry VIII, cap. 2.

52 Lords Resolution, 15 December 1768 and Commons Resolution, 16 December 1768, *Proceedings and Debates* 3:46–47, 52; *Boston Evening-Post*, 25 April 1774, p. 1, col. 3.

53 Gough, *Fundamental Law*, p. 197. Lord Coke ruled that the statute of Henry applied in such a case, leading one imperialist to assert that, "The law, therefore, was clearly settled, and perfectly known, at the era of American Colonization, in the reign of James I." [Chalmers,] *Answer from Bristol to Burke*, p. 15.

54 [Lind,] *Thirteenth Parliament*, pp. 398–99; 19 George II, cap. 9.

55 Letter from Jared Ingersoll to Governor Thomas Fitch, 6 March 1765, "Ingersoll Correspondence," p. 318.

56 Anon., *Answer to Burke*, pp. 25–27; *Gentleman's Magazine* 47 (1777): 284–85; [Chalmers,] *Answer from Bristol to Burke*, pp. 15–16.

57 Address from the House of Assembly to the King, 2 November 1769, *North Carolina Colonial Records* 8:123. Similarly, see Message from the Bur-

gesses to Governor Lord Dunmore, 11 March 1773, *Journal of Burgesses* 13:22.

58 Letter from Edmund Burke to the Sheriffs of Bristol (1777), reprinted in *Burke on American Revolution*, pp. 173–74. Similarly, see Speech of William Dowdeswell, Commons Debates, 26 January 1769, *Proceedings and Debates* 3:66. For similar argument about transferred jurisdiction in Great Britain, see Burgh, *Political Disquisitions* 3:235; Instructions of the Livery of London to their Representatives in Parliament, 10 February 1769, *Political Register* 4 (1769): 191.

59 *Monthly Review* 56 (1777): 471. The factual argument was endless. To the last point, Americans might answer:

> [I]f the people of America are so interested on one side of the question as to be unfit for judges or jurors on any trials relative to it, the people of Britain are as much, nay, if possible, more interested on the other side of the question. . . . For, clearly, the controversy is not, as in the ordinary cases of treasons or other crimes, between the prince and the subject, but between subject and subject, between the people of America and the people of Britain, which shall have the power over American property in the very important point of taxation.

Letter from William Samuel Johnson to Governor William Pitkin, 3 January 1769, *Trumbull Papers*, p. 317. "Will it not be thought on the other side of the Atlantic, at least as likely, that twelve men *may* be found here at the devotion of a ministry, capable of perjury and murder, as it can be thought here, that twelve men cannot be found there incapable of perjury and treason?" Speech of Constantine Phipps, Commons Debates, 8 February 1769, *Proceedings and Debates* 3:111.

60 Thomas, *Townshend Duties*, p. 117 (discussing arguments of William Dowdeswell); [Lind,] *Thirteenth Parliament*, pp. 322–23 (rejecting these arguments); [Lee,] *Speech Intended*, p. 28 (quoting Sir William Blackstone on the "bloody Reign"); Speeches of William Dowdeswell, Commons Debates, 26 January 1769, and Frederick Montagu, Commons Debates, 8 February 1769, *Proceedings and Debates* 3:66, 92; Letter from Charles Garth to South Carolina Commons House Committee, 9 February 1769, "Garth Correspondence" 11:47.

61 *Boston Evening-Post*, 30 July 1770, p. 2, col. 1 (motion of 9 May 1770 by Burke).

62 E.g., [Jacob,] *Laws of Liberty*, pp. 155–17 (contending that the Act of 1 George II for trial of Scottish rebels in England infringed "upon the liberty of the Subject" [p. 115]).

63 *Boston Evening-Post*, 24 July 1769, p. 2, col. 3. Also, see *Boston Evening-Post*, 23 April 1770, p. 4, col. 2 (Burke contending about colonial objections to the law of Henry that "they have reasoned better upon the constitution than us").

64 *Boston Evening-Post*, 7 September 1767, p. 3, col. 2 (Mansfield would have transported James Otis).

65 Letter from Governor Horatio Sharpe to John Ridout, 11 October 1774, Edgar, *Colonial Governor*, p. 258 *(in terrorem)*; Letter from William Samuel Johnson to Governor William Pitkin, 9 February 1769, *Trumbull Papers*, p. 317; Letter from Charles Garth to South Carolina Commons House Committee, 9 February 1769, "Garth Correspondence" 11:48 (know "executive Power of Great Britain"). Also, see Letter to Thomas Cushing, 15 September 1769, "Letters of Dennys De Berdt," p. 379; Leslie, "Gaspee Affair," p. 245. Surprisingly, the commander of British troops at Boston believed some Bostonians were "under apprehensions of a trip to England." Letter from General John Pomeroy to General Thomas Gage, 6 February 1769, Gage, *Papers*.

66 *Boston Evening-Post*, 3 July 1769, p. 3, col. 1 (attributing the phraseology to Virginia's House of Burgesses).

67 Virginia Resolutions, 16 May 1769, *Boston Post-Boy*, 12 June 1769, p. 1, col. 2; Massachusetts Resolutions, 29 June 1769, *Speeches*, p. 180; North Carolina Resolutions, 2 November 1769, *North Carolina Colonial Records* 8:122; Maryland Resolutions, November 1769, *Rhode Island Correspondence*, p. 418; New Jersey Resolutions, 6 December 1769, *New Jersey Votes and Proceedings* (1769), p. 88; Maryland Resolutions, 28 December 1769, *Boston Post-Boy*, 22 January 1770, p. 3, col. 2.

68 Resolutions of South Carolina Commons House, 19 August 1769, *Boston Chronicle*, 1 October 1769, p. 316, col. 1. Also, see Representation of New York General Assembly to the House of Commons, 25 March 1775, *Scots Magazine* 37 (1775): 236.

69 Ramsay, *History*, p. 84.

70 Letter from Governor William Tryon to Lord Hillsborough, 8 January 1770, and Letter from Lord Hillsborough to Governor William Tryon, 18 January 1770, *North Carolina Colonial Records* 8:169–70, 170–71.

71 Resolves of 16 May 1769, *Journal of Burgesses* 11:214.

72 South Carolina Resolves, 19 August 1769, *Boston Chronicle*, 1 October 1769, p. 316, col. 1. Somewhat similar resolutions were adopted in Charleston, 8 July 1774. *Boston Evening-Post*, 25 July 1774, p. 2, col. 1. Also, see Resolutions of the Lower House of Assembly, 20 December 1769, *Maryland Votes and Proceedings* (1769), p. 248; Address from the House of Burgesses to the King, 16 May 1769, *Boston Evening-Post*, 12 June 1769, p. 4, col. 1. It was even said to have been part of the emigration contract that America's settlers "whenever they were accused of any breach of law, . . . should be tried by their Peers." Patten, *Discourse at Hallifax*, pp. 13–14. A 1663 Rhode Island law claiming exclusive jurisdiction was several times printed in colonial newspapers in the 1770s. Leslie, "Gaspee Affair," p. 246.

73 Address from the House of Assembly, 17 June 1769, *Delaware House Minutes* (1765–70), p. 218; Address of the North Carolina House of Assembly to the King, October 1769, *Boston Evening-Post*, 22 January 1770, p. 4, col. 1.

74 The grievance stated in the Declaration of Independence, that accused

George III of taking trials beyond the seas, may have referred to the Act of 35 Henry VIII as well as to the Massachusetts Justice Act. The king did not sign the resolutions calling for the enforcement of the law of Henry. Also, see Minutes of 21 October 1774, *Journal of the First Congress*, p. 113; *Boston Evening-Post*, 28 January 1771, p. 1, col. 2 (*Junius Americanus* or Arthur Lee).

75 12 George III, cap. 24; Declaration of Rights, 14 October 1774, *Journal of the First Congress*, p. 64; Minutes of 3 March 1775, *Journal of New York Assembly* (1766–76), p. 54; Letter from Georgia Commons House of Assembly to Virginia Committee of Correspondence, 5 June 1773, *Journal of Burgesses* 13:51; Resolves of Westerly, R.I., 2 February 1774, Denison, *Westerly*, p. 111; Resolutions of Ipswich, 17 December 1772, *Boston Evening-Post*, 18 January 1773, p. 1, col. 3; *Authority of Rights*, pp. 54–55, 191–92.

76 Motion of 12 March 1773, Virginia House of Burgesses, *Rhode Island Colony Records* 7:226; Instructions of 5 May 1770, *Boston Town Records* 18:133; Letter from John Dickinson to Richard Henry Lee, 1773, Lee, *Richard Henry Lee* 1:91; Leslie, "Gaspee Affair," p. 250; *Authority of Rights*, p. 192.

77 Instructions of 5 May 1770, *Boston Town Records* 18:133; "John Adams' Proposed Resolutions," 30 September 1774, *Letters of Delegates to Congress* 1:131; Minutes of 21 October 1774, *Journal of the First Congress*, p. 113.

78 *Authority to Tax*, pp. 29–31, 217–22. The "govern" issue of the Townshend Acts concerns such matters as the authority of the customs commissioners created by the acts and the authority of the British ministry over those colonial officials for whom the acts specified Crown salaries.

79 Thomas, *Townshend Duties*, pp. 22–23; Thomas, *British Politics*, p. 357. During the debate on the Stamp Act, Townshend said: " . . . if some proper plan is not formed for governing as well as quieting them [the colonies] at present and for the future, it will be extremely dangerous. The magistrates [are] at present in many colonies elective, the judges dependent on the assemblies for their salaries." Speech of Charles Townshend, Commons Debates, 7 February 1766, Ryder, "Parliamentary Debates," p. 283. The act is 7 George III, cap. 46.

80 Charles Garth reporting on the Commons debates of 13 May 1767, *Proceedings and Debates* 2:470. Also, see Speech of Edmund Burke, Commons Debates, 8 November 1768, *Proceedings and Debates* 3:7; Ritcheson, *British Politics*, p. 100; Thomas, *Townshend Duties*, p. 25.

81 Speech of Thomas Pownall, Commons Debates, 8 May 1770, *Proceedings and Debates* 3:273; Speech of Richard Pennant, Commons Debates, 19 April 1774, *Proceedings and Debates* 4:181.

82 Royle & Walvin, *English Radicals*, p. 24.

83 Speech of Thomas Pownall, Commons Debates, 5 March 1770, *Proceedings and Debates* 3:218; Speech of Thomas Pownall, Commons Debates, 19 April 1769, ibid., p. 155; Dickinson, *Letters*, p. 373.

84 For a concise statement of British constitutionalism and the Townshend Acts, see Speech of Thomas Pownall, Commons Debates, 5 March 1770, *Proceedings and Debates* 3:237.

85 Resolves of New Shoreham, 2 March 1774, *Rhode Island Colony Records* 7:277; Letter from Governor William Pitkin to William Samuel Johnson, 6 June 1768, *Trumbull Papers*, pp. 277, 282 (this letter was "approved" by both branches of the legislature).

86 Letter from William Samuel Johnson to Governor William Pitkin, 3 January 1769, *Trumbull Papers*, p. 307.

87 Ibid., p. 305 (quoting Hillsborough); Letter from Lord Barrington to Governor Francis Bernard, 2 January 1769, Bernard & Barrington, *Correspondence*, p. 182; Letter from William Samuel Johnson to Governor William Pitkin, 26 April 1769, *Trumbull Papers*, pp. 336–37.

88 For a somewhat different explanation by a colonial lawyer, see Letter from William Samuel Johnson to Governor Jonathan Trumbull, 5 December 1769, *Trumbull Papers*, p. 383.

89 *Authority to Tax*, pp. 262–70.

90 Speech of Edmund Burke, Commons Debates, 9 May 1770, *Proceedings and Debates* 3:301. "This Act of Parliament imposes a duty upon them, which every man in this House allows to be contrary to all commercial principles. It is upon this law therefore that you will pin that question upon your own rights." Speech of Isaac Barré, Commons Debates, 26 January 1769, ibid., p. 78.

91 Letter from William Samuel Johnson to Governor William Pitkin, 20 October 1768, *Trumbull Papers*, p. 296.

92 Letter from William Samuel Johnson to Governor William Pitkin, 3 January 1769, ibid., p. 305.

93 Letter from William Knox to George Grenville, 15 December 1768, *Grenville Papers* 4:400.

94 Letter from William Samuel Johnson to Governor William Pitkin, 3 January 1769, *Trumbull Papers*, pp. 306–7.

95 Letter from William Knox to George Grenville, 15 December 1768, *Grenville Papers*, pp. 400–1.

96 Letter from William Samuel Johnson to Governor William Pitkin, 23 March 1769, *Trumbull Papers*, p. 324.

97 See especially Speech of Thomas Townshend, Commons Debates, 19 April 1769, *Proceedings and Debates* 3:154.

98 Letter from William Samuel Johnson to Governor Jonathan Trumbull, 3 February 1770, *Trumbull Papers*, p. 406.

99 Letter from William Samuel Johnson to Governor Jonathan Trumbull, 6 March 1770, ibid., p. 421.

100 Speech of Lord North, Commons Debates, 5 March 1770, *Proceedings and Debates* 3:213. Also, see Letter from Charles Garth to South Carolina Commons House Committee, 6 March 1770, "Garth Correspondence" 13:229–30. It was later claimed that North admitted "that the tea was as much an anti-commercial tax as any of those which were repealed on that

principle; but the authority of parliament being disputed, he could not repeal all till that was fully acknowledged." Speech of George Johnstone, Commons Debates, 23 January 1775, *Parliamentary History* 18:178. The preamble of 7 George III, cap. 46 is reprinted in Jensen, *Documents*, pp. 701-2.

101 Speeches of Thomas Pownall, Commons Debates, 5 March 1770, and 19 April 1769, *Proceedings and Debates* 3:230, 154-55.

102 Speech of Thomas Pownall, Commons Debates, 8 February 1769, ibid., p. 110; Speech of Lord North, Commons Debates, 5 March 1770, ibid., p. 229.

103 Speech of Lord Rockingham, Lords Debates, 18 May 1774, *Proceedings and Debates* 4:434.

104 Petition from the House of Burgesses to the King, 27 June 1770, *Revolution Documents* 2:129. It was "retained merely as a *Precedent.*" Nicholas, *Present State of Virginia*, p. 262.

105 Thomas, *Townshend Duties*, pp. 212-13. "[O]nce the other duties were repealed, the tea tax was more or less successfully collected, at least on tea that was legitimately imported." Countryman, *Revolution*, p. 53.

106 Thomas, *Townshend Duties*, p. 165. But see Eden's later argument (which he admitted "has not the weight I could wish") that the Tea Act of 1773 was not a precedent for taxation. *Authority to Tax*, p. 131.

107 Thomas, *Townshend Duties*, pp. 213, 137, 212.

108 For a partial explanation of the significance of precedent in eighteenth-century law, see *Authority to Tax*, pp. 122-34.

109 Speech of Edmund Burke, Commons Debates, 19 April 1774, *Proceedings and Debates* 4:230; Speech of Thomas Pownall, Commons Debates, 5 March 1770, *Proceedings and Debates* 3:235, 229, 235.

110 Speeches of Welbore Ellis and Lord George Germain, Commons Debates, 7 March 1774, *Proceedings and Debates* 4:39, 45, 39.

111 Thomas, *Townshend Duties*, pp. 247-49. For an argument that the company opposed the act, see Speech of Governor George Johnstone, Commons Debates, 23 January 1775, *Proceedings and Debates* 5:299. The Tea Act is 13 George III, cap. 44.

112 Speech of Lord North, Commons Debates, 26 April 1773, *Proceedings and Debates* 3:488. The total was later said to be "only equal to two year's [*sic*] consumption." Anon., *View of North*, p. 107 footnote.

113 Speech of Lord North, Commons Debates, 27 April 1773, *London Magazine* 43 (1774): 314; [Sewall,] *Americans Roused*, p. 16; Anon., *Arguments in Support of Supremacy*, p. 40.

114 Speeches of William Dowdeswell and Barlow Trecothick, Commons Debates, 26 April 1773, *Proceedings and Debates* 3:488, 489.

115 Speech of Lord North, Commons Debates, 26 April 1773, ibid., pp. 488-89.

116 Speeches of Charles Jenkinson and Lord North, Commons Debates, 26 April 1773, ibid., pp. 489, 490.

117 Speeches of Charles Wolfran Cornwall, 19 April 1774, *Proceedings and Debates* 4:236, 230. Also, see Anon., *View of North*, p. 8.

118 Speech of Lord North, Commons Debates, 19 February 1778, *Parliamentary History* 19:763; Speech of Lord North, Commons Debates, 23 January 1775, *Proceedings and Debates* 5:299; Speech of Lord North, Commons Debates, 17 February 1778, *Gentleman's Magazine* 48 (1778): 54.

119 Speech of Edmund Burke, Commons Debates, 19 April 1774, *Proceedings and Debates* 4:230. Benjamin Franklin's explanation was that the ministry "have no idea that any people can act from any other principle but that of interest; and they believe that threepence in a pound of tea, . . . is sufficient to overcome all the patriotism of an American." Trevelyan, *Revolution Condensation*, p. 86.

120 Speech of Charles James Fox, Commons Debates, 19 April 1774, *Proceedings and Debates* 4:238.

121 The "monopoly" grievance pertains more to the authority to govern than to the authority to legislate and cannot be developed here. See Continental Congress Memorial to the Inhabitants of the Colonies, 21 October 1774, *Commemoration Ceremony*, p. 118; Resolutions of Essex County, Virginia, 9 July 1774, *American Archives* 1:527; Resolves of Westerly, Rhode Island, 2 February 1774, Denison, *Westerly*, p. 112; *Boston News-Letter*, 30 March 1775, p. 2, col. 3; [Macfarlane,] *Second Ten Years*, p. 129; Waters, *Otis Family*, p. 182. Monopolies were a long-standing constitutional issue in England, and the Tea Act, by introducing a commercial monopoly to the colonies, added a grievance of unequal treatment. Ellys, *Tracts on Liberty* 2:70; Anon., *Review of Present Administration*, p. 20.

122 Providence Resolves, 19 January 1774, *Rhode Island Colony Records* 7:273. Also, see Richmond Resolves, 28 February 1774, New Shoreham Resolves, 2 March 1774, Barrington Resolves, 21 March 1774, ibid., pp. 276, 277, 279; Paine, *Letter to Raynal*, p. 7.

123 *Authority to Tax*, pp. 132–34.

124 Labaree, *Tea Party*, pp. 126–27; 6 George II, cap. 13, sec. 2; 7 George III, cap. 46, sec. 4; 12 George III, cap. 7; 12 George III, cap. 60; 13 George III, cap. 44.

125 Knollenberg, "Adams and Tea Party," pp. 494–99.

126 Labaree, *Tea Party*, pp. 119, 291, citing 7 & 8 William III, cap. 22, sec. 6, applying to the colonies 13 & 14 Charles II, cap. 11, sec. 4.

127 Letter from Governor Thomas Hutchinson to Sir Francis Bernard, 1 January 1774, quoted in Knollenberg, "Adams and Tea Party," p. 497.

128 Tucker & Hendrickson, *Fall*, p. 314.

129 Letters from William Samuel Johnson to Governor Jonathan Trumbull, 20 August 1770 and 15 November 1770, *Trumbull Papers*, pp. 450, 463 (quoting Burke).

130 Speech of William Dowdeswell, Commons Debates, 7 March 1774, *Proceedings and Debates* 4:38; Speech of Charles Wolfran Cornwall, Commons Debates, 19 April 1774, ibid., p. 236.

131 Speeches of Edmund Burke and Thomas Townshend, Jr., Commons Debates, 19 April 1774, ibid., pp. 204, 194, 232.

132 Speeches of John Burgoyne and George Rice, Commons Debates, 19 April

1774, ibid., pp. 232, 229; Speech of Lord George Germain, Commons Debates, 2 May 1774, ibid., p. 381. The second ranking law officer said: "The whole disturbances are owing to the factious spirit of some persons and not to the tax. If you give up the idea of taxing America we must give up more. We must give up the country." Speech of Solicitor General Alexander Wedderburn, Commons Debates, 19 April 1774, ibid., p. 232.

133 Speech of Charles James Fox, Commons Debates, 2 May 1774, ibid., p. 361. George III wrote: "I am clear that there must always be one tax to keep up the right, and as such I approve of the tea duty." Thomas, "George III," p. 28. In May 1780, Henry Seymour Conway would recall: "The miserable system of Taxation was maintained as long as it could be maintained; nay, I may say, even longer; it shewed itself through fifty disguises: first, in the shape of Regulation, then the honour of Parliament. . . . All idea of any other tax but the Tea-duty was disclaimed; but still the Tea-duty was maintained; we quarrelled for the Tea-duty, fought for the Tea-duty, for the Tea-duty was this destructive war with France, Spain and America, positively made." Conway, *Peace Speech*, pp. 8-9.

CHAPTER NINETEEN: CONCLUSION

1 Speech of Lord North, Commons Debates, 7 December 1768, *Proceedings and Debates* 3:32.

2 Speech of George Johnstone, Commons Debates, 6 February 1775, *Proceedings and Debates* 5:374.

3 "Another Origin of Judicial Review," p. 987.

4 As was suggested as a solution. Ibid., pp. 985-86; Anon., *Speech Never Intended*, pp. 27-28.

5 One proposal was a court consisting of selected English, Scots, and Irish high-court judges, as well as a member of each of the two houses of Parliament. *Scots Magazine* 36 (1774): 631; "Another Origin of Judicial Review", pp. 986-87.

6 A contention that was also made by participants in the constitutional debate: "The great difficulty attending this American controversy is, that the question changes upon us from day to day; and what would be a compleat answer one week, by the next is nothing at all to the purpose." [Ramsay,] *Thoughts on Nature of Government*, p. 6.

7 Ibid., pp. 27-28.

8 William Smith ("Cato") reprinted in [Chalmers,] *Plain Truth*, p. 81.

9 *Annual Register 1768*, p. 72*.

10 Pownall, *Administration Fifth Edition* 2:4.

11 Speech of Charles Jenkinson, Commons Debates, 6 March 1775, *Proceedings and Debates* 5:504.

12 [Chalmers,] *Answer from Bristol to Burke*, p. 73.

13 [Knox,] *Controversy*, pp. 34-35.

14 Morgan, "Colonial Ideas," p. 341. The internal-external distinction, for example, although based on the terminology of colonial constitutional

advocacy, was an imperial fabrication, not a colonial whig legalism. Ibid., pp. 318-19; *Authority to Tax*, pp. 33-34.

15 Morgan, "Colonial Ideas," p. 312.

16 Morgan, *American Revolution*, p. 5.

17 Morgan, *Challenge*, pp. 3-4.

18 Degler, "Preface 3," p. 41.

19 Bailyn, *Ideological Origins*, p. 218.

20 Morgan, *Birth*, p. 51.

21 For whigs to have stated "at the outset exactly what they believed . . . they would have had to know what they believed much better than any of us do and to have adhered to it with superhuman consistency." Ibid., pp. 51-52.

22 Bailyn, *Pamphlets*, p. 384.

23 See chap. 3, pp. 52-56.

24 These resolutions are summarized in the introduction, pp. 9-11.

25 See chap. 3, pp. 52-56.

26 See chap. 3, pp. 56, and chap. 18, pp. 286-90.

27 See chap. 18, pp. 281-86.

28 See chap. 18, pp. 276-81.

29 Resolution of 6 December 1769, *New Jersey Votes and Proceedings* (1769), p. 88; Resolves of 16 May 1769, *Journal of Burgesses* 11: 214; Resolutions of Maryland Lower House, 28 December 1769, *Boston Chronicle*, 18 January 1770, p. 22, col. 3.

30 *Authority to Tax*, pp. 132-34.

31 See chap. 18, pp. 295-98.

32 14 George III, cap. 19.

33 14 George III, cap. 45.

34 14 George III, cap. 39.

35 14 George III, cap. 54.

36 Resolves of New Shoreham Town Meeting, 2 March 1774, *Rhode Island Colony Records* 7:277.

37 Langford, "Old Whigs," p. 111; Schuyler, *Empire*, pp. 110-11.

INDEX

477

DESIGNED BY IRVING PERKINS ASSOCIATES
COMPOSED BY CONNELL-ZEKO TYPE & GRAPHICS, KANSAS CITY, MISSOURI
MANUFACTURED BY CUSHING MALLOY, INC., ANN ARBOR, MICHIGAN
TEXT AND DISPLAY LINES ARE SET IN CALEDONIA

Library of Congress Cataloging-in-Publication Data
Reid, John Phillip.
Constitutional history of the American Revolution.
The authority to legislate / John Phillip Reid.
508pp.   cm.
Part of a four vol. work on U.S. constitutional history.
Includes bibliographical references and index.
ISBN 0-299-13070-3
1. Legislative power—United States—History.
2. United States—Constitutional history.
3. United States—History—Revolution, 1775-1783.
4. Great Britain—Colonies—America—Administration—History.
I. Title.
KF4930.R45   1991
342.73'029—dc20
[347.30229]   91-50326